This superb photo of BUTCH BABY is from the collection of the late aviation historian and pilot Jeff Ethell. Lt. Julian Bertram was the pilot here. It had been Lt. Col. Joe Broadhead's MASTER MIKE. Later Lt. Jim McLane took it over until war's end and it was then re-named DAINTY DOTTIE.

TO WAR WITH
THE YOXFORD BOYS
The Complete Story of the 357th Fighter Group

By

MSGT Merle C. Olmsted, USAF (RET)

with

COL. C.E. "Bud" Anderson USAF (RET)

Dedicated to the 92 men of the 357th Fighter Group who lost their lives in the line of duty and with the greatest affection to all the men of the Group and its supporting units - to the marvelous wives of the 357th Fighter Group association and especially to Joe and Ellen DeShay who, through their efforts, kept us together for many years - and to my wife, Margreth who has shared my enthusiasm for "The Group" for four decades.

TO WAR WITH THE YOXFORD BOYS

The Complete Story of the 357th Fighter Group

First Edition

Manufactured in Korea

ISBN: 0-97210600-6-5 Standard Edition

ISBN: 0-9721060-7-3 Deluxe, autographed, limited edition

Library of Eagles
Eagle Editions Ltd.
Post Office Box 580
Hamilton MT 59840 USA
www.eagle-editions.com

COVER PAINTING © Roy Grinnell depicts then Capt. Charles E. Yeager's Ninth victory, 27 November 1944 near
Magdeburg, Germany, entitled **ONE OF FOUR THAT DAY**; The 363rd Fighter Squadron was on an escort mission, flying top cover for a group of P-51s strafing targets south of Magdeburg, Germany. Capt. "Chuck" Yeager was leading
Green Flight about 35,000 feet. Suddenly a warning of "Bandits at 11 o'clock" came through his headset. Two huge formations of German fighters darkened the sky. Flight leader Major "Bud" Anderson told Yeager to take over the lead, as
the squadron turned into the enemy. Passing the smaller group, Yeager climbed over the rear of the larger enemy formation. He fired a side deflection at a Focke-Wulf until its tail flew off. Within minutes, Yeager had downed three more
Fw 190s in furious aerial encounters, making his victory score four for that same day.

Cover image is owned by and used with permission from The American Fighter Aces Association and
The Museum of Flight, Seattle, Washington.

★★★★★★★★★★★★★★★★★ Foreword ★★★★★★★★★★★★★★★★

by BRIG/GEN CHARLES E. YEAGER, USAF (RET)

Merle Olmsted's book on the 357th Fighter Group covers the activities of one of the premier Mustang groups of WWII. Basically, it covers the forming of the Group, the training days, and then through the combat days in Europe. We trained on the Bell P-39, as discussed at length by Olmsted. I, and many other pilots loved to fly the airplane - as long as we weren't fighting in it. It was a tricycle-gear airplane, and very easy to take-off and land. It had a reputation as a "tumbler" in the air force, but I don't recall much evidence of that, and Bell test pilots reported they could not make it tumble. However, it was a tricky airplane, and if you stalled it, or snapped it, it could turn vicious. It had a 37 mm cannon firing through the prop shaft, and as I recall it worked well for me, I was usually able to deplete my ammo supply. It was a fun gun to fire!

We trained first at Tonopah, Nevada, then moved to Santa Rosa, California, and then split the Group going to Oroville, Hayward, and Marysville, all in California. In the fall of 1943, we moved to Casper, Wyoming, Ainsworth, Nebraska, and Pocatello, Idaho, before moving on again and embarking on the liner QUEEN ELIZABETH, bound for England.

We were well trained in the P-39, most pilots had about 400 hours in the airplane. We were excellent dogfighters, outstanding gunners, and we understood tactics and formation flying. So, when we got to England, we got P-51s. Merle explains very well in his book that it was probably a good example of how not to commit a unit to combat. We were thrown into battle with very little experience in the airplane - but there was not much choice, they were desperate times!

Besides our lack of experience in the P-51, we were handicapped by the 85 gallon fuselage fuel tank, not part of the original design, but added as a range extender. In the tactics we used, with the drop tanks (75 gallons at first, 108 later), the fuselage tank and 92 gallons in each wing, we took off on the left main and then switched to the fuselage tank to drain it down to about 40 gallons. With over that in the fuselage tank, the airplane was dynamically unstable. If you started a turn with tank full, the airplane would "dig in" and spin.

However, we accepted this handicap as it gave us tremendous range. In fact, the maximum endurance we could get out of the P-51 was up to 8 hours. At the altitude we flew, 35,000 feet, and with pressure breathing oxygen, we didn't really have any troubles, except for the extreme cold, but we lived with that.

When you look at today's command structure of an Air Force Fighter Wing, you have excellent command and control from the top down. In my opinion, the 357th Fighter Group was drastically handicapped by the Group leaders we had early in the war. My 363rd Squadron went through many commanders for various reasons, including one being fired because the Group commander's wife did not like him! When we went into combat, in my opinion, our leadership in the Group was poor. There were occasions when bandits were called in at 9 o'clock, the Group leader would be "investigating bogies" in another direction. I think our higher headquarters, 66th Fighter Wing recognized this and moved Colonel Spicer in as our commander. He was a marvelous leader, everyone liked and respected him. He was a brave man and a natural leader. I flew his wing several times and recall he would let down to 10 or 12,000 feet over Paris, or some other city, in order to light his old pipe. Flak would be popping all around us, and I said "Colonel, we are going to get shot down" and he replied "Laddie, don't worry, they can't hit us." Well, soon after they did shoot him down!

I have been critical of some individual leadership, but the Group's outstanding record in 14 months of combat makes it clear we also had many excellent leaders, from Group level down to Squadron Commanders, flight leaders, and element leaders. In some cases element leaders progressed through the system to become Squadron Commanders.

Basically, the whole history of the 357th, the flying problems, such as the abort rate, the trials and tribulations of the ground crews, and the mutual respect between the pilots and the ground crews - this is all spelled out very well in Olmsted's book. For the first time I read a book that explains everything that happened in the 357th Group and all parts of life, whether maintenance, combat flying and the loss of many pilots who did not return - all part of war.

I think you will enjoy this book, as it is really outstanding and one of the few really thorough histories of a WWII Mustang Group that has ever been written.

Charles E. Yeager, B/Gen, USAF (ret)
Chairman, General Chuck Yeager Foundation

★★★

Preface

This is a story about fighter pilots, fighter planes, the ground crews of many trades, and the military unit that gave them cohesion and made them an outstanding team. It is also the story of what they did in the fifth decade of the last century in a great European war. As with most military organizations, this one had a number - it was the 357th Fighter Group.

Fighter pilots stand tall as this writer's heroes, especially those of the 357th. How, you may ask, is the writer, who was not a fighter pilot, qualified to comment on the subject? First, because, at least in theory, anyone is free to express an opinion. Beyond that, as official historian for the 357th and a dedicated history "buff", I have associated with, and written about fighter pilots and "our group" for some 50 years. One of the highlights of my life is to call a great many of them my friend, as well as all the men and wives of the 357th.

Besides the story of fighter pilots, we will also attempt to show the place and function of the many "faceless" support personnel, who were vital to the mission, but who were, in no way, glamorous!

To the younger generation and aviation enthusiasts of today, fighter pilots are the epitome of glamour, which the pilots themselves like to project. This is as it should be, as the "gung-ho" attitude is a major factor in the make-up of a successful fighter pilot.

For men in the fighter business, being a genuine "tiger" is the ultimate objective, but not all of them are or were tigers, which is defined as one who looks forward to engaging the enemy, and eagerly seeks him out, and then has the skills to go with it to become a successful tiger. The tiger category, however, was only a small percentage at the top. At the other end of the scale was another very small group who should never have been in fighter cockpits, and often avoided flying combat. Some of them were so emotionally unfit that they were removed from operations as a danger to themselves and to their comrades, and they soon disappeared from the squadrons.

In the center is the large majority, who would perhaps, not qualify as tigers, who were often apprehensive before a mission, but nonetheless never shirked their duty, flew their missions as assigned, and did not hesitate to engage the enemy. In other words, they were men with the same fears, pride, and desire to do the job well, as most average people are. The lucky ones completed their tour, some as aces, some not, with a job well done and returned to the ZI. Perhaps these are the ones this writer admires the most.

Although the tigers are usually the ones who ran up the big scores of air victories, it does not tell the whole story. There are undoubtedly many genuine would-be tigers, who never had the opportunity. One does not shoot down enemy aircraft unless they are there to be shot down. In the European war, there were periods when the Luftwaffe was lying low and very difficult to find, while it recovered from devastating losses, such as the spring and summer of 1944. Good friend Harvey Mace, who had "only" three victories (two confirmed) likes to say that he shot down all he saw.

Then there are the wingmen. It was not their primary job to shoot down the enemy, although many did. Their responsibility was to protect their element leader's tail. Many of them later became element and flight leaders.

The reader will encounter William "OBee" O'Brien again and again in this tale. He was an original member of the 363rd squadron, a captain, flight leader and ace, and he provides the final word in our discussion of fighter pilots:

"As discussed above, there is a place for "tiger thinking", but we have hundreds of graves showing the fact that would-be tigers die, and many rest in unmarked graves.This stresses the importance of good judgment, which can be expressed in training. Some very good fighter pilots were killed by stupidity - their own, or someone else's. A perfect example being the death of Captain Lloyd Hubbard. (Note: Hubbard was a flight leader and considered one of the best pilots in his squadron. He was killed on 8 February, 1944, while flying with the 354th Group. They flew across a German airfield at low level and Hubbard was hit by intense flak. It was his first combat mission.)

"We all have pride and fears but we have an overriding commitment not to disgrace ourselves or fail to perform our duty. Loyalty is a ladder that goes both up and down. It is difficult to write about fighter pilots as individuals, but remember they are just part of the team, the co-captains of which the ground crews and their fellow pilots."

Looking back through the mists of time, the WWII fighter pilot does appear as a glamorous figure - jousting in the vast cold blue with an evil enemy. There was indeed an element of this as they went to war in their colorful machines. However, it was a very dangerous business, the enemy was skilled, well equipped and usually determined. The air war in Europe was a brutal deadly affair. The 8th Air Force alone lost almost 30,000 dead, mostly bomber crews. This was about half of the total USAAF deaths in WWII. RAF casualties were equally horrendous.

An official total of fighter pilot deaths has not been found, but there are over 900 fighter pilots of the 8th and 9th Air Forces buried in U.S. cemeteries in Europe, or on the Walls of the Missing. This number is by no means all of the fighter casualties, large numbers of U.S. dead were returned to their families after the war.

Roger Freeman, the eminent historian, in his book THE FIGHT FOR THE SKY, (Arms and Armour Press, 1998) says 3,950 U.S. fighter pilots were killed in the European Theater of Operations (ETO) and almost 2,000 in the Mediterranean Theater. RAF fighter pilot deaths are put at 3,600
No total casualties have been found for the Luftwaffe, but they must have been even more appalling.

While admiring the exciting machines and the extraordinary men who flew them, we should never forget the grim reality of the air war in Europe and of WWII in general. These men were only a small part of the millions who kept Europe from descending into another dark age under Adolf Hitler.

Finally, a summary of the facts and figures and group accomplishments is in order, although much of this will be covered in greater detail in the narrative.

The 357th was a late-comer in 8th Fighter Command. Of the eventual 15 groups, only three became operational after the 357th. Nevertheless, the Group soon overtook many of the older groups, partly because they were the first to have the capability (besides the two P-38 groups) to cover the bombers no matter how far afield they went. Therefore there was plenty of fighting available!

The number of aerial victories credited to each group varies by whatever source is used. The following figures for the top scoring four groups are compiled from USAF HISTORICAL STUDY NO. 85, titled USAF CREDITS FOR DESTRUCTION OF ENEMY AIRCRAFT, WWII, from the Office of Air Force History, 1978.

The 8th Air Force, alone among the numbered air forces, credited ground victories, possibly as a morale booster. Study 85, however, credits only air victories, there is no tally of ground victories.

Another high-scoring unit was the 9th Air Force's "Pioneer Mustang Group", the 354th. Figures vary on their total air victories, but Study 85 gives the figure 599.9.

GROUP	DATE OPERATIONAL	AIR VICTORIES	ACES
4th	2 October 1942	448.5	39
56th	13 April 1943	666	41
352nd	9 September 1943	579	28
357th	11 February 1944	595.5	42

(The 56th was the only group to retain P-47s until the end of the war. The 4th and 352nd converted to P-51s).

None of the other eleven groups were even close to these four. Besides being second only to the great Hub Zemke's 56th Group in air victories, the 357th distinguished itself in several other ways.

1. The most enemy aircraft destroyed in air combat in one day, 55.5 on 14 January 1945. As far as is known, no other U.S. fighter unit has come close to this, before or since.
2. More enemy jet aircraft (Me 262) destroyed in air combat than any other group, 18.5.
3. The fastest scoring fighter group during the last year of the war
4. Although in combat much less time, the 357th had 42 aces, more than any other group.

The data that made this book possible, and the author's previous books and articles, comes largely from the original 357th Group records on file at the Air Force Historical Archives at Maxwell AFB, Alabama, and some from the National Archives (when that was possible). These consist of the Mission reports, filed by the mission leader; the monthly statistical and operational reports; the pilot's individual encounter reports, filed whenever a pilot encountered-an enemy aircraft; the MACRs, (Missing aircrew reports), USAAF accident reports and British police reports on accidents.

Of at least equal importance to the official documents are the many stories, comments, incidents and hairy tales that the pilots have so freely provided the last 40 plus years. We have used as many as possible and it is these that hopefully add color, excitement and the personal touch to this tale of the 357th.

In addition to the narrative assistance, and vital to telling the story, are the hundreds of photographs that have been loaned and given to the historical files. Although the author took a few of the photos, the vast majority came from the generosity of the these men.

Some 25 years after WWII, a few veterans of THE YOXFORD BOYS began to drift together again, which soon snowballed into the 357th Fighter Group Association, ramrodded ever since by our beloved leaders, Joe and Ellen DeShay. Before they began to dwindle away, there were about 500 active members and the periodic reunions often brought 300 or more members and wives together. For the past 30 years, the Group Association has been one of the highlights of this writer's life. In the fall of the year 2001, the Group met one more time at Dayton and the Air Force Museum, and then turned out the lights and locked the hangar doors for the last time.

Many of us have been back to that island to visit the scenes of our youth, and the many friends we now have in Britain. Little remains of station F-373 as this is written. Short partial sections of runway and taxiway remain, and a few decaying gray green buildings are scattered among the trees, some used by the present land owner. A leisure caravan park occupies part of the old 363rd Squadron dispersal area. Included in the park complex is a fine club house with many photos and memorabilia of the 357th Fighter Group, and nearby is a fine granite memorial, flanked by the flags of the two countries, to all who served, and those who died there. This is the result of a small band of highly dedicated local people (and a few not so local!) who have gotten together as THE FRIENDS OF LEISTON AIRFIELD. Every spring the memorial is re-dedicated with appropriate ceremony, a military band, and when available, a P-51 flyby.

Lastly, my grateful thanks are due to a great many of the veterans of the 357th who provided photos and historical information over the years. There are far to many to list (without danger of missing a lot of them), so to all of them, I acknowledge their help. This would not have been done without them.

My grateful thanks to our own Colonel C.E. "Bud" Anderson for his valued assistance and encouragement on this project.

Also a special thanks to James E. Anderson, Bud Anderson's son, and proprietor of the marvelous 357th web site, www.cebudanderson.com, and the one who originally proposed that I write one "final, super" book on the 357th. As this is written, the 357th Fighter Group Association has "turned out the lights, and closed and locked the hangar doors". It is my hope that the men and women of that marvelous association will approve of what I have written here.

Merle C. Olmsted , 2004

A FEW WORDS ABOUT
THE MESSERSCHMITT Me 109

The reader will not find the designation Bf 109 or Bf 110 for these Messerschmitt fighters, in this book. The designation is not incorrect from a technical point of view. It was used in some Luftwaffe records, but the common term of the day "Me 109" and 110 was used in others. The Luftwaffe's own newspaper, DER ADLER, did not use Bf, but referred to these aircraft as Me 109 and Me 110, as they were called throughout the Luftwaffe.

Furthermore, to use the term Bf when writing about the USAAF or the RAF is a gross distortion of history. Hundreds of U.S. and British mission, combat and technical reports have been read over the years, and the Messerschmitt fighters are never referred to as anything but "Me".

To quote an Allied aircrew as saying he engaged a Bf 109 is a lie, he never said it, his words have been altered by someone. He invariably reported combat with an Me 109, or an Me 110.

Over the last 20 years or so, many publications, especially in Europe, have eagerly adopted the term Bf, but many prestigious organizations and authors have not. Mr Roger Freeman, one of the world's leading WWII aviation historians, agrees with this writer, and The American Fighter Aces and others still use Me 109 etc.

The Allies were well aware of the Bf designation, and we leave this subject with a final word from the British official publication AIRCRAFT RECOGNITION for March, 1944:

"In designating the Me 109 and 110, official German handbooks and documents use the contraction Bf (Bayerische Flugzeugwerke) and not "Me", but German recognition publications use "Me" and except in the handbooks and documents mentioned, the aircraft are known throughout the German Air Force by this contraction. (Me)."

Contents

The author, left, and his friend and partner, Crew Chief Ray Morrison with the P-39 at Hayward Army Air Field in the summer of 1943.

CHAPTER 1:
TO TRAIN A FIGHTER GROUP

Two of the "rookie" pilots of the 362nd Squadron with an AT-6. Leonard Carson and Joseph Broadhead (on wing) would both become aces, command the Squadron and survive the war.

"San Francisco by the Bay" - magic words that conjure up romantic visions to millions of people, most of whom have never been there. It is indeed a romantic, beautiful and fascinating city.

North across the Golden Gate Bridge, at the north end of San Francisco Bay lies San Pablo Bay, and on its western edge is Hamilton Air Force Base, long abandoned by the Air Force as this is written in the year 2000.

In the 1930s, Hamilton Field was one of the wonderful new Air Corps bases built as government purse strings loosened after a decade of congressional neglect of the armed forces. Hamilton, along with March, Randolph, Selfridge, Langley and others were either newly built or renovated with the great Art Deco architecture and state of the art quarters, hangars and shops.

During most of the 1930s, Hamilton was home to the 7th Bombardment Group with Martin B-10 bombers, but they had long ago departed to go to war by the time the 357th Fighter Group was activated at Hamilton in January 1943.

One of the most astounding aspects of World War II was the job the Roosevelt administration, the armed forces, and the American people did in response to the traumatic Pearl Harbor affair.

Without a doubt, this huge build-up was fraught with inefficiency, false starts, thousands of bad decisions, corruption, and just plain bad luck. The fact remains, however, that the country put millions of men in uniform,

The beautiful Art Deco buildings up on main base at the Air Corps lovely Hamilton Field were not for the "New Guys". The mud flats and tar paper shacks seen here was where the 357th Fighter Group came into being, on the 1st day of December, 1942

equipped them reasonably well, built hundreds of facilities to train them in thousands of specialties and then formed them into hundreds of different kinds of military and naval units. Almost all of American industry was involved and all performed miracles. Then there was the matter of logistics, getting the men and equipment to where they were needed - more miracles!

Only one year after Pearl Harbor, the 357th Fighter Group became part of this force, received the aircraft and equipment, and just ten months later, was rea-

sonably well trained and ready for combat. It was an accomplishment to be proud of.

For the 357th, it had all begun at Hamilton Field. This is where the men began to trickle in, in response to a Special Order from 4th Air Force, dated 1 December 1942, which directed that a new unit, the 357th, would be formed.

The pleasures of Hamilton's main base were not for the newcomers, however, who were shuttled off to the hastily-built tar paper shacks well off main base. Here the enlisted men began to report in, mostly from the 4th Air Force Replacement Center at nearby Hammer Field. There were no airplanes, of course, these would come later. The vital equipment at this point were pencils, typewriters and reams of standard army forms, and the administrative personnel to put it all together. A high point of the two month stay was the issue of sheep-lined leather jackets, pants and boots to the future maintenance types.

A group needs a commander, of course, and Lt. Col. Loring Stetson filled that slot until his departure for a combat command in Africa six months later. Joining also at this point were several senior officers who would remain with the Group for much of its existence. Major Donald Graham and Captain Irwin Dregne joined the team and both would one day command the Group. Of the three Squadron commanders, two were combat vets of the Pacific fighting, and two, Captains Varian K. White and Hubert Egenes would die in the service - White in an accident and Egenes in combat.

Conditions were primitive at Tonopah Army Air Field, part of the sprawling three million acre Tonopah Bombing and Gunnery Range. There were no hangars of any kind at that time (there were later). In this photo, 364th mechanics change the engine on #76 behind a make-shift wind break (left). Robert Krull, Crew Chief on #76 still recalls 55 years later, "it was a real dog".

Colonel Loring Stetson was the first Commander of the new Group. Well liked and respected by all of his officers, he was fired in July 1943 due to the large number of aircraft accidents. The man at left is unknown but believed to be the general officer who came over from 4th Air Force to do the firing.

With the men assigned to the three Squadrons, the 362nd, the 363rd and the 364th, and all the required paper work completed, it was time to get to work. It was now the end of February, 1943, and all personnel, except for a very few with POVs (privately owned vehicles), boarded a train which eventually deposited them approximately in the middle of the well known "nowhere". It had a name - Tonopah, a mining town midway in the 450 miles of sand

between the two major watering holes of Nevada, Reno and Las Vegas, both of which were little more than villages themselves in those days.

Among the massive construction projects in that busy year since Pearl Harbor, the army had built a 3,000,000 acre bombing and gunnery range some six miles east of town.

Preceding the 357th, the 354th Fighter Group, which was to become a very high scoring group in the 9th Air Force, had trained at Tonopah and one more group, the 363rd, would follow by which time it was apparent that Tonopah's 6,000 foot altitude was already about half of the P-39s limited useful altitude of 12,000 feet. From then on it became a B-24 training base. Tonopah Army Air Field long ago faded into history but the Air Force still controls much of the land in Nevada as part of its vast complex of test ranges. Tonopah, now a bit larger, is still going strong as a way station between the two major metropolises of Nevada.

In 1943 though, Tonopah AAFs job was to make some semblance of a fighter group out of a hodge podge of administrative and technical men, fresh out of Army Tech Schools, and some 75 pilots most of whom had been wearing their silver wings only a few weeks.

Except for one or two old line Air Corps NCOs, the enlisted men of many trades learned by doing. Training of the pilots fell mostly to four Flight Leaders in each Group. Assigned as 2nd Lieutenants, many from the 328th Fighter Group at Hamilton soon pinned on the silver bars of a 1st Lt. to go with their Flight Leader status. None of these men were really high time pilots but at least had been flying the

A 362nd Squadron dispersal point. All aircraft are P-39Ds. #74 at left has the long-barreled 20 mm cannon fitted to the D-1s. Refueling was done from the 50 gallon drums which had a hand pump on top.

Three P-39s of the 364th Squadron. Oddly enough, and very unusual, at least two of these do not have any tail numbers, the identifying feature of all Air Force airplanes.

Although it was "only training", the pace was hectic with much night work. Here the black desert night covers all except the flood-lighted P-39 and its lone mechanic. It should be emphasized that other than being recent graduates of Air Force mechanics schools, almost none of these men had ever worked on a "real live airplane" before Tonopah. It was a scary business!

A very clean, probably freshly-painted P-39D-1, bearing the original insignia of the 363rd Squadron. The 20 mm cannon has been removed in this photo.

P-39 for a few months and were probably viewed as crusty veterans by the new fledglings.

Flight Leaders in the 362nd were (all 1st Lts.) Joseph E. Broadhead, Maurice F. Baker, Arthur M. Lingo, Davis T. Perron and Calvert L. Williams.

In the 363rd, they were (all 1st Lts.), Clarence E. Anderson, Paul K. DeVries, Lloyd M. Hubbard, William R. O'Brien and Edwin W. Hiro. 1st Lt. John A. Storch, and 2nd Lts. George D. Currie, John L. Mediros, Glendon V. Davis, and Jack R. Warren took over Flight Leader positions in the 364th.

Squadron Commanders were Captains Hubert I. Egenes (362nd), Stuart R. Lauler (363rd), and Thomas L. Hayes Jr, (364th) who replaced Captain Varian White after his death.

In order to train a fighter group, fighters are needed and these were to be Bell P-39s, a fighter with serious problems but an admirable machine for training. Aesthetically, Bell's little fighter named AIRACOBRA, was a real triumph. In appearance it was thoroughly modern - sleek, mean and lean, with a big cannon and sundry other guns all sitting on a neat tricycle landing gear. True, it was a bit odd with the 12 cylinder Allison engine installed mid ship but this was said to have been the result of Bell's engineer's desire to mount the 37 mm cannon in the most effective way.

Sadly enough, the AIRACOBRA never lived up to its aesthetic attributes for several complicated reasons. The old aviation saying that "If it looks right, it is right", was once again proven wrong. Come to think of it, the big

Oldsmobile built cannon never lived up to its hopes either. The full story of the P-39's checkered career is not pertinent here, but some comments are, if for no other reason than the fact that eleven pilots died in the AIRACO-BRA. (Two others and one Flight Surgeon died in AT-6s). (See page 272 for a full listing of 357th fatal training casualties).

> *"Don't give me a P-39*
> *With an engine that's mounted behind*
> *It'll tumble and roll*
> *And dig a big hole*
> *Don't give me a P-39"*

This little ditty, one of several variations circulating in the AAF gives a good indication of the prevailing opinion. This was the infamous "P-39 Tumble", described as a rolling around the wing axis, tail over nose, usually ending in an inverted spin from which many pilots were unable to recover.

When the stories began to surface from the first P-39 group, the 31st, the Army asked Bell to investigate. Bell and the Army conducted extensive testing but finally reported they could not make the airplane tumble.

Nevertheless there was ample evidence of the phenomenon, as we shall see.

Also based at Tonopah in 1943 was the 444th Fighter Training Squadron whose mission is was to tran-

Most everyone who was there remembers this spectacular crash. With his engine on fire, Lt. Norman Baxter elected to land instead of bailing out. The P-39 touched down, trailing flames, at an excessive speed and went off the end of the runway where the nose wheel collapsed. Lt. Baxter jumped out and ran as the tail melted off. This was the end of P-39D-2, S/N 41-38241.

sition pilots into the P-39. Several, but by no means all, 357th pilots graduated from their school. Only one of their training manuals survives. This manual was brutally frank and we offer a few quotes from it:

"Do not attempt to impress your earthbound brothers with steep turns and maximum rates of climb close to the ground. Keep a good margin of speed to save you in case of engine failure. This applies to all aircraft, of course, but is particularly true with the P-39's high wing-loading. Rough handling of the controls will result in a stall at any altitude, at any speed, in any attitude of flight in the P-39, particularly in a turn or violent maneuvers."

The manual ends with the usual admonition about buzzing: "Acrobatics at low altitude, low flying and violation of flying regulations have cost many lives, property damage and have seriously retarded the training program. Save your cockiness for combat!"

Good advice but widely ignored by young exuberant pilots! Tom Beemer recalled: "The manual was the first step in putting my new silver wings to work - learning to fly the P-39. Reading it in recent years brings sever-

al reactions: One is the '39 was a dangerous little bird. Stall and spin characteristics and prop malfunctions made for scary reading also. Thinking back though, the ship was more forgiving than reported here. My second day at Hayward, Joe Broadhead, 362nd Operations officer, took me up to check me out. Suddenly he turned to get on my tail. We ended up nearly stalling in a left hand circle. That introduction to pressing the limits was mild compared to what we did while Broadhead and Egenes (362nd Commander) were tending to their paperwork. Maybe we were lucky, maybe the P-39 wasn't as bad as reported. Maybe both."

Bud Anderson, 363rd Sqdn. Flight Leader: "Tonopah, with its sprawling gunnery range was where we polished our shooting and bombing skills. Because the place was so remote, we flew where we wanted, often right on the deck, in between the cacti, hugging the sandy gray hills. It was good to know how. Someday, in combat, knowing how to hug the hills could be everything."

In his book YEAGER, Chuck tells of many hair-raising escapades in the P-39 and most of the other sur-

This P-39N at Hayward Army Air Field shows clearly that the Allison was not a clean running engine as indicated by the heavy exhaust staining. This was normally washed off after a flight with gasoline.

Winter in the desert. A light dusting of wind-driven snow has stuck to the sides of the this P-39D. The name of the leather-clad 362nd mechanic is long forgotten.

vivors of those times relate similar tales. It should be remembered that almost all of the pilots were "just kids", not long out of their teen years. Uncle Sam had given them a fast expensive airplane to play with and play with it they did!

All of this wild flying was against all sorts of Air Corps regulations but on the other hand it built their confidence in the airplane and in themselves and went a long way toward making them competent fighter pilots.

Chuck Yeager in his book YEAGER: "The airplane performed beautifully at low altitudes, but was under powered high up and if you stalled it, you might end up boring a deep hole because it spun like a top going down. Once you had the feel of the ship and understood it, the '39 was a fun airplane to fly. Another problem was maintenance. We flew so much, yet there were very few old hands among the ground crew. There was a lot of trial and error, both on the flight line and in the sky."

The author was a flight line mechanic in the 362nd Squadron. The only training had been at the Air Force mechanics school at Sheppard AFB which concentrated on basic, of course. In addition there had been a short course on the P-38 at the Lockheed factory school at Burbank, California. Except for one or two old time Air Corps NCO in each squadron, everyone had similar backgrounds, but at Tonopah the maintenance types were confronted by the real world - a strange fighter no one had seen before, no experience and very limited help from Tech Orders - if we even had any manuals.

Two incidents are all that are remembered from those days:

The 24 spark plugs (2 per cylinder) on the Allison V-1710 engine were fired by a magneto mounted on top of the engine accessory case, routed to the plugs by two ignition distributors, one mounted on the rear of each cylinder bank. It had been determined that one of these distributor rotors was cracked causing the engine to misfire. A new one had been obtained and installed, but the engine still refused to run properly. Finally one brilliant soul checked the part number on the rotor against the engine parts manual and it was discovered that Technical Supply had provided a distributor rotor for a left turning P-38 engine. With the proper rotor installed, the engine ran fine, but a great deal of time and effort had been expended on what should have been a simple problem.

The P-39 was a very small airplane and with the engine, guns and pilot filling up the fuselage, all fuel had to be carried in the very small wings. Total capacity on P-39s varied by the model, but the D models carried about 90 gallons in five self-sealing tanks in each wing. Five cells meant many interconnect lines that had to be fuel tight. All work on the cells was done through very small openings in the wing surface. The memory of working 24 hours straight on those dreadful cells, with time out only for meals remains vivid. All mechanical work was done outside - there were no hangars at Tonopah at that time.

Before closing our tale of the Tonopah days, we must talk about the town itself. Although Elko and Mina were other tiny towns, Tonopah was the only one of any size for off-duty soldier shenanigans and its nightlife was part of the training saga. The bar at the Mizpah Hotel, opened in 1907, was a popular gathering spot but the Tonopah Club was the major drinking and gambling establishment. It was the center of social life for soldiers and the rougher element of Tonopah (which was most of them).

A superb study of a well-used P-39L, LITTLE TONI, the white tail, nose and wing tips indicating a 362nd Sqdn. aircraft. There is considerable oil and exhaust staining and the recently applied red border to the national insignia has obviously been done hastily, with a large brush!

Then there was Taxine's house for those seeking female company. (Yeager mentions Taxine's in his book YEAGER). When Taxine died in the mid-1950s she was eulogized in the local paper in an article entitled THE END OF AN ERA. The Mizpah Hotel, in the year 2000 is still in business, but the Tonopah Club burned many years ago and town is probably more respectable now as it caters to tourists enroute to Vegas or Reno.

In his book TO FLY AND FIGHT, Clarence Anderson sums up the Tonopah experience: "Here, the pilots of the 357th having learned to fly, more or less, were taught to fight." The ground crews also had learned their jobs - "more or less".

In concluding the Nevada saga, mention should be made of the four men who died in accidents while there. Despite the P-39's well-deserved reputation for vicious stall characteristics, only one of the four may have been as a result of this and the accident report makes no mention of it. The safety record here was probably about average for the war years, but it soon would get much worse.

After about three months in the Nevada desert, the entire group moved on 2 June 1943, to various bases in north central California - back to the land of milk and honey! By that time the Army had established dozens of small training bases throughout the state. The 362nd went to Hayward AAF, the 363rd, 364th and headquarters to Santa Rosa AAF where they stayed only about six weeks. The 364th then moved to Marysville and the 363rd to Oroville. No reason has ever been found for these moves, but they undoubtedly provided good experience in unit movements.

Here the training proceeded much as in Nevada although the Group was getting newer P-39s, L and N models and finally P-39Qs.

Bud Anderson in his book TO FLY AND FIGHT: "We flew as much as we could and every day there were mock dogfights. We flew at night, we flew in formation, and we shot the hell out of ground and aerial targets. We were honed and craving excitement. Almost anything went. Oklahoman Joe Pierce, a soon-to-be ace in my flight, buzzed the Oroville runway so low that the prop actually chewed up the cement. He gathered it together somehow and stayed airborne. The stunt caused some frowns, but Joe was one of the tigers, it took more than a frown to deflate Joe Pierce. (Pierce was killed in action on 21 May 1944).

The accident rate increased dramatically after the move to California. During June and July, seven pilots died, three of them in a four day period. In addition there

After the Group transferred to California bases, many aircraft (but not all) were painted in the newly assigned Squadron colors. The nose band and tail section of this 362nd Squadron P-39Q-1 are white. The newly called-for red border on the national insignia has been crudely painted with a brush.

This P-39Q-10 with the new 363rd Squadron skull insignia bears the name OLD CROW in small letters just below the number 152. Flight Leader "Bud" Anderson's later P-51s with the same name would become much more famous. The nose band is in the Squadron color red, but not the tail section.

was a long list of bailouts, gear up landings, hitting trees, and other assorted mishaps. During September, two more men died. The appalling accident rate is thought to have precipitated the transfer of Colonel Stetson, on the old military theory that the commander is always responsible. Stetson went to the Mediterranean where he took over a P-40 group. Colonel Edwin Chickering took command of the Group. In mid-October, he collided during a gunnery pattern, with Lt. Currie who landed safely while the Colonel bailed out.

Pilot survivors today are still unhappy with Chickering as they say his solution to the accident rate was to do most flying straight and level with no shenanigans. This might be safer but probably is no way to make a fighter pilot.

Upon arrival in Europe, Colonel Chickering went to the 9th Air Force and eventually took command of the 367th Fighter Group.

We have already discussed the P-39s nasty habits, but now that the Group was in California the infamous tumble began to take its toll of unwary pilots.

Of the eleven men killed in P-39s, one was observed to perform the classic "tumble", tail over nose, a snap roll and into an inverted spin from which there was no recovery. Three others were the result of stalls, snap rolls and gyrations resembling the tumble.

Despite the fatal accidents, bailouts, belly land-

Lt. Col. Edwin Chickering took over from Stetson in July and is seen here on the left with two men who would play major parts in the story of the 357th, Donald Graham and Irwin Dregne, both of whom would command the Group within the next year.

ings and many minor incidents, a great deal of flying was done that summer of 1943. Most of the pilots had built up a very respectable 300 to 400 hours in Bell's little rasper and were well prepared to go on to a more capable fighter. To close out the P-39 saga, we will present just two of the many opinions on the aircraft.

The date is 4 August 1943, two 364th pilots, Lt. Darwin Carroll leading with Glenn Hubbard on his wing, came upon a formation of eight 363rd Squadron P-39s led by Eddie Simpson. At Hubbard's urging, Carroll led a bounce on the "enemy" P-39s, diving under them and pulling up in front of them. Unfortunately, Hubbard's judgment did not quite match his exuberance and he pulled up too soon, Simpson's propeller removing much of his fin and rudder. Both P-39s landed safely with Hubbard's yellow-tailed Cobra as seen here.

Seven pilots of the 362nd Squadron at Hayward in the summer of 1943. They are left to right: Konstantin Vogel, Elmer Rydberg, Cal Williams, Fletcher Adams, Robert Wallen, Al Lichter and James Van Dyne. Only Willams, Wallen and Lichter would survive the war, the latter as a POW.

Sgt. Robert Grupposo poses with #181 in front of the hangar at Marysville. Grupposo would become senior NCO, and was one of the many who "kept 'em flying" until the final victory. The nose band is in the Squadron color yellow and the number 181 is edged with the same color.

Flight Leader William "OBee" O'Brien: "I was never completely relaxed while flying the airplane, as I considered it aerodynamically unstable, even when you knew where the center of gravity was located (or at least you thought you knew).

"I contended the C.G. (center of gravity) on a P-39 moved around more than a party girl at a company picnic. With a full load of gas it flew differently than it did an hour later when the fuel burned off. The same was true when flying gunnery, except it got worse as we expended both fuel and ammunition, and the wandering C.G. was more noticeable. You could never trim the beast to fly hands off. There were those who say the P-39 won't tumble, but I've seen this 'changing ends' occur.

"As a trainer for fighter pilots, I would rate the P-39 as excellent. The reason being that it was so unforgiving. If you could handle this plane properly, it then became obvious that the pilot possessed a satisfactory degree of competency. There was nothing to compare with the precision of a four-plane flight's tactical approach, coming in at 50 feet elevation, 250 MPH indicated, in echelon to the leader's right and when he crossed the end of the runway, seeing the P-39s racked into a climbing chandelle without power, pulling streamers from the wing tips each plane following and spaced so all four were rolling on the runway at the same time. That was fun and flying!"

Harvey Mace, who ended his combat tour as a flight leader in the 362nd; "The P-39 was very unforgiving of careless handling. Usually it was an easy airplane to fly, even the planned stalls were quite normal but an accelerated stall or unusual attitude could result in some wild unplanned maneuvers. I've tumbled the airplane twice and have watched others tumble at least five times.

"I loved firing the P-39's 37 mm cannon. It was supposed to be fully automatic but invariably it jammed after two or three rounds. In spite of that I once destroyed a ground target with two rounds. The cannon was murder on ground targets, a great morale booster. Trying to hit an aerial target was a different matter entirely. To the best of my knowledge, no one was able to hit it with the cannon."

The big Oldsmobile cannon gave the armorers fits. Despite their best efforts they could never get it to fire more than two or three rounds.

This pile of debris had been a P-39N, s/n 42-8823 prior to the morning of 28 June 1943. Lt. Bill Overstreet was the fortunate survivor when the aircraft stalled, snapped rolled, tumbled tail over nose and into an inverted spin from which he could not recover. With difficulty he got clear, his chute depositing him among the wreckage. Not many pilots survived an out-of-control tumbling P-39.

The pilot of GOOSENECK was Lt. William Gambill. The man at the propeller is thought to be Sgt. James Walker, Crew Chief. The nose wheel and nose band are both red. "Stubby" Gambill was one of the 92 men of the 357th who died in the line of duty during WWII.

Sergeants Red Loos (L) and John Timpo, Flight Chiefs in the 362nd Squadron at Hayward. The white tailed P-39 is a Q model as can be seen by the under-wing .50 caliber gun. Only the Q models had these.

This P-39Q, 42-20750 was the first of three BILLIE'S BITCH aircraft. The other two were a P-51B and P-51D that 363rd flight leader William OBee O'Brien flew during his lengthy career with the 357th. O'Brien had a low opinion of the Bell P-39, but thought its nasty characteristics made it a good fighter trainer.

A beautiful shot of P-39Q, 42-20747 about to touch down at Hayward. It was taken by 362nd Squadron Adjutant, Lt. Lem Henslee.

The 364th hangar at Marysville, California. Although Marysville airport is in the same place, this hangar was demolished many years ago.

Flight Leader 1st Lt. C.E. Anderson with his OLD CROW is illustrating the final version of the 363rd Squadron skull insignia.

Right: Lt. William Overstreet and his beautiful 1938 Buick convertible. Photo taken at Oroville Army Airfield, summer 1943.

363rd pilot, William Overstreet who went on to fly an extended combat tour with the Squadron, has good reason to remember the 28th of June, 1943. He is the only one to provide us with a first-hand account of an escape from an out-of-control, spinning P-39. Along with three other pilots (He thinks they were Lloyd Hubbard, Hershel Pascoe and Charles Peters), he took off to engage in general rat racing and combat in the vicinity of the airfield at Santa Rosa:

"At some point in the rat race, I lost control of the airplane, possibility due to an over-control. The P-39 snap rolled to the left and then tumbled tail over nose, ending up in an inverted spin. At that moment it was obviously time to part company with the airplane. I pulled the release handle for the doors but they did not separate, possibly due to air pressure on the doors. By getting my shoulder against one door and knees against the other, I was able to push enough to get the door off. I got out immediately and pulled the rip cord. When the chute opened, it slowed my fall at the same instant my feet hit the ground. I landed standing up, didn't even bend my knees. I landed amidst the wreckage of the P-39, right beside one of the prop blades and among the 37 mm ammunition. Since the chute opened below the trees the rest of the flight went back to base and reported my demise."

The first week of October brought the California sojourn to an end when all three squadrons headed east to Idaho (362nd), Casper, Wyoming (363rd) and Ainsworth, Nebraska (364th). These final stations provided more flying and some familiarization with 2nd Air Force B-24s, but it lasted only a month. There was however, some excitement. Besides the Chickering/Currie collision, Flight Officer Chuck Yeager bellied in one P-39 and bailed out of another one which was on fire. Both incidents occurred within three days.

The Final Tactical Inspection of the Group in late October concluded "Combat fitness of training, personnel and equipment is considered very satisfactory and the unit is recommended for overseas movement on its readiness date".

The taxpayers had spent a great deal of money making the 357th into a fighting unit. The war in Europe and the hard-pressed bomber crews were waiting and it was payback time.

Leaving the P-39s on the ramps, for whom we knew not, all personnel and large amounts of equipment and supplies entrained for the east coast Ports of Embarkation. Upon arrival at Camp Shanks, everyone at least looked like a soldier, having been issued steel helmets, gas masks and M-1 carbines and laden with barracks bags containing all worldly possessions.

On the 23rd of November there was considerable surprise to find that the Group would be traveling on the largest liner in the world, the RMS (Royal Mail Ship) Queen Elizabeth. Once a luxury ship for 1,000 wealthy travelers, she was outfitted to carry an amazing 15,000 troops. Although armed with many light automatic weapons, she relied on her speed to survive and completed many wartime crossings of the dangerous Atlantic.

The Queen put out to sea at about 1600 hours on 23 November and glided into the Firth of Clyde in Scotland on the 29th. One would think that such an adventure for a mid-western boy would have left vivid memories, but they are all gone. There was a British military band welcoming the new arrivals.

Headquarters and the 362nd were first to board the soon-to-be familiar compartmented trains and with the other squadrons following, rolled away into a blackened-out land. The 357th had arrived to play its part in history.

"SO THAT'S ENGLAND! . . . . I DON'T LIKE IT!"
—Pvt. Tom Flannery

*This humorous cartoon from the Army newspaper YANK,
illustrates the first view of England of one skeptical soldier.*

REMEMBER? A SHIPFUL OF MEMORIES FOR THOUSANDS OF GIs. ONE OF THE FEW PICTURES MADE OF THE QUEEN ELIZABETH SINCE HER CONVERSION INTO A TROOP CARRIER, IT SHOWS THE LARGEST VESSEL AFLOAT TIED UP IN BOSTON FOR REFITTING.

*This photo of the QUEEN ELIZABETH is from the Army week-
ly newspaper YANK. This ship and its sister, QUEEN MARY
carried an astounding 15,000 troops per voyage and the 357th
was part of this mass of soldiers late in 1943. Both ships served
throughout the war carrying troops without a loss.*

Off He'll Go Into the Wild Blue Yonder

'daho's First Pursuits Train Here

*This clipping from a Pocatello, Idaho
newspaper features Lt. Alvin Pyeatt during
the very short time the 362nd Squadron
was at Pocatello. Al Pyeatt was killed in
action early in the combat period.*

TOMMY HAYES ON ORIGINS AND THE TRAINING DAYS

"In-the fall of 1942 a decision was made in Washington, which directed that all AAF pilots who had fought the Japanese would be brought home and assigned to units where experience was needed. The 357th, then forming, picked up Hubert Egenes and Varian White both fighter pilots from the South Pacific. This was a smart move because through 1942, it was to a degree, the 'blind leading the blind' in the U.S. training program.

"Egenes and I were with the 17th Provisional Pursuit Group in Java. At that time Varian K. White was escaping by sea from the Philippines. On February 20th, 1942, I was shot down over Bali and crash landed, but was still in the hospital when they started to evacuate non-flying pilots on February the 26th. Back on flying status, I was assigned to the 35th Fighter Group in New Guinea in early spring of '42 where we flew P-39s on ground support missions. In the fall of 1942, I returned to the States and was with the 328th Fighter group at San Francisco Airport.

"Our mission was to give a minimum of combat training to new pilots just out of flight training. It amounted to 20 hours in the P-39. But first, it was necessary to learn to fly the P-39 without 'Augering in'. The '39 was really a most unforgiving airplane, if the pilot made a mistake. It was a good program - better to lose a pilot and aircraft in the U.S. than 10,000 miles away.

"On May 21st, I'm on duty when I get a call from Operations that a Colonel Stetson will be landing shortly and would like me to meet him on the ramp. Col. Stetson, who was he? What had I done, or not done? Well, I'm on the ramp as he parks his P-39. He introduces himself and informs me he has just lost a Squadron Commander who crashed in his P-39 and said he was going to ask for me as a replacement. He then added, 'Unless you have a good reason otherwise, I suggest you start packing. See you in Tonopah'. Well, it was Captain Varian White's bad luck and my good luck.

At Tonopah, Nevada, the 357th was about to complete its first phase checking out new pilots to fly the P-39, fly formation, fire the guns etc. I inherited a good Squadron, the 364th, and no changes were necessary here. In less then two weeks, the three Squadrons would move to new bases in California. This was part of the plan, to be mobile and able to move within 48 hours notice. We made the move on 2 June and our mission here was to become a fighter group, all for one, etc.

"At Santa Rosa, our base was a new field well camouflaged and from the air no runways, hangars, or taxiways could be seen, but they were all there! A couple of times friends flew in to visit me, but had to go back to Hamilton for details on how to find it.

"The Squadron operations officers would get together and lay out the missions - one VS another, one VS two etc. These were basically flying exercises.

"The P-39 was the only fighter I flew which had bad, vicious handling characteristics and I feel it was a poor design. It stalled easily and took a long time to recover, add the panic of a new pilot and there were a lot of crashes. On one such crash, I thought the pilot had survived. The Flight Surgeon and I arrived at the site, the P-39 was lying flat on the ground with no sign of lateral movement or slide. The pilot was sitting head down in the cockpit, dead. It had come straight down, hitting the ground in a flat attitude.

"The training was intense, maybe some of the pilots should have been held over, maybe the pace was too fast. One thing for sure, most of the accidents were relatively new pilots. If we had had P-51s instead of P-39s there would have been far fewer accidents. Too bad we didn't get the P-51 earlier."

"Thanks go to the British for their marvelous engine and to North American Aviation for their airplane!"

Training Days

Color photos of the training days and the Bell P-39s are very scarce. We are fortunate to be able to present these excellent quality photos from 53-year-old color slides. They are provided by Richard Gambill whose father was 2nd Lt. William "Stubby" Gambill, who photographed the men and planes while the 363rd Squadron was at Santa Rosa and Oroville, summer of 1943. William Gambill was killed in action in March, 1944.

A handsome and colorful P-39N at Oroville where the Squadron moved to from Santa Rosa. During this period colors assigned to the Squadrons were white for the 362nd, red for the 363rd and yellow for the 364th. We do not know why this and several others sported the 362nd white tail and the red noseband of the 363rd. Possibly they had been transferred from the 362nd. In small white letters under the number 134 is the name CORN HUSKER. The national insignia has the proper red outline of the period.

A beautiful photo of P-39N-5, s/n 42-19896, flying near the great California landmark, Mount Shasta. This machine also carries the colors of both the 362nd and the 363rd, but bears the 363rd insignia on the door.

Another P-39N serial number unknown. Many P-39s bore names, but usually in small white stenciled letters, such as FERTILE GERTIE here. The Major and Sergeant are both unidentified.

This P-39 has left the paved surface and appears to be mired in the mud and may have collided with the road equipment. A large crowd contemplates the problem of getting it back on the hard surface.

This P-39, 42-20740 is a Q model but without the underwing gun packs which are probably in the armament shop. At right is an empty engine cradle and crate indicating a new engine has been installed and is being run up. The mechanic in the cockpit seems pleased with the results.

This marvelous photo from the Harvey Mace collection (Mace on right) shows the poor condition of the OD paint on what is a relatively new P-51B, when this photo of SWEET HELEN (43-6923) was taken in February or early March, 1944. Lt. Konstantin Vogel (Left) was KIA on 18 March 1944.

A fine color view of Mace with an RAF 486 Squadron Hawker Typhoon and an air-speed Oxford in the background. These were visitors to Raydon Wood airfield in January 1944. Mace is wearing a B-3 sheeplined flying jacket, which was rarely worn by fighter pilots while flying due to its excessive bulk.

CHAPTER 2:
RAYDON AIRFIELD AND THE MUSTANG ERA

The date of this mixed formation flight is unknown but possibly before becoming operational. Lt. Col. Graham is leading in B6-W which shows the damaged paint due to tape removal. The aircraft already has a Malcolm Hood, probably the first one in the Group. The 3rd P-51 in line is a 364th Squadron machine, C5-T, the first of Peterson's HURRY HOME HONEYs. Note that Graham's coolant radiator shutter is open while the others are closed.

After a night train ride from Scotland, the Group got its first look at its new home, Raydon Airfield, some ten miles southwest of the city of Ipswich. In the gray dismal dawn of a winter day, it was not an inspiring sight. The base was new, the 357th being the first occupants and where there is construction there is mud, especially in a wet English winter. As the Group prepared to settle in, it was the last part of 1943.

It was nearing the end of the fourth year of war for the British Commonwealth, most of Europe and the German Third *Reich* which was tottering on the brink of ruin. These years of war had made a deep impression on the people and the land of the British Isles. There was an overall sense of dreariness about everything. England is by nature a country of great beauty, even in what can be a miserable winter and even though the beauty is there in the countryside, it is often obscured by fog and cold rain, and sometimes snow.

It is true that the dark days of 1940 were over but the aftermath of those days was still highly visible in the cities. It was not long before the men of the 357th were allowed evening passes to visit the nearby towns and it was there that the sense of dreariness was most evident. Like most everything else, clothing was in short supply and the drabness of dress became immediately apparent. Many of the younger girls, of whom the young GIs were most interested, managed to present an attractive appearance. There was an overall sense of weariness about the people.

Food and fuel and most of the luxuries of life were scarce, plus the casualty lists of the British forces were still depressingly long. However there was no longer much likelihood of defeat in the long run. Among the changes which had come to the island was the presence of

Lt. Col Edwin Chickering, Commander since July, 1943, brought the Group to England. He may have flown a mission with the 354th in January or February, but was soon replaced by Colonel Henry Spicer who had been Executive Officer with the 66th Ftr. Wing. He took over on 17 February and is seen here with his crew SSgt. Currie and Corporal Hamilton.

the United States Army Air Forces, the 8th, and in increasing numbers, the tactical 9th Air Force. These Air Forces were becoming the dominate factor in the eastern counties, for better or worse. Near its peak strength, the Eighth sprawled across East Anglia in a vast complex of airfields, with over 70 major installations and many smaller ones, stretching north from London almost 100 miles to The Wash.

"SIX BIG AIRFIELDS OPENED IN DAY AS U.S. STARTS THIRD YEAR OF WAR." So ran the headline of a front page story in THE STARS AND STRIPES, the daily newspaper for American Forces in Britain. The story went on to say the bases had been built at a cost of 40 million dollars by the U.S. Army Corps of Engineers. One of these was station 157, which was Raydon. The date was the 7th of December and the 357th had been in residence for about a week. Although most of the paving had been laid,

runways, taxi ways, roads etc were complete, the wet weather and construction created a sea of mud. Any vehicle, truck or airplane off the paved surface was probably stuck. There were, however, no airplanes. There were two large metal RAF hangars and dozens of drab half cylinder shaped structures huddled in groups and scattered at random in the drizzle. The Nissen hut was to be the universal home for thousands of American troops in the British Isles. They were cramped, and always cold, but were a lot better than many soldiers had in the global war.

On the day the six bases were dedicated, orders were issued from the U.S. Army Forces, United Kingdom, assigning the 357th to the 9th Air Force then undergoing buildup as the primary support force for the coming invasion of the continent.

Although everything was in short supply, there was little time to be lost. A training schedule was set up and a few officers and EM departed for various schools. During the week of 12-18 December, the first airplane arrived. To an eager fighter outfit, it was a big letdown - a lowly Piper L-4B, a militarized Cub! Its purpose is obscure but was probably meant to be a courier vehicle.

On the 19th the real thing arrived and the Mustang era had begun. A single P-51B! It was an immediate object of great interest, as most had never seen one. It was not attractive in its shoddy Olive Drab and gray paint and it was not new, but a used RAF Mustang III, with its roundels still visible under the OD. It was the first of many that the Group would take to war but its serial number is unknown.

Even though the Group had come overseas with a full complement of pilots there was an influx of new ones, and undoubtedly others departed for various reasons. The continual coming and going with no surviving documentation is the reason there is no complete roster of people who served with the Group.

By the time the 357th arrived in Britain, the German air threat had receded to a low level but it was at Raydon that the first sound of gunfire in anger was heard. The never-to-be-forgotten howl of air raid sirens had brought a group outside to stare into the night sky. Nothing was to be seen but the group was rewarded by the sound of automatic weapon fire in the night, accompanied by the drone of engines. It was assumed that an RAF night fighter had fired at an intruder - and missed, as there were no flames in the sky.

Records from this period are very sparse, but they do show by the last week of the month, there were 15 P-51s on hand, presumably five for each squadron. The L-4 disappears from the records, replaced by twin-engined RAF Airspeed Oxford. 205 hours of training were flown, as a few pilots began to build time in the new machines.

A wet day at Raydon Wood airfield. As the pilots began to transition into the P-51 it was felt prudent, because of the pilot's inability to see over the long nose, to have a ground crewman ride the wing and provide another pair of eyes. As pilots became adept at "S-ing", the crewman on wing idea was abandoned.

Few photos have surfaced from the short period at Raydon Wood. This one of G4-B, 43-12151 is one of the first photos taken by the author with his $8 Kodak Jiffy camera. The man on the ground is Lt. Merlin Kehrer, who is thought to have been a transfer from the RAF. He was shot down on 25 February and became a POW.

The 357th was still at Raydon when this photo was taken at Leiston Airfield. The 358th Fighter Group was in residence and in a sea of mud. The famous brick house/photo lab is prominent in center and the big hangar would soon be occupied by the 362nd Squadron. The P-47 42-74730 survived until 7 October 1944 when it was lost in action.

Lt. Konstantin Vogel had trouble mastering the P-51 and seen here is one of several of his landing accidents January 1944. Apparently the brakes were set and when he landed the aircraft nosed over violently, tearing the prop off. Lt. Gilbreth, 362nd engineering officer rides the Cletrac crane in the one photo. Konnie Vogel finally got the hang of it, but was killed in action on 18 March 1944.

There was a heavy schedule of ground school for the pilots who had much to learn about weather flying, and standard communication practices. The author recalls being shown an indoctrination film on the 56th Fighter Group, called RAMROD TO EMDEN. Fifty years later, the man who wrote, directed and flew that mission, Colonel Hub Zemke lived only a few miles from the writer and was a good friend until his death.

Raydon Wood, like all other U.S. bases had an Officers Club, an NCO club and the Red Cross-run AERO CLUB where everyone was welcome. These clubs provided a place to get coffee and doughnuts, to read and write letters in a pleasant atmosphere. Adding to the attraction was the fact that an American girl was usually the manager, assisted by several other young ladies both American and British.

The one overpowering memory of life in wartime Britain was the blackout, both on base and throughout the country. It is still hard to imagine a large city without lights and to strangers it was a baffling experience. Actually, there was some light on the streets and on moving cars, but no projected beams, only vague soft glowing spots in the blackness. Still, everyone learned to cope.

The small number of P-51s available during the two months at Raydon severely restricted the amount of transition training. There were never more than 17 aircraft available and the bulk of the P-51s did not arrive until after departure from Raydon and shortly before the first combat mission. There was little actual training, it was mostly a matter of building up experience in the aircraft

Lt. Col. Donald Graham, seen here seated, became Deputy Group Commander when Spicer took over. They had been friends since both had been instructors at Randolph Field. Left is a young Lt. Richard Peterson, not yet an ace and standing to Graham's left is Major Irwin Dregne, Group Operations Officer.

as the pilots were already supposed to be fighter pilots. Harvey Mace, a 362 Squadron stalwart, does not recall any training and the ten hours or so that he had in the P-51 were acquired on ferry flights from the great aircraft depot at Blackpool. He never did fire the guns until he did so in combat. Most pilots seemed to transition into the Mustang with little trouble.

Some did, however. Mace was a close friend of Konstantine Vogel and Mace recalls his problems:

"Being a dyed-in-the-wool airplane nut, if I'm not flying myself, I can usually be found watching others who are flying. Consequently, I was watching Vogel during his series of mishaps that started with a dead stick landing from about 8,000 feet. His approach to the field was well planned except for not allowing for the huge reduction in glide ratio when he dropped his gear on the base leg. Consequently, he hit off base with quite a bad crash, although he was not seriously injured. It did have quite an affect on him mentally and there were a total of three landing incidents following the crash. All three were similar, but the last one was the most spectacular. It broke the prop and gearbox off and in bracing himself with the airplane in the tail high position, he leaned on the throttle and the engine, unencumbered by the gearbox and prop, screamed like no other piston engine I have ever heard.

"After the third incident, our Operations Officer, Broadhead, decided he had better give Vogel some dual time in the AT-6, which he did. Vogel finally got his confidence back and went on to continue his tour."

Lt. Konstantin Vogel was missing in action on 18 March 1944, according to an eyewitness, shot down by an Fw 190.

It was from Raydon that the first combat missions were flown, but not by the Group as a whole. A few senior pilots flew their first sorties with the 354th Group out of nearby Boxted. The 354th had preceded the 357th through the training cycle and had flown its first mission on 1 December 1943, and by now had completed fifteen. On one of these, Major James Howard, separated from the rest of the unit, was the sole defense of the 401st Bomb Group against a swarm of enemy fighters. For this action, he was awarded The Medal of Honor, the only fighter pilot in Europe to receive this highest of awards.

The 354th was the first Group to fly the Merlin Mustang and it was assigned to the tactical 9th Air Force at a time when the 8th was desperate for long range fighters. The reason for this was probably the fact that the previous Mustangs, all powered by the low altitude Allison engine, had been used in the ground attack mission both by the USAAF and the RAF. Although the two aircraft bore a strong family resemblance, the Merlin Mustang P-51B was an entirely different breed of cat, and possibly

Most of the P-51s which arrived at Leiston Air Field in January and February 1944 were very scruffy in appearance, but the efforts of the Squadron painters soon produced much more presentable aircraft. Lt. Col. Graham's B6-W later became B6-C (bar) and was wrecked at home base by Joe Pierce. The third P-51 in line is Richard Peterson's C5-T, HURRY HOME HONEY, 43-6935, in which he scored many of his victories before its loss on 20 June with Heywood Spinks.

An early photo of pilots of the 362nd. Of these men, five would die in combat and seven would be shot down to become POWs or evaders. Major Egenes, killed late in March, is at center in leather jacket with the squadron insignia on it.

C5-M did not last long, being wrecked on 9 February, two days before the Group became operational.

USAAF, United Kingdom, did not appreciate that. The 8th Air Force was very unhappy with the decision as it was clear to them the Merlin Mustang was the answer to their requirements for a long range fighter. The 9th was not willing to give up the 354th, but did loan it to the 8th on many occasions for bomber escort and an agreement was reached that the new group, the 357th would go to the 8th, their first P-51 unit.

On the 14th of January, 1944, Colonel Chickering, and Majors Graham and Egenes were the first to venture into the land of the enemy. There was no major action on this mission, but the 354th lost one aircraft and claimed six e/a (enemy aircraft). In recent years, Major General Donald Graham (ret) has told this writer that he had a clear shot at an Fw 190, but his guns refused to fire - a portent of future problems. Exactly one year later, on 14 January 1945 the 357th would shoot its way into the record books with the largest score of enemy aircraft ever shot down in one day, by any Air Force unit in any war.

Ten days later, four more pilots flew with the 354th. They were Captains Joseph Giltner, Joseph Broadhead, Edwin Hiro and John Storch. Giltner did not return from this mission - the 357th's first combat loss. Because of this fact, we provide extracts from the Missing Aircrew Report by Captain James Cannon, 354th Fighter Group:

"On 24 January 1944, I was leading Jacknife White Flight of four in mutual support, providing escort and support to a box of bombers enroute home. Captain Priser, with Captain Giltner of the 363rd Squadron on his wing, was weaving back and forth in front of the formation. We were flying just above the cloud layer, approximately 25,000 feet. At 1145 hours when in the Brussels, Ghent, Antwerp area, four white-nosed Fw 190s made an attack on Captain Priser's two ship flight from 4 o'clock below. After a short burst from one of these e/a they split-essed back into the overcast, as my flight turned into them. I saw Captain Priser and his wingman break right and drop tanks but did not see any strikes on them. I lost Captain Priser when I turned into the 190s and broke off as they went into the overcast. The attack of the e/a was apparently well planned as they appeared suddenly and disappeared rapidly."

Slightly blurred photo, but still of interest, this is the T-2 hangar occupied by the 469th Service Squadron. The much-looked-forward-to Red Cross "Doughnut Wagon" is at right center with a good crowd around it. There are two white-nosed P-51s visible (one is G4-F) and barely visible is an RAF Airspeed Oxford which was on loan to the Group for a short period.

Captain Priser's fate is unknown, but Giltner became a POW and returned after the war. On the 29th of January, Lt. Col. Egenes, and Joe Broadhead flew again with the 354th, their second and last from Raydon. Following the pattern of short stays established during the training days, it was time to move again. The next base would be more "permanent", at least until the end of WWII.

Merlin-powered P-51s were now flowing into the U.K. in ever increasing numbers and 8th Air Force was determined to get as many as possible. As related above, the 9th would not give up its only Mustang group, the 354th, but high-level negotiations led to the newly arrived 357th being traded to the 8th and the 9th got the 358th

Group, whose P-47s were more suited to the 9th's tactical role. The 358th had been at Leiston for about a month and had flown 17 missions out of Station F-373, Leiston Air Field. Located in the county of Suffolk, near the city of Ipswich, it was flanked by three small towns, Leiston, Saxmundham and Theberton. It was on occasion referred to by any of the names, Leiston being by far the most common. The base had the distinction of being the 8th Air Force base closest to the coast of the Channel and therefore the closest to enemy territory.

On the 1st of February the two groups traded bases. According to the history of the 358th Group they got the best of the deal.

A fine study of TYPHOON McGOON, 43-6628. Soon after a mission take-off on 29 March, 1944, Lt. William McGinley, flying this P-51, collided with Lt. Santiago Guitierrez. Neither pilot survived.

LOGISTICS MAGIC

The 8th Air Force was in terms of men and aircraft, the largest air striking force in history ever committed to battle. In his book THE MIGHTY EIGHTH WAR MANUAL, Roger Freeman sums it up: "The complexities of putting 2,000 bombers and fighters in a single day over Hitler's *Reich* was extraordinary and might involve, directly and indirectly, 150,000 men and women. The daily logistical requirements could be enormous; some three million gallons of fuel, 4,000 tons of bombs and 4.5 million rounds of .50 caliber ammunition." These, of course are just the major items. Then there were the vast quantities of coffee, Spam and green eggs, spark plugs, toilet paper and endless lists of aircraft and vehicle parts and hundreds of other mundane items. The effort to get them there was staggering."

Captain C.E. "Bud" Anderson with his close friend, Jim Browning. Both men flew two tours, but Browning's luck ran out on his second one when he collided with an Me 262 on 15 January 1945, killing both pilots. This is Anderson's first P-51 OLD CROW, probably 43-6723. Here it has ten missions but was lost with Al Boyle on 21 February, when he became a POW.

It was a big job to keep the Group supplied with the 100 or so drop tanks needed every day. These are the boxes that the 75 gallon tanks had come all the way from the ZI in and when empty they were very useful for building Crew Chief shacks and other small structures.

LEISTON AIRFIELD, 8TH AIR FORCE STATION F-373

All 8th Air Force bases in England were similar, but no two were exactly alike. The most visible feature was the runway layout. Most bases had three runways in a rough triangle, the main runway being 6,000 feet and the other two 4,200.

The base covered some 500 acres and was meant to house some 1700 personnel, the housing areas being off by themselves a mile or so away. Food supply was critical in wartime Britain. Government policy was to disturb agriculture as little as possible and Hill Farm was therefore located on base, with Moat Farm close by.

A perimeter track, or taxi strip circled the airfield connecting all runways and around this the three Squadrons were spaced, one on each side of the triangle. Also around the perimeter track were enough hardstands to park the Group's 75 P-51s.

Two large RAF type T-2 hangars were available, one assigned to the major maintenance support unit on the base, the 469th Service Squadron. Through some kind of chicanery, Lt. Fred Gilbreth, 362nd Engineering Officer obtained the other hangar for his Squadron. All other maintenance was done in the open or in one of the dozen or so blister hangars around the perimeter track.

All the buildings on the base were low one story Nissen Huts, or similar brick buildings all painted a dull gray green to blend into the local scenery. The control tower, the hub of all operations was located midway on the north/south runway in the 362nd Squadron area.

FEBRUARY, 1944 - THE SITUATION

Throughout the interwar years of the 1920s and '30s, the Army Air Corps primarily through its Tactical School at Langley Field and later Maxwell Field, developed the doctrine of the bomber. The theory was that a

A rather scroungy CHICAGO GUN MOLL, was 43-6556, G4-B. Lt. Robert Brown, always called "R.D.", scored a victory on 25 February but had to bail out over Switzerland on 27 May, where he was interned, returning to the Squadron at the end of the war.

Major Thomas "Tommy" Hayes, long time Commander of the 364th Squadron, and later Deputy Group Commander, is seen here with his first FRENESI, named for a popular song of the day. Hayes was one of the very few combat veterans who joined the Group from the beginning.

FIRST MISSION! 11 February 1944. Lt. Ken Hagan in 43-12173, formerly PEG-O-MY HEART with the 354th Group, waits for taxi time. Crew Chief Robert Raffen at left, ready to pull the chocks on signal.

Left: Lt. Gilbert O'Brien, who would become an ace with the 362nd Sqdn. and survive the war.

Right: The "other" 357th O'Brien, William, of the 363rd. Both O'Brien's flew a full tour and scored seven victories each. Both men in these photos are wearing RAF type C helmets and RAF MK VIII goggles as did most of the original pilots.

Right: Pilots were transported from their Squadron equipment rooms to their aircraft by whatever Squadron vehicles were available, overloaded jeeps as seen here, as well as Weapons carriers and 6x6 trucks. Man at right is holding a sponge rubber cushion - very important on long missions.

Two views of Major Irwin Dregne's first P-51, C5-Q, with an early Malcolm hood and evidence of large areas of missing paint. The names on the left, BOBBY JEANNE are for his child and wife. The name on the right side AH FUNG GOO applied by his crew chief, is said to be an Italian obscenity.

Two views of Captain Joe Broadhead's BABY MIKE (his son). It was a P-51B-1, 43-12227. It had a long life, as Broadhead flew it through his first tour scoring six victories in it. It was lost in November with Lt. Warren Corwin who was almost surely the only 357th pilot to be shot down by an Me 262.

Left: The first pilot of the 357th to become an ace was 364th Squadron's Captain Jack Warren. On the 18th of March, 1944, he vanished forever in miserable weather.

Two views of Lt. Thomas Harris's LI'L RED'S ROCKET C5-S, 43-6653 in which he scored five victories before becoming a POW on 22 May 1944. The message on the bomb TO HITLER'S KIDS is of interest.

Right: Lt. Robert Becker with his "Tiger" P-51 which later became SEBASTIAN. Becker completed his tour and went home an ace with seven victories. The small white cross on the fuselage indicated that the aircraft was fitted with the 85 gallon fuselage fuel tank.

Below: B6-E, OH BOBBY! 43-6519, was another of the original batch of P-51s but nothing is known of who the pilot was.

Right: Glen Davis's P-51B PREGNANT POLECAT 43-6867 from which he bailed out late in April, due to engine failure. Squadron code is uncertain but crew chief Wilber Reich recalls it as C5-0. One-half victory credits were usually painted as a whole which accounts for the nine symbols. Several of these were scored on the early Berlin missions.

well-armed bomber could accomplish its mission and defend itself against enemy fighters, without friendly fighter support. In those days the Air Corps had no bombers that even approached "well armed". When the first B-17 appeared in the late 1930s, it was a giant leap forward in technology but it was certainly not well armed.

The 8th Air Force flew its first mission in June, 1942, in a few A-20 light bombers borrowed from the RAF.

Fourteen months later, it had 50 bases in England and 26 heavy bomb groups. The mission, even if not stated as such, was to bomb Germany into submission.

Throughout this period, the 8th had been struggling to prove the self-defending bomber concept. By now, the bombers really were "well armed", but during the summer and fall of 1943 bomber attrition to German fighters had begun to bring the concept into doubt. After the disastrous raids on Schweinfurt in August and September, the concept was dead. It was now clear that long range fighter support was essential for escort.

Fighter strength in the 8th then stood at 11 groups, two with P-38s, the rest with P-47s. Although large, heavy and ungainly appearing in comparison with most fighters of the day, the P-47 soon proved itself a capable opponent for German fighters. Its range, however, was totally inadequate. The P-38, on the other hand, had ample range but was beset with technical problems which left its future in serious doubt. Throughout the fall of 1943, 8th Air Force Technical section was able to steadi-

ly increase the P-47's range with new drop tank development to the point where it could now battle the *Luftwaffe* up to the borders of the *Reich*.

It was at this point that the Mighty Merlin Mustang, with a radius of 750 miles appeared on the scene and immediately became the choice for 8th Air Force escort needs.

THE OPPOSITION

At this time the *Luftwaffe* had 32 fighter *Gruppen* (groups) in the west, with some 750 single engine fighters (roughly the same as 8th Fighter Command) and somewhat less than 200 twin engined Me 110s and 410s.

Even though the *Luftwaffe* had inflicted serious losses on the U.S. bomber force, it had, fighting on three fronts, taken a grievous beating itself. Although not readily apparent at the time, the *Luftwaffe* fighter force was already on the road to disaster and final defeat.

Early in 1944, it could only get worse for *Jagd-geschwadern* and for the 8th, it would slowly get better as 8th Fighter Command continued to expand and improve its equipment and tactics.

Long before the move to Leiston Airfield, 8th Air Force leaders had been planning Operation ARGUMENT, soon to be known forevermore as BIG WEEK. Along with the 15th Air Force out of Italy, its objective was a series of massive attacks on the German aircraft industry, in hopes

Major Edwin Hiro, 363rd pilot, Ops. Officer, and finally its C.O. As far as is known, all his P-51s were named HORSE'S ITCH and he is shown here with the first one. By September 1944, when he was killed, he had scored five victories all Me 109s.

F/O Charles Yeager with his first P-51, GLAMOURUS GLEN, s/n 43-6763. On 5 March he was shot down in this P-51 by an Fw 190, which was then shot down by OBee O'Brien. As is related in his book, he evaded capture and eventually returned to his unit.

2nd Lt. Alvin F. Pyeatt was considered a "hot rock" in the 362nd Squadron. After scoring two victories, he was shot down on 16 March 1944, and died several days later in a German hospital. The P-51B-7-NA is s/n 43-6960, its code was G4-S. This marvelous photo shows Al in the cockpit and the uneven faded paint job, with two victory symbols, three escort and one "sweep" symbol. Pilot and crew names are in white and the aircraft data block is in black next to the white cross indicating the airplane is fitted with the fuselage fuel tank. There is a personal memorial to Al Pyeatt on the author's wall as this is written.

One of the strangest P-51s in the 8th Air Force (?), but nothing is known of it. No visible markings and the dark/light paint job could be any one of many combinations. There appears to be a "normal" P-51 at far left. This photo came out of 362nd pilot Harry Ankeny's photo album but he has no memory of it. It may, or may not, have been taken at Leiston, and it may, or may not, be related to the 357th Fighter Group.

MSgt. Joe DeShay, at various times a flight chief and line chief in the 364th Engineering Section, another of the enlisted technicians whose job was to provide airplanes on time to perform the Group's mission. In the post-war years, Joe and Ellen DeShay were far and away the most important people leading the 357th Fighter Group Association and keeping its members together for 40 years.

Captain Glendon Davis was a Flight Leader in the 364th Squadron and had a good string of victories going (7.5) when he was forced to bail out of his P-51 due to engine failure in late April, 1944. Luckily he was immediately picked up by the French Underground and evaded capture, finally arriving in Paris six days after it was liberated. He returned to England and to the Group, but was not allowed to fly combat again, and soon returned to the ZI.

it would blunt the sharp end of the *Luftwaffe* fighter force. As February began, it awaited only a weather forecast of five days of good weather. Probably no one in Group, not even the senior leaders knew this but whenever it came the 357th's new Mustangs would be in the middle of it, ready or not.

As the Group moved into Leiston, the vital supporting units were already in place or were also in the process of moving in. These were: 50th Service Group Headquarters and its 469th Service Squadron, the largest of the units whose mission was major aircraft repair; 70th Station Complement; 18th Weather Detachment, a part of the huge 18th Weather Squadron which served all of the 8th AF; 1076th Signal Company; 1177th Quartermaster Company; 1260th Military Police Company; 1600th Ordnance Company; and 2121st Engineering Fire Fighting Platoon.

There was precious little time left now. By the end of the first week in February there were about 75 P-51s on

hand, the main occupation now for the pilots was simply to get as much "time" as possible in their new mounts, to become familiar with them.

During this time, a few senior officers and Flight Leaders managed to get in an indoctrination mission with the 354th. Captain Clarence Anderson and a half dozen others took their Mustangs to Boxted on the evening of the 7th of February. They expected that an easy break-in type mission had been planned for them. At the briefing it was with some shock that Anderson found they were to be thrown into the deep end of the pool, to swim or sink. In his book TO FLY AND FIGHT, he gives a classic description of his first mission:

"The target was Frankfurt, 360 miles from our base in East Anglia. This was not a milk run for training new pilots. This was dangerous mission. We were liable to see German planes, close up, on this kind of a mission. Focke-Wulfs and Messerschmitts, good planes manned by experienced pilots."

The Eighth was too short of escort fighters to waste time with easy missions for the 357th fledglings! Anderson's apprehension was well taken as he experienced all of the traumas and confusion of a fighter pilot's first mission, and he did see the enemy - close up! He was flying wingman for an experienced 354th pilot, and was determined to stay with him:

"I'm almost upside down now and I'm looking straight up/down at this deadly and beautiful thing, robins egg blue with big black crosses and the man I'm protecting is sliding in right behind it."

The 190 pilot lived to fight another day, however, due to poor R/T procedures by an unknown pilot who startled a sky full of Mustangs by transmitting :

"Mustang, there's one on your tail", with no identification. This bone-chilling advise to no one in particular broke up the affair with everyone frantically clearing their tails, including Anderson's leader who broke away from his intended victim. Although Anderson says the culprit was an American pilot, one cannot help but wonder if it was a German transmission.

He sums up his experience: "My first mission, on the whole, hadn't been a confidence builder exactly. But I'd seen the bad guys up close and survived the experience. I was a little bit smarter by evening than I'd been in the morning, which was all that had been hoped for"

One of the pilots who went out that day did not return. In his diary for 8 February, Lt. Fletcher Adams noted: "Captain Lloyd Hubbard of the 363rd killed strafing a German field today. Hard to believe we are so close to this thing, but we will find out real soon." Fletcher Adams, with nine victories by the 30th of May, was shot down by an Me 109 and murdered by civilians on the ground.

Small table radios were available in the shops in Ipswich and other nearby cities and most barracks had one. The BBC was listened to for the news and for good American big band music, the German propaganda stations were the best. Aimed at U.S. personnel in Britain, they mixed a steady diet of propaganda with Glenn Miller and Tommy Dorsey and their bands. William Joyce, a turncoat Englishman, commonly called "Lord Haw Haw" was the most famous of the propagandists and soon after arrival, Joyce greeted the 357th whom he tagged THE YOXFORD BOYS, threatening all kinds of dire events that awaited them.

A favorite trick of these stations was to tell such and such a base that the officer's club clock was two minutes slow (or fast). Although the base was usually referred to as Leiston and occasionally as Saxmundham or Theberton, it was never referred to as Yoxford, a small town to the northwest and further away than the others. This brings into question the accuracy of the vaunted German intelligence service but the Group has been eternally grateful ever since for the catchy name. THE SAXMUNDHAM BOYS would not have done nearly as well!

Above: LITTLE LADY was Elmer Rydberg's assigned P-51. (his name, in small letters is just under the dog's nose.) Rydberg vanished with LITTLE LADY, and his element leader Dave Perron in LITTLE BITCH on 1 April 1944.

Below: Two ground crew types, Childs and Christenson, and two pilots, Drollinger and Duncan, pose with their namesake "YOUNG-UNS". The art work was probably done by Childs.

Post war revelation brought into question the brilliance of German intelligence gathering. In 1972, Yale University Press published the previously classified Masterman Report, under the title THE DOUBLE CROSS SYSTEM. This remarkable book makes the claim and backs it up, that the German espionage system in Britain was run and totally controlled by a section of MI5, the British Internal Security Agency who supplied only what they wanted the Germans to have. The book is well worth reading. On the night of 10 February, after being on station only ten days, the teletype machine clattered out the alert for FO 240 (Field Order). Tomorrow The Group would be considered operational. It was payback time.

OPERATIONAL

When a new group in the 8th was declared operational, it was standard practice to bring in an experienced leader from another group to escort the new lads on their first two or three missions. On the morning of the 11th of February, Major James Howard came over from Boxted to do just that. Howard was a veteran of the Pacific war and was now a Squadron Commander in the 354th Group. One month previously on 11 January, having been separated from his Squadron, he engaged in a lone 30 minute running battle with some 30 enemy fighters which were attacking a force of B-17s. During this remarkable one-sided battle, he shot down three enemy fighters before gun failure and low fuel forced him to return to base. For this action, he became the only fighter pilot in the ETO (European Theatre of Operations) to be awarded The Medal of Honor.

Things would be less hectic on the 11th of February as he led 41 neophyte pilots of the 357th on their first venture into the land of the enemy. Since it was the first of well over 300 missions, we will quote Howard's mission report for the day: "FO 240, Major Howard leading. 47 P-51s, 17, 362nd, 17, 363rd, 13, 364th. Six aborts, three mechanical, one Navigation error, one broken oil line, one escort. Sweep. "LF (Land fall) FeCamp, 25,000, at 1000 hours. Meager inaccurate trailing flak at Rouen. Flak at St. Omer was intense but inaccurate in altitude and lead. LF out east of Calais 25,000 at 1050 hours. R/T (radio telephone) good except difficulty hearing Parker. (fighter controller.)"

The first effort had been nothing more than a 50 minute sight-seeing tour on the edges of the enemy's domain. They had seen flak for the first time and for most, had flown their first larger formation - over 40 P-51s.

The next day, the 12th, would be the first real mission, a bomber escort of over two hours. This time Lt. Col. Don Blakeslee, another distinguished fighter leader, came over from the 4th Group at Debden, to lead. On this day the 8th was relatively inactive with 99 B-24s of the 2nd Division, bombing V-weapon sites in France. Harry Ankeny's diary entry for this date describes the Group's second mission and his first:

"My first combat mission was a bomber escort job over the Northern France area. Lt. Col. Blakeslee led the group taking off around 0900. We headed directly south

Four of the sixteen pilots who scored victories on the first big Berlin mission on 6 March. (The Group had been to Berlin on the 4th, and Bob Wallen and Chuck Yeager both shot down Me 109s). Here (L-R) Dave Perron, Tommy Hayes, Glendon Davis, and Don Bochkay show off their claims.

Lt. Roger Pagels seen here with a 363rd Squadron dog, also scored on the Berlin mission of 6 March, shooting down an Me 110. This was his only victory of the war, as he disappeared just after take-off on D-Day, the 6th of June. No one saw what happened to him but he survived and evaded capture.

A great view of Colonel Spicer's TONY BOY with his three victory symbols which would date it between 25 February and 5 March, when he was shot down. This is a P-51B-7-NA, serial number 43-6880.

from Leiston. Was flying on Lt. William's, my flight leader's wing - R.D. Brown and Adams were also in the flight. Complete overcast over our field and nearly all over the target area. Did a nice job climbing thru the overcast 6,000 feet thick, entirely on instruments.

"Passed over North Foreland on course and picked up the first box of B-24s near Dieppe. They were bombing secret installations inland from Amiens. Saw no enemy fighters, but a little flak over the target. Took two boxes of bombers over the target and did a good job. Coming back in Squadron formation, we let down thru holes over the channel. Nearly ran into barrage balloons over Ipswich but all got back OK."

The next day, the 13th, Blakeslee led again, for the last time. This was again a three hour area patrol in the Dieppe, Rouen, Abbeville area. There was no sign of the fabled *Luftwaffe* fighter unit, "the Abbeville Kids" but Lt. R.W. Brown was forced to bail into the Channel when his engine quit."

Don Blakeslee went back to his 4th Group and immediately began to press for P-51s to replace their P-47s. Four days later he had the first three P-51s.

There was now a six day stand-down, most of the 8th being inactive. For the majority of the time the weather was bad, but preparations for OPERATION ARGUMENT, the big assault on the German aircraft industry

also kept the 8th on the ground. During this period, on the 17th, Colonel Chickering commanding since 7 July 1943, also left the group for 9th Air Force. Replacing him was Colonel Henry "Russ" Spicer, a flamboyant fire-eater.

He had been an army pilot for a long time having graduated from Kelly Field in 1934, where he remained as an instructor in both pursuit and bombers. As was common in the old army going way back to the civil war it was not unusual for an officer to remain a Lieutenant for 15 or 20 years. So, in March 1942, he was still a 1st Lieutenant.

The pressure of war broke the promotion bonds and three months later he was a Major and a full Colonel by the end of 1943. By that time Spicer was in England as Executive Officer of 66th Fighter Wing (357th's parent unit). Considering Spicer's drive, it would not come as a surprise to find that had pulled a few strings to get a combat command and what better than the new Mustang outfit?

Spicer took command on the 17th, first flew a Mustang on the 19th and the next day the 8th returned to the fray and the storm broke.

The non-operational period did not mean that the troops were sitting around. There would have been maintenance of all kinds to be done, test flights to be flown, and many of the pilots would have used this period to build up time in the Mustang. It was probably during this week

Captain Kenneth Hagan and his MY BONNIE. Hagan was leading 362nd Blue Flight on 17 June 1944, a few miles SW of Caen France, when his engine failed and he crash landed 42-106831, code G4-G. At the time of its loss it is thought to have had the "half" paint job common in the 362nd, would have had full invasion stripes and the red and yellow nose. With the help of the local Frenchmen he avoided capture and returned to the unit in August, but as was the policy did not fly combat again. We believe that Hagan was a murder victim in the late 1940s, a sad end for a valiant fighter pilot.

that 2nd Lt. Tom Beemer checked out the aircraft's altitude capability. He finally reached 39,000 feet or so and decided that the quickest way down, and also a chance to check the aircraft's behavior in a dive, was a vertical descent with full power. This worked fine but as is often the case, recovery ate up more altitude then expected and Beemer was rapidly running out of that commodity, remarkably recovering at about 6,000 feet. Considering the P-51's occasional tendency to break up under some stress conditions Beemer may have been one of the lucky ones.

OPERATION ARGUMENT
THE BIG WEEK

As mentioned previously this operation had been in the planning stage since before the 357th was even operational, and implementation had been awaiting a forecast of one week of good weather. Starting on the 20th, and ending on the 25th, ARGUMENT was carried out. The 8th, along with elements of the Italian-based 15th Air Force, smashed at the industrial centers from which came the Fw 190s and Me 109s that were the bane to the

existence of the B-17s and B-24s. The weather ranged from marginal to fair during this period. The size of the effort can be seen by the fact that, over the five days of operation there were almost 2,800 bomber sorties escorted by an overwhelming 3,800 fighter sorties. During the week, German fighters and flak shot down about 150 bombers and some 35 fighters - far from light losses, but sustainable by the now massive 8th Air Force.

Although German aircraft production did sag after ARGUMENT, the long term effect was not what had been hoped for. By far the most significant affect was the decimation of the German fighter force. Forced into sustained combat to protect the vital factories, they lost fully 1/3rd of their aircraft and almost 1/5th of their pilot strength. The aircraft could be replaced, but it was much more difficult to find and train someone to fly them.

Worse for the *Luftwaffe* was yet to come. The strength of the 8th Air Force was now so massive that they were able to keep the pressure on the faltering *Luftwaffe* throughout the rest of 1944. Operation ARGUMENT had signaled the beginning of the end for a once elite force and the 357th had arrived just in time to play its part in a momentous period.

In its first few tentative steps into occupied France, the Group had only peeked into

ALL AWAY II, B6-P, s/n 43-6393. Pilot is not certain, but thought to have been Eddie Simpson. This P-51 does not show up on any loss list so it may have been transferred to one of the new groups just getting P-51s where it served as a trainer.

the window of war. Now they would be thrown headfirst into the melee.

Colonel Spicer flew his first mission on the 20th, the day after his first P-51 flight but he did not lead as Colonel Don Blakeslee came over from 4th Group to do so once more. Since the 4th Group had a few P-51s by this time, he was probably flying one of these. Besides being the first penetration in the enemy homeland, there were other important incidents - the first combat loss on a group mission and the first of some 600 air victories.

The six-day "Big Week" assault on the German aircraft industry was really only five days. After heavy action on the 20th, 21st, and 22nd, the 23rd was a day of inactivity due to weather and the need for maintenance and repair on the bomber fleet. 20th Group P-38s flew an uneventful sweep and the 7th Photo Group flew its usual reconnaissance missions. Their F-5s and Spitfires frequently flew when no one else did.

Over these five days, the Group claimed 21 enemy aircraft destroyed and lost eight pilots - it was obviously going to be a tough war. Two of those lost, Lts. Tom Beemer and Charles McKee were victims of "friendly fire". Bomber crew operated on the theory that you shoot at anything which points its nose at you. There was no time to try to distinguish between a P-51 and an Me 109. McKee bailed out, badly wounded by .50 caliber gunfire. Beemer bailed also and sustained serious injuries on landing with a streaming parachute. Both men became POWs, but due to their serious injuries, both men were repatriated before the end of the war.

Alfred Boyle, Albert Lichter, Don Rice, Don Ross, and Merlin Kehrer all survived as POWs, but Darwin Carroll was not so lucky. German records show him as dead in the wreckage of his P-51. On balance it had not been a good week with eight pilots gone already.

During the first mission on the 20th, Lt. Calvert Williams of the 362nd Squadron was the first pilot of the Group to shoot down an enemy aircraft. Here we will quote this historic encounter report:

"Five or six Me 109s made a pass at my flight, flying north of Leipzig at 25,000 feet. They came in from out of the sun and above the formation. My wingman and I made a sharp break to the left. An Me 109 came in firing from above and behind but over-shot and ended up directly in front of me. I gave him a good burst and plainly saw tracers going directly into the fuselage whereupon the enemy plane became engulfed in a cloud of black smoke and abruptly fell off on one wing. 1st Lt. Perron, my wingman, last saw the plane smoking heavily and in a spin. 410 rounds fired. Lt. Donald Ross of the 363rd scored about the same time but apparently flew through the wreckage and had to bail out himself into POW status.

All five days of "Big Week" produced combat, losses and victory claims, the most of the latter on the 22nd, when claims for seven were submitted - all Me 109s. Colonel Spicer led a depleted group of only 30 Mustangs on that date. Harry Ankeny was one of the ten from the 362nd Squadron and we will let his diary entry serve as an example of "Big Week":

There were at least seven pilots in the 357th named Smith, two of them R.C. Smith. This is Robert C. Smith with PAPP'S ANSWER. Assuming this was C5-E 43-6813, it was later named PAPPY'S ANSWER and had a long career including "Pappy" John L. Mederios who was shot down by flak on 4 March 1944 to become a POW. This photo with the aircraft having a white nose, would have been taken in the last two weeks of March. Robert C. Smith scored 2.5 air victories and flew 140 hours of combat before being transferred out of the Group. The small plate with the cord attached was fitted over the sheltered air inlet (both sides) to keep dust out of the induction system while the aircraft was inactive. These soon fell out of favor as dust was not much of a problem in England.

Don Bochkay at the rudder of 42-103041. This was a P-51C-1-NT, thought to be his first P-51, ALICE IN WONDERLAND although no photo of it has yet surfaced. It was lost on 8 March 1944 with Lt. Wm. "Stubby" Gambill who was killed on his way to POW camp, by an allied bomb.

"My second mission and it was really rough. We were to escort two boxes over the target at Bernberg; five boxes in all went in. Took off at 11:45 after the group had started across the channel. Was flying a new ship that had just come in the night before so this was its test hop. Caught the Squadron right off the enemy coast and joined the Squadron. I set my fuel selector in the drop tank position and accidentally dropped one of my tanks (75 gallons). I was on the extreme right of the group and Adams, my element leader and I went directly over the Ruhr Valley. The flak was thick and we really sweated it out - popping all around us. Got through OK. Our target was aircraft factories 400 miles away and we flew forever it seemed, until we picked up the bombers. Almost immediately Me 109s started dropping straight down thru the bomber boxes and violent rat races began. I saw an Me 109 flying by itself below and to the right so I called Adams

and told him to get it while I covered him. He peeled off and got into a spiral and a spin. Followed him a little ways but lost him. He destroyed the 109 and the pilot bailed out. After I lost him, I started turning to the right to see if anything had jumped my tail. Sure enough, an Me 109 was firing at me. I tightened up and got on his tail - got a two second burst at him as he went into a cloud below, at 10,000 feet. Couldn't see following him any lower so I pulled off and found Adams, thank the Lord - was really worried. We headed back picking up altitude until 23,000 ft. Again we went over the Ruhr Valley and flak gave us a lot of trouble. Got through OK and landed at 1630 hours - really a long mission. Lt. Lichter, my roommate, was hit by flak and bailed out over the Dutch Islands. Our Squadron got two 109s, Group total was seven destroyed. Two boys didn't get back. Al Lichter has a good chance of escaping, I believe. Sure was good to get home."

Harry Ankeny went on to fly a full combat tour, but of the seven men who scored victories on the 22nd, none would complete a full tour. Henry Spicer, John Carder, and John Medieros would finish the war in a *Stalag Luft* (POW Camp). Hubert Egenes, Fletcher Adams, Jack Warren, Ellis Rogers and Ed Hiro would all die in action.

We will end "Big Week" with Colonel Spicer's classic encounter report which is one of the longest discovered. Although it was a deadly serious affair, Spicer lets his humor show through. He was obviously in his element and enjoying himself!

"On 24 February 1944, I was leading the Group on bomber escort (FO250). Rendezvous was made without difficulty. The B-24s, our bombers were flying directly below the B-17s and not out to the side as stated in the Field Order. Goldsmith 1-2 reported no difficulty, so we stayed on top and covered the entire mass. Eventually the two ATFs extricated themselves, going in the usual wrong directions (also not covered in the FO) so we peeled off and took the B-24s, hoping they would sooner or later find out where they were, as it was CAVU. This, fortunately, proved to be true for they turned to the left at the I/P and positioned themselves for Squadron bombing on the bomb run.

"At this time the bulk of my Squadron had aborted (engine trouble and out of oxygen) leaving myself and wingman (bless his heart) to cover some 40 or 50 bombers. Two 109s were scared off. One 190 hit the deck and we drove up on him. The bomb run was completed with excellent results, a right turn was made and the next five miles continued without incident. At this time a Ju 88 was sighted about 2,000 feet below (23,000) and two miles to the left. As Goldie said he was OK, I pulled off and gave chase. He went down fast, losing altitude in a steep spiral.

*2nd Lt. Elmer Rydberg pulls through the prop on
Dave Perron's LITTLE BITCH. Both men vanished
in miserable weather on 1 April 1944.*

"At 3,000 feet I turned tight inside of him and he obligingly straightened out, allowing me to do the same, so I closed straight down the alley and opened fire at about 600 yards in an attempt to discourage the rear gunner. Steady fire was held until he burst into flames. I overran him rapidly (cause seeming to be excessive airspeed as I was indicating 550 mph at the time) so I yanked it out to the side to watch the fun. The whole airplane was coming unbuttoned. My wingman, good old Beal, had slowed a bit and later stated he saw two men jump and their chutes open (poor shooting on my part).

"The ship continued straight ahead, diving at an angle of about 40 degrees until contact with mother earth was made, which caused the usual splendid spectacle of smoke and flame. Looking up suddenly, lo and behold, if there wasn't a Me 110 dashing across the horizon. He showed a little sense and tried to turn so I was forced to resort to deflection shooting - opening up and spraying him up and down, round and across. (I believe I was a little excited at this point). Fortunately the left engine blew up and burst into flames. As I overran him (still indicating

500 mph) the pilot dumped the canopy and started to get out. He was dressed in brown and had streaming yellow hair, the handsome devil. I lost sight of him at this point (1000 feet) and again pulled out to the side.

"No chute was seen, but the aircraft descended impolitely into the center of the town of Erfurt, causing a rather understandable confusion as it blew up and burned merrily. Again as I looked up (this is getting monotonous) an Fw 190 whistled up and just as I began to turn with him my engine quit, embarrassing me no end. Believing I had been hit by the 110 rear gunner, and being at a loss as to the next step, I opened fire (90 degrees deflection) at zero lead and pulled it around clear through him until he passed out of sight below the nose (more bad shooting), intending to frighten him off more than anything else.

"No claim is made, as I saw no more. Here the engine caught again, laboring and pounding badly. At this point I passed to the side of an airdrome, completely snowed in, but saw hangars and maybe 20 twin-engined airplanes which may have been dummies, as they appeared to be snow covered.

This photo was taken at the end of the "White Nose era". This is an early attempt to comply with the 8th Fighter Command Directive assigning nose colors to its groups. This directive was issued on (or close to) 23 March 1944 and apparently was quite vague. This is how Lt. Johnny Pugh's G4-N, 42-106473 GERONIMO looked after the painter finished with it. We assume they got the colors right - red and yellow. We don't know how long this eye-catching scheme survived but probably not long!

"Struggling to keep afloat, I increased RPM to 2500 and reduced the manifold pressure to 20 inches, (airspeed 170) and slowly but surely gained altitude to 12,000, not going higher as Beal was out of oxygen. We crossed out without further incident, comparatively speaking, going south of the Ruhr, and avoiding all towns of any size. At the coast a P-47 pulled up behind me at 1,000 feet above. I waved my wings trying to get him to join up, but he edged out to the right, apparently taking a good look, then turned back inland. I had not been hit and at the time of writing the engine difficulty is not known. I give a world of credit to my wingman, 1st Lt. Henry Beal, for his support and companionship. Further deponent sayeth not. I claim: One Ju 88 destroyed, one Me 110 destroyed, one Fw 190 scared. Ammunition expended: 533 rounds."

IN SUMMARY

As the Group was becoming operational early in February, the 8th was ready to launch ARGUMENT, and the Group was in it to the hilt. The month ended with Spicer leading 50 P-51s on a four hour escort in miserable weather to targets in the Brunswich area. There were no claims and no losses. With only six missions behind it,

there had been plenty of action and the 357th was blooded and ready. It was also plain that it was going to be a rough war.

As February ended, ten of its pilots were already gone - dead, missing or prisoners. Most of them, thanks to the skill and care of the squadron's parachute riggers were in the latter category. Thomas "Tommy" Hayes, then 364th Squadron Commander and later Deputy Group Commander, would retire from the Air Force years later as a Brigadier General. Highly respected and much loved alumni of THE YOXFORD BOYS, as this is written in the year 2001, Tommy remembers those early days:

"From our training days in California until February, 1944, we were three Squadrons but not really a Group yet. When we got the P-51s, our squadron C.O.s, Flight Leaders and element leaders got to fly missions with the 354th Group with a chance to see Europe below and most important, to fly with veterans, to see the air battle.

"Then a new Group Commander arrives and finally we begin to become a Group. Under Colonel Spicer's lead, we run up 30 victories. I like to think he continued to lead the Group from *Stalag Luft* I."

Tommy Hayes and THE YOXFORD BOYS had been flying their new long-range Mustangs on operations for two weeks as the calendar flipped over to March. What did these new P-51s with a "Damn Great Merlin" up front really look like? 8th Air Force fighters are remembered today as some of the most colorful of historic warplanes, largely triggered by the great Colonel "Hub" Zemke when he requested permission to paint the noses of his 56th Group P-47s in squadron colors. Other groups followed and Fighter Command then began assigning colored noses to all of its groups (15 eventually) that are so well-known today.

The P-51Bs and Cs that flowed into Leiston in January and February were mostly new, direct from the huge aircraft depots in the north of England although a few were hand-downs from the 354th Group.

The colors referred to above did not begin to appear until the end of March, 1944. During the period of February and March, all 8th Air Force fighters shared the same Olive Drab and gray paint with white noses and white identification bands on wings and tails.

However, even though the P-51s were new, they had had a rough sea voyage as freighter deck cargo and worse was to come at the depots when the sealing tape was removed from the joints and seams, taking large areas of paint with it. The result was that at least until the Squadron painters could get to them, they were a scruffy batch of airplanes. So, during these early days there was little about the P-51s which was colorful or handsome - they were a drab sight.

If an aircraft survived into the summer and fall, it was quite likely to have been stripped and painted several times. The Squadron painters were busy men. One man, SSgt. Louis Boudreaux of the 362nd, died in the line of duty of paint related lung problems - a non-pilot casualty of war.

THE IDES OF MARCH

On the first day of March German radar screens remained clear as the 8th Air Force stood down to lick its wounds from the traumatic days of "Big Week". The only activity were two 7th Photo Group Spitfires, one of which did not return.

The next day, it was back to battering Germany. The 8th launched a relatively small force of 3rd Division B-17s which bombed an airfield at Chartes, France and B-24s bombed a variety of targets in Germany with over 500 fighters in support of which 111 were P-51s of the 4th and 357th Groups.

Colonel Spicer, the new Commander was leading in TONY BOY with 32 P-51s of THE YOXFORD BOYS for a largely uneventful ride. Only four enemy aircraft were seen two of which evaded into the undercast. The other two made it an eventful day for Major Tom Hayes, leading the 364th squadron with John Carder as his element leader. In his encounter report Hayes describes what happened.

"I was leading Gowdy (364th) Red flight and escorting a box of B-24s on the way home just north of Frankfurt. I was crossing over the bombers at 25,000 feet when I looked back and saw two SE e/a that must have attacked the rear of the box. We dropped tanks and started down."

When the 109 pilots spotted the P-51s they went into a steep dive and split up. Carder and his wingman, LeRoy Ruder followed one and Hayes and his wingman the other. After a short chase, Hayes shot down his 109 which crashed in a wooded area near the town of Altenstadt. Carder's kill provided a more spectacular sight. From his encounter report:

"The e/a and I went into a valley, with a steep tree-lined hill on the far side. At the bottom of the hill I fired a burst and saw strikes on the right wing. The 109 pulled up sharply above the horizon and I saw his wing tip was crumpled. I believe he hit a tree, unless I had damaged his wing spar. He did a slow climbing half roll and went down again inverted and crashed on top of the hill. I took a photo of the crash.

"I could see part of the wing and a wheel that slid into the main street of the town. I did a roll and believe civilian morale is lower now."

C5-M, GEECHEE GAL (SN 43-6582 that crashed on takeoff, ending up inverted on the grass, with Ray Sparks trapped in the cockpit. The date was 16 March 1944. The cockpit was resting in the mud and a pool of gasoline. It is believed that he was dug out of the wreck by the first few ground crew men on the scene. Although relatively intact at the site, it was destroyed totally during its clearance from the field. Oddly enough, the name GEECHEE GAL, clearly visible on the wreck photos, has been painted out here or the cowl panel replaced.

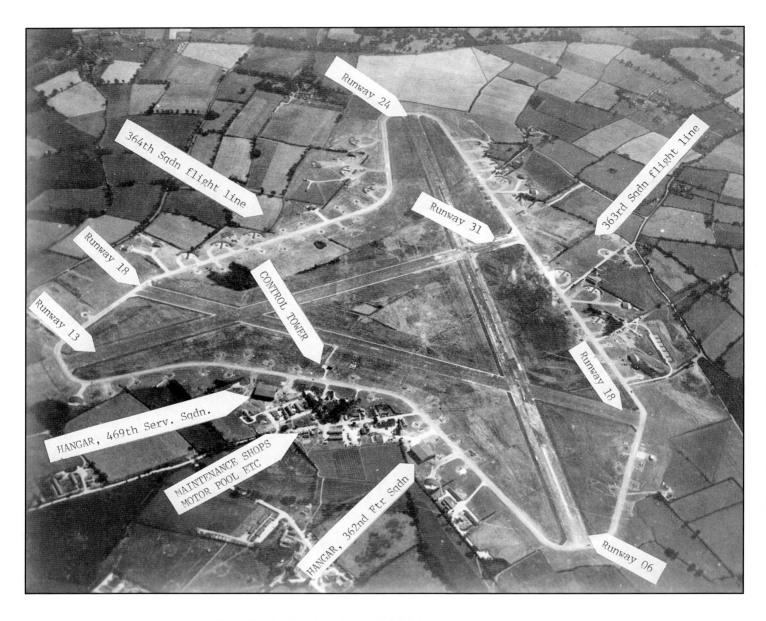

This is Station F-373, Leiston Airfield. For some 16 momentous
months, the home of THE YOXFORD BOYS.

CHAPTER 3:
BERLIN-BIG B AND ON TO D-DAY

The RAF, having been in business much longer than the 8th Air Force had been to Berlin many times at night. Berliners had long since learned what to expect when the colorful TIs (Target Indicators) blossomed in the sky.

Even though it had been two years since those few A-20s of the 15th Bomb Squadron had flown the first mission, the 8th had never been to Big B. Berlin was awash with important military targets, but it was more than that. It was the snake's head and brain of Nazisim, one of histories most evil empires and the home of Adolf Hitler its leader. It was obvious the 8th had to go to Berlin and everyone knew it. The bomber crews knew that one day the briefing mission route tapes would terminate there. The *Luftwaffe* certainly expected to do battle there with American bombers, if not with its fighters.

Lt. General Jimmie Doolittle and his planners were ready. They had a powerful bomber force and the vital buildup of long range fighters now made it possible. At this time, there were four long range fighter groups, three with P-38s and the 357th with P-51s. (The 4th Group was in transition from P-47s to P-51s.) In addition, the 9th Air Force's 354th Group was available on loan. These were

the fighters that would go to Berlin, the P-47s units would provide penetration and withdrawal support.

From Leiston, the closest to German territory, it was a long grind to Berlin some 520 miles in a straight line. For pilots, sitting on rock-hard and lumpy dinghy packs, it could seem twice as far. Then there was the strong possibility of combat and if that was survived, it was another long ride home, low on fuel and possibly with a damaged aircraft. From Leiston and return, it was an average of five hours. A fighter pilot's life in a long range fighter was not so glamorous after all. For P-38 pilots it was even worse as it was impossible in that aircraft to provide enough cockpit heat to battle the minus 50 degree outside air temperature.

Eighth Air Force planners relied heavily on their weather forecasters, but the state of the art and the rapid weather pattern changes made life difficult for the weather people. They had indicated that the 3rd of March looked good for the long-awaited Berlin mission. It wasn't. The weather over the continent turned to horrible and only 79 bombers out of 748 dropped bombs on enemy targets, none on Berlin. Nevertheless, eleven bombers and seven of 730 fighters were lost. On this date, however, U.S. fighters appeared over Berlin for the first time.

Pilots of the 362nd and 363rd Squadrons. None from the 364th have been identified. Kit Carson is kneeling on the wing, bareheaded, next to the fuselage at right. Chuck Yeager is kneeling (leather A-2 jacket) just right of the right propeller blade. Walter Corby, who was to die in an AT-6 crash in January is in the light colored trench coat sitting on the wing, at left. C.E. "Bud" Anderson is standing just below Corby, to his right, (Leather jacket). John Kirla, to be another double ace is bareheaded, sitting on the wing at right, third from the fuselage. Chuck Weaver, another ace is just below the left prop blade in leather jacket with 362nd Sqdn. insignia on it. Many of the others are known, but many are not identified.

Harry Ankeny (L), who is probably serving as OD (Officer of the Day) since he is wearing his pistol which is in a shoulder holster, worn on the hip - a common practice. At right is Lynn Drollinger (Universally known as "Junior"). He bailed out over France on 28 March 44, evaded capture, returned to the unit, and then on to the ZI.

The 20th Group had had a tough time of it in the three months they had been operational. Casualties had been heavy due to the weather and an un-ending series of mechanical problems with the P-38. The scoreboard had been heavily in favor of the *Luftwaffe*.

On the 3rd, Lt. Col. Hubbard led 33 P-38s to Berlin where they were slated to provide withdrawal support, but found no bombers. Hubbard was unable to contact the bombers so they headed home, engaging a half dozen Me 109s with no score on either side. These then were the first U.S. fighters over Berlin. One wonders if Herman Göring, the *Luftwaffe* chief saw them and what his thoughts were!

The 357th was active on the 3rd, with Colonel Spicer leading 53 P-51s. However, illustrating the mechanical problems with the new aircraft, and probably the ground crew's lack of experience on the type, eleven P-51s aborted the mission. It was, nevertheless, an ample number, since the whole force was recalled. 41 Mustangs were back on their hardstands by 1500 hours, and one, serial number 43-6998, was on the bottom of the Channel. (See DOWN IN THE DRINK, for Bob Foy's adventures.)

After the mission recall of the 3rd, the weathermen at PINETREE (8th Air Force Headquarters) must have been "sweating out" the forecast for the next day. Planning for the 4th was well under way on the 3rd, before the stragglers had returned from the recall. The decision would have been made by the Deputy Commander for Operations at the nightly operational conference at 2000 hrs (8pm). The "GO" signal filtered down through the three Division headquarters and then

to the Wings and Groups. At Horham Airfield, home of the 95th Bomb Group and some 15 miles from Leiston, the teletype machine clattered into life with the following: "Maximum forces will be dispatched against objectives in the Berlin area on 4 March". Details on the mission would follow later. The same alerting message would have come in to Leiston and dozens of other bases, including the 100th Bomb Group at Thorp Abbotts and the 4th Fighter Group at Debden. These units, the 95th and 100th Bomb Groups and the 4th and 357th Fighter Groups, would be the only ones over Berlin the next day.

On the morning of the 4th, weather was not good, but the decision had been made and over 750 B-17s and B-24s took off into the murk. However, the entire 2nd Division of B-24s was unable to assemble after takeoff and returned to their bases. The remaining 500 B-17s pressed on into the land of the enemy.

Over an hour after the bomber departure, at 1051 hours, Colonel Spicer took off leading the first section of the 357th, and Rendezvoused on time with the bombers two hours later. Twenty minutes after Spicer's first section, Lt. Col. Graham (Deputy Group Commander) led the second section off. Altogether there were 52 P-51s at take-off, but 22 aborted along the way - a very bad performance! Colonel Graham's section passed over a group of P-51s which had reversed course and were returning to base. These must have been from either the 354th Group, or part of the 363rd, the other 9th Air Force Group which had recently gotten P-51s. (The unit was broken up by the weather and lost eleven pilots to this cause.) Graham attempted to contact this group of P-51s without success

Armorer Percy Signore poses with a "big .50" in front of a classic Crew Chief shack, with names of home towns, favorite bar rooms of the past, mileages etc. The 75 gallon tanks would indicate March or April 1944. One of the P-51s has already had its paint removed from the fuselage.

This black and white mobile airfield control vehicle is built on a British army Chevrolet truck with a B-17 nose cone on top to give some protection to the controller. These vehicles had the same radios as the control tower and were often used during mission departures and returns to control traffic, as they were always parked next to the active runway, which in this case is runway 06.

and both sections of the 357th carried on with the mission. This encounter with the withdrawing P-51s was the first inkling of the big recall message fiasco of the 4th of March. About two hours into the mission, most of the B-17s turned back, supposedly in response to a recall signal from PINETREE (8th Air Force). Most of the fighters turned back as well.

There has been considerable confusion on this recall. Most historians treat it as a legitimate 8th Air Force recall signal. However, in the book B-17s OVER BERLIN, a 95th Bomb Group history, the event is told in considerable detail. Leading the First Combat Wing of the 3rd Division was Lt. Col. Harry Mumford in a B-17 named I'LL BE AROUND, with Lt. Al Brown as pilot. Shortly after crossing into Germany, T/Sgt. Frank Atterbury, Brown's radio operator reported the recall signal to Mumford and Brown. He added that the signal was not in the proper code and therefore was a bogus recall originating with a German transmitter.

On the strength of this information, Mumford elected to continue on though most of the force turned back in response to the signal. What remained was one squadron of the 100th Bomb Group and three of the 95th, a total of twenty-nine B-17s, a pitifully small force to attack Berlin for the first time.

Here, however, the miserable weather worked in their favor and they arrived in the Berlin area unmolested

by German fighters, although one B-17 was lost to flak.

The cloud cover over the city was broken, but the holes were in the wrong places to bomb and due to the extreme cold (-65F) the lead B-17's bomb bay doors were frozen shut. The crews of the pathfinder lead a deputy lead aircraft showed great skill in cobbling up a method of getting the bombs away on time, and generally on target.

The crews of the B-17s were not aware that friendly fighters were in the area, thinking all had returned on the recall. Therefore, it was with great relief that P-51s showed up about the same time as some 20 Me 109s arrived to defend their city. This Mustang force consisted of one squadron of the 4th Group (which was in the process of transitioning from P-47s), and 33 aircraft of the 357th. In many histories, including that of the 4th Group, all credit goes to the 4th for this first Berlin escort.

These eight squadrons, four bomber and four fighter, were the first to carry out an attack on the core of the *Nazi* empire. Lt. Joe Blagg a B-17 navigator later said; "We had no fighter support at the time and assumed they had been recalled along with the bombers. Then some P-51s showed up, just like the movies. I doubt if any of us would have got back to base if the P-51s had not been there." Joe Thayer, a co-pilot added "Without a shadow of a doubt, the Mustangs saved our lives that day." This of course, is what fighter escort was all about. Claims were not high, both the 4th and 357th claimed two and lost one

each, but the relief they brought to the bombers at a critical time was most important.

The 357th claims were by 363 squadron's Chuck Yeager, for his first victory. In his encounter report, he describes the Me 109 as having a "large red and black devils head on the left side". The other victory went to Lt. Robert Wallen of the 362nd, as his only victory of his combat tour. About an hour before reaching the target, his Flight Leader Capt. Dave Perron aborted the mission, taking the other three with him. Almost immediately however, he thought better of it and directed Wallen and his wingman to return to the bombers. Somehow, Wallen became separated from his wingman and as he approached the bombers, he spotted a single fighter in a shallow dive. Wallen later recalled: "I ambled over to see what he was and identified him as an Me 109. This was the first enemy aircraft I had seen close up and I guess I was a little excited."

Wallen latched onto his tail and got in two good bursts. The 109 exploded in a big ball of fire. He started to follow the wreckage when it suddenly occurred to him he was all alone in a very hostile sky, and seeing an aircraft diving toward him, he increased his downward dive. About this time his canopy departed with a loud bang. Despite damage to the right flap from the canopy departure, he came home on the deck, strafing two locomotives leaving them spouting steam. It had been a stressful few hours.

This first 8th Air Force attack on Berlin was carried out by eight B-17s of the 100th Bomb Group and 21 of the 95th Group, including one pathfinder aircraft of the 482nd BG Fighter support in the target area was approximately 40 P-51s, about 30 from the 357th and the rest from the 4th Group.

The Yoxford Boys' only loss was Captain John Mederios, hit by flak at 27,000 feet, who bailed successfully. This good shooting by a flak crew was ominous portent of an event that would occur on the following day.

If the recall signal on the 4th of March had indeed been a German attempt to deflect the Berlin attack, it was remarkably successful, except for an alert radio operator and a resolute colonel aboard a B-17 named I'LL BE AROUND. For a group that had been totally innocent of air combat in the hostile skies of Europe only a few weeks earlier, the 357th was now in the month of March, embroiled in combat almost on a daily basis.

With this mass of activity, it would be impossible to cover all the victory claims, losses, hairy escapes and wild stories; however, relating some of these will give the flavor of the Group's second month of operations.

A pristine P-51B in factory bare metal, 43-7184 which exhibits most of the post-factory modifications, a Malcolm Hood, the 85 gallon fuselage tank indicated by the small black cross under the data block, a "Spitfire" mirror and a dorsal fin, the modification shown by the small black cross on it although it is difficult to see why that was needed. A note in the records shows it as salvaged on 1 June 1944 so it must have been involved in an accident.

TO THE SOUTH OF FRANCE

The day after the first Berlin raid, the B-17s of the 1st and 3rd Divisions stayed on the ground, but some 200 B-24s were dispatched to the south of France to bomb airfields in the Bordeaux area. They were supported by over 300 fighters, 88 of them P-51s from the 4th, 357th and 363rd Groups. The losses were light, except to the crews of the four bombers and five fighters which did not return - losses were not light to them.

From Leiston, south to Bordeaux, it is about 500 miles, roughly the same distance as it is to Berlin. Even though the south of France is many miles from the hornet's nest of Berlin, the raid managed to stir up considerable opposition.

On March the 5th Col. Russ Spicer led his third mission in three days, and his last of WWII. Forty-five P-51s followed him with only seven aborts on this day, a big improvement from the previous day. Most of the Group was back at base by 1440 hours, with eight or ten landing at various RAF bases.

For Lt. Harvey Mace, the mission was mostly boredom. He was assigned as radio relay and spent some five hours circling just off the coast of France (on deep penetrations the Group was out of radio range so radio relay aircraft were used to pass on messages.) Mace's boredom was relieved when two homebound P-38s took an interest in him as a possible bogey, or bandit. This was soon sort-ed out and the P-38s went on home and Mace continued to orbit. Meanwhile the rest of the Group rendezvoused with the B-24s at 1027 hours, escorting them to separate airfield targets.

Captain William "OBee" O'Brien was an original member of the 363rd Squadron, and a Flight Leader from the P-39 training days in Nevada and California. He tells the story of his first victory: "At the RV point with the B-24s, Colonel Spicer (call sign "DRYDEN") requested the 363rd Squadron (CEMENT Squadron) furnish fighter support for a box of straggling bombers. My flight went back to pick up the stragglers. I was leading the flight with Lt. Bob Moore as wingman, and Lt. William McGinley as element leader. Flight Officer Charles Yeager, who was a spare, moved up as McGinley's wingman when Lt. L.D. Wood aborted.

"As we approached the stragglers, I searched the sky for enemy aircraft, but saw none. We moved in to about the three o'clock position on the bombers at their altitude, but out of range of their guns. This is where the bomber crews liked us to be 'nice and close', even if it was the wrong tactics for fighters. We should have been about 5,000 feet above, and a couple of miles ahead of them."

Author's note: The Christmas, 1943 message from General Hap Arnold, Chief of the AAF, directed the 8th to destroy the *Luftwaffe* where ever he could be found. Lt. General Jimmie Dootlittle had taken command of the 8th in February, and with General Kepner at Fighter Command, the "Shackles" keeping the fighters close to the bombers became, about this time, much more flexible.

O'Brien continues: "We'd been with the stragglers less than a minute when I spotted an Me 109 attacking the bomber box from a six o'clock position. I'd just started to drop my left wing to attack the 109 when a call came from Yeager, 'Break, Break'! We broke to the left, and about 180 degrees into the break I latched onto an Fw 190 which was in a diving turn. Yeager's call had saved us From being clobbered, but not himself!

"I opened fire at fairly close range which resulted in some pieces coming off the 190. Both of us were now diving nearly vertical, when something large went flying by my cockpit. I did not recognize the object at the time, but apparently it was the German pilot who had bailed out. I then saw that I was fast approaching a solid undercast, and since I had no idea how thick it was, it was time to pull out of the dive as the 190 was going straight down. I pulled out of the dive into a climb and at this point I did something really stupid - I let the P-51 go straight up till its airspeed dropped well below 200 mph. When I rolled into a left turn, there was 'ole Jerry, an Me 109 on our tail. We broke into a tight circle and lost the 109. Moore and I, unable to communicate due to radio failure, headed for England, the weather getting worse the further we went, and low on fuel, we just made it in to the RAF base at Ford.

"After our flight of two landed, we watched eight P-47s peel off and land, except for one which crashed. While in base operations phoning in our location and a damaged claim to Leiston, the P-47 pilots came in and we noticed that two of them were wearing RAF uniforms and U.S. leather jackets with Captain's rank bars.

"Later on at the RAF officers club we met the Jug pilots. Ours were the first P-51s they had seen, and we got into a discussion with one of them on the relative merits of the two aircraft. I told him I thought the P-51 could whip his P-47 in an air fight, at which time he suggested we get together the next day about 0800 and find out which was better. About this time I had gone to the bar for a refill, where I was joined by one of the American P-47 pilots who asked me if I knew who I was talking to. When I said 'no', he told me he was a Polish pilot by the name of Gladych and the other pole was Andersz. They had both fought in Poland, Norway, France and the RAF. It seems Gladych was several times over an ace!"

Author's note: Michael Gladych, who held the rank of Squadron Leader in the RAF was one of five Polish pilots who were on loan to Colonel Hub Zemke's 56th Fighter Group. The other man with him was Flight Lieutenant Tadeusz Andersz, who had been with him since their days in the Polish Air Force. Gladych was one of two who stayed with the 56th until the end of the war. 56th Group records show him with ten victories and he is generally credited with another 16 having been achieved while serving with the other air forces.

O'Brien takes up the story: "With this information I started to think maybe it wasn't a good idea to challenge him. The next morning I was up and at the flight line at 0600 where I looked over Gladych's P-47 and sure enough there were a bunch of German crosses on it! My P-51 had nothing but a serial number!

"I got Moore and we took off for Leiston. To this day Gladych does not know how good a pilot I may have been - we'll just keep it that way." Maybe Obee did the right thing - but then, who knows??

The Fw 190 that O'Brien claimed as a damaged was upgraded from damaged to Probably Destroyed by Fighter Command, undoubtedly after gun camera film evaluation. He would not know for another 52 years that the 190 was destroyed, upping his victory total from six to seven although Air Force records still show six.

For many years a French dentist and historian named Didier Fuentes has researched the air battle of that day and has found the crash sites of both Yeager's P-51, and the 190 that shot him down and was in turn destroyed

by O'Brien. As is well known, Yeager evaded capture and eventually returned to England and rejoined the Yoxford Boys. Dr. Fuentes was able to identify the 190 pilot through German records as *Unteroffizier* Irmfried Klotz, who bailed out, but was killed when his chute did not open. O'Brien's adventures on the Bordeaux mission were not the only note worthy events of the day, as we shall see.

Apart from a few unfortunate He 111s, Ju 88s and a *Storch* or two, all of the enemy aircraft destroyed by the 357th Group were the usual 109s and 190s (plus 18.5 Me 262s, more than any other group). On 5 March, a type not seen before or again was encountered. The big graceful four engined Fw 200 Condor had been an airliner, but when war came along it was converted into a very successful maritime commerce raider. The *Luftwaffe* operated them out of French bases attacking allied shipping in the Atlantic and the Bay of Biscay.

On this day, Gowdy (364th Squadron) Blue flight led by Captain Glendon Davis with Lt. Morris Stanley and F/O Tom McKinney came upon a lair of the big Condors, on an airfield SE of Caholet, near Parthenay (This is a small town about 120 miles due north of Bordeaux, and handy to the Bay of Biscay).

In his encounter report, Morris Stanley describes the results: "Through a hole in the clouds, Captain Davis spotted three large aircraft taking off from a field near Parthenay. We started a steep dive in trail formation. On the way down I spotted two Me 109s at approximately 5,000 feet, but kept them in sight. Capt. Davis made contact at the edge of the field at approximately 200

It is mid-April, 1944, and "Pete" Peterson (left), already an old-timer with 3.5 victories, talks to a group of new pilots. The tall man Peterson is speaking to is James Colburn who was to die in action. At far right Morris Stanley talks to Nick Frederick (wearing chute).

feet altitude. I observed strikes by Davis and as he pulled up to avoid collision, I noticed the left landing gear of the e/a fell down. I fired at the same aircraft, but observed no strikes. The flight then circled the airdrome to the left. During this time the Fw 200K, which Captain Davis damaged, crashed into the landing mat, first ground looping, then cartwheeling until it was completely wrecked. On completing the 360 degree turn contact was made with the remaining Fw 200Ks.

"Captain Davis closed on the ship to the right and fired a long burst, closing fast. I observed strikes on the wing and engine nacelles followed by flame and smoke from the #3 engine. As Davis pulled up, I closed to 250 yards behind the remaining ship and started firing from dead astern and continued to fire to approximately 25 yards observing strikes on wings and fuselage. After pulling off I was in position to see Captain Davis's Fw 200K hit the ground and explode, and a few seconds later I noticed the Fw 200K I had shot at start a slow turn to the left and hit the ground and explode."

Among the burning wreckage of the three Condors, there were other targets and Flight Leader Glen Davis was tempted but common sense prevailed, as he relates at the end of his encounter report: "There were four more Fw 200s parked in front of the hangar on the northeast corner and one more out on the field ready to take-off to the southwest. A single engine aircraft was parked on the southeast corner. I wanted to go in and strafe it but as we had stirred everything up and I had noted a flak tower on the west side of the field, I decided to let well enough alone and get out of there. We climbed back to 15,000 feet and proceeded home without incident."

Total claims for the day were only six with four damaged. Included besides the Fw 200s, was an Me 109 to Ellis Rogers and an Fw 190 to Gilbert O'Brien of the 362nd Squadron, and one of the formidable "long nose" 190s[1] to Richard "Pete" Peterson, the first of his eventual 15.5 victories. Captain Irwin Dregne, one day to be Group Commander, punched a few .50 caliber holes in another "long nose" before it outran him. The persistent gun problems with the early P-51 were much in evidence, and Gil O'Brien's 190 was shot down with only one gun working.

The claims for the day hardly made up for the losses. Flight Officer Chuck Yeager, one day to be very famous indeed, was shot down, as told above, and the Group lost its dynamic new leader, Colonel Henry Spicer. By this date, 5 March, Spicer already had three victories, but was a victim of gun problems. He did however, manage to damage a 190 before the guns quit.

Spicer was flying with the 362nd Squadron and after the dogfight was joined by Lt. John Pugh, who tucked in as his wingman.

This is believed to be Kit Carson's first NOOKY BOOKY, although it bears no name. It is G4-C, the code Carson used through the war and it is thought to be 43-6634, which went MIA with Roger Hilsted on 12 May 1944. The crew is Livingston Blauvelt III, Jewell Williams and John Warner, Crew Chief on the right.

Lt. John Schlossberg smiles for the author's camera. Many details of the B model cockpit show up. The fuel gauge for the 85 gallon fuselage tank is barely visible at center right - very difficult to see from the pilot's position.

John B. England (L), and Harry Ankeny are both happy because the latter has just shot an Me 109 off England's tail - the date is 11 April 1944.

The mission report gives the basic facts of his loss:

"Colonel Spicer and Lt. Pugh, his wingman, came out from Bordeaux at 10,000 feet headed north. They let down to the deck upon crossing out at the Loire. Coming out near Caen on the deck, Colonel Spicer was hit by white bursting tracer flak. They climbed to 4,000 feet still headed north, when the Colonel's plane caught fire."

Johnny Pugh's statement in Spicer's MACR (Missing Aircrew Report) tells what happened then: "He told me he was going to bail out after riding it as far as could over water. He said 'be sure to May Day' and get me a fix". He again told me to give a May Day, then bailed out about ten miles off the French coast. I saw the Colonel's chute in the water and his dinghy inflate. I climbed to 12,000 and gave a May Day at 1315 hours BST. I gave more May Days and then switched to D channel and told Parker I had received no acknowledgment. Then I switched back to B channel and gave five more May Days at 15,000 feet. Being low on gas, I landed at Tangmere and gave my report to Shoreham."

Spicer's decision to go to the deck before crossing out at Caen was certainly a bad decision. He is known to have told his pilots, "don't worry about flak, lads, they can't hit you". Being in the Air Corps in the 1930s he may have participated in periodic exercises with the army anti-aircraft artillery and was aware of the fact that triple A was not very effective. In Europe he had not flown very many missions and possibly did not realize that German flak had become very effective due to excellent equipment and a great deal of practice!

Major General Donald Graham (ret) was an old friend of Spicer's, they had served as instructors together at Randolph Field. Now Graham was deputy group commander. In a recent letter to the author, he says: "Spicer wanted to lead all of the missions after he managed to get out of 66th Fighter Wing, and I went along on all of them. On the milkrun to France (which turned out not to be), my aircraft had damage and I did not go." Graham speculates that if he had been along, he might have been able to advise Spicer to keep off the deck. With Spicer's departure, Graham became Group Commander and remained so until he finished his tour in the fall.

It is a puzzle why ASR did not launch a rescue effort. Spicer was in the water about ten miles off enemy coast and about 100 miles south of Portsmouth and other bases in southern England. General Graham says no search was made because Spicer was too close to the enemy coast. However, the ASR service had in the past and would again go in very close to enemy coasts to snatch fliers from under the muzzles of German guns.

The fact that John Pugh received no answer to his May Days would seem to indicate they simply were not receiving his transmissions. Later, possibly after Pugh landed at Tangmere, two Typhoons were sent to the area but found nothing. Spicer was in bad condition when he eventually drifted ashore, was captured, and spent the rest of the war in *Stalag Luft I* (along with a dozen or so other YOXFORD BOYS). Major General Henry Spicer died in December of 1968.

BACK TO BIG B

The 6th of March was to be the first of many big raids on Hitler's jewel city. In March alone the 8th would go there five times and the 357th would be there every time. The *Luftwaffe*, of course, was well aware of the impending strikes and heavily committed their fighter force to oppose them. Doolittle dispatched some 700 bombers and almost as many fighters. The *Luftwaffe* fighter force was nearly as large and included a great many Me 110s and Me 410s.

This was a big mistake as these twin engined types were decimated. Both sides suffered heavy losses, but we will not attempt to cover this huge air battle, except as it relates to the 357th. Suffice to say, the 8th lost 69 bombers and 11 fighters and the *Luftwaffe* lost some 90 aircraft. For the full story of this battle, the reader is urged to read Ethell and Price's TARGET BERLIN (Arms & Armourer Press, 1999).

Tommy Hayes, commanding the 364th Squadron, was to lead the mission by default when Colonel Graham had to abort; Hayes recalls how it all started: "In the night

Major Tommy Hayes, the highly respected and well liked C.O. of the 364th Squadron and later Deputy Group Commander.

the Operations people worked while the pilots slept. The pilots were unaware of the target until the curtain was opened and the tapes seen. Usually there was emotion shown when the curtain was opened, happiness over the deep penetrations and obvious groaning over the probable milk runs. On this particular morning the noise level was at its highest. It was psychological - the first big raid on Berlin and it was logical to expect an intense German air defense.

"Group briefing was followed by short Squadron briefing, then to the aircraft, start engines, take-off, form up and the long penetration to the R/V. The 357th seemed to always get the escort for the last seventy to 100 miles to the target. Hence we had to overfly (overtake) the bomber stream, say two hours before arriving at our escort point, some 400 or 500 miles from base. On this mission for diversion and because of flak, the bombers took a route to the north via Hamburg area and then southeast to Berlin. Our route was a straight line from base to rendezvous northwest of Berlin. Because of solid undercast navigation was strictly time and vector as briefed. There was no way to correct for drift. As time goes on, in and out of clouds, a psychosis sets in and pilots begin to question our position. What did worry me was a large column of smoke rising in the distance on our left. It was, in fact, Hamburg still burning from the RAF raid the previous night."

On the morning of the 6th, Captain O'Brien and Bob Moore returned to home base about 0700 from RAF Ford where they had spent the night after the Bordeaux mission on the 5th. His Crew Chief, Sgt. Jim Loter would

have had time for a cursory post flight inspection (from yesterday) and a preflight on BILLY'S BITCH, B6-G before start engine time shortly after 1000 hours. In addition, drop tanks would have to be installed serviced and then run in to be sure they fed properly. On deep penetrations you wanted all 485 gallons of fuel available. His Armorer, Tom Quinn would have made a quick inspection of the guns, run a cleaning patch through the bores and replaced ammunition expended the day before.

O'Brien describes his day that 6th of March, 1944: "While the Group had performed well during 'Big Week', it had not had a 'big day', which can be described as a day when the Group tallied twenty or more victories. In truth, our losses had been severe, involving the loss of Group, Squadron and Flight Leaders. All things considered we were not yet setting the world on fire! In fact, the previous day we lost our Group Commander, Colonel Russ Spicer.

"On 6 March, things started off with a bang. Lt. Col. Graham, the new Group Commander had to abort shortly after take-off. He was leading with my squadron, the 363rd. Old 'Lucky Pierre', OBee O'Brien was now the Squadron Leader. On top of that I was leading it with Captain C.E. 'Bud' Anderson's flight and not my regular flight. It could and probably would have been worse for me if Major Tommy Hayes, C.O. of the 364th Squadron had not been present. He assumed command and led the Group. I thank God every day for Tommy Hayes!

"Weather at take-off was good, which was unique for England. The penetration was flown over low scattered clouds which prevented me and other leaders from being able to navigate with precision. In fact, I hadn't seen a recognizable landmark since the Zuyder Zee in Holland. By now the undercast had increased to about 8/10 solid."

It was time for the rendezvous with the bombers when Tommy Hayes broke radio silence to ask me "Where is Berlin, OBee?". This was the first and only time during an operation that I was ever consulted during an on-going mission! I told Tommy, "I think Berlin is behind us". Tommy said we would hold course for two minutes. We did just that, then we made the well-known 180 degree turn which had us flying into Berlin from THE EAST. And guess what? There, 20 to 30 miles away, was a wonderful sight, the 8th Air Force bomber stream. About the same time we had more company in the form of forty plus enemy aircraft on a convergent course with the bombers and us.

"At this point, on the Rules of War scale, leadership had done its job, the enemy was in our vicinity and we immediately attacked. Fortunately for us the Germans had committed their twin engine night fighters to defend Berlin. We headed for a group of e/a attacking the bombers. The Me 110 that I latched onto was easy pick-

Awaiting transport to their aircraft are 362nd pilots Gilbert O'Brien and Tom Norris, who scored 2.5 victories while O'Brien made the ace list, and both survived their combat tours.

ings, which was O.K. with me, I got him burning in his left engine area and we were in a very steep diving right turn, when my machine guns started jamming. I had four functioning .50 caliber guns when the fight started but now I did not know how many were working.

"I found myself going too fast and pulling quite a bit of 'Gs'. The Me 110 is heading vertically for the deck. I pulled up and rolled a bit and watched the 110 crash into a large structure resembling a factory. You never saw such an explosion! It was plainly visible from 20,000 feet. I tested my guns with negative results, none were working. Having no wingman I headed for England, knowing it is not smart to hang out by oneself in the area of a firefight.

"When I had climbed to 20,000 feet I saw a P-51 approaching me from the 4 o'clock position, and observed it to be a 'Yoxford' mustang. It took a position on my wing and radioed 'who are you?' He identified himself as LeRoy Ruder, and I told him to hang around and I would get him back to England. A few minutes later LeRoy called. 'Bogey at 2 o'clock'. Sure enough it was an Me 110, so I told him to get it. He did, and I had a first class seat to watch him shoot it down." According to Ethell and Price in TARGET BERLIN, this 110 was from III. *Gruppe* of the

night fighter *Geschwader* 5, the pilot was Lt. G. Wolf, and he managed to crash land the aircraft near Bernau. The 110 that O'Brien shot down earlier was probably from this same unit.

O'Brien continues: "We made it back to Leiston in good shape, and I never did tell LeRoy that my guns weren't working. I guess he just went on thinking that 'ole OBee was a real nice guy. The big day could not have come at a better time. The next day General Woodbury, commanding 66th Fighter Wing, flew into Leiston. He said he came to congratulate us for the work at Berlin, but I always thought he came to find out what happened to his friend and former chief of staff, Colonel Russ Spicer, whom we had lost the previous day.

"Why were we so fortunate? I think there were a number of reasons. First, was that we had trained together for two years as a unit. Next, getting the new long-range fighter, and finally having Major Tommy Hayes leading us into battle from the east of Berlin, all combined to make the Berlin mission a great success, with no losses on our side."

Claims for the day included three Me 109s, three Fw 190s, one Me 410, one Me 210 and twelve Me 110s. Since the Me 210 had been a dismal failure and had seen only limited production, which had stopped two years before, it is likely the 210 was probably a 410 (they were very similar in appearance).

Captain Davis Perron, a 362nd Squadron Flight Leader, was holder of the high score for the day with three claims. Perron and his wingman 2nd Lt. Rod Starkey had come across a crippled B-17 under attack by two Fw 190s. When the 190 pilots saw the two P-51s they broke away from the bomber. Perron reported: "I picked the lead 190 and dived on his tail. I caught him at around 15,000 feet and began to fire three long bursts from 600 yards range. I kept closing to 300 yards and continued firing. I saw strikes on his left wing. His wing tank blew up and he caught fire and he went into an inverted spin, disappearing as I broke off. I saw no chute."

Immediately after this, the other 190 blundered in front of Perron who fired two long bursts, resulting in fire and pieces blowing off. Climbing back to the bombers he spotted a Me 210 (410?) and shot it down as well. Starkey had stayed behind to deal with several Me 109s, one of which he shot down, with only one gun firing. This was Starkey's only victory of the war, although he flew a full tour and survived. These also were Perron's only victories, for three weeks later he disappeared in bad weather over the channel and was never found.

One occurrence of interest during the melee was an "almost" friendly fire casualty. At the height of the affair, Captain Glendon Davis and his wingman, Lt. Tom

"Little Red" Harris were taking turns shooting parts off of an Me 110. Davis was covering Harris on the 110's tail when a 362nd Squadron P-51 cut in front of Harris and fired at the 110. Davis reported: "The P-51 pilot can thank Lt. Harris for not shooting him down, as the range was only about 100 yards. Moral: When someone else is firing don't cut in front of him if you want to live".

The 362nd pilot may have been Captain Gilbert O'Brien and it is unlikely he did it knowingly, but saw only a "cold meat" 110 and not Harris. In any case, O'Brien did not claim a victory on that day, while both Davis and Harris claimed one each.

It is almost impossible to re-assemble Groups and Squadrons after a big rat race, and the P-51s often returned singly or in small groups. Major Tommy Hayes was headed home with four other P-51s and they were about 100 miles NW of Berlin. They were on the deck after chasing two Me 109s away from some B-24s. The 109s managed to evade, but Hayes, shortly thereafter, caught one of them attempting to land at an airfield near Uzlen. Hayes tells the rest in his encounter report:

"I was about to strafe a containment of about 500 white pyramidal tents when I observed an Me 109. I cut him short and started firing at 300 yards. Suddenly I noticed he was over a field at 300 feet. He was burning and smoking with wheels semi-lowered. I overshot him and went under him by 50 feet, pulled off to the right and watched him crash 1000 yards from the perimeter of the field. Went back to strafe the plane and see if the pilot had survived. When almost in position, another 109 crossed over me evidently trying to look at the crash which must have looked like it had spun out.

"I fired at him but he had the speed on me and poured on the coal. He headed east and was out of range, so, afraid of gas shortage, I gave up the attack and turned toward home." The pilot of the first 190 was Uffz K. Pelz, of JG 302 - he was killed in the crash.

A few minutes after Hayes had shot down Pelz, he had re-formed his depleted Squadron of four aircraft and headed home. One of these stalwart four, Lt. John C. Howell, called in another Me 109. Hayes told him to get it, and with Lt. John Carder covering, Howell closed on the 109 and fired a long burst before overrunning.

He then broke off and Carder hit it with a burst. John Howell's gun camera film seems to show a large object breaking away from the 109, so Carder may have fired at an empty aircraft. However, for reasons unknown, Carder got full credit for the shoot down. The pilot, *Oberleutnant* Gerhard Loos, fell from his chute and was killed. He had seen extensive combat on the Russian front. Now early in March, with 92 victories he was a *Staffelkapitän* in JG 54.

In mid 1999, Friedrich Ludecke, a former German fighter pilot was successful in contacting John Howell, seeking information about the death of Loos, whom he had taught to fly in 1942 and they had become close friends. John Carder was killed in a plane crash in 1961. John Howell was able to provide memories of that event 55 years ago when he and Ludecke had been enemies.

The 6th of March mission was noteworthy for the catastrophic losses inflicted on the Me 110s by the 357th and other fighter groups operating that day. *Geschwader* 26 and 76 lost 21 Me 110s and seven Me 410s between them and night fighter *Geschwader* 5 lost another eight.

Me 110s were seldom encountered in daylight again after this date, although Tommy Hayes and Bill Reese shot down two of them late in March and in the latter part of April, the 362nd Squadron caught a gaggle of them in daylight and shot down nine with another eight damaged.

All aircraft were on the ground at home base before 1600 hours. There was time before evening mess for pilots to be debriefed and meet in their Operations pilots rooms and tell each other what great pilots they were and generate jealousy among those who were not on the mission. Later most would meet at the Officers Club for cool ones and to hash it all over between the three squadrons.

Tomorrow the pilots could sleep in. The entire 8th Air Force, except for five leaflet dropping B-17s, remained on the ground. The crew chiefs, mechanics and technicians would not sleep in - they would be servicing and working on their P-51s which had gone through three major missions on the 4th, 5th and 6th. Although no one knew it there would be another major effort on the 8th.

On the morning of 8 March, it was almost 1130 hours when 49 P-51s took off, formed up, and headed into the land of the enemy. Eleven aircraft aborted at various points however - another bad show. The remaining 33 RVed with 2nd Division B-24s north of Brunswick almost two hours later and stayed with them through the targets in Berlin. After only one day of stand-down, Doolittle had launched about 600 bombers of all three divisions with the major target being the VKF Bearing works in the Berlin suburb of Erkner. The 3rd Division took the heaviest loss, losing 23 B-17s. Almost 600 fighters provided support, mostly P-47s, of which Colonel Hub Zemke's 56th Group had the best score of the day with 28 claims.

THE YOXFORD BOYS came home with only moderate claims of seven destroyed, while losing Lt. William "Stubby" Gambill. As is often the case, he just disappeared. He had been in Colonel Graham's flight but no one saw what happened to him after Graham shot down a 190. Many years later his son was able to trace his fate.

Somehow he had been shot down and became a POW. He was in a German transit camp, enroute to a *Stalag Luft* on 23 March when the area was heavily bombed by the RAF. Stubby was killed by a bomb hitting the shelter he was in, a sad incident of war.

To illustrate the events of the 8th of March, we will quote two encounter reports of particular interest.

The first of these is by Captain Jack Warren, a flight leader in the 364th Squadron, who engaged in a long-running see-saw battle with a Long Nose Fw 190. For some reason Warren was not leading his flight, but was wingman to Gowdy (364th) leader, Major Dregne, when they spotted two Long Nose 190s (probably Fw 190 Ds) 50 miles SE of Berlin.[1]

Warren reported: "We turned toward the 190s and they split 'essed. They pulled out at about 10,000 feet and Major Dregne made a pass at one and I got a head-on shot at the other as he kicked into a violent spiral and then spun to a lower altitude. Major Dregne overshot the first 190 and our #3 man, Lt. Strode made several passes. Each time the e/a would loop with a full roll on top. On the third time he ended up on the tail of our #3 man, who went into a Lufbury to the left. I came in on the e/a and he broke off his attack on our #3 man. The enemy aircraft then headed for the deck. I was indicating about 400 mph and began to pull up on him. I closed to about 300 yards and gave him a long burst with only two guns firing. He pulled up into a loop with a roll on top. I followed him up and then rolled out and came back on his tail. He dove for the deck again and I closed to about 300 yards and gave him a long burst with only two guns firing. He again looped and rolled, this time on top of the loop in a roll he fired at Major Dregne who was covering me.

"I followed, rolled out and come in again. He dove for the deck again flying between trees, houses and under power lines. I closed to about 300 yards and a long burst this time with only one gun firing. I noted smoke pouring out as he got lower and lower and I passed over him, he crashed in a field about 50 miles southeast of Berlin. I pulled up and came around to strafe the plane when I noticed the pilot jump out and start running. I started shooting at him and the plane when my last gun gave out. We joined formation and came home. Both Major Dregne and Lt. Strode saw the plane crash and all three will admit the long nose 190 is a fast and maneuverable plane and this pilot was way above average."

Ten days later, Jack Warren, the Group's first ace, was swallowed up in miserable weather and was never seen again. Although Jack Warren had been able to shoot down "his" Long Nose 190 with only one gun operating, his experience was all too typical of the period. It was, of course, a serious waste of all resources to send fighters 500

miles into the enemy's heartland, to destroy his air force, only to find that the weapons would not function. (see the section on guns and gunsights.)

1st. Lt. John B. England was flying his fifth mission on this date and would score the first of a long string of victories which would total 17.5, only one less than the Group's high scorer Leonard "Kit" Carson. In ten months he would be a Major commanding the 362nd squadron and be the recipient of a Silver Star.

On this day, England was probably on his way home alone or had possibly joined Anderson's Chambers (363rd) White flight. In his encounter report, England describes the event:

"I saw three Me 109s attacking a B-17 straggler near Steinhuder Lake northwest of Hannover. I was at 25,000 feet and the enemy planes at about 20,000. They were making a head-on attack on the bomber. I turned around to go back and the enemy ships went around and fell in on the rear of the bomber. Two Me 109s broke away. I went after the lead man who was shooting at the B-17 from 100 yards range. I came in from behind and underneath, closing to about 50 yards and commenced firing. I saw a big piece fly off his left wing and observed strikes underneath the fuselage between the wheel wells. He split 'essed and rolled down to about 4,000 feet. I saw the pilot bail out. The last I saw of it, the plane was smoking and in a slow spiral to the ground. I claim one Me 109 destroyed. 161 rounds fired."

Captain Clarence Anderson was a frustrated fighter pilot/flight leader. During the "Big Week" in February, the neophyte group had done fairly well, 18 pilots had scored one or more victories, but the best Anderson had been able to do was to punch a few .50 caliber holes in an Fw 190 which apparently accomplished nothing except to make work for a *Luftwaffe* sheet metalworker. Anderson recalls those early days and his eventual success: "The procedure that we adopted in our Squadron for mission scheduling was for the operations officer to post the next day's schedule the afternoon before the next mission. This way each pilot knew what he was going to be doing the next day and could schedule his activities accordingly. You had no idea what tomorrow's mission would be or where the target was. Squadron lead would be passed around to the various Flight Leaders in the same manner. The Group Commander and his staff were each assigned to one of the Squadrons for flying and we worked them into the schedule the same way.

"Now we were into March. I have seven missions under my belt and have gained some confidence but still have no victory to claim and our Group score was starting to rise. I missed the first attempt of 8th Air Force to bomb Berlin on 6 March, but was on the big raid on the 8th. On withdrawal from the target area two of our flights were returning when we came on some straggling B-17s under attack by three Me 109s. I took one and the other Flight Leader took the others. After several non-concentric circles neither I nor the 109 could get into a decent firing position. Finally I pulled so much lead I could not even see him under my nose, and fired a burst hoping he would fly through the bullet stream.

"It worked, because when he appeared again he was streaming coolant and he bailed out. The next moment John England from the 362nd tucked onto my wing and gave a big OK sign. I wondered what he meant. I knew that if I had hit the 109 it was a very lucky shot and thought that maybe John had shot him down from under me! It wasn't until we were back on base that I found out what happened. When I walked into the officer's club that evening, John rushed up to me and congratulated me on the fantastic high angle off shot he had seen. I sloughed it off with an 'Aw, shucks Johnny, lucky shot'. Then I hurried to the phone and called intelligence to claim my first victory."

As we have seen above, John England had shot down the other 109 of three that were attacking the B-17s.

Anderson concludes: "By the end of March, I had flown 15 of the 25 missions and had gained the necessary confidence and experience to cope with what was in store for me over the coming months."

On the 9th, the target was again in the Berlin area. The weather was very bad, and although the mission was flown, the target and the affects of the bombing were hidden under the overcast. No enemy aircraft were seen, but Harry Ankeny's diary entry is an excellent commentary on the day:

"Briefed again for Berlin, the trip on paper being 1050 miles. Took off on Col. Graham's, our group C.O.s, wing and he led us through the overcast with precision - best job of instrument flying I have ever seen. He just took his time, kept his airspeed at 170 mph and we really sailed through fine. Being #2 man in red flight, it was my job to stay on the bomber fighter channel, reporting anything unusual to RIGHT FIELD. Our Group leader, Colonel Graham's windshield frosted up quite badly when we hit the enemy coast and he had to turn back. Captain Broadhead took over RIGHT FIELD and I tacked onto his wing. Since the bombers were 50 minutes late, we met them very early and started escorting them, our Squadron taking the lead box of bombers.

There was a complete overcast over the continent, so much so that not a single enemy aircraft came up. Captain Broadhead really is a rough leader - terrible! He really wore us out, the boys in his flight. Returning we crossed some terrible heavy flak at Hannover. For a

minute I thought they were going to get all of us. I made a sharp diving turn to the right and luckily nothing hit me. Lt. Adams, who was right behind me, got two good-sized flak holes in his plane. Was sure tired after this mission. It wasn't the 1300 miles we covered, but Captain Broadhead gave me such a rough time, it wore me out. You couldn't tell what he was going to do next."

It is, of course, essential for a Flight Leader to be a "smooth" pilot. Joe Broadhead became a Major, Squadron Commander, and an ace with eight victories, but he was not a "smooth" pilot!

After the 9th, there was a stand-down for six days, with no missions flown. This was part of a general reduction in effort by the 8th Air Force. On two of those days, there were no U.S. heavy bombers over the continent, except for a very few night leaflet-dropping B-24s. On one day, 52 B-24s bombed targets in France, and the other two days, a small force of bombers were out striking secondary targets, all escorted by P-47s and P-38s only.

MSgt Joe DeShay was a Flight Chief in the 364th squadron at this time. He kept a wartime diary which consisted of only a few words each day. His entries for these five days are of interest: "10 March, 24 hour pass, rode bike to Saxmundam. 11 March, no mission, no mail. 12 March, No mission, raining, no mail. 13 March, No mission, released for three days, slept till noon. 14 March, Pulled all engine bolts last night. Slept till noon. No mail, no flying. 15 March, worked all day and night and next day."

These brief entries provide a good picture of the period as lived by the ground crews. They show, for one thing, how important mail was to troops so far from home. They also show that it was not all work, there were periods when the work level allowed some crews to be released from duty. Work in progress on other aircraft meant that not all crews were released from duty. DeShay's short entry on the 14th shows why no P-51s were flying - they were all grounded. This was the result of a catastrophic failure of the four engine mount bolts on a 354th Group P-51 over its base at Boxted - the entire engine assembly broke away and the pilot was killed.

All P-51s were grounded, and as DeShay indicates, a crash program to replace all P-51 engine mount bolts was begun. Generally, the P-51 was relatively easy aircraft for the mechanics. John Warner, a Crew Chief in the 362nd Squadron recalls a few points.

The thing that stands out most in his memory is how cold it was on the hands when pulling the fuel strainer. Rough running engines were common, usually due to spark plugs (British plugs were better than their U.S. counterpart.) Warner: "What kept a Mustang performing well was changing plugs and checking timing, (magnetos)

very often. Also a must was to perform the preflight inspection item by item, which included pulling that darn fuel strainer and freezing your hands! Having Kit Carson for a pilot meant I seldom had to change tires or brakes."

Oddly enough, what sticks in this writer's memory is not cold, but burned hands from changing the intake spark plugs on a hot Merlin. By the 16th, the P-51s were serviceable again and it was back to the war. (See page 314 for further discussion)

The 16th was a good day - and a bad day. First of all, one aircraft crashed on take-off, 11 aborted, reducing the force, led by Lt. Col. Egenes, to 33 P-51s. Lt. Robert Meyer and Lt. Alvin Pyeatt were lost in combat, the former a POW, and Pyeatt, a promising fighter pilot with two victories, was KIA. (Note, Al Pyeatt's wings, his medals and photos are framed on the author's wall - a tribute to a gallant fighter pilot). In addition, one P-51 came home with a wing damaged by an exploding enemy aircraft. It was a good day as the Group claimed 12 enemy aircraft destroyed, plus a probable and several damaged.

These included four Me 109s, one Fw 190, five Me 110s and a Do 217 claimed by Lt. William Reese. At this stage of the war any *Luftwaffe* bomber flying in daylight was in great peril. Reese reported that two men bailed out before the inevitable burning hole in the ground.

The relatively large number of twin engine types (five Me 110s, a Do 217, plus three 110s, a 410 and a Ju 88 damaged seems to indicate that the *Luftwaffe* had not learned its lesson, or they were desperate for fighters.

Tommy Hayes leading the 364th Squadron was one of those claiming a 110. We quote part of his encounter report: "At 300 yards, my first burst had not enough lead, but the e/a did nothing. Still closing my second burst caught him square and started the left engine to burn. He reacted now by straightening out where he caught the full effect of all guns. This was about 50-100 yards and I observed the canopy and other debris leave the plane. I went under him by 50 feet and noticed both engines burning. Also the black cross on underside of the left wing was trimmed heavy with bright yellow. His belly was robin's egg blue and top a rusty brown. I broke away to come back again when I saw one parachute open and the aircraft go straight down where it crashed and exploded in a snow field."

All of the twin engine types were not cold meat, however, as shown by Joe Broadhead's experience with an Me 410, whose pilot was determined not to be shot down:

"I was flying behind a box of bombers at 20,000 feet, when I saw an Me 410 on the right side of the bombers preparing to attack. He pulled in front of me and I started to chase him, but my wing tanks prevented me from getting in range, so I dropped them. Then followed

vicious maneuvering from 25,000 to the deck. The enemy pilot was undoubtedly very experienced, for he allowed me only a few good shots. One time I observed strikes on his wings from close range, but for the most part his evasive tactics were too effective. After dog-fighting for around ten minutes, the enemy plane broke through a hole in the clouds and I never contacted him again. I claim one Me 410 damaged."

Two days later, on the 18th, a five hour mission was flown but the weather was very bad which cost the 357th two pilots, Lt. Konstantin Vogel and Capt. Jack Warren, who had just reached the exalted position of ace two days before. Neither were ever found and the two 109s shot down did not make up for the loss.

Harry Ankeny's day on the 22nd illustrates another aspect of Group duties. All 8th Air Force fighter groups were expected to provide pilots and aircraft on short notice to assist the ASR (Air Sea Rescue) service searching for aircraft down in the drink, and to give cover over rescue operations in progress.

Harry Ankeny recorded in his diary: "Took off for Berlin. Weather not too good. Got half way across the channel and my oil temp got very high - went up to the red line twice and so I decided to come back. That afternoon, Lt. Pascoe, 363rd Squadron and I took off to act as spotters for Air Sea Rescue. We stood by on 'B' channel (Air Sea Rescue) and waited around Great Yarmouth for them to vector us out to circle someone in the channel. They vectored us clear across to the enemy coast to pick up a bomber in distress but did not see them. A P-47 ditched in the channel - we could hear him giving his MAY DAY (distress call) but his buddies stayed with him and we weren't sent out. Spent three hours just flying around over the channel but didn't see anything. Weather was terrible - very low ceiling - clear down in the water in some spots." The P-47 was probably serial number 42-8512 of the 361st Group. The pilot, Lt. James Rogers was not found.

There were missions on the 23rd, 27th, 28th and 29th, closing out the month of March, 1944. All of them were long tiring missions usually in appalling weather and none were easy. On each of these missions, pilots were lost including Lts. Gutierrez and McGinley who collided when one flight flew thru another in the overcast. ASR, quickly on the scene, found nothing. On the 28th Lt. Col. Hubert Egenes, Deputy Group Commander and veteran of the early fighting in the Pacific was shot down and killed while strafing an airfield on which five Ju 88s and a hangar were burned.

Allied fighter pilots lost in strafing attacks must run into the hundreds. It is true that vast amounts of German lives and material were destroyed in these low

This photo of Lt. John Carder, who scored his third victory (out of seven) on 6 March 1944 shows the N-3B gunsight, which had the type A-1 bomb sight assembly attached. This apparatus was for use in horizontal bombing, but the mirror has been removed from it's forward bracket here, making the bomb sight portion unusable.

level attacks, but were the results worth the cost? We will never know the answer, of course as opinions vary, but in a 1995 letter to this writer, Donald Graham expressed his thoughts:

"When I was C.O., the three of us (Commander, Deputy Commander and Group Operations Officer), took lead on a regular basis, no matter to where. Egenes led on an airfield strafing deal and got the flak. I was in London on time off. Saw his young wife later in the States, another sad deal. I did not think the gains were worth the cost on those missions, a few aircraft on the ground were worth nothing in the big picture."

There was a bizarre incident with a happy ending on the 27th during a mission to the south of France. William Overstreet tells what happened: "The mission was to Mont De Marson, near Bordeaux. Flak severed my oxygen line while I was at about 25,000 feet and I passed out. The next thing I knew I was in a spin, dead engine and it was an hour and a half later. I recovered from the spin, switched to fuel tank with gas, got the engine restarted and pulled up just before I was in the trees. There was no way to know where I was so I assumed that I had generally followed the heading we were using for the mission and reversed it. I was able to find the coast of France, cross the channel, but by the time I got to the base of the 4th Ftr.

Grp. (author's note; this was Debden, about 60 miles SW of Leiston). I was low on gas and horrible weather in the direction of Leiston, I landed there and was put in the hospital. The debriefing officer Captain Mead, was a neighbor of my parents in Clifton Forge, Va, and the mechanic who fixed my airplane was a buddy I had played with on high school teams, "Hotcha" Tucker. Apparently their PR man released the story as Lowell Thomas used it on his radio show and the June issue of TIME carried it."

The third month of 1944 had been a very hectic period. Missions had been flown on 16 days, many four and five hours - a long time in the cramped cockpit over a land full of enemies. There had been combat on many of these. At the end of six weeks of operations 24 pilots were gone, eight dead, 16 POWs and two evaders. There was never a significant drop in pilot strength, however, due to the inflow of replacements. The victory score stood at 75.

At this time, Joe Broadhead was Commander of the 362nd Squadron, with Montgomery Throop at 363rd, and Tommy Hayes leading the 364th. The war in the air had escalated into a brutal slugging match with both sides hammering at each other, resulting in heavy losses on both sides. Although callous, from a military point of view, 8th Air Force could absorb and sustain its losses. The *Luftwaffe*, although it managed to sustain aircraft pro-

duction to make up its losses, could not do the same with pilots. During the summer there would be long periods in which the German air force did not react to 8th Air Force incursions. Although no one doubted that Germany would be defeated, no one knew there were still 13 months of fighting before Germany would lie in ruins, and the rest of Europe drained and exhausted after a war that cost over 13,000,000 lives.

TO ABORT, OR NOT TO ABORT

"Abort" was a dirty word in the 8th Air Force, but almost all pilots did it when they felt it was the thing to do. From the word "abortion", to terminate prematurely, it is defined in military terms as an early return from a mission, usually caused by an aircraft systems malfunction. The vast majority of aborts were for legitimate causes, but there were a few pilots, unable to overcome their apprehension about the all-too-real dangers of the mission, used imaginary mechanical defects as an excuse to leave the formation and return early. These few soon became known to their flight leaders, fellow pilots and the ground crews. A "rough engine", common enough with the Merlin, was a favorite reason, and often enough, mechanics could find no defect.

Joe DeShay, flight chief, and line chief, in the 364th Squadron, recalls: "There was a time in the latter part of the combat tour when we had a spate of problems with tail wheel tires blowing out during taxi on the perimeter track, or turning onto the runway. At these points a sharp turn was made, which tended to roll the tire off the rim, or blow it out.

"Now, it was not for we of the ground crews to determine if the situation was accidental, or created intentionally. However, we did not want to see an aircraft abort the mission in this manner, so we assembled a spare tail wheel and tire. We took a team of three men and the Cletrac out to the runway marshalling area, and waited for any tail wheel failures. When such occurred, the Cletrac driver ran the machine up close to the aft fuselage a sling was placed around the fuselage and the tail winched off the ground. The third man replaced the wheel and tire quickly, and the pilot was signaled to take off. It did not take long before the blowing of tail wheel tires became a thing of the past."

(Author's note: For the technically inclined - an explanation of the tail wheel locking system: With the control stick fully forward, the tail wheel was unlocked and free swiveling. With the stick aft of neutral, the tail wheel had only six degrees of swiveling, right or left, controlled by the rudder pedals. If the stick was back (tail wheel locked), and one brake held to make a tight turn, it

was possible to roll the tail wheel tire off the rim - accidentally, or on purpose.)

Squadron and Group Command, who were very sensitive to the "abort" problem, often unfairly "chewed out" pilots who aborted for legitimate reasons, of which there were many, especially early in operations. Many pilots, determined to protect their reputations in the future, often continued with a mission when they should have turned back and a few were undoubtedly lost as a result.

Many pilots and ground crews had enviable records of many missions flown without aborts and a few Crew Chiefs were awarded The Bronze Star for a specified number of missions completed. (number uncertain, but thought to be 100). Without taking anything away from these awards, which were certainly deserved in any case, luck had a large part to play in it. There were many parts of an aircraft which could fail without warnings, despite excellent maintenance.

As time went by, the P-51 became increasingly reliable. A 362nd Squadron analysis for February, 1945, indicated an acceptable rate of 14 aborts for the month - five due to engine, three for propeller malfunction, two for drop tanks, two for cooling system and one each for oxygen and electrical defects.

As the calendars were flipped over to April in the orderly rooms, shops and operations centers, there were only about nine weeks remaining until the biggest event of the European war - the return to the continent, D-Day. By now everyone knew it was coming, and the latrine rumors said it would be in May. They weren't far off.

April and May were the lead-in to OPERATION OVERLORD. During this period no less than 47 missions were flown. On many days early in May, there were two and three in one day. At least 23 of these missions produced "no joy", to use an RAF phrase - there was no sign of the *Luftwaffe*. Yet on other days there was violent combat, enough to provide 154 victory claims, and cause the loss of 31 pilots. There were many noteworthy events of this period, too many to cover in detail so we will endeavor to provide the flavor of those pre-invasion days.

2nd Lt. Henry Pfeiffer's first combat mission was not filled with heart stopping encounters with enemy aircraft and was not even very exciting. Yet it illustrates the tensions and traumas of a brand new fighter pilot, alone over a hostile land, possibly with a Focke-Wulf lurking behind every cloud. The date is uncertain, but it was almost certainly either the 18th or 29th of April - the Group and most of the 8th Air Force had gone to Berlin on both days.

Henry Pfeiffer: "I was scheduled for a two-ship radio relay with Flight Leader 'Stormy' Fairweather. The range of VHF radios was such that on deep penetrations, radio relay aircraft were provided to orbit just off the coast of Holland, and to relay communications between the Group Leader and home base. This was especially needed if the Group ended up at low altitude in the target area. As newly assigned pilots, our P-51 experience was certainly minimal, some of us had never been above 20,000 feet, and did not know all we should have about the bird, including instrument and weather flying.

"We took off shortly after the Group had departed, and were about to go into the soup when Fairweather aborted, leaving me alone. The Group Leader decided I was to proceed as briefed, to climb to 20,000 or as high as required to maintain contact, and to orbit north of Holland over the North Sea. I climbed through many layers of clouds and came into the open between layers at about 25,000. I could see land below about 50-75 miles out. I was getting a little cold, but with my sheepskin flight suit and boots, I'd be OK.

"Then to my concern and amazement two P-38s came climbing out of the overcast below me, and toward me. Since the P-51s were new to the theatre and they looked similar to Me 109s, we were briefed to beware and not let them get into firing range. Here I am a lone Mustang over enemy territory, so I thought I would give them a little altitude and began to climb. However, they seemed to have identified me and stayed in the same area. They probably had a similar mission, but we hadn't been briefed that other aircraft were to be in this area.

'I then climbed to 32,000 to just below the high overcast and stayed there, freezing until the Group Leader released me to return to base. I had remained on point for about three hours, scared and frozen the entire time. I returned, through poor weather, to base with no other problems, my first mission accomplished."

Pfeiffer's wariness of the P-38s was well advised, as witness from the Group leader's report on 11 April: "A P-38 pilot fired on our pilot while he was destroying an Me 109, which had just fired on bomber crews in chutes. P-38s also fired on other P-51s while they engaged e/a. In addition, P-38s bounced our group while it was flying in formation with belly tanks." While some bomber gunners went by the theory - "if it doesn't have four engines, shoot at it", some P-38s operated on the similar theory, "If it doesn't have four or two engines, shoot at it." As the year wore on and more P-38 units switched to P-51s, this problem became less acute.

March ended with the Group having flown 25 missions (15 of them in March), often in atrocious weather. Twenty-four pilots were gone, eight dead, 16 prisoners

Lts. Ollie Harris, Tom Norris and Gil O'Brien, plus a skeptical squadron dog pose in the 362nd pilot's room.

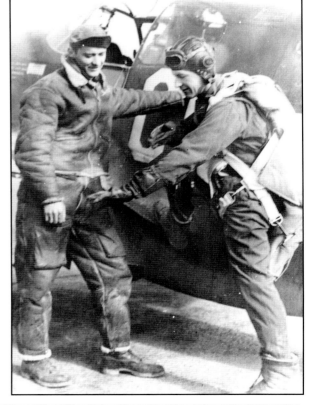

Right: A classic posed fighter pilot photo. Captain John Howell shows how it is done to Sgt. Lyle Olson, a Crew Chief who has heard it all before.

of war, two had evaded capture and returned, and Lt. Edwin Sutton was still missing and would be so listed at the conclusion of the war. 75 enemy aircraft had been shot down. By the end of March, the Group had settled into the pattern that would continue until the end.

We think of March as the learning period. In truth, of course, the learning never ended. New pilots, new tactics, (ours and the enemy), new equipment and changing conditions, all contributed to the constant effort to "keep on top of the situation". It is, of course, impossible to tell of the many missions flown, the many triumphs and the often tragic loss of comrades. Instead, we will relate some of the happenings of that spring and early summer, 1944.

THE FIRST OF APRIL - APRIL FOOL'S DAY

The 1st of April was a bad day for THE YOXFORD BOYS. The mission took off as scheduled, but the weather was so bad that the whole thing turned into a fiasco, nothing was accomplished, and two men had vanished into the murk.

No mission report has been found for that day, but Harry Ankeny's vivid description in his diary, tells the story better than a mission report could: "We were on a fighter sweep into France. Had Lt."Rocky" Hill on my wing in Lt. Adam's flight. Target for the bombers was Frankfurt, just below the Ruhr Valley. We were supposed to hit the target the same time the bombers dropped their bombs. Started into the overcast at 8,000 ft. Lt. Adams got a little slow (150 mph) in the overcast, so I took Lt. Hill and decided to climb thru alone.

"We climbed to 23,000, still in the overcast, and I heard some one say they were at 28,000 and still in it. I decided to turn back and everyone did. The radio relay ship was the only one to hit the top, 35,000 feet. Found the southern coast of England and made my way back to the field flying along the coast dodging barrage balloons. Captain Perron and Lt. Rydberg never did get thru the weather and probably spun into the channel. Was terrible weather - they should never have sent us on the mission."

John England adds his comments on the loss of Perron and Rydberg: "I was flying element leader in Judson (362) blue flight at 24,000 feet in the vicinity of Doullens, France, when I heard over the RT, the order from my flight commander, Capt. Perron, to drop tanks and turn homeward. Shortly after, I heard a scream, 'I've got to bail out'."

Right: These 364th pilots are L-R, Mark Stepelton, Frank Koko, Captain John Storch, the senior man here; LeRoy Ruder, and Cyril Conklin. Koko and Ruder would die in combat and Conklin would become a POW. Both Stepelton and Storch would complete their tours.

Left: 1st Lt. Tom McKinney, the regular pilot of ROUND TRIP JR. He flew a complete tour, scoring four victories, and returned to the Zone of the Interior.

THE MYSTERY OF

WING COMMANDER WARBURTON, RAF

A very insignificant mission took place on the 12th of April, but it is of interest due to one of the men involved, and the fact that it ended in a mystery which has never been solved.

On the morning of the 12th, two Lockheed F-5s (The photo reconnaissance version of the P-38), took off from Mount Farm Airfield, home of the 7th Photo Group, and one of them did not return. Its loss caused a major furor at Mount Farm Airfield, and in the higher levels of the RAF because the pilot of this USAAF airplane was an RAF officer who should not have been flying the mission. Captain Carl Chapman, Operations Officer of the 7th Group, was leading and his companion was Wing Commander Adrian Warburton, the RAF's most highly decorated photo recon pilot. He had flown a remarkable 400 reconnaissance missions out of Malta over a three year period when it had been under constant attack. Now, early in 1944, recovering from a jeep accident, he was the RAF liaison officer with the 7th Group, and not medically cleared to fly, nor was he qualified in the F-5 aircraft. As Operations Officer, Chapman would have planned the mission, apparently with the approval of B/Gen Elliott Roosevelt, the Wing Commander, and a close friend of Chapman's.

The field order (#297) for 12 April assigned eight P-51s to "escort PRUs". (PRU actually meant "Photo Reconnaissance Unit", but was often used referring a PR aircraft.) The eight P-51s, led by Lt. Leonard Carson, took off at 0905 hours, and rendezvoused with the F-5s as planned. In his mission report Carson says that the P-51s, carrying drop tanks, had trouble keeping up with the F-5s, and in fact, six of them lost contact and returned to base, leaving Carson and Lt. Ollie Harris. The targets are uncertain, but the two F-5s separated to cover different targets in the Augsburg area, one P-51 going with each.

The mission report implies that all four aircraft rejoined at Lake Constance, the two F-5s heading south, presumably to Sardinia where Warburton had friends. In recent correspondence, Harris disputes this, saying the two F-5s did not return to Lake Constance at all. He and Carson were to meet there, but were unable to make contact except by radio, and each returned to base alone. Almost surely the two F-5s did not rejoin either, each proceeding south by itself. So much for the very simple story of a routine mission from the view-point of the 357th. Surely no one in Group Ops knew (or cared) who the F-5 pilots were, and certainly Carson and Harris did not. Carson once told this writer he did not recall having any radio contact with "his" F-5 pilot.

From here the story gets very murky. The author had considerable correspondence with Squadron Leader Tony Spooner, Warburton's friend and author of his biography WARBURTON'S WAR, and with Colonel George Lawson, Commander of the 7th Photo Group. Before his death, Chapman also contributed to the controversy, although not much. All disagree on major points of the story.

Lawson, in a letter to the writer, expresses surprise that the two F-5s had a P-51 escort. He states that recon pilots did not want escorts as they just attracted attention to themselves. Lawson says: "It was our policy to avoid other airplanes at any cost, we were as afraid of P-51s and P-47s as we were of 109s and 190s." (Later in the war however, as recon losses mounted, the 7th Photo Group actually acquired some P-51s to escort their recon aircraft.)

All that remains is the bottom line, Warburton did not arrive in Sardinia, and in fact, was never seen again. So, this very minor 357th mission ended with the disappearance of a famous RAF flyer, who was not medically cleared to fly and was not qualified in the P-38 type aircraft, and why was he flying the mission and what was his fate?

In August of 2002, the remains of a U.S. Lockheed P-38 type aircraft, with the remains of its pilot was found near Egling, Germany some 30 miles south of Munich. Since the P-38 was a U.S. type, German authorities turned the remains over to the U.S. Army, whose forensic laboratories were able to identify the remains as that of Adrian Warburton.

Almost 60 years after his disappearance, Wing Commander Warburton was buried in the British military cemetery at Durnbach, Germany, with his widow and high ranking RAF personnel in attendance. The aircraft remains were donated to the aviation museum on the island of Malta, where Warburton had such a distinguished career in the early years of WWII. So ended the 357th Fighter Group mission of 12 April 1944.

"However, I saw both Perron and Rydberg after the call came thru. They were both with the flight in heavy overcast with very limited visibility, struggling, as we all were, to maintain level flight by instruments."

After the pilots and aircraft had returned to base, an immediate search was launched for the two pilots. Captain Don Pickerall, 362nd Squadron Intelligence Officer: "On 1 April a search for Captain Perron and Lt. Rydberg was made from station F-373. Six P-51s, led by Captain Broadhead, took off at 1230 BST and landed at 1500 BST: The Channel area from Boulogne to Dieppe on the French side and Dover to Beachey Head on the English side was covered. The search planes zigzagged diagonally back and forth across the channel without discovering any trace of the missing pilots."

With the coming of spring, more men were taking advantage of what was a very generous pass policy, allowing some men off from their crews as long as it did not affect the work load. Many headed for London, but nearby towns and villages were also popular where the culture could be absorbed, and also the favorite pastime could be pursued - pub crawling and girl chasing.

John "J.J." Hoefner, an Armorer in the 362nd, does not mention whether he engaged in the latter two pursuits, but he does tell us about his views on life in a fighter Squadron, and just being in England: "Being sent overseas caused me to have feelings in several different and opposite ways. There was one of concern, the fear of the unknown and what really awaited us. It was, after all, wartime, with everything that war represented. Then there was a feeling of excitement and wonder that I was going to see things and places that I had read about, but never dreamt I would see. I thought we must have the most wonderful job in the world, working around airplanes. I had wanted to be involved in ordnance and had applied for OCS in that branch while at Tonopah. However, the fact that I wore glasses ruled me out. Being an armorer in a fighter squadron made up for my disappointment and I really thought there was no better job.

"We really had a good situation, a good squadron, a good base, and while we worked hard with long hours, we always had a dry place to sleep, food, plus many other things the combat troops did not. Obviously my feelings were influenced by knowing I was not in the dangerous part of war as our pilots were. I'm sure they did not all think of the war in the same way, even though they had wanted to fly military airplanes.

"My worst memory was when I saw Jenkins crash because I knew there could be no surviving. I was sick to my stomach and could not sleep that night. The other one which was nearly as bad was watching the P-38 crash after the pilot tried to slow roll on takeoff. Here it was not quite as bad, as he was a stranger, and not one of ours. The English and Scottish people that I met were great and little different than we were. They reacted well to their problems and the hardships they had gone through. There was a severe shortage of everything, but they coped very well. They had a sense of humor and kept it through the trying times and needed it to be able to put up with the great invasion of 'the yanks'."

It is 11 April, 20,000 feet over Hannover-Brunswick and the 357th is about to fight it out with over 50 aggressive 109s and 190s, losing Lingo, Currie, and Gray, and going home to claim 25 victories. C.E. Anderson is leading 363 Squadron White Flight, and his fuselage tank is still full when the melee begins. In such a state the P-51s C.G. is dangerously far aft, and the airplane does not take kindly to attempts at aerobatics. Anderson is definitely not ready to mix it up with 109s, but the choice is not his, and he finds himself trying to out-turn one, directly in the path of the oncoming bomber stream.

Anderson, in his book TO FLY AND FIGHT: "The bombers' gunners are not picky. The P-51 looked enough like an Me 109 that they weren't going to bother getting second or third opinions about which was which. Looking back, I can see 60 plus airplanes, and behind those there will be 60 more, and in back of those another box of 60, and another, all filled with fuel and bombs and men who will shoot first and ask questions later.

"We are playing chicken out here, this German and me. The first one to break out of the circle will lose. He surely has noticed the bombers bearing down, has calculated the odds, and come up with the same sort of answers that I have. His breath is coming in short gasps, like mine. His palms are wet like mine. And suddenly he rolls and goes down, I follow him happily. He goes straight to the deck, 20,000 feet down at full power. Peeling off first, he has opened some distance between us. I'm closing it up, fire a burst, get some hits. He breaks hard, I go by and wheel about, see a large moving shadow on the ground which I don't have time to check out, and I see my opponent reversing his turn, trying to come at me head-on. He doesn't quite make it. Almost but not quite head-on, before he can fire, I put a withering burst into him. The propeller flies off. The engine cowling is blown away. Then off comes the canopy, and out comes the pilot."

"Now - what the hell was that shadow? I had seen it out of the corner of my eye, but I knew it was something big, something that shouldn't have been there."

At this moment, the rest of his flight has caught up, and they spread out to find the shadow, and there he is - "A Heinkel 111 twin-engine bomber scooting along right on the deck. He is trying to use his camouflage to

TAXPAYERS DELIGHT was a P-51B, 42-106777, 364th code C5-J. Flight Leader John Carder had seven victories as seen here before he was shot down 12 May 1944, to become a POW. Carder also served in Korea, became a crop duster and was killed in a mountain crash in Arkansas in 1961.

blend into the countryside, but in the bright sun his shadow betrays him. "I go in first, set an engine to smoking, then roll out and watch the rest go through, one by one. Eddie Simpson goes for the smoking left engine and blows it to hell. Bill Overstreet rakes the bomber from as close as 100 yards. Henry Kayser comes in from an angle and hoses the cockpit until he runs out of ammo. I come around for a second pass, this time right to left, and hit him from tail to cockpit until mine is gone too.

"The Heinkel is too low for a bailout now, and losing altitude quickly with one engine gone, the pilot tries setting it down in a field, but there's a pole in his path, and it tears the left wing away. The bomber slides along, slews around, and explodes in flame. We swing around, pass over the wreckage, and see two men jump out. One takes off running like hell. The other just stands there, looking up at us, as if he were waiting for a bus and trying to decide whether or not it might rain. It was both brave and stupid. There are plenty of guys on both sides who would strafe a downed airman, on the theory that he could kill you tomorrow."

Anderson was right, there were many pilots who subscribed to this theory, and possibly rightly so. There are many such strafing of downed airmen by 357th pilots. However, Anderson did not believe in the practice so this unknown German crewman lived - for that day anyhow. If he continued to fly He 111s in daylight in a combat zone, he probably did not live much longer.

During two tours, Robert Foy became one of the top-scoring aces of the 357th, with 15 victories. On the 19th of May he started his scoring with three in a day, the last two without firing a shot. After shooting down the first Me 109, Foy was closing on two more, and observed two other 109s attempting ahead-on pass at him. In his encounter report he tells what happened next: "The two Me 109s on which I was closing apparently saw me for the first time and immediately pulled into a sharp turn to the left. The lead ship of this two-ship formation collided with the outside 109 attempting a head-on pass. The wing of this ship struck squarely in the propeller of the ship making the head-on pass and was shorn off at the fuselage. The ship burst into flames and I saw no chute. The e/a which collided head-on lost its prop and the engine nacelle seemed to be crushed and the 109 started into what might be described as an irregular spin. I started after this ship but two Me 109s were turning on my tail and I started into a Lufbury. I made six 360 degree turns with the 109s still following when a gray nosed P-51 attack the rear ship, shooting it down in flames. The other e/a broke off. I claim two 109s destroyed."

This remarkable still from John England's gun camera film shows a spread eagled German pilot who has just bailed out of his Me 109. The date is probably 15 May 1944, as England describes such a scene in his encounter report for that day.

Another excellent "still" from John England's gun camera film where he closes in on an Me 109 which is pursuing a B-17 with #2 prop feathered. This may be 15 May 1944, as it resembles England's account of a combat he had that day.

1st Lt. William D. Michaely, 363rd Squadron, shot down by flak, 21 May 1944. Lt. Ray Staudte reported: "A silver P-51 on my right passed me. I noticed white smoke streaming from the plane. The pilot climbed to safe altitude and bailed out. I believe the letters on the ship were B6-R, which was flown by Lt. Michaely." The Germans put Michaely on trial for shooting at civilians but gave up on it as he had not fired his guns that day. He was released from POW camp after the war.

21 May 1944. Two weeks before D-Day, John Howell in SHOO SHOO BABY, C5-L, 42-106447, along with others of the 364th were shooting up a train which turned out to have some flak cars included, which shredded his rudder and aft fuselage with a burst of 20 mm shells. Here it has been towed to the 469th Service Sqdn. for repairs.

The other end of C5-L, SHOO SHOO BABY. John Howell contemplates the damage inflicted by an expert German flak crew. C5-L is 42-106477.

364th pilot Joe Sullivan was shot down by light flak over a French airfield on 24 May. No details are known, but apparently he evaded capture.

On 30 May, Major Dregne led a four hour mission to Bernberg, which resulted in some vicious combat and claims for 18 Me 109s, Fw 190s and Me 410s shot down. The Group Leader reported: "In vicinity of Celle, four Me 109s bounced one of our flights, shooting down our Flight Leader and damaging two others. This flight of three then destroyed the four 109s." The Flight Leader lost was Captain Fletcher Adams, a nine-victory ace who was murdered on the ground by civilians. The other loss was Lt. Robert Foy who bailed into the sea and rescued by ASR.

With OVERLORD coming up fast, all of the Allied air forces were literally "workin' on the railroad" - and the highways, and the airfields, and the canals too, for that matter. All of this was to reduce the enemy's ability to move his forces, and reached a crescendo on 21 May when all of the Eighth was engaged in Operation CHATTANOOGA (aptly named after the popular song of the day CHATTANOOGA CHOO CHOO). It was a very dangerous business as German anti-aircraft weapons were both numerous, and up to their usual efficiency. Lt. John C. Howell was with 364's Green flight, and came very close to being a casualty statistic. He was flying his SHOO SHOO BABY, code C5-L. It was AAF s/n 42-106447, and despite the beating it took that day, it gave very long service to the Group, surviving until February, 1945 when it was lost in a local crash. As this is written, a piece of 447's rudder pedal lies on my desk.

John Howell: "My memories of the mission are not the best. As I recall we went down to the deck and headed north (from Berlin), spotting a train which appeared to be in a marshalling yard. We were in a spread formation and started the strafing run when I smelled a rat and called "flak train, lets get out of here!" About the same instant, Bill Reese got hit and went into the water immediately, just off shore from the town of Stralsund. At the same time, my plane was hit, and was responding poorly to the controls. While looking for an area to crash-land, I got the bird under control with throttle and trim

tab and headed for home. The old Mustang stayed together and it was throttle and trim tab all the way home. Losing Bill Reese was a severe blow, he was a fine person, outstanding pilot, and a true friend." (Reese's P-51 was C5-F, and carried the name BEAR RIVER BETSY.) There was extensive damage to the tail section and aft fuselage on Howell's airplane, and it was a remarkable feat to fly it from southern Germany to England.

Encounter and mission reports often contain bits and pieces of out-of-the-ordinary and interesting information. We present two here: On 8 April, Tommy Hayes was leading the usual escort type mission to Brunswick, and the after action report mentions enemy aircraft in colors not usually associated with German fighters: "4-6 black Fw 190s, 8 to 10 Me 109s, painted silver gray undersides and black on top, observed in target area." Five of these black aircraft were claimed shot down.

364th pilot Joe Sullivan claimed an unusual victim on the 13th of May. He had just gotten hits on an Me 410 (which he claimed damaged), when: "We saw a Fw 44 flying about 1,000 feet off the ground 90 degrees from us and about 50 yards away. I circled in behind him and fired at about 300 yards, and broke off at 30 yards. I fired two bursts and the aircraft broke into flames, and crashed immediately and burned on the ground. I claim one Fw 44 destroyed with pilot and occupant."

The Fw 44 was a light two seat biplane trainer, similar to a U.S. PT13 or a British Tiger Moth. There were few safe havens left in German air space, and the crew of this Focke-Wulf, which may or may not have been instructor and student, stood little chance of survival in a sky full of Allied fighters. The end of May brought promotion to full Colonel for Don Graham and Lt. Col. to Tom Hayes, now Deputy Group Commander. About this same time, carbines, .45s and Thompson Sub Machine guns appeared out of dusty corners, as fears of a possible German airborne assault brought an order for all personnel to be armed at all times.

During May 1944, Base Air Depot #2 (B.A.D. 2) in northern England, responsible for processing P-51s coming in country, held a war bond contest. The three winners would be allowed to name a P-51. The three P-51Cs were all dedicated on 30 May and two of them were then delivered to the 357th. We see all three of them here at the depot probably on 30 May.

SOME THOUGHTS AT THE END OF MAY

The following poetic thoughts and reminiscences of the recent past are from the records of the 362nd Squadron, author unknown but probably someone in the Operations Section:

"We looked into cloudless skies, watching the fields of rye rippling like a deep green sea -knew the satisfying tingle of a hot sun as our bodies seemed to hungrily reach out for its rays. We began to recall the Coca-Cola box back at Hayward, California, to long for a good big league double-header on Sunday, to take better care of the too-few bicycles belonging to the squadron.We witnessed the coming of spring to England-and we were glad.

"Most of us expected D-Day during May but even though it did not take place, we felt that as a squadron, we had matured, had come of age, during the period. Hell, any way you looked at it, there could be but one conclusion.

"Statistically, for instance, we hadn't done at all badly. We had flown 25 missions, destroyed 30 e/a, while our losses amounted to three. Fellows who harken to the names of Broadhead, Roberson, Carson, O'Brien had become eligible for the most cherished of all fighter pilot epithets - 'ACE'. We had matured, too, when Captain Brown didn't return on the 27th. This was one of those long-feared losses for 'R.D.' was the Pepper Martin of our squadron - capable and buoyant, personal spark plug who knew how to make others laugh. Remember how he had been fished out of Frisco Bay by seven women in a boat after the tail of his P-39 came off and how he proceeded to get blind drunk with his rescuers? Remember his mock western duels with Tex Hill?"

"This was the month of May and we had been overseas half a year. We had become used to abominable plumbing, the drone of bombers early in the morning, the lack of hamburgers and strawberry milk shakes, the black out, V-mail and English colloquialisms; we were carrying .45s and carbines and Tommy guns to the hard-benched movies.

"Over in France the farmers were busy in the fields and they would pause in the midst of their labors to wave the victory sign. Small towns seemed peaceful in miniature and girls riding their bicycles turned eyes upward and smiled. Our pilots wagged their wings and rolled over so that the white stars could be clearly seen. Viva La France!

"An enlisted man managed to share some of the glory on the 12th when the Crew Chief of Lt. Norris's ship watched it land, shot up like a sieve with a 175 hours of non-abortive time logged. SSGT George Roepke had sweated this one out as few have sweated." (Norris is said to have over-partied that night and Roepke later received the Bronze Star.)

The other war bond P-51 received by the 357th was PRIDE OF THE YANKS and it became C5-Z with Charles Sumner as pilot (at prop). Lee Henley was the Crew Chief (next to fuselage). Flight Chief, Joe DeShay is on the upper cowl. DeShay's wartime diary records that it was received on 31 May, the day after the dedication at the depot. DeShay also notes it was damaged in a ground loop accident on 16 July. It was repaired by the 469th Service Sqdn. but there the trail ends on 42-103502 and there is no record of its loss in combat.

OLD CROW shows nine victory symbols here which would date it about the 1st of June 1944. His Crew Chief has dressed up the tires with white walls, and in a few days the airplane would be resplendent with invasion stripes.

JUNE - THE "LONGEST DAY" MONTH

June 1944, was one of the most momentous months in world history with the Allies achieving a permanent foothold on the shores of Europe. During the early month run up to "The Longest Day", the Group flew missions on the 2nd (2), 3rd, 4th and 5th. Two of these were full strength, roughly four hour, bomber escorts. There were no engagements with enemy aircraft and in fact none were even seen. The mission on 2 June was noteworthy - of the 49 P-51s, there were no aborts, a notation rarely seen in mission reports.

The 3rd of June saw another unusual operation, twelve P-51s led by Major Gates escorted a single B-17, tail marking Square D to the Brussels area. This was a 100th Bomb Group aircraft and 8th Air Force records say it was doing radio counter measures in the Pas De Calais area. (This is the stretch of water which the English call The Straits of Dover.) This was undoubtedly part of the massive cover up plan to convince the Germans the invasion would be in that area.

We will cover the D-Day (Operation OVER-LORD) in some detail but will first list a few events of interest that took place during June, 1944.

2 June; 489th Bomb Group B-24 crash-lands, Leiston, two wounded aboard.
5 June; Base closed, no one allowed to leave or enter 2000 hours, work started to paint invasion stripes on P-51s, into the night until all aircraft painted.
6 June; D-Day, eight missions flown, three pilots missing.
7 June; Four missions flown, Luftwaffe strikes back.
8 June; 16 P-51s escort photo recon P-38s on early evening mission.
10 June; Lt Childs shot down accidentally by Lt. George.
15 June; First of what would be many V-1 buzz bombs, passed over base.
Between 6th and 15th, Group dropped 469 bombs in support of OVERLORD.
16 June; Lt. Col. Tommy Hayes leads group on the first belly tank fire bomb attack on marshalling yards.
20 June; Invasion support ended, Group returns to normal missions. Nick Frederick and Merle Allen shoot down Fieseler Storch, the only one of its type on the victory list.
21 June; 50th Fighter Group (P-47s) stage through Leiston.
Both Groups took off within minutes of each other but on different missions.
29 June; 20 enemy aircraft shot down.

Note: Six pilots killed in action during June. 362nd Mechanics completed eight engine changes in month, a new record.

OVERLORD - THE GREAT ENDEAVOR

Bomber leaders of the 8th Air Force and the RAF, both strategic forces had always resisted efforts to divert them to tactical attacks in direct or close support of troops on the ground. They believed that their bombers could contribute more to victory by constant hammering at industrial targets.

However, as the Great Endeavor, Operation Overlord, came to fruition early in June, it was obvious that all Allied air power must support the greatest sea borne invasion of all time. It was crucial that the troops not only get a foothold on the continent but that they stay there and not be pushed back into the sea. So it was that for approximately two weeks after D-Day the 8th applied its considerable power to that objective.

By the night of the fifth it was plain to everyone that the big day was about to dawn. The base was sealed off - no one entered, no one left. Down on the flight line, there was feverish painting activity in progress. The squadron painters with spray guns and most everyone else with paint brushes and cans of black and white paint and flashlights. The resulting so-called invasion strips were not very even but they served their purpose.

Leonard "Kit" Carson recalls the scene in the officer's club: "The Officer's club looked like the Last Chance Saloon on Saturday night. Every officer had either a shoulder holster or one on his hip with a .45 Colt in it or a carbine and the smoke filled room needed only the reclining figure of Lillian Russell or Goya's DUCHESS to complete the picture." (author's note: Due to the possibility of a German airborne attack, all personnel had been ordered to be armed at all times. For the officers it was the familiar Model 1911 service pistol and for the enlisted men the issue M1 carbine. Senior NCOs were armed with the Thompson Sub-machine gun. With little training in their use it is fortunate that they were not needed!)

For D-Day each of the 8th's Fighter Groups had its own assigned area forming a wide curve inland of the French coast. The 357th had two areas. The Group flew eight missions on D-day, the first departing Leiston Air field at 0215 hours. Colonel Graham led and his brief mission report stated: "Up 0215, 363rd & 364th Squadrons, sweep west of Guernsey. No e/a seen. Captain Ruder crash-landed five miles SE Cherbourg. Lt. Pagels last seen at take-off. Solid overcast to 12,000."

Captain William O'Brien was part of this first mission and his vivid memory describes the affair somewhat better than the official report: "The idea for the mission required a night take off and night formation work. The weather was poor and the result was no one got into formation at low altitude circling the field. We got on top of the clouds and started looking for our respective flights and Squadrons. I couldn't find anyone who was supposed to be with me. About that time a P-51 came strolling by with his navigation lights on, so I tacked onto to him. The two of us were joined by another lonesome P-51 so that the guy in the 'lighted' airplane set out on course.

Captain Richard C. Smith with his MR. PERIOD, C5-K, s/n 43-6974. Smith had scored two victories. On 29 June, after a dogfight with 109s and 190s, Capt. "Bud" Anderson heard Smith say on the radio that he was bailing out. However, he is listed as KIA.

"As the 363rd was the lead squadron I felt comfortable with whomever I was flying with. Well, away we go! Finally the sun comes up and we are stooging around somewhere. I slid in close to observe the guy in the lead trying to orient a map with what coast line we could see. I felt sorry for him, Magellan couldn't have helped us.

"After horsing around like this for six hours and 50 minutes, we are back at Leiston. All planes taxi to the 363rd dispersal area and out steps Graham, the leader and his wingmen, Anderson and O'Brien.

"How wonderful, a Group leader without a Group, who also is a Squadron leader without a Squadron, and two Flight Leaders without flights.

"You can appreciate the facial expression displayed in the picture. I assume Anderson and I were trying to answer Graham's question 'Where in hell did everyone go?'."

Bud Anderson from his book TO FLY AND FIGHT: "Some guys got so lost they wound up in Spain. Jim Browning said later, when the light came up that morning he looked down and saw a coast line that ran east to west. He decided it had to be Spain, turned north and flew for two hours to get back to England. On the way home, we (Graham and his small flight) had a quick glimpse of history through the breaks in cloud cover, the vast armada and beaches besieged. As it turned out, this was the longest mission I ever flew-six hours, 55 minutes."

Armament sergeant Willard Bierly lost his pocket knife on D-Day. As the first mission prepared to take-off, Captain LeRoy Ruder arrived at C5-X, LINDA LOU, having forgotten his knife and asked to borrow Bierly's. (A knife was important in the unlikely event that the pilot's dinghy might inflate in the cockpit.)

Ruder's flight ended up somewhere near the southern tip of France where his engine failed. He called his element leader and said he saw land and was going to crash land. He was never seen or heard from again although his element leader, Mark Stepelton searched the air and ground for him.

Lt. Roger Pagels and Lt. Irving Smith were the other two losses on D-Day, the latter just disappearing and Pagels later listed as "escapee". The first two missions were patrol searches but all other six were dive bombing and strafing of transport targets. This was the pattern until the third week in June when the mission gradually reverted to the usual escort jobs. The troops were solidly on the continent and there to stay.

Meanwhile, back at the 362nd Squadron Operations and Pilot's room, an unknown person probably an enlisted man working in Ops, or Intelligence wrote an eight page, single spaced narrative on Squadron events of the period. The same would have been going on at the 363rd and the 364th, so for a "You are there" look, we will quote parts of his story:

"Around 1300 hours, just after noon chow on the fifth the TANNOY blared out an announcement which further heightened the air of mystery. 'No personnel, military or civilian, will be permitted to leave the base. Civilians may purchase soap and cigarettes from the PX.'

"The voice sounded rhythmical and precise as usual but there was a note of crisis in it as the proclamation was repeated. 'Limey' workers leaned on their shovels and looked at each other, wondering. Even the chance to buy Camels and Lucky Strikes was not worth a night away from home and the missus.

"Then they went back to digging as though nothing had happened - these men who had lived through the blitz. In the Group briefing room at 4 o'clock the next morning were all the pilots, all the 'Paddle feet'. (author's note. This is a fliers derogatory name for non-flying personnel.) The black out curtains were still tightly drawn and the air was thick with cigarette smoke which gave a dull glow to the lights above.

"Small bunches of men formed, discussion was animated, this must be the pay-off. Forgotten now were the personal differences, the rank, the fact that this fellow was an ace and that one a virgin, that this one hailed from Georgia and that one from Brooklyn, that this one belonged to the 362nd and that one to the 364th; forgotten was the fact that this one was Phi Betta Kappa and that one an ex-coal-miner, that this one had flown with the RAF and that that one had been an instructor in AT-6s for two solid years back in the states.

"Then, like a shot, someone bawled ATTEN-SHUN! And everyone arose hurriedly, standing in awkward rigidity as the Group C.O. walked briskly towards the front. This time it was more than perfunctory formality, it was an expression of unity and purpose. Young and slim, his face seemed a bit older this morning, drawn and intense. 'Be seated, please, gentlemen', he said, and the stillness became oppressive, quickening the pulses.

"Nervously fingering a sealed envelope, Colonel Graham peered around the room into the expectant faces sensing the drama of the moment. Then in a slow subdued voice he said, 'Under the command of General Eisenhower, Allied naval forces, supported by strong air forces, will begin landing Allied armies this morning on the northern coast of France.' D-Day!

"Major Broadhead, our commanding officer led 16 planes out onto runway 35. At exactly 0512 hours the P-51s were airborne. We were to patrol area 22 in France. Higher headquarters had carefully planned the whole thing, assigning certain regions and duties to certain groups, well aware that scrupulous organization was more than ever important, for an unprecedented number of Allied planes would be operating in a limited area.

"We patrolled the area encountering neither Allied nor the vaunted *Luftwaffe* and came back home. Just short of seven hours in the air. The pilots rubbed their butts and shouted for hot coffee.

"Fifty-one minutes later, we had 14 planes loaded with 250 lb. general purpose bombs, streaking back towards the same area. We bombed a highway bridge crossing the Mayenne river west of Chateau Gontier, or tried to bomb it, for results were poor. But we tore up some railroad tracks in the same vicinity. Nobody saw anything of battles, ground or air. All planes were down by 1643 hours.

"The pilots' room was a mess. Iron cots were all over the place, covered with gray lumps which were the pilots buried under English gray blankets for some much needed rest. The new radio was tuned in constantly for latest reports of Allied progress. PFC Ayers, in supreme command of the snack bar, forgot the hours for serving and set a new record for eggs and hotcakes prepared. The Operations board had new schedules prepared before the preceding mission had been completed. Intelligence officers Captain Pickrell and Lt. Brown were barely through calling in their reports and recording interrogations before another four flights were wearily straggling into the S-2 office. The chips were down and each fellow on the field was more than willing to forego sleep, meals, entertainment, in order to work.

Men at work in the control tower on D-Day, although none are identified.

Major Dregne catches a nap between the many missions on 6 June.

Major Alfred Craven, Group Intelligence Officer and Major Dregne at work during the D-Day period.

A marvelous portrait of John Brooke England, a major player in the 357th for whom England Air Force Base was named (now closed). John England was killed in an F-86 crash in the 1950s.

"If you happened to be up in the control tower at 0350 hours on 7 June, you'd have felt a curious thrill running up and down your spine. Sixteen of our planes loaded with bombs were taking off in the darkness. You couldn't see the planes, only the navigation lights as they streaked down the runway, bobbing a little and then slowly getting higher off the ground as you held your breath. When they were airborne you'd have sighed in relief and listened to the R/T conversation, trying to recognize the individual voices. 'Blink those lights ROUGH ' That must be Captain Williams calling. And then someone saying 'Hell, I can't see a damn thing', exasperatedly - sure you couldn't mistake Carson. A slow drawl, then, 'That ain't me below you, Mitch, that's the field, cause I'm above you all' -- good ol' Tex. Somebody laughed. 'Roger, good luck men'."

June with its D-Day operation was one of the most momentous times of WWII and it brought with it a different kind of war. For THE YOXFORD BOYS, it had been a "machine gun" war but now there were a large number of bombs on the racks to be dumped on all kinds of rail, road and airfield targets - glide bombing, skip bombing and dive bombing, they were all tried sometimes even with good results. From the 6th through the 15th of June, 469 bombs were dropped, mostly 250 lb. general purpose type. During the two weeks until the 20th there were only two brief skirmishes with enemy aircraft with nine claims. For all of the month there were only 29 claims of e/a destroyed, 20 of these in a big battle on the 29th. During the month nine pilots were lost.

It was a very stressful time for pilots. There were missions every day of the month, except on the first and often two or three a day. Although the *Luftwaffe* was unable to make any significant response and there was little air combat, there was a great deal of dangerous ground attack. To add to the stress, six and seven hour missions were not unusual.

This is a very long time to sit in the cramped confines of a WWII fighter. Simple fatigue was a real problem for many pilots. This, of course was something the squadron flight surgeons monitored closely.

Kit Carson, with tips to new pilots on how to prepare and how to cope with the problem: "Think strategic escort, get in the habit of thinking about five and six and even seven hour missions. Dress for the missions as though you were going to walk out of Germany, make sure you have a good pair of boots. Above all, make sure you have a good foam rubber pad to sit on; that Goddamed dinghy pack is like a slab of concrete and it will ruin you if you don't have a good pad.

Sgts. Wilber Reich and Tom Aurio check out the engine while Anton Froehlich services the fuselage tank on C5-0. Harry Hermanson was the regular pilot who completed his tour but the airplane was lost on 18 September at Arnhem with Captain Bernard Seitzinger who became a POW.

Another veteran P-51B, Anderson's OLD CROW served him through the D-Day period and in fact until he completed his tour in August. It then went to Bill Overstreet as BERLIN EXPRESS when the "S" was changed to an "O".

This beautiful white-wall tired P-51C, BERLIN EXPRESS is B6-0, 42-103309. This is the first BERLIN EXPRESS. It is one of the few of this model in bare metal and it has full invasion stripes. The pilot Bill Overstreet, pipe and all poses with his crew for the official photographer. There are two victory symbols and at least 25 mission "bombs". There is no record of a loss of this lovely machine and we don't know its eventual fate. Late in August, Overstreet took over Bud Anderson's P-51B OLD CROW, renaming it BERLIN EXPRESS and flew it until the end of his tour.

Richard Peterson (on wing pointing) was still flying his highly successful P-51B during the D-Day period. Like all of his aircraft, this one was named HURRY HOME HONEY, C5-T and it was 43-6935. On 20 June, Heywood Spinks was shot down in this aircraft but evaded capture. Pete then got his first D model.

"Regarding the fatigue problem on long missions - four hour missions are not so bad, in fact they don't bother me at all. Five hours and up is where it gets you in the legs and fanny. When you fly six and seven hour missions, the ground crew will probably have to lift you out of the cockpit! The retarded circulation in your legs and being stuck in one position is what does it. Stamp your feet, massage your legs with one hand and get the circulation going in any way you can.

"One final note, the relief tube on this airplane freezes up on the first time you use it at altitude. The second time you might as well pee on the floor because that's where it will wind up anyhow, so consume your breakfast coffee accordingly."

The vigor of youth helped, of course, and allowed pilots to "bounce back" rapidly. Ray Conlin, often Car-son's wingman: "I found that my long legs had a tendency to cramp due to limited leg room. After several hours and when the opportunity afforded itself, I would light up a cigarette and my jittery nerves would settle down. When we reached home base and I was on the ground, my tiredness seemed to fade away instantly and I was ready for a party or whatever." John Skara, 363rd, also does not recall any problems and along with Conlin was ready to party at the end of the day. (Incidentally, this writer is pleased to say that close to 60 years later both Conlin and Skara are still ready to "party", although in a somewhat more subdued manner!)

Nick Frederick and Henry Pfeiffer, both 364th, remember that long missions did reduce their ability and slow down their reaction times. As in most anything else, people varied in their reaction to fatigue.

It is not known how many, if any of the new P-51Ds reached the 357th before D-Day. This is Kit Carson's 44-13316, with the half paint job. Since it has full invasion stripes we assume it was there by 6 June, but this might not be true. The records show it did not reach England and 8th Air Force until 4 June. It is possible the depot rushed it through and it was in Leiston the next day but the odds are it arrived a few days later. It bears five victory symbols and the name MILDRED. In later years, Carson told the author he had no idea where the name came from. In any case, it shortly became NOOKY BOOKY II. Man is Asst. Crew Chief Livingston Blauvelt III.

MISS MARVEL, G4-D, 43-6710 still has its full invasion stripes putting this photo in June or early July. Lt. Lloyd Mitchell (on wing) and his crew; Armorer J.J. Hoefner (L), Ken Lane, and Crew Chief Bob Raffen.

Since Colonel Graham is shooting a German Schmeisser machine pistol, we can assume it is after the successful invasion of the continent. Somehow the weapon found its way back to Leiston. In the original print the empty cartridge cases be seen as they are ejected. The P-51 is LIBBY B and was lost with Captain William Mooney on 24 December 1944. Mooney was one of several 357th pilots who was murdered by German civilians.

SOME VIGNETTES OF JUNE 1944

16 June: Harry Ankeny, 362 squadron: "I was breezing down the runway when the fuel connection on my left drop tank broke and really started shooting gasoline. I left a vapor trail all around the pattern and on landing, my other connection on the right tank broke."

20 June: P-47s of the 50th Fighter Group (9th AF) staged through Leiston to refuel. The base's proximity to German occupied land caused it to be used by other Groups, sometimes staying overnight and departing with full tanks the next day. During this time frame, P-38s of the 474th, P-47s of the 358th and P-51s of the 355th, all staged through F-373. It made for crowded conditions on the taxiways and in the messing and lodging facilities.

20 June: The apprehension of the crew of an unarmed *Luftwaffe* observation type, a Fieseler *Storch* in a sky full of Mustangs can well be imagined and on this date, the worst fears of one such crew were realized. Nick Frederick in his encounter report: "I was flying Greenhouse Red 3. After I had destroyed an Me 109, I saw several P-51s chasing a Fieseler *Storch* on the deck. I got behind Lt. Merle Allen and saw him fire, observing strikes on the fuselage. The *Storch* kept flying and since my guns were jammed, I forced the *Storch* into the ground by flying several feet above him. The prop wash evidently spun him in. The plane broke into many pieces." Merle Allen

then strafed the wreck and the two shared the claim.

16 June: The "D" model Mustang was still a novelty in June, having just begun to arrive in theatre. Although clearly a great advance over the "B" in most ways, some pilots were not so sure. Lt. Col. Tommy Hayes had become involved in a turning battle with an Me 109: "I had the advantage but could not get inside him because the fuselage tank was still full, spoiling the C.G. (center of gravity). Neither would give on altitude and I found that with the later engine I could not climb above him in a circle. It seemed to me this P-51D doesn't maneuver quite as well as the P-51B and it has no guts above 25,000 as the P-51B had with the high altitude engine.

"Well, I'm getting nowhere, so I pulled the nose through and gave him a burst. He did what I wanted him to do by split essing. Now I got on his tail and got strikes on him as we both hit the clouds around 11,000 feet. I had no idea I was going so fast; pulled back on the stick, snapped and spun once or twice, and broke out. Saw the 109 crash at a fairly steep angle."

24 June: More on Nick Frederick from Joe DeShay's diary for this day: "Nick lands 'Y' in Normandy and returns." Joe is referring to C5-Y, the aircraft's Squadron code. Years later, Frederick recalls: "A voice on the radio told me I was losing coolant. I didn't notice anything unusual on the instruments, but John Storch, who was leading Greenhouse, told me to get it on the ground.

"I called 'Oilskin' for directions and was steered to an RCAF base near Caen, which was still under construction. They were waiting for me and I landed OK, but ran out of runway. I hit a pile of dirt which was about 20 feet high and bent my new prop blades.

"The RCAF commander wanted me to stay until they could get me a new prop. Spitfires and Fw 190s were battling overhea, and I could hear cannon fire nearby - it didn't seem like a good place to stay! I had a cup of 'tea' with him and asked for a sledge hammer. No hammer, but they had a rope and many strong backs, and we did our best to pull the blades into something like the right position. I said 'Fellows, it's as good as new.'

"They thought I was nuts and the C.O. advised me not to fly it. I then signed something which relieved them of responsibility. I started the engine and it sounded like a cement mixer, but I flew it back to Leiston anyhow. I landed and 'Tex' Crawford (his Crew cCief) had tears in his eyes and welcomed me home. I had some sand from the beachhead for him, and I think I had tears myself."

During this period of mostly tactical support missions, the Group as indicated above, dropped 469 bombs. Harvey Mace injects a bit of humor in an otherwise serious business as he describes his expertise at the art of putting bombs on a target: "Being one of the charter members of the 362nd Squadron, I had oodles of gunnery and skip bombing in the P-39 and was proud of my ability to hit what I shot at and to put bombs where I wanted them. I was Flight Leader by this time and was leading a flight of three replacements. We stooged around for awhile looking for something better than a rail line, and found a village with a good sized marshalling yard and decided it was well worth working over.

"I brought the boys down and started firing at long range - first at anything that looked like it might shoot back, and then concentrated on engines and box cars. The shooting was going great and I decided - Hell, I'll give them 37 mm also - and pressed the button on top of the stick. The instant I did I realized that I was a victim of habit-the P-51 didn't have a cannon! I had just prematurely released the bombs. I groaned in agony as I watched the left bomb blow harmlessly in a field - all I could hope was that it was Brussel Sprouts! Fortunately the right bomb rolled up on the track and took out a good sized section.

"Back on the ground I got the boys together and asked them how they did. One of them said, 'Fine Captain Mace, but how long will it be before we can place a bomb like you can?' I figuratively kicked the dirt, and said, 'Oh, you'll get the hang of it.' A Flight Leader should not show weakness, right?"

As the month of June ran down to an end, there were several small engagements on the 20th when four Me 109s attacking a crippled B-24 were shot down, plus another in a separate action. The *Luftwaffe* was still committing its twin engined Me 410s to daylight battle and four were shot down in a big battle on the 29th along with 17 single engine fighters. Captain Richard C. Smith was the only loss who reported he was bailing out, but nothing more is known and he is listed as KIA.

The encounter reports often provide tidbits of interesting information. 364th Squadron's Captain Bryce McIntyre caught a big He 177 bomber, the only one ever encountered by THE YOXFORD BOYS. The crew of this one was lucky however, as all McIntyre could claim was a damaged.

It was sometimes not necessary to use the P-51's weapons to achieve a victory, as Captain Charles Sumner Jr reported: "I was flying Greenhouse Blue Three and after a series of dogfights, became separated from my leader. I then sighted an Fw 190 diving through the clouds to the deck and I gave chase. After I had chased him for a few minutes and was preparing, to open fire he started a steep turn and then reversed his turn and crashed in a field. I claim one Fw 190 destroyed."

Captain John C. Howell: "I was leading Greenhouse White Flight when we contacted flights of 109s and

190s coming in towards the bombers. I broke into several that hit the clouds and then found one at 15,000 feet who tried to turn with me at high speed. I reefed it in to get a shot and he tried to pull in tighter. He snapped over into a vicious spin and I followed him until I saw the right wing come off and I think it hit the tail. Pieces flew and he went down. No chute seen. I claim one Me 109 destroyed."

Although the Group had returned to its primary mission of bomber escort about mid-month, on at least six occasions the Group engaged in widespread strafing and bombing attacks after breaking off escort. On one mission, they apparently carried bombs instead of tanks during the escort and then deposited these bombs on various targets.

THE GREAT *LUFTWAFFE* ATTACK ON LEISTON AIRFIELD

Perhaps stung by the thousands of Allied aircraft over "their" beaches on the morning of 6th of June, the *Luftwaffe* struck back at THE YOXFORD BOYS on the night of 6/7 June - and it was a pathetic effort! According to RAF records, several bombs fell on Tuddenham and five bombs were dropped in the vicinity of Parham and Framlingham (both only a few miles from Leiston). Three B-24s returning late from a mission were attacked and at least one was shot down shortly after midnight. An RAF 25 Squadron Mosquito shot down an Me 410 40 miles east of Southwold.

Why Leiston Airfield? Possibly because the German pilot was "stooging" around over a blacked-out England looking for something to shoot at. (It is possible it was the same aircraft involved in the B-24 attacks.) The big communal mess hall was serving midnight chow for those work kept them up at night. Some careless person left the door open, providing a beautiful shaft of light and a target for the marauder. A burst of 20 mm shells punched a few holes in the mess hall roof, causing pandemonium among the late night diners.

Sergeant Emery Gaal was one of those in the mess hall. We will let him describe the scene: "I was having midnight chow with Karnicke (probably Richard Karnicke), we heard the plane coming and then a big boom like a cannon and it blew a big hole just below the roof. All of us hit the deck and the benches and tables flew all over and we were hollering at the cooks to shut off the lights, which they did. Lying across my legs was a heavy object and I thought it was Karnicke. I kept calling his name, thinking he had been hit.

"After the lights came on, I found the weight on my legs was a table and I had a cut on my leg, but that was the extent of the injuries."

Elsewhere on base, many dramas were taking place when the strange engines were heard and the gunfire erupted. The author should say that although he was there, he can contribute nothing to the story as he was asleep in his bunk until the appalling sound of cannon fire, and it was all over before he could get out of his bunk.

Another man having trouble getting out of his bunk was Captain OBee O'Brien, who provides a different slant on life on a wartime airfield: "I remember that it was almost impossible not to hear aircraft engines. The 8th bombers started their engine checkouts long before the sun was up. A little later our ground crews cranked up the Merlins and a still later yet, we started engines and listened to the Merlins attentively until we returned to England. After we were home we could watch and hear our bombers coming back which overlapped with RAF bombers firing up for their night's work. What does this have to do with the strafing? It sets forth the sound pattern we lived with.

"On the night we got strafed, I heard the Kraut winding up in his pass on Leiston. I remember that I'd never heard engines that sounded so unsynchronized. I knew we were in for something different."

O'Brien struggled out of his bunk, turned it over, grabbed his pistol and ran outside, only to find it was too late to have the satisfaction of getting off a .45 caliber bullet at the intruder.

Sergeant James Frary seems to have been one of the few who made a detailed entry in his diary: "I was standing outside the orderly room (I was C.Q. that night) and there was a red alert on at the time. I heard the plane coming in low from the south. I didn't think about it being German until he reached the edge of the field and I could see him silhouetted against the sky. Just as a precaution, I crouched down in front of the door. About then our AA guns started to fire. Pink tracers were going all around the enemy ship.

"Just as he got almost out of my range of vision he banked around to the east and cut across the communal site. It was then that he cut loose with his guns, putting three holes in the mess hall and plowing up the baseball field with his 20 mm guns. The AA fired about 300 rounds

Another of the first batch of P-51D-5s that arrived at Leiston about the 1st of June. Captain Robert Beeker was pilot on SEBASTIAN JR. G4-0, s/n 44-13517. The presence of a variety of bombs at the handstand, plus full invasion stripes dates this photo to within a week or so of D-Day. Bombs were normally not kept on the hardstands but during the D-Day period the Group did a lot of bombing.

1st Lt. Arval Roberson on the wing of his first PASSION WAGON, which served him well into the summer when he received a new D-5 to fly on the Shuttle Mission, 6 August. This P-51B was G4-R, serial number 43-6688.
It was still flying missions in December and was finally salvaged in June, 1945.

When this photo was taken, C5-A, ROUND TRIP JR. had flown about 25 missions most of them probably with Lt. Tom McKinney. Here one of the 364th Squadron dogs poses dramatically with the ground crew of 42-106843. On 29 July, Lt. Daniel Finley bailed out due to engine failure. He was captured but sadly enough, he died in POW camp near the war's end from illness contacted during the long winter forced marches, as the Germans moved POWs from one camp to another to prevent their liberation.

Major Thomas Gates was a real old timer, having graduated from cadets in 1931. He then left the army and became a CAA inspector. WWII brought him back to the army where he served a tour with the 357th, where he scored two victories.

Charles K. "DADDY RABBIT" Peters ran his score to four during his combat tour. The P-51s code was B6-J, and its s/n may have been 43-6594, but that is uncertain.

It was not all work - here we see a British bus optimistically named WOLF WAGON, used to transport soldiers to nearby towns in search of girls and other entertainment.

An everyday scene, ground crew waiting for the first sight and sound of the mission returning - these are 362nd Sqdn. men.

The man serving as Officer of the Day was assigned a jeep to pursue his duties. Harry Ankeny (Note the OD arm band) poses in his jeep in front of 362nd Sqdn. Operations.

of .50 caliber and eight rounds of 40 mm at him as he crossed the field. They apparently hit him as a gas cap and some scraps of metal were found later." The only man known to have returned fire was Sgt. Jack Summers, a member of the base defense team about which we know very little. Summers was manning a .50 caliber machine gun mounted on a British armorer car and he fired a 25 to 50 round burst, but does not believe he got any hits.

Sgt. Claude Allen, 364th Armorer, was driving a 2 1/2 ton truck on the perimeter track when he heard the strange engines and gunfire. He and his partner abandoned the truck, leaving it in gear, for the dubious safety of a shallow ditch (the truck soon stopped on its own). 363rd Squadron's Ken Sylvester was on the flight line working on a P-51 and recalls that they had a truck with a ring-mounted fifty, but all dived under the truck and no one went near the gun!

Among those who were there, there has always been much confusion and disagreement about the details. The type of German aircraft has never been determined for sure. Group records say it was an Me 410, but two men who were outside and got a close look at it say it was a single engine type. However, they, Sergeants Will Bierly and Jerry Huritz do not agree on the type, one says an Me 109 the other an Fw 190. Since neither of these types were really suitable, an Me 410 sounds most likely, but who knows??!

In any case, the raid was considered of so little importance that it rated only a one sentence mention in the Group Operational Summary for June.

The only known full photo of Peterson's first HURRY HOME HONEY. Like C.E. Anderson he later switched to a D model P-51, but both men scored the majority of their victories in the P-51B. Here it is parked in front of the 469th Service Sqdn. hangar and the canopy has been removed. It is probably in the process of having a Malcolm Hood installed.

Captain Herschel Pascoe with DESERT RAT (actually two rats). The aircraft is 44-13714. He was shot down in this aircraft on 12 October, 1944, by Oberst (Colonel) Josef "Pips" Priller, **Kommodore** of JG 26. Priller ended the war with 101 victories. Pascoe survived as a POW.

Lt. Tanner Laine, Public Relations Officer. He was the man responsible for all the press releases that went out to home town newspapers, extolling the accomplishments of the men of the 357th.

Someone in the 362nd Squadron thought it would be a good idea to write to some Hollywood stars and ask for some autographed underwear. It is believed that 8 or 10 responded, including Rita Hayworth. Kit Carson is seen here contemplating some lacy panties from Marjorie Riorden. The pilots' room wall carving is thought to have been done by pilot Tom Beemer.

Endnotes:
1. No Fw 190 D aircraft were flying in March 1944. The "long nose" Fw 190 D did not go into production until August 1944.

CHAPTER 4:
THE SUMMER WAR

A view of "downtown" Leiston Airfield. This is the main street in the communal area where the mess halls, clubs, barber shop, gym, and most other important installations were located. The use of discarded paper drop tanks as decorations is noteworthy.

The Group flew 27 missions during July, many of them two and three a day. Due to the lack of *Luftwaffe* opposition, some missions were flown at reduced strength.

The miserable weather of the winter of 1943/44 was now gone and July recorded a high of 75 and a low of 50 degrees, a very pleasant change. This, of course, does not in any way indicate that mission weather was also good. Even in summer very low temperatures are encountered at 30,000 feet and many mission reports mention solid undercast or overcast. These notes were found in the Operational Summary for July:

"Few enemy aircraft were seen. Many avoided combat. Thirty one e/a were claimed destroyed. Five P-51s were lost on operations and 21 new pilots were assigned during the month. Pilots and mechanics were on station for training as 55th Group was converting from P-38s to P-51s. Lts. Frank Koka and Paul Holmberg were killed in action during the month. Rollin Carter and Daniel Finley became POWs, the latter later died in POW camp. Lt. Don Vogel bailed out over enemy territory but evaded capture."

Although the *Luftwaffe* was elusive in early summer, combat on the 1st and 5th resulted in four victories on each of those days. Captain "Pete" Peterson had only recently been assigned one of the new P-51Ds and was obviously pleased with the new armament, as he commented at the end of his encounter report; "I claim one Me 109 destroyed - thanks to the upright guns of the P-51D."

Even when the P-51s were not fending off German fighters they were often of service to the bombers. On 12 July, Colonel Graham reported two straggling B-24s in trouble. He escorted them out of Germany to within 150 miles of the enemy coast, where other escorts took over. On the same day, four other B-24s were escorted to the Swiss border.

Again on the 21st, Graham reported: "Three bombers which were lost, were escorted to Walcheren Island by one of our elements, and then at their request, told where they were."

On the 17th, Captain Howell led four P-51s on a curious task, the mission report saying: "Escort B-17 to mid channel and return." No indication of the B-17's mission but it may have been a routine weather recon."

Lt. William Overbeck, co-pilot on a 486th Bomb Group B-24, relates another service by THE YOXFORD BOYS: "As we approached the target, Saarbrucken, we were in the tail-end Charlie position in the low squadron. Our Liberator took several flak hits - a rather common occurrence when flying that position. I was checking the crew by intercom for reports of injury and extent of damage. Everyone was OK, but the tail was well ventilated.

"Suddenly we lost power on numbers 3 and 4. With six 1,000 pound bombs still hanging in the shackles,

the B-24 dropped like an anvil from 24,000 feet to 18,000. In the face of dire threats, navigator Lt. Ed Kurpieski stopped looking for a target of opportunity and jettisoned the heavy load. This gave us a fighting chance to adjust power and slow our rate of descent considerably. While I handled the engines, Butts (the pilot) called for 'Little Friends' and we were assured that they had us in sight.

"Until now we had been too busy to realize that no fighters were in sight. The crew began to get nervous at the thought of our crippled condition, and the possibility that our fighters may be escorting other cripples in a different sector. There can't be a much lonelier feeling than that of limping along deep in enemy territory at half-power with no friendly aircraft in sight. Butts called again for reassurance that the escort had us in sight and four of the prettiest P-51s dropped out of the sun, streaked past and hurtled back to their vantage point. During this brief glimpse we noted that the fighters had red and yellow checkered noses and that the top side of the natural metal planes were O.D.

"We now had some sense of security as we pointed the B-24 toward England. With No. 3 engine out, we had no generator, leaving us without power turrets. Four manually operated turrets and two waist guns were hard-

ly effective against 109s and 190s, so we were doubly grateful for our bodyguards.

"Butts alerted ASR as we approached the Channel losing altitude continuously and the navigator gave us a course to Woodbridge. We felt it wise to have two miles of runway at our disposal. Because of tail damage we would have to put the B-24 down, without hydraulics, and with a one-shot application of brakes available. The Liberator hit hard and stuck, but not without loud complaining from the tires. After an exceptionally long roll, I pulled the brake handle and brought the battered monster to a halt.

"It occurred to us that the P-51s were low on fuel after hanging back to stay with us and they also landed at Woodbridge. The Flight Leader's plane bore the name MISS FLORIDA and G4-Y. We met the pilots over tea, and learned they were from the 357th Fighter Group. We also learned from Flight Leader Captain Jim Badger that the fighters would be of little help at our altitude. They had to stay high to be effective.

"Forty plus years have not erased the vivid memory of an outstanding performance of escort duty by THE YOXFORD BOYS. Their effort probably prevented some *Luftwaffe* pilot from collecting four points toward his Knight's Cross with Diamonds!"

One of the more unusual combat occurrences was when a single bullet of unknown origin passed the cockpit of Carson's C4-C, hitting the canopy release and ejecting the canopy. Here Carson sits on the wing after a long cold ride home from Germany.

A very attractive RAF green P-51 B, B6-E, $BLACKPOOL BAT. This is not a dollar sign, but are the initials "I" and "S", the logo of George G. George's pre-war employer. Although married to a girl from Blackpool, England, the BAT does not refer to her, but the winged mammal. The object in the center of the bottom photo is a fire extinquisher with a canvas cover. The P-51 vanished in bad weather with Kenneth Graeff, who probably collided with Lt. Louis Nowlin, also missing at the same time. George George completed his tour with the 363rd, stayed in the military after the war, and was killed many years later in an F-100 crash.

The reputed statement by Badger about them being of little help at low altitude is puzzling, considering the capabilities of the Mustang both high and low.

Earlier in the month, on both the 6th and the 7th, a single flight (four P-51s) of the 363rd Squadron was dispatched on an Air Sea Rescue search for an airman down at sea. Robert Foy led on the 7th, finding only an empty dinghy, but Lt. Eddie Simpson stirred up some excitement on the 6th. The flight found a dinghy, believed empty, which was being circled by an RAF Wellington. The flight therefore turned for home. Simpson's wingman, Lt. Hershel Pascoe tells what happened: "I was flying #2 on an ASR patrol when we saw a Ju 88 flying at about 150 feet altitude and 180 degrees to our line of flight. Lt. Simpson, flying #1, peeled down and closed behind the e/a which turned in toward the enemy coast 'balls out'.

"The e/a went into a thin layer of cloud at about 100 feet altitude. I observed strikes on the fuselage. The e/a kept trying to hide in the clouds but they were too low to the water. The second time Lt. Simpson fired, the e/a hit the water at high speed and broke into pieces."

Ju 88s did occasionally attack Air Sea Rescue boats and this one was probably on that mission. There is, however, more to the story of this Ju 88's destruction. Although both the mission report and Simpson's encounter report cover the action (and are in the author's files), Eddie Simpson and probably Hershel Pascoe, were nowhere near Borkum Island on the 6th of July. Here is the real story of the event.

F.O. Chuck Yeager had been shot down on 5 March, evaded capture and traveling through Spain, as related in his book, YEAGER, had arrived back in London in mid-May. The regulations said that no evader would be allowed to return to combat, as, if shot down again, he might be "persuaded" by the enemy to reveal information on the French Underground. Yeager, however, had no desire to return to the ZI as an instructor. Determined to return to his unit and to combat, he worked his way up through the chain of command to the Supreme Commander himself, General Eisenhower. Ike was sympathetic but indicated he did not have authority to change the regulations.

He would, however, pass it along to USAAF Headquarters in Washington for a decision. Yeager, therefore, returned to Leiston where he was allowed to fly and to train pilots but not fly combat. On 6 July, he was aloft with three trainee pilots and in audio tape to this writer, in January 2001, he tells what remembers of the incident.

While rat-racing in the vicinity of base he was queried by control as to how much fuel he had. When he replied about three and a half hours, he was directed to take his flight and proceed to the Heligoland area, near Borkum Island to cover a B-17 crew in a dinghy while a rescue operation was in progress. Arriving in the area, the dinghy was spotted and then Yeager saw a twin engined aircraft approaching at low level which he identified as a Ju 88 or 188.

When the pilot of the '88 saw Yeager approaching he reversed course and turned back toward land, "laying black smoke from both engines". After a ten-mile chase, Yeager caught him and "rolled him up in a ball" on the beach.

Upon return to base, he reported the facts to Major Ed Hiro, 363rd Squadron C.O., who was furious that Yeager had violated his ban on combat. When Yeager pointed out that he was following orders to protect the ASR operation, he had to agree that Yeager was clearly in the right.

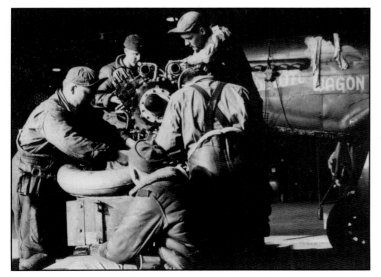

Night work for the ground crews was common throughout the 8th Air Force. Here TSgt. Red Loos's hangar crew work on a Merlin engine. The kidney shaped object is the coolant header tank. In the background is a P-51 well known through photos and drawings - PASSION WAGON.

Peterson's second HURRY HOME HONEY, with the famous "half" paint job and 14 victory symbols, indicating the photo was taken about mid-June, 1944. Later Pete Howell flew it re-named FLAK HAPPY and still later, George Kouris was assigned to it, now named GREECE LIGHTNING. It was lost with him on 3 February 1945.

362nd armorers Moores, Rafferty, and Parmer (kneeling) pose with Gilbert O'Brien's SHANTY IRISH. This aircraft had an interesting career, ending up as a two seater (see chapter 11 Colors and Markings.)

Now what to do? The choices were, to report the facts to Group/ 66th Fighter Wing, Fighter Command and on up to 8th Air Force Headquarters, and take the resulting storm of paperwork - or to simply alter some of the paperwork and get on with the war.

The second choice was adopted. Lt. Edward Simpson's name replaced Yeager's on the mission report and the victory claim. Pascoe was given the combat time. Of course, Yeager never did get credit for the destruction of the Ju 88 while Simpson is credited with it in the USAF Victory Credits for WWII.

Three months later Eddie Simpson was dead, killed on the ground in a battle zone after surviving a collision with fellow pilot Donald Ferron. Pascoe was shot down two days later, on 12 October and became a POW.

Captain Clarence Anderson in the cockpit of his faithful B model OLD CROW, with which he completed his first tour with 12 victories in July 1944. He went back to the states for a 30 day leave, reporting back to the 363rd for his 2nd tour which ended in January, 1945.

Soon after this episode, a favorable reply was received from Washington and Yeager returned to combat, thereby changing his life forever.

There was a brief flurry of activity on the morning of the seventh. Lt. Col. Tom Hayes led a typical mission for some 300 B-17s bombing Merseberg. Although this target was much hated by bomber crews due to its fierce flak defenses, on this day only two B-17s were lost.

Three Me 109s were engaged and shot down by Captain "Bud" Anderson, Lt. Fennell and Eddie Simpson. Before being shot down however, one of the 109s damaged Lt. Frank Koka's engine. He reported that he was bailing out but he did not survive. As the month wound down, there was an interesting operation on the 14th and significant missions on both the 25th and the 29th.

On the 14th of July, 1944, (Bastille Day in France), the Group flew a familiar bomber escort mission (Usually listed as "Target, penetration, and withdrawal support"), but with an unusual aspect. The 350 B-17s of the 3rd Air Division were carrying out OPERATION CADILLAC, dropping almost 4,000 containers of arms and equipment to the French underground forces in the St. Lo, Vercorse and Limoges regions. This daylight "drop" went well with no bomber losses and the resistance radioed "very successful results".

Lt. Col. Tom Hayes led Group's 40 P-51s escorting the "drop" and engaged ten Me 109s which had taken off from an airfield five miles west of Valence. Four were claimed shot down, one by Hayes. Captain Mark Stepelton in his encounter report: "Just after the bombers had completed their run, I saw two ships make a pass at the bombers so I broke off toward them with my wingman. When I approached the e/a, we were attacked by about ten Me 109s which then kept on going so we again went after the Fw 190s. I fired a burst at one and hit his right wing root which began to leave a large vapor trail. The e/a hit the deck and we gave chase firing at him several times but out of range. After a long run, I finally closed on the tail of the e/a and gave him a long burst after which he crashed into the ground and rolled up into a ball of flame on the edge of a little town."

In his report, the mission leader observed that there were 25 single engined planes, without engines, on an airfield 10 miles North of St. Vallier identified as Curtiss Hawks.

The P-51s were back at home base by 1220 hours and in the late afternoon Colonel Graham led some 50 P-51s escorting B-24s which bombed airfields at Perronne and Mont Didier. No enemy aircraft were seen and all aircraft were back at base in early evening. It had been a busy day.

Right: A veteran P-51B with distinctive nose art and over 100 missions. It is a 362nd Squadron aircraft but its code and tail number are unknown. Armorer John Hoefner is the man in the picture.

Left: Major Tommy Hayes with his Crew Chief, Robert Krull (far right) and Sgts. Gene Basalou and Fred Keiper. Hayes' final score of nine victories in Europe is shown here, but the Japanese victories are not in the USAF official score list, probably because of the chaotic conditions and record keeping in the early days of the Pacific war.

Lt. Lloyd Zacharaie, 364th pilot of the oddly named MOM SMITH'S LITTLE ANGEL. Mom Smith was his college fraternity house mother.

THE BOULEVARDS OF PARIS

Paris - The City of Light was the scene of several area patrols during the latter part of July. Despite the approach of Allied forces, Paris was still German after four years of occupation, but one month later it would again be French. Late in July, however, the Germans were still there and full of fight.

Lt. Col. Tom Hayes led-51 Mustangs on an area patrol in the Paris vicinity on the 25th. From Hayes' mission report:

"Arrived area 0900 and patrolled 15,000 to 19,000, to 1115, then swept area from Angers to LeMans to Paris. On NW outskirts of Paris, intercepted 25 plus Me 109 and Fw 190s attacking an unidentified P-38 at 20,000, 1150. Group engaged these e/a which dove for the deck over Paris. Combat was from 8,000 to Paris rooftops with above results. Heavy traffic headed south on all highways on areas patrolled. Heavy small arms fire encountered over Paris."

Claims for this low level melee over the city were not high. Donald Bochkay and Robert Foy of the 363rd claiming one each, with Johnny Pugh, Robert Becker and Kit Carson shooting down one each for the 362nd. We will look at Carson's interesting tale from his book PURSUE AND DESTROY:

"A mixed group of 109s and 190s came down out of a high cirrus overcast, which was at about 32,000 feet and attacked a group of P-38s below us just west of Paris. They went past my squadron vertically like a controlled avalanche and I barely saw them in my peripheral vision to the right. I chased a 190 clear across the city of Paris and finally nailed him after a weird rat race past the Eiffel Tower. You could identify the major boulevards in my combat film. It wasn't until the shooting was over that I fully realized where I was and then I clearly recall asking myself, 'How the hell am I going to get out of this place?' I shoved everything forward - throttle, mixture, RPM and stick. The Merlin was laying down black smoke out of both rows of exhaust stacks. It was one of the few times that I asked Rolls Royce to deliver everything advertised. I almost never ran an engine at full power in combat. I was at house top level, flat out at 72 inches of HG (Mercury, manifold pressure) and 3,000 RPM. Half the flak in Paris was coming up. I can also recall another desperate invocation to the Merlin 'Run, you son-of-a-bitch, or quit, today is the day - or I walk.' It ran and we all made it back, no losses."

Raymond "Ted" Conlin was Carson's wing man that day and the passage of time has not dimmed his recollection of the Paris escapade: "Dollar blue and green flights were enjoying one of those rare '*Freie Jagd*' missions, a free hunt, a fighter sweep, as our enemies would call it. We made landfall near the invasion beaches and were ranging south down near Kennes. Captain Becker was leading blue flight and Captain Carson, green flight. After about 15 minutes, Becker began a sweeping left turn to head back north. The two flights came on the western edges of Paris - the glamour city of all Europe. In that area were large marshalling yards. It was noon when one of our guys called in that P-38s were bombing and strafing below. At that moment, a gaggle of 109s and 190s appeared dead ahead and at our level. I don't believe they ever saw us as they rolled over to attack the P-38s below. I was flying #2 on Carson's wing. He rolled over and I followed him down as he tacked on the rear 190. The element leader in Green flight, Captain John Pugh broke away and jumped on the tail of an Me 109 that was headed down. The game was on and I was on a wild ride earthward trying to stay in position on Carson. At that time it seemed we were diving almost vertical and the 190 pilot was doing big barrel rolls, and we were right with him.

"As Carson closed the range, he started getting strikes on the 190. This and the ground coming up caused the German pilot to flare and level off. We were now at about 300 feet and Kit was getting hits all over the Focke-Wulf when its engine failed. We were headed east just above the Grand Armee - Champs Ellysees Blvd. It looked like the 190 was going to crash into the Arch de Triumph. The pilot must have been dead because he did not try to jump.

"Carson broke away and I was fascinated watching the prop wind milling as the 190 headed toward its demise. All of a sudden I realized Carson was gone and there I was at 300 feet and every soldier with a weapon was firing at me. (I even saw one officer whip out a pistol and shoot at us.) The Germans had AA weapons on the roofs and in the parks - they all were concentrating on me! I saw the Seine River off to my right and swung over and down into it, hugging the north bank which is about 50 feet high. The guns could not repress enough to reach me that way.

"I flew about two miles along the river until it looked safe for me to break out for home, and I started a gradual climb for the French coast, then on to Leiston. When I arrived home I found that Carson had taken the same route out. I then confirmed Carson's victory.

"In summing up, I had a new appreciation of the daring and flying skills of the man who would ultimately become the leading ace of the 357th, Leonard K. Carson."

Becker's, Bochkay's and Johnny Pugh's victims all crashed within the city of Paris. Pugh had a new K-14 gun sight and had some troubles with it: "I tried to use the K-14, but do not find myself smooth enough on the controls to use it successfully. This e/a was shot down from very close range - it was impossible to miss."

Although Capt Becker's Fw 190 did crash in the city of Paris and he made a claim for its destruction, it was not to be:

"I was about 800 yards and closing on the enemy aircraft when he went straight into the ground and exploded in the N.E. section of Paris. Apparently he had been hit by his own anti-aircraft fire. From the time I first sighted this plane until he crashed, I saw no shots fired at him. We seemed to be the only Allied planes in the vicinity. Even if he had not crashed, he would have been a dead duck. I was catching him and there were eight other P-51s to render assistance if necessary. I feel that my pursuit of the 190 was responsible with fog its destruction

Victory claims in which no shots had been fired were common and often accepted, but in this case, Becker's claim was disallowed. He went on to complete his tour with a total eight victories.

DADDY RABBIT, B6-J, was Charles Peters' second aircraft to carry this name and cartoon. It was 44-13897.

This is thought to be the same airplane as above with Yeager in the cockpit, and now with the famous name applied. It was lost on 18 October 1944 with Horace Roycroft.

Left: This is B6-Y, thought to be Chuck Yeager's elusive GLAMOROUS GLEN II, identity not known, but it may have been 44-13897, which was also DADDY RABBIT, either before or after this. Later the aircraft did have the name.

Lt. Joe Cannon's rather scruffy B6-B, LITTLE JOE, 44-13887 and a group of happy ground crew pose for the camera.

Joe Cannon's earlier LITTLE JOE, B6-C shows hard usage with its chipped RAF green paint.

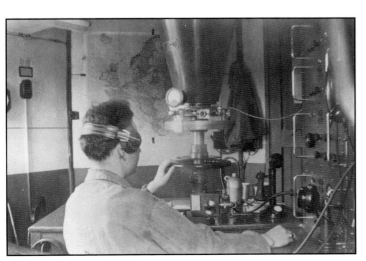

Seldom seen was in the inside of the station DF (Direction Finding) silo, which was off base in a farmer's field. Here Sgt. Robert Shearer operates the direction finder.

This fine photo of a 371st Fighter Group (9th Air Force) P-47 flying over very rough country, was taken by Donald Bochkay from his P-51.

A BEAUTIFUL AND DEADLY LAND

From 30,000 feet, continental Europe can be a thing of beauty, whether in spring greenery, or under a mantle of snow. Under the beauty, was a deadly threat. Clarence Anderson in his book TO FLY AND FIGHT:

"The sky above was bright crystal blue and the land below a green-on-green checkerboard divided by a silver blue ribbon. Below was occupied France, beyond the river lay Germany and it all looked the same, rolling and peaceful and bursting with spring.

"But it was an overpoweringly sinister place. From our perch six miles up, we couldn't see the enemy, some huddling over their guns taking aim, some climbing into their airplanes to fly up and get us, and some, on the far side of the river, waiting with pitchforks and hoping we'd fall somewhere close. All we could see was the green of the fields and forests. But we knew they were there, watching us come and thinking how they could kill us."

Anderson was talking about the view from a healthy airplane - consider how much more threatening it would have been from a parachute - as many found out.

From Leiston to targets in central Germany, the natural route was over the Netherlands. In five years of constant air battles, Holland and the waters surrounding it became the graveyard for an astounding 7,000 airplanes, British, American, and German - and many of their crews.

There were two prominent lakes along this route to central Germany, Dummer Lake about 65 miles west of Hannover and Steinhuder Lake, quite close to the that city. Because of their high visibility both were used as rendezvous points, by both sides.

On the 29th of July, Colonel Dregne leading 57 Mustangs, rendezvoused at Dummer Lake with a force of 3rd Division B-17s and from there on to bomb oil targets at Merseberg, one of the most hated targets by bomber crews due to its reputation for especially deadly flak. In his mission report, Dregne lists flak as "Heavy, intense, and accurate at the target".

The lead box of B-17s was hit by a small force of 109s and 190s in the target area and six of these were shot down. Three pilots, however, were lost, with Rollin Carter and Daniel Finley bailing out. Lt. Paul Holmberg was the victim of an unusual accident - while firing at an Me 109

his P-51 exploded for unknown reasons. There is no other known incident of this kind in 357th records.

During the withdrawal from the target, a 390th Bomb Group B-17 was hit by flak, knocking out #1 engine and their oxygen supply. Before the day was over, this crew would also be grateful for the presence of red and yellow-nosed Mustangs. Sergeant Walter McElroy was "toggler" on the B-17 and 45 years later he recalls the details:

"Fortunately, none of the crew of ten were injured. Losing an engine naturally caused us to lose air speed, so we had to drop out of formation and straggled along for awhile. Shortly thereafter, two P-51s joined us and proceeded to fly escort on our wings. I shall never forget the sight! They would try to fly as slowly as us, then one at a time would peel off and "sweep" the area. Both pilots waved to us while in formation. One of the aircraft had the name RELUCTANT REBEL, and the other was either COBBER or COBBER II. Both had invasion stripes on them. We were escorted back across the North Sea without any enemy aircraft attacking us and made an emergency landing at Woodbridge."

Both P-51s were from the 363rd Squadron. The assigned pilot of RELUCTANT REBEL was Robert Foy and Lawrence Wood was probably the pilot of COBBER II. It is not known if they were flying them that day.

D model Mustangs were now coming in fairly large numbers. In his diary for 8 July, Harry Ankeny recorded: "Got a new P-51D-5 today and my Crew Chief just finished last minute touches on it. Took BETSY on a test hop and really ran her thru the paces, from 500 MPH straight down to straight and level. Its better to find out if you have a good ship over here then to wait until you really have to press her in combat deep in enemy territory. She performed like a charm even though I wore myself out!"

BETSY was squadron code G4-S, AAF serial number 44-13596. Four days later, while cruising at 23,000 over Augsburg, BETSY took a burst of flak causing considerable damage to the airplane and Ankeny's confidence but she brought him home, and he was to complete his combat tour flying BETSY who was named for his wife.

On the Merseberg mission on the 29th, Captain Harvey Mace was leading Dollar Blue Flight - until someone called in "bogies". By the time he had disposed of his drop tanks, which were reluctant to release, the rest of the outfit had departed the area like a pack of hounds after a rabbit, leaving Mace and his wingman Flt. Lt. Eric Woolley RAF all alone with the bombers.

A short time later a flash of sun off a polished surface caught his attention and he was able to make out a B-17 far below, dog fighting "something", which revealed itself as a small speck. With Woolley following, Mace peeled off in an attempt to interfere in the B-17/Me 109 dog fight. Still far out of range, he fired a burst hoping the tracers would cool the 109 pilot's ambition - which indeed it did, the 109 streaking for a cloud deck below.

Mace takes up the story: "Since it was the first e/a I had ever seen and he had been attacking a lone B-17, I was determined to get him if at all possible. But the chances were looking glum with the head start he had and I pushed the dive a little harder than I should have. I soon felt the classic symptoms of compressibility, much buffeting and tightening up of the controls.

"This dictated an immediate throttling back and a slight pull-up. In continuing the chase, it became obvious the e/a was about to enter the clouds and I was still out of range. Not wanting to give up easily, I leveled out over where he should be. There he was, just near enough to the surface that I could easily make out the 109 and the pilot hunched over his flight instruments, just as tense as we were when on instruments."

Knowing the German pilot would go either up or down when he felt safe, Mace followed until the 109 began to drop thru the clouds. Then jammed the stick forward and dove through the cloud coming out just behind the 109. Half blind from the brightness of the cloud tops and then going into the murk, he could make out only a shadowy figure of an airplane.

Harvey Mace again: "When you're going to shoot someone with six .50 caliber guns, you should make sure it's the right party. So I eased down and to the right until I could see the cross and the outline of the 109. I slid back and fired a short burst, which missed. I adjusted the sight pip and fired a good burst. I was amazed at the amount of damage wrought by six .50s.

"So much trash and smoke came off him it obscured vision, so I slowed and pulled over him, rolling inverted so I could see him. Looking down (up) through my canopy for a moment we were canopy to canopy and there he was looking up at me while he was busily getting out of his harness preparing to bail out. I quickly rolled over to the right hoping to swing out and back in for a killing shot before he bailed out. It was to no avail however, as he was already in his chute by the time I got my nose back on him."

364th Squadron's Lt. Wallace Reid was "on the board" for the 29 July mission, but got no further than the take-off end of the runway. According to the USAAF accident report: "The pilot ran his engine up to check the maps, the engine was very rough so he decided not to takeoff and began to taxi back.

"The left wing tank began to leak at which time a spark of carbon from the exhaust ignited the gasoline on the plane. The aircraft was loaded with 485 gallons of 150 octane fuel which resulted in total loss before being extinguished by the station fire-fighting facilities."

Reid exited the cockpit with only a slight burn to the neck. Under "Recommendations", the accident board, Lt. Cols. Hayes and Dregne, and Major Storch wrote: "The use of compressed paper tanks be discontinued because of the tendency to leak. This contributes to a large number of early returns from missions as well as contributing an extreme fire hazard."

The recommendation was apparently not accepted by higher authority probably because the tanks, although leak prone and dangerous, were vital to the accomplishment of fighter missions of the 8th Air Force.

"No enemy aircraft seen" and poor weather were dominate themes in the mission reports for the month of August, 1944. The *Luftwaffe* had all but disappeared. The question was however; "are they gone forever, or is it a temporary respite?"

Of course, no one knew for sure.

From his book PURSUE AND DESTROY, Kit Carson comments on this period: "Two months after the Normandy landings, German fighter units in France had ceased to exist, period. Shot up on the ground, knocked out of the air, grounded for lack of fuel because trucks could not move on the roads, they simply disappeared. Just as their land forces were retreating, so was Germany's defensive fighter arm pulled back to the borders of the Fatherland itself."

Even on deep escort missions into Germany, the *Luftwaffe* was seldom seen. It had become a relatively "safe" war, temporarily at least. Despite considerable bombing and strafing, no one was shot down by ground fire and no one was shot down by e/a. Seven aircraft were lost, with three pilots killed. Eddie Simpson and Donald Ferron collided over the battle area with the latter dying in the crash. Simpson survived but was later killed on the ground while attempting to cross the battle lines. Harold Kenney of the 362nd bailed out during this period, but evaded capture.

Lt. Wallace Reid's war ended when his engine caught fire over northern Germany on 4 August and he bailed out: "Just as we approached Kiel, at 32,000 feet, my engine caught fire and I knew it was real trouble. Going a bit further I switched the engine off and started to let down over the Baltic. The fire and smoke was so bad that I trimmed it down, rolled over and bailed out. I went into the water about 100 yards from a German freighter and within a very few minutes they had a boat in the water and picked me up.

"I was taken aboard the freighter, notified that I was a POW and thereafter treated royally! They gave me

dry clothes, cognac, cigarettes, excellent food and cigars. The next day a launch came out from Kiel, picked me up and took me back to the city clink. From then on the royal treatment was over for sure!"

Reid was a guest of the Third *Reich* for the next nine months until Patton's troops turned him loose.

SUMMER DOLDRUMS

The Group flew 17 missions in August so there was ample activity. However, for an eager fighter pilot hoping to add to his score, it was the doldrums. No enemy aircraft were even seen until the 18th.

Was the *Luftwaffe* gone - "*Kaput*"? Only time would tell. Meanwhile the bombers went about their business smashing at the infrastructure of the 3rd *Reich*, grateful for the absence of German fighters but still exposed to the deadly flak.

The main event of August was the memorable Operation Frantic V, the shuttle mission to the Soviet Union - the land of the Russian Bear. This will be covered separately and we will look at activities at and out of Leiston air field, with brief extracts for the early part of the month from the mission leaders reports:

1 August: Vectored by Oilskin to Everaux area, 1530 but found no e/a. Provided withdrawal support to force to enemy coast, leaving them SW Leharve at 1600 at 25,000. Vectored back to Everaux area by Oilskin, where only Spits and P-38s were seen. One B-17 seen to go down vicinity Orleans from flak, two others collided in air, several chutes seen. Down, 1750 hours.

2 August: Area support: No strafing because of poor visibility and group leaders decision to land before field at home base closed in due to weather conditions. No e/a seen.

3 August: Gave close support to bombers thru targets as briefed. No e/a seen. No bombers in distress

4 August: two missions: Colonel Graham led 53 P-51s, no e/a seen, no Bs in distress. Marred only by the loss of Lt. Wallace Reid, who bailed due to engine failure and spent the next 10 months as a POW. A week earlier Reid's P-51 had burned on the runway at home base.

4 August: 2nd mission: Lt. Col. Hayes, 10 P-51s, joint mission with the 353rd Group P-47s, searching for a reported truck convoy. Hayes reported; "Difficulty maintaining formation with P-47s. P-51s without tanks were unable to fly slow enough without engines running rough and stay in formation with P-47s, with tanks." The truck convoy was nowhere to be found.

From the Operational Summary for August: "The weather was pretty nasty for the next mission. Lt. Col. Hayes and 13 other Mustang pilots did get off late, but got

off in spite of the weather. Over the continent everything was SNAFU because of limited visibility. Our mission joined in supporting bombers that were already heavily escorted. The bombers themselves were looking for something to attack. The skies were full of planes, all Allied." (Author's note: SNAFU was an obscene saying of the time, meaning, in general, that the situation was all messed up. Situation Normal All Fouled Up.)

With most of the Group still on the Russian expedition, there were only a limited number of aircraft and pilots available,and on the 10th, 14 of them again led by Hayes, joined the 55th Group on a five hour B-24 escort. It was generally uneventful except for the tragic loss of Lts. Edward Simpson and Donald Ferron which will be covered later.

The 11th and 12th of August brought two more uneventful missions and on the 14th, the Group was again at full strength with the main force having returned from the Russian odyssey.

There was still no sign of the *Luftwaffe* on the 14th through the 17th. On the latter day, it was dive and skip bombing of marshalling yards and bridges, where a long list of targets were hit, including two water towers. As might be expected, the light flak claimed a victim Lt. Harold Kenny who bailed out. German records say pilot dead and presumed burned. They were wrong however, as Kenny evaded capture and returned to Allied control.

As the month ran down to the end, there was still little sign of the enemy. No large gaggles were seen, but a few 109s flying singly, in pairs, or very small groups were found.

On the 18th, "two silver Me 109s" were encountered NE of Paris and both were dispatched. Captain John England and Lt. Walter Perry shared one of them. Perry was to die five days later when his P-51K, TOOLIN' FOOL, shed its wings in an apparently uncontrolled vertical dive, cause unknown. Perry had just been promoted to captain, and an amendment to his Missing Aircrew Report dated 31 January 1945, duly makes note of the fact.

On the 24th six 109s were found near Brunswick and Lt. Hermanson (who was leading the Group due to Colonel Dregne's early return to base) destroyed one and Lt. Gerald Tyler the second one. Both men highly praised the new K-14 gun sight, Hermanson saying he had gotten hits at 400 yards while the 109 was doing violent evasive maneuvers. Both men recommended that new pilots fly a practice mission before trying to use it in combat.

Group losses had been Harold Kenny, an evader Reid, a POW and Simpson and Ferron, both KIA. There were three further losses however. 2nd Lt. Charles O. Campbell was a newcomer and had probably flown no missions. On the 17th, he was killed in a crash near home

base. East Suffolk Police constable William Martin reported: "I beg to report that at 3:15 P.M. on Thursday the 17th August, 1944, a Mustang fighter plane crashed at Middleton, map ref M880853.

"Whilst the machine was in mid-air the nearside wing became detached, the plane crashed and burst into flames immediately when it struck the ground. The pilot was killed and badly burned and the plane was totally destroyed. The wing fell a few hundred yards away from the main plane.

"The machine fell in a wheat field which was cut and shocked owned by Walter Hatcher, Rose Farm, Middleton. About 40 shocks were destroyed by fire. Personnel from the airfield, Leiston, were quickly on the scene with mobile fire fighting apparatus and extinguished the flames and removed the dead pilot."

In the autumn of 1988, British aviation historian, writer and archaeologist, and a friend of this writer, Ian McLachlan, was walking across the field where P-51B, 43-6999 plunged to earth 44 years ago. He was astounded to find on the crest of a freshly ploughed furrow, a pair of distorted silver pilot wings.

There is little doubt that these had belonged to Lt. Charles Campbell who was probably very proud of his achievement in earning them. However, as in so many other cases it had all been for nothing.

HISTORICAL STATISTICS

Confirmed Group victory score as of 1 August 1944
Destroyed - 279.5
Probable - 20
Damaged - 63
Group Losses; Aircraft - 74   Pilots - 71

Aircraft (P-51) status, flying time 1 August 1944
For period November 1943 to 1 August 1944

P-51s assigned during period	218
P-51s missing in action	74
P-51 crashes, total loss	13
P-51s transferred (includes for battle damage	52
P-51s assigned as of 31 July,'44	79
Total operational hours flown	23,630
Total non-operational hours	4,300
Total gasoline consumed	2,602,132.8 gallons

THE BURTNER/BARON AFFAIR

The Group lost the services of two other pilots in August. Lt. George Morris who was leading Greenhouse (364th) Green flight reported: "Greenhouse Blue 1 (Lt. Walter Baron) called in that his engine had cut out and had started again, but was too rough to make it back to base. He asked for a course to Sweden. I gave him the course of 20 degrees. At this time we were at 20,000, 20 miles east of Rostock. I last saw Baron heading away from our formation for Sweden with Lt. Burtner, Greenhouse Blue 2, on his wing. Lt. Burtner's radio was out and we did not have contact with him."

This affair has always had an air of mystery about it, which continues to this day. Morris states that Baron was leading Blue flight with Burtner as his #2, but Burtner tells an entirely different story. After this writer had published the story in one of his books, he was contacted by Charles Burtner and we later had a long discussion of the incident during his visit to our home.

Burtner says he was not Baron's wingman and he did not even know him. In fact he thought Baron was flying an aircraft from another squadron. He further stated that soon after take-off his engine had begun running badly but he elected to continue the mission. Eventually, near the target, his engine quit and although he managed to get a re-start, it would run only at low power. His only option was to land in Sweden. Since his radio was inoperative, he was not in contact with anyone.

As he approached his landing, he noticed another P-51 on a roughly converging course which bellied into the same field in which he landed normally, wheels down. Swedish soldiers soon arrived and both men were interned. Burtner recalls that the Swedes were surprised to see him but seemed to be expecting Baron.

Burtner's P-51 was 44-13345, code C5-I (bar) which he had also flown on the shuttle mission. Baron's P-51B, according to his Missing Aircrew Report was 42-106854, which had been PEABODY'S PET (also given in this MACR). The squadron code is unknown but it was a 364th aircraft with Sgt Dick Eagan as Crew Chief. At the time Baron put it down on its belly in Sweden it was fully painted in green and gray, but whether it had the name is unknown as the only known photos of it in Sweden are not clear. In the discussions with Burtner, there seemed to be quite a lot of information he did not wish to discuss, but it appears as though Baron was involved in some kind of clandestine activities with the Swedes and may have continued in that business in the post war years.

Both Baron and Burtner show up on two 364th Squadron rosters of the period. Burtner states he joined the 357th on 7 June 1944. One roster shows him with 130 hours of combat time by 25 August and Baron had 109. Both men were released in about two months, but neither returned to the 357th except to pick up their belongings. The Swedes retained the two P-51s.

At the time of this writing, Baron shows up on our roster as deceased. Burtner, who was a retired Air Force Lt. Col., is no longer on our rosters. The bottom line is that we do not know what Baron was doing in Sweden or Burtner either for that matter, and are not likely to find out.

On the 25th of August, 364th pilots Walter Baron and Charles Burtner left the formation and landed in Sweden for reasons still not clear. The only photos we have of the P-51s in Sweden are these copied from a Swedish newspaper. C5-I (bar) was Burtner's.

In this photo by the author, two P-51Ds taxi in a light rain with the control tower in the background.

MISSION TO THE LAND OF THE RUSSIAN BEAR

Operation FRANTIC, the shuttle escort to Russia, was the major event of the month of August and one of the highlights of Group history.

In retrospect, it is at first difficult to see why the idea of shuttle bombing missions to Russia so enthralled government and air force leaders. Although the results were never worth the effort and losses, looked at in the context of the times the idea did seem to have potential merit.

By the end of 1943, German industry was working hard to relocate much of its war-making capacity to the east - hopefully beyond the range of Allied bombers. It did seem reasonable that U.S. bombers flying out of Russian bases could strike these targets in eastern Germany. Even more important was the desire to show the Russians the Allied will to strike at Germany from all sides, and the hope that the Soviets would be impressed with the capabilities of strategic bombing. The Russians never did really "buy" into either idea. They were never enthusiastic about the idea basing U.S. Aircraft on Russian soil and it required great diplomatic effort at the highest levels to finally get Stalin's reluctant approval in

February, 1944. By May, after a logistics nightmare, three bases were ready to receive the U.S. strike forces.

By August of 1944, there had been four previous FRANTIC missions, three by the 15th Air Force out of Italy, the other in June by 8th Air Force bombers and fighters. This had ended in disaster when *Luftwaffe* bombers caught the B-17s on the ground and in a night raid, wiped out about half the force.

The first FRANTIC mission from Italy had come as a surprise to the Germans, but they took immediate action to ready for the next which they were sure would come. Four bomber *Geschwadern*, KG4, KG27, KG53, and KG55 were transferred to Minsk, a German occupied city in White Russia and some 400 miles NW of the American bases in Russia, at Mirgorod, Poltava and Piryatin (the main fighter base).

Oberst (Colonel) Wilhelm Antrop, C.O. of KG 55, was notified at mid-day on the 21st of June of the passage of the B-17s headed east. By evening, the *Luftwaffe* force was bombed-up and ready. About 80 He 111s and Ju 88s took off shortly after 2100 hours, arriving over Poltava at about 30 minutes after midnight. For some two hours the bombers ravaged that base and Mirgorod with 110 tons of bombs. Dawn the next day made it clear that the *Luftwaffe* had conducted a very efficient strike. Fifty U.S. bombers and a few fighters were destroyed; two Americans and 30 Russians were dead.

Half of the U.S. force, however, survived due to the prudent actions of the 13th Wing Commander and his deputy and group leaders. The 13th Wing was the occupant of Mirgorod. Soon after landing, Colonels Edgar Wittan and Joe Moller observed a German aircraft orbiting the base at high altitude. This caused a great deal of concern and Wittan, unable to contact General Archie Olds at Poltava, decided on his own to remove his aircraft. With reluctant approval of the Russians all 13th Wing B-17s took off at night and dispersed to three other Russian bases where they escaped the attention of the *Luftwaffe*.

Even though Wittan had outwitted the Germans and saved half the force, a major blow had been struck at the FRANTIC idea. Although the Germans never repeated their success, FRANTIC went down hill from this point. The next two were flown out of Italy by fighters only, with minimal results. Possibly because of the loss of 50 B-17s on the June mission and the already cooling ardor for the shuttle idea, the fifth FRANTIC mission was flown by only about half the number of bombers with only the 95th and 390th Bomb Groups participating.

Fighter escort was to be the same, however, four Squadrons of P-51s, all provided by the 357th. The 4th "victory" Squadron to be made up of spares from the other three.

There was little advance notice to Group Headquarters. With take-off scheduled for 0930, Sunday the 6th of August, the first warning arrived on the evening of the 4th. The period inbetween can only be described as hectic, with most departments and sections involved in one way or another. 72 P-51s were required, more than had ever taken off on one mission. When the time came, 72 Mustangs were ready - maintenance had done its job well.

Realizing the historic aspects of the operation most pilots were eager to be a part of it. 362nd Squadron's Ted Conlin had been on leave in London and returned to base on the 5th of June where he found that he was scheduled but would have to take all of his shots, in both arms, at one time. Anxious to go, he agreed. The next morning his arms were like lead. It was a chore to handle the controls but he was ready and part of the great adventure.

As on previous FRANTIC missions the fighter ground crews were assigned to fly in the bombers, some as waist gunners. One suspects that both the neophyte gunners and the regular crew members sincerely hoped they would not have to fulfill their new duties. It was the only time in Group history that other than pilots would fly a combat mission. There were 35 of them, four being officers. The others were all enlisted technicians. Before dawn on the 6th, these men reported to the 390th Bomb Group at nearby Parham with whom they would fly.

T/Sgt Leo Kiselewski remembers the sketchy briefing: "When we arrived at the base, everything was ready. All our belly tanks and spare parts were already aboard. We didn't get much briefing. When we got aboard, I was assigned the left waist gun and a regular crew member gave me a fast run-down on loading the

The briefing room on 6 August 1944, departure date for the OPERATION FRANTIC V mission to Russia. Note that the mission tape goes off the right side of the map of Europe and does not show a return route. The sign at the top left gives ASR procedures, the blackboard at left gives the Field Order number, order of take-off, wind information and checkpoints. The one at right gives call signs and other communication information. There are many black ID models hanging from the ceiling.

gun, and how to clear a jam, and all the rest was up to me. He said 'pull the trigger and fire'. We did get some practice as we flew over the channel."

At 0922 hours, 72 Merlins coughed blue smoke and rumbled into life. At 0930, Colonel Don Graham got the show on the road and the other 71 followed in good order. All, however, did not continue on as seven of these were spares only two of which were needed. Lt. Norbert Fisher, Green 2 in 363 Squadron, found that his oxygen regulator was inop and he was replaced by Flt. Lt. Jack Cleland, RNZAF, who moved in as wingman to Green flight's leader, Lt. Bill Overstreet. Captain Thomas Hughes was replaced by Lt. Ray Staude and the other spares returned to base. The remaining 64 P-51s set course on what would be a very long ride. FRANTIC 5 mission #1 was underway.

The course track took DRYDEN GROUP (357th code call sign) out to sea to the northeast, along the Frision Islands passing below the German island of Heligoland, crossing into the narrow neck of Germany where the first enemy aircraft were sighted - by one man at least. Lt.

Harvey Mace was flying element lead in John England's 362 flight. 45 years later Mace recalled: "We had rounded the bend crossed near the flak saturated island of Heligoland and were crossing the Danish peninsula when I saw nine Fw 190s. Coming from the opposite direction a little to our right and a little lower were the nine 190s in a very tight echelon show-type formation, a very pretty formation. Obviously they were totally unaware of our presence. None of our group made a move and there was no mention on the R/T of the 190s. The target was so tempting I actually started to push over to go for them, but then had to remind myself that we were given strict orders not to attack enemy fighters unless they were a threat to the bombers. All I could do was watch them disappear to our rear. I don't know if anyone else saw them or not."

After leaving Mace's 190s behind, the force stayed out to sea over the Baltic for another 250 Km or so until they RVed with the bombers over "Leva See", a small coastal lake some 75 Km NW of the target at Gdynia, Poland. At this point the bombers were under escort by the 55th and 339th Fighter Groups both of which turned

Colonel Graham led the mission to Russia in his P-51D-5, B6-W, BODACIOUS, s/n 44-13388.
Some references say this airplane has a special paint job but there is no evidence of it here,
where it appears in the common RAF green and gray.

In these two photos by Sergeant Jim Frary, it is shortly after 0930 hours on the 6th of August, 1944. Col. Don Graham has already taken off at the head of 72 Mustangs (seven were spares and would return to base) bound for far away Russia. Here we see Captain John England in G4-H, tail number 413735 (it had no name at this time). Just visible behind G4-H is G4-M, a P51B with Tom Martinek as pilot. Note that all visible P-51s in this photo are painted in RAF green. The aircraft in the left background are 363rd squadron aircraft, with Captain Don Bochkay's WINGED ACE OF CLUBS just visible under the spinner of G4-H.

Although taken within a few minutes of the England photo, below is a partial change of scene which provides some fascinating information. G4-0, SEBASTIAN JR. was Captain Robert Becker's P-51 and his total seven victories are seen under the cockpit. However, Becker did not fly the mission and the man in the cockpit is Captain Maurice Baker. G4-0 did not return from the mission, Baker having crashed it without injury to himself on take-off in Italy. (the white slash on the photo is a defect in the original negative) In this photo we have examples of three different paint schemes. SEBASTIAN JR. is in the "half" paint scheme, Olive Drab (possibly RAF green) upper surfaces with fuselage sides in bare metal. Some but not all 362nd Squadron aircraft were painted as such and a few 364th Squadron aircraft, but none from the 363rd. Just in front of G4-0, is G4-X and it is in the late war bare metal scheme, except that the visible portions of the rudder and fin are in a dark color (OD?) as is a short section of the rear fuselage. Even though the tail number is not visible this P-51 is almost surely 44-13738 which had been received from the 55th Fighter Group only two days earlier. This was part of the augmentation of aircraft to make up the equivalent of four Squadrons for the mission. The pilot of G4-X was Lt. John Schlossberg. The partially painted tail would suggest the airplane had been damaged and the entire tail section replaced with that from a painted aircraft. Again Bochkay's B6-F, WINGED ACE OF CLUBS, can be seen in the same spot just ahead of G4-X although he was not flying it this day the pilot being Ernest Tiede.

On the Ground in Russia, pilots and crews "just waiting". C5-I in the foreground BOBBY MARILYN, 44-13783. 1st Lt. George Morris is the pilot. Next in line is Johnny Pugh's P-51B GERONIMO, G4-N. He is reclining on the wing. By the time of the Shuttle in August there were many of the new P-51D-5s on hand, but the older P-51Bs made up about half of the force that went to Russia.

This photo is the result of international intrigue by SSgt. Dick Eagan and an unknown Russian officer. The photo of a Russian Pe-2 bomber with Russian and U.S. Airmen was taken by a Russian official photographer. Prints were not made available to the Americans, but a Russian officer that Eagan had become friendly with knew the location of the photos and the two broke into a photo lab to obtain this (and one other) print. Hopefully the statute of limitations has run out. Eagan is on the wing 4th from left to the right of the Russian officer.

back to home base when the force arrived in the target area (an Fw 190 assembly plant at Gdynia). As the 55th turned back, a curious and very much unbriefed occurrence took place. Lt. Clifford Sherman of the 38th Sqdn, 55th Group, called Hellcat Leader, reporting engine trouble, and saying he would be going on to Russia, taking his wingman, Lt. David Jewell with him.

As far as can be determined, Sherman and Jewell not only went on to Russian bases, but stayed with the force all the way, going on to Italy, and returning to England. Whether they attached themselves to the bombers as a flight of two, or joined the 357th is unknown. None of the 357th pilots questioned recall the two 55th Group P-51s.

Luftwaffe reaction would be weak throughout the seven day mission, with claims for only six enemy aircraft destroyed, plus one other that will be discussed later. From the target onward, enemy fighters did appear in small numbers, but all prudently retired without engaging. There was however, one brief combat in which two 109s were shot down, and this incident would have repercussions 45 years later.

Greenhouse White Flight, with Lt. Robert Shaw leading, spotted the 109s first, and was able to turn them away from the bombers. Shaw got numerous hits on one of them, with a gratifying display of smoke and fire and he claimed this one as destroyed. Lt. Hollis "Bud" Nowlin, element leader in White Flight, looking back over the years, remembers:

"I wasn't prepared for combat, I had too much loose stuff in my plane. On the left side of the windshield were two oranges; on the right side were 6 or 9 navigation charts covering half of Europe, along with a canteen of water. Under the seat was a set of spark plugs which Dennis Green (his crew chief) suggested I take, also a ditty bag with the usual items for travel. None of these things were tied down."

Ready or not, Nowlin took on the other 109.

The two Messerchmitts were from *Luftwaffe* fighter unit JG 51, the leader being a man named Günther Schack, one of the stars of JG 51 with over 100 victories on the Russian front. He was *Staffelkapitän* of the 9th *Staffel*, III *Gruppe*, JG 51. His wingman was Lt. Besekau.

Schack still has vivid memories of that summer day: "The 3rd *Gruppe* of Fighter Wing Mölders (JG 51) was stationed at Lyke, East Prussia on 6 August, 1944. We were greatly astounded at the report that a hundred American "Furniture vans" (German slang for four engine bombers) were flying east from Danzig. Every available plane must intercept - all nine of us! We met the reported "big herd" at the (for us) unusual height of 18,000 feet, very close to the front line.

1st Lt. Hollis "Bud" Nowlin shot down an Me 109 on the flight to Russian bases, but he did not know it until 40 years later when he met the pilot. He had gotten strikes on the 109s coolant system, but then broke off to re-join his unit, fast fading away in the distance.

"It was reported to us by ground control that no escort fighters were with the bombers. But before we could begin our attack, Mustangs came out of the sun. In a turn, my Me 109 received a hit in the cooler, and I had nothing more in my thoughts than to continue west to make a belly landing in German territory. In a dive I thought to escape "the boys" and somewhat to cool my engine. As I was concentrating on a place to belly land a Mustang flew very close past me, and turned to the east. After I was on the ground I received artillery fire and was hustled to safety by an infantryman. I had landed almost on the front line, in a small salient with the Russians on three sides."

We are fortunate in this case to have the view from both sides of the gun sight. Catching up with the 109 he opened fire and after this first burst the 109 did a split

"S", with Nowlin following getting more strikes and being rewarded with the typical white cloud associated with coolant pouring from a dying engine. Nowlin, overrunning the now-gliding 109, pulled off to the side to watch. At this time, he suddenly realized he was alone, short on fuel and with the rest of the group long out of sight. Waving to Schack he broke away heading for a healthier climate.

Nowlin claimed only a "damaged", as the 109 was still flying when he last saw it. Even though the Messerschmitt was lost, it was over 40 years before Nowlin learned this fact, so his claim for shooting down Schack remains as a "damaged".

In the late 1980s, historian Bill Graham brought the two together again when Bud Nowlin and his wife paid a visit to Schack at his home in Germany. In the fall of 1991, Günther Schack was an honored guest of the Nowlins and the 357th Fighter Group at their fall reunion in Georgia. For over four decades, Schack had wondered why the P-51 pilot had not finished him off. After meeting Bud Nowlin, he now has come to the conclusion that Nowlin was a good man who did not desire to finish off a crippled fellow airman. Bud Nowlin certainly fits the description of a "good man", but there were other factors at work that day also. Nowlin recalls: "I was a bit late finding out that he had reduced power and as a result I gave what I call a wave-off (somewhere between a wave and a salute). From that time I proceeded with a sharp climbing turn to the left and unable to see my wingman, decided it was time to head toward our destination, east of Kiev." Thus ended his brief encounter with *Hauptmann* Günther Schack.

About the same time as the Nowlin/Schack combat, Lts. Nick Frederick and Kirky Brown spotted a potential victim of a different type, and their encounter has interesting aspects. From their Encounter Report of 6 August, 1345 hours, 50 miles NE of Warsaw:

"We were flying Greenhouse Blue 3 & 4 and a black Ju 88 flew past our formation at 22,000 feet. We turned 100 degrees and pursued it. The e/a started a violent dive to evade us and was headed for the only patch of woods in the vicinity. The woods were surrounded by wheat fields. We were about 1,000 yards behind the e/a going over 500 mph and we cut throttles and started to level off around 6,000 feet. We then went down to 3,000 feet and kept our eye on the e/a and it kept on diving at about a 70 degree angle, doing approximately 500 mph.

"The e/a failed to level off and was last seen at 1,000 feet still in its dive. We know the e/a did not pull out as we would have seen it crossing the wheat fields. We believe the e/a crashed in the woods, and due to the blackness of the woods we failed to observe any results of

Hauptmann *Günther Schack was an ace with 100 victories on the 6th of August when he led the 3rd* **Gruppe** *of JG 51 (which could only muster nine Me 109s) off from its base in East Prussia to intercept the FRANTIC force. However, the Mustangs drove them away, shooting down at least two, one of which was Schack, hit in the coolant system by Nowlin. In the late 1980s, the two pilots met in Germany and in 1991, Gunther Schack was a guest at the 357th Fighter Group reunion.*

the crash. We claim one Ju 88 and crew destroyed. Ammunition expended: 0."

Their claim was accepted, and is so credited in the USAF victory records for WWII. Kirby Brown was to be killed in action a month later. The confirmation of victories was simply a judgment call by now unknown persons, and this confirmation of the Ju 88 in which no shots were fired and the e/a not seen to crash, can be compared to the 25 July claim of Captain Robert Becker in which he and two flights of the 362nd squadron were chasing an Fw

190 over Paris. As in the Frederick/Brown case, no shots were fired, but the 190 was seen to crash and explode in NE Paris. Becker's claim was rejected.

After this brief flurry of action, the force continued without incident until 1630 hours when the P-51s finally left the bombers 10 miles east of Kiev. Thirty minutes later the Mustangs arrived over their airfield at Piryatin, but not without some difficulty. General Graham recently told this writer that the field was well camouflaged and difficult to see.

By shortly after 1700 hours, all Mustangs were on the ground, after seven and a half hours of sitting on a lumpy dinghy and the B-17s were safely down on their base with 35 YOXFORD BOY technicians, probably relieved that they had survived their first combat mission with no ill affects.

The time spent on Russian soil was to be very short. Having arrived on the evening of the 6th of August, the force would depart on the morning of the 8th. There was little of Russian life to be seen but several men have recorded their impressions. Lt. Henry "Hank" Pfeiffer's impressions were probably typical: "The camp was very primitive with slit trenches and Russian guards, all old combat veterans who would shoot everything. Needless to say, a trip to the slit trench was a mini-combat mission and hair-raising to say the least! Some of us were offered a trip to the nearest village. Other than seeing the native Russian people, (all old or children) the trip was not much. Nothing was available to buy or they would not sell it to us. The area we drove through had been fought over several times and was devastated, much old war equipment, guns, cannons, carts, etc, were littered everywhere. These people had had a very hard time of it."

Back at home base in far away England, the following teletype arrived in the evening: "Confidential 8 FC A810D report rec'd from Eastern bases via A-2 Pinetree on Frantic mission, F.O. 487, 6 August, 1944. 75 B-17s escorted by 64 P-51s of the 357th Grp bombed Fw 190 factory at Rahmel with good to excellent results. 74 B-17s and 64 P-51s landed Eastern bases. 1 B-17 believed to be in Russia. I crewman wounded. All fighters arrived safely with no battle damage. Claims for fighters are 0-2-2, claims for bombers 0-2-2. No information available on two pilots of 55th Grp believed to have gone to Russia."

The claims listed are incorrect for the fighters and should have been 2-0-2.

Minor maintenance and servicing at Piryatin was done by a small group of U.S. mechanics, each with a Russian helper. On the night of arrival, or the next day, someone in the fuel servicing section committed a major blunder, and an unknown, but significant number of P-51s were serviced with a low grade fuel, probably 80 or 90

octane. The error might have been avoided if the 357th mechanics had been present, but for reasons now unknown, none of them ever made it to the fighter base, but remained with the B-17s at Poltava, and throughout the rest of the mission.

Ray "Ted" Conlin's P-51 was one of those serviced with the wrong fuel: "When I got down to G4-C, I found the Russian ground crew had mistakenly filled my tanks with 90 octane instead of 130. When the Russian 3rd Lt. in charge learned of the error, he drew his pistol and threatened to execute the man responsible. I jumped off the wing and my American Sergeant and I pleaded with the Russian to relent. He did, and it left an impression on me that life in that part of the world was not held in high esteem."

The problem was much more widespread than Conlin's G4-C, but the extent did not become apparent until take off on the morning of the 8th when the Group departed Russia for Italy.

Harry Ankeny and several others got air borne only with difficulty, and one aircraft was destroyed in a crash. To Henry Pfeiffer goes the distinction of having accomplished the what had to be the "hairiest" take off in the history of the Group, and maybe in all of 8th Fighter Command!

Henry Pfeiffer: "My aircraft, C5-E, was one of those refueled with the bad fuel. On this grass field, several flights would take off at once, with my flight being one of the last to go. On my take-off roll I added power very slowly, in order to keep the flight together. Upon reaching 40 to 45 hg (inches of Mercury) manifold pressure my engine cut out. I eased the throttle back and it started again. Again I added power and again it cut out. Now I was committed and found that I could run at about 40 hg, so decided to go and give it a shot on getting airborne.

"All the rest of the flight went screaming by like a covey of quail. At this time I caught sight of a P-51 skidding gear up into a revetment, hitting a power unit and on fire. My attention was on the end of the field, I knew I did not have flying speed and something had to be done. I bounced PAPPY'S ANSWER over the ditch into the next field and kept going, this field being about as long as our landing field, but rough. I noted that the airspeed was picking up slowly but I was coming to the end with no place to go if I didn't fly so I added some more flap. With the stick all the way back, it bounced into the air and didn't settle back. Now I was airborne about a foot off the ground at just about stall speed. I couldn't turn, but it was gaining speed, and after about ten miles I had enough speed to start easing up the flaps. I had retracted the gear when I honked it off the ground."

EDWARD K. SIMPSON AND DONALD J. FERRON

Simpson and Ferron were both fighter pilots. Ferron died in a fighter but Eddie Simpson died as an infantry machine gunner. This is his story.

On the 10th of August, while most of the 357th Group's P-51s and pilots were in sunny Italy on their way home from the shuttle mission, those pilots and aircraft left at home base continued to fly missions at reduced strength of course.

Lt. Col. Tom Hayes led the mission on the 10th, 14 Mustangs on a five hour escort of an equally small group of B-24s bombing targets in France. Hayes reported no enemy aircraft seen. It would have been a routine operation if it had not been the mid-air collision of two 363rd Squadron P-51s.

Lt. Marion Burnett was a witness: "We were escorting B-24s at approx. 1110 hours, at 22,000 feet, ten miles east of Sens, France. Lt. Simpson was leading the flight and he started a medium turn to the left. Lt. Donald Ferron immediately crossed from the left to the right and I began to slowly move my element in trail. I had nearly completed the move when Lt. Ferron, apparently thinking I wasn't going to cross over, did a sharp turn to the left and over Lt. Simpson. The two ships collided and locked together and one caught fire. After spinning once or twice, the planes separated and the fuselage tank in the burning plane exploded, practically destroying the ship.

The other plane began a slow spiral seemingly under full control. I was a few miles behind and above this plane and started to follow him, but after dropping down to 14,000 feet I lost him in the haze." Both Lts. Simpson and Ferron were listed as Missing in Action although in fact, Ferron had died in the burning P-51.

Almost a month later, early in September a bracelet with the name of Edward K. Simpson was delivered to the 357th, which had come down through channels from the Office of Director of Intelligence of U.S. Strategic Air Forces in Europe. It was endorsed to 8th Air Force, 8th Fighter Command, 66th Fighter Wing and finally to the 357th. That exact action that was to be taken is unknown but all endorsements say the same thing; "For your information and necessary action". Perhaps it was meant to be sent on to Simpson's wife in Pomona, California. What happened to the bracelet is unknown.

About a month later on the 9th of October, a report from the Intelligence Officer of the 302nd Air Transport Wing, based in France, provided the facts of Simpson's death. The report states that Simpson survived the accident uninjured, but was killed in action four days later on 14 August. After the crash he had made contact with the FFI (the French underground resistance forces). Little more was known except that, four days later, Simpson was killed while fighting with the French.

Fifteen years later under date of 31 March, 1960 the casualty Section of the Adjutant General's Office wrote to the Chief, Personnel Services Branch. It relates the above facts and adds that the 25 November, 1959 issue of STARS AND STRIPES newspaper had a detailed article about the action in which Simpson died, titled THE DEAD YANK OF ORLEANS FOREST. After a great deal of effort, a copy of the 1959 STARS AND STRIPES article was obtained and it provided more details on Simpson's death. After contacting the FFI they took him to one of their camps deep in Orleans Forest. There were about 200 men and women in this force. Soon after Simpson's arrival they were attacked by German troops. The French were well armed and beat off the attack, but it was now obvious that they must make an attempt to break through to approaching Allied lines.

Using captured German vehicles they set off, hotly pursued by German forces. It was plain that if they were to escape the enemy must be delayed. Five Frenchmen jumped off the last truck with a machine gun to attempt the delay and Simpson joined them. All six were killed, but they did delay the Germans long enough for the remaining group to reach Allied lines which included seven other Americans. After the war, the French erected a monument honoring the six in the village of Ouzouer-sur-Loire and another in the Orleans Forest. Simpson's name is on both, considered to be a hero to the people of the French resistance none of whom he really knew.

In 1960, with this information, the Casualty Branch sent investigators to the area searching for eyewitnesses. None were found but two people with knowledge of the event were interviewed. The final statement said: "It is recommended that a report of death be issued showing that Captain Edward K. Simpson was killed in action on 14 August, 1944, in ground combat with German forces, while fighting with the French Maquis."

All humans make decisions which turn out to have been the wrong choice. Eddie Simpson made a bad choice when he decided not to go on the shuttle mission to Russia, which was a long and potentially dangerous operation. With only a few hours left to complete his combat tour, he elected to remain at home base, fly out his few hours and then return to the ZI. It was a tragic mistake as he was killed on a "milk run" type mission while no pilots were lost on the Russian operation.

The P-51 that Pfeiffer saw slide into a revetment was that flown by Lt. Howard Egeland. Unable to get airborne he had cracked up as seen by Pfeiffer, wrecking the P-51B (s/n 43-6721), but with slight injury to himself.

After Pfeiffer had managed to struggle into the air, the rest of the Group was long gone, of course, but he found them "as little gnats about 30 miles ahead and far above." By staying low and climbing very slowly at low power, he finally joined up in the target area and went on in to San Severo, the next stop in Italy.

For the enlisted crews in the B-17s it had been a fascinating but relatively uneventful experience up to now. On the run from Poltava down to Foggia in Italy, some of them would get a taste of the real air war. In his mission report for the 8th, Colonel Graham reported flak as "very inaccurate". From his waist gun position Leo Kiselewski had a different view: "We didn't seem to meet much resistance in the target area, a little flak came our way, but not much. We did get a surprise after we left the oil fields, when a few batteries of flak raked us over good, with two engines shot out. We were flying over the mountains when the order came to throw everything overboard, so all the guns ammo, spare parts etc went out the window.

"Then the order came to bail out, but it was apparent that we were too low, so it was rescinded. It seemed like we could reach out and touch the mountains, but we managed to scrape over, and suddenly could see the beautiful blue water of the Adriatic. It was beautiful and made us feel good about the whole mission! After landing we found the plane was only good for scrapping, and we had to wait around a week to get transport back to England."

The sojourn in Italy turned out to be the most pleasant of the trip - like a vacation said Leo Kiselewski. The balmy weather, the blue Adriatic and its beaches, the ample supply of cantaloupe and ice cream and the hospitality of the San Severo base P-38 group, made it the high point of the journey. It was also the longest stay - having arrived on the 8th, they did not depart until the 12th.

One operation only was flown from Italy, and a very rewarding one. Heavy escort was provided for 12 C-47s picking up escapees and evaders from a mountain top field in Yugoslavia.

Homeward bound on the 12th, and support of the invasion of Southern France. One P-51 crashed on take-off, and its pilot, Captain Maurice Baker returned to home base much later, wearing a red fez and telling tales about Casablanca and Algiers.

Tragic cases of aircraft and crews lost to "friendly fire" are nothing new in air warfare - it has been happening since WWI. On this last mission of the Grand Tour, a weather scout Mosquito of the 25th Bomb Group was mistaken for a Ju 88, and shot down by 357th Group P-51s. The navigator bailed out and survived - the pilot did not.

By 1400 hours, the force was back on the ground at Leiston. It had been a fascinating adventure for those lucky enough to take part, they had flown over much of Europe, visited two countries none had ever seen before, and came back with many stories of their adventures. THE YOXFORD BOYS' part in FRANTIC V was over.

For their part as amateur B-17 crew members, 35 men of the ground crews were awarded the Air Medal - the only enlisted men of the 357th to be so honored. One of these men, however, was to wait some 50 years before receiving his. SSgt Richard Eagan, 364th Squadron, who went to Poltava as waist gunner on the one of the B-17s, like all the other enlisted men, arriving there on the 6th of August. Two days later the B-17s and the 357th P-51 flew to Italy, on their way home.

Eagan's B-17, however, became mired in the mud and was unable to take off until three days later, when it finally departed, but not for Italy. The Russians insisted they go instead to Teheran, Persia (now Iran). They spent two days there and then went on to Cairo, Egypt. Engine trouble kept them there until the 28th of August when they finally got away to Tunis, Marrakish and finally to the B-17's home base at Horham on 1 September.

No one in the 364th Squadron knew what had happened to him and when he reported in 1st Sergeant Clifton Fergusan was preparing to list him as missing. By that time the Air Medal list had been forwarded and Eagan, of course was not on it.

Some 50 years later, Eagan decided he should have his Air Medal, and wrote to the 357th Fighter Group Association asking for help. His timing was fortuitous, as at this time the Government had announced that it would accept applications from veterans who thought they should have received medals. Through the effort of Colonel C.E. Anderson, then president of the 357th Association, Richard Eagan did receive his Air Medal - 50 years later!

PASSION WAGON and pilot Arval Roberson wait for engine start time. Crew Chief Sgt. Lybarger at left, and Armorer Ernie Seeley at far right, all smile for the camera. Other two men's names forgotton. Below, a close up with Lybarger.

A beautiful weapon of war, Arval Roberson's PASSION WAGON, G4-A, 44-13691 a D-5 without the dorsal fin which was added later. After Roberson completed his tour, Charles Weaver flew it and it was finally transferred to the 364th Squadron as GYPSY, with the nude remaining.

Another view of PASSION WAGON in RAF green. Although it has invasion stripes on the bottom of the fuselage, that does not mean it flew over the D-Day beaches. It did not, in fact, depart the U.S until the 23rd of June and would have arrived at Leiston late in July, just in time for Roberson to fly it on the Russian shuttle.

Right; 362nd Squadron Armorer John Hoefner charges the guns on PASSION WAGON. The cable with T-handle was used to retract the breech block and feed a cartridge into the chamber. The guns were then "hot".

For amusement 364th Squadron armament personnel sometimes mounted a .50 machine gun on their Weapons Carrier and drove it out to the nearby beaches of the North Sea where they enjoyed blasting away at small objects on the beach. Surely this must have been against some British laws??

AUTUMN SKIES

The Operational Summary for September tells us: "Operations for the month of September became more intense than they had been since D-Day. A total of 25 missions were flown by the Group in spite of the bad weather. On those 25 missions a score of 60-1-3 brought the Group's score to 390 1/2-20-88. (Destroyed - Probably Destroyed - Damaged.)

"The good combat record of the unit was marred to some extent by an unusually large number of accidents at home. The first coming at the end of the first mission when a pilot landed long on the runway and couldn't stop before running into a tree at the end of the strip. The others were scattered throughout the month of operations and training."

The absence of the *Luftwaffe* led some to wonder if the war was about over. On the 3rd, Capt Howell (Probably John C.) led 16 P-51s on an escort, where the B-17s made repeated bomb runs at the usually suicidal altitude of 8,000 feet. There was no flak or enemy fighters.

Operation APHRODITE was the experimental attempt to use radio-controlled drone bombers, loaded with 20,000 pounds of explosives, to strike at hardened targets. About 20 missions were flown, starting in July or August. Almost none hit their intended targets and several crews were obliterated in premature triggering of the explosives.

The 388th Bomb Group was the primary unit that carried these out, but the U.S. Navy also had a small detachment flying PB4Ys (B-24s), and Joseph Kennedy, brother of the late president, John F. Kennedy was killed when his aircraft exploded in flight in August.

The 357th provided escort for several of these missions, such as the one on 3 September when Major Hiro led 15 Mustangs escorting a Navy Liberator bomber. The mission was uneventful, although Hiro reported a huge blast in the vicinity of the target.

Most of the intense activity mentioned in the Operational Summary took place in the second half of the month. The nine missions flown in the first half of the month were similar to Operation GRASSY, which held the attention of Major Hiro and 32 other pilots on the 9th, 68 B-17s dropped supply canisters to the French Underground forces. No losses, no flak, no enemy aircraft seen, no claims. A pleasant ride over southern France.

Eighth Air Force flew its third FRANTIC shuttle run to Russia on 11 September, two groups of B-17s with the escort this time provided by the 20th Fighter Group. The 357th, with Captain John England leading a strong force of P-51s (55 after six had aborted), escorted the bombers to Dresden, where the 20th Fighter Group took over.

The 11th was significant because it was the first time since late May that the *Luftwaffe* reacted strongly against about 1,000 B-17s and B-24s, with some 500 fighters. The vicious battle cost the 8th some 40 bombers while the *Luftwaffe* lost over 1/5th of the fighters committed. The 357th, however, did not share a "piece of the pie". Only three enemy fighters were seen, which attack and shot down a bomber, but not before its gunners had destroyed two of them. The other evaded before THE YOXFORD BOYS could intervene. Captain England and his 55 P-51s had to be content with a few ground targets, the claims of which included "Two German officers". It would be interesting to know the circumstances of this, but the mission report is silent on details.

The next day, a large force of enemy fighters were seen, but chose not to fight. Colonel Dregne reported: "150 plus e/a observed at approximately 1040 approaching bomber from NE at Salzwedel. When 10 miles out e/a made 180 degree turn and were not seen again."

The next day, the 13th, the German fighter force was ready again and this time THE YOXFORD BOYS collided with several gaggles of Me 109s.

Even with the losses of the day before, the 8th sent over 1,000 bombers to oil and industrial targets in southern Germany. The 109s and 190s were again airborne in defense of the *Reich*, but the efforts were scattered, and the 357th claimed 15 destroyed, but in three different formations and one lonely 109 all by itself. Captain John England, who was leading the mission added 2.5 to bring his mounting score to eleven. From his encounter report:

"I placed the e/a properly in my K-14 sight and squeezed the trigger. I got strikes all over the engine and cockpit. The enemy aircraft, burning, went out of control and crashed in a river. Without the K-14 sight and my G suit, I don't think I would have gotten this Jerry, as he was headed for a heavily defended airdrome. My wingman said later that I was pulling 6 'G's when I got this Jerry." 364th Squadron's Lt. Horace "Pete" Howell also shot down a 109 - "I used the new gyro sight, which I found very effective and easy to use."

Statistically, the 357th was on the right side of the ledger, but the cost had been high, with five P-51s lost, and three pilots dead. Lt. Goldsworthy bailed into the channel but was soon fished out by rescue service and returned to base, as was Lt. Johnson who had bailed over Belgium. No one knows what happened to Marion Burnett or James Valkwitch, but German records show the latter as dead in the wreckage of his P-51. Lt. Kirby Brown was the other loss, and his fate has been learned only in recent years.

Lt. Merle Allen was element leader in Greenhouse (364th) Blue flight with Brown on his wing, when they ran through a gaggle of forty Me 109s headed for the bombers. Allen tacked onto a straggler and shot it down. After this,

Brown had disappeared, and although Allen later contaced him on the R/T when he stated he was OK, Brown was not seen again and did not return to base.

In the author's previous book (THE 357TH OVER EUROPE), the death of Brown is covered with information from German historian, Konrad Rudolph; however, in the year 2001, Rudolph reported that this information was incorrect, and that he and fellow historian Stafan Sander had learned the true facts: Brown had bailed out (reason unknown) and landed near the village of Schoenau about 30 km east of Kassel. Brown was captured by a farmer and then taken to the city of Heiligenstadt, where he was turned over to an SS officer named Karl Gebhardt, who then killed Brown with his pistol.

Kirby Brown was buried in the city cemetery, and his remains were removed in 1952 by U.S. Army authorities. Since he is not listed as being buried in any of the European American cemeteries, it is likely his remains were returned to his family.

In the year 2000, historian Stefan Sandes and a group of villagers erected a simple memorial to a former enemy who had been murdered by a German officer.

After the mission of the 13th of September, the ensuing three days of relative inactivity provided some rest, in prepartion for the traumatic events which would soon take place - OPERATION MARKET GARDEN.

After he completed his tour with the 357th and returned to the RAF, Flight Lieutenant Jack Cleland, Royal New Zealand Air Force, returned to Leiston flying a Spitfire to visit his old friends. Here he is on the wing of the Spitfire with Lt. John Skara trying out the cockpit.

363rd pilots pose on the wing of a P-51. First two on the left are unknown but third from left is Captain Pasquale Caracciolo, the Group dentist wearing the garrison hat. Others L-R - Donald Bochkay, Charles Peters, Jack Cleland (RNZAF), Hershel Pascoe and George G. George.

No high quality photos of OBee O'Brien's BILLY'S BITCH have ever been found. This back lighted shot shows the code B6-G, but little else.

G4-U, BUFFALO BELLE, lifts off with its element leader slightly ahead. Both aircraft have 20 degrees down flaps, standard for take-off. This airplane had at least three different names and survived the war.

Left: Nose art was seldom seen on drop tanks but here we see a rare example on G4-P, ROLLA U (bar). The writer has a vague memory of having painted this face himself.

ARMAGEDDON AT ARNHEM

During a period of about a week or so in mid-September, Armageddon had surely come to the innocent people of the central Netherlands and to soldiers and airmen of four armies, and three air forces - this was the affair at Arnhem.

Operation MARKET GARDEN was one of the most momentous events of the last year of the war. It had the potential for a great success and also for a major disaster. It came closer to the latter. One of the most interesting combat operations of the war, it has spawned several excellent books, of which the most notable is Cornelius Ryan's A BRIDGE TOO FAR. This and other books are recommended for those desiring the story in detail. We will lay out only the bare bones of the story to relate the part played by the 357th Group.

MARKET GARDEN was to be a huge airborne assault using both parachute and glider-borne troops. The objective of the plan, originated by the flamboyant British Field Marshal Montgomery, was to capture the required bridges, and cross two canals and three rivers in The Netherlands, out-flank the German Siegfried line and provide a springboard into Germany. It was an extremely complex plan needing precise timing of uncounted events. As with most complex battle plans, much of the timing became unraveled and the overall operation was a failure.

The assault force consisted of some 35,000 troops of the 82nd and 101st U.S. airborne divisions, the British 1st Airborne Division and the Polish Independent Parachute Brigade. Because there were only 1750 transport aircraft available -not nearly enough, the troops had to be delivered on successive days. This factor alone was bad enough, but with miserable weather, communications breakdowns and dozens of other major problems, the makings of a major disaster were there. The result was the loss of most of the British 1st Airborne and the Polish Paras. The 82nd and 101st did achieve some of their objectives and suffered less severely.

Air support was to be massive, and for a week or more in mid-September, the skies of The Netherlands saw what was probably the densest concentration of airplanes in history. A few figures will be given as an indication of this incredible concentration of air power.

The British Air Ministry War Room summary for 17 September, the first day of the operation, lists 1452 glider tugs and transports involved. In addition there were about 700 RAF fighters and light bombers providing support. The 8th Air Force was heavily committed with over 800 bombers and 600 fighters, this huge mass of aircraft all operating in the general area of Arnhem, Eindhoven, and Nijmegen.

The 357th was part of this mass on the 17th, but the *Luftwaffe* was nowhere to be seen, and there were no

PRINCESS PAT, 44-14648, whose pilot was Lt. Ed Fry, but Robert Muller was flying it when it was shot down by flak on 17 April 1945. Muller spent only a few days as a POW before war's end.

losses. It would be a new ball game the next two days as the *Luftwaffe* reacted. There was, however, one aircraft destroyed, and one pilot shaken, but unhurt on this first day of MARKET GARDEN.

Even though the P-51D was the dominant model, there were still many B model Mustangs left in the fall of 1944. The Operational Summary for September comments on the many accidents "at home", and several of these were B models. DAM-PHY-NO! was 43-6510, 363rd squadron code B6-0. Norbert Fisher recalls the demise of this colorful old timer.

"It was the 17th of September, (the first MARKET GARDEN mission). On take-off the engine completely lost power. The landing gear was already coming up, but I had to get rid of the drop tanks. The mechanical salvo lever had a safety on it. I flipped the safety off, but it flipped right back on again. It took three attempts before I felt the tanks drop. At the same time the tanks fell off, the air scoop caught the railroad tracks on top of an eight foot embankment, moving the tracks about six feet and tearing the tail off. The rest of the plane pancaked into a brussel sprout field, staying pretty much together. There was no

fire and I walked away from the wreck with minor facial injuries from hitting the gun sight. I thank God they built the P-51 as strong as they did!"

It was normal procedure for police constables to submit written reports of aircraft crashes in their jurisdiction. This extract is from the one on the Fisher crash: "The aircraft first struck the tracks of the LNER, (London North Eastern Railway) pulling the tracks out of alignment and bringing down the telephone lines. It then rebounded into a field of marigolds, uprooting same.

These are the property of Herbert and Sydney Tyrrell of West House Farm, Leiston. The remaining damage was all to property of the LNER Company. The pilot was quickly attended to by the medical officer from Leiston airdrome, and Lt Pelton of the Provost Marshall's office posted a guard of MPs. The damage to the railway was repaired the same day and trains were running normally on Monday."

By noon on the 18th, when the 357th became airborne, the situation around Arnhem was already in an advanced state of deterioration, and in a desperate attempt to salvage the situation, Eighth Air Force provid-

BUTCH BABY had two pilots, J.H. Bertram and then Jim McLane until after the war. 44-14798 had been Lt. Col. Joe Broadhead's airplane on his second tour, when it was MASTER MIKE. This photo shows the formation lights (center of the star and just aft of the name) which were installed on a few P-51s late in the war. They were orange in color and supposed to assist in bad weather formation flying. There is an RAF battery cart in the foreground. These had a small engine for charging the batteries. Note that the flaps were always down when the aircraft was parked to keep people from walking on them, and make it easier for the armorers to reach the gun bays.

ed some 250 B-24s to drop supplies to the beleaguered troops from a very low altitude. The 50 Mustangs with red and yellow noses were numerically insignificant among the mass of airplanes in the area, but they were to play a role in an attempt to stave off disaster.

Major Thomas Gates led his force into the area shortly after 1300 hours, at 13,000 feet, making landfall at Westhove, ancient castle on Walcheren Island. "Tackline", the fighter controller, vectored the Mustangs neatly around the flak concentrations at Eindhoven, and they patrolled the southern area for about two hours, until at 1505 hours, they intercepted and dispersed some 60 109s and 190s, north of Maastricht. Two P-51s were lost in the melee, but claims of 26 e/a destroyed were made.

Tom Gates, from his encounter report: "I was leading Dryden (357th) on free lance patrol, under MEW control, over airborne drop zones. "Tackline" vectored to intercept several groups of "bogies" but all were Little Friends. "Tackline" then directed us to patrol on our own. Over the DZ we saw a gaggle of 109s and 190s flying our reciprocal course to our right and about 2,000 feet above. I turned the group to intercept and called "drop tanks" after clearing the gliders below. By the time the tanks were off and climb started, the first gaggle of 190s were passing overhead and up into the sun. I turned DOLLAR squadron back head-on into the second bunch and the fight was on. I picked six 109s, they broke left, then sharp right. I got on one, but he spun out under me.

Another was in the turn so I latched onto him. He was most aggressive and after much maneuvering he straightened out and I got short burst which knocked some parts from his ship. The second burst set him on fire, and the third finished him. He dived in from 500 feet on fire. My wingman was still with me and we climbed back to 10,000 feet. We saw five 109s flying close formation with a flight of P-51s bouncing them. One 109 split-essed out and went to the deck in aileron turns. The others turned into the bounce. I took after the one on the deck and let him have a burst from 1,000 yards, but no strikes seen. When he came to an airdrome he made a turn. I closed enough to see American markings on the upper surfaces of both wings and it was a P-51 painted same as the 109s. There were no group markings on the nose. When I saw it was a P-51, and to avoid the flak from the field I widened my turn and the P-51 leveled out and beaded S.E. at full throttle. There is no doubt that it was flown by a German pilot."

Shortly after 1630 hours, the Mustangs were back on their hardstands at Leiston, with the ground crews beginning the task of making them mission ready again.

Besides Gates' 109 there were 25 other claims for 109s or 190s shot down, all singles except for Lts. R.L.

Smith and Gerald Tyler of the 364th who both claimed doubles. Two men did not return - Captain Bernard Seitsinger (POW), and Lt. Robert Fandray who was KIA. The Air Ministry War Room summary for the 19th again shows heavy Allied air activity, with 612 transports and glider tugs operating, with swarms of fighters and bombers in support. *Luftwaffe* fighters, brought in from other areas were aloft in large numbers and the stage was set for another day of extensive combat.

Take-off time for the 357th was again late in the day, at 1415 hours. Major Edwin Hiro, C.O. of the 363rd Squadron was leading the mission, which was to complete his tour of combat. It was, indeed, to be Ed Hiro's last mission. Although the mission report does not say so, it is apparent that each squadron was operating on its own in separate areas. Captain Arval Roberson was leading Dollar Green flight with Charlie Goss on his wing, in company with one other Dollar flight (8 P-51s). Roberson was an old timer by September, being one of the original members of the 362nd Squadron, with four victories. The desperate air battles over Holland on this day were vividly different, for Roberson than other engagements he had fought.

"The first sight of the engagement left one of the strongest impressions of my operational tour, for it was more like the aerial dogfights that are depicted on artist's canvases and in movies of yesteryear. The scenarios for most of the encounters that I had had, involved a large stream of bomber formations being threatened by a gaggle of enemy fighters, who in turn were hit by smaller groups of escort fighters. The subsequent boiling mass of aircraft would soon spread all over the sky, with one pilot firing on another, or a wingman covering the one doing the firing. Then, with amazing suddenness one could not locate another plane of any kind!

It is hard to visualize that at one moment there would be aircraft numbering in the hundreds "ginning" around and then just minutes later the sky could be completely devoid of aircraft.

"However, on this day, although the engagement was the same boiling "mass of aircraft, I'd estimate between 30 and 40, the weather was acting as a barrier, containing them in one general area. It seemed as if the cloud cover came up from the deck like a wall on the east to about 20,000 feet where it shelved westward, almost solid, to the coastline of the Low Countries. It had a purple to lavender coloring that is associated with storm scenes in paintings and made the whole arena sunless and fairly dim.

"It was the dimness that actually helped me to get the first glimpse of the action. Whenever .50 cal ammo made contact with a solid object, a flash would emanate.

In this dim light it was a strobe and the large amount of flickering that was occurring could be seen like a fireworks display many miles away."

Dutch aviation historian John R. Manrho has done extensive research into that great air battle over Arnhem, and especially as it relates to U.S. and German losses and to the activities of *Luftwaffe* fighter units. John Manrho: "The II *Gruppe* of *Jagdgeschwader* 11 took off at approximately 1745 hours from Breitscheid Airfield, which lies about 40 miles NE of Koblenz. The *Gruppe* had arrived at this base only the day before. They took off with approximately twenty Me 109s to attack the supply forces of Market Garden. After three attacks, low on fuel and ammo, they turned east. Just a few seconds later they discovered about 40 plus Mustangs above them. The time is then 1805 hours (1705 British time). The pilots desperately tried to gain height and in the following battle at least ten 109s were shot down or made crash landings."

Arval Roberson continues: "We checked sights and armament switches and prepared to drop our tanks. I decided not to barge into the melee, but to "street fight" on the outside edge and started to look for a target. I spotted a 109 under me going from my left to my right. I made a diving steep bank and lead the gun sight ahead of his nose and fired. A ball of "fire developed where the canopy had been, and I observed black smoke trailing the aircraft as it headed straight toward the ground. I did not see the pilot bail out."

Meanwhile, JG 11's Me 109 pilots, caught at low level by the 357th P-51s, were attempting to extricate themselves from deep trouble. Dutch Historian John Manrho: "*Leutnant* Georg Wroblewski of 8th *Staffel* was attack by several Mustangs and while turning like a madman he suddenly saw a P-51 climbing in front of him at a distance of about 200 feet. The Mustang pilot obviously had not seen him. Lt. Wroblewski fired a few rounds from his 20 mm cannon and observed hits. The P-51 went down vertically and dived into a canal. A few moments later his Me 109 was also hit and he was forced bail out. Seriously injured he landed near Bathmen just east of Deventer."

THE YOXFORD BOYS lost five P-51s and pilots this day, three of the latter survived, and two did not. Wroblewski's victim was almost surely Lt. James Blanchard of 62 Squadron, whose remains were found along a canal bank and identified after the war. Blanchard was a recent replacement who had been a staff pilot for a general officer until he talked his way into a combat slot. On the previous day he had shot down a 109, his only victory.

Major Ed Hiro was leading 363 squadron, and was to complete his combat tour with the mission of the 19th. However, it was not to be and he was killed in the violent combat over Holland. Seven enemy aircraft were claimed by Cement Squadron, all 109s, with Lts. Roper and Pasaka claiming two each. It is of interest to note that three pilots saw fit to express their pleasure with the new K-14 gun sight, Donald Pasaka's comment being typical: "The K-14 sight is really perfect. In fact it is hard to miss after you once get it on him. I hope all the planes are equipped with it soon."

One of the 109s claimed was shot down by Major Hiro, his 5th confirmed victory. His encounter report, claiming the 109, was filed for him by his wingman, F.O. Johnnie Carter, who reported: "I was on Major Hiro's wing when we entered the fight, but was forced to break up and out slightly to avoid hitting a ship coming head on to me. Major Hiro made a sharp turn to the left and got on the tail of an enemy ship. There were so many planes in a lufbury that I had to pull out and over in order to get back in position on Major Hiro's wing. About this time the plane that I thought was Major Hiro broke out and headed for the deck on the tail of a 109. I took out after him and followed all the way to the deck and saw the 109 crash in flames."

Dollar Squadron's Ray "Ted" Conlin still vividly remembers the strange weather conditions of the day as described by Arval Roberson, and the loss of Blanchard and Hiro also remain clearly after 5 decades:

"Jim Blanchard was my wingman that day. When we arrived in the area we heard considerable RT chatter from our guys, probably Hiro and his squadron. Just as we dropped our tanks, we were bounced by 109s that came out of the sun and cloud cover. A 109 being chased by a P-51 went across my nose, but the '51 had a 109 on his ass so I rolled into attack headed straight down. As I closed on the 109 I took cannon fire on my left side. I had to break off to handle my problem. It was at that moment that my wingman Jim Blanchard was shot down. I had thought at the time that Major Hiro was the P-51 and I tried to re-locate him and Blanchard. After several minutes the enemy broke away and we returned to base. I then gave my account at briefing and I am certain Major Hiro was the man in the middle of our attack."

Greenhouse White flight was the big loser in the day's action, with all three being shot down (probably by Me 109s from JG 26). All however, survived and more than evened the score before being overwhelmed, submitting claims for 5 enemy aircraft destroyed, after their return to U.S. forces. Captain Bryce McIntyre was leading White flight with Lts. Jerome Jacobs and Howard Moebius as numbers 2 and 3. Moebius remembers the day: "On that day I had the misfortune of having our flight become separated from the entire group, and one of the wing men had to abort. The three of us were flying at approximately 10,000 when attacked by 35 or 40 German fighters. It all happened so fast I don't recall in which direction my flight leader or the other wing man went. I do know I ended up with at least 12 or 14 German fighters in a very tight circle. I opened fire as I closed in on the tail of one ship, and saw parts of his plane come off and smoke come out. I did not see him bail out, and the airplane nosed over and dove for the ground. I tightened my turn and got in behind a second ship in the circle and after a few turns was able to set him on fire. In the meantime there were two or three enemy ships that stayed out of the circle and were taking pot shots by making dives at me from head on and right angles.

"All of a sudden my left wing seemed to explode. The doors on the gun bay popped open and the wing was in flames. We were in a tight turn to the right and our speed was considerably reduced. I pulled the handle and popped the canopy, and jumped out on the inside of the turn, delaying the opening of my chute. Since there were airborne troops parachuting into the area, I am sure the Germans would not hesitate to open fire on me in the chute. When I thought I was down to about 1500 feet, I pulled the cord.

"It wasn't long before two planes were diving, at me, it was hard to tell whether they were P-51s or 109s, until they opened fire! By dumping air from the chute I came down faster and spoiled their run. Because I was so close to ground they did not make a second pass."

This was the beginning for Howard Moebius of five months with the Dutch underground, whose members continually risked their lives to assist his escape, until his return to U.S. forces.

Jerome Jacob's experience in the one-sided battle was similar to that of Moebius. After shooting down a 109, his P-51B (code C5-E, PAPPY'S ANSWER) was hit hard by fire from other 109s, forcing him to bail out.

With badly a burned face and left wrist plus several wounds, he was to spend the remaining seven months of the war in a *Stalag Luft*. Although the Group flew support mission over Holland several more times, there was no further contact with the *Luftwaffe*. During the two days of intense combat on the 18th and 19th, claims for the destruction of fifty 109s and 190s were made. Seven Mustangs were lost, with three pilots dead, three prisoners and one evader.

THE YOXFORD BOYS' participation in the bloody Arnhem affairs was over.

At home base, the enemy was also seen, although with minimum threat. A Group diary reported: "Buzz bomb flights started over the base this month. Concern is expressed over possibility of one crashing on base. Average of two every 24 hours pass over at less than 1,000 feet."

The noisy little bombs also brought a windfall of good fortune, the many British girls who worked on the AA guns and associated equipment which now occupied the coastal areas. They were a welcome addition to the weekly Red Cross Club dances.

Colonel Dregne at right in C5-Q, 44-13408. B model at left is unidentified. The lack of drop tanks would indicate a local flight.

Armorer Christenson stands next to pilot Jesse Frey, with Jack Nickolson and Crew Chief Pat Buzzeo at right. AIN'T MISBEHAVIN, G4-M was 44-15267.

Lt. Col. Thomas Hayes, one of the many who made the 357th so successful and one of its great leaders. Here he tempts fate by smoking his cigarette next to 108 gallons of aviation fuel in a paper tank!

The mighty Merlin, hanging from a Cletrac crane, ready for installation.

Clinton Maag, a 364th Armorer and a patchwork line shack complete with chimney and stove. Note there is a victory symbol swastika on the wall next to his elbow.

L-R, Hollis Nowlin, Mark Stepelton, Richard Peterson and Lewis Fecher in the fall of 1944. All except Nowlin are carrying sidearms, not a normal practice except during the D-Day period.

SSgt. Ray Morrison works on the brakes on G4-P. The jacking provisions would not pass today's safety regulations.

Nothing is known of PERRY LOU, 44-13681, except that it had previously been Bochkay's famous WINGED ACE OF CLUBS.

Captain Morris Stanley and C5-V on a crowded taxi strip. 44-13681 survived the war and probably ended its days as scrap in 1945.

AFTER ARNHEM

On two more occasions the Group patrolled the Arnhem area. On only one mission for the rest of the month, were e/a seen and they avoided combat. Jet and Rocket sightings are now common in the mission reports, but always some distance away. A single 109 was seen on the last mission of the month, in the target area, in a steep dive, with an unidentified P-51 on its tail. (See chapter on jets for more on Me 262s and Me 163s.)

On the 28th, 362nd pilot, Lt. John Templin bailed out over Germany when the engine failed on BOWLEGS a P-51B. He survived and spent the rest of the war in Stalag Luft 13 with Jim Sloan and other Yoxford Boys. German researchers excavated the wreckage of BOW-LEGS in the 1980s, and bits and pieces of 43-6698 are now in the author's collection.

Worse was to come some three hours later. Not much is known of 2nd Lt. James Leek. The AAF accident report shows he had 17 hours in P-51s. Most of this was probably accumulated at the 8th Air Force fighter Training center at Goxhill. Most fighter pilots went thru their course until the "Clobber Colleges" were formed at Group level, where the Group familiarized their own new pilots. It is unlikely he had flown any missions prior to his death.

Leek was flying #2 in a two ship training exercise with veteran 364th pilot Bob Schimanski, who went through a series of aerobatic maneuvers with Leek following. After passing through a haze layer, Schimanski was unable to locate his wingman, and returned to base. #2795 Squadron, of the RAF Regiment was stationed on Foulness Island, a close-in island about 50 miles south of Leiston. Gunner R. Davenport's eyewitness account from the AAF accident report:

"At approximately 1515 hours I was on duty as spotter in the watch tower. I heard the sound of an aircraft diving but because of low cloud base could not see anything for a moment. Suddenly in a westerly direction from my post I saw an aircraft break through the clouds.

"It was diving absolutely vertically at a speed I estimated at about 600 miles an hour, and turning slightly as it dived. About midway between the clouds and the ground, a main plane (wing) broke away from the fuselage. The fuselage was diving at a greater speed than the main plane, the latter being slightly left behind. After this my view was obstructed by trees.

"There was the sound of a very slight explosion, and I saw a black column of smoke rise." (author's note: The RAF Regiment is an infantry-like unit whose mission was - and is - to provide security for RAF installations.) The tail unit was not found with the wreckage.

The accident board consisting of John Storch, John England and Henry Beal, reported that with 35 gallons of fuel in the fuselage tank, and no drop tanks, the center of gravity would have been proper. However, the aircraft had not been modified with a dorsal fin and rudder bob-weight, but "since the empennage has not been found, it may be assumed to have failed early in the dive originating as an inexperienced pilot lost control in the haze."

The aircraft was serial number 43-6971, 364th squadron code C5-U. James Leek joined the ranks of many other fliers who died before they could confront the enemy.

1st Lt. Bill Dunlop's adventures in mid-month were audacious, foolish (?) and with a touch of humor, all of which make good stories. Dunlop's adventure four months later would have no humor, but the story of his miraculous survival will be told later.

For reasons obscure, Dunlop decided it would be great to make an aerial tour of Norway. Therefore, on the 14th of September, he asked his operations section to put him on the mission as a spare. All went well, and not needed to fill in for an abort, he took a NE heading, alone, on his way to the coast of Norway across 400 plus miles of very cold water.

As would be expected the weather gods did not co-operate and he struggled through a variety of nasty conditions, finally arriving at an unknown point on the Norwegian coast. He then spent an hour or so frolicking among the coastal fjords finally arriving another 100 miles north at the town of Horton a bit south of Oslo.

There, in the bay he found several juicy targets in the form of a He 115 seaplane and several Dornier flying boats. To make the trip worth while he made one strafing run, with only half his guns working. Although one of the Dorniers shows up well in his gun camera film it is not likely he did much damage.

The arrival of a P-51 so far from its normal habitat must have given the Germans quite a surprise, but they recovered enough to shoot back. Possibly it was this that convinced him it was time to go home. After seven hours of flying he landed at the first Allied field he could find, at Crail in northern Scotland, just south of Dundee. His tanks contained about 4 gallons of fuel.

He might have gotten away with a "lost" excuse if he had not asked for the appropriate maps the day before. Dunlop recalls that his Operations Officer, Don Bochkay, grounded him for a week for the escapade. However, apparently the grounding did not "take" as he was over Arnhem on both the 18th and 19th where he shot down an Me 109 on each day.

*Above: Tyler's second LITTLE DUCKFOOT, 44-14660
in the fall of 1944, showing all of his seven victories.*

*Right: 1st Lt. Gerald Tyler and
the first LITTLE DUCKFOOT,
43-6376, C5-J also seen here with
full invasion stripes, somewhat
worn around the gun muzzles.*

John Skara flew a full tour in DOODLE BUG,
a P-51B, 42-106458. Here in bare metal it also
at one time had a full OD/gray paint job.

C5-Z about to touch down. Donald Kocher, along with three friends, all named their P-51s "4 BOLTS" on the right side. Kocher's name LITTLE POOPSIE appeared on the left side.

MAZIE R, s/n 42-103601 became C5-C, with pilot John Salsman, Crew Chief John Shultz and Dick Spicer Asst. Crew Chief. Originally delivered in bare metal, MAZIE R is seen here rather crudely painted in green or Olive Drab leaving the name on the cowl visible and now with a Malcolm hood. Salsman flew this for a long time. There is no record of its loss in combat.

Lt. Howard Moebius scored three victories, all during the violent Arnhem affair, but after shooting down two Me 109s on the 19th of September he was in turn shot down, along with the other two men of his flight. All survived but Moebius was to spend five months with the Dutch Underground before returning to Allied forces.

Statistics for September 1944
Average number aircraft on hand - - - - - -67.6
Percentage aircraft operational - - - - - - - 88.8
Percentage operational aircraft airborne - - -63
Rounds fired - - - - - - - - - - - - - - - - 11,535
Stoppages - - - - - - - - - - - - - - - - - - - 21
Rounds fired per stoppage - - - - - - - - - 549.2
Total aborts - - - - - - - - - - - - - - - - - - 48
Total aborts, non mechanical - - - - - - - - - 33

Major Ed Hiro tucks in close to the camera plane, in B6-D. Although nose appears to be white, this writer believes it is the standard red and yellow (which is very faintly visible on the bottom of the cowl). It is thought the type of film, lighting and other factors have washed out the red and yellow colors.

B6-Q, s/n 43-6510 carried the clever name DAM-PHY-NO! Little is known about it, but Lt. Norbert Fisher was scheduled to fly it on the big Arnhem mission of 18 September 1944. However, the Group went to Arnhem without him, as his engine quit on take-off and the aircraft was totally demolished, dislodging some railway tracks at the same time. The cockpit section remained intact and Fisher emerged with no more than a few bumps.

Lt. Keenhn Landis on the wing of Bill Fricker's 'OL FLAK JOE, B6-0, s/n 44-14532 waits for ground crew to complete some last minute maintenance.

Close up of 'OL FLAK JOE, another marvelous example of nose art. Joe's suit was, of course red and yellow.

Kit Carson's NOOKY BOOKY II is the first of his three D models. It is G4-C, 44-13316. Carson flew it until the end of his first combat tour when it went to Ted Conlin as OLIVIA DeH.

Majors Donald Bochkay (L), and Donald McGee, both of whom commanded the 363rd Squadron. Bochkay has victory symbols painted around his 363rd Squadron patch. McGee is wearing the jacket patch of the HEADHUNTERS, the 80th Fighter Squadron, 8th Fighter Group where he scored two of his total of 6 victories before coming to the 363rd where he scored his 6th.

Don Bochkay's well known WINGED ACE OF CLUBS, carried on all of his D model airplanes. This is 44-15422 which was wrecked in a belly landing by Lt. John Casey on 15 February 1945 due to overheated coolant.

Another of the early batch of P-51D-5s without the dorsal fin, Colonel Dregne's C5-Q with crewman Jim Enright taking his ease on the wing.

This fine photo of MSgt. Ralph Crawford, 363rd Armament Chief is an excellent example of how a "well used" P-51 looks. The basic paint is RAF Green, but oil from the breather (just below the word "Little") has carried away some of the paint leaving the national insignia and squadron codes badly faded and stained to a gray color from exhaust, oil and washing the aircraft with aviation fuel. 44-13887

Another beautiful P-51 of the 357th, Major Tom Hayes' D-5 FRENESI and the ground crew, Bob Krull (L),
Gene Barsalou and Fred Keiper who really owned the airplane and only loaned it to Hayes to fly missions!

A fine take-off shot of Broadhead's MASTER MIKE, and an unknown wingman. Broadhead
has already activated landing gear retraction as the inner doors are coming down.

There is much to learn from this photo as a troop carrying C-46 "buzzes" the control tower. (Note another C-46 on the ground at far right.) The hardstand, with its rack of "ready" drop tanks belongs to G4-Z, HOT SHOT. The Crew Chief shack is especially well built, and the number "36" on the tower indicates the runway in use.

HOT SHOT CHARLIE John Duncan in G4-Z with his crew chief, George Roepke (RT), Armorer Barcala, and Ed Duggen, ACC. The aircraft data block is unusually clear in this photo. Four of the victory symbols are for air victories, his total.

As far as is known, only two sets of brothers served with the 357th. Lloyd and Glenn Hubbard's service time was a sad one after the death of Lloyd. Here we see a happier ending, Joe and G.A. Robinson both flew with the 362nd and both survived the war.

Lt. Irving Snedecker was the pilot of ROVIN' RHODA, 44-13783, seen here in its earthen revetment in the 364th Squadron area. Snedecker was shot down by flak on 17 April 1945 and spent a month or so as POW before war's end.

C5-R is probably John Storch's SHILLELAGH (left side only), 44-13546, lost with Zetterouist on 5 December 1944. The man in the photo is Lt. Robert Stewart 364th Squadron Armament Officer. The odd structure in the background is one of the dozen or so blister hangars on the base.

Major John Storch's SHILLELAGH, C5-R, probably 44-13546. It had been bare metal as were all D models on delivery and has been painted in RAF green, with the name taped off to avoid having to repaint it.

DOODLE BUGS, THE V-1s

"20 September, about 7 pm a buzz bomb roared directly across our hut, not over 75 or 100 feet high. Terrifying roar and yellow red flames had me plenty scared. Saw two others go over, one exploding a few miles from our base. At 5 am another roared across the base and exploded six miles away. I have a piece of that one.

"25 September. For about the last ten days we've had two red air raid alerts each night, one at 9 pm, and the other at 5 am

"9 October. Was awakened at 1 am by a red alert, saw a buzz bomb come over the tree tops and exploded less than one mile away. In the morning, I went out to see it, and brought several pieces back. Two farm homes were destroyed and many windows broken in Saxmundem."

Don Marner's diary descriptions of the Buzz Bombs, or Doodle Bugs, will be familiar to all who were on station F-373 from September until the end.

Although many of them passed over Leiston and vicinity during that fall and winter, only one remains in the memory of this writer - the first one he saw which appeared over the roof of the latrine toward which he was headed. It was a spectacular sight, with the ear-splitting roar and the long trailing flame from its pulse jet engine. Though they became a familiar sight mostly at night, few people knew much about them. To flesh out the memories, we give some facts and figures from FLYING BOMB, by Peter Cooksley, (Scribner's sons, New York, 1979)

"They first appeared over Britain a few days after D-Day, all fired from land launching sites in France, mostly aimed at London. None of these would have been seen in the Leiston area. By the end of August, most of the launch sites had been captured by Allied troops. Anticipating this, the Germans had been working hard on an air launched version. The Air Launch phase began early in September and was in full swing by about mid-month. The last one was launched on 14 Januar 1945.

The launch platform was the *Luftwaffe's* work-horse bomber, the He 111 and the unit was KG 53 which flew from two bases in Holland. The bomb was carried (usually) under the right wing, inboard of the engine. In all, about 1200 V-1s were air launched of which 638 were actually plotted as crossing the English coast. Of those coming in during September and early October few were shot down because the anti-aircraft gun belt which had been protecting London from the French base sites was in the process of moving north to counter the new threat. Eventually there were 1,045 guns of all calibers in a belt running from Ipswich north to Yarmouth. These were supported by a great many searchlight batteries. By early October the guns were in place and very effective. Of the total number of V-ls shot down from June through January 1945, fighters destroyed 1,846, and AA guns 1,859. A large percentage of the gun and searchlight crews were women, a welcome addition on their off duty time, to the social life of Station F-373.

Although there were no known casualties to those on base a total of 23,000 houses were destroyed, mostly in London and 5,500 people were killed.

Each Squadron had a pilot's lounge located near the Squadron Operations Office. This is the 364th as can be seen by the fireplace decorations. There is a copy of the British magazine FLIGHT hanging on the window at left and there is an unidentified trophy on the mantel.

CHAPTER 5: AUTUMN DAYS

*"The Sky was never still", as seen by these everyday "Contrails" (condensation trails)
in the sky over Leiston as hundreds of fighters and bombers set off on their missions.*

"The Least Active Month", so says the operational summary for October, 1944. It goes on to say that "the pilots of the Group were over Germany only 19 times, of which one was a strafing - mission in rough weather. For the first month in many the Group also failed to keep its average monthly total of 50 enemy aircraft destroyed."

The operational summary, of course, is referring to "inactivity as far as the number of missions flown and the absence of the *Luftwaffe*. There was ample activity in other respects and for many people. By the end of the first week in October, the red and yellow nosed Mustangs had been to Kassel, Frankfurt, Munster, Berlin, and Liepzig - a grand tour in itself, plus two tangles with the 109s and 190s. There were no losses that first week, but several pilots made precautionary landings on the continent before returning to base.

The mission leader's observations often provide tidbits of interesting information such as:

2 October: B-17 with ball turret missing and two engines feathered escorted to 25 miles east of Lille, where he took a 120 degree heading. Escort broken due to lack of fuel.

3 October: B-17 down at Munster, no chutes.

6 October: Enemy aircraft encountered were very aggressive in combat. Eight to ten feighters heading north from Whilhelmshaven.

7 October: Contrails, apparently jet aircraft at 35,000 over target. 18 balloons over NE part of Erfurt. P-47 with 78th Group markings but apparently without squadron letters, trailed group and bombers SW of target. Red nosed P-51, JS-3, flew to Zuider Zee with one element where it turned back into Germany at 1250 hours.

The red nose on the P-51 would indicate 4th Fighter Group, but JS-3 fuselage code does not match any 8th or 9th Air Force Fighter or recon unit. It is likely both the P-51 and 78th Group-marked P-47 were German operated.

Even though 8th Air Force was capable of launching a very powerful fighter force to escort its bombers, the system did not always work. The B-17s and B-24s and their scheduled escort did not always rendezvous as briefed. This left some combat wings without fighter support. *Luftwaffe* fighter controllers, watching their radar screens for any vulnerable sections of the bomber stream, were quick to vector their fighters into this area.

This occurred on 6 October, and Captain John England, leading the mission, describes the situation and the results:

"I was leading Dryden Group at 28,000 feet, escorting the combat wing of bombers which had just turned on their initial point. About three minutes later I looked back and saw enemy fighters going through two combat wings several miles behind us. I immediately turned and headed for the enemy planes, taking two

squadrons along and leaving one squadron to protect our assigned bombers. Before we could reach the harassed bombers, the enemy fighters had made about six company front passes from the rear and shot down six of them. The attacks were both aggressive and effective; I believe that if we had reached them five minutes later, the whole combat wing would have been wiped out."

England got strikes on an Me 109, but was forced to break off after being fired on by another 109, which was shot down by either Jenkins, Mooney or Gilbert. England then shot two 109s in rapid succession, "using my K-14 gun sight for 30 degree deflection shots, observing numerous strikes on wings and cockpit. The pilot jettisoned his canopy, but did not bail out." John England's score was now a respectable 12.5.

The next day, the 7th, almost the same scenario was repeated. Major Tom Gates was leading this time: "Escorting the first four combat wings. About 1200 hours, 40-60 enemy aircraft made tail end pass at fifth box, attacking in waves of 15-20 line abreast. Group turned back to defend and combat ensued east of Jenal. Five to ten bombers down, 25 chutes seen."

All three squadrons shared in the somewhat meager list of claims. John Salsman was leading Greenhouse (364th) squadron, and Richard "Pete" Peterson was leading Blue flight, and both provided interesting comments. John Salsman: "I saw an Me 109 coming at me, and he was joined by two more. They rolled under me and I turned on their tails. I was closing and about to shoot when the two outside ones split essed and the middle one bailed out. One of the others was shot down by Captain Peterson, the other disappeared in the clouds."

Richard Peterson: "I made a head-on pass at an Fw 190 with no effect and then singled out an Me 109. I closed to 350 yards and did some mighty lousy shooting. After a few practice bursts, I found him and got some effective strikes - hitting cockpit, coolant and wings. He jerked his canopy and then snap-rolled about three times and crashed. The enemy aircraft seemed to take separate directions, but we should have had more."

362's Lt. Tom Martinek's solitary P-51 war against the *Luftwaffe* is a remarkable story in itself. He took off with the rest of the group on the 7th bound for targets in the Leipzig area. However, he soon aborted due to a rough engine.

On letting down to a lower altitude, the engine smoothed out and he also discovered that he left his carburetor air control in the "filtered" position, which apparently had caused the problem. Returning the carb control to "ram air", he then made the remarkable decision to turn back into the land of the enemy and fly his own mission! He soon spotted a group of bombers, and about 100

enemy fighters about to attack them from the rear. The numbers did not deter him and he waded into the gaggle of Fw 190s, immediately shooting down one and then tacking onto another. From his encounter report: "The pilot must have been killed with my first burst, for such gyrations as he went into could never have been equaled. I almost spun out trying to follow. I was about to break and run for it, when the 190 went into the ground and exploded. I saw no chute, and took a picture of the wreck." After shooting down two 190s he went home from his one man escort mission and his tangle with 100 190s.

On the 9th, Flight Officer Otto "Dittie" Jenkins was escorting Lt. Delager home because of a mechanical problem, when his own engine failed, some 50 miles from the city of Brussels, Belgium. From 20,000 feet he attempted to glide to the city, but did not make it. From his statement: "I spotted a large airfield and belly landed in it. I did not put down my wheels due to low airspeed and altitude. The field was a Spitfire base, with Norwegian pilots.

They had just moved in, causing all kinds of confusion for all, including myself. I tried to talk to the commanding officer, but he seemed to be angry because Lt. Delager had continued to circle to see if I was alright. I finally walked five miles to a town and engaged a civilian for 100 francs to take me to Brussels. Instead he took me to Antwerp. Finding this out, I gave him another 200 francs to take me to Brussels. There I reported to a Lt. Col. Foot, who got my statement about the condition of my plane and where it was. He sent me home on a C-47 the next day." Jenkins was to achieve double ace status and die in a crash at home base the following March.

This was the end of a veteran P-51B, code G4-P, s/n 42-106829, named JOAN by its first pilot in February, and re-named FLOOGIE, by Jenkins. It had served well for ten months of operations.

A full strength mission to Breman on the 12th brought the last contact with the *Luftwaffe* in October, and two events of note. This was the date Chuck Yeager claimed five Me 109s. (see chapter ACE IN A DAY.) In the summer of 2000, Yeager wrote to this writer asking "did I shoot down an Me 109 on 12 October? I can't remember" He was reminded that 12 October was the day he got five of them. Frank Gailer and Jack Roper added three more to Yeager's total.

The mission report for the same day says "One NYR (not yet returned), Captain Pascoe, 63rd, last seen 1125 vicinity Steinhuder Lake." Hershel Pascoe's service in the 357th had ended, along with P-51D 44-13714, DESERT RAT.

Yeager's 363rd squadron had turned to engage the 22 Me 109s, at which time Peter Pielich, flying Pascoe's wing, lost him due to a problem with his drop tanks. No one saw Pascoe after that.

His MACR however, tells the following events. German documents, under "Final report of enemy airborne equipment and airplane crews" tells us the aircraft was a P-51 with B6 markings, and it was 90% destroyed. Under "Kind of capture" it says; "By fighter, Lt. Col. Priller, at Kolensfeld, 4.5 km south of Wundsdorf, pilot captured." It does not indicate whether he crash landed or bailed out.

This is the only MACR seen in which the victorious pilot's name is given. *Oberstleutnant* (Lt. Col.) Josef "Pip's" Priller had been a *Luftwaffe* pilot since 1936, and a member of JG 26 since 1940, taking command of that unit in January, 1943. In January, 1945 he was relieved of that command to become Inspector of Day Fighters (West), ending his combat career.

Historian Donald Caldwell, biographer of the *Luftwaffe's* JG 26 has determined that it was they who Yeager and the 363rd engaged on 12 October. Although the 363rd claimed seven 109s, JG 26 reported six losses, two of whom were killed. One of those six was *Leutnant* (Lt.) Heinrich Schild of the III *Gruppe*, JG 26.

He recalls: "Fate overtook me on 12 October 1944, at high altitude over Bremen at about 1130 hours, when I lost my controls after being struck from long range by a single Mustang. After many futile attempts to leave the aircraft, I was able to bail out at low altitude. I landed in the teufelsmoor. I came to four days later, lay in the hospital for two months, and resumed my military career in December, 1944."

Schild returned to his unit but was restricted to ground duties. He did not fly combat again until the following April, at which time the war was coming to an end. He had survived 307 combat sorties, all in the west against RAF and USAAF opposition and had tallied 101 air victories.

Hershel Pascoe went to a *Stalag Luft* POW camp and returned after the war. He died in 1984.

On the 14th of the month, Captain Pete Peterson had taken 15 other pilots and their P-51s to an advanced base, probably Fersfield (north of Norwich), home of the APHRODITE experiment.

As mentioned elsewhere, this was conducted with B-17s loaded with 20,000 pounds of explosives and after the take-off crew had bailed out, became a radio controlled bomb. Its primary targets were the almost invulnerable German submarine pens.

The program had begun in August and was beset with disaster with several B-17s exploding prematurely, killing their crews and as far as is known, none of the bombs had ever hit their targets. The 357th had provided escort on several of these affairs. When Peterson and his lads provided escort on the 15th, the program was already moribund and was abandoned soon after.

On this day Peterson reported one of the B-17 bombs missed and the other hit on the NW tip of the island (Heligoland), with a concussion ring of 1,000 feet.

*Returning to base from escorting one of the APHRODITE "flying bomb B-17"
missions on 15 October 1944. Captain Peterson, here flying C5-E led the mission
to Heligoland. The B-17 missiles both missed their targets. The other pilots are:
C5-P, Ed Fry; C5-R, Herman Zetterquist and 4th in line C5-C, with Ed Juszczyk.*

Right: Nothing is known about this P-51, MINNIESOTA, but it is probable that all of the men are from that state. The only one identified is Doctor (Major) John Barker, Group Flight Surgeon, second from left.

Lt. Alden E. Smith was one of the many little known pilots, who flew his tour, scored 2 victories and went home, all of it in G4-K, AMERICAN GIRL, 43-6637.

Yet another P-51B with an illustrious record. This is John England's G4-H, 42-106462 still showing full invasion stripes and nine victory symbols. SSgt. Currie left, Crew Chief, Cpl. Hamilton, on wing, armorer. Later the airplane became G4-Y and was salvaged for battle damage in October.

On this same date, Major Gates led eighteen 362nd Squadron aircraft to the same target, in which the 26 B-1 7s bombed Heligoland through 10/10 cloud. On the 18th, Lt. Col. John Landers led the mission to Kassel - no enemy aircraft seen, but Lt. Horace Roycroft was last seen spinning into the overcast NE of Ghent (Belgium). If he was very far NE of Ghent, he was over water. Nothing more is known.

This mission was the beginning of John Lander's short stint as 357th commander. Colonel Graham, after commanding for eight hectic months when the Group was still learning the game and then into a violent spring, had completed his combat tour and returned to the Zone of the Interior. Graham stayed in the Air Force, retired as a Major General and as this is written lives in Florida and corresponds with this writer quite frequently.

Irwin Dregne was to be the new commander, but was on leave in the U.S. and Landers was assigned during the 7 week period before Dregne returned. An ace, Landers served in several fighter groups, and is best known today as pilot of P-51 BIG BEAUTIFUL DOLL when he was in command of the 78th Group in the waning days of the war.

There was one other loss during the month, but with a happy ending. 362 Squadron's 1st Lt. Charles Goss had planned a three day pass in London with his fellow pilot Chuck Weaver. However, Weaver's name showed up on the mission list for the 19th, so Goss, not wanting to go to The City by himself asked to be scheduled also. It turned out to be a bad decision.

As Goss says, "Chuck came back, I didn't".

In the vicinity of the target, Ludwigshafen, Goss called Gilbert that his engine was cutting out and he was heading home, with his wingman. Gilbert decided that the whole flight would head home, but about 20 minutes later, Goss's engine "quit cold". With no other viable option, Goss bailed out. For the next month he managed to evade capture, heading all the time toward Allied lines, walking only at night, and using the compass from his escape kit.

On the 4th day, he was lucky to be "caught" by a group of Polish workers who were doing forced labor for the Germans. At the risk of their own lives, they gave him food and took him to a hay barn where he stayed for 15 days.

It was then decided it was time to try to make the Allied lines. Goss and five Poles left at midnight. They had a rifle, but no bolt for it. Nevertheless, it was useful to threaten two Frenchman who caught them in their house, eating their food. The next day, as they made their way toward Allied lines, one of the Poles was captured by the Germans, but Goss and the other four continued, surviving a massive Allied artillery barrage, and finally being picked up by a half track of the U.S. 121st Cavalry Recon. Squadron. It was the 19th of November - Goss had been on the run for a month.

He now returned briefly to his unit and then returned to the ZI. The Poles joined a Polish unit of the British army, and Goss remained in contact with one of them, who settled in Chicago after the war.

A veteran P-51 with a checkered career. 43-6787 served Gilbert O'Brien for a full tour as SHANTY IRISH, then went to James Kenney as LITTLE FEETIE. Damaged in landing accident on 2 November 1944, the 469th Service Sqdn. rebuilt it as two-seater, and named it EAGER BEAVER. It was then assigned to the 364th Squadron as C5-H (bar), and they took it to Germany with them after the war . It is seen here at Attlebridge, where Earl Wassem, 466th Bomb Group, photographed it. Above the tail number 36787 are the letters "WW" for War Weary. It finally met its end at the hands of the salvage crews in 1945.

"CLOBBER COLLEGE"

During October, the first 13 replacement pilots arrived direct from training in the ZI. The fighter training unit at Goxhill which had been responsible for initial fighter transition was phasing out. From now on each group would transition its own pilots in a section soon to be called "Clobber College" ("Clobber" was an RAF slang term meaning the shooting up hostile aircraft and ground installations.) Sufficient war weary P-51s were set aside for this, and high time pilots assigned to do the training.

In a letter to this writer in 1998, Richard "Pete" Peterson recalls his stint as "Dean of Clobber College": "Your letter brought back memories of my beginnings with Clobber College. I believe the program of training our own pilots began about November, I was not directly involved until after 20 January, 1945. That day we had arrived home after being missing for five days after we landed at Auxerre, France, short of fuel. Visibility at home base was 0/0 and Major Gates thought we ought to bail out. However, using a "seat of the pants" navigation system I had developed, we all landed. No one on the field could see us until we taxied by the control tower. I got word that day that I was to be the next prexy of Clobber College.

"We spent time looking at combat film, flying typical formations, briefing them on instrument conditions, geography of the continent, the importance of orientation if ending up alone, importance of cockpit checks, parachute, dinghy, oxygen check - all basic stuff for survival, as well as what one should expect from a wingman. To my recollection, we used an independent building on the flight line, and I am not sure where the planes were parked. I thought we were on the 364th flight line, but it could have been near the big hangar (469th Serv. Sqdn) by the tower.

"I remember in the training how I emphasized the buildup of speed by the Mustang in dives and in a short time you could become mesmerized by concentrating on the target longer than you should. In a short time, you could be out of control or flying into the target. I went back on operations after about a month and finished my second tour about the middle of March, 1945. "Just before completing my tour, an opportunity came to go to Sweden to check Swedish pilots out in the Mustang. They had a few, including a couple of ours. I chose not to go because I was going home to get married to another Swede!"

Very little is known about the operation of CLOBBER COLLEGE, but William Blystone was a member of the maintenance crews, and sheds a little light on the subject. He had spent most of 1944 at the fighter training base at Goxhill, maintaining the P-38 and P-51 training aircraft. When Goxhill closed out training and the individual fighter groups took over, Blystone came to Leiston with his Goxhill unit, the 554th Fighter Training Squadron, which operated as such for a short time, before being disbanded, and the men were re-assigned to the 362nd Squadron. Bill Blystone: "We had a blister hangar for use in bad weather, but did most of our maintenance in the open. I'm not sure as to the number of aircraft that we had, but don't think it was ever over ten or so. The number of men varied, but we were not a large outfit."

During October Joe Broadhead, and Richard Peterson both returned to the Group after a months leave in the ZI. Some of the original pilots had such an attachment to the Group, their fellow pilots, and the desire to fly combat, they volunteered for a second tour. On his return, Joe Broadhead became Group Operations officer, and Peterson returned to his squadron the 364th. Tom Gates, an old time pre-war Air Corps pilot, and an old man now well into his thirties, became deputy Group Commander when Tommy Hayes completed his tour and departed.

The Operational Summary also commented: "The second winter promises to be more pleasant than the first dreary winter. The mud situation is more in hand, quarters are better. The Zebra Club (NCOs), the Aero Club (Red Cross) and the Officers club all help toward high morale."

The Group lost another well-known aircraft early in October, but luckily not its Pilot. P-51D, 44-13316, G4-C had been Kit Carson's NOOKY¯BOOKY II. When he completed his first tour and returned to the ZI on leave, it went to Ray Conlin, who had often been his wingman.

On the 5th of October, Conlin was leading the 362nd Squadron - for the first and only` time. He had a high-ranking wingman, Major Lawrence Giarrizzo, recently assigned to the Group. Conlin remembers: "My normal reaction when it came time to drop tanks, was to drop and then run out of fuel before I would realize I had forgotten to switch to inboard tanks. For some reason, maybe because I was squadron leader, or the good Lord was watching over me, I tried to switch tanks first. This is when I found out that I was unable to turn the selector to internal tanks. I was afraid that if I forced it, the thing would stick half way and I would be out of fuel. I turned the squadron over to my element leader and had London control give me a fix to somewhere.

They advised Antwerp so the Major and I took off for there. On arrival, after losing altitude down to about 3,000, I circled the field and saw that there was quite a bit of infantry action taking place, so I had the Major, who was at 15,000, call for a new fix. They sent me to Brussels, but when I got there, the field was under British control and C-47s were coming in one after another carrying fuel cans for the ground forces.

"Landing was being handled by someone with a biscuit gun (a light). I flew over him and went around once but my fuel was about gone, so I forced my way into final approach and the engine quit. Because of the muddy terrain I could not put my gear down until certain of the runway. I was between two C-47s on final and one in front caused so much turbulence that it forced me down earlier then I wanted.

"I slid along on those two paper tanks until the kite stopped. I had dumped the canopy because I did not want to burn up in the thing. I had full internal tanks when I crashed.

"The RAF sent out a big crane and wrapped a chain around the fuselage and over my protests, started to raise it to clear the runway. Naturally, the damn kite broke her back with heavy tail section and that was the end of G4-C. I was taken to the city, fed and returned to the base and given a ride back to London in one of the C-47s."

Less than a month later, Major Lawrence Giarrizzo was dead, when his P-51 shed a wing. As this is written, my good friend Ted Conlin is still going well!

For a month that had been characterized as "least active", there had indeed been a great deal of activity during October.

In mid-October, one of the original pilots, and one of the eventual high scorers, flight leader Clarence Anderson returned from two months in the ZI after completing his first tour. With 13 victories, Anderson was already well on his way to being one of the stars of THE YOXFORD BOYS. He had hoped to return as squadron commander of the 363rd, but that slot had recently been filled, and he became Operations Officer for his second tour.

Although of poor quality, this is the only photo we have of a Clobber College P-51. It was once a 363rd aircraft, but carries the numeral seven instead of the normal code letter. It is thought to be 43-6686, and carries the letters "WW" (war weary) just above the tail number.

Left: A typical group of 363rd Squadron mechanics. The P-51 is one of Donald Bochkay's WINGED ACE OF CLUBS, possibly 44-13681, due to the small size of the winged emblem.

These two 364th mechanics on Lt. Gil Weber's ALIBABSANDI (named for his wife and daughters) are probably wondering "where that oil is coming from!" 44-72372.

ACE IN A DAY

To an ambitious fighter pilot, making Ace was the pinnacle of success. Double ace, Triple Ace etc. were steps up in the profession. There was, however, another category reached by only a few - destroying five enemy aircraft in one day thereby becoming "An ace in a day".

Of the thousands of fighter pilots who flew under the banner of the "winged 8", only 19 became aces in a day, and two of these belonged to the 357th Fighter Group. They were Leonard K. "Kit" Carson (362nd Squadron), and

Charles E. "Chuck" Yeager, 363rd Squadron.

Four YOXFORD BOYS almost made it to ace in a day, with four victories. These were Andrew Evans, John England, John Kirla, and Otto Jenkins. In Addition, Chuck Yeager also scored four in one day.

Because of the unique distinction, we present in full, Carson's and Yeager's encounter reports for the occasion on which they became Ace in a Day. At the time, Carson had 6.5 victories and Yeager 1.5.

PILOT: CHARLES E. YEAGER, 1ST LT. AC 0-387005

A. COMBAT

B. 12 OCTOBER 1944   FIELD ORDER #1235A

C. 363RD FIGHTER SQUADRON, 357TH FIGHTER GROUP.

D. 1130

E. STEINHUDER LAKE TO HANNOVER, GERMANY

F. 5/10 CUMULUS FROM 3,000 TO 5,000 FEET.

G. ME 109S ;

H. FIVE ME 109S DESTROYED

L. I WAS LEADING THE GROUP WITH CEMENT SQUADRON AND WAS ROVING OUT TO THE RIGHT OF THE FIRST BOX OF BOMBERS. I WAS OVER STEINHUDER LAKE WHEN 22 ME 109S CROSSED IN FRONT OF MY SQUADRON FROM 11:00 O'CLOCK TO 1:00 O'CLOCK. I WAS COMING OUT OF THE SUN AND THEY WERE ABOUT 1 ½ MILES AWAY AT THE SAME LEVEL OF 28,000 FEET. I FELL IN BEHIND THE ENEMY FORMATION AND FOLLOWED THEM FOR ABOUT 3 MINUTES, CLIMBING TO 30,000 FEET. I STILL HAD MY WING TANKS AND HAD CLOSED UP TO ABOUT 1,000 YARDS COMING WITHIN FIRING RANGE AND POSITIONING THE SQUADRON BEHIND THE ENTIRE ENEMY FORMATION. TWO OF THE ME 109S WERE LAGGING OVER TO THE RIGHT. ONE SLOWED UP AND BEFORE I COULD START FIRING, ROLLED OVER AND BAILED OUT. THE OTHER ME 109 FLYING HIS WING, BAILED OUT IMMEDIATLY AFTER AS I WAS READY TO LINE HIM IN MY SIGHTS. I WAS CLOSEST TO THE TAIL-END OF THE ENEMY FORMATION AND NO ONE BUT MYSELF WAS IN SHOOTING RANGE AND NO ONE WAS FIRING. I DROPPED MY TANKS AND THEN CLOSED UP TO THE LAST JERRY AND OPENED FIRE FROM 600 YARDS, USING THE K-14 SIGHT. I OBSERVED STRIKES ALL OVER HIS SHIP, PARTICULARILY HEAVY IN THE COCKPIT. HE SKIDDED OFF TO THE LEFT AND WAS SMOKING AND STREAMING COOLANT AND WENT INTO A SLOW DIVING TURN TO THE LEFT. I WAS CLOSING ON ANOTHER 109 SO I DID NOT FOLLOW HIM DOWN. LT. STERN, FLYING IN BLUE FLIGHT, REPORTS THAT THIS E/A IS ON FIRE AS IT PASSED HIM AND WENT INTO A SPIN. I CLOSED ON THE NEXT ME 109 TO 100 YARDS, SKIDDED TO THE RIGHT AND TOOK A DEFLECTION SHOT OF ABOUT 10 DEGREES. I GAVE ABOUT A 3 SECOND BURST AND THE WHOLE FUSELAGE SPLIT OPEN AND BLEW UP AFTER WE PASSED. ANOTHER 109 TO THE RIGHT HAD CUT HIS THROTTLE AND WAS TRYING TO GET BEHIND. I BROKE TO THE RIGHT AND QUICKLY ROLLED TO THE LEFT ON HIS TAIL. HE STARTED PULLING IT IN AND I WAS PULLING 6 "GS". I GOT A LEAD FROM AROUND 300 YARDS AND GAVE HIM A SHORT BURST. THERE WERE HITS ON HIS WINGS AND TAIL SECTION. HE SNAPPED TO THE RIGHT THREE TIMES AND BAILED OUT WHEN HE QUIT SNAPPING AT AROUND 18,000 FEET. I DID NOT BLACK OUT DURING THIS ENGAGEMENT DUE TO THE EFFICIENCY OF THE "G" SUIT. EVEN THOUGH I WAS SKIDDING I HIT THE SECOND 109 BY KEEPING THE BEAD AND RANGE ON THE E/A. TO MY ESTIMATION THE K-14 SIGHT IS THE BIGGEST IMPROVEMENT TO COMBAT EQUIPMENT FOR FIGHTERS TO THIS DATE. THE ME 109S APPEARED TO HAVE A TYPE OF BUBBLE CANOPY AND HAD PURPLE NOSES AND WERE A MOUSEY BROWN ALL OVER.

I CLAIM FIVE ME 109S DESTROYED.   AMMUNTION EXPENDED: 587 ROUNDS .50 CAL MG

CHARLES E. YEAGER lst LT. AC

CAPTAIN LEONARD K. CARSON

A. COMBAT
B. 27 NOVEMBER 1944.   F.O. #1343, HQ, EIGHTH AIR FORCE.
C. 362ND FIGHTER SQUADRON, 357TH FIGHTER GROUP
D. 1300 B.S.T.
E. SOUTH OF MAGDEBURG, GERMANY
F. CAVU
G. FIVE Fw 190s (5)   (AIR)
H. THREE PILOTS BAILED OUT, TWO DIDN'T
I. I WAS LEADING BLUE FLIGHT OF DOLLAR SQUADRON, PROVIDING ESCORT FOR ANOTHER FIGHTER GROUP. WE WERE IN THE VICINITY OF MAGDEBURG, WHEN TWO LARGE FORMATIONS OF BANDITS WERE REPORTED. ONE OF THE FORMATION, STILL UNIDENTIFIED, MADE A TURN AND CAME TOWARDS US AT 8 0'CLOCK. WE DROPPED TANKS AND TURNED TO MEET THEM. WE TACKED ONTO THE REAR OF THE FORMATION, WHICH CONSISTED OF 50 PLUS Fw 190s. I CLOSED TO ABOUT 300 YARDS ON THE NEAREST ONE AND FIRED A MEDIUM BURST WITH NO LEAD, GETTING NUMEROUS STRIKES. HE STARTED TO BURN AND WENT INTO A TURNING DIVE TO THE LEFT. I BELIEVE THE PILOT WAS KILLED, HE NEVER RECOVERED BUT CRASHED INTO THE GROUND AND EXPLODED. I RETURNED TO THE MAIN FORMATION, AGAIN CLOSING TO THE NEAREST ONE ON THE REAR. I OPENED FIRE AT ABOUT 300 YARDS, FIRING TWO SHORT BURSTS, GETTING STRIKES ALL OVER THE FUSELAGE. HE STARTED TO SMOKE AND BURN. HE DROPPED OUT OF FORMATION AND TURNED TO THE RIGHT UNTIL HE WAS IN A SORT OF HALF SPLIT ESS POSITION, NEVER RECOVERING FROM THIS ATTITUDE. I SAW HIM CRASH AND BURN. THE PILOT DID NOT GET OUT. I COULD STILL SEE THE MAIN FORMATION, ABOUT A HALF MILE AHEAD OF ME. STARTING TO CATCH THEM, I SAW A STRAGGLER ON THE DECK. I DROPPED DOWN TO ENGAGE HIM, BUT HE SAW ME COMING. HE TURNED LEFT AWAY FROM ME AND I GAVE CHASE FOR ABOUT THREE MINUTES BEFORE I CAUGHT HIM. I OPENED FIRE AT ABOUT 400 YARDS, GETTING STRIKES ON THE RIGHT SIDE OF THE FUSELAGE. HE TURNED SHARPLY TO THE RIGHT AND I FIRED ON A FEW DEGREES LEAD, FIRING TWO MORE BURSTS, GETTING STRIKES ON THE FUSELAGE. THE PILOT JETTISONED HIS CANOPY AND BAILED OUT. AS I WAS CHASING THIS ONE, ANOTHER FORMATION OF 30 OR 40 Fw 190s PASSED ABOUT 500 FEET ABOVE AND 400 YARDS IN FRONT OF ME. THEY MADE NO ATTEMPT TO ENGAGE OR TO HELP THEIR FELLOW JERRY. THEY CONTINUED ON A HEADING OF 20 OR 30 DEGREES. I PULLED UP AFTER MY LAST ENGAGEMENT AND SET COURSE FOR HOME WHEN ANOTHER Fw 190 MADE AN ATTACK ON US FROM 7 O'CLOCK HIGH. WE BROKE INTO HIM AND HE STARTED A ZOOMING CLIMB. I CHASED HIM, GAINING SLOWLY. SUDDENLY HE DROPPED HIS NOSE AND HEADED FOR THE DECK. I GAVE CHASE AND CAUGHT HIM IN FOUR OR FIVE MINUTES. I OPENED FIRE AT 400-450 YARDS, BUT MISSED. I CLOSED FURTHER AND FIRED ANOTHER BURST, GETTING SEVERAL STRIKES ON THE FUSELAGE. THE PLANE STARTED TO SMOKE. I FIRED AGAIN AS HE MADE A SLIGHT TURN TO THE RIGHT, OBSERVING MORE STRIKES ON THE FUSELAGE. THEN THE PILOT JETTISONED HIS CANOPY AND I BROKE OFF MY ATTACK TO THE RIGHT. I WAITED FOR HIM TO BAIL OUT BUT HE DIDN'T, SO I TURNED BACK TO ENGAGE HIM AGAIN. I WAS STILL ABOUT 700 YARDS AWAY WHEN THE PULLED HIS NOSE UP SHARPLY AND LEFT HIS SHIP. HIS CHUTE OPENED A COUPLE OF MINUTES LATER. DURING THE ENTIRE ENCOUNTER MY WINGMAN, F/O RIDLEY REMAINED WITH ME. I DO NOT BELEIVE HIS PERFORMANCE AS A WINGMAN COULD BE SURPASSED.
I CLAIM FIVE (5) Fw 190s DESTROYED IN THE AIR. 1,620 ROUNDS FIRED.

LEONARD K. CARSON CAPTAIN, AIR CORPS.

HARVEY MACE ON " WEATHER"

Miserable weather was a way of life in wartime Europe. Some pilots became quite skilled at weather flying. Others did not and some paid for the lack of skill with their lives. In his book THE HIGHS AND LOWS OF FLYING, Harvey Mace describes "one of those days".

"After being forced to fly many hours on instruments, I felt fairly comfortable with my ability to handle any reasonably miserable weather. Underline 'reasonably'. Not included were nerve-jangling times trying to find home base in zero zero weather! At least they didn't seem better than zero zero at the time and I never felt comfortable with that kind of flying.

"Once we awoke to weather so dastardly that even the usually cold-hearted mission planners were stymied! They sent up a request to our squadron asking for a volunteer to fly up through the horrible mess to see how high and bad the weather was. No one else raised their hand, so after as long a pause as I thought could be gracefully accepted, I raised mine. I don't know why. Maybe it was because I felt more qualified for the job than the others, or maybe I just hated the idea that someone would think the 362nd was not up to a challenge. Or maybe I was just dumb.

"At any rate I soon found myself taxiing out to the end of the runway through the muck. When I reached the end of the runway I could see a black mass of rain bearing down on me that was even worse than what I had been taxiing through, it was a gully washer, worse than zero zero. In spite of the conditions they cleared me for take-off. I quickly countered that I was going to hold for a couple of minutes to see if the mess was going to pass or be a permanent feature of the day. Fortunately, while I sat there agonizing over the stupidity of my volunteering, I was thankfully interrupted by a recall. The big wheels had sensibly decided to scrub all operations for the day and my relief knew no bounds."

A quiet period inside the 363rd Squadron Operations Office. SSgt. Robert Smith (L) was Operations NCO under the Operations Officer. Man at right is Lt. George Rice who was one of those killed in the C-47 crash in October 1945.

The pilot of MARYMAE was Lt. Richard "Rip" Potter. Photo taken at the intersection of Harrow Lane (a pre-war road) and the perimeter track. The other smaller sign says "Perimeter track speed 25 mph. All aircraft have the right of way."

DEADLY AUTUMN

With 19 missions flown in October and three encounters with enemy aircraft, November produced only 18 missions, with five encounters, one of which resulted in a big rat race with claims for 30 destroyed and only one loss, the victim of a "friendly" P-51. Five pilots were killed in November, and one, Lt. Frank Gailer, became a POW.

By now, in the late fall of 1944, 8th Air Force had been augmenting its fighter groups, and during November the 15 groups averaged 86 aircraft, finally reaching over 100 for some units. Missions were now flown in greater strength, often split into A and B Groups. On the 2nd of the month John England led 63 P-51s, minus ten aborts, which mixed it up with twenty 109s caught attacking the bombers. Air claims were modest, one each to Kit Carson, Harold Hand, Tom Hughes and Pete Peterson, plus an array of ground targets.

As usual, even on days of no contact, the Group Leaders' observations often provided a vivid picture of the air war - a few examples of the many:

2 Nov: P-51, minus tail, SW Merseberg, pilot bailed.
P-51, no markings, seen heading east from Naunberg, taking evasive action. Believe German Two B-17s down over target, 8 chutes.

6 Nov: l Me 163 at 25,000 vicinity Hengale, Holland, flying east. B-24s bombed through 10/10 cloud.

8 Nov: White nosed P-51 exploded in the air.
100 barrage balloons up to 4,000 feet at Wesel.
Black nosed P-51 destroyed an Me 262 SW Dummer Lake.

10 Nov: B-17 broke in two target area, no chutes.
Explosion at 8,000 feet west Koblenz.
Tudor 52 reported he was going to belly land, engine cut out,: (Note: Tudor 52 would have been a 55th Group P-51.)

20 Nov: 9th Air Force P-47s dive bombing oil storage tanks and warehouses west Koblenz.

21 Nov: B-17, spinning through undercast with tail off west Frankfort.

26 Nov: B-24 crashed NW Dummer Lake, J in square, marked RN-J. No chutes, appeared to be on auto-pilot.
Fighter hit by flak heading straight down, smoking, 2 chutes seen, north of Hamm.

27 Nov: Green nosed P-51 marked CV-Q shot down two 109s SE Magdeburg. One silver P-51 bellied in east Celle.

30 Nov: 8 B-17s down over target, 4 from flak, 4 from mid-air collision. 5 chutes seen.

No attempt will be made to chronicle all missions, but those with significant interest will be related.

NAUGHTY AUTY with pilot Jim Sehl on the wing and Crew Chief
Pete Dana next to him. Note the control tower in the background.
Lt. Sam Fuller went MIA in this airplane on 18 November 1944.

This attractive nose art of a cartoon hillbilly adorned P-51D, 44-63168, B6-C of West Virginian Paul Bowles. A late replacement, Bowles flew it till the end of the war and then it went to Germany with the Group.

1st Lt. Carroll Ofsthun was the pilot of THE COUNT, B6-Y, 44-14977. The aircraft is in a blister hangar undergoing landing gear retraction test.

Captain Mark Stepelton, sometime after he scored his fourth victory (credited with 3.5). The mission scoreboard may not be accurate for this late date. In the early days, most ground crews faithfully recorded each mission, but later the practice became less common. 42 106978

November saw several battles with the formidable Me 262 jet fighters, with several victory claims and one man (Warren Corwin) killed in action with the jets. See the chapter BATTLE WITH THE JETS, as we will not discuss them here.

There were many factors involved which could contribute to any number of things going wrong on a mission. For some reason the 364th Squadron did not participate in the 5 November bomber escort job, on which Major Joe Broadhead led 39 P-51s of the 362nd and 363rd Squadrons. Although there was little opposition and no losses, it was not a good day.

Broadhead, Group Ops officer: "Landfall in Ostend 21,000. Arrived RV point 1033 and orbited awaiting bombers. Rved with 93rd Combat Wing at 1045, SE Sedan, 26,000. Sighting another wing of bombers approaching from west five minutes later, 362nd investigated and found they were 1st CW of the 3rd force. 2nd Force had disappeared so it escorted this wing through target breaking escort 1245 south of Brussels. LF out Ostend 1300. 363rd continued with 93rd. Wing through target, breaking off to meet approaching gaggle which were found to be friendly fighters. Apparently after targets, Bs had left briefed course, so sqdn escorted B-24s from target to Reims. LF out Dunkirk.

"Bomber formations poor. Fighters and bombers were probably blown about by high winds which forced changes in course, but confusion of planes in southern target areas was pronounced."

By the end of the first eight days, two men were already dead. Major Lawrence Giarrizzo had been with the 362nd only a short time. Not much is known of him, although he is thought to have come from Training Command, probably having wrangled a combat assignment, not wanting to miss out on the war.

The report from Captain Don Pickrell, 362nd Intelligence Officer gives the details: "Captain John B. England was flying about 1,000 yards directly behind Major Giarrizzo when the Me 109 with which he was engaged broke sharply to the left. Giarrizzo did the same. At this point his left wing broke completely off, about two feet out from the fuselage.

"Captain England watched the rest of the plane plunge straight down from 6,000 feet at approximately 450 mph, hit the ground and explode. Major Giarrizzo did not get out. There is not the slightest doubt in England's mind about his death."

The 8th of November brought a relatively routine escort ride for the 62 P-51s led by newly promoted Lt. Col. Tom Gates. However, major dramas were played out on the sidelines resulting in the destruction of two Me 262s, one of which there is still uncertainty about the victor and the death of Lt Warren Corwin also still shrouded in mystery.

*The name AIN'T MISBEHAVIN' originated with a musical number by fame jazz musician Fats Waller and also expressed the hope of its pilot, Jesse Frey also a musician, that he wouldn't "mess up". He didn't, scored two victories (see little **Nazi** flags under windshield) and completed his tour. The airplane continued to fly to the end of the war without an abort, thanks to Crew Chief Pat Buzzeo and his crew. There are two 353rd Group P-47s in the background.*

The 363rd Squadron, after leaving the bombers, crossed out over the coast of Holland flying quite low (the mission report says 8,000 feet). It was somewhere near the coast that Lt. Warren Doranski was hit by flak and reported "in trouble" as he reached mid-channel. Lt. Col. Gates told him to get out of it, and presumably radioed a MAY DAY for ASR. Probably reluctant to leave his aircraft for the cold waters of the channel, he delayed, attempting to re-start his engine. Unsuccessful at this, he bailed out his chute blossoming as he hit the water. The squadron orbited for about 30 minutes but Warren Doranski was not seen, joining the hundreds of airmen who died in the channel and the North Sea in two wars.

The 362nd Squadron's operational history recorded: "Major Evans, our West Point grad who was stationed in Iceland awhile flew mission number one on his birthday, November 11th, flying an escort mission to Oberlahnstein. Nine new pilots were assigned and they seemed to be eager beavers. Their names - J. Dunn, R. Dunn, Schlieker, Ziebell, Gasser, Ridley, Ecker, Duncan, Becraft. Most of them came directly from the states and had a lot of training to do before their first mission.

Lt. Goss returned to the squadron, not saying much about his experiences. He had bailed out over German occupied Haguenau, France on 19 October a month before. He informed Corporal Duggan, well-oiled, that he intended to get married on reaching the states.

Duggan, with a disgusted expression exclaimed, "Married? From de 'flying' pan, into de fyah!"

After the 11th of the month, there was an unusual span of four days during which no operation was flown by the 357th. Europe's killer weather had intervened again and other than a few weather reconnaissance and other special probing flights, The Eighth remained on its bases probably to the intense relief of the *Luftwaffe* and people living in likely target areas.

On the 16th, the three Air Divisions launched well over 1,000 bombers to strike tactical targets in support of ground forces. Despite its four day respite, the *Luftwaffe* failed to appear and no bombers were lost either to flak or fighters. The weather, however, claimed its victims as usual and a fourth name was added to the month's casualty list. 2nd Lt. Robert Wiser of the 364th was killed letting down through the overcast a few miles south of Norwich. A Home Guard soldier who witnessed the crash said the plane appeared to be flying nose high/tail low attitude, with flaps down. Engine sounded as though it were running flat out but aircraft was flying very slow and low. Aircraft crashed through some trees, and was completely demolished. Conditions were poor with light fog.

A witness said he saw three small swastikas painted on a piece of metal. No record of the aircraft serial number has been found.

This photo by the author shows the 362nd Squadron waiting their turn to take off with their noses into the wind to assist cooling. Kit Carson's NOOKY BOOKY IV, at left and John Duncan in G4-Z, HOT SHOT.

Lt. Dwaine Sandborn, 364th Squadron who flew PRIDE OF THE YANKS, one of the two war bond P-51Cs that were issued to the 364th.

With its engine cowl off, there is no clue as to this P-51's name, if any and nothing is known about it. The placement of the tail number is unique possibly due to the Crew Chief's desire to "be different". Removal of the lower fuselage panels suggest coolant radiator problems. The fin of the UC-64 Norseman can be seen behind the '51.

The skies over the continent were a bit unusual on the 18th as they were totally clear of B-17s and B-24s, and seven fighter groups had the war to themselves, losing seven aircraft and claiming 26 e/a shot down with another 69 destroyed on the ground. Only four of these belonged to the 357th, all going to the 364th Sqdn, which caught a gaggle of Me 109s taking off.

Lt. Robert Winks claimed one of these - from his encounter report: "I was leading Green flight when I saw a lone 109 on the deck and on a 180 degree course to me. I dropped down on its tail from 5,000 feet and proceeded to chase it through a series of gullies giving it intermittent bursts and observing strikes. Finally the e/a pulled straight up, jettisoned his canopy and whip stalled. I saw many pieces fall off as I clobbered him while he sat there. He then dived again for the deck, regained control and started once more into a zoom. Again I clobbered him, again chunks came off. He bailed out at about 2,000 feet. I took pictures of the crashed plane. Ammo expended, 1500 rounds."

Meanwhile, John England leading Blue and Green flights of Dollar Squadron, attempted to strafe a train, but was forced to break off due to heavy Mustang traffic already working that target. He then formed his eight P-51s in line abreast and strafed the airfield at Mengen. This turned out to be a lucrative target, and was left with ten Me 109s and an He 111 burning in dispersal areas with another in a blister hangar, with three aircraft, all on fire. Nine pilots shared in the carnage.

Lt. Edward "Buddy" Haydon, involved on the 8th in the Me 262/Nowotny affair, also found friendly traffic to congested at Neuhausen Airfield, but soon found another small airfield on top of a hill a few miles away. As soon as he came up from behind the trees he was exposed to intensive flak which inflicted damage to his windscreen and wings, forcing his wingman to shear off. Nevertheless, he completed his run, clobbering a parked Fw 190. He ends his report: "The e/a was later seen burning furiously. A second pass was not attempted."

The eleven aircraft destroyed by England's crowd cost the life of Lt. Sam Fuller. John Sublett heard him on the R/T saying: "This is Fuller, I think I've been hit. I'm having trouble with my oil pressure". Due to radio chatter Sublett heard no more. German documents with his MACR say aircraft 80% destroyed without burning, pilot dead. The markings are given as G4-S and the name as SCREAMIN' DEMON, s/n 44-13596. This P-51 had carried at least two other names, BETSY, with Harry Ankeny, and NAUGHTY AUTY, pilot probably Jim Sehl.

25 November: Kit Carson and John Sublett reduced the *Luftwaffe's* aircraft inventory by two. The victims were Focke-Wulf 44s, a neat bi-plane trainer similar in function to our own PT-13/17 series. Although not a major threat to Allied Air Forces, they were nevertheless,

part of the *Lutwaffe's* assets. Carson reported: "I was leading Dollar White flight. We had dropped beneath the bombers to about 12,000 feet and we saw that railway traffic was exceedingly heavy in this area. We dropped our tanks and made our first attack on a double-header diesel freight. After we had destroyed it we pulled up and spotted two Fw 44s in a sod field about a mile north of the RR tracks. I took my flight to the field and made two passes. I set one on fire during the first pass, Lt. Sublett set fire to the second. We attack from 2,000 feet opening fire from 800 yards doing 350 MPH closing to about 50 yards. We then returned to the railroad and caught a 20 car passenger train going west. We blew the locomotive on the first pass. The passengers were bailing out from doors and windows in the meantime. On the second pass we raked it fore and aft hitting every car and then pulled off. We flew a heading of 220 degrees for a few minutes and spotted two more freights which we shot up beyond repair."

The end of the month brought two events of note. One was a major battle with a force of Fw 190s and a few 109s, on the 27th. Two days before this, however, it was "party time", in celebration of, or at least recognition of the end of the first year of service in the ETO.

Considerable planning had gone into the affair. On Saturday the 25th, a big time up-to-date movie DOUBLE INDEMNITY was shown. In the evening there were dances at both the Officers Club and the Aero Club, which drew many civilian girls as well as those from the nearby AA batteries. Music was provided by Leiston's own part time soldier dance band, THE BUZZ BOYS. At the Officers Club, a "stag show" with a genuine, and very attractive "stripper" was presented.

All of this helped to forget the war for awhile. The whole affair would have engendered much envy among the millions of servicemen who were serving in less civilized areas!

The war, of course did not stop. Captain Foy led a full strength four hour escort of 3rd Division B-17s which proved to be uneventful. Field Order 1343A for the 27th of November spelled out a mission somewhat different than usual - escort and strafing, but it was not bomber escort. The field order itself is not available and the mission report is not clear, but apparently the 357th was briefed to provide escort for the 353rd Fighter Group which would do the straffing. Rendezvous was made with the black and yellow nosed Mustangs over England, the two groups making landfall at 1150 hours at the Hague. Forty-five minutes later, the briefed mission fell apart when MEW (Microwave Early Warning) reported that bandits were forming up 40 miles ahead. Ten minutes later, with bigger game afoot, the strafing was abandoned and a big air battle was on.

When John Landers came to the 8th Air Force in mid-1944, he already had 6 victories scored in the Southwest Pacific. He scored four more with the 55th Fighter Group, then took command of the 357th Group for about six weeks while Colonel Dregne was on leave in the ZI. He scored one victory with the 357th then left to command the 78th Group, where he scored 3.5 more - an impressive career! He is seen here in a jovial mood at a 362nd Squadron hangar party in November.

There were over 700 8th Air Force fighters over Germany on the 27th, as all 15 fighter groups were operating. All were P-51s except for the 56th Group's P-47s. Nine of the groups scored victories, totaling 98, but the biggest number fell to the 357th with thirty while the 353rd claimed 18.

The two forces collided a few miles southwest of Magdeburg. Dollar Squadron (362nd) being in the right place, claimed the bulk of the victories with 22, the 363rd with nine and the 364th was almost "shut out". Lt. Bob Schmanski, the only one from that squadron to score tells why: "I was leading Gree House Squadron, flying to the right of Dryden (the Group code name). Very accurate and intense flak forced me to the south, away from the group. Nuthouse (the controller) vectored the Group to the bandits with my 364th Squadron trailing."

Above: A close up of the nude, probably done by an enlisted man named Childs. Armorer Cpl. Meley admires the artwork.

*Left: Chuck Weaver's "no name" nude, G4-A, s/n 72199, D-20. Instead of the usual swastika victory symbols, here small **Nazi** flags are used to show his eight credits.*

Lt. Jacob Giel joined the Group sometime late in 1944 and was killed in a freak accident three weeks before the end of the war. Returning from a mission to Kiel and crossing out near the Island of Terschelling, Dollar Red Two called that he was dropping his wing tanks. Giel, White Two, was hit by one of these on his right wing with tremendous force. With part of the wing missing, the aircraft named WINNIE GAL, snap rolled twice and went into the overcast. Although Red Flight searched, they found nothing but an oil slick. We don't know who Winnie Gal was but she had lost her man.

1st Lt. Sam Fuller is one of THE YOXFORD BOYS who flew from Leiston's runways and one day did not return. Not much is known of Fuller. He shared an Me 109 on 13 September 1944 with John England, his only credit. On 18 November he reported over the R/T that he had been hit. He was flying a P-51D named SCREAMIN' DEMON, 44-13596. German documents with his Missing Aircrew Report say aircraft 80% destroyed, and pilot dead. He is another of the "faceless" thousands dead of WW II remembered now by no one except a few aging descendants.

Schimanski did, however, find a small group of 109s and shot a wing off one of them. The dominant theme in most of the encounter reports is the extreme reluctance of such a large group of German fighters to engage in combat.

Major Andy Evans: "The e/a were making every effort to get away, evading any encounter with us." Lt. Frank Gailer: "The 190s held no formation, just a large gaggle of 150 or more." Captain John England: "There were approximately 40 to 50 190s flying more or less in a bunch, as far as I could observe, in no particular type of formation." Lt. Charles Weaver: "I followed the gaggle to the deck, they made no attempt to turn or break up." Lt. John Sublett: "I was expecting the Jerries to turn into us, but they just kept going down and stayed in formation."

Sublett was flying wing to John England, who was leading Dollar Green flight. Between the two of them, they claimed seven Fw 190s destroyed.

There were many multiples. Captain Leonard Carson made "Ace in a Day" with five. Besides England, Chuck Yeager claimed four, and Captain "Bud" Anderson three. Chuck Weaver claimed two, another probable, and a "damaged".

Lt. Clifford Anderson: "I was flying Dollar White four position. At 3,000 feet an Fw 190 pulled directly in front of me from the right and crossed to the left and slightly lower. I latched onto him, but before I could fire he rolled into me to the left and split-essed. He was too low and could not pull out. He crashed and burned in the yard of a large German house. I counted over thirty aircraft burning on the ground in the immediate vicinity."

Major Andrew Evans: "I saw an Fw 190 turning left in an attempt to get away. He was at 2,000 feet and I was at 3,500. I turned as tight as I could, rolled to the left and down, firing as I came out of the turn. Before I could fix my sights on him and get off a good burst, he rolled into the ground from 1500 feet, exploding as he hit."

Lt. James Sloan was one of four pilots of Cement Squadron who scored. Although the mission and encounter report call it an Fw 190, he remembers it as a Me 109. Many years later it is still vivid in his memory.

"The visibility was unusually good, very few clouds. We encountered a small flight of Me 109s. My first thoughts were that since I was flying 'tail end Charlie', it wasn't too likely that I would be directly involved. How wrong I was! My guns had yet to be fired at an enemy target. Suddenly I found myself engaged in a 'one-on-one' aerial combat. It happened so fast there was no time to think, just react.

"The 109s did not want to engage us, and tried to run for it. The squadron broke up in pursuit. My element leader did not stay with our flight leader, but proceed on

his own and was quickly on the tail of an Me 109. His guns would not fire, so he told me to take him. My guns were OK but my gun sight was out. After firing several short bursts in a very tight left turn with no hits, my thoughts were; what if I run out of ammo? How can I part company? Maybe he will dive for the deck and I'll just let him go. But by using the path of the tracers, I managed to pull enough lead and destroyed most of his right wing. He crashed in an open field.

"Upon returning to base, I did a slow roll, too low to make the Sqdn. C.O. happy who told me never to do that again. The aircraft I was flying had just been assigned to me. The crew and I were practically strangers. They had never crewed for anyone who had scored a victory, and they were more fired up than I was. Regretfully I cannot remember their names, but 'Thanks fellows, you did an excellent job, and I'm sorry I was not around at the end to thank you personally'. (Sloan was a POW at war's end.)

For 1st Lt. Frank Gailer, it was a very traumatic day as he was THE YOXFORD BOYS only loss. In his encounter report filed some six months later after his release from POW camp, he tells what happened. He had shot down two 190s (which put him over the top and onto the Ace list.):

"I climbed back up to 12,000 feet where a pilot from the 55th Group tagged onto my wing. We climbed up to 28,000 trying to find some stragglers from the other enemy gaggle. An element of two ships made a head-on pass at me. I thought they were P-51s, but not being sure, I did not break, but kept ready to fire in case they were bandits.

"As we closed, the lead plane coming at us fired, shattering my canopy, knocking out my oil line and wounding me in the right shoulder. They were P-51s that knocked me down, of the 352nd Group. I got back as far as Kassel where my prop and engine froze. I bailed out at about 7,000 feet. The 55th Group pilot stayed with me all the time. I called my squadron before bailing out and told them of my victories." (Gailer claimed two Fw 190s, which were confirmed.)

Gailer thought he had been shot down by a blue-nosed 352nd Group P-51. The writer checked with Robert "Punchy" Powell, pilot and now historian, and author of THE BLUE-NOSED BASTARDS OF BODNEY who made a search of 352nd records, but could find nothing that matched Gailer's case.

Another possibility is that Gailer's tormentor may have been a 359th Group pilot, as the 359th had a similar nose design but in a medium green. 359th aircraft were in the area, as Major Broadhead observed a green-nosed P-51 shoot down two 109s. In addition, a green nosed P-51 shot up Major Juntilla's P-51. Leading the 353rd Group, he managed to return to his base at Raydon. It is of little consequence, of course, but it would have easy for Gailer to mistake a green nosed P-51 for a blue nosed one.

John England sums up the 27th of November: "This was one of the best shows I have ever seen, since being in combat. Our whole squadron had tacked on the rear of the enemy aircraft and opened fire simultaneously. I believe these enemy planes were part of a huge force intending to rendezvous with another force and attack our bombers, which were bombing south west of this vicinity."

German historians have determined that the 357th's opponents on the 27th of November were mostly from the two Home Defense units, JG 300 and JG 301. Why did such a large group of formidable fighters perform so poorly. The answer seems obvious - untrained, inexperienced pilots. German historian Werner Girbig in his book on the last days of the *Luftwaffe*, titled SIX

MONTHS TO OBLIVION gives a graphic description of the plight of the pilots of the 109s and 190s:

"The sky was full of well-trained enemy pilots, and on the German side there were too few fighter pilots with the experience called for by an all-out dogfight. At this stage, many pilots quite simply lacked the training for this type of operation.

"For the first time they were seeing the gruesome downward plunge of a friend who had managed to jump clear of his blazing 'crate' only to find that his parachute would not open. For the first time they were confronted with death, and with the reality of war.

"And then it happened. While the novice, fresh from flying school, was trying to grasp all these incomprehensible things and was staring wide-eyed at machines dropping out of the sky beside him and exploding as they hit the ground, he too, paralyzed by what he had seen, fell prey to the Mustangs."

G4-D, GASH-HOUND already has its gear up here while wingman just lifts off. Lt. Pete Pelon was the pilot of GASH-HOUND, 44-14848, but Oliver Boch flew it for the last 40 missions to the end of the war. On the left side, it had a large painting of hound dog.

A pleasant scene on the 364th flight line with Lt. Ivan McGuire, and TSgt. George St. Onge.

A mixed group of 363rd Squadron officers. They are L-R, standing: John Meyer (Intelligence Off.), Hal Reynolds (Communications), Norman Badger, (Engineering), Paul DeVries (pilot), John Swan (Ordnance). Kneeling are; Ernie Denigris (Intelligence Off), Jim Browning (pilot), Dave Willet (Adjutant), Chuck Yeager (pilot), Dan Evander (Sqdn Exec. Officer), Paul Tramp (Flight Surgeon).

Ingenuity at work. Using a bicycle, a 75 gallon drop tank, and the engine from a battery cart, Sgts. Devince Bienvenu and Clarence Parker produced their own side-car equipped motor bike.

This 95th Bomb Group B-17 went off the end of the runway for unknown reasons, ending up in the weeds. Damage does not appear to be severe so it was probably repaired and returned to service. If so, it survived the war as it is not on any loss lists.

Captain Ernest Tiede flew a full tour ending with this colorfully named machine. Its serial number was 44-63763, but we don't know its 363rd Sqdn code.

Major Leonard Carson's colorful NOOKY BOOKY IV, a P-51K, being run by a crew member. It has its full total of 23 Swastikas -- 18.5 of which were air victories. When the war ended, the use of the 108 gallon paper drop tanks stopped immediately, replaced by the less dangerous 75 gallon steel type as seen here. This aircraft had both formation lights and tail warning radar.

For such a well known P-51, there are not many photos of OLD CROW. Although published many times before, it is used here because no other good ones have been found in the bare metal finish. It was received at the 8th Air Force depot at Warton in the first week of September, 1944, just off the freighter from Newark N.J. It would have arrived at Leiston a week or two later, where it was apparently immediately painted in RAF green and Anderson flew it like that until winter came on, when his crew stripped it back to bare metal. It was eventually scrapped in November, 1945.

The above comments on OLD CROW are also applicable to Chuck Yeager's equally famous GLAMOROUS GLEN III. It arrived from the states about a week after Anderson's 44-14450, and no other good photos are known of it either. It was missing in action on 2 March 1945, after Yeager had returned to the ZI. The pilot, Patrick Mallione, was killed. It was 44-14888.

Right: 362nd Armorers SSgt. Parmer and Sgt. Morrisey pass belts of .50 caliber ammunition up to a colleague on the wing and into the ammo cans of NOOKY BOOKY IV.

Below: Captain Alva Murphy flew with the 362nd Squadron. In the fall of 1944, he was transferred to the 364th. He is seen here with G4-U, 44-13334, which displays six victory symbols, four of which are air victories. He added two more Me 109s on 2 March 1945, only minutes before he was shot down while strafing an airfield. His wingman Howard Wesling saw him bail out, but he did not survive. A week later his promotion to Major came through.

Although the date is unknown, this is undoubtedly an award ceremony, with Major General Earle Partridge (Left), Commander of the 3rd Bomb Division and Major Joseph Broadhead, C.O. of the 362nd Squadron, and later Group Ops Officer. Note that the two men wear different versions of the 8th Air Force patch Broadhead wears the official "long wing" type, and Partridge weard the British-made "short wing" version preferred by most 8th AF troops.

A well known photo of TANGERINE (a popular song of the day), which was published in the press in the fall of 1944. This was the second TANGERINE, the first being lost with Bryce McIntyre on 19 September. No photo of it has ever surfaced. Lt. Henry Pfeiffer then got this new one (44-14507) and flew it through his tour when it went to Lt. John Salsman who finished the war with it. It is another of those in RAF green paint, the name in yellow.

Lt. Wallace Reid was apparently hit by flak on 4 August 1944. Having a damaged cooling system and overheaded engine, Reid was forced to bail out into the Baltic near Kiel, Germany. The crew of a freighter fished him out of the water, gave him dry clothes and treated him royally with fine food, cigars and a good night's sleep! The next day the royal treatment ended when a launch picked him up and took him ashore into captivity.

CHAPTER 6:
DEEP WINTER

After Alden Smith departed, 6637 became RUBBER CHECK, seen here with many mission symbols and three victory marks, probably those credited to Lt. Walter Perry.

As the pages of the desk calenders at station F-373 flipped over to the last month of 1944, going from the bad weather of November to the even more miserable conditions of deep winter, it signaled a frustrating but very active month ahead.

Basic statistics: 19 missions, 64 enemy aircraft shot down, plus many ground targets; seven pilots lost, with only Zetterquist and "Smilin' Jack" Martin surviving in POW status where they joined Colonel Russ Spicer, and many other 357th pilots, under the 56th Group's Hub Zemke, senior Allied officer at *Stalag Luft* I.

At the end of the month the station weather office summed up the situation for December and although the figures changed somewhat, it is an excellent commentary on the general weather conditions pilots had to put up with. The miracle is that more weren't lost to this cause.

"During the month of December, 1944, our planes were grounded 42% of the time - 13 days out of 31, by adverse weather conditions, either in base area or in the target area or a combination of both. Out of the 13 days in which the planes did not fly, operations were prevented on six days due to fog with visibilities averaging about 100-200 yards for several hours at a time. During the whole of the month, from the 6th to the 30th, there were 16 days of fog, ten days of which the visibility was reduced to 100 to 200 yards or less for the whole day. The longest single day of fog lasted from the evening of the 18th to the morning of the 23rd. During this period the

Apparently RUBBER CHECK always brought Walter Perry home but it was finally burnt out in a home base accident on 2 December, as seen in this photo. Three weeks later Perry died when his P-51D shed a wing during combat.

heaviest fog occured, and operations were impossible for four of the five days. An added hazard to both ground and flying operations occurred with the deposit of coats of frost on runways and roadways during this period, with temperatures dropping to a very near minimum record, 21 degrees F, on the mornings of the 26th and 27th. With additional "coatings of frost; the roads and runways were soon coated with about a quarter inch of clear ice.

"Of the remaining seven days, operational flying was prevented by bad weather in base area on four days, with ceilings of 400-800 feet at times, and poor visibility, in rain and drizzle. On three days, although the base areas were operational, conditions over the continent and in the target area were too poor for operations."

Despite the abominable weather, none of the seven pilots lost in December were due to these conditions. During the combat period of 14 months, about 12 pilots were lost due to weather-related causes and it is a miracle it was not more.

All pilots had received rudimentary instrument training – no one recalls it as being comprehensive. During the eight months the unit trained on the P-39, all pilots were required to fly an hour os so "under the hood" on instruments, but this was not done in the P-39 rather in a BT-13 or an AT-6. Even this was done in good weather where the safety pilot could take over. As a consequence, no one had actually done much, if any, flying in nasty weather.

Many realized this deficiency and made a determined effort to learn not only the procedures, but also all the prominent landmarks around Leiston Airfield and the coastal area and then do time and distance checks from these to Leiston's runways. Many of them, Pete Peterson was one, became very good at getting home "when the ducks were walking".

From the 6th through the 18th of December, missions were flown to Merseburg, Koblenz, Geissen, Darmstadt, Kassel and Mainz. No enemy aircraft were sighted and there were no losses. Prior to this long period, earlier in the month, there had been action on two days, the 2nd and the 5th.

All three bomb divisions were operating on the 2nd but for the 3rd Division it was wasted effort. Koblenz was the target but as the 357th leader, Captain Foy, reported: "10 miles east of the target, our combat wing made a 180 degree turn and returned. No reason for abort was given to group leader over the R/T."

Free of the bombers, the controller then vectored Foy's 52 Mustangs to a gaggle of Me 109s where the 362nd Squadron had all "the joy" with two each to Alva Murphy and Kit Carson, and one each to Delager and Schlieker. Of these four men only Carson survived the war.

Foy, however, with his wingman Joe Cannon had the most interesting encounter of the day and his report tells the story of his unfortunate victim: "As I approached the Me 109s, I observed a Ju 88 directly beneath me and I peeled off onto his tail. The Ju 88 was all silver and had no visible markings. To make certain of his identity, I pulled up in formation with it and only then could see a cross on the fuselage near the tail and a small swastika on the stabilizer. I then made a 360 degree turn and pulled up astern e/a giving short burst at about 50 yards. Observed several strikes on left wing, then right wing and pieces flew off the e/a. the Ju 88 lowered flaps and I lowered flaps following him in close trail.

"He crash landed in a field and I pulled off making two strafing passes. The first pass after he crashed I fired a short burst setting the left engine on fire and hitting a crew member attempting to clear the aircraft. The second pass I made set the right engine on fire.

"As I flew formation with the e/a, I could distinctly see several shafts protruding from the nose of the ship - three slender shafts extending down, one on either side of nose extending forward and two extending up. "There was also a slender shaft on each wing about five feet from the wing tip and extending forward. Appeared to be only one machine gun in use on the E/A. This was directly behind and above the pilot"

His wingman Joe Cannon, had stayed with him and confirmed destruction of the aircraft and said he believed all of the crew were killed.

Three days later it was back to Berlin with some 450 B-17s of the 1st and 3rd Divisions, bombing through the overcast. Over 300 P-51s kept large numbers of *Luftwaffe* fighters away from the bombers, who lost only three. Seventeen P-51s, however did not return; two of these from the 357th and 91 e/a were claimed. This time, all three squadrons shared in the 22 claims for 109s and 190s. Captains Anderson and Bochkay of the 363rd and Lt. McCall of the 364th all scored doubles on Fw 190s.

Sometime during the engagement, Captain Herman Zettergiuist was forced to bail out of C5-R, SHIL-LELAGH to become a POW. After his release from POW status he entered a claim for one e/a destroyed on the 5th, which was allowed - his only victory of WWII.

Lt. Mathew Martin called "Smilin' Jack" due to his resemblence to the comic strip hero of that name, has reason to remember this period:

"On the 4th I was censoring officer. Normally I would have had to sign a few letters and then be free to go on a mission. On this day, one of the men who worked in group was found in his hut with a copy of the Field Order for that day's mission (probably that of the 2nd). He was placed under arrest in his quarters, and that night shot

This is 44-15385, although the red rudder on 363rd airplanes often makes it impossible to read the tail numbers. Lt. Warner Roberts was the pilot, who scored one victory during his tour, that during the big air battle of Christmas Eve 1944. The small antenna for the tail warning radar is visible as a light colored spot on the vertical fin.

The author was ground crew for Lt. Edward Hyman on ROLLA (U-bar) (a girl's name and ranch brand) and postwar friend. Hyman scored two on the massive mission of 24 December.

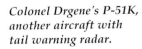

Colonel Drgene's P-51K, another aircraft with tail warning radar.

himself with his carbine. I had to read every outgoing letter to be sure no one mentioned it." (author's note: As far as is known, no one in the Group, except for those in command, ever found out any details of whether the man was actually a spy or just made a stupid mistake. He is buried in the American cemetery at Cambridge).

Jack Martin continues: "On the 5th I was OD (Officer of the Day). I went to briefing and it was a straight line to Big B and we always saw enemy fighters when we went there. I was complaining about staying home when my buddy, Willie Gilbert suggested I ask one of the new pilots to take my place as OD, which I did so I could go on the mission.

"I was flying wing to John Kirla when we had a report that enemy fighters were climbing up some 15 miles ahead. Kirla's plane began syphoning a liquid. Since the vent pipes for fuel and coolant were close together, I moved up under him close enough to see it was fuel, and told John to switch tanks. At that moment my engine backfired, cut out, caught again and then quit and caught fire. Kirla told Willie to stay with me, but I told him to go on as I obviously had to bail out."

Martin ended the war where so many other 357th pilots did, at *Stalag Luft* I.

The living sites at Leiston Airfield were about two miles from the airfield proper and were made up in small sections dispersed from one another. Each squadron had its own site. Site 6 was that of the 364th squadron and it was in his Nissen hut here that Joe DeShay recorded the events of the day in his diary. All entries were very brief, but taken together, they give a good picture of life among the ground crews and of their jobs, in December 1944:

"3 Dec. Released. (means no mission) Steam-cleaned Cletrac and tug and scalded foot. Hard to walk and quite irritating, but went back to work after the medics bandaged me up. 3 letters from Ellen.

"4 Dec. Foot don't hurt, but badly blistered. Just a fair amount of work today, for a change."

"5 Dec. Not much work in AM, but ships came back in bad shape from mission. Two wing changes, engine change, two radiator and one carburetor change. Had to take Hughes' ship all apart to change an oil line.

"6 Dec. Mission. Wing change on Pete's ship, worked until 10 PM.

"7 Dec. Released. Worked on "D" engine change, got new compressor.

"9 Dec. No mail, no mission. Got a new P-51D-20. Saw show "When our Hearts Were Young and Gay"

"15 Dec. Came back from London, squadron party at Aldeburgh (a small coastal town near the base.)

"21 Dec. Released. - Foggy. No mail, built room instrument and electrical crews behind hangar wall. Feel fine after good hot shower and shave."

"22 Dec. Released, still foggy. Only flew two days out of last ten. Troops need our help in Belgium as Jerry broke through, back 40 miles in counter attack."

In his entry for the 22nd, he records one of the most momentous events of WWII, now generally referred to as THE BATTLE OF THE BULGE. By the time DeShay made his diary entry, the battle had already been won, although it was not yet apparent to those doing the fighting.

Vast numbers of books and articles had been written on the Battle of the Bulge, and the reader is referred to them for details on this pivotal battle. A short dissertation is needed as a background for the actvities of the 8th Air Force and the 357th Fighter Group.

By December of 1944, the Allied armies had been on the offensive pushing closer to the German heartland. Most everyone thought the Germans were beaten and the war all but over. Those in command positions were thinking "offensively" not "defensively". The Germans did a masterful job of covering their intentions which were to smash through the Ardennes Forest in Holland, to the Channel ports and reverse Germany's downward slide. Allied intelligence certainly failed in this case although a few astute individuals in the intelligence field suspected that all was not right.

U.S. troops in the Ardennes area were mostly in a "rest" status after heavy fighting and were understrength and heavy with raw recruits. So when Von Rundstedt's three armies burst forth on the morning of the 16th they made good progress against three thinly spread U.S. Army Corps. At the beginning everything was in the German's favor; surprise, overwhelming force, and miserable weather which they had counted on to negate Allied air power.

For most of this battle, U.S. troops had little or no air support. Nevertheless, only two days into the battle the German timetable had begun to unravel. Although surprised and overwhelmed, U.S. soldiers mostly in small groups and often without proper clothing in bitter cold weather, stood their ground and stopped or delayed many of the German columns. Many of these small groups did not even have a designation as they were made of ragtag groups of men from any unit that was handy, combat or non-combat. The 291st Engineer Combat Battalion is a good example of the many stellar small units often commanded by an NCO which dug in their heels and held on until the massive reinforcements began to arrive in a few days. On the 22nd, six days into the battle, Combat Cargo C-47s began to air drop supplies to entrapped units. On the 26th, Von Rundstedt signalled Hitler that the gamble was lost.

Casualties had been horrendous, German estimated at between 100,000 and 125,000. Almost 9,000 U.S. soldiers died, with 47,000 wounded and 21,000 missing or POWs.

*Lt. Otto "Dittie" Jenkins scored four of his total of 8.5 victories in the big Christmas Eve air battle. This photo would have been taken sometime after that and before his death in this airplane on 28 March 1945. The name TOOLIN' FOOLS REVENGE is yellow and does not show up well. The black circle behind the top row of **Swastikas** is the outlet port for the flare pistol which clipped into place on the cockpit wall. As far as is known these were never used and in fact flare pistols were not even carried in the aircraft.*

After a five day hiatus, Colonel Dregne led 65 Mustangs, escorting B-24s bombing communications centers. Only Bob Foy scored, shooting down an Me 109 caught taking off from an airfield. For that, the Group traded Lt. Walter Perry (who probably was unaware that he had just been promoted to Captain).

William Mooney was a witness: "I was flying white 3 in Dollar squadron when we made a pass at some bogies at 1240 from 15,000 feet near Prum, Germany. I saw a silver P-51 which was undoubtedly Lt. Perry heading straight down at approximately 15,000 feet. As I watched, it started snapping and at approximately 5,000 feet, both wings came off at the roots. The fuselage dove straight into the ground and exploded. I did not see the pilot bail out."

Perry was flying a P-51 K, named TOOLIN' FOOL. Bill Mooney's statement is dated the 24th of December. By the evening of that day, Bill Mooney was dead, murdered by a German policeman. (See under Casualty section.)

The next day, Christmas Eve, the holiday was not forgotten. In the evening there was a party at the Aeroclub. There was a good turnout of local children,

with presents and foods not generally available in wartime Britain.

However, the war and the beleaguered troops in Holland and Belgium had priority and the Group put up 76 P-51s (with only four aborts) under Colonel Dregne (25 aircraft of the 363rd) and Major Peterson (51 aircraft of 62 and 64 Squadrons).

There is much to tell of the big affair on Christmas Eve. It is a long story, but worth telling. The word came down from the highest levels to use "everything that would fly", and the result was that 8th Air Force launched the largest number of warplanes in one day in the history of air war. Freeman in his MIGHTY EIGHTH WAR DIARY, shows 2,046 B-17s and B-24s (of which 1,884 were effective - dropped bombs on targets), and 853 fighters. (the 78th and 339th Groups were fogged in and did not participate.)

Targets for the entire force were airfields and communication centers that were supporting the German armies in Holland and Belgium. The 357th were escorting their usual charges, B-17s of the 3rd Division. Takeoff time for both sections was shortly after 1100 hours. Dregne's group was fully engaged by 1240 in the Kassel area with

some 35 enemy fighters. During this melee the only loss occurred. Lt. Wendall Helwig and his wingman Saul Sitzer flew through a flight of 55th Group P-51s. Sitzer was lucky and emerged unscathed, but Helwig smashed broadside into Lt. Kenneth Mix of the 55th Group's 343rd Squadron. Neither pilot had the slightest chance for survival.

On this day before the holy holiday, THE YOXFORD BOYS out-scored all other fighter groups with claims for 31, with an almost even spread between the squadrons as to the number of pilots who scored - eight for the 362nd, and the 363rd, and seven for the 364th.

The cost was three pilots killed in action. Besides Helwig, Bill Mooney and William Gilbert did not return. Ozz Howes and Bob Foy made emergency landings on 9th Air Fields on the continent and returned to base later.

Under "Observations", Colonel Dregne inserted this curious note: "L-5 hit in wing tip at 1250, landed safely approximately 20 miles west of Arlon." Since a liaison type aircraft such as an L-5 would have been operating "on the deck", it is difficult to understand how Dregne could have seen it from his altitude!

Peterson's force of the 362nd and the 364th tangled with the largest gaggle of enemy aircraft. From his mission report: "60-70 Fw 190s and Me 109s at 26,000 with 40-50 giving top cover were intercepted in vicinity Fulda, before reaching the bombers. Enemy was flying in flights of four with flights in close trail formation. As we engaged they turned sharply trying to close up in a Lufbery of flights. We attack before maneuver was completed. Enemy was very agressive but no other improvement in quality of pilots was noted."

The 362nd Squadron did exceptionaly well with many multiplies, all 190s. Dittie Jenkins with four, John Kirla with three, Gilbert, Ed Hyman and Paul Pelon two each, and Kit Carson, George Behling and Jesse Frey with one each. On the tally board for the 364th were Ray Banks, Dale Karger, Ivan McGuire, Fred McCall, Bob Schimanski, Byron Braley, and Bob Winks, all with one each, a mixture of 109s and 190s.

Dregne's group took off a few minutes earlier and engaged some 35 109s and 190s in the Koblenz area. Johnnie Carter claimed two and Dregne, Major Carlisle, James Crump, Bill Dunlop, Warner Roberts and Jim Sloan all claimed one.

In recording these events of more than a half century ago, a major (and often the only) source of information are the official documents of that time - the mission leaders' reports and the individual pilot's encounter reports. The reader should realize, however, that these often contain major and minor errors of fact. This is to be expected considering the hectic events, man's varying powers of observation, and the methods used to compile these documents.

A case in point is the mission report for Dregne's 363rd Squadron, which credits James Sloan with an Me 109. Sloan's encounter report, which, like all such was dictated hurridly and taken down by a harrased clerk in the Intelligence Section, typed and later signed by him, also claims an Me 109.

In many letters to the author in recent years, Jim Sloan is adamant that his victim was a long-nose Fw 190, not an Me 109, and the mission report does not even record that part of the affair. Here is Sloan's story, still vivid in his memory after 50 plus years: "Our course was well west of the bombers. The flight of four Fw 190s was west and south of us heading 90 degrees, with an altitude advantage of more than 1,000 feet. Evidently they did not see us until we changed course to intercept them. Two of them immediatly dove, still heading east. The other two maintained altitude.

"Colonel Dregne dropped tanks and began pursuit of the two that were diving. I also dropped tanks and from my position on the Colonel's left I kept the other two in sight. In a few seconds, one of the remaining two dropped down in trail of the Colonel. I chopped throttle and was quickly on his tail and the 190 broke to the left. I had him on film, but no hits. In the tight turn I hit his dropwash and went into a high speed stall and spun off to the right. After recovering from the spit, my air-speed was in excess of 450 mph.

"When I pulled out, the 190 was directly in front of and above me. With the speed that I had I closed the gap quickly and raked the aircraft full length, knocking out his engine. His prop began windmilling and he began a series of 90 degree left turns.

"It was impossible for me to get into a firing position and I circled about 1,000 feet above him. The direction of his let down was easterly, and I'm sure that he knew where he was and was trying to reach German lines in the area of the 'bulge'. At about 1,500 feet he started a steep dive to the east from which he never pulled out and exploded on contact.

"At the point where the fight ended, I climbed at a zero degree heading and intercepted the bombers just before they made landfall. This was a sight to behold. Under sunny skies the bombers could be seen in three directions for 50-60 miles or more."

Dregne's mission summary has another cryptic note left unexplained: "After engagement with e/a west of Koblenz, four flights had insufficient gas to continue." Presumably these 16 aircraft had disposed of their drop tanks early in the mission. The remaining two flights (eight P-51s) remained with the bombers.

MAN O WAR, an old P-51B looks out of place in the late war context, but it flew combat through-out the year 1944, and finally ended up, now war weary as a training aircraft with Clobber College. In this winter 1944 scene it displays a vast number of mission symbols. A great deal of effort has gone into an attempt to discover its identity and its pilot, but without success. This detective work has shown that it may be G4-E, 43-6448, but there is no photographic proof.

Fighter-to-fighter combat usually resulted in a winner with the other man either dead in his machine or hanging from his parachute, perhaps to fight another day. Occasionally there was no winner, only two losers. Sometimes it ended in a draw with both pilots going home to "Happy Hour" in the officer's club.

On the 24th of December, one of these one-on-one combats produced two men who lost. This is that story:

1st Lt. William T. Gilbert, of the 362nd Squadron took off from Leiston Airfield, flying P-51D, 44-15620, as element leader in 1st Lt. John Kirla's Blue flight. Soon after Blue 2 and 4 aborted. Gilbert became Kirla's wingman, all in the group led by Major Peterson.

At about 1400 hours, Gefr. (Corporal) Hans Hufnagel was airborne from an airfield in the Dresden area with his unit the 7th *Staffel* of home defense unit JG 300. He was flying an Fw 190, W.Nr. 739441 bearing the fuselage code "White 6".

Gilbert and Hufnagel met at about 1430 that after-noon over the villages of Gorzhain and Machtlos, some 25 km NW of Fulda.

John Kirla reported: "Lt. Gilbert had moved up my wing after numbers 2 and 4 aborted, but I lost him during the ensuing combat and never saw him again. However, after the squadron had destroyed 16 Fw 190s and we were trying to re-assemble the formation, I called over the R/T saying, 'I got three! How about you guys?' The other pilots told me their individual scores; Jenkins four, Pelon two, Behling two, Hyman two, etc. Lt. Gilbert called that he had destroyed two 190s. The conversation took place over 'A' channel. After that his radio must have gone dead and he must have been attacked, for none of us heard nor saw him again.

"Since Lt. Gilbert is reported missing in action and cannot make his own claims, I would like to claim two Fw 190s destroyed on his behalf. He was a cool, steady pilot and if he claimed the enemy planes destroyed, they were destroyed. Of that I have not the slightest doubt."

The claim submitted by John Kirla was accepted and Gilbert is credited with these two victories in the offi-cial USAF credits for WWII, giving him a total of four.

On the 30th of December, the commander of the 7th *Staffel* of JG 300, *Hauptmann* (Captain) Gerhardt Seidlitz wrote to Hans Hugnagel's mother and we quote a portion of that letter: "Please accept my and the Squadron's deepest svmpathy at the death in action of your son, Gefr. Hans Hufnagel. On December 24th at 2 PM, our formation took off in order to fight a squadron of terror bombers that was flying in. There has been an air combat against superior hostile fighters in the area west of Eisenach.

"As a result, your son's plane must have been badly hit so that he decided to bail out. He was found in a near distance to the place where his plane hit the ground."

Hauptmann Seidlitz probably had other letters to write that day. Although losses of his 7th *Staffel* are unknown, JG 300 lost eleven pilots killed and 7 wounded. (see SIX MONTHS TO OBLIVION, by Werner Girbig).

William Gilbert's Missing Aircrew Report says he was last seen in the vicinity of Fulda and German documents with his MACR pinpoint the location of his crash as the western edge of the village of Machtlos. These same *Luftwaffe* documents report "Pilot unknown, supposedly escaped".

Hugnagel's Fw 190 fell in open country about one km east of the village of Gorshain about 1 km from Gilbert's P-51. Hufnagel had bailed out, but too low for his chute to open and his body was found some 400 meters from his aircraft.

It now seems clear that Gilbert and Hufnagel shot each other down and it is due to the efforts of a dedicated researcher living in the area of the combat, that the details of this incident and its aftermath, are now known.

His name is Konrad Rudolph and he was a boy of ten in 1944, when aerial combat was common in the skies over his home. To him goes the credit for pinpointing the sites of the crashes, and for finding an eyewitness to the events of that day.

The witness's name is Adam Biedebach, a *Panzer* (tank) soldier who had been wounded on the Russian front and was home on leave. Following is a translation of his account of the duel between Gilbert and Hufnagel.

"A German and an American fighter fight against each other. The U.S. fighter burned but he nevertheless shot the Fw 190 down. The pilot from the 190 bailed out, but his parachute did not open because of the low height (about 150 meters). He was dead. Also the Amercian pilot bailed out, we searched for him, but could not find him. Some weeks later we found him, the parachute hanging from a tree. He was dead."

In his letter to Hufnagel's mother, *Hauptmann* Seidlitz closes with; "Unfortunately, neither myself nor

any of his Squadron fellow pilots will be able to take leave of our Cpl. Hans Hufnagel and pay him the honors personally, as we are in readiness for missions every day and are not allowed to leave our place of action so that our attendance at the funeral is impossible."

A similar letter to Willie Gilbert's parents would probably have gone out from Major John England, commanding the 362nd Fighter Squadron.

It appears to have been German policy to bury fallen airmen, both their own and the enemy in the nearest cemetery and such was the case here, both Gilbert and Hufnagel being buried in the village cemetery at Gorshain. One of the village women, a *Frau* Flohr, is said to have maintained both graves, until in the post war years when Gilbert's remains were removed to the American cemetery at Margraten in the Netherlands, where it remains today.

Two other JG 300 pilots killed on the 24th, may very well have fallen in combat with the 357th. *Leutnant* Klaus Bretschneider, an Fw 190 pilot and high scoring ace, and *Leutnant* George Schmitt, leader of the 6th *Staffel*, whose 109 crashed only 5 km from where Hufnagel's 190 fell.

World War II produced millions of casualties and against this background, the deaths of two obscure airmen, Gilbert and Hufnagel are of little consequence but worth remembering, if only briefly.

There is no better way to end our story of the big Christmas Eve affair of 1944, then to quote a letter from Bob Schimanski written to his fellow pilots at Christmas 32 years later:

"The Battle of the Bulge was on and England was blanketed with fog. The P-51s were not flying until December the 24th, 1944. On that day the Eighth Air Force flew the largest mission ever flown in the war.

"Approximately 2,500 bombers, formed a bomber train of 200 miles into Germany. The 357th Fighter Group was divided into two divisions, and half of you escorted the lead bombers, while Pete (Peterson) and I brought up the rear.

"As we crossed into Germany there were extreme headwinds of around 125 miles and hour and the B-17s were barely crawling along. The free air temperature was 60 degrees below, the sun was shining and Germany was covered with a new blanket of snow.

"As Pete and I joined the bomber groups, we contacted the lead group that had escorted the lead bombers, and were told that there was no action - it was a dry run. Well, it wasn't for Pete and I. As soon as the last bombers left the target, the fighters hit and we started fighting. I don't know what Pete did, but I was credited with one victory and shared another with Karger.

"As you will recall, when we crossed the coast line we were to call in NUTHOUSE and identify ourselves. I remember calling in and telling them that Greenhouse 62 was crossing over into the channel at 24,000 feet with remnants of the 364th. NUTHOUSE answered and replied, 'We've been listening to you Greenhouse, and you put on another good show. Merry Christmas, Greenhouse 62.' And I replied with 'Merry Christmas NUTHOUSE'.

"Suddenly, the stark realization of where I was, and what I had done and where I was going hit me. Strapped into the cockpit of a P-51, crossing the channel, returning to base after destroying two aircraft and killing two Germans and talking to a radio station in Luxembourg and exchanging Christmas greetings, made an indelible impression on my mind."

After the traumatic affair on the 24th, the pace did not slacken although *Luftwaffe* opposition did for the 357th. Missions were flown every day (seven days!) through the 31st. The weather was foul and there were no claims and one loss. Lt. Harold Chandler was reported hit by flak in the Koblenz area and although he bailed out, he did not survive - the last casualty of the year 1944.

Lt. Col. Dregne, who had just returned from leave in the ZI, took up his new post as commander and jumped into the game with vigor, leading seven of the 11 missions in the last half of the month. Peterson and Carlisle led two each, and Foy and Broadhead one each.

On the 26th, "The other enemy", the weather gods, took a hand. On return from a five and a half hour run to Koblenz, the returning Mustangs found Leiston socked in solid with fog and all 57 landed at the 55th Fighter Group base at Wormingford, where they remained grounded until the 28th.

During these last few days of the year, no enemy aircraft were brought to battle by the 357th, but other groups who were in the right place, scored well on the 25th, 27th and 31st.

With most of the Group's airplanes parked at Wormingford, there were not many left at Leiston on the morning of the 27th but Major Carlisle scraped up 14 planes and pilots for an area patrol, where two locomotives and six trucks were claimed destroyed- hardly worth the effort.

Still, every truck or loco destroyed was one less to deliver supplies to German forces in the Ardennes.

From the photo album of the late Donald Bochkay, comes this photo of two unknown 363rd Squadron pilots synchronizing their watches - or having their picture taken.

This photo by the author clearly illustrates the weather conditions in which the Group had to operate in the winter of 44/45. Taken at the time of the Battle of Bulge when the troops on the ground needed all the help they could get, the runway control officer waves two more P-51s into take-off position, in near zero visibility. Other aircraft on the runway are obscured by rain and fog.

Carlisle's mission report says: "One crash landed due to battle damage on return." This was almost surely John England, who did indeed crash land that day, after hitting "something" while strafing, jamming the landing gear in a partly extended position.

On 28 December, 51 aircraft departed Wormingford and joined 12 home based P-51s for a normal mission. NUTHOUSE reported no enemy activity and all pilots were back on base by mid-afternoon. Meanwhile, at home base, the mundane activities went on. Headquarters, 8th Air Force passed the word that used engine oil would not be used as fuel for stoves, as it "is dangerous and extravagant. Used oil will be salvaged and turned in".

In his brief period as commander, Colonel Spicer had started the tradition of a drink of cognac for every victory and records say the tradition was still carried on - some ten months after Spicer had gone to *Stalag Luft* 1. Few recall this ritual, but it was official policy for Flight Surgeons to dispense a small drink of OLD OVERHOLD rye whisky to each pilot after a mission - a totally unacceptable practice by today's standards!

The 2nd Gunnery and Tow Target Flight arrived for a brief stay with an A-20 and several A-35s, but little is known of their activities.

The Operational Summary for December could not resist a considerable amount of justifiable bragging about the Group's accomplishments. 64 enemy aircraft were destroyed that month for a total of 469 air victories.

At the beginning of December, the Allied mood from top to bottom was one of optimism that the war was almost over. The deadly German offensive in the Ardennes, although blunted and stopped, had shaken that quick victory hope.

The *Luftwaffe's* OPERATION *BODENPLATTE*, of New Year's Day, on 16 Allied airfields in France, Holland and Belgium, also did not help the feeling of optimism! (this massive attack discussed later.)

The Operational Summary for December, 1944: "At the end of 1944, not quite the end of the 11th month of operations, the Group had a total of 39 aces. Thirty Nine aces and not one of them with so many that a few good days in bagging Jerries by the others would not put them ahead. The very fact that they are human would make all of them want to be the top-scorer, it is a tribute to their thought of the team that the total scores are so close together, not a few with a lot, and the others with a few.

"The Groups' total claims are pretty well divided among the squadrons and individual claims are pretty well distributed within the squadron, the aces are not all in one division."

In SIX MONTHS TO OBLIVION, Werner Girbig sums up the state of the *Luftwaffe* at the end of December:

"Bombing raids on German airfields had destroyed 129 aircraft and damaged 140 more. Although Germans shot down 63 U.S. bombers and 23 fighters during the last four days of the month, they lost 128 fighters.

"Total German casualties for the month amounted to some 500 pilots killed or missing, 35 POWs and 194 wounded. The High command now realized that the *Luftwaffe* was no longer capable of influencing the course of events."

THE NEW YEAR - AND FOUR MONTHS TO VICTORY

1945 started off with a BANG for the 9th Air Force and the RAF's 2nd Tactical Air Force on bases in France, Holland and Belgium, but the 357th and in fact, the 8th Air Force as a whole were not involved at all. (The single exception is the 8th Air Force's 352nd Fighter Group, which had been temporarily transferred to Y-29 airfield, near Asch Belgium. They were heavily involved and did very well in the big air battle of New Years day.)

The BANG referred to was the *Luftwaffe's* OPERATION *BODENPLATTE* (BASEPLATE), which had been in planning for some time. Since THE YOXFORD BOYS were not involved, we will only describe it briefly as it was a major event in the air war.

Taking off from many German airfields were some 800 to 900 Me 109s and Fw 190s led by navigating Ju 88s. The force stayed on the deck and struck some 16 Allied airfields in the low countries at around 9 AM. The objective was to cripple the U.S. and British fighter force and to return the faltering *Luftwaffe* to a point where it was better able to deal with Allied bombers which were devastating German industry and cities. It is worth noting that even with total success, it would have had no effect on 8th Air Force fighters which were the main nemisis of the *Luftwaffe* fighter force.

The scene must have been right out of Dante's Inferno, with the roar of hundreds of aircraft engines, exploding bombs, over-worked anti-aircraft guns, and burning and exploding airplanes, both on the ground and in the air.

BODENPLATTE did destroy a large number of Allied aircraft on the ground (anywhere between 200 and 800 depending on which figures you choose) but the effect on the *Luftwaffe* was far worse. German loses, like Allied, are by no means exact, but Girbig says around 300 Me 109s and Fw 190s were lost and 151 pilots killed. 63 became Allied prisoners. The effect on the *Luftwaffe* fighter force was devastating, but the Allied losses in aircraft were easily replaced in a week or two and the raid caused hardly a ripple on their operations.

An AT-6D belonging to the 364th Squadron, seen here with some very nasty weather moving in from the back. With its red and yellow nose, spinner, wheels and the name ANITA THERESA in the same colors, it was a very attractive machine.

JANUARY - TO THE "BIG DAY"!

150 miles or so west of the Low Countries, where hundreds of 109s and 190s battled P-47s, P-51s, Spitfires and Tempests that had gotten airborne, all was proceeding normally at Leiston Airfield and scores of other 8th Air Force bases as they prepared for their day's mission.

After the scattered survivors of the *BODENPLATTE* attackers had straggled back to their bases and the fires were still burning in Holland and Belgium, Major Peterson led 43 P-51s of the 363rd and 364th Squadrons on the first escort of the new year. Other than one B-24 group being badly strung out, there was little for Peterson to report.

A few minutes before Peterson's departure, John England led 18 pilots of the 362nd Squadron, escorting two explosive laden B-17s on another APHRODITE mission to an unknown target in Oldenburg, a small city in NW Germany and some 50 miles inland from the East Frisian Islands. The target did not matter anyway, as England reported that "both babies missed target and blew up in open fields" which was probably good fortune for the people of Oldenburg. This may have been the last gasp of OPERATION APHRODITE which had been a dismal failure from the beginning.

On this same day, the 1st, Joe DeShay wrote in his diary: "Cold day, put sand on runway. Got ship back that had bellied in on continent."

It seemed like the Operational Summary for every month reported the weather that month had been worse then the preceding one. Because the weather is so often overlooked as a major factor in the air war, and was so important, it is worthwhile to quote Lt. E.D. Rhoads, the Station Weather Officer: "January 1945, proved to be the coldest and one of the most difficult months for flying the Group has so far experienced in this theatre. Minimum temperature for the month, 16 degrees F, was reached on two days. Mean temperature for the entire month was 33, with the ground and runways either frozen or covered with snow and ice on eighteen days - 58% of the time.

"Precipitation occurred in the form of rain, drizzle, or snow on 21 days of the month. Average cloud cover for the month was 9/10 with ceilings less than 2,000 all or most of the time for 21 days. Fog or heavy haze appeared on 12 days, reducing visibility at one time or another to less than 1,000 yards, and on many occasions to less then 100 yards. Takeoff was made on three days with visibility less than 1500 yards in fog. On one occasion, the 16th of January, the group diverted to the continent because of sudden fog at home base. On this day, some 30 stray planes from other bases in the British Isles were landed at this field in visibility rapidly dropping from 1,000 yards to less than 100 yards.

"Combination of poor visibility in the base area and on the continent served to ground our planes 17 days of the month, some 55% of the time."

January was a very bad month for casualties, the Group losing thirteen men, five of whom were lucky enough to return from POW status after the war. They were Saul Sitzer, Ed Haydon, Bill Dunlop, Jim Sloan and George Behling. Of the other eight, Fred McCall, lost to flak, was the only combat death. The remaining seven were accident victims near home base and the miserable weather was a factor in all.

On the 13th, shortly after mission takeoff, as the Group was climbing through the scud, Robert Schlieker lost control and crashed near the emergency field at Woodbridge. In the next six days, Richard Anderson (still in Clobber College), William Thompson, Herman Delager and Morris Gallant were all killed in conditions of fog, drizzle, and low cloud. Delager and Gallant both disappeared over water on the same day, the 19th. On the 27th Walter Corby and Sgt. Mel Schueneman died in the crash of the AT-6 when they flew into the ground near Dover.

Flight Officer Saul Sitzer had been in the 363rd since October. On the 23rd of December, while part of a small escort for a PRU Spitfire, he shot down a 109, his only victory of the war. On his 22nd mission, 2 January, he was hit by flak while strafing a truck and joined Frank Gailer, Col. Spicer and other pilots in *Stalag Luft* I for the next several months. 1st Lt. Ed Hayden was also a victim of flak on the 20th.

Casualty-wise, it was a very bad month. To replace these losses, there was an influx of new pilots on the 24th; 2nd Lts. Ed Gordon, Gilbert Robinson Jr., Joe Shea, Holsey Johnson, Frank Kyle, Gene Lasswell, Will Foard, and Flight Officers Anton Schoepke, William Holmes, Charles Schneider and James Steiger.

About two weeks later, on 10 February, Major Peterson was leading a Clobber College practice dive bombing mission during which Johnson's war-weary P-51B, 43-6755WW disintegrated in flight. ASR found only an inflated dinghy.

On New Years Day, when most of the *Luftwaffe* fighter force were engaged in *BODENPLATTE*, enough were left to contest the bombers and 23 were destroyed by 8th fighters and bombers (none by the 357th). It was the last major contact with the enemy for two weeks. During the period, all of the 8th Air Force could claim only nine e/a, two of these to the 357th's Tom Adams, an Fw 190 on the 5th and an Me 109 on the 10th.

Three days later Major Anderson led a small force on an uneventful escort, the *Luftwaffe* making no reaction to the 900 bombers and 400 P-51s. Anderson and his lads were home by mid-afternoon in plenty of time to make evening chow.

Tomorrow, the 14th of January, would be different!

Colonel Dregne led a five hour mission on 10 January. Probably fatigue and an icy runway caused Lt. Rocco LePore to lose control of C5-C which skidded into an empty 363rd revetment. Here the guns have been cleared and the crowd dispersed. The other P-51, at left is Q-PEE, probably B6-Q, lost with Lt. Jim Sloan four days later when he was forced to bail out near Berlin to become a POW. Faintly visible at upper right is a Vultee A-35 of the 2nd Gunnery and Tow Target flight and at least one P-47.

CHAPTER 7:
THE GREAT RAT RACE - THE BIG DAY

Another famous P-51, John England's MISSOURI ARMADA with 18 victory symbols. His official score is 17.5.

As the year 1944 came to an end, it is proper to review the situation as regarding the war in general and the 357th Fighter Group in particular. As December brought that year to an end there were still four months remaining of a deadly European war which had left much of the continent bloodied and in ruins. No one knew that the war was that close to the end. There was still a great deal of fighting to be done.

On the ground the last major *Nazi* effort to turn back the invading Allied armies with a powerful surprise offensive on the U.S. 1st Army front, through the Ardennes Forrest, was shuddering to a halt. German General Von Runstedt's 18 divisions had scored impressive early successes but by the end of December, the momentum had gone. Slowed by desperate resistance of scattered American troops, under appalling winter conditions and battered by an incredible array of Allied tactical air, the Battle of the Bulge was nearing its end.

In the air, the 8th Air Force was at the peak of its awesome power and had in fact, flown the largest mission in history the day before Christmas when over 2,000 of its

bombers, escorted by some 1,000 fighters had applied their weight to stop the German offensive.

The rampaging U.S. 9th Air Force and the RAF 2nd Tactical Air Force, with considerable assistance from 8th Air Force fighers, had made daylight movement of German transport an extremely hazardous proposition. This was one reason the *Luftwaffe* laid on a massive strike, in hopes of blunting Allied tactical air. This operation was launched on New Years Day by close to 800 *Nazi* fighters against British and American air fields. Although the attackers scored heavily in some areas, they lost even more to defending fighters and triple A guns - losses the *Luftwaffe* could not afford.

Such was the general situation at year's end. The weather that winter had been foul throughout Europe and there were many days when flying was all but impossible. At bases scattered across England, hundreds of fighters seemed to huddle under their canopy covers, shrouded in mist and freezing rain. Hundreds of equally miserable mechanics trudged to their aircraft each morning to chip ice from wings, crank and warm stubborn engines, only to cover them again and dash for the meagre warmth of line shack or Nissen hut.

At station F-373, Leiston Airfield, home for all of 1944 to THE YOXFORD BOYS, the 357th Fighter Group there was a Christmas Eve party for the children of the surrounding area. Many 8th Air Force stations provided these parties along with candy, gifts, and ice cream for children who seldom or never got them in those austere years. That same day the Group had taken part in the massive 8th Air Force effort, claiming 31 victories and losing three pilots, all dead. They would fly another mission on Christmas day with no enemy contact or losses.

The Operational Summary for December included a re-cap of the year and the end of 11 months of combat operations. Letting his pride of unit show, the unknown author wrote: "Becoming operational months after eleven of the other fighter groups in the 8th Air Force and during the roughest part of the European air war, the 357th Group rapidly forged ahead in claims and in the confidence and respect of their ability by higher headquarters. This confidence and respect caused the unit to be assigned on missions alone, or in the important spots when several units were on the mission.

"Assignments that should have gone to one of the older groups, but in accordance with general military policy - the best units get the most important, and often the hardest jobs."

At this time the Group had claimed 517 air victories and had 39 aces on its rosters. By the end of the first week in January, with their part in the Ardennes affair tapering off, the bombers returned to their primary mission of strategic bombing and the 357th returned to its normal escort duties.

Prior to the 14th of the month, the appalling weather conditions had restricted missions to only seven days, with claims for only two air victories while losing three pilots killed - two in weather related crashes near base.

Near the end of that first week in January 8th Air Force weather forecasters became aware of an impending change which would take place about the 10th of January. A high pressure center was forming over northern Sweden and Finland while another was taking shape in the North Atlantic west of Ireland. These two high pressure centers soon joined producing a long ridge from the North Atlantic to Russia. This, in turn, tended to divert storm centers north of the British Isles and brought dry cold air over northwest Europe.

By the 14th, the weather was ideal for what was to be "The Big Day" in 357th Fighter Group history, resulting in the largest number of enemy aircraft shot down by one group, in one day, in 8th Air Force history.

G4-E, MISSOURI ARMADA, with crew chief Robert Currie (left), Flight Chief Lewis Moye, and armorer Forrest Highland. Apparently in mid-winter to judge by the leather clothing.

From an unpublished manuscript, Leornard "Kit" Carson, already an ace several times over, describes the dreary beginning of the day: "The 357th Fighter Group came to life by the clatter of the teleprinter machine in Group Operations, punching out Field Order 1515A from 8th Fighter Command Headquarters, northwest of London, 100 miles away. The night watch at Group Ops scanned it and then cranked the field phone and the one in our squadron orderly room buzzed lightly.

"The Charge of Quarters picked it up and heard, 'Roust 'em, briefing in one hour'. The CQ, irreverently known as 'the company queer', knocked cautiously at our door as if he knew the hostility inside to being roused at such an uncivilized hour. In the blackest part of the January night we groped our way to consciousness, pulled on cold boots and stumbled to the mess hall through the half frozen mud that comprised the local real estate. Life in an English garden? You bet, chum, violins and all!. The Nissen huts that were our home looked like igloo-shaped freighters, floating in a sea of mud. The freezing cold was the wet kind that permeates the soul. The only good thing about this morning was that the weather wasn't as rotten as it could have been.

"After bacon, pancakes and coffee, the pilots took the dirt path that had been scuffed across a small meadow and walked almost idly, in clumps of three or four to group operations for the briefing. As the 66 pilots of the three squadrons filed into the briefing room they were watched by Doc Barker, our group flight surgeon, checking for red eyeballs, sniffles, and bronchial coughs.

"I walked in with John Sublett and my wingman, 'Hot Shot Charlie' Duncan - both aces. Damned comforting to have an ace for a wingman. That kid's got his head screwed on real good and as fine as any shooter and rudder stomper that ever came down the pike. 'Is it scrubbed yet?' someone asks. 'Nope, still on.' The ominous red ribbon that marked our route and target ran eight feet across the large briefing map of Europe pasted to the wall at the rear of the speaker's stage.

"Briefing time. Over six thousand fuzzy-faced kids and a few old timers over 30, in Mustangs and Fortresses were converging on a single purpose. The bombers had indeed already taken off and a corps of crew chiefs, armorers and radio men were in a last minute hustle to get the fighter escort off. The name of the village, Derben, at the end of the red ribbon, really didn't matter. It was Berlin - in January."

There were 66 red and yellow nosed Mustangs at take-off, 22 each from the 362nd (Dollar), the 363rd (Cement), and the 364th (Greenhouse) squadrons. However, three of those landed again due to various troubles and seven others turned back before the Group was committed, so that the force had dwindled to 56 by the time of rendezvous with the leading bombers of the first three Combat Groups, north of Cuxhaven at 1150 hours.

Kit Carson on the run into the target: "The mission was to be a North coast of Denmark, avoiding land fall and flak to the last minute and turning southeast to Derben/Stendahl just west of Berlin. The target was 180,000 tons of oil storage. The weather was clear over the target. The 357th was assigned the lead escort position to the 13th Combat Wing of B-17s which was leading the 3rd Air Division. Within the 13th Wing, the 95th Bomb Group was leading the whole force, followed by the "bloody" 100th and the 390th. All three of these veteran groups had participated in the Schweinfurt ball bearing plant raids in October 1943, and the 95th had been the first group to bomb Berlin in March, 1944. We were at Berlin too, that day, as the first P-51 group assigned to General Doolittle's 8th Air Force. Now we were to rendezvous again west of Denmark over the North Sea."

As the First Force neared the target with the B-17s at about 24,000 feet, the 357th escort was as follows: On high cover at about 30,000 and somewhat further back on the bomber stream, was the 363rd Sqdn. led by Major Robert Foy; providing close support at about 26,000 were the remaining two Squadrons. With the target coming up on the horizon, the mission leader Colonel Dregne, and the Squadron leaders were especialy alert for a tactic they had been warned of earlier in the week. This report, the result of Prisoner of war interrogations, had alerted all groups that the *Luftwaffe* was about to try the "company front assault". Although not a new tactic, there were indications it was to be tried on a larger scale.

Twenty miles north of Brandenburg, Colonel Dregne spotted two large gaggles of e/a approaching the lead box of bombers from 1 o'clock high, (or roughly from the southwest). It was 45 minutes past noon.

Kit Carson: "We hadn't been in escort position more than 30 minutes when the enemy force was sighted pulling condensation trails and approaching from Brandenburg. They were coming at us at about 32,000 feet.

Lt. Joe Shea reported in to the 362nd Sqdn. late in January, 1945 and named his P-51 MY BONNIE. Only bad luck prevented him from shooting down an Me 262 in the last days of the war. Control Tower is in the background, and an RAF battery cart is at left.

The briefing room map on a historic date, 14 January 1945, when the Group shattered all records for the number of enemy aircraft shot down. The map shows the mission track tape from Leiston to the target (Berlin) and return.

'Judson leader, contrails at 11 o'clock high, about 100 of 'em'. 'Judson leader here, roger. Dollar, Cement and Greenhouse drop your tanks.'

"Switch to internal fuel, punch the red button on top of the stick and away they drop; 116 wing tanks streaming fuel out of the broken connections into the stratosphere, as a prelude to the clash. It was a reassuring sight to the crews of the Forts below. They knew we were springloaded and ready to go. Flick on your gun and camera switches. It all took about 5 seconds."

Taking Greenhouse squadron with him, Dregne turned to intercept but then spotted a third group of e/a at his own level which he had missed at first. The two large gaggles whose contrails he had spotted first were now seen to be perhaps 100 Me 109s on top cover at about 32,000 feet. Ignoring these, Dregne's 18 Mustangs turned into the low gaggle which now proved to be Fw 190s in the expected company front waves of about eight aircraft each. The 190s immediatly abandoned their company front formation, most breaking right into a Lufbery. One of the biggest fighter battles of the war was on.

Dollar Squadron led by Major John B. England (already an ace three times over) had now dived into the middle of the mixup and this set up the mouse trap play that had been hoped for. Although a tactic as old as war, it worked again and drew the Me 109 top cover into the battle leaving Cement Squadron (363rd) free to spring the trap.

From this point on, it is not possible to follow the rat race in any semblance of order because the P-51 formations broke up about the same time the 190 company front disintergrated. In a savage brawl like this it was frequently impossible for even the best wingmen to stay with their leader and often it became every man for himself. However, most re-joined and returned to base together.

The two major *Luftwaffe* home defense units were JG 300 and JG 301. Several reliable sources indicate these two *Geschwadern* were the primary opponents of The Yoxford Boys, both suffering very heavy casualties.

Oberfeldwebel (Master Sergeant) Willi Reschke, who ended the war still alive, with 26 victories and a Knights Cross, was a pilot in Staff section of JG 301. In a

This P-51 PAPPY'S ANSWER was on the big day mission of 14 January. Its pilot, John Stern scored three victories to bring his total to four, as seen under the windshield.

recent letter to fellow *Luftwaffe* pilot Helmut Peter Rix (a long time friend of this writer, now deceased), Reschke recalls the 14th of January, 1945:

"The JG 301 started from Platzen-Welzow-Finsterwald and Alteno, takeoff at 1150 hours. The course was, immediatly after take-off in the direction of Berllin, and reached Berlin at 1230 hours at an altitude below 8,000 meters. The course was NW. The squadron was in a slight climb when reaching Berlin. Shortly after, the thick contrails from exhuasts were visibly recognized. A short time later we could see the thinner condensation trails of the escort fighters - more and more, pointed directly at us. Within a few minutes the following situation took place: JG 301 was attacked from higher flying and very numerous escort P-51s and a great majority of our squadron did not come out of the battle with the P-51s.

"Right at the beginning of the battle I shot down a P-51 which shortly before had shot down an Fw 190 A-8 "Yellow 3", pilot *Oberleutnant* Herzog of 11 *Staffel*, who was injured in the encounter. I could not observe further the P-51 which tumbled down because I had to defend myself constantly not to be shot down by the other P-51s. The formation of our squadron in the encounter scattered and a few pilots were able to escape the encounter with the escort fighters."

From the Group Leader's mission report and the encounter reports of the individual pilots, it is possible to glimpse the action for the next 30 minutes. Colonel Dregne himself opened the affair when he fired at a 190, getting strikes on the tail and fuselage. Although it fell off into a spin, he did not see it again, so claimed only a "damaged". At this point he found himself in a Lufbery with eight or ten 190s. He managed to climb above them, went to the aid of a bomber box under attack and here found a stray P-51 which turned out to be Andy Evans. Dregne, who had long since lost his wingman ordered Evans to fly his wing and the two of them again took up their escort duties.

Prior to this chance meeting with the Group Leader, Evans had been extremely busy. Although Lt. Col. Evans was Deputy Group Commander, he had been a spare when the mission took off. At rendezvous point, Lt. Dittie Jenkins turned back with a rough engine, taking White 3 with him as escort. Evans moved into white flight, where he stayed until, as he put it, "all hell broke loose". In quick order Evans shot down an Me 109 and a 190, faked another Fw 190 into flying into the ground, and then turned to engage another 190 which promptly "collided with somebody". Then, "thoroughly shaken up", he climbed to 31,000 where he joined Colonel Dregne on

A fine portrait of G4-P FLOOGIE II. Like most other painted D models it is in RAF green. Its identification was 44-14245 and Lt. Otto Jenkins was the pilot. It was damaged in belly landing in December, repaired and then destroyed on 13 January 1945 in a crash near base killing Lt. Robert Schlieker.

Lt. Walter Corby liked to fly, and used to "hang around" 363rd Squadron Operations, hoping a test, or ferry flight might come up. In January, 1945, returning from a maintenance flight to France in the AT-6, Corby and SSgt. Schuneman were killed in a bad weather crash.

Walter Corby KIC

Salt Lake City resident, Lt. Roland Wright, who scored his first victory six days after the Big Day, here with his MORMON MUSTANG, probably C5-T, 44-14868, Peterson's old HURRY HOME HONEY. Wright was later the commander of the Utah ANG and retired as a Major General.

withdrawal support for the bombers. Soon after the two had joined, an Me 109 was seen far below and Dregne shot it down in flames. Evans concludes his encounter report with: "From then on the mission was uneventful."

1st Lt. "Big John" Kirla was leading Dollar (362nd) Green flight with Jim Gasser on his wing. When the melee started, Kirla quickly shot down two Fw 190s and then an Me 109 which caught fire and began shedding parts until, as Kirla put it: "there wasn't enough left of the ship to crash".

Evans and Kirla were the only two to claim four victories each, but no less than six pilots claimed triples. One of the latter was Captain Leonard "Kit" Carson who was to end the war as top scoring pilot of the 357th Group. From his book PURSUE AND DESTROY (Sentry Books, 1978), Carson takes up the story: "Hot Shot Charlie" had kicked his Mustang about four wing spans out to my right where he could see me in his peripheral vision and watch the 190s come in. He was waiting for my first move.

"We both fired as we met them and just a half second before the first wave passed, I hauled it around at full power in a steep, tight chandelle to reverse course and attack from the rear. I closed to about 200 yards on a Focke-Wulf and fired a good burst getting strikes all over the fuselage and closed the range to about 50 years. No long range gunnery here. Shove all six guns up his butt, pull the trigger and watch him fly apart. I hit him again and he rolled to the right and peeled down and started a series of rolls which became more and more violent. He was smoking badly and the ship was obviously out of control. I pulled up and watched him hit the dirt. The pilot did not get out, in fact he didn't even release the canopy."

After being joined by a stray P-51, the three of them waded head-on into a group of 20 or 30 190s, one of which became his second victim of the day. Having lost "Hot Shot Charlie" and the other Mustang, Carson climbed back to 14,000 feet where he came upon two Me 109s with "barbor pole spinners" and after a difficult time with them, destroyed one at point blank range. The "Big Day" was over for him, and these three victories closed out his score at 18.5 victories.

Major John Storch, leading Blue Flight of Greenhouse squadron, claimed two 190s and a single 109, the latter being unlucky enough to be shot down after Storch's K-14 gunsight burned out. "I was a picture of confusion," says Storch, "trying to turn, fire, fix my sight, put down flaps, pull up flaps, and work my throttle. Finally, after giving up on my gunsight, I once again got close enough so I couldn't miss and got strikes; coolant and smoke came from the e/a. He tried to belly in just short of a forest, hit and bounced almost over the clearing, but hit the last few trees on the fringe of the forest, and the

Matthew "Smilin' Jack" Martin was the pilot of TEMPTA-TION, with its lovely bathing beauty. It was G4-N, 44-14722, but Martin and the bathing beauty parted company on 5 December 1944 when the engine failed deep over Germany, and he joined many other YOXFORD BOYS in **Stalag Luft I** *for the rest of the war.*

pieces scattered into the clearing. I claim one Me 109 and two Fw 190s destroyed. Ammunition expended, 1725 rounds."

Major Robert Foy was leading Cement Squadron and the following is quoted from his encounter report: "The 190s dove toward the bombers and we attempted to cut them off, meeting them head-on just before they were in range of the bombers. The 190s broke their company front formation and headed in every way imaginable. I turned to the right and lined up up with a 190, closing in to a good firing position, giving him short bursts while in a shallow turn and about 30 degrees deflection. Strikes were observed on both wings of the e/a and he immediately straightened out, flew level for a second or two, when suddenly the pilot jettisoned his canopy and bailed out. This took place at about 22,000 feet and I had to pull up sharply to avoid colliding with the hun pilot.

Big Day aftermath. Here Colonel Dregne who led the mission, chalks up the day's score and the Group's total while Robert Foy, John Storch and Andy Evans look on.

"I observed another 190 flying 90 degrees to my path and directly beneath me at about 3,000 feet. I did a quick wingover and split-essed onto his tail. He apparently saw me coming and did a split-ess toward the deck. I followed giving him short bursts observing strikes on the left wing. He continued his dive and must have been indicating over 500 mph. He made no move to pull out of his dive, so I started a gradual pullout at about 4,000 but kept his ship in view off to one side. The e/a dived straight into the ground and I made a 360 degree turn, diving to get a picture of his ship burning on the ground.

"I then leveled out and made a climbing turn toward the bombers and giving my flight the opportunity to pull up into formation. My No. 2 man (Lt. Ralph Mann) joined up, but somewhere enroute and during the fun I apparently lost my second element."

Foy and Mann stayed with the bombers on withdrawal until, low on fuel and oxygen, they headed for home. On the way they found a train and Foy shot its locomotive full of holes, chased a 190 which they lost in a haze, and finally burned another Fw 190 which he found on a "beat up airdrome."

Although the Group Leader's mission report indicates the enemy force was composed of several hundred 190s and 109s, several Greenhouse pilots had an inconclusive encounter with a jet propelled Me 262. Lt. Dale Karger spotted the 262 first, which was making a pass at the No. 2 man (Lt. Westphal) in Maxwell's Green flight. The 262 pilot however overshot, and Lt. Ray Banks, element leader in Green flight fired one burst at the jet, but

observed no strikes and the 262 flew away and was not seen again. (Two of the 262s were, however, shot down by pilots of the 353rd group on this date.)

Also out of the ordinary was the 109 that Lt. Charles Weaver became involved with early in the rat-race. Another 109 had dived between him and his element leader. While attempting to rejoin, he happened upon another 109 painted olive drab with black and white invasion stripes around the fuselage. Weaver immediatly tacked onto his tail, firing a short burst at long range which forced the 109 into a steep left turn. From a semi-inverted position, Weaver fired again with no apparent results. Nevertheless, the strange OD 109 dived straight into the ground in a massive explosion. (What Weaver took to be invasion stripes may have been the blue and white "Defense of the *Reich*" fuselage stripes carried by JG 300.[1]) The huge battle that day over the Berlin area was not exclusively a Yoxford Boys/*Luftwaffe* affair.

The 20th Fighter Group escorting combat wings further back on the bomber stream also claimed 19.5 victories in the scramble and the 353rd Group was also involved, claiming nine. It is a safe bet also that the 361st Group was also in the area, as two 357th pilots had considerable trouble with yellow nosed P-51s. Captain Chester Maxwell, flight leader in Greenhouse Squadron had shot down three Fw 190s and then had his traumtic encounter with the yellow nosed Mustang. (See LAST SEEN IN COMBAT AREA, for his story).

The scope of the battle can be seen from the rather dry "Observations" of the Group Leader in his mission report. One surprising comment, considering the late date is that some of the Me 109s were "E" models. Twenty five miles north of Brandenburg an unidentified P-47 was seen to shoot down an unidentified P-51. Fifteen minutes later, three B-17s went down NW of Berlin with only five chutes observed. A 20th Group P-51 was seen to to shoot down an Fw 190 and then meet the same fate from another 190 (the 20th Group records show no loss for this day).Finally, a 357th pilot in the heat of battle, fired on another 20th Group Mustang, observing strikes on the wing but the P-51 headed home apparently OK.

Lt. Robert Winks, Greenhouse Yellow flight leader, who had just shot down one Fw 190: "I began circling for altitude and came across another 190 doing the same thing. He was damned aggressive so we started our affair with a head-on pass. Neither fired as I remember. Soon we found ourselves essing back and forth on a common course, chopping throttle, adding throttle, and dropping flaps, both trying to get the advantage. Sad situation! Finally, I out essed him, got on his tail, fired and watched as he obligingly blew up. I therefore claim one Fw 190 destroyed and possibly pilot also."

WHAT OF THE BOMBERS - ON THE BIG DAY?

So far it had been a day of stunning success for The Yoxford Boys and equally a disaster for JG 300 and JG 301, but what of the bombers which had come to Berlin on a cold winter day to drop 550 tons of bombs on oil installations? Was it a highly successful day for them also? The answer has to be the old reliable "yes & no".

Lt. Col. Irwin Dregne, leading the 357th, says in his after action mission report: "None of the formations of e/a attacked believed to have reached the bombers although some may have filtered through."

In a citation awarded the Group some two weeks later, B/General Harbold says: "Not one of the bombers of the formation they (the 357th) were escorting failed to release its bombs because of hostile fighter activities." This statement is difficult to support by the available documents.

In his mission report, Dregne states: "R/V 1150 north Cuxhaven 25,000 ft with lst three combat grps of 1st Force." The first three bomb groups in the bomber column then, were those escorted by the 357th.

There is no doubt that the pilots of the 357th did an outstanding job of keeping enemy fighters away from the Big Friends of the first two combat groups, but for the crews of the third group, it was going to be a bad day. The force that went to Derben that day to bomb oil installations, was not large by 8th Air Force standards - only 186 B-17s of the 3rd Air Division were involved. There were however, another 600 heavies striking other targets in the German heartland. They were supported by almost 800 fighters - seemingly enough to keep the entire *Luftwaffe* fighter force apprehensive about what was behind them at their 6 o'clock position. However, bad timing and bad luck allowed the German fighter controllers to vector their 190s and 109s into a patch of sky devoid of P-51s and hack down eight B-17s while losing a few of their own to bomber guns.

The first three combat groups made up the 13th Combat Wing, which was an old friend of the 357th, (they had gone to Russia together on the shuttle mission in August) and consisted of our closest neighbors, the 390th Bomb Grp at nearby Franlingham and the 95th and 100th Groups. These were the units assigned to the 357th for escort.

The 95th's 32 B-17s led both the 13th CW, and the 3rd Division, crossed the enemy coast at 1144, rendezvousing with the the 357th one minute before noon. For the 95th it was almost a textbook operation, bombing from 26,000 feet, most of the bombs were on the underground oil installations. The 95th mission report describes the fighter escort as excellent, keeping most e/a away. Ten to fifteen Fw 190s did make a pass at them, but caused no losses to the 95th while its gunners claimed five, including the only Me 262 which was seen. These would have been the few that Dregne mentions as "filtering through".

The 100th Group, which had had its share of bad luck in the past and been tagged "The Bloody Hundreth" was second in the 13th Wing with 34 B-17s behind the 95th. One squadron missed the primary target but the other two bombed with good results. Although their mission report tells us that enemy fighters were seen, "fighter support was very good. It broke up the enemy formations, was on time, and as briefed." The 100th Group, like the 95th, lost no aircraft.

The 390th was third and last in the 13th CW, but was lagging well behind the 100th, by about five minutes or ten miles. This gap apparently left the 390th without fighter cover and it was during this time that German fighters hit the formation. The low squadron of the 390th lost all six of its B-17s and another two from the lead Squadron. Fourteen chutes were seen. The only aircraft returning from the low Squadron were three which had aborted early. This was the last sustained attack of the war by German fighters on a single 8th Air Force unit.

Regardless of the loss and in apparent contradiction, the 390th mission report says: "Friendly fighters gave good support but were unable to keep off attacking enemy fighters."

The 390th had been the responsibility of the 357th, so what went wrong? The deadly gap between the 100th Group and the 390th was a major factor, but a close look at the clock may provide another. The 390th mission report says their low squadron came under attack "about 1240 hours". This is within a couple of minutes of the time Dregne spotted swarms of 109s and 190s and during the 30 minutes the 390th was being hacked down, the 357th's entire attention was devoted to dealing with several gaggles of aggressive enemy fighters, three times their own number.

By the time this massive dogfight had simmered down, the 357th P-51s were scattered across many miles of Europe, in singles, twos and threes, and they and the 390th were on their way home. As we have seen above, the 390th mission report comments on good support from friendly fighters. These were almost surely not 357th, since they were all involved at the head of the bomber

stream. Whose P-51s, then, did provide support for the 390th?

The 4th and 5th Combat Groups of B-17s, behind the 390th were under escort by the 20th Fighter Group. This entry in the 20th Group's diary shows clearly that it was Major Merle Nichol's 79th Squadron which engaged the 390th's tormenters and prevented further loss. They were also the ones referred to in the 390th's report that "provided good support".

The 20th Group diary entry: "Major Nichols who was leading the 79th squadron out in front of the bombers, engaged a gaggle of 100+ e/a which had apparently been attacking the combat groups ahead of our bombers and in the battle that followed the 79th accounted for six destroyed and three damaged, one of the destroyed being accounted for by Major Nichols."

It would appear then that the bombers under 357th escort did not fare as well as the initial reports would indicate. The reasons being the fact that the 390th was lagging badly and had the misfortune to be hit just as THE YOXFORD BOYS were fully engaged at the head of the column. 20th Group P-51s then intervened and prevented a worse loss.

Besides the eight pilots who claimed four or three victories, five scored doubles. The total Group claims for the day were 57 1/2. One of this number was Foys grounded Fw 190, but the other 56.5 were all air claims, a total unapproached before, or after, by any allied fighter group in Europe or possibly anywhere else. Like most air combat claims, it is not possible to determine whether these are totally accurate. However a perusal of all pilot's encounter reports indicate a large majority of the victims were seen to bail out, crash, or break up in the air.

Werner Girbig, in his authoritative book SIX MONTHS TO OBLIVION, lists total casualties for JG 300 and JG 301, at 69, of which 55 were killed or missing. Of these 56 1/2 claims, later re-evaluation denied credit for three. Lt. Col. W.C. Clark's credit was transferred to 66th Fighter Wing, his assigned unit. Two of Captain James Browning's claims were denied, reducing his to one for the day. (His total for the war was seven.)

This brought the approved claims to 531/2; however, when the war ended in May, 1945, returning POWs Jim Sloan and Bill Dunlop entered claims for one each for 14 January. Both of these claims were accepted, and the total of 55 is now official, and is listed as such in "USAF CREDITS FOR DESTRUCTION OF ENEMY AIRCRAFT, WORLD WAR II." Commonly referred to as "study 85", it was produced and published by the Office of Air Force History in 1978, and since updated with later wars. THE YOXFORD BOYS' losses were just as amazing. Five P-51s failed to land at home base, but one of these landed in

allied territory and soon returned to base. Another was Maxwell's wreck at Antwerp. The three lost, George Behling of the 362nd, and Sloan and Dunlop of the 363rd, reported as "last seen in combat area" all survived their POW days and returned at the end of the war. (See the section LAST SEEN IN COMBAT AREA for stories of their adventures.)

By 1445 hours, all aircraft, except the five referred to, had landed at home base. When the preliminary claims went in there was considerable disbelief at 66th Fighter Wing, and at 8th Air Force Headquarters, but re-counts came up with the same figures, and later as celebrations went on at Leiston, a teletype message arrived from General Jimmie Doolittle, which said "you have given the hun the most humiliating beating he has ever taken in the air."

Two of the men who were there, sum it up. John England as a comment at the end of his encounter report: "Our squadron (362nd) racked up a wonderful score this day and established further proof that good spirit, good formation, discipline and teamwork pays dividends. The wingmen did fine work, only one pilot returned alone."

John Stern, in a letter written four days later, to former 363rd pilot John Skara, who had completed his tour and returned to the ZI: "We sure had a big day on the 14th, we got 57! What a sight. We were over near Big B, it was as clear as a bell. They came in about a hundred and fifty strong. I was leading White flight, Foy Red, Browning Green and Dunlop Blue. After we got ahold of them, and couldn't let go, it was fight it out! You never saw such a sight. Every place you could look you could see planes going down. All over the ground you could see pillars of black smoke coming up. I got three Me 109s, Foy got three and so did Browning. We got 13 in the squadron. Andy and Yeager were down around Switzerland goofing off. It was their next to last mission. Andy and Yeager are finished now, Andy has 19 Krauts and Yeager 12."

Although never unbeatable, the *Luftwaffe* fighter force had seldom been a pushover and it is appropriate to try to find the reason for the lopsided defeat. Even at this late stage of the war the *Luftwaffe* was a potent fighting force, but it was running along the edge of its grave. Many of the experienced pilots and leaders were dead and their replacements had received only sketchy training due to the lack of time, fuel, facilities etc. On the 8th side, its groups were at the peak of their form, heavily laced with experienced veterans, confident and aggressive, and flying one of the great fighters in existence. The Fw 190 and the aged Me 109 were still good fighters, the Mustang was simply better.

As John Stern said:
"We sure had a big day on the 14th!"

HEADQUARTERS AAF STATION F-373
Office of the Operations Officer
APO 559   US Army

MISSION SUMMARY 253

DATE: 14 JANUARY 1945. FO NO.1515A TYPE MISSION: RAMROD, LOCALITY, DERBEN
GROUP CLAIMS: 56 1/2-0-3(air). AIRBORNE 68; COMPLETING MISSION, 58. 1-0-1 (ground)

PILOT	OPN'L TIME	CLAIMS	REMARKS (abortions A)
364th			
DREGNE, IRWIN	4:40	1-0-1 (group Leader)	1 Me 109 dest 1 Fw 190 dam
CLARK, W.C.	4:35	1-0-0	1 Fw 190 dest
JOHNSON, E.W.	4:45	1-0-0	1 Fw 190 dest
FITCH, A.W.	2:40		(A) Escort Braley
WINKS, R.P.	4:35	2 1/2-0-0	2 Fw 190 DEST 1/2 unident grp.
ZACHARIAE, L.E.	4:50		
GALLANT, M.E.	:15		(A) landing gear trouble
KOURIS, G.C.	4:30		
ADAMS, T.H.	4:50	2-0-0	2 Fw 190 dest
ZETTLER, V.V.	4:40	0-0-1	1 Fw 190 dam
WEBER, G.L.	4:25		
SNEDEKER, I.E.	4:25	1-0-0	1 Fw dest
STORCH, J.A.	4:50	3-0-0	2 Fw 190, 1 Me 109 dest
WILLIAMS, D.R.	4:50	1-0-0	1 Fw dest
HATALA, P.R.	4:50	2-0-0	2 Fw 190 dest
BRALEY, B.K.	2:45		(A) rough engine
MAXWELL, C.K.	6:15	3-0-0	3 Fw dest
WESTPHAL, L.A.	4:30		
BANK, R.M.	4:35	3-0-0	3 Fw dest
KARGER, D.E.	4:25	1-0-0	1 Me 109 dest
KOCHER, D.C.	1:30		(A) DROPPED TANKS
WESLING, H. (NMI)	4:15		
362nd			
ENGLAND, J.B.	4:40	1-0-0	1 Me 109 dest
DUNN, R.	3:55		
CHEEVER, D.W.	4:40	1-0-0	1 Fw 190 dest
POTTER, R.I.	4:25		
BROADHEAD, J.E.	4:55	1-0-0	1 Fw 190 dest
HYMAN, E.D.	4:55		
JENKINS, O.D.	2:45		(A) rough engine
CASTER, C.R.	2:50		(A) escort Lt. Jenkins
CARSON, L.K.	4:25	3-0-0	2 Fw 190, 1 Me 109 dest
DUNCAN, J.F.	5:15	2-0-0	2 Fw 190 dest
WYATT, H.A.	4:55	1-0-0	1 Me 109 dest
BECRAFT, MA.	4:25		

PILOT	OPN'L TIME	CLAIMS	REMARKS (abortions A)
362nd continued			
KIRLA, J.A.	4:35	4-0-0	2 Me 109, 2 Fw 190 dest
DUNN, J.W.	4:30		
BEHLING, G.A.	4:30		(M.I.A.)
GASSER, J.A.	4:30	1-0-0	1 Fw 190 dest
SUBLETT, J.L.	4:30	2-0-0	2 Me 109 dest
GRUBER, W.W.	4:50		
DELAGER, H.H.	4:50		
FREY, J.R.	5:25	1-0-0	1 Me 109 dest
EVANS, A.J.	4:45	4-0-0	2 Fw 190, 2 Me 109 dest
WEAVER, C.E.	4:30	2-0-0	1 Fw 190, 1 Me 109 dest
363rd			
CARLISLE, G.I.	1:10		(A) coolant hot
CORBY, W.E.	1:10		(A) escort Carlisle
DUNLOP, W.R.	2:30		M.I.A.
STERN, J.R.	4:20	3-0-0	3 Me 109 dest
RICE, G.J.	4:05	1-0-0	1 Me 109 dest
WOLF, R.E.	4:20	1-0-1	1 Me 109 dest, 1 Me 109 dam
MYERS, D.N.	4:20		
FOY, R.W.	4:50	3-0-0	2 Fw 190 (air) 1 Fw 190 (Grd) dest
MANN, R.W.	4:50		
FIFIELD, R.S.	4:35		
PIELICH, PETER (NMI)	:50		(A) left mag bad, rough engine
BOCHKAY, D.H.	:10		(A) landing gear inop.
THOMPSON, W.B.	4:20		
SLOAN, J.R.	2:30		M.I.A.
HARE, H.L.	3:55		
BROWNING, J.W.	4:20	3-0-1	3 Me 109 dest, 1 Me 109 dam
TAYLOR, J.E.	4:30	1-0-0	1 Me 109 dest
WINDHAM, J.T.	4:40	1/2-0-0	1/2 Me 109 dest
ZARNKE, J.A.	4:25	1/2-0-0	1/2 Me 109 dest
ANDERSON, C.E.	4:30		
YEAGER, C.E.	4:30		
CARR, E.J.	4:15		Radio Relay
THORKELSEN, R.L.	4:25		Radio Relay

Signed *Robert W. Foy*, Captain, Air Corps, Operations Officer

NOTES BY AUTHOR; This is a copy of the original 357th Group Operational summary.
1. FO NO 1515A, refers to the Field Order from 8th Air Force Hdqers, for that particular mission.
2. OPN'L time, refers to the time credited to each pilot toward his 300 hour combat tour.
3. Underline names are flight leaders
4. Re-evaluation transferred W.C. Clarks claim to 66th Fighter Wing, his assigned unit.
5. J.W. Browning's claims were reduced to 1 from 3.
6. When POWs W.R. Dunlop and J.R. Sloan returned, they put in claims for one each, which were allowed.

LAST SEEN IN COMBAT AREA

Statistically, it had been stunning victory for THE YOXFORD BOYS, with 56.5 victories and three P-51s and pilots lost. Statistics, however, are of little comfort if you are one of those on the debit side. On the credit side, there were no 357th fatalities - all three losses survived as POWs, and their stories are well worth telling.

1st Lt. George Behling was a midwesterner from Chicago and on this mid-January day was flying his 42nd mission, having joined the 357th the previous August. On the 24 December mission, he had shot down an Fw 190. On the 14th of January he was flying element leader (#3) in John Kirla's Dollar Green flight. Lt. Jim Gasser was his wingman. The *Luftwaffe* was about to even the score for the 190 he had shot down in December.

George Behling tells his story of "The Big Day": "Berlin is easily descernible by the heavy black flak smoke at our altitude. Suddenly a mass of German planes came screaming down on us from above. The sky is filled with airplanes. I jettison my wing tanks and take a bead on an enemy fighter. A P-51 drifts across my nose at a 30 degree angle in slow motion, so close I still don't know why I didn't tear off his tail with my propeller. I'm completely distracted and lose sight of my quarry.

"I bank to the left and look behind. There is a plane on my tail and it isn't my wingman. It has a large radial engine and is easily idenitified as an Fw 190. What happened to my wingman who was supposed to cover my tail?" Jim Gasser was having his own problems. As Behling broke left into the 190s, with Gasser following, the latter had blacked out, due to disconnected G-suit hose, and when he recovered, Behling was nowhere in sight.

With his wingman gone due to a disconnected G-suit hose, and an Fw 190 on his tail, we return to Behling's own words to describe the traumatic events of the day.

"Now I turn to the left, I've got to out-turn him. I see his cannon bursts, but apparently he can't lead me enough. I wonder what I'm doing here; a person could get killed. Why did I ever want to be a pilot? I'm only 20 years old and should be home, going to school and returning in the evening to my parent's comfortable home.

"I pull into a tighter turn, feeling so many 'G's I can hardly turn my head. Then the stick goes limp, I'm spinning - but you never spin a P-51, it might not come out. My primary training instinctively takes over. I kick hard right rudder, the plane stops spinning and I pop the stick forward. I'm flying again at 20,000 feet.

"This time I turn to the right and look behind. The son-of-a-bitch is still there. He followed me through a spin and 10,000 feet. It can't be, these German pilots are supposed to be undertrained wet-behind-the-ears kids. Same scenerio. Tighter and tighter to the right. More cannon bursts. Another spin, coming out at 10,000. He's still there.

"Well, if I can't out-turn him, surely I can out-run him. I shudder at the thought of one of those cannon shells tearing through my plane. In fact, I'm utterly para-

Another view of Rocco LePore's PRETTY PAT after its landing accident on 10 January 1945. Here an armorer is clearing the guns.

lyzed with fear. I point the plane at an approximate 10 degree angle toward the ground and open the throttle full. It's working, he's falling behind, out of range. Now I'm at tree top level just west of Berlin passing over the Elbe river. My engine sputters, intermittently spewing white clouds. I cut back on the throttle and lean the mixture, but it gets worse. Suddenly the engine goes dead streaming two contrail like bands from each side.

"I'm directly over a dense forest, no place to land. Pull up and bail out. But I'm going less than 200 mph, not enough speed to pull up to an altitude that will give my chute time to open. Look for a place to put this baby down dead stick - it was my worst thing in basic training!

"There - 20 degrees to the left is an open field running parallel to a railroad track. I'm barely flying, so don't turn too sharp, the stick is mushy. I'm lined up, 50 feet, gear up. Then, in front of me - high tension wires. I close my eyes and pull back on the stick, bounce over the wires and hit the ground with a thud. Its a frozen plowed field and my plane skids along like a sled, stopping 50 feet short of a line of trees. Open the canopy, no one around, but I hear an engine, and look around, there's the 190 coming right at me. He doesn't fire and passes overhead."

Since no one was in sight, Behling headed for the tree-line, but was soon captured by four homeguardsmen, who marched him back to his P-51 "Chi-Lassie". There he found it swarming with people, and with children already playing in the cockpit! Behling remembers: "It was a sad sight, that beautiful airplane that had been my faithful companion for so long just sitting there with its torn undercarriage and twisted propeller just as helpless and forlorn as I. This 'Little friend' was down and out. Then a horrible thought crossed my mind - I had not turned off the gun switches. If one of those children pressed the switch on the stick it would cut at least ten Germans in half.

"An officer approached me. He was a Colonel, home on leave from the Russian front, and he spoke English. He said: 'For you the war is over, I bet when you took off this morning you didn't think you would be here this afternoon'. I don't think I ever heard truer words. I told him about the hot guns, but he shrugged and led me off the field."

So began George Behling's journey to *Stalag Luft III*, where he remained until liberated by the Russians, who threatened to send all the POWs home via Moscow. Whether they ever did or not, is unknown, as Behling and a friend did not wait to find out, but left camp on their own, eventually arriving back in Chicago at his "parent's comfortable home".

Lt. George Behling's handsome G4-J, which was not so handsome after its engine failed while Behling was being chased by an Fw 190 on the BIG DAY. Behling put it down on its belly and went off to a miserable few months as a POW.

THE AMAZING SURVIVAL
OF JIM SLOAN AND BILL DUNLOP

Major Guernsey Carlisle took off on the 14th leading Cement Squadron, but soon aborted with an overheating engine. His wingman, Walter Corby, who was to die in an AT-6 crash two weeks later, returned with him as escort.

Other aborts in Cement Green and Blue flights caused considerable confusion, with the result that the two seemed to have combined with Jim Sloan leading, Henry Hare on his wing, and Bill Dunlop as No. 3 with Bill Thompson, who was to die two days later in a crash near home base, as No. 4. For Sloan and Dunlop, it was going to be the most exciting day of their life.

Lt. James R. Sloan was flying his first mission in ten days - his idleness the result of a back sprain suffered during a basketball game on 5 January. He was one of the fall replacement pilots, having joined the Group in October. He had shot down an Fw 190 on 27 November, and during the great Christmas Eve air battle, had knocked a 109 off Colonel Dregne's tail. This was his 43rd mission and he was flying his P-51 Q-PEE, s/n 44-14784. It must have been quite distinctive, as its tail section had been damaged and replaced but not painted to match the rest of the aircraft.

Jim Sloan, writing 40 years later, remembers: "Although my plane was running smoothly, my flight was falling behind even at full throttle. I motioned Dunlop to take the lead and was about to abort when the action began ahead and below our altitude of 26,000 feet. Dunlop dove into the melee and I was too far back to give him cover and did not follow."

Sloan then spotted a flight of four Me 109s about 500 feet below and headed into the bomber stream. A 270 degree diving turn brought him in behind the 109s, where he got numerous strikes on one of the 109s. At this point he became aware of a single 109 making a pass at him from the 4 o'clock position. "I broke right into him, but he shot away my canopy and the fuselage was severed behind the cockpit. I recall hitting the seatbelt release and being thrown clear." In a report written after his escape in 1945, and in a recent letter to the author, Sloan says he may have collided with the 109, as they were "very, very close".

"When I came to, I was falling face up. After several attempts to turn over so that I could determine my altitude failed, I pulled the rip-cord. When the chute popped open, the engine and wings crashed on the ice of a small pond, and the tail section was second, and I was a close third, just seconds apart. My free fall was nearly 25,000 feet.

With no handicapping injuries, Sloan was able to avoid capture until early evening, when he was arrested by a city policeman in a nearby town. Lt. William Dunlop was, like Sloan, an old hand. by January. He had flown a noteworthy, planned, but unauthorized solo mission to Norway the previous September. He had scored two victories during the confused fighting during the airborne invasion at Arnhem, and had added a third on the 24 December mission.

There is no better way to tell of the events after Dunlop dived into the swirling mass of enemy aircraft, than to quote in its entirety, the encounter report he filed soon after the war.

There were many miraculous escapes from death in WWII, but Dunlop's is certainly one of the most amazing: "I was leading Cement Blue flight at 21,000 in trail of white and red, when large bogie gaggles were called in at 12 o'clock heading for the bombers. I jettisoned tanks and climbed at full throttle, reaching 30,000 feet as the enemy contacted Cement. 109s were in the sun above, so I dove into the main gaggle below, passed through two groups of 109s and 190s, firing and being fired at. I then tacked onto a gaggle of approximately 30 109s, somewhere around 20,000 or lower. I lost Blue 3 and 4 at the very first gaggle, but believed Blue 2 was still with me. I began firing at the apparently tail-end-charlie 109 in the gaggle and he began a fairly steep dive, kicking rudder violently. I had to cut throttle to avoid over-running and I fired each time he skidded through my sights.

"I hit him repeatedly from wing tip to wing tip. The canopy flew off to the right and the pilot came out the same side, barely missing my wing as I passed between him and the smoking 109. One fraction of a second later, it felt as if my guns were firing without me pressing the trigger, and the controls went out, completely dead. I watched one of my left hand .50s blow out through the wing skin and my fuselage tank caught fire. The ship was in a drifting dive and going straight in.

"The pressure held me in the right of the cockpit and was powerful enough so that I couldn't raise my hand to release the canopy. Then everything blew - wings, canopy, tail section and fuselage seperated and seemed to blow in different directions. The canopy must have left first, as I felt flame sucked in the cockpit, was cooked on the forehead and then felt the cool air as I was blown from the rest. I landed still in the bucket seat with armor attached and shoulder straps neatly in place. The engine and one wing lay together about 50 feet away, and the pieces were still floating down all about. Another 100 yards away, lay the Me 109 ammo still popping."

Although the above narrative does not say so, Dunlop did bail out after a fashion. When the P-51 flew

into pieces, throwing him clear, he was at about 5,000 feet. Although badly disoriented he finally managed to find and pull the ripcord, after which he immediatly hit the ground. As he says in his statement he was still in his seat (with the armor plate attached) when he landed. The most amazing aspect of his escape was that, although still strapped in the seat, the back pack chute was able to deploy in the small space available and dump him on the ground with minor injuries.

Dunlop managed to untangle himself from the wreckage and travel a short distance before he was captured. He and Jim Sloan were united the next day at the German airfield at Stendal. From there they went through the usual POW routine, ending up at *Stalag Luft* 13, Nuremburg where they met 357th pilot John Templin, and a week later Edward Haydon.

Both Sloan and Templin escaped from the infamous 75 mile march of 5,000 POWs to the Munich area, and after traveling 10 nights and over 100 Km, they finally made contact with U.S. troops of the 12th Armored Division.

364th pilot Captain Chester Maxwell was having an exciting day also. In the midst of the huge aerial struggle, having lost the rest of his flight, he drove several gaggles of e/a away from the bombers, shot down three 190s, and was chasing a 4th. At this point a yellow-nosed P-51 shot away some of his controls, knocked off his canopy and tore large holes in his wings through which ammo belts were flapping in the wind. Realizing his mistake, the yellow nosed P-51 flew away leaving Maxwell to struggle on with a faltering engine, towards friendly territory. After a long slow trip he arrived at tree top level at the city of Antwerp and bellied the P-51 into a British army parking lot.

Two of 363 Squadron's old hands, Bud Anderson and Chuck Yeager, had taken off with the mission that morning. Why neither are found on the victory list for the day, makes a fitting end to the story of "The Big Day".

Both men were completing their second and voluntary, combat tours - time to go home. Anderson, being squadron operations officer scheduled the two as spares, but since they believed there was little chance of combat with e/a they had hatched a plan. They would leave the formation after take-off, and if not needed, go off on an aerial tour of Europe. They followed this plan. Among the delights of the tour was the dropping of their tanks on Mont Blanc and straffing them, and the buzzing of a hotel on Lake Annecy. Both are near the Swiss/Italian/French border and far south of all the action.

In his book TO FLY AND FIGHT, Anderson wraps up the story: "We'd just shot up a mountain in a neutral country, buzzed half of Europe, and probably could have been court-martialed on any one of a half-dozen charges. It didn't matter, we were aglow. It was over, we had survived, we were finished, and now we would go home together. What a way to go! It had been one hell of a wonderful day.

"It was late when we landed at Leiston. Ours were the last two planes back from the big raid on Berlin. We'd flown more than a thousand miles. A small crowd had gathered as I taxied up to the hardstand. Nice gesture, I thought, a celebration. They knew I'd flown my last mission.

"What they also knew, which I didn't, because we been out of radio range, was that the Group had set some kind of record, they had handed the *Luftwaffe* its greatest defeat of the whole *dammed* war, and we'd been goofing off! Heino (his crew chief) jumped up on the wing almost before the plane stopped rolling. 'Group got more than 50 today', my crew chief said as he helped me unbuckle. '*Must* have been something, how many did you get?' 'None' I confessed in a small strangled voice. I felt sick".

LIFE ON LEISTON AIRFIELD 1944/45

Dawn has not yet broken through the cold swirling mist at Leiston Airfield in the county of Suffolk, on England's North Sea coast. It is January, 1945, and many of the 1500 men of the fighter group and its supporting units are still secure in their cots. However, many others have been awake all night as numerous shops and offices require 24 hour manning.

Among those awake and hopefully alert, were the CQs, which meant "Charge of Quarters", an old army term for the NCO who manned the unit's Orderly Room during off duty hours. It was a duty that rotated among all the unit's NCOs and for eons, the CQ has been irreverently referred to by several other rude terms. As dawn approaches the three squadron CQs go forth from the orderly room to rouse their comrades, the pilots and ground crews, to face the coming day. He had been jarred from late-night lethargy from Group Operations, which at some time during the night had received, by teletype machine, from 66th Fighter Wing, the Field Order for the coming mission.

The Field Order (FO) originating from 8th Air Force Headquarters, spelled out the mission objectives, units involved, bomber routes to the target, fighter rendezvous times and locations, radio codes and all other necessary information for the unit to play its part in the continuing air assault on Germany.

As the CQ went from nissen hut to nissen hut, the routine was about the same. He stepped in the door, flipped on the light switch, and said in a loud voice;

"Briefing 0700, maximum range, maximum effort". Normally only the time varied depending on pilot's briefing time. In the case of the pilots' huts, he woke only those scheduled to fly that day.

The first item on the agenda was breakfast at the big consolidated mess hall or the officer's mess. From there it was off to the flight line via GI truck, bicycle, or on foot (it was a mile or less). With the crews on their way to the Mustangs huddled under their cockpit covers and the pilots drifting into Group briefing, the day's activities were beginning to accelerate. For centuries, large military bases have tended to be self-contained cities, and Leiston Airfield, station F-373, like dozens of other 8th Air Force installations which sprawled across East Anglia was no different. The 1500 men (and the few women nurses and a half dozen others who manned the Red Cross club) provided all of the usual town services and a few others of a more war-like nature.

The mission of these 1500 men was to provide as many P-51 fighters and their pilots over Europe, as they were ordered to that they might smite the enemy and so win the war. The dominate factor on Leiston and all other fighter fields, were some 75 to 85 fighter aircraft and a roughly equal number of pilots. Everything else and everyone else was in existence to support them, and for no other reason. Therefore, the primary function of this book is to tell the story of these few pilots and their machines. However, the support crews were of vital importance, and we have tried to tell their story also. Here we will present some insight into "A day on the flight line and other comments".

Our narrative started on a cold misty January day in 1945. The weather was entirely typical of that winter. The weather office for station F-373 reported at the end of the month: "January, 1945, proved to be the coldest, and one of the most difficult months for flying weather the group has so far experienced, minimum temperature for the month, 16 degrees F, was reached on two days, the 25th and the 27th. Average temperature for the three days was 25F, with fog on all three days. Mean temperature for the entire month was 33, with ground and runways either frozen or covered with snow and ice on 18 days."

The report continues with equally dreary facts, but this is enough to give the weather background for the period.

We have chosen January, 1945 as our lead-in as it was a fairly typical month except for one day. The 14th of the month was not typical, as on that day - since known as "the big day", the 357th shot down 55.5 enemy fighters in a great air battle in the Berlin area - the highest score ever in USAF history for one group.

We have left the ground crews on their way to their individual aircraft, and it might be instructive to discuss maintaining of an aircraft in a flyable state. It is not always obvious to those outside aviation (and to some in it), the critical importance of quality maintenance in the operation of airplanes. In military operations it can mean the difference between success and failure of the mission, and the spectre of aircraft and crew loss always hangs over operations due to mechanical failure of some part of the machine.

Another view of HURRY HOME HONEY, taken from the waist window of a 34th Bomb Grp. B-17, which Peterson had come upon and stayed with due to their battle damage. Please note the tail number is blurred, it should be 414868.

Across the North Sea from Leiston Airfield and throughout Central Europe, the ground crews of another air force - the *Luftwaffe*, were doing much the same as those at Leiston. Of them, their commander, Hermann Goering, said:, "Without their service nothing can be achieved. I must say that their endurance, their skill, their patience, although different, is in every way the equal of that of the aircrews." Although one of the major villains of WWII, his words are still a great compliment to ground crews of all air forces.

In the 357th, there were two levels of maintenance, the flight line crews assigned to individual aircraft, and the hangar crews which handled heavy maintenance, such as engine changes etc. A third higher level on base the 469th Service Sqdn. which did the more complicated jobs that the Squadrons were not equipped for such as wing changes, major battle damage etc. When ground crews are mentioned, which is seldom, it usually refers to the Crew Chiefs, but most 8th Air Force fighter units assigned three men to each airplane. Besides the Crew Chief usually a Staff Sergeant, there was an Assistant Crew Chief, a Sergeant, or "buck Sergeant", and an Armament man, a Corporal or Sergeant. Those picked as Crew Chiefs were usually in their '20s, or the very elderly - in their 30s. The writer was 19 and assigned as an Assistant Crew Chief. Unless one was on "other duty", both the Crew Chief and Assistant arrived at their aircraft at the same time.

Cockpit and wing covers and the pitot tube cover were removed first. The propeller was then pulled through a few times and the pre-flight inspection begun. Compared to military aircraft of later years, the P-51 was remarkably simple. Nevertheless the pre-flight as laid out in the manual was quite lengthy. Most of this consisted of visual inspections, many of which had been completed on the post flight the previous day. All reservoirs were checked for fluid level, coolant, hydraulics, battery, engine oil and fuel. An inspection was always made under the aircraft for coolant leaks which often occurred due to temperature changes. It was often difficult to tell coolant from water, but touching a bit of the fluid to the tongue would reveal the difference, as coolant had a bitter taste (and was poison if consumed).

If all visual and servicing checks were satisfactory, the engine run was done, using the battery cart to save the internal battery. Because the seat was rather deep to accomodate the pilot's dinghy pack, a cushion in the seat helped to reach the brakes and provide better vision. Brakes were set and the seatbelt fastened around the control stick to provide up elevators during power check. Flaps were left down, fuel selector to either main tank, throttle cracked open and mixture control to idle cutoff.

After yelling "clear" to be sure there was no one around the nose, the starter switch was engaged (the P-51 had a direct drive starter), along with engine prime. As soon as the cylinders began to fire, mixture control was moved to "run". Propeller was already in full increase RPM, and the throttle was set at 1300 RPM for warmup.

Since this book is not a manual on the P-51 the various checks will not be detailed but the major ones will be mentioned. After engine oil and coolant temperatures were in the green, the engine was run to 2300 RPM and magnetos checked. With each mag off, the maximum allowable RPM drop was 100. Propeller governor was also checked at this RPM. Maximum RPM was 3,000 but this was for takeoff and not used on ground run.

After the engine was shut down and everything checked OK, it was mostly a matter of waiting. Fuel and oil trucks cruised the taxiway and all tanks were topped off after the run. Windshield, canopy and rear view mirror were polished for the tenth time or so. The Armament man had long since arrived and charged his guns, so all aircraft on the field had "hot" guns long before takeoff. Gun switches in the cockpit were off of course, but occassionaly one had been left on and the pilot gripping the stick could fire a burst, terrifying everyone within range including himself.

Pilots usually arrived 15-20 minutes before engine start time, via overloaded jeep or weapons carrier. After the pilot was strapped in with the help of the crew, his goggles and windshield were given a final swipe as engine start time came and some 60 Merlins coughed into life around the airfield hardstands. Then chocks out, and with a wave of the hand to the crew, each aircraft took its proper place on the taxi strip, in a snake-like procession toward the active runway.

The ground crews, and everyone else in the airfield area, usually sought a vantage point to watch the take-off - always an exciting event, the sound and sight of 60 or more overloaded Mustangs getting airborne remains a vivid memory.

Mostly responsible for the heavily loaded condition were the two long-range fuel drop tanks. "For want of a nail", the old saying goes, "the battle was lost". (reference is made to horseshoe nails, of course). Almost as humble as the horseshoe nail, was the droppable fuel tank, so vital to the successes of the U.S. fighters in Europe. Most of these were of paper composition (some were metal) units holding 108 U.S. gallons, built in huge quantities by British companies. They were installed and filled the night before the next day's mission. During operation they were pressurized to insure positive feeding at altitude, by the exhaust side of the engine vacuum pump. The piping for this and fuel flow were rubber tubes with glass elbows which would break away cleanly when the tanks were dropped. Even though they were pressurized, it was necessary to coax fuel into the system during preflight.

After switching to drop tank position, the engine would often die and the selector switch was quickly put back to main and then back to drop tanks until they fed properly. On the mission they were always dropped when empty or earlier, if combat demanded it. With all 15 fighter groups operating, 8th Air Force fighters could require 1800 tanks per day.

During mid-day, while the mission was out, the line crews were in a state of suspended animation. It was mostly free time, to attend to laundry, read the squadron bulletin board to see when mail call was and to check to see if your name had appeared on any unwanted, but unaviodable extra duty rosters. There was also time to check in to the Post Exchange for a candy bar and to take in noon chow at the big consolidated mess hall.

Regardless of what they had been doing during the time the mission was out, the aircraft crews always "sweated out" the return of "their" airplane and pilot, and when both returned safely, it was a great relief.

Whether crews had a close relationship with their pilot or not, depended on several factors such as how long they had been together, the pilots general atitude toward enlisted men and whether or not he was an outgoing individual. In later years, several pilots told this writer they regretted not have been closer to their crews, but that they had been too engrossed in the realities of combat and possible death to do so, certainly a reasonable point! Few pilots seldom thought about such concerns and looked forward to combat.

Although the word "hero" probably never occurred to the crews, they were well aware that the pilot was the one doing the fighting and sometimes dying, not they. In most cases there was considerable affection for their pilot and they were proud of his achievements. There was always a period of depression when an aircraft and pilot failed to return, and in many cases the cause never filtered down to the ground crews. In a day or two, a new P-51 arrived and a new pilot, and the war went on.

The average mission was four or five hours and by the time of the ETR (estimated time of return), everyone was back on their hardstand. If the Group came into sight in proper formation and to the rising snarl of many Merlins, it was probable that there had been no combat. If they straggled back in small groups or individually, it was certain there had some kind of action. Missing red tape on the gun muzzles was a final confirmation.

This fine view of Peterson's famous HURRY HOME HONEY was probably taken on the continent in January, 1945, when bad weather forced the Group to lay over in France several times. Its serial number was 44-14868 and the exhaust staining is very evident which has also dulled the national insignia on the fuselage.

As each P-51 turned into its proper parking place, blasted the tail around, shut down the engine and chocked the wheels, the mission was over for another day - one more toward completion of pilot's tour. After the pilot had brought any malfunctions to the attention of the crew and departed for de-briefing, there was considerable work ahead to complete the post-flight inspection and repair the discrepancies. If luck was with them, the airplane could be "put to bed" in time for evening chow and the work day had come to an end. Often it did not work out that way with work continuing into the night.

Our narrative started before dawn on a dreary January day and we will close out this month with a typical mission report from that month, again illustrating the bad weather of that period.

On 16 January, two days after the Group's astounding success over Berlin, Major Carlisle led 54 P-51s on a heavy bomber escort. He reported: "Take off 0924, down approx 1600 at various bases on continent. Group RVed (rendezvoused) with bombers at 1100 Zwolle at 24,000. Left bombers at 1400 at Strasbourg. Weather bad. 10/10 cloud over target. Group instructed to land on continent, returned to UK on 19 Jan. Lt. William Thompson, 363rd, killed in crash near Framlingham."

Thompson was a victim of the bad weather, only a few miles from home base. He was one of the seven who died during January. One of these was SSgt. Melvin Schuneman, a Crew Chief and the only ground crew man to die in an aircraft accident. He was killed on the 27th in another weather related crash, along with pilot Lt. Walter Corby in the Group's AT-6.

Whatever else they may be, wartime airfields, of any era, are seldom boring. Dramatic and memorable events are played out almost on a daily basis. The word "memorable" is used with some trepidation, since many of these WWII events are gone from the writer's memory. However, surviving documents, photos, and input from those with better memories make it possible to relate some of these.

Leiston Airfield was within a few miles of the coast of the North sea. As such it was often the first airfield seen by pilots of battle-damaged aircraft and many such cripples landed there, some with no further incident, others with various degrees of crashes. One of these which ended in a fiery spectacle occurred late in May

1944. Captain William "Obee" O'Brien describes what happened: "After a mission flown in the early afternoon, I was in the cockpit of my plane and my Crew Chief, Jim Loter, was standing on the wing. We saw a P-47 taxiing from south to north on the perimeter track on the 363rd squadron side of the field. The Jug was moving fairly slowly and he then pulled into an empty hardstand just across from where I was parked.

"As he turned, I could see white smoke starting to come from the lower fuselage, well back from the engine, about where the turbo supercharger exit was located. I told Jim to try and get to the Jug with our fire extinquisher as the pilot shut down the engine.

"The smoking aircraft was facing to the west and about this time, its guns started to fire and the pilot was out of the plane and standing on the hardstand. It is well known that the Jugs had eight .50s. All eight were firing and believe me that was the first and only time I've ever heard that much firepower released. Needless to say, neither Loter nor I could get to the jug which proceeded to burn and fire its guns. I imagine everyone within four miles wondered what the hell happened.

"The story I got was, the Jug pilot was short on fuel, to the extent that he might not make it, landed at the first base he saw, planning to refuel and then proceed to his home base. He got refueled alright and was taxiing to takeoff when he heard a loud bang, so he pulled into the nearest hardstand. He had been doing some strafing on the way home from his mission. The loud bang was probably a 20 mm, or larger shell that had lodged in the fuselage and finally exploded possibly caused by taxiing across a rough spot, which was enough to activate the fuse. This Jug pilot was one lucky man!"

The writer was present and like everyone else, headed for a low spot in the terrain. The P-47, its unit and pilot still unknown, was a total loss. Group records are silent in regards to any damage from the runaway firepower. Gunfire of a more sinister nature had hit Lieston Airfield during the D-Day period. (described elsewhere.)

We have discussed here only briefly, some of the daily activity at a typical fighter station in those long-gone years. It was, of course, a much more comlplex and interlocking society, but it is hoped this will have given the flavor of the times.

End Notes:
1. JG 4 carried Black and White stripes on the rear fuselage.

CHAPTER 8:
AFTER THE BIG DAY

Taken in the winter of 1944/45, this attractive group stands in front of B6-W TEXAN. Lt. Col. Guernsey Carlisle (left) was one of several senior officers who joined the Group during this period. He commanded the 363rd Squadron from late September into January. We don't know who the beautiful women are, however, Bud Anderson (center) and Chuck Yeager (RT) profess not to recall their identities.

The *Luftwaffe* again disappeared from the skies after the debacle of the 14th, but Bob Winks who had claimed 2.5 victories on the 14th, caught an inattentive Me 262 pilot the next day doing slow rolls over an airfield near Augsburg and added its flaming wreckage to his final score, bringing it to 5.5 and putting him solidly on the ace list.

The horrendous weather especially manifested itself on the 16th when most of the bombers, after lengthy assembly and a long tiring ride to the targets, found them covered with 10/10 cloud. At the end of the day, B-17s were scattered all over western England at various bases other than their own and some 70 B-24s were forced to land on the continent. Joining them were most of Major Carlisle's 54 P-51s, which spent the night with the 9th Air Force's 416th Bomb Grp (A-20s) and in fact, did not return to base until the 19th.

The weather gods continued to disrupt any semblance of normal operations and during the period 20-27

January, there were aircraft dispersed around the continent some examples of superb flying, a "well done" for the men of the DF (Direction Finding) section in their little wooden silo in a farmer's field near base and finally, the death of two more men.

With the aircraft and pilots returning from three days in France on the 19th, the mission on the 20th started out normally with Lt. Col. Andy Evans leading the usual escort. The 8th had put up over 700 bombers all of whom bombed thru 10/10 cloud with radar.

1st Lt. Dale Karger was leading Greenhouse White Flight with Lloyd Zachariae on his wing. Dale Karger recalls his big day: "As I remember it was a clear, blue sky, probably about 50 to 80 miles west of Munich. There was snow on the ground, and we soon spotted a train. We did a strafing run on the train and then spread out a little as was proper for this kind of an attack. When I was within range and started firing, one of my guns 'ran away' (would not stop firing when the trigger was released). I turned a few degrees to keep from hitting anyone and started to climb. I did not realize my wingman

Zachariae was still with me (He was). As I reached six or seven thousand feet, the gun still firing, someone called out 'two jets circling above us'. Peterson had already started a climb, but I was ahead of him and my runaway gun had stopped now - out of ammo.

"The two jets continued to circle at about 20,000 feet, but when we got to about 1,000 feet below them, they split up and started a descent. The one I had latched onto headed east toward Munich in a slow let-down. Having a good speed advantage he began to slowly pull away from me. He was about four or five miles ahead of me and I was about to give up, when he started a left hand turn. He was over Munich by this time at about 5,000 feet, and I thought he might be trying to draw me over the flak zones in the city. Anyway, when he started his left turn, I did the same, hoping I could cut him off, and it worked, except that he was crossing in front of me. I had the diamonds on the gun sight all the way closed (maximum range) and decided to lead him a little. Almost instantly when I fired, I thought I saw a strike around the cockpit area and he immediately bailed out.

"On this mission my own plane was in for repair, therefore I was flying Steve Wasylyk's MY LADY DIANE. He told me it had a smooth running engine and to be sure to bring it back in one piece. As fate would have it, I did not! As Zack and I started home, we found the weather was now IFR (Instrument Flight Rules) in eastern France and we went on instruments in snow and cloud.

"By this time we were aware we were not going to get anywhere near England, as we had used a lot of fuel in the jet chase and probably were down to about 50 gallons. I called for a vector, but he was 125 miles away, so I gingerly started a let-down, not having any idea of the terrain in this area.

We broke out at about 500 feet in a snowstorm, but there were no airfields in sight and Zach's fuel gages were bouncing on empty. I told him to belly it in while I looked for a 9th Air Force airfield. Zach did so and reported he was down and OK, just as I spotted an airfield on which P-47s were parked. I landed on the steel mat runway with snow and it felt like I was on a sled. The brakes did no good and I went off the runway into a pile of frozen dirt. That took care of Wasylyk's MY LADY DIANE.

"I retrieved my gun camera film and after an interrogation, I found I was near Rheims where I spent the night in a hotel after I had done some pub crawling. Very strange, I thought, as we were probably within 60 miles of the front lines. The next day, Zach and I were taken to Paris where we caught a ride back to England on a C-47."

This was Karger's fifth victory, (of a total of 7.5) making him an ace, and one of only three who became

aces while still teenagers. He did not turn 20 until several weeks later. One Me 262 destroyed - one to go.

Richard "Pete" Peterson, Greenhouse Red Flight Leader: "With the upper jet eliminated, the lower one headed down for home in a hurry. I rolled over, split-essed and poured on the power. In no time, compressibility with no control at speeds in excess of 650 mph. After finally getting control at the lower denser altitudes, I pulled out in a wide sweeping arc just over the treetops and pulled up behind the 262 for a perfect 6 o'clock shot. Unfortunately, I was out of trim and my tracers went right over the top of his canopy. He left me in a cloud of kerosene exhaust as if I were standing still. In the meantime, my flight had caught up with me and we headed for Lechfeld Airbase which I anticipated was his home field. We flew over Lechfeld at about 6,000 feet. The field bristled with flak emplacements. There were about 100 jets nose to tail parked on the inactive side of the field which meant they were out of fuel, or pilots, or both. We were not sure of the traffic pattern or which end of the runway the jet would use.

"Tiede and I cruised toward the south end. Haydon and Wright spotted him on the approach at the north end. Haydon headed for the jet, but he was too high and made an easy target for the flak guns. When they opened up, I swear they put three or four 20 mm shells in the same hole - in the engine! On the R/T, Haydon said he was on fire. He pulled up and bailed from about 400 feet and landed on the airbase, ending up as POW. Roland Wright, following Haydon, was fence post high and the flak never caught him. He wiped out the 262 on its approach.

"The remaining three of us re-assembled south of Lechfeld and I called for them to check their fuel. We were briefed before the mission that our minimum gas to get home that day would be 135 gallons, due to strong headwinds. I had 135 gallons, but Wright, who was tail-end-charlie, was down to 85 or less. It was pretty obvious that we were not going to make it home so it was imperative that we find a "friendly" airport.

"Flying at 8,000 feet, deep in Germany in nasty weather, we headed west through a weather front with icing and instrument flying conditions. We finally broke out and spotted a large town near a river and we turned to it. Lo and behold there was an airfield covered with snow, no tracks from aircraft traffic but there appeared to be an Me 109 near a hangar. I told Wright to land, tail first because of the unknown depth of the snow and wave his arms if they were friendly. If they were not, then get the hell away from the plane so that I could shoot it up. Out came a Citroen full of people to the airplane as I circled with Tiede. Finally Wright waved his arms and Tiede and I landed. We were southwest of Paris at Auxerre, and the

A well known 362nd Squadron P-51, 44-13691, still bearing its nude and
Roberson's victory symbols, but with the name PASSION WAGON removed.
Sometime in the fall of 1944 it was transferred to the 364th Squadron where
it became C5-V and later with the name GYPSY, the nude remaining.

Inspection time for ROLLA U-bar.
Here the author (rt) and SSgt. Ray
Morrison wash the engine with a
spray gun and an ammo can of aviation fuel. Those were primitive
days!

front lines were 60 km down the road at Dijon. When Wright landed, his engine quit. The 109 I had seen was gutted and abandoned.

"Auxerre had a small company of Military Police and the town had been only recently liberated. I asked the MPs for help with communications to get fuel so we could get out of there. But in the meantime we got rooms in a hotel and some food. Our fuel would be coming from Patton's armored units and there was no telling when that would be. The small contingent of French aviation cadets on the airfield pushed Wright's P-51 to the hangar while we waited."

At the 0942 takeoff on the 20th, Andy Evans had 42 P-51s with him, but combat, bad weather and ground strafing broke up the formations after leaving the bombers. Besides Peterson, Tiede, Wright, Karger, and Zach, at least eight others landed on the continent at various airfields. The remaining 30 or so straggled back to home base.

Robert Schimanski, in a recent narrative tells how he did it: "I had helped chase the jets and tried to box them in but never did get close enough to fire my guns. Instead I used up a lot of fuel and then had to think about getting home through absolutely horrible weather. Some of my squadron, the 364th, elected to return with me rather than setting down on the continent. I flew on instruments in a solid overcast for a long time at about 25,000 feet.

"Miraculously, as I crossed the coastline, a single hole appeared through the clouds. I could see the coastline and elected to descend and cross the channel at an altitude of about 200 feet. The ceiling got lower and lower and lower, however, and at about 50 feet I went back on instruments and climbed to about 500 feet. I then called Leiston tower and asked for a heading home and was told that the base was closed and that I should return to the continent, as all other fields in England were closed. I was low on fuel and knew I could not return to the continent, and did not want to ditch in the channel.

"I continued on with the other P-51s on my wing and told DRYDEN (357th code name) that I did not know who closed the field, but as leader of part of Greenhouse Squadron I ordered the field to be re-opened and all operations would proceed as normal. The flare truck was to be in full operations at the end of the runway. Pilots flying with me were advised that we would first try to land under my instructions, and if I could not make it, they were to climb to 1,000 feet, make sure they were over land and bail out.

"After all these years I now find it interesting to note that after hearing my decision to re-open the field, no superior officer on the ground countermanded my order."

Dryden gave me a heading and I approached the base at an altitude of about 250 feet on instruments with my wing man tucked in close. Flares were fired through the overcast and I knew I was over the beginning of runway 24. I then made a single needle width turn of 180 degrees heading into the downwind leg at 60 degrees climbing on instruments to about 400 feet to give me a little breathing room (at 200 feet on instruments it is difficult to breath normally - now is the time for self discipline!).

"I then flew an extra long down wind leg in order to have extra time to again line up on the runway. I completed another 180 degree single needle width turn, got another heading from Dryden and discovered I was exactly on course. Lowered partial flaps, dropped gear, cut throttle and started descent from 400 feet very carefully. At 300 and 200 feet I could see nothing but slop all around me. At about 150 feet I couldn't see ahead, but I got the first glimpse of mother earth straight down below me. Full flaps, cut throttle, and saw the beginning of a runway while looking straight down. I sat down on the left side of the runway, with number two on the right etc. We landed without mishap, and then had extreme difficulty in taxing to our revetments because of rotten visibility.

"My loyal crew chief, Sgt. Wilbur Reich was there waiting for me. I had brought his airplane home once more. Reich was one of the more experienced Crew Chiefs, but had already lost two pilots and two P-51s through no fault of his own. He and I got a new P-51D, code C5-0, serial number 44-14334 and he and I successfully finished my tour of 70 missions without a scratch, bullet hole or flak damage. Later I discovered that my aircraft ended up in a scrap yard in England and was bulldozed flat by a D-8 cat. Seems like the 8th Air Force should have given it to me and told me to fly it home!"

One other pilot who has left us his impressions of the period is Don Kocher, then 1st Lt. 364th Squadron: "Due to low fuel state, several pilots had already left the formation, searching for an emergency field at which to refuel. With my flight leader's permission, I left also, Lts. George Kouris and Dave Williams joining me. We were vectored to an RAF base at Antwerp. We were well recieved and refueled, but they would not clear us to return to England due to the weather. They put us up at a hotel in Antwerp which was fine except for the incoming German missles. The Germans were trying to knock out the port of Antwerp and cut off the supplies for the Allied armies. These V2 rockets were falling all over the place with some hitting the port. We were in a very nice room on the eighth floor, but it felt like it was right in the line of fire.

"We went exploring the city and found a bar in a cellar where the action seemed to be. There were lots of young people and plenty of beer which we proceeded to sample. While in the bar, several rockets had landed and sent clouds of dust and plaster from the ceiling. The only reaction from the natives was to cover their glasses and pay no attention to the explosions.

"The next morning after breakfast, we were taken back to the airfield, but a ground fog prevented any flying. There was an Me 109 parked on the field and we were on the wing looking at it when the earth suddenly erupted a few hundred feet from us, leaving a crater 30 feet in diameter.

"With the fog clearing, the tower cleared us to leave. I was checking the mags on the edge of the runway when a small building on the other side of the field went up in a cloud of dust. That made my engine run just fine and I turned on the runway and took off with the other two close behind.

"After a couple of hours on instruments, I called Earlduke (Leiston flying control) for landing instructions. Capt Botti answered with 'Boy, are we glad to hear your voice, welcome back'. That made me wonder what was going on as no one had ever greeted me that enthusiastically before! That night in the club, Botti told me he thought I was Col. Dregne, that I sounded just like him on the radio. I never got that welcome again."

Joe DeShay's diary: "20 Jan. 1945. 17 ships (364th) on mission. 12 didn't return, including Pete. Out of gas or something"'

We have devoted considerable space to the period in late January because we are fortunate to have so much input and these wonderful stories go a long way to show what it was like in the last months as the war wound down. However, we are not yet finished with that period in late January, 1945.

21 January: The AT-6, with Lt. Walter Corby and SSgt. Melvin Schueneman departs Leiston, bound for airfields in France to repair three of the Groups' P-51s. A few days later, both men died in the crash of the AT-6.

The AAF accident report and surviving documents are sparse, but the story of the two men has been compiled as closely as we will ever know. The AAF accident report says that after their arrival on the continent they were held over for several days at Melun. The AAF Form 1A shows the date as 21 January, at which time the airplane, an AT-6D, serial number 42-84593, had 376.5 hours flying time, with two minor discrepancies. Under remarks, PILOTS AND MECHANICS, is the terse statement "Missing."

The Group mission on the 21st did not return to base until 1430 hours, so it is likely that they had gone to France to repair aircraft from a previous mission. On the 21st, Captain Fifield and Lt. Myers had landed, according

to the mission report, "north of Lille". However, in recent correspondence, Dan Myers recalls that they needed no assistance and returned to base the next day, never having seen the AT-6 or its crew.

The accident summary reports that after being held up at Melun for "several days", they went on to Amiens where they landed to avoid a cold front. This would probably have been the 25th or 26th.

The only pilot we know who had his aircraft repaired by Schueneman was Lt. Joe Cannon who had blown a tail wheel tire on his P-51 LITTLE JOE, B6-B while landing on a grass strip near Fontainbleau (possibly Melun). In any case Schueneman would have replaced Cannon's tail wheel sometime between the 21st and the 25th, after which they proceeded to Amiens, some 60 miles north of Paris and on a straight line to Leiston. On the 27th, Corby was cleared by 363rd Operations to proceed to home base. The Operations orders show they took off from Amiens at 1330 hours.

The weather in southern England was not good, but as any airmen knows, they may have been afflicted with "get-home-itis". At approximately 1430 hours, the aircraft crashed at Swingate near Dover. Visibility is given as 1,000 yards with light fog and 10/10 cloud at 200 feet. The accident report says it is assumed the pilot was on instruments, but he may well have been staying below the overcast at 200 feet, attempting to remain VFR when contact with the terrain brought the flight to an end.

Under NATURE OF ACCIDENT, the report ends with "undetermined" Other than those who died in the C-47 crash after the war, Melvin Schueneman was the only 357th enlisted man to die in an aircraft accident.

DeShay's diary: 25 January 1945. Cold! 16 degrees F. Released from combat mission schedule. Pete Peterson in C5-T, along with V, F, and another P-51 came back after landing in France."

We had left Major Peterson and several others awaiting fuel in France. Peterson takes up the story on their return home: "Finally, after a five day wait, on January 25th, a truck with a trailer full of five gallon Jerry Cans arrived and the French cadets filled up our planes. The weather was beautiful in Auxerre and we were anxious to get home, so we took off for England. The first knowledge I had of the weather in Leiston was when we were about mid-channel, and I contacted the tower for an altimeter barometric setting so I could have an accurate reading of altitude in an instrument let-down. The weather in mid-channel was a solid wall of fog from 1500 feet down to the water. It looked like a wall of concrete along a straight vertical line. There was quite a roar on the radio when they heard from us because the last anyone knew was that we were in a dogfight with Me 262s five

days ago. Major Gates got on the radio and said that there was no way that we could get in because the field was socked in with fog. He thought we might have to bail out. I thought I would give an instrument approach a try even though we had no GCA (Ground Controlled Approach) or instrument landing equipment on the field.

"At mid-channel we were flying in a "V" formation with both wingmen stacked above me as I started a let-down in an attempt to get under the soup. I got down where the altimeter read "0" and one of the guys said; "Pete, you better get up - a wave just went by!" At that point, discretion was a better part of valor so we climbed back up above the fog to about 2,000 feet. When I guessestimated that we were within the general area of the field, I asked the tower to fire a rocket so we could get a fix on position relative to the field. The rocket came up just above the fog so I told the guys to circle the area of the rocket because I was going to try an instrument approach.

"Since our longest runway had a bearing of 240 degrees, it gave me a clue that maybe I could apply my high school geometry to an instrument let-down and we could make it in. So I headed out a little way toward the channel and turned straight north at 0 degrees. As I kept talking on the radio for bearings, they fed me bearing to the field back of me. First, 300, then 290, then 280. When they gave me 270 degrees (making a 90 degree angle with my heading true north) I clocked the time that it took for the bearing to change to 240 degrees. Twice that time was the time it would take to reach the field on a heading of 240 degrees, which was the runway alignment.

"The runway 240 heading and a heading of 270 makes a 30/60 degree right triangle as I flew north. In a 30/60 degree right triangle, the side opposite the 30 degree angle is half the length of the hypotenuse. In this case, the 'hypotenuse' would be the line of approach toward a 240 degree bearing, turning toward the landing on the runway. As I descended toward the runway and got to about 50 feet above ground, I could see straight down and spotted the end of the runway. I knew then that we could make it in by just repeating what I had done. I climbed back up on instruments and picked up Roland Wright who flew off my right wing and we went through the same trianglulation.

As we turned on the approach and started the let-down on instruments, I let down my wheels, and Wright lowered his wheels and stayed back just far enough to keep me in sight and follow my instrument flying. I dropped flaps, he dropped flaps. As I got to about 50 feet,

One of the ever-busy refueling crewmen pumps fuel into the right wing tank of NEVADA SKAT KAT. The drop tank is steel, not the familiar paper type, although the capacity is the same at 108 gallons.

I spotted the runway and called it out to him. He picked up the sight of the runway and landed. I did the same thing with Tiede and he landed. I then did a tight 360 turn about 50 feet off the ground and landed.

"The people in the tower could hear us, could hear the tires squeal on landing, could hear me powering up to go back up, but could not see us. At no time did the tower see us until we taxied by. The tower and the DF guys did a helluva job or we could not have made it. It was the best flying that I had ever done — or ever since!"

2nd Lt. Will Foard was in the control tower, and "Observed" (or heard) Peterson, Wright and Teide return to base: "The day after our group of eleven replacement pilots arrived at Leiston, we were on a tour of the base. We were in the control tower seeing how they operate when a flight of P-51s radioed that they were preparing to land. This flight had been delayed in France waiting for fuel after a mission. From the tower we could see nothing of the runway or any of the field. We could hear a plane land and the leader gun his engine to climb back up to get another wingman.

"The first sight we had of any of the planes was when they taxied by the tower on the perimeter track. The flight leader brought all the planes in safely while us 'fledglings' stood on the balcony gripping the cold iron rail with white knuckles and holding our breath.

"You can imagine the effect that episode had on us green pilots! You can also understand the admiration of the flight leader with his flying ability and guts. Pete Peterson was to be the dean of "Clobber College" who would check us out in the P-51 and instruct us in combat flying. Our training in the states didn't prepare us for this kind of flying - it was a real good lesson on the importance of instrument flying!"

We have devoted much space to the events of late January, the shooting down of two Me 262s, the crash of the AT-6, and Bob Schimanski and Pete Peterson have given us their stories on how they penetrated the zero zero weather and returned home.

"During that period, and under similar conditions, other pilots had returned to Leiston instead of landing on the continent. Possibly some of them used similar tactics to return safely to runway 24 (the longest of Leiston's three runways, at 6,000 feet). However, we have no input from them, and will let Peterson and Schimanski's superb job of flying stand for any others that might have come home under similar conditions.

This is ace Donald Bochkay's B6-F on the morning of 15 February, 1945. Lt. John Casey was the pilot. After a lengthy taxi period and a hurried takeoff, the coolant overheated and the relief valve "popped open", leaving a trail of coolant vapor. Unable to make it to a runway, Casey put it down on the field on its belly. The accident report blamed 60% pilot error and 40% supervisory error.

This panoramic view of Leiston Airfield looks very peaceful, but probably is not. G4-Z HOT SHOT's engine is running chocks have been pulled. George Roepke, Crew Chief and his assistant are right, waiting for the aircraft to taxi onto the perimeter track. Across the way, Kit Carson's Crew Chief, John Warner and his partner have just seen Carson leave the hardstand and taxi out of camera range. Although there are no other P-51s visible, there are undoubtedly 60 or so of them forming up for takeoff, out of the camera's view. The large number "24" on the tower indicates the runway in use.

FEBRUARY, 1945 - THE END OF WINTER?

The Group's only excuse for existance, of course, was to fly and fight the common enemy. Station F-373 was its "Hometown", and like all hometowns, many events of life went on there surrounded always by THE MISSION. As the January desk calender pages were torn off and discarded, we provide some observations of interest from the month of February:

FEB 1; LtCol. Dregne, the Group commander was promoted to Colonel.

FEB 2; Joseph Broadhead was promoted Lt. Col.

FEB 3; Robert Foy became a Major

FEB 4; John Kirla and Otto "Dittie" Jenkins appeared on orders dated 3 Feb as official aces.

FEB 5; Kit Carson received a Silver Star (the Army's third highest decoration) for achieving five victories in one day, and driving the enemy away from the bombers.

FEB 6; The Daily Bulletin announced that a Spitfire would be on display at the control tower with pilot available, on Thursday, the 22nd.

FEB 7; The base had its first formal parade, in class A uniform, for the inspection visit of General Partridge (Commander 3rd Air Division), and General Woodbury, (Commander 66th Fighter Wing) on 16 February. The parade is said to have gone off well, despite the unfamilarity with parading.

FEB 8; An unusually large amount of corned beef was delivered from depot, making it difficult for the Mess halls to come up with variety.

FEB 9; Due to the heavy losses to infantry units in the Battle of the Bulge, voluntary and non-voluntary selections were made to replace them.

FEB 10; Flying control announced that in the year since February 1944, 150 aircraft had been saved from gear-up landings by red flares from the mobile control van. (author's note: An amazing number!)

FEB 11; The Flying Evaluation Board met during the month and considered two cases, one for inherent lack of flying ability and lack of confidence, the other was extremely nervous and tense while flying. The board recommended that both be removed from flying status.

FEB 12; At this time there are between 1600 and 1700 people assigned to the base.

It was not a good month as losses totaled six pilots, only Lt. George Kouris surviving as a POW. Richard W. Taylor was KIA as was Captain James Browning, on his second tour. (See Casualty chapter for details of Browning's collision with an Me 262.) Lt. Holsey Johnson was killed while still in Clobber College, as were Ralph Eisert Jr. and Robert Hoffman, who collided during a training flight led by Captain Carson. (author's Note: On a visit to England in 1988, our small group of 357th veterans were invited to join a "dig" at the crash site of Hoffman and Eisert. Engines, guns and other wreckage was recovered, much of which went to local museums.)

On the credit side, Lts. Roy Anthony and Dan Myers were recovered from the North Sea by Air Sea Rescue units. It was also not a good month for adding to the victory score. The Operational Summary makes note of February's first mission on which the B-17s were out to knock down a rail bridge at Wessel - which they missed. Not surprising as the mission leader reported 10/10 cloud over the target. On the 11th they tried again on the bridge, but the records are silent as to results.

February the 3rd saw the most destructive raid of the war by the 8th, on Berlin. The targets were not just the city area but specific military headquarter buildings, the Air Ministry and other important goverment buildings. Besides widespread damage to these, there were heavy civilian casualties as would be expected. With over 2400 bombers and fighters involved it was a massive raid, but for the 357th, it was mostly a five hour ride marred by the loss of George Kouris to flak. Only the 55th and 56th Fighter Groups found enemy aircraft to mix it with, claiming 19 between them. The 357th had to be content to vent their hostility on a few German vehicles.

Bad weather, as usual, restricted activity during the first half of the month with most of the 19 missions being flown in the second half. At this stage of the war, most of the 8th's bombs were falling on communication and oil targets, with the 357th's part mostly routine - if any war activity causing widespread destruction can be called routine. Most missions were a combination of escort, and, weather permitting, ground strafing of a wide variety of ground targets.

German property shot up on the ground was mostly the usual locomotives, rail rolling stock, road traffic, radar buildings, military barracks and few aircraft (on the 25th, two He 111s, a Ju 88 and an Fw 190).

There were however, a few targets of interest, such as:
A motorcycle
15 Soldiers
Staff car and Jerry officer
10 flat cars with unassembled aircraft
A bread truck
One crew chief shack
One windmill
High tension lines (twice)

Questions that come to mind: How did they know it was a bread truck? Since it is very difficult to hit high tension lines with gunfire, how was this done? It is suspected that part of the lines came back to Leiston attached to a P-51.

There was on the 4th of February a brief flurry of aerial activity. With little need at this stage of the war for bombers (which in any case had little chance of survival in the daylight skies), the *Luftwaffe* converted two of its bomber units to fly the Me 262. These were KG 51 and KG 54, which became KG(J) 51 and KG(J) 54, the "J" indicating fighters.

On this date the 1st *Gruppe* of KG(J) 54 took off from Giebelstadt on its first mission since transitioning from Ju 88s. Leading was *Oberstleutnant* (Lt. Col.) Volprecht Riesdsel *Freiherr* (Baron) zu Eisenach. Before they could get to the bombers the leader was killed when he collided with Jim Browning. Captain Don Bochkay shot down one of the former bomber pilots bringing his score to a 12.5. (Details on Browning and Bochkay can be found in the chapter on the jets).

Lt Johnnie Carter describes his efforts to bring one of the speedy jets to bay: "I was leading Cement Squadron, Green flight when we encountered some Me 262s in the vicinity of Fulda at about 24,000 feet. Cement Blue flight leader dropped his tanks immediately and made an attack on the four 262s that were low and to our left. Cement Blue Leader took one of the 262s that went to the right and I took the other. I followed him for ten or 15 minutes.

He was out of range and gaining distance on me all the time. I was still after this one when I spotted another Me 262 about 12 to 15,000 feet below me and he appeared to be in a glide. I gave up on the one I was chasing, rolled over and split-essed on the one below me. I gained on him very rapidly and gave him several bursts. I was out of range but saw a few strikes.

I was still closing on him when the pilot bailed out. The 262 appeared to have his jets off and was gliding, probably to land. The pilot bailed out at about 12,000 feet and the plane went down thru the clouds. My entire flight had lost me during this encounter. Ammunition expended: 753 rounds."

Although not the assigned pilot, Lt. Joe Black takes it easy on the wing of BUTCH BABY which had been Broadhead's MASTER MIKE, G4-V, 44-11798.

Robert Foy, now a Major, "was there" also on the 9th of February, leading Cement blue flight. Although pilots did not normally write their own encounter reports, a few pilots often provided very lengthy detailed narratives, which they might have written themselves. Foy was one such, as was 364th's Pete Peterson.

Foy's quest to add a formidable "jet job" to his mounting score was frustrated on the 9th. Although he bounced a flight of them and managed to get many strikes on one, resulting a heavy smoke trail from one engine, he could claim only a Probable. Foy's lengthy report ends with: "I had to pull off as my engine was extremely rough, vibrating so that I could hardly read the instruments. I pulled 64 inches of Mercury (manifold pressure) at 3,000 RPM for over 10 minutes.

"If the Me 262 did land safely, he weighed considerably more than he did when he took off and his ship will not fly until they do an extensive repair job. I fired all my ammunition and from appearances of strikes on e/a, fully half of the rounds hit him. I claim an Me 262 probable." Alas, the powers that be did not give him credit for that 262 - that would have to wait a month or so.

M.E.W.

In the 1930s the Army Air Corps experimented with ground and air control of fighters, using radio, but without radar, little was accomplished. The big breakthrough on radar fighter control came with the RAF system used during the Battle of Britain, which played a large part in winning that battle. When the 8th Air Force arrived in England with almost zero knowledge of the subject, they merged with the British and learned rapidly.

The ground-based fighter controller was of very great importance and assistance to the fighter leaders and the technology rapidly improved, so that by the beginning of 1945, the improved MEW (Micro Wave Early Warning) system was in operation and in fact, 357th attached personnel such as Claude Early, were heavily involved (See Communications section). By February, the MEW controllers had moved to the continent, giving their equipment the range to cover most of the battle area with their mobile sets.

The Operational Summary for February comments on the use of MEW: "M.E.W. has proved an invaluable aid to successful operations, not only in helping fighters to make a rendezvous with bombers, but also in giving warning and direction of enemy action and as emergency fixing stations. The problem of bomber escort, the primary work of 8th Air Force fighters at this time, has been greatly simplified by M.E.W. directing the fighters, not only to the bomber stream but to the proper box or boxes."

Lt. Col. Jack Hayes, Group Operations Officer, also outlined the new tactics to deal with the formidable Me 262 jets: "Two factors were considered: (a) Jet aircraft are always encountered in comparatively small formations, (b) the prime objective of this type aircraft has been to get to the bombers and their only tactic against our fighters has been outrunning them. Considering the above, it was decided that jet propelled aircraft would not be attacked unless attacking the bombers or in dangerous proximity to them. If the jet propelled aircraft were attacked, instead of an entire squadron making the "bounce", as on former occasions, the squadron leaders will delegate a flight or flights, maintaining a ratio of two friendly to one enemy aircraft. Furthermore, aircraft making a "bounce" will not drop wing tanks until it is evident that enemy aircraft are going to press attacks against the bombers or will be overtaken. By using this procedure a maximum amount of escort is kept in close support of bombers and long range is maintained by eliminating useless and premature dropping of combat tanks."

Although the Group had little luck finding airborne enemy aircraft, they managed to reduce the *Luftwaffe's* aircraft inventory by burning a few of them on the ground. On the 28th, Major Foy, leading Cement Squadron, spotted a large number of all silver Fw 200 Condors parked on Lubeck/Blankensee Airfield. As he circled the field he spotted 40 or 50 other aircraft hidden and dispersed among the trees. Foy and his flight made two passes with Foy himself doing most of the damage, destroying two Ju 88s, an Fw 190 and an Me 109. Pete Peterson also took two flights across the field adding to the carnage. Total claims were five twin engine and two single engine aircraft destroyed and a number claimed as damaged, and assorted other targets. Not a great total, but worth the effort as there were no losses to the considerable amount of flak.

Thus ended the month of February, 1945.

MARCH - IN LIKE A LION

Except for the isolated encounters with Me 262s, there had been little contact with enemy fighters since "The Big Day" - until the 2nd day of March.

Six weeks of "no e/a seen" ended abruptly when mission #278 exploded into combat NE of Leipzig when enemy fighters were intercepted and driven away from the "big friends".

The 8th Air Force was out in force, with hundreds of heavy bombers striking mostly oil targets in the Magdeburg, Dresden, Leipzig areas, and under escort by a swarm of Mustangs. These P-51s from five fighter groups were to be responsible for another day of disaster for *Luftwaffe* units JG 300 and JG 301, which attempted to intercept. It is difficult to give exact figures after a span of 40 plus years, but one *Luftwaffe* casualty list thought to be accurate, lists 30 aircraft lost. Seven of the pilots are listed as wounded, the rest dead or missing. In the German book *START IM MORGENGRAUEN* (Take off at Dawn), Werner Girbig says JG 300 and 301 lost 23 pilots dead, one missing, and seven wounded.

The escorting Mustangs did their job well and few of the 109s or 190s got through to the bombers, the general area of combat taking place on a line from Magdeburg southeast to Dresden. The five fighter groups with some 300 Mustangs, were engaged in this area and although each group can be plotted as to its area of engagement, the action was by no means this neat. Reading the pilots' encounter reports, one finds many comments concerning

the confusion and mixing of the groups once the melee began.

Captain Donald McGee was leading the 357th and he reported: "R/V 0950 Rheine with 3rd, 4th, and 5th combat groups, 2nd force. Intercepted 25/30 Fw 190s and Me 109s behind and below bombers, 1010 NE of Leipzig and combat ensued to deck."

Of the air-to-air claims by the 357th, one was a long nose Fw 190D shot down at low altitude by Captain John Sublett. The remaining twelve were all 109s one of which was jointly shared by Captain Robert Schimanski and Lt. Dale Karger both 364th Squadron. Their encounter reports are of considerable interest because both make comment on the aircraft markings of their victim, a fairly uncommon occurrence.

Their reports are quoted here. Schimanski seems to have engaged first: "I was leading Greenhouse Blue Flight escorting Vinegrove 2-4 when enemy fighters were called in east of Magdeburg at about 1000 hours. I saw an explosion below me and started spiraling down with my section following. At about 10,000 feet I recognized an Me 109, dropped tanks and started to attack. This single 109 was chasing four P-51s from the 339th Group. He had a black and white barber pole spinner, OD color ship, with a large red and yellow stripe on the fuselage. This guy was exceptionaly good as he could really handle that ship. After about five minutes of torrid combat, one of the 339th boys got some good strikes and the 109 snap-rolled and started spinning. The 339th then left and I followed the e/a down.

"Below the clouds he recovered and then he and I had another go at it. After five more minutes of head-on passes I was joined by Lt. Karger. Both of us started to work on him which proved sufficient. Lt. Karger hit him in the cockpit area and the e/a dove in with me hot on his tail strafing him on the ground. I claim one Me 109 destroyed together with pilot, shared with Lt. Karger."

Dale Karger had mixed it up with a 109 with no results, lost his wingman and dived below the cloud deck, where he got into a turning duel with another 109: "With the 109 still turning, I pulled thru him in a slight stall, enough to give him a good burst right in the cockpit. It was just about this time that I saw Captain Schimanski get behind him and then drop out again, so I got on him again. When I hit him it must have killed the pilot because the plane dished out and pancaked into the ground, its wings came off and it caught fire. Then Captain Schimanski strafed him and I followed taking pictures. I claim one Me 109 destroyed, shared by Captain Schimanski.

"The 109 had a black and white barber pole nose and bluish gray paint job with large red stripe and a yellow one on each side, and a big number "7" on the fuselage." Four plus decades later, Dale Karger still remem-

These two wonderful photos show MAN O WAR co-starring in some publicity activities. Although the P-51 was a 362nd Squadron machine, all four pilots (all aces) were from the 364th. In the photo above we see Bob Winks comforting the horse while Paul "Shorty" Hatala helps Don McGee mount the steed. In the photo below, we have a change of riders, still with Bob Winks leading and Richard "Pete" Peterson mounted, while the other two observe the strange sight. We don't know the date, but it is late in the war, as Peterson is a Major here.

bers; "This German was a rather good fighter pilot, and really tested my skill. I give a great deal of credit to having a superior aircraft. In a vertical turn I actually pulled my nose through the 109 in a high speed stall while pulling quite a few 'G's. When I couldn't see him anymore, I started firing and then slacked off my turn and when he reappeared he ran through my gunfire. I don't think I could have got him any other way."

From these encounter reports we know that the 109 had a red and yellow stripe on the fuselage and a number seven. The red and yellow stripes would be the late war identification bands carried by JG 301, just forward of the tailplane. The *Luftwaffe* casualty report referred to above shows only one lost aircraft with a tactical number "7", actually "Yellow 7". This was Harald Ruh, an NCO pilot of the 15th *Staffel*, IV *Gruppe*, JG 301. The *werknummer* of Ruh's 109 was 491200 and his loss is listed as near Stresow, in the vicinity of Magdeburg.

Werner Girbig, in SIX MONTHS TO OBLIVION, lists the fate of several 15th *Staffel* pilots and confirms that Harald Ruh and his "Yellow 7" were shot down near Stresow. In their encounter reports, Karger and Schimanski seem to disagree on the color of Ruh's airplane with the latter saying it was O.D. and Karger remembers it as bluish gray. O.D. would be unlikely, but the upper surface may have been oversprayed in varying shades of green. This may have been what Schimanski saw, while the lower surfaces could have been gray. After so many years, Schimanski still remembers the skill with which the pilot of "Yellow 7" handled his Me 109.

While there is no way to prove conclusively that Harald Ruh was the tiger who fought it out with Schimanski, Karger and several 339th Group Mustangs, the evidence is strong that this is indeed the story of how Harald Ruh met his death one morning in March, south east of Magdeburg. Although it is not part of this story, it is a strange quirk of fate that another *Luftwaffe* pilot of JG 301 who was shot down during this same general engagement, and was one of the lucky few to survive, is today a good friend of this writer.

The 357th Group suffered heavily on this date also, losing five Mustangs. F.O. Mallione, was last seen south of Magdeburg and was almost surely shot down in combat with JG 301. He did not survive. The other four were victims of ground fire during strafing attacks after the air battle. Captain Alva Murphy and Lt. Mathew Crawford were KIA, while Lts. Ray Bank and Rocco Lepore survived as POWs.

Although March had "come in like a lion" with extensive combat and the heaviest one day loss, it was not typical of the rest of the month. There was only one more occasion that brought contact with German fighters.

Mission-wise, March was a busy month with 21 flown, often with the Group split further into A and B Groups. On one day to Hamburg, the Group put 60 Mustangs on the mission (one loss, no claims). On the 3rd of the month, there was contact of a sorts with Me 262s, the Group managing to fend off most of the six but they did succeed in shooting down one B-17. Captain John Sublett did put a few rounds of API into one of the 262s which; "poured on the coal and took off at an astounding hurry".

From the 4th through the 18th, the monthly Operational Summary shows a long list of zeros under losses, claims and ground targets. This does not imply that these missions were without drama. As usual, the Mission leader continued to report fascinating events under the heading "Observations": 5th of March, Major Foy "On withdrawal in vicinity of Namur, a flight led by Lt. Col. Hayes encountered a B-17 doing lazy 8s on a heading of about 350 degrees. This aircraft, tail number 297322 had the wing markings and Square A on the tail of 94th Bomb Grp. In addition, tail painted yellow with a broad red stripe around fuselage at waist door. The bomber fired green/green flares at our flight. Col. Hayes flew alongside the B-17 whose engines were OK and showed no flak damage. Believing it lost, he indicated correct heading to co-pilot then had to slip under B-17 to avoid being rammed. As they were low on gas, the flight set course for base thinking the bomber would follow. However, when last seen NW of Aachen this B-17 was on a heading of 30 degrees."

These were indeed the markings of the 94th Bomb Group, but the USAAF loss list for B-17s does not show this one so it must have returned to its base at Bury St. Edmonds.

In March, Colonel Irwin Dregne, the Group Commander, was awarded The Distinguished Service Cross (DSC), the second highest ranking gallantry medal, and the first to a member of the 357th.

During this month Lt. Tom Beemer returned from German POW camps. Beemer had been shot down by a B-17 gunner over a year before and was repatriated to Allied control due to extensive injuries sustained in his bailout.

By late March the 3rd *Reich* was tottering - Allied and Soviet armies were compressing what remained, in a huge deadly vise. Soviet forces had broken through in the Lower Vistula and were racing for Berlin. Earlier in the month U.S. and British troops had crossed the last great barrier, the Rhine.

As U.S./British and Soviet forces converged, there was the potential for clashes between the two, especialy in the confusion of the air war with hundreds of aircraft milling around in a confined space, all looking for something to shoot at. This potential became a reality on

the 18th of March. The 357th mission report: "One flight escorted a B-17 of the 379th Bomb Group, serial number 338420 to north Stettin on the way to Sweden. Plane was having trouble with three engines. Flight was fired on by three Yak fighters near Stettin, who broke away after identifying our aircraft."

There was considerably more to it then that! The main U.S. unit involved was the 359th Group, which apparently shot down several Soviet fighters (The Russians said six) of the Yak 9 and La 5 types, with several pilots killed.

357th pilots involved were Capt. Alan Crump, Lts. Ernest Tiede, Frank Kyle and Floyd Atkins who were escorting the B-17. They spotted three Russian fighters, one of which fired a burst at Kyle and then broke off and flew away; 357th pilots fired no shots. There were no casualties on either side.

The Russians chose to make a major international event out of it and high level messages flew back and forth for two weeks before General Hap Arnold, Chief of Army Air Forces, sent a formal apology to General Antonov, Chief of Staff of the Soviet Army. The event then became a minor forgotten event in the last days of the war.

The next day, the 19th, there was a clash with more formidable opponents, Me 262s, this time in formations much larger than previously. These were, according to author Bill Hess, in his book THE GERMAN JETS VS USAAF, from the *Luftwaffe*'s premier jet unit JG 7. Remarkably, they were able to put 45 aircraft aloft this day. Lt. Col. Andy Evan's report describes the events: "36 Me 262s attacked bombers at 1408 hours, at Chemnitz. They came in at B-17s from 6 o'clock, slightly high, in waves of 12, each wave consisting of four flights of 12 each in V formation. The 262s seemed to be attacking at relatively low speed.

"Our 63rd squadron leader Col. Hayes was able to prevent the last two waves from hitting the bombers, these jets broke and went into a slight dive breaking into two ship elements which easily out-distanced pursuit. No other attacks were made on our combat groups. The weather was ideal for jet attacks as they attacked out of cloud cover thereby preventing our proper positioning and early interception.

"After leaving the bombers, a flight led by Major Foy observed a flight of P-51s being pursued by three Me 262s in a V formation. The jets were in a flat dive and passed over our flight evidently not seeing them. Major Foy opened fire on one at 600 to 800 yards. After two short bursts the left nacelle started smoking. The jet split-essed to the left and crashed west of Giessen. This combat occurred at 1510, at 6,000 ft in heavy haze." This was Foy's 14th-victory, and his first "jet job".

An hour before Foy's shoot-down, during the initial 262 attack on the bombers, Captain Robert Fifield had knocked down one of the attackers using the same tactics Foy did later - he lobbed some .50 caliber API projectiles at one of the 262s at very long range. To his surprise he got enough hits on one engine to slow the jet down, allowing him to close in and finish it off. Lts. Joe Cannon and Johnnie Carter got hits on two jets but "no joy".

The jet attack on the bombers had been successful, with four B-17s shot down. Evans counted 19 chutes. A few of the more interesting "Observations" by the mission leader during the month:

2 March: Wreckage of two aircraft, believed B-24s, observed one mile off Ostend with ASR boats standing by.

9 March: One chute east of Frankfurt at 8,000, 1010 hours. No plane visible.

9 March: B-17, tail number 297844 crashed west Weisbaden, 4 chutes.

12 March: 2 large Motor vessels in Flensburg harbor and 1 very large ship at Rendberg. 1130 hours, 8 mine sweepers sweeping ahead of 6 cargo ships heading NW thru Fehmarn Belt. 4 Mine sweeps, moving off coast north of Roskock.

15 March: B-17 marked square K with "P" on yellow tail, hit by flak 1550 over Salswedel, bellied in near Steinhuder Lake.

15 March: An airfield north of target and believed to east of Paarchim with single east-west runway, contained 20 plus He 111Ks, one B-24.

19 March: One green nosed P-51 crashed 20 mi east of Leipzig (359th)

21 March: B-17 headed for Russian territory, exploded due to jet attack.

21 March: North of Erfurt, approx 4 blocks of buildings with letter POW in white on roof.

22 March: P-47s observed dive bombing airfield, large fires resulted.

23 March: B-17 shot down by flak, Hamm. No chutes. This bomber spun down hitting another B-17 which lost wing tip, but recovered and continued on course.

We have listed only a few of these observations, most of which will remain a mystery, but they did give a vivid picture of the scope of the air war.

On the 20th, the German pilots of two Fw 190s and a single Me 109 showed a distinct deficiency in aircraft recognition. Colonel Dregne: "Me 109 leading two Fw 190s encountered west of Dummer Lake at 1745, 12,000 feet and engaged. Apparently they believed our planes were friendly." Two were shot down, one 190 escaping, its pilot to bone up on recognition. Lt. Col. John Storch on the 23rd: "Two tail gun positions in bombers of 95th BG, fired on P-38 in target area at 1150. The P-38 had solid red vertical stabilizers. At least ten strikes seen." By this time of the war, the 8th Air Force had no fighter groups flying P-38s. It may have been an F-5 from the 7th Photo Group.

During March, another technical innovation arrived at Leiston Airfield in the form of AN/APS-13 tail warning radar. Some P-51Ds in the 20 and 25 production block had the sets installed at the factory, but other sets were installed on base. Aircraft with this set can be identified by the three small rod antennas (appx 4" long) on each side of the vertical fin. The set gave a visual (red light) and audio signal when any aircraft approached within four miles of the tail. The limitations can be imagined and it is uncertain how well it worked. With the war winding down, only a few 357th aircraft had it. Photo evidence indicates at least 20 sets installed.

B6-J WHOLE HAWG (name probably in red) was the mount of Major Donald McGee, who commanded the 363rd Sqdn. for about a month early in 1945. It was 44-15888.

OPERATION VARSITY - THE RHINE

By the third week in March, the Allied armies occupied the west bank of the Rhine River - the last great barrier to Germany itself. Earlier in the month elements of the 9th Armored Division had found, to their astonishment, that the Ludendorff rail bridge at Remagen was still standing and intact, although in fragile condition and laden with explosive charges. Showing great dash and daring, small units of infantry and engineers raced across, cutting and removing explosive wires and charges.

By evening, tanks and infantry of the 9th had a strong bridgehead on the east side. By the 23rd, the time had come for the major assualt and crossing of that great river. On the afternoon of that day, Colonel Dregne attended a group commander's conference and on the morning of the 24th, briefing for the first mission was at the very early hour of 0300.

The next days' massive thrust across the Rhine could not have been much of a secret (the Germans would have been well aware of it anyhow!). The news had already filtered down to the flight line, as Joe DeShay's diary entry for 23 March records: "Big Day tommorrow as "Monty" (British General Sir Bernard Montgomery) is all set and all ships to be ready."

The Rhine crossing was the third great airborne operation of western Europe (D-Day and the Arnhem affair were the others). The 8th Air Force was out in force and many of the targets of the 1700 bomber sorties were *Luftwaffe* airfields. All 15 fighter groups were operating

with a total of 1800 fighter sorties. Many groups flew two or more missions on the 24th and during the day claimed 53 enemy aircraft shot down with nine losses. THE YOX-FORD BOYS' first mission, a small group of 27 P-51s led by the Group Commander, took off a minute before 0600 and returned five hours later having encountered little of interest.

1st Lt. Otto D. Jenkins had joined the Group as a Flight Officer the previous September. (His army nickname was "Dittie", although his wife and family did not call him that.) He had been with Colonel Dregne on the early mission and was killed on return to base. The following is from the AAF accident report, by the accident board, Lt. Cols. Jack Hayes and John Storch, and Major Robert Foy.

"Otto Jenkins, 1st Lt. 0-1998554, was dispatched on an operational mission on 24 March 1945, as white flight leader of the 362nd Squadron, flying P-51D-20 aircraft number 44-63199. This was to be the last mission of Lt. Jenkin's tour of combat. Upon return to the field, Lt. Jenkins proceeded to "buzz" the field at a low altitude. On several occasions he flew over the building area at such low altitude that personnel in the vicinity were forced to lay flat on the ground to avoid being hit; trees and buildings were narrowly missed.

After the third pass, Lt. Jenkins pulled up sharply and attempted to split-ess from approximately 1500 feet. The aircraft was observed to mush at the bottom of the pull-out and one wing hit a tree. Wing was torn off, aircraft flipped over on its back and hit the ground catching fire and sliding over 100 yards before coming to a stop. Aircraft was demolished and Lt. Jenkins killed instantly"

"Dittie" Jenkins was a good fighter pilot. This writer had been on his crew. He had 354 hours in P-51s and was an ace with 8.5 victories, four in one day. He let his exuberance overcome his discipline and as many pilots before and since, he paid with his life.

Almost everyone on the base, including this writer, were witness to the "buzz jobs" and ran to the scene, but of course, nothing could be done. The accident board had little choice but to charge the accident to 100% pilot error.

Although there were hundreds of 8th Air Force and RAF heavy bombers operating over Germany, the 357th was not assigned to escort duties. Both missions were area patrols, sweeping their assigned segment of German airspace, watching for enemy aircraft that ventured out from the tree lines they had been hiding under in recent months.

The second group, some 35 P-51s, led by John Storch, took off an hour before the the first group returned to base and they hit "Pay dirt"! The three squadrons had

split up, each on its own and shortly after noon the 364th, about 13 strong, spotted 20 Me 109s flying below them on the deck and dove to the attack. We will quote two of the pilots who claimed one each of the eleven destroyed by that squadron. Capt Paul "Shorty" Hatala:

"I was leading Greenhouse blue flight, flying at about 6,000 feet, when we spotted about 20 e/a on the deck. I picked out a 109 and started turning with him. I got some strikes on the wing. Pieces came off and it went into into a dive. The pilot bailed out and his chute opened. I then saw an Me 109 on the tail of a P-51 and got on his tail and started shooting. After some strikes on his wing and fuselage, he then leveled out and I gave him another burst. Pieces came off and the pilot bailed. As he bailed I tried to shoot the pilot as he cleared the plane, but missed. His chute opened just before he hit the ground. He's a lucky man. I claim two Me 109s destroyed."

Lt. Gilman Weber had taken off as a spare and would normally return to base if there were no aborts. However, he elected to continue on the mission even though not needed:

"I was flying Greenhouse spare when we saw about 20 Me 109s headed west on the deck. We bounced them and as we closed to within firing range they broke into a tight turn to the left. I joined the Lufberry and found it hard to tack on a Jerry and stay because I had no wingman which made me very busy trying to cover my own tail. I finally singled out a 109 that had left the scrap, making numerous turns to the left with him, ending up on his tail and noticed strikes on the wings and fuselage. He started smoking and bellied in, crashing through some trees. I claim one Me 109 destroyed."

Lt. Roland Wright saw the combat, joined up with Weber to come home and confirmed his victory. (Wright had also destroyed one 109 and damaged another). As indicated, the other two Squadrons were patrolling in other areas. Lt. Col. Andy Evans was leading ten Dollar Squadron P-51s of 362 Squadron. "We were flying east of Munster when the 364th Squadron spotted 15-20 Me 109s headed west in the vivinity of Gutersloh. After considerable pleading, I was able to extract from the 364th leader, their position and altitude, immediatly heading toward the area with all possible haste.

"When we arrived there we found that Squadron already engaged and doing a good job, but we were able to plunge in and get a few of the remains. I jumped two 109s who were flying a perfect element formation riding a P-51's tail. They broke as I fired from extreme range to scare them off. As I closed, I fired another burst at one of them and found my guns running away in an uncontrollable fashion. Turning off the switch, they stopped, but when I again squeezed the trigger, the results were the

A lineup of 364th P-51s late in the war. Peterson's HURRY HOME HONEY is third in line. Second in line is probably C5-C, WES'S WICKED WENCH, the pilot may have been Howard Wesling. MARY ALICE, MAD PAPPY identity is unknown, but it may be the 363rd aircraft of Captain Atlee Manthos who did fly a P-51 named MARY ALICE.

Near the end of the war, Donald Bochkay poses with his WINGED ACE OF CLUBS. His final total was 13.88.

This photo from Bill Blystone, (far left, back row) shows ground crews of the 554th Ftr. Trng. Sqdn. Originally based at the fighter training base at Goxhill, the 554th moved south to Leiston in December, 1944, when Goxhill phased out training and the fighter groups took over their own training in their CLOBBER COLLEGES. The 357th supplied the "Dean" and instructor pilots and the 554th maintained the ten or so war-weary P-51s used in the College. Attached to the 362nd Squadron, they were all eventually transferred to the 362nd and the 554th phased out.

same, so I wasted ammo and threw lead all over the sky. After getting several strikes around the cockpit, I observed that, before he crashed into the trees, the aircraft was out of control, so I presume one of my shots had hit the pilot.

At this time, my engine began belching flame and black smoke, making a terrific racket, so as I pulled into the other 109 I was unable to check to see if my guns were firing. However, I gave chase for a few moments, until my engine had me thoroughly worried, finally giving up."

With his ammunition scattered across the countryside and a sick engine, Evans concludes with: "Then I started the long ride home sweating out every mile with just enough power to keep it flying." Mechanically speaking, Evans had had a bad day, but had added one Me 109 to bring his final score to six.

Cement Squadron, too far away to get in on the scrap, arrived too late, but Bob Foy, his usual "tiger" self, managed to knock down a 109 (the mission report says an Fw 190) and then attempting to strafe the wreck and pilot, "My ship continued to mush toward the ground. I pulled back more on the stick and the aircraft snapped to the left and hit a fair-sized tree, growing in a most inconvenient

spot. The impact swung the ship around and my right wing struck a smaller tree."

After this hair-raising experience, Foy regained a semblence of control and, like Evans, brought his battered P-51 home. We don't know what the engineering officer and ground crews thoughts were when they saw it.

Other than Evans, Weaver, Duncan and Gruber added to the 362nd's share, for a total of 16, probably all from JG 27, which lost heavily about this time.

The 30th of March brought a routine bomber escort - nothing of note until the Group made "land fall out" over enemy coast at mid-afternoon. No one knows what caused Lt. Dan Myers' engine coolant system to fail, but fail it did, setting off one of the biggest ASR operations of the war.

Before it ended, partially successful, 93 Mustangs, 38 P-47s, 25 RAF Warwicks, 6 Mosquitos, 3 B-17s, 8 Beaufighters and at least one OA-10 (PBY Catalina) were involved in the effort to retrieve Myers from the North Sea. One Beaufighter and its crew were lost, and the OA-10 was sunk. (for the full story, see chapter DOWN IN THE DRINK.)

CHAPTER 9:
BATTLE WITH JETS AND VICTORY!

Captain Ivan McGuire poses with his "unusually" named P-51D-25, C5-J, s/n 44-72056, which can be seen stenciled on the landing gear fairing door. McGuire almost made it to the ace list with 4.5, the "point 5" being an Me 262 shared with Lt. Gilman Weber.

By the end of WWII, pilots of the 357th Group had shot down 18.5 Me 262s in air combat, nine of these in April - the last month of Hitler's Third *Reich*. However, the struggle against the jets began some nine months before when Major Joe Myers, 78th Fighter Group, shot down the first of the magnificent Messerschmitt Me 262s with his P-47.

Before covering the Group activities during April 1945, we will go back and examine some of the background of the *Luftwaffe*'s Jets and some of the early 357th successes against them. Because of space limitations, only a few of these encounters can be covered in detail.

"I spotted a lone 262 approaching the field from the south at 500 feet. He was going very slow (around 200 mph). I split-essed on it and was going around 500 mph at 500 feet. The flak started coming up very thick and accurate. I fired a short burst from around 400 yards and got

hits on the wings. I had to break off at 300 yards because the flak was getting too close. I broke straight up and looking back saw the e/a crash about 400 yards short of the field in a wooded field. A wing flew off. I claim one Me 262 destroyed."

The above described incident is part of Chuck Yeager's encounter report in which he also claims two other 262s damaged. The date was 6 November 1944, and the location was an airfield six miles east of Assen, Germany. It was the first 357th victory over the elusive enemy jet aircraft. Ultimately, the 357th was to be the most successful 8th Air Force group in the destruction of the jets.

The jet principle, as applied to turbine powered aircraft was well known and by the summer of 1944 when the 262 reached operational status, British jets had been flying for about three years. The Gloster Meteor F.III, in fact, became operational about the same time as the 262. RAF 616 Squadron was the first to be equipped with

Two curious GIs examine part of what looks like the engine tail pipe of a V-1 Buzz Bomb which crashed on base. Many of these passed over the Leiston area and a few crashed on base, but there is no record of any damage from them.

Meteors, and had shot down its first "Buzz Bomb" in August. By January, 1945, 616 had deployed to the continent and become operational. Apparently, the Meteor encountered no enemy aircraft before the war's end, although many "Buzz Bombs" were shot down. If the war had continued through 1945, the Meteor would undoubtedly have become a factor in the Me 262 problem, although it was somewhat slower than the 262.

The U.S. jet effort began with the Bell P-59, but it was in no way a combat airplane, or in the same league with the Me 262. That slot was to be filled with the Lockheed P-80, but that program was beset with problems and it would have been much later before it became operational.

Messerschmitt's Me 262 must rate as one of the great aeronautical achievements of WWII, even with its faults. Its endurance was short and it was not very maneuverable. Its most serious fault however was the unreliability of its powerplants. This was true of all turbine engines, but the Junkers engines also suffered from the unavailability of high temperature resistant metals, reducing their life span even more.

The few faults, however, cannot obscure the fact that this airplane was one of the great aircraft of its era. With very heavy firepower and a speed advantage of almost 100 miles per hour over the best of the Allied fighters, it posed a difficult problem for the Allied fighter force the last eight or ten months of the war.

The 357th was relatively late in coming to grips with the jets and as far as is known, 357th pilots never did actually engage any of the rocket-powered Me 163s. About 300 of these were built and although very fast, it achieved little due to its very short endurance and its dan-

gerous flight and ground characteristics. Although a few were shot down, it is said that fully 80% of their losses were during take-off and landings.

The Me 262 remained elusive after Myers had destroyed the first of the line, and there were no conclusive contacts during September. By the first of October, *Kommando Nowotny*, the *Luftwaffe*'s first jet unit for the defense of the *Reich*, became operational with about 30 aircraft. The unit was organized with two *Staffeln* (squadrons) based at Achmer and Hesepe, near Osnabruck. From this point on, the jet war became a real concern, the bombers were again at extreme risk from German fighters. During October U.S. fighters reported 27 combats with the jets and claimed five destroyed, in addition to two known shot down by RAF units, one by a Spitfire and another by a Tempest.

There was, however, "no joy" for THE YOXFORD BOYS until Yeager broke the ice early in November, as related at the beginning.

The mission on the 6th of November was assigned as a target support and sweep of some four hour duration. Led by Captain Robert Foy, the 55 Mustangs were logged off at 0911 hours. By 1030 they were sweeping the target areas over NW Germany and then provided support for 2nd Division B-24s which were bombing the Mittland Canal and targets in the Minden area (a town some 60 km west of Hannover). Foy then led the P-51s on another sweep in the area north and east of Minden specifically in search of jet aircraft. Foy reported the events as follows:

"Contacted five jets (Me 262s) N of Osnabruck flying in elements of two and three respectively at 10,000. Two flights followed two jets in climb towards Bremen, but jets pulled away after leveling off and believed to have landed at an AD at Delmenhorst (4RW5796), 15 plus Me 262s observed on field which has a green metal hangar and is very heavily defended by lite flak. Flights went in to strafe, shot up three flak emplacements and were driven off by very heavy fire from machine guns mounted on house tops adjoining AD. Same flights observed at 1150, three Me 262 on military highway with evidence of highway being used for take-off and landings. Did not strafe because of gas shortage.

"Another flight followed the other three 262s at 10,000 to AD at 4VR8060. Destroyed one at 1,000 over field, heavily defended by flak and damaging two in vicinity of field. Flight saw four other 262s on field, whose run-ways were estimated to be 6,000 ft long. Two flight straffed AF at 4RW850 on which ten of 20 U/I acft were damaged. The SE enemy aircraft were well camouflaged and some were dispersed in plowed field adjacent to AD. No jets or other enemy aircraft seen in target area. LF out 1230 Egmond."

Foy, the mission leader, had his first chance at the jets but failed to score. In his tactical report, Foy says: "Just north of Achmer airdrome, I recieved a call on R/T at 1100 hours stating that bandits were engaged in area north of Osnabruck. I retraced my course and returned to the area. Flying at 10,000 feet, I saw five Me 262s at 8,000 feet, two of these were about 100 feet lower than the others. I dispatched Cement White and Green flights after the high e/a and turned to engage the low two Me 262s. The e/a were closing in on two P-51s who were apparently unaware that they were about to be attacked. I dove on to the 262s and was closing when the tail end 262 apparently saw me. He started a gradual climbing turn to the left and it appeared he climbed at a steeper angle as he gained altitude. During the climb at an altitude of 15,000 feet, I was closing in on him and always gaining during the climb.

"He continued turning to the left, levelling off as he did so, pulled away from me gradually. He continued to pull away going into a shallow dive on a straight course. He dived into the clouds and I immediately dove under the undercast. The two 262s appeared beneath the clouds and just ahead of me. I took chase but in level flight their speed was obviously greater than ours. I followed them for several minutes and saw them land on an airfield just southwest of Bremen and very close to town.

"I hit the deck and started a run to strafe the field. Immediately a wall of flak came between myself and the airfield. I turned off to the right and passed over a small town named Mahndorf. I observed as I passed over the town that the houses closest to the airfield were used as gun positions (machine guns). I hung to the deck and

made 180 degree turn in toward the field. It was during this run that I strafed two flak emplacements and one machine gun emplacement. The flak emplacement personnel were eliminated but heavy accurate fire from the other emplacements made it impossible to hit the field."

One of the two jets pursued by Foy was almost surely flown by a man named Helmut Lennartz. At the time they encountered Foy, the two had been aloft long enough to be very low on fuel and had hoped to land at Achmer or Hesepe. However, a swarm of U.S. fighters in these areas precluded this and the two made for Bremen, using only enough power to keep ahead of Foy. As Lennartz was on final to Bremen, both engines quit due to fuel starvation and he made a rough landing, damaging the landing gear.

Other than a few ASR P-47s and photo reconn Mosquitos, the 8th Air Force conducted no operations on the 7th of November.

On 8 November, the 3rd Division was recalled and only the 1st and 2nd Division put a few bombs on marshalling yards, canals etc. with light losses. All 15 fighter groups were operating but managed only four victories among them, losing 11 aircraft - hardly a fair exchange.

Four 357th pilots were involved in two separate actions both encounters being in the same general area and within a few minutes of each other. One was near the well-known check point of Dummer Lake, and the other in the Quakenbruck vicinity, a few miles NW of Dummer Lake.

Lt. Warren Corwin, 362nd Squadron, had developed a rough engine in his P-51, 43-12227, in the target area and had taken a course for home escorted by Lt. James Kenney. About an hour into the return, at about 1230 hours, they came upon a box of B-17s with no escort. With Corwin's engine running reasonably well, Kenney suggested they provide escort. His encounter report takes up the story: "As we climbed above them to 22,000 feet, we saw a lone bogey going 180 degrees to the bombers. We broke into it and saw that it was an Me 262. It climbed, turned towards the bombers and passed them. Then it turned to make a pass from ten o'clock. I got on its tail, with Corwin behind me. I began firing from about 400 yards at 30 to 0 degrees deflection. I saw a puff of red smoke come from him. He dove for the deck and Corwin split-essed. I rolled down on him and got on his tail again. He was diving very shallowly and I over-shot him twice, doing 300 mph.

"The first time he kept straight ahead, but the second time he made a medium turn to the left. I out-turned him and got behind him again, firing from 250 yards to zero yards, dead astern, with no observed strikes. Smoke

was coming from the right nacelle, however, and the pilot bailed out at 4,000 feet. The ship was dirty gray with a blue tail and the wings were swept back and narrow."

During this flurry of action, Corwin was hit by gunfire of unknown origin but almost surely from the 262. At the time, Kenney was not aware that the 262 pilot had fired at either of them. However, Corwin had split-essed and disappeared from Kenney's view. We can only speculate that Corwin was attempting to get into firing position on the jet, misjudged his timing and instead became the target. Corwin reported on the RT that he had lost a foot or so of wing and had been hit himself. Kenney never saw him again. He has been reported as landing near Brussels and later dying of his wounds. Despite considerable effort, this writer has never been able to trace Corwin's fate. There was much correspondence between 8th Air Force and Washington, but as late as July, 1945 he was still listed as missing. He is not buried in any of the military cemeteries in Europe nor is his name on any of the Walls of the Missing.

The Me 262 pilot, whose aircraft was hit moments later by Kenney and who bailed out, has been identified as *Oberleutnant* Franz Schall, from *Kommando Nowotny,* and an ace with some 100 victories. Later in the war he was again shot down in an Me 262 and killed in the crash.

A few miles away, at 30,000 feet near Dummer Lake, Captain Merle Allen and his wingman, Lt. Edward Haydon were about to play a part in the elimination of one of the *Luftwaffe*'s great stars.

Greenhouse Squadron had had a good day strafing targets west of Hanover, and during the melee, Allen and Haydon had become separated from the unit and were headed home alone when they spotted the lone Me 262 below them. Both went to max power and gave chase, with Haydon now in the lead. Merle Allen recalls: "As I remember, I saw the 262 from about 25,000 feet and he was flying on the deck going in the opposite direction. We split-essed and had no trouble overtaking the 262 as he probably was returning to base at a slow cruise speed."

The skies were crowded with P-51s and others were also hounding the 262, with Captain Ernest Fiebelkorn of the 20th Group and his wingman also converging on the 262, which led the P-51s over an airfield. The immediate flak response momentarily scattered the Mustangs. However, Haydon and Allen, and possibly the 20th Group machines, again caught up with the Messerschmitt at low altitude and apparently very near *Kommando Nowotny's* airfield at Achmer. Although Allen and Haydon were about to open fire, neither did as the 262 rolled inverted and hit the ground in a giant fireball. Since none of the P-51s had fired, the cause remains unknown, but there was a great deal of flak and the 262 may have

been a victim of this. The pilot of this aircraft had been *Major* Walter Nowotny himself. His death soon spelled the end of the unit bearing his name. Merle Allen did not submit a claim since he had not fired his guns and the victory was credited jointly to Haydon and Fiebelkorn.

In later years here has been considerable confusion and controversy over who eliminated Nowotny. Although Haydon and Fiebelkorn (20th Grp) were credited with it, Bill Hess in his book THE GERMAN JETS VS THE U.S. ARMY AIR FORCE, presents evidence that the victor was Lt. Richard Stevens of the 364th Group. However, neither Stevens or his wingman actually saw the 262 crash, so it seems to remain an open question.

The end of 1944 found the *Luftwaffe* attempting to bring order out of the best way to bring their new weapon into service. By late December the three *Gruppen* of JG 7 were dispersed to three different bases and soon after the first of the year, a second unit, JV 44 was activated (It was of a size between a *Gruppe* and a *Geschwader*). Also close to operational status were three former bomber units being reformed as fighter wings. These were KG(J) 6, 51 and 54. The KG (*Kampfgeschwader*) indicated their former status as bomber wings, and the J indicated their new mission as fighters, (*Jagd*).

Naturally these new outfits were beset with difficulties as it was not easy to retrain bomber pilots to fly the new jets, especialy under the constant threat and actuality of air raids on their bases, shortages of fuel, spare parts etc. It was to be late February before either unit flew its first combat sorties and encountered the swarms of Mustangs in their skies.

Considering the great effort Hitler demanded into making the Me 262 a bomber (against the *Luftwaffe*'s wishes), it is probable that most of the jet sorties in December were hauling iron bombs in support of the German's Ardennes offensive.

Sometime in December or January, Colonel Dregne analyzed the meager information on the Me 262 tactics and wrote the following: "It was found that a flight of four P-51s could box in an Me 262 and prevent it from evading. This tactic is being developed by the Group and will be used when possible. It is considered that if P-51s have initial advantage of altitude and position and a numerical superiority of four to one, jet propelled planes can be destroyed on every encounter."

In retrospect, it sounds a bit optomistic, but if the 262 pilot co-operated and made the requried mistakes, it was certainly possible. In fact, over the next several months these tactics in general did work many times.

By January of 1945, the skies of Germany had long since become very hazardous for any German aircraft. A moment's inattention by a *Luftwaffe* pilot or crew, could be instantly fatal. Such was the case on the 15th. An Me 262 pilot, probably exhibiting his joy at flying such a machine, was spotted doing a series of slow rolls at low altitude SW of Munich paying for it with his life.

On that day the Group was escorting 2nd Division B-24s, which had, due to 10/10 weather over the primary targets, bombed some secondaries. There had been no sign of enemy fighters. Lt. Robert Winks was leading Greenhouse green flight when someone called in an airdrome with some 15 262s parked in a neat row. In his encounter report, Winks tells us what happened: "Major Peterson was leading, but had instructions not to strafe as the Field Order for the day so specified, so he orbited the squadron over the airfield to take photos. While doing this I sighted an enemy aircraft doing a series of slow rolls on the deck and immediately called it in. No one could locate it so I went down from about 15,000 feet, got on his tail, and fired a good burst just as the aircraft was approaching the airfield.

"I observed many strikes, and the fuselage burst into flames. The enemy aircraft crashed on the edge of the field and blew up. The pilot was not seen to get out. Because of camouflage I was not certain of the enemy aircraft's identity until landing at home base when I was informed it was an Me 262."

9 February 1945 - Captain Donald Bochkay: "I was flying wing to Captain Browning who was leading Cement Spares on an escort mission of B-17s to Leipzig, Germany. We were doing nicely on our escort job at 26,000 feet, crossing over bombers and holding a very good formation.

"At 1115, around the Fulda area, four Me 262s were called in by one of our flights, under us about 4,000 feet below, heading toward the bombers. We dropped our tanks and Captain Browning dove to the left for attack. The four 262s broke up, two dove to the right and two to the left. Captain Browning never did get within range of the two going left and down. I climbed high, balls out, keeping the Me 262s in sight as well as covering Captain Browning. I climbed to 28,000 feet and leveled off. Just as I leveled off the two 262s broke right in a steep climbing turn.

"I called Captain Browning and told him I was cutting them off. I dove my ship to gain more speed. The sun was in my favor and I believe the 262s did not see me. I came in on the lead 262 but could not get my sights on him. I passed under the lead 262 and broke hard to the right, coming out on the second 262's tail at a very good range of 300 yards. I fired a long burst as he was pulling away from me, but I observed some very good hits about the canopy and right engine. That really slowed him down.

"The lead 262 headed straight down, the one I hit broke to the left in a gentle turn so I opened fire on him

Lt. Myron Becraft was the pilot of MOOSE. Although it shows seven victory symbols, six of these were for ground claims, his only air victory was in the big battle of 2 March 1945.

again at about 400 yards, and kept firing all the way in on him. I saw many strikes all over him and his canopy shattered, along with large pieces flying off the enemy aircraft. I broke to the right to keep from running into him. As I passed very close to him the pilot was half-way out of his cockpit. The ship then rolled over on its back and the pilot fell out.

"He never opened his chute and the plane went straight in. I then pulled up in a climbing left turn to rejoin Captain Browning, but we got separated because of so many P-51s the area with the same colored tails. I found myself alone so I set off to join up with someone from our own bunch."

Bochkay then spotted another Jet being chased by five out-of-range P-51s, cut it off in a turn and opened fire - only to have one gun stutter out six or seven rounds and quit. On the 18th of April, Bochkay would shoot down another 262, one of only two men in the Group to score a double on the jets.

Captain James Browning, an original member of the 363rd Squadron since the very beginning in Nevada and California, did not return from this mission. No one saw him after he and Bochkay engaged the Me 262s. It was not until the end of 1994 that his fate was learned.

In response to a letter written by the author to the appropriate U.S. Army agency, some 50 pages of documents, consisting of reports of army MIA investigating teams, eyewitness reports, and even medical reports, were received. What follows is the story of Jim Browning's death on that day in early February, 1945.

Browning was one of the gung-ho types who had come back to the group for a second combat tour - entirely voluntarily. An ace with five victories before he had departed for the ZI in mid 1944, he returned near the end of the year and scored two more victories.

The mission on 9 February was the usual bomber escort, the 357th providing 62 Mustangs in two groups, led by Colonel Dregne and Major Peterson. *Luftwaffe* opposition was in the form of the formidable Me 262, one group of three which used their superior speed to evade Greenhouse Sqdn. Fifteen minutes prior to that, at 1140 hours, Cement Sqdn. (363rd) engaged nine 262s. From the mission report: "The Squadron dropped tanks and dived on the jets which broke into elements of two and scattered. The lead jet, although under attack, turned into the bomber formation and made an attack through the box, one of our elements in pursuit. The remainder were driven away from the bombers with the above results."(this refers to 262s destroyed by Bochkay and Carter with a probable by Foy.)

The mission report also states; "One NYR (Not Yet Returned), CPT Browning, last seen vicinity of Fulda."

Bochkay's later statement: "At 1145 hours, Captain Browning was on the tail of two Me 262s and was chasing them. I was covering Browning at that time and continued to cover him until it was in our favor for me to be the attacker. I then called him and told him that I was cutting him off and for him to cover me. As I was making the attack on the last Me 262, Captain Browning called me and told me to keep going as he had me covered. That was the last I heard or saw of him. This happened at 24,000 feet over Fulda, Germany. There were a large number of P-51s in the area at the time."

So there the matter rested, there was no further information forthcoming on Browning - he had simply disappeared. There are German documents attached to his Missing Aircrew Report, but they merely indicate: 1140 hours, one Mustang shot down 3 Km SW Wuerger, 20 Km SW Limburg after fighting with German day fighters. Pilot, Captain James Willey Browning, s/n 0-740361, and aircraft totally destroyed."

The army's efforts to identify and recover the remains of its dead were very thorough and painstaking. Investigating teams had fanned out throughout Europe even before the end of the war. German police and town officials were interviewed and many statements of eye witnesses taken. After complete analysis, a board then decided if the remains were recoverable and if so, they were moved to one of the several military cemeteries, and then to the ZI if next of kin desired it. The investigation in this case did solve the mystery of what happened to Jim Browning.

In a statement dated 5 August 1947, one Adolf Keller, Burgermeister of the town of Woersdorf says: "On 9 February 1945, at noontime I saw a dogfight in the vicinity of Wuerger. Besides a German fighter which was engaged in the fight, there were several other planes in the air. The German fighter rammed an airplane and both of them catched (sic) fire and crashed down."

Keller goes on to say a German Sergeant in charge of Russian prisoners later brought him several items from the wreck which included a gold ring, an ID tag with Browning's name, a photo with his name on it and some currency. That afternoon Keller went to the wreck site and saw the remains of both aircraft. "The body of the German pilot, Volprecht Riesdsel *Freiherr* (Baron) zu Eisenach. *Oberstleutnant* (Lt. Colonel), was evacuated already."

The following comments are extracted from a statement dated 6 August 1947, by one Wilhelm Manrer: "I was a railway employee. On 9 Feb 1945, I was in my office when I heard firing from weapons of a plane, followed by an explosion. I went outside and saw a cloud of smoke about 600 meters from the station. When I was relieved at 1800 hours, I went to the place of the crash.

"There I saw the wreckage of a plane scattered over an area of 400 meters. I could not recognize the plane type. On one part I found painted the letters 'ZANKE'. The plane was burnt. I did not see any remains or parts of a body. Approximately 600 meters from the place of the crash, a German plane had crashed. I however, did not see the crash."

The "ZANKE" that Manrer reported was undoubtedly the canopy rim and the name was "ZARNKE", since Browning was flying Glenn Zarnke's P-51 JUNIOR MISS II on that date. At some point then, after Bochkay had taken the lead, Browning had collided with an Me 262, both pilots dying as described.

Of interest is the very high rank and title of the German pilot (*Freiherr* means Baron). Contacts in Germany and the U.S. have identified Riedesel as the Commander of KG(J) 54, flying Me 262 W. Nr. 500042. This unit was a former bomber *Gruppe* (same as our wing), as shown by the KG designation, which had re-equipped as a fighter unit (J) at a time when Germany needed fighters much more than bombers. KG(J) 54 lost five Me 262s this date to the 78th and 357th Groups.

Jim Browning knew the risks of returning for a second tour when he could have remained in the states, but he came back to "the old outfit" (as many soldiers have a way of doing).

Two views of the handsome Mustang, Joe Cannon's LITTLE JOE, A P-51D-20, 44-72258. As with all late war 363rd aircraft, the rudder is red. The object on the post behind it is a "Tannoy" loud speaker, many of which were scattered about the field.

The odds caught up with him however. In May, 1949, Hdqters. American Graves Registration Command, Europe, issued its synopsis of his case recommending that his remains be declared non-recoverable. Because there were no recoverable remains, James Browning's name is listed on THE WALL OF THE MISSING at the American military cemetery in Luxembourge.

It should be noted that there are many other 357th missing whose fate may very well be detailed in obscure U.S. Army files.

As March came in the *Luftwaffe* was beginning to achieve its goal of getting the jets into action in large numbers, making co-ordinated attacks on the bombers and trying to avoid the fighters. On the 19th, Lt. Col. Andy Evans reported the largest number yet seen at one time when 36 Me 262s attacked the bombers from six o'clock high in waves of twelve. Lt. Col. Jack Hayes, leading Cement Squadron was able to turn away the last two waves but the first wave had been lethal enough with four B-17s going down.

Major Bob Foy frustrated on previous occassions with the jets, caught one of them this time, the pilot of which was almost surely *Oberfeldwebel* Mattuschka of JG 7 who was KIA at about this time and place. Another of those turned away by the 363rd was also shot down. Captain Robert Fifield showing considerable perseverance, reported: "I was leading the 2nd element of Cement blue flight when 20 plus 262s attacked our box. I dropped my tanks and tried to beat them to the bombers. I got there just as they hit. I shot at about four different ones and finally singled one out. They were all diving to the left, and since they were getting away from me I tried lobbing some long range shots in and finally got some black smoke trailing from him. After that he slowed down and I started closing in on him. After I got some more hits, his wingman got close to him and then took off again when I got some more hits. I closed to about 400 yards and got many hits. He trailed white smoke and then went straight in and exploded."

Sometime in March, Colonel Dregne wrote a tactics report on the changing scene of the air war: "The German Air Force fighters have been inactive in the defense role, the burden of the bomber interception falling on the 262. The number of jet propelled aircraft and the aggressiveness and frequency of their attacks has increased markedly during this month of March. It has been necessary for the Group to devise and develop new escort tactics to protect the bomber columns from attacks by these jet propelled huns.

"The Group now flies rather close escort to the bombers, keeping in flights and sections. The former tactic of having squadrons forming a loose perimeter around the bomber boxes has been abandoned. The new method of defense permits our fighters to turn into the attacking jets and drive them off before they break through. It has been found that our formations must not permit the maneuvers of the jets to draw them too far away from the bombers, because the jets, with their superior speed are able to pull up and turn back so swiftly into the now unprotected bomber boxes, leaving the P-51 pilots far behind and therefore helpless as a defender."

As has been described, March ended with the beginning of the massive Myer's rescue attempt. Oddly enough, a pair of Me 262s dealt themselves a hand in this affair. In his book PURSUE AND DESTROY, Kit Carson describes in vivid detail his encounter with these machines over the cold waters of the North Sea: "We found the PBY without difficulty, but no sign of Myers unless he was on board. A few minutes later two Me 262s came storming out from the mainland at a much lower altitude than ours, possibly a thousand feet off the water.

"They took no time to scout the situation; obviously they were well informed before arriving. Their course was dead into the Catalina. I didn't see them before they passed below me and even though I yelled out over the radio to my two remaining wingmen and we pulled out all the stops, it was impossible to effect an interception that would cut them off. Both of the 262s were firing at the Catalina by the time I could get my sights on the lead ship, even though it was a long range deflection shot. I went in for whatever it was worth, trying to get a few hits. The 262s peeled off to the right and made a wide, high speed circle back to the mainland.

"Certainly not wishing our troops in the Catalina any bad luck, I was hoping that bastard in the lead 262 would tighten up his turn and try to come back, because if he had I was going to nail his ass. I had the throttle through the gate at 72 inches of mercury and 3,000. My speed was up and I had a 3,000 foot altitude advantage so I could easily have reached 400 mph, maybe more. If I could get my sights on him for three seconds at 200 yards, that's all I needed. He didn't do it though, and there wasn't anything more I could do about it. At least they knew we were there and it wasn't an easy setup."

Later in April, Carson would get hits on two more 262s, but he never was able to add one to his impressive victory list.

By late in March, with all the rail lines cut, the important Ruhr Valley was isolated and by mid-April the Allies had smashed their way to the Elbe, and as far south as Stuttgart and Nuremberg. However, much of southern Germany, Austria and Czechoslovakia were yet to be subdued, and it was to this area that the remnants of the *Luftwaffe* were withdrawing. Many of these units on airfields in the Prague area - some 600 miles from Leiston - the remaining missions would be long ones.

By now the entire air defense of the crumbling *Reich* had been taken over by the Me 262 - piston engine fighters were seldom seem anymore. An exception was the 7th of April when the *Luftwaffe* high command committed a volunteer ramming unit, about 100 volunteer pilots, many of whom were barely able to fly their 109 or 190. Although a few bombers were rammed, it was another disaster as P-51s shot down 59 of them and the bomber gunners claiming another 40.

The Operational Summary for April, 1945: "With the bright outlook that is now being presented by the speed of the Allied armies in Germany and Italy, the part that the 357th is to play henceforth in this theatre appears to be confined to waiting for last minute breaks by the enemy or the order to pack."

It was not quite time to pack - there was still a little fighting to be done. However, the 357th missed out on most of the action on the 7th, although Ivan McGuire and James Windham caught two straggling Me 109s, the last of these classic fighters to be shot down by the 357th.

The Group also missed out on the "Great jet massacre" on the 10th, when the *Luftwaffe* launched the largest number of Me 262s of the war. It was a remarkable achievement for the ground and air crews of the most important jet *Geschwader* JG 7. With their airfields devastated, a desperate shortage of fuel, and their supply lines in ruins, 55 Me 262s took off that day in defense of the *Reich*. A few of these broke through the Mustang screen and shot down ten bombers, but JG 7 lost 27 262s, more than half their strength. From this point on it was all down hill. Most 8th Air Force fighter groups had a share in this, but the 357th was busy at a lower level, where they burned 23 assorted aircraft on Neuruppin Airfield.

Meanwhile the efficient pipeline was still delivering replacment pilots, some of whom arrived too late to fly a mission. The mixed feelings of these men is remembered many years later by 2nd Lt. James McLane:

"Upon arrival at Leiston, it was a real blow to find out that several weeks in Major Bochkay's 'Clobber College' would be required before being permitted to fly combat. It began to look as if all the practice and learning were to be for naught. Finally, on April 16th, the dozen of us who had arrived three weeks earlier were told that we could either fly the next days mission or take a three day pass to London. Fearing it might be all over at any time, I flew the missions on April 17th, 18th, 19th and 20th. The reality of it all was quickly established when two of my fellow replacement pilots were shot down on this, their first mission, along with another fellow while strafing on the way home. I did manage to fire my guns once at an

Frank Kyle was a late war replacement pilot in the 363rd and named his green P-51 from his wife's nickname, "Pony". Note the mustache.

out-of-range Me 262 while flying wing for Kit Carson. What a disappointment when it didn't even show up on the film!"

The 357th would fight its last battles on the 17th through the 19th - all in the area around Prague. By this time the fields around the city were jammed with aircraft and the skies crowded with Allied aircraft. Colonel Dregne reported some 200 planes, including twelve 262s, on a field east of the city and 150 more on Prague-Ruzyne. John Duncan and Anton Shoepke destroyed two of these grounded 262s.

We will attempt to provide the "feel" of these last few days with the words of several men who "were there".

Flight Officer James Steiger was, like McLane, a new comer to the Group. He was flying only his second mission on the 17th of April, but was more fortunate than Mclane - he got a very close look at the speedy Me 262"

"I was flying Greenhouse Blue four when we sighted an Me 262 going 180 degrees to the bomber stream. We turned into the enemy aircraft as he turned into the bombers. The flight spread out and gave chase and I was on the extreme left. The enemy aircraft flew

Lt. Stephen Wasylyk joined the 363rd Squadron at an unknown date but probably somewhere around the lst of 1945 as he shot down an Me 109 on 24 March. In April, a Squadron listing shows him as an element leader. His P-51, PHILLY-DILLIES, started out as a D-5 without dorsal fin, but it has been retrofitted here along with a tail warning antenna.

over Prague and I passed north of the town. At this time I sighted another 262 at 6,000 feet going in a northerly direction east of Prague. I tried to turn into the 262, but he turned inside me. I then pulled up into a wingover and rolled over onto his tail. As I closed I began firing at approximately 600 yards and continued right up till approximately 15 yards away. At this time the enemy aircraft fell off on its left wing and dove straight into the ground and exploded."

The Field Order for the next day, the 18th, called for an area patrol. The area again being Prague - the purpose being to keep the Me 262s on the ground while the "Big Friends" were in the area, or to destroy them if they took off. Major Leonard Carson was on the board as mission leader, and there is no better way to get the picture of the times than to quote portions of Carson's book PURSUE AND DESTROY: "Prague was 600 miles away by the devious route that was plotted for us. To avoid revealing our target and intentions to the enemy we were going to make a couple of zig-zags in our course and go in on the deck to avoid radar detection. My problem then was to navigate 54 airplanes 600 miles down about 200 feet off the ground and improvise tactics to keep the jets down after we got there. Between now and time over the target gave me about four hours to think it over. The one piece

of concrete intelligence I had was that the flak at Prague would be brutal. They were absolutely correct."

It must have been a thrilling sight for the school boys of the Low Countries - 54 Mustangs "on the deck", to the music of 54 Merlins. For the first 300 miles or so the weather was perfect and the Group hit Frankfurt on time and on course. After a course change at that city, the weather turned hazy and it was necessary for Carson to put the flights in trail and tighten up the formations: "Since we were hitting our checkpoints dead center and on time, I decided to keep the Group on the deck and pull up to 10,000 feet. At 1250, ten minutes before we were due over Prague, I still hadn't come up with a brilliant strategy. The flak was there and nothing would make it go away.

"At 1250 we pulled up and the gods of war were on our side. At 1300 we came up dead center on Prague-Ruzyne Airfield and nothing was stirring."

Carson split the Group at this point and sent Major Don Bochkay and Cement and Greenhouse Squadrons to cover airfields to the east of the city, while he kept Dollar Squadron orbiting to the southwest, out of the intense flak, waiting for the *Luftwaffe* to make a move:

"It soon came. Under cover of the flak umbrella, the Me 262 pilots cranked up and taxied one by one to the

Lt. Vincent Zettler (rt) was pilot of C5-F, CANTON CAN. There are eight victory symbols on the canopy rim, but seven of these are ground scores. On 2 March 1945, the 357th had a bad day losing five pilots, three dead, and claiming 13 e/a destroyed, mostly Me 109s. One of these was Zettlers. On the same day he claimed four He 111s destroyed on the ground.

Three of the late war period Group leaders. Left is Lt. Col. Jack Hayes, who shot down an Me 262 in the last days of the war. Later he commanded the 55th Group. Center is Lt. Col. Andrew Evans, an ace and future Group Commander. Right is Colonel Dregne, who led the Group the last six months of the war. Both Evans and Dregne are wearing the Group insignia on their jackets.

north end of the airdrome for take-off. The moment of truth had arrived. They were going to try to punch their way through and get to the bombers anyhow. Our opposing strategy was now clear. My squadron would go down by flights of four, well spread out to dilute the flak on each of us. As the first 262 started his take-off roll, we dropped our king tanks and I started down with red flight from 13,000 feet with an easy wing-over and about 50 inches of mercury and 2700 rpm.

"The Mustang would accelerate like a banshee going down hill. The 262 had his gear up and was going past the field boundry when we plowed through the intense light flak. As I came astern of him and leveled off at 400 plus, I firewalled it to hold my speed and centered the bulls eye of the optical sight on the fuselage and hit him with a two second burst. My timing had been off. If I'd split from 13,000 about five seconds earlier I could have had all six fifties up his tail pipes. Even though I scored only a few strikes. It's an even bet that he was too busy checking for leaks to make it to the bomber column."

With the squadron reformed, Carson took them back over Ruzyne where they found four jets airborne and Carson got a few strikes on one before it pulled away. Lts. Dellorote and Bradner also claimed one damaged. Jet

activity on this day was not extensive. Besides the three damaged claims, there were two kills, one to Captain Chuck Weaver, and one to Don Bochkay, his second jet victory. The bombers suffered no losses to jets. While flying Chuck Weaver's wing during the brief flurry of action, Lt. Oscar T. Ridley took a flak hit in the engine, bailed out and spent some six weeks with the Czech underground until war's end.

Tomorrow it would be back to Prague - with more success.

The mission report 19 April 1945: "Heavy bomber escort, 8th A.F. Field Order 2024A. L/F in 0959 Schouwen 20,000. R/V with Vinegrove 2-3 and 2-4 18,000. 'A' Group (Lt. Col. Jack Hayes) 1 squadron, swept ahead of bombers and 'B' Group (Lt. Col. John Storch) 2 squadrons, gave close escort through target, leaving bombers 1407 NE Frankfort, 15,000. One man seen to bail out of B-17 with yellow tail and red stripe 1240. Bomber was apparently OK and on course."

So read a portion of the mission report for the final occassion when The Yoxford Boys would engage enemy aircraft. It was a good day - there were no casualties and six Me 262s were claimed destroyed, with five damaged. We will close out the combat record of the 357th

On the last big "rat-race" with Me 262s on 19 April 1945 Lt. Joe Shea "almost" got one of them. He had, however, forgotten to turn on his gun's switches so all he got was this excellent photo of the 262 as it streaked away.

with the words of two men, first with Captain Robert Fifield: "I was leading Cement White flight when we arrived at Prague. Some jets were called in while taking off. I watched two elements take off and saw two more ships start to roll down the runway in formation. I couldn't see any more jets taxiing on the field so called 'Cement Sqdn. white flight dropping tanks.' We were then at 16,000 feet. There was no reply so I dropped and started down on a jet about three miles from the field.

"I started firing when I got in range and continued until I over-ran him. I pulled up slightly and then dropped back down on him, and shot some more pieces off. He started burning in the left jet unit, pulled up, did a half roll and went straight in and exploded. I was then at about 2,000 feet. I couldn't see any of my flight so I started climbing and said I would meet them over the field.

"I got up to 10,000 when I saw another jet below me. I went down on him and got some hits but I was also being hit by light flak so I hit the deck and let him go. I saw two Squadrons of bombers with red tipped rudders coming in from Prague. There were some stragglers and I thought I saw one of them go down in flames. I couldn't see any escort for them and figured they were being hit so I headed for them alone and called my group leader about it. I didn't hear an answer from him, but Lt. Zarnke said he was at 3:00 o'clock to me.

"I saw a jet coming up behind one of the stragglers so I went down on him and he headed east after shooting at the bomber which he did not get. He started a turn to the left and I cut him off and gained slightly on him. He headed north and I figured he would try for Prague so I just kept him in sight and got between him and Prague. I positioned Lt. Zarnke between me and Prague so he could come down if I missed. The jet made another turn and I fired with only two guns and missed."

Glen Zarnke also got a few hits, but as Fifield says; "Our engines couldn't take it anymore, so we throttled back and set course for home." It had been a busy time for Fifield - with a little more luck he might have been the only man to shoot down three or even four of the jets. Although neither Zarnke or Fifield mentions it, the mission report says that the two collided a short time later and both bailed out but returned to base. Fifield had only about three weeks to live, as he died after the end of the war in a collision with an RAF Mustang.

Four decades later, Gilman Weber still has vivid memories of "his" Me 262: "The bomber's target was in the Dresden area. We were close to the target, above and to the east side of the bombers when I spotted two Me 262s coming in on a box of B-17s just ahead and to the right. They flashed under my nose from left to right. I called them out, dropped tanks, broke down and to the

Runway Control Officer Kit Carson flags off two 363rd Sqdn. P-51s on what is thought to be the last escort mission of the war, B-24s bombing railway marshalling yards. The P-51 in the foreground is PAPPY'S ANSWER, 44-14736, which may have had the name YANKEES on the right side. Lt. John Stern was the regular pilot, but it is not known who was flying it here.

Two late war replacement pilots, Eddie Carr in ALICE MARIE III, and Frank Kyle in B6-D.

Lt. James T. Windham reported to the 496th Fighter Training Sqdn. at Goxhill in August, 1944, for transition into P-51s and would have arrived at Leiston late in September. As an element leader in Yellow Flight, 363rd Sqdn. he shared an Me 109 with his wingman Glen Zarnke on the historic mission on 14 January 1945. In April, 1945 now a Captain and flight leader, he added another to his score.

VICTORY CREDITS FOR JETS (ALL ME 262)

1. Captain Charles E. Yeager   6 November 1944
2. 1st Lt. Edward R. Haydon   8 November 1944
    1/2 credit, shared with Capt Ernest Fiebelkorn, 20th Grp.
           Victim was Major Walter Nowotny
3. 1st Lt. James W. Kenney   8 November 1944
      Victim was Franz Schall, who bailed out. Later KIA
4. Captain Robert P. Winks   15 January 1945
5. Ist Lt. Dale E. Karger   20 January 1945
6. 1st Lt. Roland K. Wright   20 January 1945
7. Captain Donald H. Bochkay   9 February 1945
8. 1st Lt. Johnnie L. Carter   9 February 1945
9. Major Robert W. Foy   19 March 1945
10. Captain Robert S. Fifield   19 March 1945
11. FJO James A. Steiger   17 April 1945
12. Captain Charles E. Weaver   18 April 1945
13. Major Donald H. Bochkay   18 April 1945
14. Captain Robert S. Fifield   19 April 1945
15. Ist Lt. Paul Bowles   19 April 1945
16. 1st Lt. Carroll Ofsthun   19 April 1945
17. 1st Lt. James P. McMullen   19 April 1945
18. 1st Lt. Gilman L. Weber   19 April 1945 credit, shared
        with Captain Ivan McGuire
19. Lt. Col. Jack Hayes   19 April 1945

PROBABLY DESTROYED

1. Major Robert W. Foy, 9 February 1945
NOTE: In addition, three men were credited with 262s destroyed on the ground.
They are: Colonel Irwin Dregne, Lt. Anton Schoepke, and Lt. John Duncan.

right after them. They went thru and under the box of B-17s. I stayed just above the bombers.

"One 262 broke away to the right and made a pass at a straggler. His right turn and his break away to the left gave me a chance to get close enough to get a shot that hit him in the cockpit area. It was a hell of a long shot even then. We continued in a shallow turn and went down quite rapidly. He apparently tried to make it to the airfield at Prague, but bellied in west of the field about a mile. I then pulled up, spotted another 262, and covered my wingman (Lt. James McMullen) while he shot him down. He caught fire, rolled over and the pilot bailed out. It was the first time I had ever seen a ribbon chute. I can still see it as though it just happened."

The encounter report and the official records give Captain Ivan McGuire one half credit for Weber's 262, but the evidence suggests that Weber was the principle "shooter". The other four who scored against the 262s on

the 19th were Lt. Col. Jack Hayes, Lts. Paul Bowles, Carroll Ofsthun and James McMullen. The latter's victory at 1300 hours was the last enemy aircraft to fall in combat with the 357th Fighter Group.

The three final combat missions of the Group were on the 20th, 21st and 25th. They were generally uneventful, the last being distinquished by the fact that the 54 P-51s flew a five and a half hour mission without a single abort.

One of these missions - on the 20th, was to show Lt. Don Kocher a side of the war seldom seen by fighter pilots - the ground war. With a failing engine he made a belly landing a few miles north east of Hanover, not knowing whose territory he was in. The appearance of a 6x6 truck from a combat engineer unit brought relief on that count: "The major and two staff Sergeants took me to their base just in time for chow. Then the major got a message that a crew of his men had been ambushed and

killed. He asked if I would like to go along with him to check on the men. I told him I would love to but I didn't have a steel helmet or rifle. He said 'Oh, hell, take the captain's.' Thus I found myself in the back seat of a jeep with a rifle I had never seen before on a mission of revenge. We found the men, all dead, but no Germans. From there we visited an abandoned and deserted German airfield. In a partially wrecked hangar I found an Arado 234 bomber that appeared undamaged. I found several cannisters containing performance records of the Arado jet. There were also lots of photos, all of which I packed up to take back to Leiston."

Upon Kocher's return to home base, via various C-47s, the bomber prints and photos were turned over to the 364th Squadron intelligence officer. The last few weeks of the war had seen dramatic changes in the air campaign. The traditional enemy - the Me 109 and the Fw 190 had all but vanished from the skies. The jet fighter was the new enemy but by the end of April it had also been vanquished. Although the Me 262 was encountered by other units, in small numbers well into May, it too had passed into history.

In reading the available U.S. and RAF records, it is clear that, despite the now inferior performance of their aircraft, Allied fighter pilots were eager to engage the jets and often overstressed their powerplants to do so. The 262 was a tough opponent, but it could be, and was, caught and destroyed.

On the 25th of April several hours after the 54 Mustangs were back on their hardstands, a signal came down from 66th Fighter Wing to provide four P-51s for an ASR operation. Group passed it down to the 362nd Squadron, and Lt. Ed Hyman was tagged by the Operations Officer to lead it, in an effort to find an unknown airman - down at sea. Since this was the last operational mission, we will quote Hyman's mission report: "Two planes RV with Warwick approx 1855 Great Yarmouth 1,000 feet. Other two planes RV with Catalina at 1855. Escorted Catalina and Warwick to search area. Wreckage of aircraft, oil slick and one capsized dinghy partially inflated, sighted. No sign of life. Catalina made numerous passes on deck over wreckage. Also searched surrounding area by our planes at 100 feet. Nothing else seen.

"Colgate (Fighter Controller) advised Catalina not to land unless some sign of life as getting late and sea choppy. Catalina therefore left and was escorted by entire flight to vicinity of 53 degrees north 04 degrees east. Warwick remained in search area."

2nd Lt. Jack Bussard's engine coolant temperature had been running high, so Hyman directed him to land first, followed by the other two (identities unknown). When the wheels of Ed Hyman's P-51, code G4-P, serial number 44-72489, touched the runway at Leiston, the Yoxford Boy's war was over.

It was 1015 PM, the 25th of April, 1945.

One of the final parades of the 357th - an unfamiliar activity, but they all look like soldiers here. G4-P ROLLA U (bar) in back with a stack of "ready" drop tanks. The brick house (right center) is a pre-war structure, used as the photo lab. Sixty years later it is still there and occupied by the manager of the farm that replaced Leiston airfield.

GERMANY QUITS, shouts the headline of the Stars and Stripes newspaper, displayed here by 364th ground crew John Moriarity, Ken Thompson and Bill Wilkes.

PEACE - THE BEGINNING OF THE END FOR THE YOXFORD BOYS

With the last mission flown on 25 April, the Group had fulfilled the mission assigned to it when it was first slated to join the 8th Air Force in the fall of 1943. Now it entered a period of uncertainty - the question on everyone's mind was "What now?" It would be some weeks before the Group's fate would be announced, until then life went on Leiston airfield, although with different objectives and at a different pace.

Long before the last shot was fired, the Government and the military services had begun planning for the vast demobilization of somewhere around ten million men. In the army a system of points was developed in which many factors were considered, such as length of service, time overseas, age etc. Soldiers who had been involved in combat received extra points.

The magic number at war's end was 85 points, and in May and June, old timers who had the points plus all men over 42 yars of age, began to leave the unit. There was considerable shuffling among the command slots and some pilots who had almost completed their combat tours were transferred out to other units. Airplanes also began to depart, all of the new P-51s with less than 100 hours of time on them were transferred, soon followed by those with less than 200 hours. Also departing were the remaining eight "War Weary" P-51s which had been in use in Clobber College.

On 1 May, a message from General H.H. Arnold, Chief of Army Air Forces, provided encouragement when he stated that "You will be moved just as rapidly as available troop ships and air transport can ply the seas and the air". Not so encouraging was his further statement that many troops would be needed for occupation duty and some would begin direct movement to the Pacific to join a war not yet over.

For brevity, we will list some of the noteworthy events of May and June:

3 May: Four days before the official end to the war, Captain Robert Fifield, 363rd Squadron was killed when his P-51 spun in at King's Farm, near the town of Westleton. The British police report says it is thought he had collided with another aircraft, but there is no confirmation. Fifield was on his third tour extension and had 376 hours of combat time with 2.5 victories. Two of these were Me 262s.

7 May: Teletype message from General Partridge providing details on the final surrender of German forces.

8 May: Message from General Doolittle, Commander 8th Air Force: **"EFF IMMIEDIATELY, 1ST, 2ND, 3RD AIR DIVISIONS ARE STOOD DOWN FROM ANY FURTHER BOMBER AND FIGHTER OFFENSIVE OPR IN EUROPEAN THEATER."**

9 May: Ceremony and service in the 362nd Squadron hangar, led by Colonel Dregne and Chaplain, Captain Berl A. Lewis, honoring the Group's dead.

13 May: 48 P-51s joined aircraft from dozens of other Allied units in a fly over review above London.

16 May: Big Parade! A review of all units, with Colonel Dregne presenting medals to 48 officers.

21 May: lst Lt. Alfred Bierweiler, 362nd Squadron, was killed while doing aerobatics in the vicinity of the city of Ipswich. The P-51 entered a spin from which it did not recover.

29 May: lst Lt. Manual K. Soo was killed on a navigational flight to Germany. Pilot lost control in bad weather.

14 June: lst Lt. George P. Barrett, was killed on this date when his P-51 collided with an RAF Mustang which he had bounced. Barrett bailed into the sea without dinghy or Mae Nest. Rescue services found nothing.

Having obtained a B-17, a twice a week "rest and recreation" flight was made to the city of Edinburgh. Aircraft strength soared with the arrival of high time P-51s from other groups, with 105 aircraft assigned.

During this period, the infamous blackout ended as did mail censorship and three ice cream machines arrived, welcomed by all! (When the Group packed its equipment to go to Germany, the ice cream machines went with it!)

On 14 June, "The other shoe dropped", and the waiting was over. A warning order arrived alerting the Group for movement to Germany for occupation duty. The move was to be on or about 1 July 1945 - only two weeks away. All activities accelerated, including the transfer of all men qualified and there was more shuffling of high time/low time P-51s. It was a massive job to prepare for the move, shipping tons of equipment and supplies, much of which needed to have boxes and crates built - the carpenters were busy men.

There was also the job of turning in and disposing of un-needed equipment, much of it undocumented due to the wide spread practice of "squirreling" away extra supplies obtained by illegal means (called "moonlight requisition"), to have in case of need. Another huge job was cleaning up the base in preparation for its return to the RAF.

By mid-July, advance air parties had gone on to the new base at Neubiberg, a former *Luftwaffe* base near Munich. The final road convoy of vehicles and equipment left Leiston on 19 July, arriving at Neubiberg on the 31st of July.

It was the end of an era, Station F-373, Leiston Airfield had been more than adequate as a base of operations and it had been home for almost 18 months. Now it was history.

Although the 357th Fighter Group had departed, many ghosts were left behind.

These are repatriated POWs who briefly returned to the Group after the war. The only one identified is the man facing the camera, he is Lt. Charles E. McKee, who lost his arm when shot down by a B-17.

Captain Tom Adams was another late arrival who managed to tally 5.5 victories between December and the end of the war. ARKANSAS TRAVELLER was C5-L, 44-63099. At the end of the war, 8th Air Force decreed that fighter codes should be applied to the bottom of the wing, as seen here, to discourage indiscriminate "buzzing".

In March, 1953, British farmer Roger A. Freeman, not yet the world's foremost 8th Air Force Historian, visited Leiston Airfield to search for the Otto Jenkins Crash site. At that time he took this photo of the control tower, empty and abandoned. It was torn down soon after and Leiston Airfield, Station F-373, was well on its way to return to farmland.

One of the great aircraft engines of its day was the Pratt & Whitney Wasp, R-1340, of some 600 HP, seen here installed in the Norseman, also with its name SPIRIT OF ST. LOUIS visible.

During the first months at Leiston, the Group had several RAF utility type airplanes on loan. All of these were soon replaced by several AT-6s, in the 363rd and 364th Squadrons. The 362nd got a Canadian built Noorduyn Norseman UC-64. Its eight passenger capacity made it a very useful aircraft and the Group took it to Germany after the war where it hauled passengers to Paris and other exotic places. It is seen here resplendent in its red and yellow nose.

These are high-time P-51s which are having their original group nose colors removed, ready to be repainted in 357th colors. SSgt. Robert Bignell, the author's "buddy" is applying the paint remover.

In late 1945 and early 1946, the salvaging of surplus aircraft really got into high gear. In this scene at Neubiberg, Germany, we see the end of Kit Carson's NOOKY BOOKY IV, reduced to junk - a sad sight.

Another gallant warrior on the scrap heap of history at Neubiberg, Germany, late in 1945 or early 1946. Identity of this one is uncertain. Enough of the data block (forward of the victory flags) can be made out to indicate it may be a P-51D-10, s/n 44-14372. This P-51 may not have seen wartime service with the 357th, but was one that came from another group in the big shuffle of aircraft after the war ended. The 12 victory symbols would seem to narrow its pilot down to John Storch, or Dale Karger, both of whom qualify if ground victories are counted, as they often were. This photo came to the author from historian SFC Jim Crow, U.S. Army ret.

Combat missions now over, the bomb groups had little to do and sometimes provided a B-17 and crew so that ground crews could have a joyride. This l00th Bomb Group B-17 was photographed from a similar B-17 by 364th Squadron Armorer Robert Prante. The airfield below does not look like Leiston.

Captain John Sublett's LADY OVELLA, seen here with all eight of his victory credits. It was code G4-Q, s/n 44-11190. It was destroyed after war's end in a fatal crash with Lt. Alfred Beirweiler.

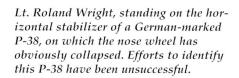

Lt. Roland Wright, standing on the horizontal stabilizer of a German-marked P-38, on which the nose wheel has obviously collapsed. Efforts to identify this P-38 have been unsuccessful.

THE END OF THE ROAD

As the 357th took up station in a conquered Germany, it had a new Commander. Colonel Irwin Dregne, who had led the Group the last six months of the war, was ordered to attend the Army Command and Staff School at Fort leavenworth, Kansas. Lt. Col. Andrew Evans, the Group's only West Pointer and ace himself, took command of the Group.

During the 1930s, Hermann Göring was not only Hitler's number two man, he was head of the *Luftwaffe*, and in those heady days for the *Nazis*, nothing was too good for the *Luftwaffe*. When the 357th arrived at Neubiberg Air Field (9th Air Force station R-85), they found first class facilities. After Leiston, which had been a hastily-built temporary wartime installation, Neubiberg's barracks (two man rooms for the enlisted men) and mess halls seemed a soldier's heaven. In addition there was ample free time to explore the countryside and on Saturdays many Squadrons held beer parties on the tree-shaded lawns.

The Groups' aircraft strength soared after the arrival in Germany with many assorted non-fighter type machines assigned - primarily because no one knew what to do with the vast glut of now useless airplanes. Most of these would soon join the thousands of aircraft slated to destruction and salvage.

Personnel was a different story. True to Arnold's promise, many were headed for home, with only a trickle of replacements. Only two months after arrival in Germany, only 23 P-51s could be flown due to the lack of mechanics. In October, 1945, 300 men left for the ZI, with only 15 replacements arriving. Only ten to 15 P-51s were now being flown.

In October, this writer was one of those who left the Group, assigned to the 558th AAA (Anti-Aircraft Artillery) Battalion, for the trip home.

On the 30th of October, 1945, the Group suffered its worst aircraft accident when its C-47 crashed in the Alps, with a heavy loss of life. (See BRENNER ROUTE CLOSED).

In November, all three squadrons were consolidated in the 362nd under Captain Robert D. Brown, an original member of the 362nd who had recently returned from internment in Switzerland. In December, only five or six P-51s could be flown and this condition continued into the new year of 1946. In January, the records show that that the Group had one Stinson L-5, four Piper L-4s, one UC-64, and four to six P-51s flyable.

In August of 1946, the 357th Fighter Group ceased to exist replaced by the 33rd Fighter Group, which in turn became the 86th Fighter Group. (In 1948, the author returned to Neubiberg for another hitch with the P-47 equipped 86th Group, now fully staffed and with an appropriate number of P-47s.)

Thus, we end the story of the 357th Fighter Group. Fortunately, however, its colors and traditions were handed over the Ohio Air National Guard still operating today. See chapter on the 178th Fighter Wing for details.

With the war over, there were literally thousands of now useless aircraft to dispose of - these once beautiful airplanes were now junk. At first, however, there was an effort to separate low time P-51s from high time ones. The low time aircraft went to an unknown destination, probably to depot at Warton. High time P-51s came in from other groups for the 357th to take to Germany on occupation duty. This is a line-up of low time P-51s awaiting pickup. Some of these were sold to Sweden and Switzerland.

CHAPTER 10:
THE MEN OF THE 357TH

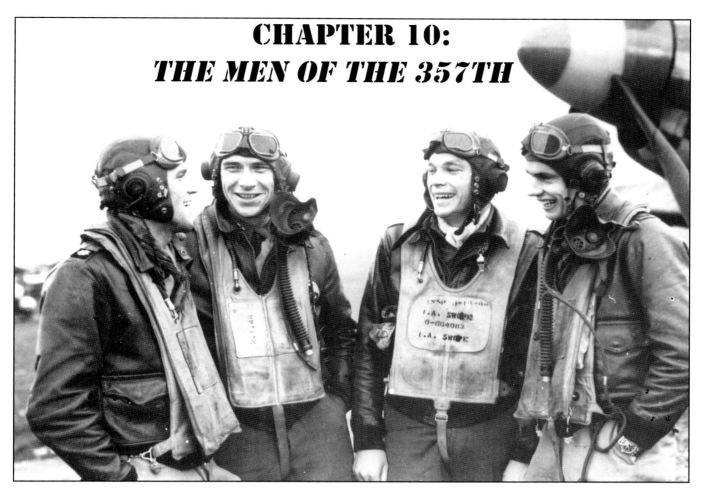

The 357th Fighter Group produced 42 aces, more than any other 8th Air Force Group. These are the top four (although several others were close), photographed by the press sometime late in 1944. They are L-R, Richard Peterson, Leonard Carson, John B. England, Clarence E. Anderson. All were Majors by this time, or would be soon. The photo session may have been set up hastily as England is wearing Ira Swope's MAE WEST. This photo is one of the author's favorite wartime shots.

The fifteen fighter groups which eventually made up the fighter force of MIGHTY EIGHTH AIR FORCE, had two basic missions. In the early days, they were primarily concerned with protection of the bomber force from *Luftwaffe* fighters.

After General Jimmie Doolittle took command at the beginning of 1944, with General William Kepner at Fighter Command, the mission slowly expanded and destruction of the German fighter force became the main thrust, although bomber protection remained a high priority.

With destruction of the *Luftwaffe* fighter force as a main objective which could only be achieved by shooting down enemy aircraft, the 357th was extremely adept at this, destroying 595 enemy aircraft in air combat, second only to the 56th Fighter Group which had about 60 more, but had been in combat much longer.

To a gung-ho fighter pilot then, shooting down the enemy was a major point of his profession and to be an ace, the pinnacle of that profession. The 357th ended the war with a long list of aces. If one counts only those who scored all, or most of their victories with the Group, the figure is 42. Using the same criteria, the 56th Group had 41, and the 4th Group, 39 - all very close.

However, the term "ace" is largely an artificial dividing line which says that if have five air victories, you are a genuine hero, but if you have four or less - "sorry, you don't qualify as a hero"! The ace phenomenon originated with the French Air Service in WWI, when for the first time a pilot was cited in Army orders. That man was Jean Mavarre and the date was 26 February, 1916. Mavarre had shot down two German aircraft in one day, bringing his total to five.

The number apparently was purely accidental, but coincided with his being cited in Army orders. Thereby giving us the magic number five to indicate ace

status. "Ace", however, means different things in different air forces.

The British never did actually adopt the term ace, either in WWI or WWII. In the *Luftwaffe*, it took 10 kills, not five, to become an "Experten" (ace). The official status in the USAF is somewhat hazy. Starting in 1959, with "Project Ace", the USAF Historical Division at Maxwell AFB began a series of listings on all U.S. Air Service (WWI), and USAAF, and USAF claims for destruction of enemy aircraft. This culminated in 1978 with "Study 85" listing all credits for WWII. (This has since then be re-published and incorporated with other wars).

In the records of the 357th we have found only one document which actually confirms ace status for two pilots of the 362nd Squadron. This Special Order 34, Hdqters, AAF Station F-373, dated 3 February 1945, and it states Captain John Kirla and 1st Lt. Otto Jenkins are "Hereby designated "Fighter Ace", effective date indicated" (24 December 1944). Authority is given as 66th Fighter Wing Memo 35-1.

Aces and victories have provided endless articles and discussions in books and magazines for years. All of this gives historians and enthusiasts something to argue about over coffee or beer. The ace status is probably over-emphasized, which does an injustice to many skilled fighter pilots who flew full combat tours (or more) did their job, survived (no mean feat!) and scored a few victories, or none. Many of these men were assigned as wingmen, and it was not their job to shoot down enemy aircraft but to guard their leader's tail.

Pure chance and opportunity also played a part. If there were no enemy aircraft in your part of the sky, there were none to be shot down. Good friend Harvey Mace, who has "only three" likes to say that he shot down every one had the chance to engage!

In this listing of 357th Aces, we have included only those who meet the criteria with five air victories. Ground victories are not included. This is not to imply that those with ground victories were not just as brave or skillful. It is true that 8th Air Force did credit ground victories to a pilot's total. The reason may have been twofold. First, ground strafing was often as deadly as air combat, although this was not always so, as many airfields were not defended by flak.

Another reason 8th Air Force counted ground victories may have been for political reasons - this provided a much higher level of enemy aircraft destroyed for home consumption. (The same "body count" situation seems to have applied during the Vietnam war.) It is true, of course, that these destroyed on the ground were of no further use to the enemy. The 8th Air Force was virtually unique in counting ground claims, neither the RAF or the *Luftwaffe* did this, nor did the other numbered air forces.

Lastly, the present day American Fighter Aces Association admits only those fighter pilots with five or more air victories. There are several men on the wartime ace list who would not qualify now. "Study 85" is the only official listing of credits for the destruction of enemy aircraft and all 357th victories listed here are to be found in this study.

NOTE: Major Donald C. McGee was flying a tour with the 357th at the end of the war and is an ace with six victories. However, we did not include him since he scored five of his victories in the Southwest Pacific.

357th FIGHTER GROUP ACES

1. Carson, Leonard K. - 18.5	15. Sublett, John L. - 8	29. Roberson, Arval J. - 6
2. England, John B. - 17.5	16. Weaver, Charles E. - 8	30. Schimanski, Robert G. - 6
3. Anderson, Clarence E, Jr - 16.25	17. Karger, Dale E. - 7.5	31. Gailer, Frank L. - 5.5
4. Peterson, Richard A. - 15.5	18. Davis, Glendon V. - 7.5	32. Hatala, Paul R. - 5.5
5. Foy, Robert W. - 15	19. Becker, Robert H. - 7	33. Ruder, LeRoy A. - 5.5
6. Bochkay, Donald H. - 13.75	20. Browning, James W. - 7	34. Winks, Robert P. - 5.5
7. Kirla, John A. - 11.5	21. Carder, John B. - 7	35. Bank, Raymond M. - 5
8. Yeager, Charles E. - 11.5	22. O'Brien, Gilbert M. - 7	36. Dregne, Irwin H. - 5
9. Storch, John A. - 10.5	23. Pierce, Joseph E. - 7	37. Harris, Thomas L. - 5
10. Adams, Fletcher E. - 9	24. Tyler, Gerald E. - 7	38. Hiro, Edwin W. - 5
11. Hayes, Thomas L, Jr - 8.5	25. Evans, Andrew J, Jr - 6	39. Maxwell, Chester K. - 5
12. Jenkins, Otto D. - 8.5	26. Murphy, Alva C. - 6	40. Reese, William C. - 5
13. Broadhead, Joseph E. - 8	27. O'Brien, William R. - 6	41. Stanley, Morris A. - 5
14. Shaw, Robert M. - 8	28. Pugh, John F. - 6	42. Warren, Jack R. - 5

A GALLERY OF DOUBLE AND TRIPLE ACES

CLARENCE E. "BUD" ANDERSON

CLARENCE E. "BUD" ANDERSON, born in 1922 Oakland, CA, soloed a J-3 Cub before WW II. Enlisted January, 1942, as Aviation Cadet. After graduation and commissioning, went to 328th Ftr. Grp, Hamilton Field, CA, where he became proficient in the "cranky" P-39.

In Spring of 1943, joined the new 357th Ftr. Grp. as a Flight Leader in the 363rd Squadron, where he remained thru the war, later as Operations Officer. At the end of his first combat tour, he had scored 12 victories. Returned to the U.S. on leave and then came back to the 357th for another tour, scoring four more victories. Anderson remained in the USAF until retirement and spent many years in research and development, as detailed in his highly recommended book, TO FLY AND FIGHT.

DONALD H. BOCHKAY

Among the 63 newly graduated 2nd Lts., DONALD H. BOCHKAY, of North Hollywood, California was directed by Special Orders dated 13 April 1943, Luke Field, AZ, to report to Commander, Hamilton Field, CA. From there he was assigned to the new 357th, which was to be his "home" for the rest of the war. He served two tours and is credited with the destruction of 13.5 enemy aircraft. He is one of the very few 8th Air Force pilots to shoot down two of the formidable Me 262 jets. In February, 1945, as a Major he became the last wartime Commander of the 363rd Squadron.

Donald Bochkay died in January 1981.

LEONARD K. "KIT" CARSON

As with most of the Group's double and triple aces, LEONARD K. "KIT" CARSON was an original member of the Group, who flew two combat tours. An Iowa farm boy attending The University of Iowa when war came, he enlisted in April 1942 at age 19. Graduated Luke Field summer of 1943 and joined the 362nd Squadron at Tonopah, ending up as its Commander in 1945. Flew 115 combat missions with 18.5 air victories, highest in the Group. Finished his education after the war and worked as an aeronautical engineer until retirement. Kit Carson died in March 1994. This author with Colonel C.E. Anderson and wives represented the 357th Group at his funeral.

JOHN BROOKE ENGLAND

Born in Carurthersville, Missouri, in 1923, JOHN BROOKE ENGLAND was the second highest scoring ace in the 357th Ftr Grp with 17.5 victories. As with many of the original pilots, he served more than one tour, flying 108 missions without a break. Served as a Flight Leader, Operations Officer and Commander of the 362nd Sqdn. He was a Major by December, 1944, at age 21. He remained in the Air Force after the war in many different Command positions until his death in the crash of an F-86 in France in November,1954. In May, 1955, Alexandria Air Force Base in Louisiana,was re-named England Air Force Base in his honor.

"THE MISSOURI ARMADA - this P-51 was the fourth and final plane that I used during my tour of duty in England. It completed over 30 missions over the German Reich without an abort before I returned to the states. The man chiefly responsible for this plane's consistant record was SSgt. Robert Currie. He was a wonderful Crew Chief and a credit to our great unheralded Army Air Forces ground crews."

ROBERT W. FOY

ROBERT W. FOY was born in 1916 and grew up in Johnson City and Oswego, New York. In learning to fly he had, according to one source, some 1400 hours when he joined the army. He graduated from Luke Field in May, 1943, joining the the 357th at Tonopah. He flew two complete tours, 118 missions, 502 hours of combat, scored 15 victories, held a Silver Star and had the distinction of being rescued twice from the waters of the North Sea. Foy was one of the few - a real "Tiger". After the war, having had enough flying, he joined North American Aviation as a Public Relations Rep and in March, 1950, was killed along with six other North American employees in the in-flight explosion of a company B-25.

JOHN A. KIRLA

CAPTAIN JOHN A. KIRLA was the only one of the double and triple aces who was not one of the original members of the Group. He was born and grew up in the Port Chester, NY area spending much of his early life around boats. He was working in a Connecticut shipyard building sub-chasers when he was drafted at the end of 1942 and assigned to an artillery unit. He immediately applied for transfer to the Air Corps and four months later became an aviation cadet. He graduated in class 44-A, finally arriving at Leiston and the 362nd Squadron late in May, 1944. He completed one tour and after ZI leave, returned for a second combat tour. Of his total of 11.5 victories, four were on the Big Day and three on 24 March 1945. He went to Neubiberg with the Group but when it was de-activated he returned to the ZI and to civilian life.

RICHARD A. "PETE' PETERSON

RICHARD A. PETERSON joined the fledgling 357th Fighter Group at Tonopah, a newly commissioned 2nd Lt. and pilot. When the group reached England and became operational in February, 1944, "Pete" or "Bud" soon began his rise to high scoring pilot in the 364th Squadron, ending the war with 15.5 victories after flying 150 combat missions in two tours. At 21 he was a Major and held several DFCs and a Silver Star. After the war he became a distinquished architect in Minnesota. Highly respected and loved by all who knew him or had served with him, he died early in the year 2000.

JOHN A. STORCH

JOHN A. STORCH joined the Group during training days and was a Captain in the 364th Sqdn. as the Group sailed for Europe. He became Group Operations Officer, but was out of action for awhile due to a broken arm. By the end of March, 1944, he was flying again and was Commander of the 364th, a position he retained until the end of the war. Of his total of 11 victories, three were scored on the Big Day. John A. Storch died of a stroke on 18 May 1985.

CHARLES E. YEAGER

CHARLES E. YEAGER was born in West Virginia in 1923 and joined the U.S. Army in 1941 to become an aircraft mechanic. He served as such until the opportunity came to join the new "Flying Sergeants" program. He graduated, however, as a Flight Officer from Luke Field in 1942 and along with 32 other 2nd Lts. and Flight Officers, reported to the 328th Ftr. Grp., Hamilton Field, CA. Sixteen of these men including Yeager were then assigned to the new 357th Ftr. Grp., where he served throughout the war. Although out of combat for several months due to being shot down and evading capture, he still scored an official 11.5 victories and completed an extended combat tour in January, 1945. Yeager's subsequent Air Force career during which he rose to Brigadier General and became the first man in history to exceed the speed of sound in an aircraft, is well told in his book YEAGER and many other publications.

THE COMMANDERS

Henry Spicer

Donald Graham

Irwin Dregne

THE GROUND OFFICERS

A FEW OF OUR GROUND OFFICERS
TOP: GILBRETH, 362 Eng. off; PAUL BROWN, I.O. 362nd; Doc BARKER
CNTR: ROBT STEWART, 364 ARM; JIM SWEENEY, 364 COMM.
Bttm: NORM BAXTER, 363 Eng off; LEM HENSLEE, 362 EXEC

MEN AT WORK

TOP: HOOD & SCHMIDT; SIEB & KUBISAK

CENTER: LANIER, SHEARER, JOHNSON; MSGT SAM MILLER; 1ST SGT HENRY RAMM

BOTTOM: C/C McKAIN & LT. BURNETT (KIA); AUGUGLIARO

MEN AT WORK

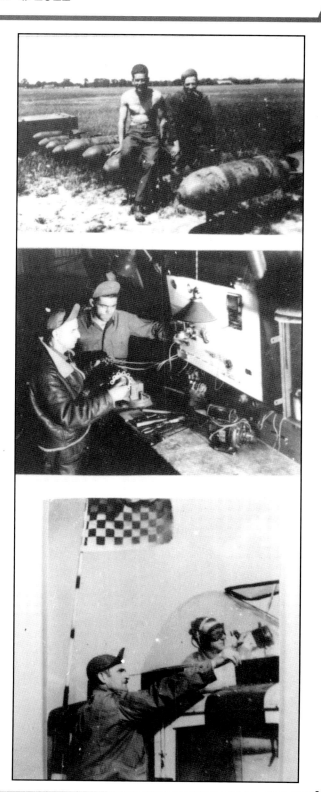

STALWARTS OF THE YOXFORD BOYS

TOP: OVERSTREET, ANKENY, SITZER
CENTER: CONLIN, CARDER, MAXWELL
BOTTOM: (corners) MACE, FREY
GROUP: STEPELTON, KOKO (KIA)
STORCH, RUDER (KIA) CONKLIN (POW)

MORE STALWART YOXFORD BOYS

STALWART YOXFORD BOYS
TOP: HERSHEL HILL, PETE PELON, HAL WYATT
CENTER: FLOYD MAYNARD, PAUL HATALA, IVAN MCGUIRE
BOTTOM: B. WILLIAMS, "HANK" GRUBER, JAMES KENNEY

MORE STALWART YOXFORD BOYS

MORE STALWART YOXFORD BOYS
TOP: BOB SCHIMANSKI, PETE HOWELL, DWAINE SANBORN
CENTER: JOHN HOWELL, WILL FOARD
BOTTOM: NORB FISHER, GERALD TYLER, LLOYD MITCHELL

MORE STALWART YOXFORD BOYS

A FEW STALWARTS OF THE YOXFORD BOYS

NICK FREDERICK, OZZ HOWES, GEORGE REHLING, HUGH MOORHOUSE
BOB WINKS, IRV SNEDECKER, TOM HUGHES, "JACK" MARTIN
TOM RIDELY, GEORGE KOURIS, C. R. CASTER, MAURICE BAKER

RAF EXCHANGE PILOTS

By mid 1944, RAF Bomber Command began to plan for the time when they could switch some of their effort from nighttime to daylight. This would increase bombing accuracy and would be feasible due to the decline of the German fighter force. This may have been the reason why two experienced RAF fighter pilots were assigned to the 357th Fighter Group - in order to gain experience on long range escort.

For reasons unknown, the practice wasn't wide spread and as far as is known, Flight Lieutenants Eric Woolley and Jack Cleland were the only RAF pilots to fly with the 8th Air Force fighters.

By all accounts, both Cleland and Woolley were favorably impressed by their service with THE YOXFORD BOYS, and both were highly regarded by all in the 357th with whom they had contact.

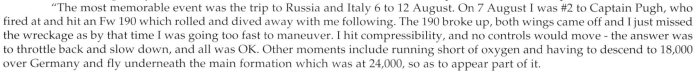

FLIGHT LIEUTENANT ERIC B.H. WOOLLEY

Eric Woolley had enlisted in the British army in 1939 at age 17 and was assigned to the crew on the 3.7" anti-aircraft guns during the Battle of Britain. After that epic battle was won, Woolley applied for and was accepted for pilot training in the RAF. In August 1941, he came to the U.S. to train in one of the USAAF schools, graduating in class 42C. He was kept on at Selma, Alabama as an instructor until January 1943 when he returned to England. He flew Spitfires in several squadrons and then in July 1944 was chosen for assignment to the 362nd Squadron.

He describes his service with the 357th Group: "The opportunity to go to the 8th Air Force for training in long range escort was a very memorable occasion. I arrived at the 362nd Squadron on 10 July 1944. My first flight in a P-51 was on 12 July and my first mission was to Munich on 16 July, flying G4-T a P-51D. According to my records I flew 21 missions, and returned to RAF 131 Squadron around 17 September 1944.

"The most memorable event was the trip to Russia and Italy 6 to 12 August. On 7 August I was #2 to Captain Pugh, who fired at and hit an Fw 190 which rolled and dived away with me following. The 190 broke up, both wings came off and I just missed the wreckage as by that time I was going too fast to maneuver. I hit compressibility, and no controls would move - the answer was to throttle back and slow down, and all was OK. Other moments include running short of oxygen and having to descend to 18,000 over Germany and fly underneath the main formation which was at 24,000, so as to appear part of it.

"The pilots and ground crews were great and easy to get on with, and it was a real pleasure to meet Harvey Mace and other former colleagues at the reunion at Louisville in 1996.

"After leaving 131 Squadron where I flew Spitfires, I was attached to a unit training pilots on the Mustang. In January 1945 I was ferrying Spitfires to Africa via western France, Sardinia and finally Algiers. I then went to Central Flying School at Trenton, Ontario, Canada, to learn to be an instructor. I was demobilized in January, 1946, and went into the family business producing lace. I came to Sark, Channel Islands in 1975. My total flying time was 1616 hours, all single engine apart from 45 minutes in an Avro Anson."

FLIGHT LIEUTENANT JACK CLELAND, RNZAF

Jack Cleland was born and raised in New Zealand. With the war in its second year, he joined the Royal New Zealand Air Force (RNZAF) in March 1941. In four months he had completed his primary training and received his wings. In August of the same year he arrived in England, where he spent most of the next year completing his training. In June 1942, Cleland went to war with 616 Squadron, flying the immortal Spitfire on channel patrols and escorts. After a two month stint in Africa for unknown reaons, he returned to 616 Squadron and on 12 June 1944, shot down two Fw 190s. With his Spitfire damaged by flak, he bailed into the channel and was picked up by ASR.

Early in July, along with Eric Woolley, he joined the 357th posted to the 363rd Squadron, serving there until September. During this period he was assigned P-51, serial number 44-13573, code B6-V, which he named Isobel for his wife. Like Woolley, Cleland also flew the Shuttle mission to Russia in August, and next month he returned to the RAF. After the war he went back to New Zealand and into a business life. He died in Feburary, 1970.

OPERATIONAL AND ACCIDENT DEATHS

EUROPE - JAN. 1944 - MAY 1945

After the Group arrived in England in the fall of 1943, there was about a three month delay before the unit was combat ready. During the approximate month of transition into P-51s, there were no losses. However, losses began before the 11th of February when the Group became operational. Two pilots, Captains Lloyd Hubbard and Joe Giltner were lost while flying familiarization missions with the 354th Group. Giltner was the first, shot down by an Fw 190, but surviving as a POW. Hubbard was hit by flak while strafing an airfield and died in a huge fireball. It was unfortunate that his brother Glenn was also a pilot in the Group and naturally took his brother's death very hard.

It was rapidly brought home with a jolt that this was, indeed, the "Big League", and that the enemy was competent and tough. In his diary for 25 February 1944, Fletcher Adams wrote, after only two weeks in combat: "This has got to come to a close. Another member of the Sad Shack went down today, Beemer bailed out over Germany." Adams had gone through training with Beemer and Don Rice (another loss he refers to), and was close to both of them, now after two weeks, two men from his barracks were gone. By the end of May, Adams had eight victories, but was shot down by an Me 109 on the 30th. Achieving a successful bailout, he was murdered by German civilians, two of whom were tried and convicted after the war. Air Crews on both sides were well aware they should make every effort to surrender to military men, not civilians. This was not always a salvation, but was the best choice of the two.

In addition to the many other hazards to be faced, there was the eternal FLAK! It was the great nemesis of Allied bombers and no small threat to fighters. German anti-aircraft artillery (FLAK is a shortened version of the German for this English term) was the responsibility of *Luftwaffe*, not the army (*Wehrmacht*), as in other countries. No effort or expense was spared in developing and providing the best guns, radar ammunition and other equipment for the flak arm. As the war ran down in 1944, about 1.5 million men and women were employed in this branch, about half of all *Luftwaffe* personnel.

From 1942 on, these units had ample practice as British and U.S. air raids increased in volume and tempo. The heavy flak guns (75 mm and bigger) were not the major threat to fighters, although it was not unusual for a fighter pilot, thinking he was safe at 25,000 feet, to be hit by these heavy guns. The most serious threat to fighters, other than weather and German fighters, were the light automatic weapons (light and heavy machine guns, 20 and 37 mm cannon) used to defend airfields and any other likely target. These weapons took a heavy toll of Allied fighters after ground attack became a common practice. A study of the casualty lists will confirm this.

Throughout the text of this book, when pilots failed to return it is often mentioned, but not always in detail. Here we will examine the fate of some of these men and all losses listed.

Disaster could strike in many ways and one of the worst enemies to be faced was the weather. Often bad over England, The Channel, the North Sea, and the continent, it could also change with dismaying suddenness. The ability to fly well on instruments was a vital key to survival and many pilots were deficient in this skill. Although difficult to say for sure, it is thought that ten pilots were missing in weather related losses. Often these were combined with collisions.

Captain Davis Perron and his wingman, Lt. Elmer Rydberg disappeared in dirty weather on 1 April 1944, and fellow pilots have told this writer that Perron was a poor instrument pilot, and Rydberg a below average formation flier - a lethal combination. Most of these losses occurred over water, resulting in these men being carried as Missing in Action forever. Most collisions took place between aircraft flying in the same formation, but Frank Connaghan perished in a mid-air with an Me 110. Ralph Donnell, who was also involved in a collision with a 110, was luckier. He bailed out and survived as a POW.

An especially violent collision took place on Christmas Eve, 1944. Lt. Wendell Helwig was flying a P-51 named BIG BEAUTIFUL DOLL on what was one of the biggest missions of the war. Flight Officer Saul Sitzer was a witness, and later reported: "We made RV with the bombers at about 1212 hours. Cement Blue Flight in which I was flying #4 position gave chase to an unknown aircraft. While we were reforming, bogies were called in south of the bombers. Lt. Helwig, flying Cement Blue 3, gave chase. I followed and started closing with Lt. Helwig and we ran through two flights of P-51s. Lt. Helwig crashed into the #4 man of a second flight of the oncoming P-51s. Both airplanes burst into flames immediately I watched Lt. Helwig fall about 2,000 feet and saw no parachutes. The collision occurred about ten miles north of Daun, Germany, at 1230 hours and at 21,000 feet. I could not see the markings on the other P-51s."

Although Sitzer was unable to see any markings on the flight of P-51s they tangled with, pilots of that flight were able to identify Helvig's aircraft as having red and yellow nose, B6 codes and red rudder. The unfortunate victim in the other flight was 2nd Lt. Kenneth Mix, of the 343rd Ftr. Sqdn., 55th. Ftr. Grp. Mix was wingman in a half flight of two P-51s, led by 1st Lt. Vincent Gordon.

They were spares on this date and positioned in the middle of a box of four 55th Grp. flights, when Helwig and Sitzer slashed through their formation resulting in the catastrophic collision on which killed both Mix and Helwig.

Lts. William McGinley and Santiago Gutierrez, of the 363rd Sqdn. died in a very similar accident on 29 March 1944. Captain Clarence Anderson was leading Blue flight on climb out through overcast, 20 miles off the British coast when White flight, doing the same thing, flew through Blue flight. Lt. Edward Simpson, Blue 1, reported: "Blue 2 was struck broadside by White 3 (Gutierrez)." Simpson climbed out of the melee, then let down to sea level in the area of the crash, but saw nothing and returned to base, his left drop tank having been hit by "something unknown".

No one knows what happened to Herman Delager. He had been dispatched to nearby Stansted to ferry a P-51 to home base. 1st. Lt. Tillie Botti, Leiston's Flying Control Officer, EARL DUKE to scores of 357th pilots, reported: "I was on duty at the control tower at 1815 hours B.S.T. on 19 January 1945, when Lt. Delager called. 'EARL DUKE', he asked, 'Are you receiving me, this is Dollar 43'. I answered, 'Roger, we're receiving you fine.' He then wanted to know if we were firing flares. I answered in the negative. 'Dollar 43, do you want a steer.' I then inquired. He said, 'No, I'm OK.' He was obviously in complete control of himself and his ship.

"About seven minutes later he called again saying he was over water and could see searchlights. 'I'm coming back to base', Delager said. In a short while I began trying to contact him over the R/T, but he did not answer. I called and called, but Dollar 43 failed to reply. Nobody has seen or heard from Lt. Delager since. He and his plane just disappeared, and to date his fate remains a mystery." Forty six years later it remains so.

Whether an airman is killed on his first mission or his last makes no practical difference - he is just as dead either way. Nevertheless, it always seems more tragic when an airman has flown a full combat tour (or more) and then "buys the farm" on his last sortie. Major Edwin Hiro, C.O. of the 363rd Sgdn., was the victim of such an occurrence. A group document of the period says he "lacked only returning home from the mission to complete a tour of duty when he became MIA during the air-

borne invasion of Holland, 19 September 1944". There was, and is, confusion on the whereabouts of Ed Hiro's remains. He is listed on The Wall of the Missing at the American Cemetery at Margraten in the Netherlands, near where he was shot down by 109s of JG 26. Yet, German documents with his Missing Aircrew Report (MACR) clearly state that he was buried in the Catholic cemetery at Vreden. When his nephew tried to visit his grave at Margraten in the early 1970s, he was told the remains had been returned to the U.S. The confusion of war often carries on in its aftermath.

Pilots who survived a bailout or a crash landing in enemy territory and reached a POW camp - usually a *Stalag Luft*, had an excellent chance of surviving the war, but at least two pilots of the 357th were an exception. Lt. William Gambill was shot down in a dogfight with 109s, and had reached a POW transient station at Frankfurt, a waypoint on his way to a *Stalag Luft*. There, on 23 March 1945, he was killed by an Allied bomb.

Another death in POW status was Daniel L. Finley. On the morning of 29 July 1944, Finley's P-51B suffered engine failure, and he took to his chute over Germany. Captured by rural police, he ended up in *Stalag Luft* III near Sagan. As Germany struggled for survival in the spring of 1945, their prison administration moved thousands of Allied prisoners deeper into Germany to avoid liberation by advancing Russian armies. Most of this movement was by foot, often in bitter weather and many died. Two of these long forced marches resulted in drastic deterioration of Finley's health. Wallace Reid, who had been a member of Finley's flight in the 364th Sqdn. and went down five days after Finley, recorded in his diary: "April 15 1945, a chaplain brought the news that Dan Finley died from illness that he developed 'on the trip' (the forced marches)." Two days later Reid served as a pallbearer at Moosburg *Stalag* Cemetery.

During this same period, with the war winding down, Lt. Jacob Geil was the victim of an unusual accident, his P-51 was hit by a drop tank from another P-51 above. With part of its right wing missing, aircraft and pilot went into the North Sea 15 miles off Tershelling Island. His name is on the Wall of the Missing at Margraten in the Netherlands.

One phenomenon of air combat, often reported by pilots and aircrew in both world wars, was how suddenly a sky full of airplanes could became a sky empty of airplanes. Flight Officer Patrick Mallione was a 357th pilot who vanished in one of these empty skies and 363 squadron mate Glen Zarnke later reported: "On March 2 1945, on a combat mission under F.O. 1683A, I was flying #3 position in Cement Yellow flight. Captain Robert Moore was flying in #1 position. The last time I saw Lt.

Mallione was when he sighted an Me 109 coming in from 11 o'clock. Capt. Moore dropped his tanks as I dropped mine and I looked back at F/O Mallione behind me. He had not dropped his tanks as yet, but I presumed he did and followed us. Both Capt. Moore and I went into compressibility in the dive after the 109. When we recovered, F/O Mallione wasn't to be seen. We both called to him on the R/T but received no answer. We presumed he had joined another aircraft and came on home. I called him several times on the way out, but still received no answer. These events took place at 1020 hours at a point 10 miles south of Wittenburg."

German records indicate the location where Malione's Mustang struck the ground and the fact he was dead in the wreck, but give no further clues. Two weeks after his death, his commission as a 2nd Lieutenant came through channels and a supplement to his MACR routinely made note of this fact.

All of those lost in the course of aerial flight in Europe died in Mustangs, with only one exception. The mission on the 20th of January was noteworthy for several reasons. It was a long mission on which heavy bomber escort was the main job, although ground targets were strafed, during which Lt. Edward Haydon was shot down (he survived as POW). The highlight of the day was the downing of two Me 262s by Lts. Wright and Karger. On return to base one P-51 skidded off an icy runway and was wrecked and another bellied in near base, out of fuel.

Thirteen aircraft landed on continental air strips, low on fuel and for various other reasons. The next day, the 21st, the 363rd Squadron dispatched a mechanic and pilot to France to replace parts and repair three aircraft. The mechanic was SSgt. Melvin Schueneman and the aircraft was an AT-6D, one of the group's utility machines. The pilot was Lt. Walter Corby. Richard Smith was 363rd Operations NCO, and he remembers that Corby was a "time hog". He liked to fly and hung around Ops, ready to test hops, ferry flights or administrative flights that came up.

Corby and Schueneran flew to France without incident on 21 Jan. 1945, and spent several days there repairing P-51s, one of which was Joe Cannon's, which had a blown tail wheel tire due to a rough landing. On the 27th, 363rd Ops cleared Corby for return to home base. The weather in southern England was not good, but as any airman knows, they may have been afflicted with "get-home-itis". At approximately 1430 hours, the aircraft crashed at Swingate, near Dover. Visibility was 1,000 yards with light fog, and 10/10 cloud at 200 feet.

The accident report says it is assumed the pilot was on instruments but he may well have been staying below the 200 foot overcast, attempting to remain VFR

when contact with terrain brought the flight to an end. The accident report lists the cause as "undetermined".

We have highlighted here, only a few of those who did not survive. The majority of those lost in the combat zone died as a result of enemy action in the form of flak or were shot down by fighters, either the Me 109 or the Fw 190. As far as is known, only one pilot was shot down by an Me 262. We close this chapter with a particularly sad case, but felt that it must be included, as there were undoubtedly others who felt as Jim Colburn did but managed to carry on to the end.

War is violence, and even if everyone plays by the "rules", it is depressing game. It is perhaps sad that most soldiers adapt to the violence to a certain degree, varying widely from individual to individual and do things they would not consider in more peaceful times. If none could adapt, there would be no war.

"Civilized" rules of war say that civilians are not legitimate targets, but this has never been strictly observed in any war and in WWII, a case was made that civilian targets are part of a nation's war making potential and therefore legitimate for attack. During WWII, all nations attack targets which may not have been civilian targets, but did put civilians at risk. Tens of thousands died because they were unlucky enough to be in the proximity of genuine military installations. *Nazi* and Japanese forces were especially flagrant violators of this, but the Allied nations also did not hesitate to strike targets if they were thought to have military potential.

Many fighter pilots of all nations, possibly carried away by the normal violence of war, often attack targets that clearly had no relationship to the military. During the *Nazi* attacks on Britain in 1940, German fighters sometimes attacked small villages, especially in the coastal areas. Allied fighters often strafed farm trucks and wagons, villages and isolated farm houses and even single bicyclists, throughout Europe on the theory that they right be German soldiers.

Many men engaged in the aerial campaign could not accept this, but most did their duty avoiding as much as possible those targets which were not military. One pilot of the 357th Group who was repulsed by these tactics, and wrote his thoughts, was Lt. James E. Colburn of the 364th Squadron. Sometime in the spring of 1944, Colburn's flight had strafed the main street of a village in Germany in which there were many civilians and also in the line fire, a church. At this late date, it is impossible to tell but there may well have been legitimate military targets in the area. Armies tend to use villages and towns as bases for obvious reasons. In any case, Colburn was considerably shaken by the incident, especially after viewing his gun camera film.

One of his hut mates, and close friend was Lt. John Salsman who had known him during training and had come overseas with him. Over four decades later, Salsman recalls: "That night Colburn wouldn't have a beer, and he loved beer. He talked and talked. I went to sleep and awoke about 3 a.m., and he was writing a letter, he said to his sister. It turned out to be to me. The next day he was shot down by an Me 109. I heard someone screaming to him to break and then said "My God, he didn't do anything."

Colburn was KIA on 14 June 1944. According to a statement by his element leader, Robert Shaw, Colburn had shot down a long nose 190 (he is credited with this victory in the USAAF victory credits) and was then hit by gunfire from another e/a, crashing and exploding near Claye Souilly, east of Paris.

Colburn's sister, a Red Cross girl came up from London to pick up his belongings and found the letter to Salsman, along with his .45, his watch, and a liquor flask, which were to go to Salsman. He still has the watch and the flask.

James Colburn's poignant letter is given here in full, another sad aspect of war:

> *"This is one of those rare occasions when I feel that my thoughts are worthy of being put or paper! Perhaps it will also give me a clearer picture. Never have I felt that I was a narrow ended person or a guy who was very religious. I've always seemed quite sinful - but there is nothing finer to me than honesty and fair mindedness and high principles. That is what this war is being fought for. The Germans and the Japanese violated these things. We are fighting this by the principle of an eye for an eye and a tooth for a tooth. In some degree it has to be so and men against men is life. However, in the short time I have been flying, I have been given the chance to see that in our aerial warfare against Germany we have brought ourselves down to their level and have murdered women and children of Germany. If this is tactical war and has to be, may God have mercy on us.*
>
> *"Within this group with which I am flying we strafed houses, villages, and what came before our guns, but even though I didn't do it myself, I'm as guilty, for I do not have the courage to quit before I do kill innocent people.*
>
> *"Bombing cities to ruins is not right by any means. I can only think one thing that this U.S. Army Air Force is a force in the fact that it is against real American principles that we all claim to have.*
>
> *"Men in the trenches is one thing, but killing women and children is sinful to the highest degree. It is as bad as what the Germans did to occupied countries and Japs to English and American women. Some people will say 'it is only right' - they are heathens without any better instincts than a maniac. What is to come of it all?"*
>
> *James L. Colburn*
>
> *"P.S. Perhaps I'll be lucky and be killed in aerial combat and won't live to see the results of this war."*

There is one other category of casualty which must be mentioned. There is evidence that at least one pilot of the 357th was executed by German Troops.

On 27 May 1944, Major John Storch was leading 364th Blue flight with Tom "Little Red" Harris as element leader and Dean Post as #4 man. Storch led his flight into a dogfight with an Me 109 in which P-51s from both the 357th and 352nd Groups were involved. When the confusion cleared, both Harris and Post had disappeared. Although Storch did manage to contact Harris on the R/T briefly, neither man was seen again. Harris was captured and spent the rest of the war as a POW.

At one of our 357th Fighter Group re-unions, this writer was given an evasion narrative by Steve Miller (the son of the great band leader, Glenn Miller). Written by William M. Baker, a gunner in the 388th Bomb Grp, who was shot down in September, 1944, and remained with the French underground until liberated in December. During this time he was given a letter from Lt. Dean Post, to his mother, along with his Lt. bars, dog tags and wings. The French told him that Post had been badly burned in an air to air collision and was being treated by them. A few days later the Germans took him away and he was shot, along with another (Unknown) fighter pilot. The items were sent to his mother after the war. At this time we have no official record to confirm or deny.

A week before that, on the 21st of May, Joe Pierce, 363rd Squadron, was shot down by flak while strafing a locomotive near Anklam. Robert Foy reported: "The ship turned violently to the left immediately after it was hit and plane struck ground breaking into a huge burst of flame. The pilot did not leave the ship before it hit the ground."

Bill Overstreet also observed the crash and felt that no one could have survived. However, for many years after the war, the story went around that he had survived the crash and had been executed by the Germans.

In 1999 this writer obtained, from the appropriate U.S. Army agency, the entire file on Pierce relating to his death, the investigation and the recovery of his remains, and the eventual shipment of them to Oklahoma. No where in these records is there any indication that his death was caused by anything but the affects of the crash. Therefore, in this case at least, it appears we can discount the rumors of his execution.

DIED IN THE LINE OF DUTY

DIED IN THE LINE OF DUTY.
TOP: MATHEW CRAWFORD, ART LINGO, WM MOONEY
CENTER: WALTER PERRY, FRED MCCALL, WM GILBERT
BOTTOM: ROBT SCHLIEKER; ROBT WISER, WM TOMPSON

IN MEMORY - EUROPE

The European air war was a brutal affair, as discussed elsewhere. All three air forces engaged, the USAAF, The RAF, and the *Luftwaffe* suffered heavy losses. 8th Air Force alone lists about 30,000 men dead or missing. Most of these were bomber crewmen, but among the fighters lost, about 1200 were P-51s.

The 357th Fighter Group killed or missing roster presented here lists 78 names. This was about average for 8th Air Force fighter units, with the 4th Group suffering 131 dead and the 361st with 63.

Of these 78, two were enlisted men, one killed in an aircraft accident, the other of duty related illness. The remaining 76 were pilots. Although we believe this is the complete listing, it should be remembered that wartime records (or any records, for that matter!) are not always correct and there may be some we have overlooked.

In addition, the date of death may not be correct, but reflects the date the pilot went missing. Date of death may be later. Aircraft serial numbers are, in most cases from the Missing Aircrew Report, but in a few cases, the s/n had to be "deduced" and may not be correct.

Lastly, in the composite photos of our dead, these are by no means all of them. For many there are no photos available and those presented represent all.

DIED IN LINE OF DUTY
TOP: OTTO JENKINS, GEORGE RICE
CENTER: WM. REESE, LEROY RUDER
BOTTOM: JAMES STRODE, MERLE CEDOZ

DIED IN THE LINE OF DUTY

DIED IN THE LINE OF DUTY
TOP: RICHARD C. SMITH, KIRBY BROWN
CENTER: CHARLES CAMPBELL, WENDALL HELWIG, M. GALLANT
BOTTOM: ELLIS ROGERS, ROBT FIFIELD

DIED IN THE LINE OF DUTY

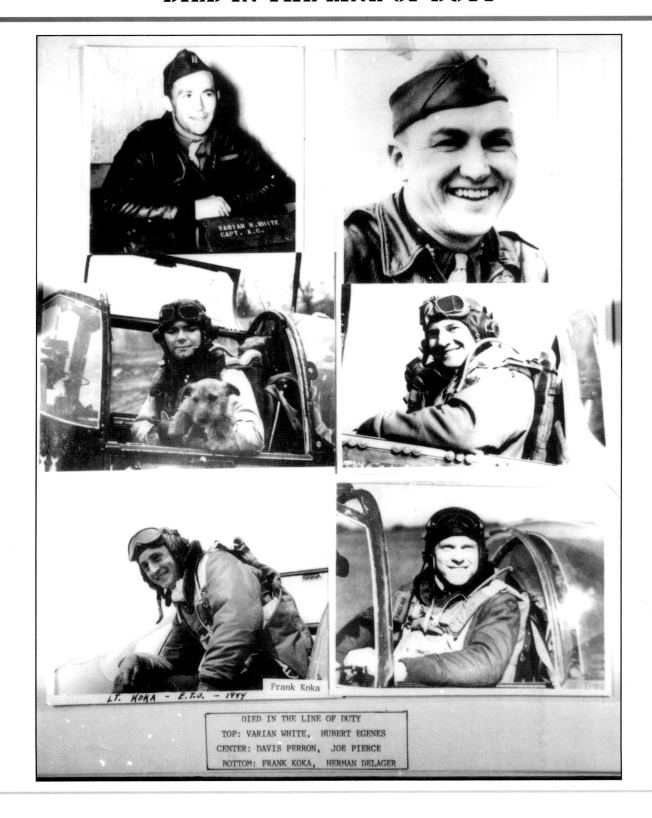

Frank Koka

LT. KOKA - E.T.O. - 1944

DIED IN THE LINE OF DUTY
TOP: VARIAN WHITE, HUBERT EGENES
CENTER: DAVIS PERRON, JOE PIERCE
BOTTOM: FRANK KOKA, HERMAN DELAGER

DIED IN THE LINE OF DUTY

DIED IN THE LINE OF DUTY
TOP: IRVING SMITH, SANTIAGO GUTIERREZ
CENTER: JIM BROWNING, WM. GAMBILL, LLOYD HUBBARD
BOTTOM: WALTER CORBY, WM. McGINLEY

DIED IN THE LINE OF DUTY

DIED IN THE LINE OF DUTY
TOP: ROBERT FANDRY - ALVIN F. PYEATT
CENTER: JAMES COLBURN - MANUAL SOO
BOTTOM: PAUL HOLMBERG - MARION BURNETT

DIED IN THE LINE OF DUTY

DIED IN THE LINE OF DUTY

TOP: EDDIE SIMPSON,   RICHARD W. TAYLOR
CENTER: A. BIEREILER, WARREN DORANSKI, WARREN CORWIN
BOTTOM: P. MALLIONE,   D. SIVERTS

NAME	DATE	ACFT S/N	FINAL FATE
Adams, Fletcher E.	30 May 44	43-1246	KIA Shot down by Me 109, murdered by civilians
Anderson, Richard A.	13 Jan 45	43-6987	KIT Killed in training crash, UK
Barrett, George	14 June 45		Collision. Bailed into sea.
Bierweiler, Alfred W.	21 May 44	44-1119	KIT Killed in training crash, UK
Blanchard, James L.	19 Sept 44	44-13741	KIA Shot down by fighters, Arnhem
Brown, Kirby M.	13 Sept 44	44-13698	MIA Shot down by light flak
Browning, James W.	9 Feb 45	44-15630	KIA Collided with Me 262, both killed.
Burnett, Marion E.	3 Sept 44	44-15630	MIA Unknown, probably shot down by fighter.
Campbell, Charles O.	17 Aug 44	43-6999	KIT Killed in training crash, UK
Carroll, Darwin J.	22 Feb 44	43-6576	KIA Cause Unknown.
Chandler, Harold D.	30 Dec 44	44-13719	KIA Cause Unknown
Childs, John K.	10 Jun 44	43-6563	KIA Hit by gunfire as he passed in front of Lt.George, who was strafing a truck.
Colburn, James E.	14 Jun 44	43-24763	KIA Shot down by fighter.
Connaghan, Frank J.	24 Apr 44	43-7176	KIA Collided with Me 110.
Corby, Walter E.	27 Jan 45	42-84593	KIT Killed in AT-6 crash, UK, with SSgt Schuneman
Corwin, Warren B.	8 Nov 44	43-12227	KIA Probably shot down by Me 262
Crawford, Mathew	2 Mar 45	44-15161	KIA Shot down by flak
Delager, Herman R.	19 Jan 45	44-6365	MIA Vanished on final approach into home base, over water
Denesha, John H.	7 Jun 44	42-106652	MIA Shot down by flak
Doranski, Warren J.	8 Nov 44	Unknown	MIA Engine failure, in channel, no MACR located.
Egenes, Hubert I.	28 Mar 44	43-6794	KIA Shot down by flak
Eisert, Ralph: E.	27 Feb 44	42-106447	KIT Collided with Hoffman, near base.
Fandray, Robert J.	8 Sept 44	44-13543	KIA Shot down by fighter, Arnhem.
Ferron, Donald J.	10 Aug 44	42-106696	KIA Collided with Simpson
Fifield, Robert S.	3 May 45	44-63710	KIT Collided with RAF Mustang
Finley, Daniel L.	30 July 44	42-106843	Died Engine failure, died in POW camp
Fuller, Sam C.	18 Nov 44	44-13546	KIA Engine failure, possible flak
Gallant, Morris E.	Unknown	42-106721	MIA Cause unknown.
Gambill, William W.	8 March 44	42-103041	KIA Shot down by fighter, died as POW from Allied bomb.
Giarrizzo, Lawrence P.	2 Nov 44	44-13735	KIA Wing failure over enemy territory
Giel, Jacob	3 April 45	44-14682	KIA Hit by drop tank, lost in North Sea
Gilbert, William T.	24 Dec 44	44-15620	KIA Shot down by Fw 190, which he also shot down, both killed
Graeff, Kenneth F.	15 Sept 44	43-24842	MIA Vanished climbing thru overcast, probable collision w/Nowlin.
Gutierrez, Santiago R.	29 Mar 44	43-7052	MIA Collided w/McGinley in o'cast when 1 flight flew thru another
Helwig, Wendall D.	24 Dec 44	44-13932	KIA Collided with 352nd Grp P-51. Lt. Kenneth Mix also killed
Hilsted, Roger A.	12 May 44	43-6634	KIA Shot down by fighter
Hiro, Edwin W.	18 Sept 44	44-13518	KIA Shot down by fighter, Arnhem
Hoffman, Robert R.	27 Feb 45	43-24766	KIT Collided with Eisert near base
Holmberg, Paul E.	30 July 44	43-6727	KIA Aircraft exploded for unknown reason during mission.
Hubbard, Lloyd M.	9 Feb 44	43-12368	KIA Shot down by flak while flying with 354th Group.
Jenkins, Joseph M.	24 May 44	42-103389	KIA Shot down by flak.
Jenkins, Otto D.	24 Mar 45	44-63199	KIA Killed in crash, home base, returning from mission
Johnson, Holsey C. Jr.	10 Feb 45	43-6755	KIT Aircraft disintegrated during dive bombing practice.
Koka, Frank	7 July 44	43-6858	KIA Shot down by fighter
Leek, James W.	28 Sept .44	43-6971	KIT Killed in crash, near base
Lingo, Arthur M.	11 April 44	43-12122	MIA Unknown, probably shot down by fighter
McCall, Frederick C.	10 Jan 45	44-15026	KIA Shot down by flak
McGinley, William R.	29 Mar 44	43-6628	MIA collided with Gutierrez
Mallione, Patrick J.	2 Mar 45	44-14888	KIA Unknown
Mooney, William H.	24 Dec 44	44-11198	KIA Shot down and captured. Shot to death by as German policeman named Hoffman, while in captivity. Tried by an Allied court, Hoffman was executed in 1948.
Murphy, Alva C.	2 Mar 45	44-63765	KIA shot down by flak.
Nowlin, Louis E.	15 Sept 44	42-106783	MIA Collided with Graeff
Perron, Davis T.	1 Apr 44	43-6792	MIA Vanished in bad weather with Rydberg
Perry, Walter H.	23 Dec 44	44-11689	KIA Wing failure during combat
Pierce, Joseph F.	21 May 44	43-6429	KIA Shot down by flak
Post, Dean W.	27 May 44	42-106632	KIA Probable collision with Tom Harris
Pyeatt, Alvin F.	16 Mar 44	43-6960	KIA shot down by fighter, died in German hospital
Reese, William C.	21 May 44	43-12313	KIA Shot down by flak
Rogers, Ellis A.	8 May 44	42-106793	KIA Wing failure
Roycroft, Horace M.	18 Oct 44	44-13897	KIA lost in bad weather
Ruder, LeRoy A.	6 June 44	42-106768	KIA Engine failure, may have been killed on ground after bailout
Rydberg, Elmer D.	1 Apr 44	43-6929	MIA Vanished with Perron
Schlieker, Robert L.	13 Jan 45	44-14245	KIA Killed in crash near base on mission return.
Schuneman, Melvin	27 Jan 45	42-84593	KIC SSgt, crew chief, killed in AT-6 crash with Corby
Simpson, Edward K.	14 Aug 44	4413712	KIA Collided with Ferron, killed on ground in battle zone.
Siverts, Donovan D.	9 May 44	43-6427	KIA Shot down by fighter
Smith, Irving A.	6 June 44	43-6947	MIA Unknown, vanished on D-Day
Smith, Richard C.	29 June 44	43-6974	KIA Probably shot down by fighter
Soo, Manuel K.	29 May 45	44-13578	KIT Crashed, lost control in overcast
Strode, James R.	27 Mar 44	43-6978	MIA Unknown, dropped out of formation in overcast
Sutton, Edwin R.	29 Mar 44	43-6454	MIA Left formation for unknown reason
Taylor, Richard W.	23 Feb 45	44-14762	KIA Dropped out of formation, crashed Holland, Unknown reason
Thompson, William R.	16 Jan 45	44-63220	KIA Killed in crash near base.
Valkwitch, James A.	13 Sept 44	42-106473	KIA Engine failure
Vogel, Konstantin, J.	18 Mar 44	43-12442	KIA Shot down by fighter
Warren, Jack R.	18 Mar 44	43-12124	MIA Vanished in bad weather
Wiser, Robert	16 Nov 44	Unknown	KIA Weather crash near base returning from mission.

NOTE: In addition, SSGT Louis Boudreaux, died, unknown date, duty related illness.

CAPT. WILLIAM H. MOONEY - MURDERED

It is Christmas Eve, 1944. The weather has been miserable all month. In the Ardennes Forest of Belgium, American troops - short of winter clothing and everything else, have been fighting desperately for a week to stem Germany's last massive attempt to change the course of the war. Their efforts will ultimately be successful - the powerful German offensive will fail.

The 8th Air Force is out in huge numbers (the largest of the war) to help the beleaguered ground troops, and so is the 357th. Colonel Dregne and Major Peterson lead 75 P-51s, in two groups, off Leiston's runways shortly before noon. The *Luftwaffe* is also out in force and it will be an eventful Christmas Eve.

Before evening chow, the Mustangs have returned and it has been a good day with claims of 31 enemy fighters shot down. Statistically the cost has been reasonable - three pilots fail to return, all are dead. However, for those lost and their families, it is not a reasonable statistic.

Captain William H. Mooney Jr., 362nd FS, along with Lt. Jesse Frey were spares and would not have had to fly the mission. Both continued however, flying above and behind Dollar red leader. Jesse Frey's statement from the Missing Aircrew Report: "Captain William H. Mooney Jr., and I were flying Dollar spare, above and behind Dollar Red leader. When the Fw 190s were called in below us in the vicinity of Fulda, Germany, Captain Mooney split-essed into the trailing gaggle of 190s. A 190 from the right side crossed in between Mooney and me and broke into me. I broke into him, but the 190 reversed his turn into another P-51. By this time I had lost Mooney. When I last saw him, he was tacked onto an Fw 190. Several pilots of this Sqdn. testify that they saw an Olive Drab P-51 of this unit on fire and saw its pilot bail out. Since Mooney's ship was painted this color, it was possibly he. All of the foregoing took place around 1425 BST."

There are several translations of *Luftwaffe* documents with Mooney's MACR, all of which indicate the aircraft was totally destroyed and the pilot dead. He was buried in the village cemetery of Laubach. There was no marker on the grave. As an unknown U.S. soldier, the case was investigated postwar by a Quartermaster Graves Registration Company so his identity could be established. The final report was dated 5 August 1947. During the investigation in August, 1945, the team obtained the following statement from the Mayor of Laubach: "The pilot, unknown, made a crash landing and was then shot in the back by a man by the name of Hoffman who is now in a prison camp in the vicinity of Marburg."

Although initially carried as an unknown by U.S. authorities, several *Luftwaffe* reports date 31 December 1944, give his full name and service number. Whether they were aware of the circumstances of his death are unknown.

In the latter part of 1993, this writer was contacted by a Hans-Peter Koller of Offenbach, Germany. Koller was researching the death of Mooney and asked for my assistance. In December, 1944, he had been a school boy about 11 years old and lived in the area where Mooney landed. He had been a school mate of the son of Hoffman referred to above.

The results of Koller's research were published in 1995 in the form of a small book titled "*Der Fliegermard Von Freiensen*". Mr. Koller has kindly sent copies of the book to myself and to Arch Mooney, William's brother. It is well illustrated with photos and appears well done. It is, of course, in German. Arch Mooney, however, financed a translation of the book.

Koller sent a copy of the original trial transcript, which is of course in English. We will quote here the evidence of the prosecution. All references to "the accused" refer to Emil Hoffman."The accused and *Ortgruppenleiter* in the NSDAP since 1933, arrested an American flyer, 24 December 1944 at Freiensen, Germany. The American flyer was in the custody of Heene (Otto). After winning an argument with a German noncommissioned officer for the custody of the flyer, the accused left the flyer in the custody of Heene while he returned to his home.

"Shortly thereafter the accused reappeared in his party uniform carrying a revolver in his hand. The accused and Heene together with another German then marched the flyer toward Lubach, Germany where the flyer was turned over to the *Kreisleiter's* office. Heene was on the left of the flyer and the accused was on his right. Suddenly the accused jumped up behind the flyer and fired a shot into him. The flyer staggered and the accused grabbed him by the arm and shot him again. The flyer fell to the ground. The accused returned to Freiensen, secured his horse and wagon, and returned to fetch the flyer to Lubach where the victim was buried. The pathologist's report shows only two gunshot wounds in the victim's body. The flyer at no time tried to escape on the way to Lubach."

Heene and Hartman were both acquitted, but despite a skilled presentation by the defense (A U.S. Army Captain Morse), Hoffman was convicted of the murder and sentenced to be hanged. He was executed by hanging at the Landsberg War Crimes Prison in August, 1948.

Mooney was the second 357th pilot known to have been murdered
by a German civilian, the first being Captain Fletcher Adams in May, 1944.

THE AMERICAN CEMETERIES IN EUROPE

After the war it was a monumental task to collect American Forces dead from the many places they had fallen across Europe. This was the responsibility of the War Department Graves Registration Service, under The Quartermaster General. Under public law, the next of kin of deceased servicemen could elect to have internment in an American cemetery in Europe or return the remains to the U.S. for final internment in private or national cemeteries.

The collection of these remains after the war was a massive job. Apparently it was German policy to bury dead airmen, enemy and their own, in the nearest village or town cemetery. This would mean, of course, that American airmen would have been in thousands of different cemeteries throughout Europe.

There are eight American cemeteries in Northern Europe, plus one in Italy and one in England, all under the administration of the American Battle Monuments Commission. 357th dead are present in all of these except Italy.

Three of these are interned at large installation near Cambridge, England. Two of these were pilots killed in training crashes and the third an enlisted man - a suicide. There are over 3800 graves at this cemetery and over 5,000 names on the Wall of the Missing, those with no known grave. Twelve of these are 357th pilots.

We list here all 357th combat and training dead who remain in European cemeteries or on the various Walls of the Missing. All of these marvelously maintained installations are worth a visit for anyone in these areas.

CAMBRIDGE - Situated 3 miles west of Cambridge, England
ROBERT L. HOFFMAN, 364TH F.S. Killed in collision, 27 February 1945, with Ralph Eisert.
WILLIAM B. THOMPSON, 363rd F.S. Killed in crash, 16 January 1945.

The following are listed on **Wall of the Missing, Cambridge:**
GEORGE P. BARRETT. 363rd F.S. Missing, 14 June 1945, training loss.
HERMAN H. DELAGER, 362nd F.S. Missing, 19 January 1945.
WARREN J. DORANSKI, 363rd F.S. Missing, 8 November 1944.
MORRIS E. GALLANT, 364th F.S. Missing unknown date.
KENNETH F. GRAEFF, 363rd F.S. Collision with Louis Nowlin, missing, 15 September 1944. .
SANTIAGO R. GUTIERREZ, 363rd F.S. Collision with William McGinley, missing, 29 March 1944.
WILLIAM R. McGINLEY, 363rd F.S. Collision with Gutierrez, missing.
LOUIS E. NOWLIN, 363rd F.S. Collision with Kenneth Graeff, missing.
DAVIS T. PERRON., 362nd F.S. Missing 1 April 1944.
ELMER D. RYDBERG, 362nd F.S. Missing 1 April 1944.
JAMES E. STRODE, 364th F.S. Missing 27 March 1944.
JACK R. WARREN, 364th F.S. Missing 18 March 1944.
NOTE: All of these men lost in the Channel or the North Sea.

NORMANDY - Situated on a cliff overlooking Omaha Beach, just east of St-Laurent-sur-Mer.
JOSEPH M. JENKINS, 364TH F.S.MIA, 24 May 1944.

BRITTANY - Situated one mile southeast of the village of St. James, Manche, France.
JOHN N. DENESHA, 364th F.S. MIA, 7 June 1944

NETHERLANDS - Situated in the southeast corner of The Netherlands in the village of Margraten.
JACOB F. GIEL, 362nd F.S. MIA, 2 April 1945. On Wall of the Missing.
WILLIAM T. GILBERT, 362nd F.S. MIA, 24 December 1944.
ARTHUR M. LINGO, 362nd F.S. MIA, 11 April 1944. On Wall of the Missing.
EDWIN W. HIRO, 363rd F.S. MIA, 19 September 1944. On Wall of the Missing.
LLOYD M. HUBBARD, 363rd F.S. MIA, 8 February 1944.
DARWIN J. CARROLL, 364th F.S. MIA, 22 February 1944.
FRED C. McCALL, 364th F.S. MIA, 10 January 1945.
RICHARD C. SMITH, 364th F.S. MIA, 29 June 1944.

ARDENNES - Situated near the village of Neupre, 12 miles southeast of Liege, Belgium.
MARION E. BURNETT, 363rd F.S. MIA, 13 September 1946.
ELLIS A. ROGERS, 363rd F.S. MIA, 8 May 1944.
DONOVAN D. SIVERTS, 363rd F.S. MIA, 9 May 1944.
WILLIAM C. REESE, 364th F.S. MIA, 21 May 1944.

EPINAL - Situated four miles south of Epinal, Vosages, France.
EDWARD K. SIMPSON, 363rd F.S MIA, 11 August 1944
DEAN H. POST, 364TH F.S. MIA, 27 May 1944.

LUXEMBOURG - Situated in the capitol city of Luxembourg
WALTER N. PERRY, 362nd F.S. MIA, 23 December 1944.
JAMES W. DROWNING, 363rd F.S.MIA, 9 February 1945.
    On Wall of the Missing.
ALVA C. MURPHY, 364th F.S. MIA, 2 March 1945.

LORRAINE - Situated 3/4 mile north of St. Alvold, France.
FRANK 0. CONNAGHAN, 362nd F.S. MIA, 24 April 1944.
SAM G. FULLER, 362nd F.S. MIA, 18 November 1944.
MATTHEW CRAWFORD, 363rd F.S. MIA, 2 March 1945.

357TH PILOTS DOWN IN ENEMY TERRITORY

All of the below listed pilots either bailed out or made crash landings in the land of the enemy. Unless otherwise noted, all returned to Allied hands, either as evaders or at the end of the war. The cause of many of these are listed as "engine failure". However most of these cannot be certain and an unknown number could have been caused by enemy gunfire - possibly not even realized by the pilot involved.

NAME	SQDN	DATE	ACFT S/N	STATUS
Bank, Raymond M.	364	2 Mar 45	44-15266	POW Bellied in after combat
Baron, Walter,	364	25 Aug 44	42-106854	Interned Landed Sweden under mysterious circumstances. Released after about 3 months.
Behling, George A.	362	14 Jan 45	44-15527	POW Chased by 190, not hit, overstressed engine failed.
Beemer, Thomas A.	362	25 Feb 44	43-6927	POW Shot down by B-17 gunner, bailed, chute streamed, landed in trees. Later repatriated.
Boyle, Alfred R.	363	21 Feb 44	43-6723	Evaded Cause of loss unknown.
Breunig, John J.	362			Evaded Cause and other data unknown.
Bridges, Archie F.	364	19 May 44	42-106648	POW Cause unknown.
Brown, Robert D.	362	13 Sept 44	43-6556	Interned in Switzerland after bailout. Shot down by fighter.
Burtner, Charles D.	364	25 Aug 44	44-13345	Interned in Sweden, engine trouble, released after about 3 months.
Carder, John B.	364	12 May 44	42-106777	POW Cause unknown, bellied in Germany.
Carter, Rollin L.	362	30 Jul 44	43-7143	POW Engine failure, possible combat damage
Conklin, Cyril D.	364	27 May 44	42-106640	POW Shot down by fighter
Currie, George D.	364	11 Apr 44	43-6773	POW Shot down by flak
Davis, Glendon V.	364	28 Apr 44	43-6867	POW Engine failure, possible flak
Donnell, Ralph H.	363	24 Apr 44	43-6986	POW Collided with Me 110
Drollinger, Lynn H.	362	28 Mar 44	43-6729	Evader Engine failure over France
Dunlop, William R.	363	14 Jan 45	44-15370	POW Shot down by fighter
Elliott, Benjamin F.	364	27 Apr 44	42-106790	POW Engine failure
Finley, Daniel L.	364	30 Jul 44	42-106843	POW Engine failure. Died in prison camp.
Gailer, Frank L.	363	27 Nov 44	44-11331	POW Shot down by P-51 from another group
Gambill, Willian W.	363	8 Mar 44	42-103041	POW Shot down by fighter. Killed by allied bomb.
Giltner, Joe H.	363	5 Jan 44	43-12187	POW Shot down by fighter flying with 354th Grp.
Goss, Charles G.	362	19 Oct 44	44-13963	Evader Engine failure
Gray, William J.A.	364	11 Apr 44	43-6515	POW Engine failure
Haack, William B.	363	9 Apr 45	44-13570	POW Engine failure
Hagan, Kenneth E.	362	17 Jun 44	42-106831	Evader Engine failure
Harris, Thomas L.	364	22 May 44	43-6653	POW Probable collision with wingman, Dean Post
Haydon, Edward R.	364	20 Jan 45	44-11165	POW Shot down by flak
Hinman, Howard S.	363	24 Apr 44	43-6624	POW Shot down by fighter
Humphrey, Robert P.	364	23 Mar 44	43-7019	POW Shot down by fighter
Jacobs, Jerome	364	19 Sept 44	43-6813	POW Shot down by fighter
Jones, Carter L.	363	22 Mar 44	43-12315	POW Shot down by flak
Kehrer, Merlin R.	362	25 Feb 44	43-6625	POW Shot down by fighter, which was then shot down by R.D. Brown
Kenney, Harold M.	363	17 Aug 44	44-13522	Evader Shot down by flak
Kouris, George C.	364	3 Feb 45	44-13586	POW Engine failure
Lepore, Rocco R.	364	2 Mar 45	44-14555	POW Shot down by flak
Lichter, Albert C.	362	22 Feb 44	43-6741	POW Shot down by flak
McKee, Charles E.	363	24 Feb 44	43-6940	POW Shot down by B-24. Later repatriated due to injuries
McIntyre, Bryce W.	364	19 Sep 44	44-14429	POW Shot down by fighter
Martin, Mathew S.	362	5 Dee 44	44-14722	POW Engine failure.
Medieros, John L.	364	4 Mar 44	43-6853	POW Shot down by flak
Meyer, Robert A.	362	16 Mar 44	43-6956	POW Shot down by fighter
Mickaely, William D.	363	4 May 44	42-103286	POW Shot down by flak
Moebius, Howard E.	364	19 Sept 44	44-13801	Evader Shot down by fighter
Monahan, James C.	364	17 Apr 45	44-14900	POW Engine failure
Muller, Robert .W.	364	17 Apr 45	44-14648	POW Shot down by flak
Myers, Daniel N.	363	30 Mar 45	44-72328	POW UNK, ditched in channel/North Sea, subject of massive rescue attempt, which failed. Drifted ashore and captured.

357TH PILOTS DOWN IN ENEMY TERRITORY, CONT'D.

NAME	SQDN	DATE	ACFT S/N	STATUS
Omernik, Stanley M.	363	9 May 44	43-701x1	POW Shot down by fighter
Pagels, Roger E.	363	6 Jun 44	43-6397	Evader Unknown cause
Pascoe. Herschel T.	363	12 Oct 44	44-13714	POW Shot down by fighter
Postle, Maurice A.	364	15 Apr 44	43-6413	POW Unknown mechanical failure
Reid, Wallace J.	364	8 Apr 44	42-106978	POW Shot down by flak
Reust, Frederick W.	363	12 Apr 44	43-6720	POW Engine failure
Rice, Donald R.	362	24 Feb 44	43-6743	POW Shot down by fighter
Ridley, Oscar T.	362	18 Apr 45	44-14789	POW Shot down by flak
Ross, Donald H.	363	20 Feb 44	43-12131	POW Cause unknown
Seitzinger, Bernard K.	364	18,Sep 44	42-106923	POW Shot down by fighter
Sitzer, Saul	363	2 Jan 45	44-14490	POW Shot down by flak
Sloan, James R.	363	14 Jan 45	44-14784	POW Shot down by fighter
Snedecker, Irving E.	364	17 Apr 45	44-13783	POW Shot down by flak
Sparks, Ray	364	8 May 44	43-6801	POW Shot down by fighter
Spicer, Henry R.	Grp Cmdr	5 Mar 44	43-6880	POW Shot down by flak
Spinks, Heyward C.	364	20 Jun 44	43-6935	Evader Shot down by flak
Stager, Joseph F.	364	24 Apr 44	42-106470	POW Shot down by flak
Summers, Cordell L	364	30 Apr 44	43-6701	Evader Shot down by fighter
Sullivan, Joseph C.	364	24 May 44	42-106884	Evader Shot down by flak
Templin, John S.	362	28 Sep 44	43-6698	POW Engine failure
Vogel, Don W.	362	1 Jul 44	43-12455	Evader Shot down by fighter
Yeager, Charles E.	363	5 Mar 44	43-6763	Evader Shot down by fighter
Zetterquist, Herman R.	364	5 Dec 44	44-13546	POW Cause unknown.

MEN WHO DIED IN TRAINING

The training phase for the 357th Fighter Group spanned some eight months from March to November, 1943. As near as can be determined, 15 men were killed during this period, all pilots except for one flight surgeon. Twelve of the fifteen were killed in P-39s, the other three in AT-6 trainers.

Their names are little known to veterans of the 357th, as most of those who died had been in the Group only a short time. Nevertheless, they died in the line of duty while serving with the 357th and deserve to be remembered. It was a lengthy and expensive effort to even find out who they were and obtain the following data, all of which came from USAAF accident reports.

Tonopah, Nevada, 27 March 1943: The first to die was not a pilot, but 1st Lt. Ralph Sullivan, Flight Surgeon of the 362nd Sqdn. While flying as a passenger with 2nd Lt. Davis Perron, in AT-6, serial number 40-2149. The engine failed and Perron landed on a highway. The left wing hit a car and aircraft cart wheeled and was destroyed. Sullivan was killed and Perron suffered major injuries,

from which he recovered and re-joined his unit. A year later he disappeared over the North Sea.

Tonopah, Nevada, 6 April, 1943: Like most of the training deaths, 2nd Lt. Rudolf W. Bisterfeldt, was recently out of flight school. He took off as part of a flight of five P-39s on a high altitude formation exercise, in P-39D, serial number 41-38258 with only 93 flying hours on it. While flying through a small cloud he lost control and entered a vertical dive from which he did not recover.

Tonopah Nevada/Studio City, CA. 18 May 1943: Captain Varian K. White, Commanding, 364th Sqdn. A survivor of the Pacific fighting with a Silver Star. He departed Tonopah and flew to Burbank, where he was to meet with the parents of his fiancée, a singer in one of the era's big bands. On takeoff from Burbank to return to Tonopah, the engine failed on P-39D, serial number 41-28274, and the aircraft crashed in a residential area of Studio City. Although it struck a house and Captain White was killed, no one on the ground was injured.

Tonopah, Nevada, 27 May 1943: 2nd Lt. Bryce Van Cott. Van Cott was one of a flight of three P-39s led by 1st Lt. Glendon Davis on a gunnery and dive bombing mission. After dropping their bombs, Davis led the three on several passes at a target sleeve being towed by F/O Tom McKinney in another P-39. During this exercise, Van Cott struck Davis' aircraft from the bottom. Davis bailed out and Van Cott was killed in the ensuing crash.

Note: on 2 June, the 357th moved to bases in north central California.

Santa Rosa, 9 June 1943: 2nd Lt. Virgil E. Wyss. At this time Lt. Wyss had only nine hours in fighter type aircraft, four in the P-39. According to eye witnesses, the P-39Q, 42-19561, entered a stall, then into a flat spin from which it did not recover. Wyss was undoubtedly a victim of the P-39's vicious characteristics.

Santa Rosa, 11 June 1943: 2nd Lt. Gail Palmer, in P-39Q, s/n 42-19561. Palmer, like Wyss had only four hours in the P-39. Witnesses stated the aircraft appeared to stall, the nose dropped and the aircraft tumbled tail over nose, did not recover and crashed near the town of Healdsburg. Palmer had attempted to bail out but too late.

Santa Rosa, 26 June 1943: 2nd Lts. Joseph Osborn and Fenemore Saxton took off from Santa Rosa in AT-6 41-186 on a local instrument training flight. The left wing failed in flight and both men were killed. The AT-6 had 3,300 hours of flight time.

Santa Rosa, 4 July 1943: 2nd Lt. Donald Stager, in P-39N, 42-8849. Leading a flight of four, they were flying very low over Clear Lake California. It was, in those days a "fun thing" for pilots to fly low over water, with the prop picking up a water spray. Stager hit the water, pulled up and hit the water again in a flat attitude, the aircraft disappearing beneath the water immediately. As far as is known, both are still there.

Hayward, 6 July 1943: 2nd Lt. Hal G. Plummer, P-39Q, 42-19560. Plummer had 43 hours in the P-39, when he took off with six others on a formation flight. At 14,000 feet the flight peeled off, Plummer's aircraft entering a spin, recovered three times but each time snapped into a spin the other direction finally crashing into the water. Plummer did not bail out. The accident report blamed 25% pilot error and 75% aircraft handling defects.

Santa Rosa, 7 July 1943: Captain Clay Davis and Lt. Lyle S. Maher. Captain Davis was leading a flight of four, firing aerial gunnery on a towed sleeve. Davis and Maher were both making passes at the target and were unable to see each other. The resulting collision caused disintegration of one aircraft, the other losing a wing and part of the tail. One man bailed out with his chute on fire, both men were killed.

Oroville, 23 August 1943: 2nd Lt. Donald Mickelson, P-39Q, 42-19593. Mickelson, with Lt. Ray Staude took off on a night navigation flight, flew to Mather Field and returned to Oroville. During landing, Mickelson struck a hill and was killed instantly.

Marysville, 18 September 1943: 2nd Lt. Donald Soens, P-39Q, 42-20755. With 149 hours in the P-39, Soens was on an aerobatics mission with F/O Tom McKinney. During this period, they spotted a B-25 and Soens began a series of slow rolls in the vicinity of the bomber. The P-39 stalled and went into an inverted spin from which it did not recover.

Hamilton Field, 6 October 1943: 2nd Lt. James Van Dyne. Van Dyne had been assigned to the 357th, but at the time of his death was apparently assigned to the 328th Fighter Grp. Therefore, his death should not be charged to the 357th, but we list him here as if he had been a member. On the date above, Van Dyne lost control in overcast and was killed in the crash.

DOWN IN THE DRINK

Probably a typical Walrus crew. These are Royal Navy personnel, pilot Harpy Cox (in cockpit), Observer Johnny Johnson (rt), and Air Gunner "Taff" Jones.

During the European war of 1939-45, thousands of airmen, British, German, and American, ditched, bailed out, or crashed into the cold waters of the North Sea and the English Channel. For most it was their final resting place.

When war came to Britain neither the RAF or the Royal Navy were prepared to rescue airmen down at sea - there simply was no rescue service worthy of the name and they were forced to begin building such a service from scratch.

The Germans were a bit quicker off the mark in that category, and had organized their *SEENOTRET-TUNGSDIENST AUS DER LUFT* (Air Sea Emergency Rescue Service) and had it on stations in 1940, equipped with boats and using the handsome He 59, a twin engined biplane on floats, as their primary rescue aircraft. With the development of the British service these two often competed for the same "customers".

The origins and build-up of the British Air Sea Rescue service is beyond the scope of this work, but a short description of what was in place when the U.S. Air Forces began operating out of the British Isles, is in order. It was, of course, a combination of several different types of high speed armed launches and different types of short and long range search aircraft and fighter type "spotters", all of which worked together with the primary rescue aircraft, the Supermarine Walrus, a single engine biplane flying boat and amphibian first ordered in 1933 as a gunfire director for the Royal Navy.

It was in no way, an ideal aircraft for the job, but it was available and it served valiantly right up to the end of the war. Thousands of airmen owe their lives to this antiquated aircraft and its courageous crews.

British ASR historian Sid Harvey has provided some figures for the early years of WWII - the Battle of Britain period. *Luftwaffe* records show 1,800 airmen missing in the period April, December, 1940, and about 1,000 British, mostly from Bomber Command. Almost all of these were in the waters between Britain and the continent. Shockingly, less than 300 were rescued.

Total number of U.S./Royal Air Force crews rescued according to Harvey were 1,998 U.S. and about 6,000 British, plus 450 airborne and glider troops. Percentagewise this is about 66% of U.S. water losses and about 33% British. (This low figure is due to the longer period for the British, the less efficient rescue service in the early years and the fact that the RAF operated mostly at night.)

Although many men were rescued, thousands were not and of the 5,000 names on the Wall of the Missing at the American cemetery at Cambridge, most are those missing at sea. When U.S. forces began operating from the British Isles, they had no rescue service of their own and relied entirely on the British system already in place. As time went on, however, the 8th Air Force became more and more involved and by the end of the war, U.S. personnel were operating the central locator and fixer station at Saffron Walden, and providing spotter aircraft (P-47s) and rescue flying boats, (OA-10 Catalina).

The purpose of this chapter is to highlight those pilots of the 357th Fighter Group who went "into the drink" and were rescued. During some 14 months of combat, approximately twenty-eight 357th pilots crashed or bailed out over the waters of the English Channel or the North Sea. The number is approximate because others went missing and were never found, and some of these may have also gone to a watery grave. Of these 28 men, there were nine rescues. Of these nine, one man was rescued twice, and two were picked up by the Germans.

On the 13th of February the Group flew its third mission, led by Lt. Col. Don Blakeslee who was on loan from the 4th Group, on an uneventful three hour tour of France. At the end of Blakeslee's short mission report, he added "Lt. R.W. Brown bailed out near English coast and was later rescued."

Brown was the first of the 357th to go down in the drink. It was also his first and last combat mission and the end of his operational career. Fifty years later, Brown recalled: "At Raydon I got ten hours in the '51 and on a training mission over The Wash, got my first kill - flew into a flock of ducks and put a dent in the wing root. On 13 February, I finally got my chance to fly from Leiston, but never landed there ."

In a December, 1995 letter to the author, Brown continues: "After my engine quit over the Channel, I tried re-starting, but with no luck. Made calls on the two channels that I was bailing out. Plane was now diving. Rolled the plane over and bailed out. I am falling and remember to pull the rip cord. It was very quiet. I could hear a plane but did not see it. Inflated Mae West and remembered caution about releasing chute buckle before hitting the water. A short time later I saw a launch and tried, but failed to get the whistle for signaling, from my pocket. The next thing I remember was lying on the deck freezing."

Brown's bailout was not a textbook exit however, as he hit some part of the aircraft, probably the tail, with damage to his legs which would plague him for years.

YANK, the soldier weekly newspaper published in the UK carried an extensive article on Brown's trials and reported that he was in the water more than a half hour when the crew of the RAF launch pulled him from the water, and this was ten minutes longer than anyone else had ever survived in the paralyzing cold of the sea.

RAF Coastal Command weekly ASR records for the period reported: "Air Rescue Boat #4 picked up '66 (Sawston Hall) pilot' (author's note; This refers to 66th Fighter Wing, hdqtered at Sawston Hall). Four miles SE Clacton at 1658. Pilot rescued had broken both legs."

When the launch arrived in port he was taken to the nearest hospital, a very small eight bed facility at Clacton-On-Sea. The rest of the Brown story is a medical one. Kept alive by the hospital staff until U.S. Army doctors and nurses arrived two days later, Brown was to spend many months recovering from his ordeal and his eventual release from the Army. He had however, survived his bailout over the waters of the North Sea, when many did not.

"VERY COOL & COLLECTED"

Among fighter pilots, the real gung-ho tigers are usually the most successful at their trade. It helps also if they have a strong sense of survival. Lt. Robert Foy, initially of the 363rd Squadron but later Group Operations Officer, was both a tiger and a survivor. Although a large percentage of 357th pilots who went into the sea did not survive, Foy was rescued twice.

On the 3rd of March, he was just another pilot, and had not yet started his impressive victory list. On that date the new Group Commander Colonel Henry Spicer,

led 53 Mustangs on the primary mission - bomber escort. Soon after rendezvous with the bombers north of Hamburg, the bomber leader reported he was turning back due to severe weather conditions. Three hours and 15 minutes after take-off, 52 Mustangs were on the ground at Leiston, and one, P-51B, 43-6998, was on the bottom of the Channel. The mission report says: "One ditched in Channel, engine failure. Lt. Foy, rescued five miles off Manston."

SHEPHERD OF THE SEAS, the 65th Fighter Wing History (which controlled all ASR) tell us; "3 March 44, CHAMBERS 54 (Foy's call sign) Maydayed at 1158 hours stating that his engine quit and was burning. Very cool and collected, he gave excellent calls at intervals and at 7,000 feet, gave his last call and bailed out. PECTIN 37 (a 4th Group pilot) overheard the distress call and asked if he could be of assistance. Since he was closer than any of the spotters, he was given a steer to the position."

The 4th Group pilot was Lt. Howard "Deacon" Hively, later a Major with 12 victories. Hively knew the loneliness of sitting in a wave - tossed dinghy waiting for a Walrus or an HSL (High Speed Launch). He tells the story in the book ESCORT TO BERLIN and winds up saying: "As you might have guessed, the cigarettes and chocolate bars and respect and admiration and comradeship that passed from one fighter pilots to that HSL crew and the whole RAF rescue service."

While Hively was orbiting Foy in his dinghy, an RAF 277 Squadron Walrus arrived on the scene, but was unable to land due to sea conditions. The Walrus crew, however, were able to direct an HSL to the scenethereby adding another satisfied customer to their list.

For the rest of March, April, and May, the Group flew 46 missions, losing 48 pilots - dead, missing, captured, or evader, and claimed 198 aerial victories. It had been a busy and deadly spring.

On 30 May, Foy again left his burning P-51, parachuting into the sea 50 miles off base. SHEPHERD OF THE SEA has this to say. "Greenhouse 30 (Richard Peterson) and Cement 54 (Foy) started across the North Sea at 1258 hours. Foy, having serious engine trouble had to bail out at 1331 hours when his airplane caught fire. Greenhouse 30 Maydayed, and HSL SEAGULL 46, was vectored to the position 12 miles away. Lt. Foy was rescued at 1405 unhurt."

The mission that last day of May had been filled with action - a real rat race. The mission report says: "Approximately 75 Fw 190s, Me 109s, and 410s were engaged in the Magdeburg/Bernburg area from 30,000 to deck, 14 of them were destroyed."

Somewhere in the melee, Foy developed mechanical problems and called flight leader, Capt. "OBee"

O'Brien, saying his prop had gone out. OBee however, was involved with a gaggle of 109s and replied he would get to him as soon as possible. After he had disengaged with the 109s, he called Foy but got no reply. However, Richard "Pete" Peterson did reply saying "Never mind OBee, I've got him".

In the rat race that day Peterson had lost not only his wingman, but his entire squadron and was returning home alone. He recalls: "I was almost to the Zuider Zee when I heard O"Brien call. I asked Foy where he was and he responded that he was near Leipzig at 11,000 with a prop stuck in low pitch. Though I was low on fuel, I headed back to find him. I soon spotted this lonesome looking P-51 barely cruising along at 180 mph, with a red and yellow nose. It was Foy and he appreciated my company. I coaxed him to hang in there and we would make it home. We cruised along about four or five miles away and parallel with the bomber stream.

"We crossed out of Holland and over the Channel, and I reminded him to switch to 'B' channel so we would both be on the ASR. I radioed a 'fix' and ASR came back loud and clear - 'Roger, we have you and we're on the way.' It was a great relief to hear that reassuring English feminine voice!"

Since it was now getting hot in the cockpit and Foy smelled smoke, he rolled the P-51 over and dropped out - just like last time!

He got into his dinghy with no problem and Peterson stayed with him until he saw a launch approaching, then headed home with nearly empty fuel tanks. His fuel ran out and the engine quit as he was taxiing to his hardstand. Peterson ends: "I took a deep breath and headed for a tall one at the club - another day, another dollar!"

Foy was in his dinghy only a short time before being picked up by a High Speed Launch, call sign SEAGULL 46. This was boat #2551 out of the station at Great Yarmouth.

A month later, this same boat was on station about 60 miles out of Great Yarmouth and responded to an imminent ditching from a 390th Bomb Grp B-17. With a swarm of U.S. fighters giving cover, the boat picked up the B-17 crew.

Radio contact with the boat was then lost, until fighters found it wrecked and burning with many men in dinghies. Other HSLs arrived and rescued 21 men of the B-17 and launch crew who reported they had been strafed by a Ju 88 after the fighter cover had left. Flight Lieutenant George Linday, its coxswain and several crewmen were killed. It was he and his crew who had rescued Foy a month earlier, and now they were gone. It was a dangerous business.

Major Robert Foy's ability to survive deserted him in the post war years as he was killed in a B-25 in which he was a passenger.

A SILVER STAR FOR RAY SPARKS

A month before Foy's second bailout over water and in a very similar engine failure condition, Lt. Charles J. Schreiber joined the all too slim ranks of those who survived a water bailout.

On that 30th of April, Colonel Donald Graham led the Group to targets around Claremont, France. Twenty enemy fighters were engaged and nine shot down. Schreiber, however, was headed home with an engine problem and escorted by his element leader, Lt. Ray Sparks. Fifty plus years later, Sparks recalled: "Just as we crossed the coast his aircraft burst into flames. He made two attempts to roll over and bail out. By that time we were about a quarter of a mile off shore and the shore batteries opened up on his parachute and my aircraft.

"I would dive toward the shore and the tracers would stop but would start again when I pulled up to circle the parachute and later to circle his dinghy in the water. I went through the MAY DAY procedure and the ASR answered immediately and took a fix on me. They instructed me to circle the pilot at about 2,500 feet. The Germans twice sent boats out but I was able to turn them back. In a few minutes I spotted two Spitfires coming in low and strafing the coast line. Then I saw the Walrus, which landed and picked up Schreiber. Then it and the Spitfires departed to their base."

RAF records show that the Walrus and the Spitfires were from 277 Squadron based at Hawkinge, only about 30 miles from Schreiber's position. This was a classic example of when everything went right. For his part in drawing the fire of the shore batteries, Ray Sparks was awarded Silver Star for gallantry.

THEY KNEW THEY COULDN'T TAKE OFF AGAIN WHEN THEY LANDED

Two days after D-Day, five missions were flown, the second airborne in mid-morning, consisting of 16 P-51s of the 362nd Sqaudron led by Captain Calvert Williams. The mission report does does not waste words on details: "Straf Laval area. Lt. O.E. Harris last seen Montegre (probably means Montagne), at 1317 hours."

1st Lt. Ollie E. Harris Jr, had come to the UK with the Group and by D-Day was a veteran fighter pilot having shot down an Me 410 on the Berlin mission of 30 May.

On the 8 June mission the 16 P-51s had bombed rail targets and Harris had shot up a freight train. He then found himself alone and was climbing toward some cloud cover when he encountered a gaggle of Fw 190s. Too close to escape he turned into them and flew thru their foramtion. He doesn't recall if he fired his guns or not, but they did, hitting his engine and shooting off his wrist watch, leaving a shallow gash in his wrist, his only injury.

He evaded the 190s in a cloud, but his engine was failing fast and he was just able to make it to the Channel where he bailed out at about 750 feet altitude. Cold and half drowned, he was able with great difficulty to inflate and get into his dinghy.

Shock, the stress of events, the numbing cold and the passing of time have erased much of the subsequent details from his memory. How long he was in the water is uncertain - the squadron diary says 45 minutes, but he believes it was much longer.

There is no doubt that he was pulled from the water by the crew of a Walrus. Due to rough seas and his inability to help, they had great difficulty getting him aboard, and due to wingtip and float damage, they were unable to take off again.

British Historian Sid Harvey: "The Walrus, with Harris aboard was taken in tow by two RAF seaplane tenders, #1515 (skipper Eddie Ross) and #1506, (skipper L. Newling). These vessels had been pressed into service due to the heavy traffic of the D-Day period. At the time of the call, were on their way to search for B-24 and RAF crews of a Warwick and a Lancaster, none of whom were found. These same boats had rescued many troops and crews of C-47s which had ditched on D-Day."

Historian Harvey has found that during the ten days after D-Day, 163 aircrew, 58 "others", and two Germans were picked up by ASR services.

Harris continues: "The Walrus that picked me up fractured a pontoon on landing, but the sea was to rough to take-off anyway. It took us about ten hours to get back to base, about 100 miles. We had started out under our own power. I guess I had fallen alseep when the two boats arrived. That was a very brave crew to do what they did. I was a very sea sick kid!"

Lt. Ollie Harris (left) with fellow pilots Tom Norris and Gilbert O'Brien, and dog "Butch". After he was picked up by a Walrus, it took ten hours of taxiing and being under tow to return to shore.

DOWN IN THE DRINK TWICE - RESCUED ONCE

1st Lt. Daniel N, Myers joined the Group in the fall of 1944. He does not remember the date, but it was the same day that British anti-aircraft guns shot down a B-17 over the base. We know then that it was 30 October and by the 27th of February, 1945, he was a veteran with 35 missions behind him. On that day he was flying P-51, 44-14356, which at one time had been named LONESOME POLECAT.

Other than some strafing of rail targets the mission was uneventful. On the way home however, Myers was the victim of an "almost" mid-air collision. Flying in formation, he looked up to see another Mustang dropping down onto him and he broke away into a dive, avoiding collison.

Now with the formation lost, he headed home alone, keeping a wary eye for enemy fighters. He crossed out over the enemy coast confident that he would soon be home, until he discovered that his fuel selector valve was jammed and he could not switch to a full tank. Myers remembers: "Now I was scared! The water down there looked very cold. Flying with my left hand and trying to turn the valve with my right, I almost made it across the water. Emerging from the twilight mist I saw a boat directly in front of me. I started to circle the boat just as my engine began to sputter. I climbed to about 1500 feet and bailed out, releasing my chute harness when I hit the water. I inflated my Mae West, but not my dinghy, as I could see the boat coming. In a few minutes one of the crew went overboard and hoisted me on deck."

The vessel was the fishing trawler RETAKO, out of Grimsby. The captain was William Watson who was a Royal Navy Reserve Officer, and he had taken his ship into a known minefield to rescue Myers. Both he and the crewman who had jumped in the water to assist Myers were decorated for their efforts. Myers returned to base the next day. Next time it would not be so easy.

By the end of March, 1945, it was apparent to even the most uninformed, that a momentous event could not be far away - the end of the war in Europe. After only some ten years, Adolf Hitler's 1,000 year *Reich* was collapsing under an avalanche of Allied explosives. Millions had died and now the survivors were looking forward to the imminent end of it all.

During March, seven pilots were lost, four of whom were killed in action. On the 30th, the Group launched 60 Mustangs on an uneventful escort to Ham-

This is RAF seaplane tender #1515, the very same boat which took Harris aboard from the Walrus and brought him home. This small vessel rescued many airmen during the D-Day period.

burg. Two Me 262s were seen, but not engaged. However, the loss of Lt. Dan Myers into the sea was to trigger one of the largest North Sea/Channel rescue efforts.

Before it was over, Group records indicate that 173 aircraft were involved and a continuous fighter cover by many different groups was maintained over the area from 30 March through the 4th of April. One Beaufighter with its crew was lost and an OA-10 Catalina was sunk without crew loss.

Myers was completing his 42nd mission as the Group crossed out near Heide, a small coastal town about 50 miles north of Hamburg.

As the Group crossed over the Frisian Islands. Myers was flying a new P-51D, 44-72328, on its 4th mission. It had less than 100 flying hours on it, but at this point the engine blew out a cloud of coolant vapor and screeched to a stop. There was only one choice - for the second time in a month, Myers went over the side. Except for hitting the stabilizer (no injury) the bailout went reasonably well. After he hit the water and got rid of the chute, he inflated his dinghy, which was upside down. He was unable to right it, so climbed on it inverted, to await rescue.

The mission returned to base at 645 hours and 30 minutes later, Captain John Stern took off with three others to provide cover. They RVed with a Catalina at 1845 hours and were directed to Myer's dinghy by two 359th Group P-51s which were orbiting. The Catalina landed on the water at 1900 hours, close to the dinghy. Shortly thereafter, darkness and bad weather forced Stern and his flight to return to base. They could not tell if Myers had been picked up or not.

Unfortunately, the Catalina crew had been unable to do so. Myers at one time had been under one wing, but they were unable to hook him due to rough sea and rising winds. About the time Myers and the Catalina drifted apart, two Me 109s arrived and strafed the flying boat, causing enough damage to make it unflyable.

Early the next morning Myers was awakened when his dinghy drifted ashore on Borkum Island. He then walked to a neaby power plant where the local police picked him up. He was on his way to *Stalag Luft* I. With the end of the war, he was back at Leiston in about two months. Of course no one knew what had happened to him, and now all attention was directed at retrieving the Catalina crew. This turned out to be knotty problem with many pickup attempts going wrong but with eventual success.

The next morning three P-51s led by Kit Carson arrived to provide cover to the now derelict flying boat, and found three dinghies with five men in them. Shortly after Carson arrived, so did two Me 262s which made one strafing run on the Catalina. (For details on this see chapter on combat with the jets.)

During the five days the Catalina crew were adrift, three airborne life boats were dropped, but none were successfully retrieved by the crew. There was available, in England, an experimental B-17 modified to drop rafts and boat, and it was able to successfully drop rafts with outboard motors which the crew boarded. Finally on the 4th of April, Royal Navy boats homed in on the raft's "Gibson girl" radios and Lt. John Lapenus and his crew were finally picked up.

Group records indicate that 93 P-51s, 38 P-47s, three B-17s, 25 Warwicks six Mosquitos, and eight Beau-fighters (one of which was lost in full view of the Catalina crews) had been involved at one time or another.

Another pilot who bailed out into the sea and survived, was the Group Commander Colonel Henry Spicer, who was captured by the Germans. See the chapter THE IDES OF MARCH. There were two further rescues of 357th pilots from the sea, but little is known of these two except for the brief mention in the mission reports.

The 13th of September, 1944, was not a good day for the Group. Although 15 enemy fighters were claimed destroyed, five pilots did not return, with three dead or missing. One bailed over Allied territory and Lt. Robert Goldsworthy, flying P-51B, serial number 43-6795 bailed into the Channel only a few minutes after take-off. The mission report says simply: "Picked up by ASR."

The other incident occurred on 26 February 1945. Colonel Dregne, the mission leader reported: "One plane hit by flak NW of Delemenhorst caught fire and Lt. Roy Anthony bailed ten miles off Southwold. Picked up by ASR".

In summary, approximately 28 pilots of the 357th Fighter Group went into the sea. In only ten cases did the pilots survive. Two drifted into the enemy shore and were captured. (One had been rescued previously). Eight men were rescued, one of them twice.

It was not a good percentage, and illustrates that, despite the most valiant efforts of British/U.S. Air Sea Rescue services, the odds were heavily against those who found themselves with an unairworthy aircraft over the unforgiving waters of the English Channel or the North Sea.

Lt. Daniel Myers who bailed into the sea twice, was rescued once and captured by the Germans the second time. Fortune was with him, however, as he survived both.

Lt. Roy Anthony. Little is known about his bailout over the sea, except that the ever vigilant Air Sea Rescue service "fished" him out of the water.

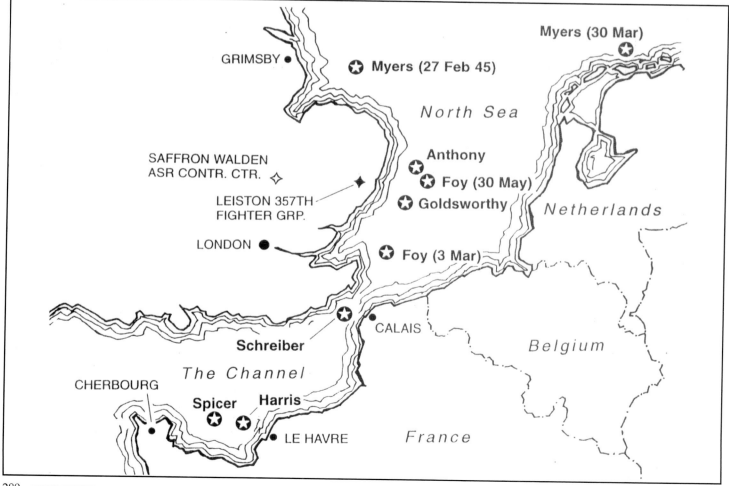

"BRENNER ROUTE CLOSED"

This is the story of the worst accident that befell the 357th Fighter Group and its supporting units, plus it took place long after the guns had become silent. The old enemy, weather, was still in business and as deadly as ever especially with a bit of human error thrown in. It was these factors that would cause the loss of C-47A 829 and all aboard.

With the war over and everyone wanting to go home, it came as a shock to the 357th and some of its supporting units, that those without enough points would not be going to the ZI, but would go to Germany as one of two fighter groups tagged for occupation duty in defeated Germany. It seemed to be punishment for a job well done. Much of the big transfer had been completed by mid-summer, both by surface and air movement, and as it turned out, occupation duty had much to commend it. Duties were not burdensome and the quarters, all ex-*Luftwaffe* were absolutely plush compared to Leiston.

The scenery was great, there were many interesting German airplanes to see and photograph, there were frequent beer parties on tree shaded lawns, and there was hunting and shooting for those inclined. There were also friendly *frauleins* despite the ban on fraternization. Soon after arrival, there were R & R (rest and recreation) flights to various spas of Europe, some of which were already beginning to revive from the wartime ordeal.

Although the records do not say so, it is quite certain that C-47A, serial number 42-100829 was on an R&R mission when it was lost at the end of October. The aircraft departed Neubiberg on the morning of 30 October with its destination listed on the flight plan as Nice, France, and Florence, Italy as alternate. There were 14 people aboard, and they are listed on AAF form 14 "Report of Aircraft Accident" as follows:

Capt. George J. Rice, pilot	Cpl. Raymond E. Stoll, pass.
lst Lt. Merle F. Cedoz, pass.	1st Lt. Jack Bussard, pass.
1st Lt. Raymond E. Wolf, co-pilot	Miss Mary C. Rhodes, pass.
MSgt. Charles Kruger, pass.	1st Lt. Anton O. Rosengreen, pass.
SSgt. Albert A. Nordone, engineer	Miss Ruth Murdock, pass.
Sgt. Charles I. Nelson, pass.	lst Lt. Harold R. Arrendale, pass.
Cpl. Edward C. Niedzwiecki, R.O.	Miss Naomi Steed, pass.

Units for all personnel is given as XII TAC and for the women as ARC. We know that Rice and Wolf were 363rd Squadron, and oddly enough, both had scored two victories each during the war, an Me 109 and a Fw 190 each, and both had scored one victory on THE BIG DAY, 14 January 1945.

SSgt. Albert Nordone listed as engineer, was an aircraft mechanic with the 469th Service Squadron; MSgt. Kruger (Krueger) was also from the 469th as Chief of Instrument Repair Shop; Rosengreen's unit is unknown; Jack Bussard was 362nd Squadron and Cedoz and Arrendale were 364th, all pilots. Units unknown for the others.

Proposed departure time from Neubiberg is listed on the clearance form as 0900, with 2.4 hours flight time to Nice, but actual departure was about 0915. Rice filed direct, contact conditions (VFR) at 12,000 feet. He had logged some eleven hours of instrument time in the previous six months, and had 31.2 hours flight time in C-47s, some 17 as first pilot. His total flying time was 1.403 hours.

The weather forecast on the clearance is brief, giving 1,000/2,000 foot ceiling at destination with 2/5 miles visibility. The more comprehensive weather forecast from 70th Fighter Wing, for 30 October, gives 8/10 to 10/l0 cloud over the Riviera, lowering to less than 1,000 feet in rain in the Rhone valley. It ends ominously with the statement: "Brenner route closed".

We do not know the route that Rice flew, but his forecast flight time matched very closely the time from take-off to 829's crash point. A direct flight from Munich to Nice, however, would go through the Brenner Pass area, which may be why Rice filed for 12,000 feet - he may have planned to go through on top. (Having flown a few years later thru the Brenner Pass area in overloaded C-47s, this writer found the topography spectacular but scary!)

By early afternoon when an arrival message had not been received at home station, a communication search was begun, but fruitless, as all communication with Nice was inop. Apparently no further action was taken until the evening of the next day, the 31st, when Florence was queried for information on the C-47. No reply was receivedd to this signal and on the morning of the lst November, further signals to Continental Flying Safety at Istres, France, also produced no information.

On the morning of the 2nd, a P-51 was dispatched to search the route, but very bad weather forced the Mustang to return with no results. Istres finally responded the same day saying that an aircraft had crashed on Mount Bramand near Cuneo, Italy, confirmation soon following that it C-47A, 829. Weather was reported as extremely bad at the time of the crash with heavy rain, low fog, and very poor visibility. Mount Bramand rises to over 2,300 meters (7,500 feet) lies about 16 miles west by southwest of the town of Cuneo - 829 and its occupants impacted about 100 feet below the summit.

The Allied Military Government in Cuneo first learned of the incident at about 1930 hours on the evening of the 30th, and soon learned that all personnel were dead. Due to the bad weather and inaccessible location, it was not until 7 November that all bodies had been found and identified. Italian mountain troops with U.S. medical assistance carried out the recovery and all bodies were interned in the U.S. military cemetery at Mirandole, Italy. The investigating officer had contacted an Italian photographer to photograph the scene and these pictures show the aircraft to be completely burnt out except the tail section and outer wing panels.

A final point, as so often happens - they almost made it, Nice is only some 30 miles from the crash scene. To close the story, a related tale is worth telling. A week or so before the Riviera flight, 364th Squadron pilots, Ed Fry and Howard Ireland flew the UC-64 NORSEMAN on R&R to Paris. Due to return the next day, the crew used the old "weathered in" ploy to stay longer, taking off one day late. Now the weather was really stinking and they were forced to put down at a French field near Stuttgart, finally returning to Neubiberg two days late. Command decided that Ireland should be punished and he was therefore scratched from the roster for the Riviera flight, sparing him for a much longer life than his comrades who made the flight.

EARLDUKE, RDF, AND MEW

TSgt. Arthur Schalick, Acting Chief, Group Communications: "We were always proud of the fact that we never had a breakdown when we had planes in the air or when we were required to be operational."

The science of radio communications had advanced, between the wars, to the point where it was an essential part of any air force. Yet, in the many excellent Air Force unit histories, the role of the men who made it work are seldom mentioned. We intend to correct this here, and will give an overview of the communications and radar section as it applied to the 357th Group and pay tribute to the small group of men who kept it working.

Each squadron had its own communications section, whose efforts were devoted entirely to maintaining the radios in the aircraft. Overseeing the squadrons was Group Communications, under Captain John Anderson, with about 35 men, most of whom had been drawn from the Squadrons. These men manned the airfield transmitter and receivers, and the RDF (radio direction finding) unit, all on a round-the-clock basis. Ten of these men were assigned to man the control tower and the RDF unit at RAF Woodbridge, whose only purpose was to provide a haven for crippled or weather-bound aircraft.

"**EARLDUKE**, this is Dollar 66, give me a homing please, over." "Dollar 66, this is EARLDUKE, steer 180, repeat, steer 180." Who was EARLDUKE answering Dollar 66 and where was the voice coming from?

All 8th Air Force Squadrons and Groups had radio call signs and the one at Leiston was EARLDUKE, as was the Flying Control Officer, Captain Tillie Botti. As with many operational and daily life aspects, the **RDF** system was part of the British network for the detection and control of enemy and friendly aircraft. The extensive radar system was for the detection of enemy aircraft, while the radio network was for the control of friendly aircraft. Compared to the communication equipment of later years, a P-51 pilot's radio gear was primitive - only a single VHF radio with four channels; "A" channel was the operational band used for contact with base, "B" was for Air-Sea rescue fixes only, "C" was for fighter/bomber communications, and "D" was for homing and position "fixes".

Leiston's RDF facility was located off base. The control station, a wooden structure resembling a short silo, was located on the Wood farm operated by the Frank Snowdon family. Robert Shearer, one of the operators, became friendly with and maintained contact with the Snowdons for many years. There was little about the structure to give away its true identity except for a short rotating antenna on top and possibly some bicycles parked next to it - the crews primary means of transport. There were two other structures, bunker-like shelters housing the transmitter and receiver, about a mile apart and both had tall antenna towers, all tied together by telephone and VHF radio.

During the time the Group was engaged in operations, normally two or three men were on duty in the DF station. Their main duty was to monitor 357th radio frequencies and to provide assistance to Mayday calls plus obtain position fixes on any aircraft asking for them. The operator at the antenna wheel wore a headset with one side tuned to "A" channel, the other side to "B" channel. A third channel was connected to a speaker on the panel. This three channel modification had been designed by Arthur Schalick. Duty at the antenna wheel was tricky and a high stress job during intensive operations.

There were nine men on the RDF crew, not all are known, but besides Bob Shearer, Roy Johnson, Leonard Stiglitz,

and Bill Lanier are known to have been some of the wizards who worked the RDF.

As mentioned previously, other Leiston communications men were further afield, with ten at the Emergency Landing Ground at Woodbridge.There were three of these installations with 10,000 foot runways, which were over 700 feet wide, enough for three landing lanes. The fields were also equipped with FIDO (fog dispersal equipment), a system of pipes running the length of the runway which contained a fuel oil. When lighted and the wind was right, FIDO would burn away the fog, leaving a long oblong hole for desperate pilots to let down through.

Bill Staples was one of the 357th men operating the control tower, and remembers one day that FIDO really paid off. The weather had been rotten and only a small force of bombers and fighters had gone to targets in Germany, returning to find all of England "socked in tight". He does not recall the date, but remembers over 100 aircraft landed that day. Although the numbers do not match his memory exactly, it may have been a day in October 1944 when Woodbridge landed 84 aircraft in one day.

Bill Staples: "The wind was from the north that day, and the fog rolled in about as fast as FIDO burned it off. We had to 'talk' many of the planes in. When the day was over, we had landed every plane on the mission, even though some of them were still parked on the runway. It was a most hectic day for me in the control tower but it must have been a lot worse for the aircrews trying to get down through the murk. Without FIDO doing its job it could have been a disaster. There were other occasions when we used FIDO but that day made it all worth while." During the time Woodbridge was in service, it handled well over 4,000 emergency landings, 1200 of which used FIDO and men of the 357th had a major part in this operation.

MEW - another of the mysterious acronyms so much a part of military life - then and now. This one stood for Microwave Early Warning, in other words, radar control of aircraft. It brings to mind a scene of men hunkered down in bunkers or mobile control vans, peering into radar scopes. These were the men who answered to such strange names as NUTHOUSE, COLGATE, PARKER, TACKLINE, and other code names. Their job was to keep track of Allied and enemy aircraft and to provide control and warning information for U.S. fighters and bombers.

The primary unit involved was the 1076th Signal Company which had arrived at Leiston before the 357th. Soon after, detachment A of the 1076th, departed and moved eventually to the coastal area around Dunwich where they set up their 30 foot antenna towers, control rooms and bunkers. With a 225 mile range they became operational before D-Day and soon NUTHOUSE became a familiar name to Allied fighter pilots. Claude Early was one of the eight radar men at NUTHOUSE. He remembers the massive foul up when the unit went to France on a Liberty ship soon after D-Day. Oddly enough, starvation was their worst peril, as the two day trip turned out to be eleven days in the hold of the ship with no rations.

The installation in England had been a fixed unit but through their own efforts, they converted to a mobile unit on flatbed trucks and vans. Eventually they arrived in Holland where they set up and continued to operate for the rest of the war. Later in the war, they received a citation for their part in the destruction of several hundred German aircraft.

There were not many of them, but the men of EARLDUKE and the NUTHOUSE - men peering into their scopes - were of vital importance in the success of the Group.

CHAPTER 11:
THE AIRCRAFT

Photographed from an AT-6 in late July or early August 1944, these four P-51 D-5s in RAF green, were four of the illustrious stalwarts of the 363rd Squadron. Leading in B6-D is Edwin Hiro (destined to die at Arnhem) in HORSE'S ITCH. Next is Donald Bochkay's WINGED ACE OF CLUBS, third in line is OBee O'Brien's BILLY'S BITCH, and last is B6-V, Bob Foy's RELUCTANT REBEL - aces all. Although all of these P-51s appear to have white noses, the writer does not believe this is so. A combination of lighting, type of film, type of camera filter, etc. have 'washed out' all traces of red and yellow on the noses. Close examination with a powerful magnifier shows the checks faintly in some places. White noses are totally inappropriate for this late date.

WARPAINT NOTES AND PUZZLES

The fighters of THE MIGHTY EIGHTH were among the most colorful of historic aircraft devoted to battle - and there were a great many of them! Not usually realized is the fact that the colors and markings on these warplanes seldom stayed the same for long, they were in a constant state of change adding to the variety and the confusion. Sorting them out can be a real can of worms, but it is a subject of great interest to model builders, historians, and enthusiasts in general.

The subject of U.S. Army aircraft painting and colors is extremely complex throughout the 1920s, 1930s, and through World War II. The "bible" for most of these years was Air Corps Technical Order 07-1-1, copies of which can be obtained (with difficulty) from the National Archives and other sources. For those who wish to delve deeper into the subject, there are several useful recent books:

THE OFFICIAL MONOGRAM U.S. ARMY AIR SERVICE AND AIR CORPS AIRCRAFT COLOR GUIDE, by Robert D. Archer. Monogram publications 1995. This book is very detailed as to paints etc., but carries the story only up to 1942.
AIR FORCE COLORS, VOL 1, 1926-1942 by Dana Bell. Squadron Signal Publications, 1979. Volume II,
AIR FORCE COLORS, ETO, MTO, 1942-45. MIGHTY EIGHTH WAR PAINT AND HERALDRY, by Roger Freeman, Arms and Armour Press, London, 1997.

The WWII enthusiast and model builders are an orderly lot, they demand their history be in the form of neat listings of aircraft serial numbers, each followed by a pilot's name, unit markings and an aircraft name. They also speak of tech order, specifications, directives and other official documents. These are all very useful as long as it is realized that all of these aircraft markings are variables, except the serial numbers. All others could and did change often if an aircraft survived for very long. Also it should be realized that regulations, directives, orders etc. also changed often and were not often followed rigidly anyway. Circumstances often caused them to be followed loosely, if at all. It would have been difficult to keep up with the changes at the time, even if anyone cared, and is beyond the realm of possibility today. Nevertheless, all of this information is useful and interesting if kept in the proper perspective.

It is also a fact that many questions about these long gone airplanes that exist only in black and white photos can never be answered positively. All of us can express an opinion, often educated, but no one knows for sure. In this chapter, we will try to provide some facts, interesting aspects, and opinions, some substantiated, some not. All we hope will be of interest and useful.

Who was responsible for those paint schemes so important to historians, model builders and others? The basic paint, of course, came from the factory of origin, or possibly from the big depots in the north of England but the details were all done at squadron level, by that now faceless unknown person - the squadron painter.

Considering how often things changed, he was a busy man. SSgt. Louis Boudreaux was that man in the 362nd Squadron, but the identity of the painters in the other two Squadrons are unknown. Boudreaux was a casualty of war, dying of a paint related lung disorder.

Early in 1944 when the 357th arrived, fighter colors and markings were quite straight forward. All were Dark Olive Drab upper surfaces and Neutral Gray undersurfaces. All had white noses and white ID bands on wings and horizontal and vertical tail surfaces. Squadron codes, in the RAF fashion were assigned. Most of the P-51Bs which arrived at Leiston were a sorry sight, due to the removal of large areas of paint when the trans-Atlantic shipping tape was removed. This is well illustrated in the close-up, rear photo of JOAN, code G4-P, serial number 42-106829.

From photographic evidence, it appears that many of these scruffy aircraft were soon repainted, although still in standard OD and gray. One wonders why the effort was expended, these were after all, "throw away" airplanes, whose efficiency was not affected by their scarred paint.

Soon after this, however, major changes began to appear. Triggered by Colonel Hub Zemke's request to higher headquarters for permission to paint the noses of his P-47s in squadron colors, and the almost immediate follow up requests from other commanders, Fighter Command decided to assign nose colors to all its groups. There were three Fighter Wings, the 65, 66th, and 67th, each of which would soon have five groups each. The 357th was part of 66th Wing, whose five groups were given checkerboard designs of varying colors. This then was the origin of the red and yellow noses of THE YOXFORD BOYS. Only a narrow band forward of the exhaust stacks were in checkerboard, the spinner merely being banded in red and yellow. These instructions were issued late in March, and sometime around the first part of April, the white noses disappeared under the attractive red and yellow paint.

We don't know the exact wording of the nose color directive, but it may have been vague because there was considerable confusion at first. In the 362nd Squadron, Johnny Pugh's P-51B, 42-106473, code G4-N, was painted yellow on the nose clear back to the cockpit, and then large red diamonds were applied. Pugh flew it a few times like this, but never on operations. In his diary for 26 March Lt. Fletcher Adams wrote: "All ships to be painted yellow with big red checks on it."

Roger Freeman, 8th Air Force historian remembers something similar. "When I was in school, on 28 March, 1944, I saw two OD P-51s fly past the schoolhouse window. They had yellow noses extending well back on the cowling. The codes were G4. For many years I thought I was in error on this, but in recent years I saw a reference in the diary of another 'boy aircraft spotter' of those days, in which he reported four yellow nosed P-51s coded G4. This was in late March, 1944. No photograph has emerged showing these."

There was, in addition, one of the strangest of all, a P-51B or C, with no visible markings. The photo is from the album of pilot Harry Ankeny. Its colors are unknown, and Ankeny has no memory of it whatsoever, nor does anyone else who was there. There appears to be a standard colored P-51 in the background.

TO PAINT OR NOT TO PAINT

From the early days of the Army Air Service in WWI, and then into the Army Air Corps from 1926 forward, most airplanes were fabric covered and were therefore painted - olive drab, then olive drab and yellow and then some aircraft in blue and yellow in the '30s. During these years there was extensive testing on camouflage schemes, which were not adopted.

364th Squadron P-51 D-5s, all in RAF green paint. From front to rear, they are C5-T, 44-13586, this had been Peterson's second HURRY HOME HONEY, but here without name. It is probably after Pete Howell took it over and before the name FLAK HAPPY was applied; C5-R, 44-13546, THE SHILLELAGH, Major John Storch, squadron commander; C5-E, a P-51B, 43-6813, PAPPY'S ANSWER, a veteran aircraft with a long string of mission symbols. Henry Pfeiffer was pilot. Last in line is C5-V, 44-13678, Morris Stanley, pilot.

When all metal aircraft such as the P-35, P-36, and the C-39 (the first of the wonderful "gooney Birds") entered service in the late 1930s, the Army made a major change decreeing that all tactical aircraft would be in bare metal or painted aluminum. This lasted only until April, 1941, when with war imminent, Tech Ord 07-1-1 now called for all tactical aircraft to be painted in Olive Drab and gray except for trainers and a few exceptions. This was to remain standard for several years and is the way, as pointed out, all P-51s were coming out of the factories when the 357th began to equip with them.

However - In October, 1943, AAF Material Command decided that the slight advantage gained by camouflage was not worth the cost, weight and slight performance loss and that henceforth, all combat aircraft would, again be bare metal.

The change took time, of course, for the manufacturers to change over and bare metal P-51Bs did not begin to reach 8th Air Force units until March, 1944. Less then two months later, the pendulum swung the other way again. With the invasion of the continent imminent, 8th Fighter Command advised that, since some fighter groups might be moving to the continent, it was suggested that aircraft be camouflaged. Very few bare metal P-51Bs came thru the pipeline, only a hand full to the 357th. In the end, only one 8th Air Force group, the 352nd, moved to continental airfields for a short time.

Instructions do not appear to have been very detailed, leaving it up to the groups how they did it. From this point, we enter a period of some controversy - Olive Drab, or RAF green??

Many 357th P-51s, both B and D models appear in

photographs, from that summer and autumn in a dark color which has to be either Olive Drab or RAF green. Since bare metal aircraft were coming through the pipeline, these dark colors are surely the result of the directive (suggestion?) that all aircraft which might move to the continent after the invasion, be camouflaged. This writer gets many questions from historians and model builders whether specific aircraft were Olive Drab or one of the RAF greens. The simple answer is that no one knows for sure, but there is a factor which makes it probable that they were RAF green.

The Lend Lease Program had been set up before the U.S. was in the war, to supply Britain with much needed military equipment without the need to pay for it at the time. When U.S. forces began to arrive in England in large numbers, Lend Lease worked both ways with the British providing much material to U.S. forces. The primary reason for this was the critical shortage of shipping space in cargo vessels. Paint was one of the items involved in reverse Lend Lease, as it would make no sense to bring paint to Britain. The closest to Olive Drab were varying shades of RAF green, and this is what we see on many U.S. aircraft. It is this writer's opinion that RAF green shows up darker in black and white photos then Olive Drab.

It is emphasized that this is only an opinion and if others see the reverse, so be it, they might be right. At about the time as the directive (or suggestion) that aircraft which might operate from continental airfields be camouflaged, someone (we wish we knew who) in the 357th, came up with a paint scheme which did not appear to have any practical basis, but resulted in some very handsome P-51s. This is what the writer calls "the half paint job" in which the upper surfaces of the wings and fuselage and the tail surfaces were left in Olive Drab, (or RAF green) and the sides of the fuselage were stripped and left in bare metal. It is uncertain whether the undersurfaces were in gray or bare metal. The method was in little use in other groups and was by no means universal in the 357th. Both B models and some D-5s arriving around the time of invasion had it. A photographic search has shown 12 aircraft of the 362nd, and six of the 364th in this scheme, but only one so far in the 363rd Squadron.

Oddly enough, these "half paint" aircraft served along side many B and D model aircraft which were almost surely in RAF green. This leaves us with undersurface gray. The question is often asked if this was U.S. natural gray or one of the RAF shades. This is even more difficult then the upper surfaces, but, for the same reason as the RAF green, it was probably RAF gray.

The national insignia and sometimes codes show up as gray instead of white. Although this dulling was official on bombers for a year during 1942/43, it was not meant to be applied to fighters. Nevertheless, it is seen on a few.

Invasion stripes, or more properly "Distinctive Marking, Aircraft", was initiated by a memo dated 3 June 1944 to be effective the next day. (The weather delay pushed this back one day). On the 5th of June, the main occupation on fighter bases of the 8th, 9th, and the RAF, was the painting of these 18 inch black and white stripes on wings and fuselage. The squadron painters would have been the leaders in this effort but most of the flight line crews took a hand also, all after dark.

Although this writer was one of those doing the painting on the night of 5 June, few details remain in the memory. As can be seen from photos, the quality of the painting ran from neat to sloppy but all served the purpose - to prevent the invasion forces from shooting at Allied aircraft, which they did in many cases anyway.

There is one obscure aspect of invasion stripes that is of interest. Many P-51D-5 and D-10 airplanes had invasion stripes on the bottom of their fuselages during the fall of 1944. This does not, however, indicate that these planes took part in D-Day operations and it does not mean that these are the remnants of full invasion stripes on wings and fuselage, which these machines never had. We will use two famous aircraft as examples:

The first is C.E. "Bud" Anderson's well-known OLD CROW. This P-51, s/n 44-14450, was delivered to the USAAF at the factory in Inglewood, California, 9 August 1944. It arrived, after a ferry flight, at Newark, NJ on 16 August and departed the U.S. as deck cargo on the 23rd of August. It would have arrived in England about ten days later and was taken on charge by 8th Air Force on 7 September. Although the exact date is not known, it would have arrived at Leiston about the third week in September, two and a half months after D-Day

The other example is serial number 44-14888, the famous GLAMOROUS GLEN III, the last P-51 of Captain Chuck Yeager. This aircraft was delivered at the factory on 31 August, ferried to Newark, left the U.S. on on 18 September, and was finally taken on charge by 8th Air Force on 10 October. (It went missing on 2 March 1945 with Lt. Patrick Mallione, who was KIA.)

There were numerous other P-51Ds with these same markings, so why were invasion stripes applied to aircraft that did not even arrive until long after the apparent need was gone? No documentation has been found, but it was official policy, as Base Air Depot #2, through

These 362nd Squadron P-51 D-5 aircraft, all in the 'half paint' scheme, are seen here in the fall of 1944. They are, front to rear: G4-B, SWEET HELEN, 44-13558, pilot Harvey Mace; G4-U, WEE WILLIE, 44-13334, pilot Charles Weaver; G4-G, no name, 44-13719, pilot Tom Martinek; G4-S, 44-13596, pilot Charles Goss. Note, that except for Mace, these are not necessarily the regular pilots of these aircraft.

which over 4,300 P-51s were processed was applying these stripes well into the fall, before delivery to the operational units. Another case of things not always being as they seemed.

It is estimated that the 357th Group, during its 14 months of ops, "used up" some 400 P-51s, a lot of airplanes! (Figures are available for the first half of this period, but not the second half.) There are no official lists of aircraft serial numbers, squadron codes, or names, all of this is assembled from photos, memories and a few fragmentary records.

One aspect of aircraft markings perhaps not always realized is just how often they changed, as new pilots arrived and the machines were shuffled around in the squadrons, and sometimes between squadrons. As an example we will follow the history of a few of them.

Two well known P-51Bs of the 363rd Squadron were C.E. "Bud" Anderson's OLD CROW, and BERLIN EXPRESS, with the flying mustang horse on the right side, flown by Bill Overstreet. Many historians do not realize that these two were the same airplane. The tail number, of course, tells the tale and the reason is simple: Anderson

completed his tour and Overstreet took it over. A recent (year 2000) book on the 357th shows these two with different tail numbers and is also incorrect on at least 15 other tail numbers on otherwise well done color profiles.

One of the interesting aspects of these colorful machines that is not often realized is how often their appearance changed. Many, in fact most, of the P-51s (if they survived long enough) carried several different names and codes during their service.

Many of these are difficult to document, but we present here a brief story on how events and the passage of time affected P-51B-10, serial number 43-6787. It rolled out of the North American factory in California and was accepted by the USAAF on 20 November 1943. It was the 29th of December before it reached Newark, New Jersey, the destination for all P-51s headed for Europe. After a ten day sea voyage and going through one of the big depots in northern England, it was taken on charge by 8th Air Force on 27 January 1944 and soon arrived at Leiston air field to become one of the original batches of P-51s assigned to the new 357th Group.

Here it became G4-Q, 2nd Lt. Gilbert O'Brien was its pilot and he named it SHANTY IRISH. O'Brien flew it for his full combat tour and scored seven victories in it. In August, it had made the long flight to Russia and back with another pilot.

When O'Brien completed his tour, probably in September, it had eight standard 362nd Squadron victory symbols (*Swastika* on white circle, with red outer ring), and over 200 mission markers along the upper left engine cowl. 2nd Lt. James W. Kenney was the next pilot and he gave it the odd name LITTLE FEETIE (on both sides). At this point its Crew Chief, SSgt. Avery Goodrich made it into an airplane probably unique in the 357th Group. He transferred six of O'Brien's victory symbols and the many mission markers to the right side of the aircraft, and started a new mission tally for Kenney in the normal position on the left side. It is a puzzle why only six victory symbols were moved to the right side when there had been eight on the left side - six plus O'Brien's two shared, giving him an official total of seven.

Early in November, LITTLE FEETIE was damaged in a landing accident. The exact date is unknown as the accident report mentioned three different dates. 9 November seems the most reasonable because on the date of the accident it had one victory symbol on the left side, for Kenney's shoot-down the previous day of *Luftwaffe* ace Franz Schall who bailed out of his mangled Me 262.

To summarize, on the day it was wrecked, it had six victory symbols and about 250 mission marks on the right side (O'Brien), and one victory symbol and about 25 mission "bombs" on the left side (Kenney).

At that time the airplane had been modified with a fin fillet and a Malcolm Hood. James Kenney went on to a D model and 6787 went to the 469th Service Squadron hangar for repair. It was then rebuilt as a two-seater, with removal of the 85 gallon fuselage fuel tank. It emerged with the new name EAGER BEAVER, named by the crews for their engineering officer, Capt. Robert Lynch and was assigned to the 364th Squadron where its new code was C5-H.

It apparently went to Germany with the Group in the summer of 1945, finally coming to the end of long useful life in September, 1945, when it was condemned and salvaged.

SERIAL NUMBERS AND TAIL NUMBERS

Mention was made earlier of a 357th Fighter Group book published in the year 2000. The book is well done, with many attractive color profiles of 357th P-51s, but at least 15 of these have incorrect tail numbers. The reason is either sloppy research or the artist or a staff member are not familiar with the system used by the USAAF/USAF for tail numbers and serial numbers.

In 1922, the U.S. Army Air Service adopted the system still used today. Each new aircraft was assigned a number beginning with the last two digits of the fiscal year in which it was ordered, followed by a dash and then the sequential number of that aircraft in the fiscal year in which it was ordered. For instance, the first aircraft ordered in fiscal year 1922, would have been 22-1. Throughout the peacetime years the numbers never got very high due to the very limited budget allowed to acquire new airplanes.

The gigantic orders of WWII for aircraft resulted in some very high serial numbers. 1942 saw the largest orders, and the last aircraft to carry a 1942 serial number was B-24J, number 42-110183. No higher numbers were ever, or ever will be reached again.

The "tail number" is not the serial number, but it is derived from the it. (The tail number is more properly called "Radio Call Number", but in reality in radio communications, only the last three numbers are used as a radio call number.) On the tail number, the first digit of the fiscal year is dropped, as is the dash in the serial number. Hence, P-51D, serial number 44-13316 would have the tail number on both sides of the fin and rudder of 41-3316.

Although all other markings would and did change, the serial number and tail number never changed (except by error), they stayed with the airplane through its service life. (The writer was once, briefly, associated with a black B-17 that had the capability of displaying several

A superb shot of HAIRLESS JOE, a B-24 J, 44-40437, of the 493rd Bomb Group and three P-51s of the 363rd Squadron led by Don Bochkay in B6-F.

different false tail numbers on the fin. In the clandestine world, anything goes.)

To add to the problems of the historian/modeler attempting to deduce colors from photographs, there are many things which can influence it such as the type and age of the film, how it was processed and printed, the lighting conditions at the time of the photo and the changes to the original paints from light, rain, snow, abrasion, mud and washing the surface with gasoline and the affects of exhaust stains.

As this is written, there are two color photographs on the desk, both taken only a month ago of a model of a P-51. The two photos were taken within a few minutes of each other, at the same location, with the same lighting, same camera position, but with two different kinds of fresh color film with two different cameras and processed by two different photo labs. In one photo the color of the

P-51 model is clearly Olive Drab, and in the other color is without doubt, RAF green.

Included here is a page of photos titled "The Many Faces of Joan" (see page 291) which we present to show the many changes some P-51s went through in a relatively short period. This took place with many 357th airplanes, but we chose JOAN because of the availability of photos of its "faces".

CONCLUSION

The study of aircraft markings and colors is a fascinating one, but for much of the area of study, there are no definitive answers. Each must do his own detective work from all the evidence and then draw his own conclusions. We hope this chapter has provided a few clues to that study.

Unfortunately, there are no good photos of TRUSTY RUSTY. It was a P-51D-5, s/n 44-13578, with the dorsal fin added later. With the 364th Squadron code C5-W, Lt. Robert Winks was the pilot (left in the photo). Delivered in bare metal, it has acquired the RAF green and gray paint scheme. Winks did well in it, scoring 5.5 victories. Both winks and the airplane survived the war.

JOAN, G4-P, on the runway with pilot Robert Wallen. It was a P-51B, s/n 42-106829 and later became FLOOGIE with pilot Otto Jenkins who left it in a field in Belgium in October 1944 after engine failure. See next page for an interesting evolution of this aircraft.

THE MANY FACES OF JOAN: *Two P-51s carried the rather mundane name, JOAN and each had other names. The top two photos and left center (originally SWOOSE), was a P-51 C, 42-103007. Damaged in a ground accident in April, 1944, it was replaced with P-51B, 42-106829, the remaining three photos. Pilot of JOAN was Robert Wallen and later Otto "Dittie" Jenkins, who renamed it FLOOGIE. He left it on its belly in Belgium in October. Note the variations in the presentation of the name JOAN, all painted by the author as was FLOOGIE.*

MORE 357TH PHOTO GALLERY

Not as sharp a photo as we would like, but the only one available showing a full side view of BERLIN EXPRESS, B6-O, 43-24823.

A close up of the winged mustang on the right side of Bill Overstreet's BERLIN EXPRESS. Neither Overstreet or his crew chief remembered any of the colors, but they were probably red and yellow.

The left side of BERLIN EXPRESS probably in RAF green with partial invasion stripes. This is probably Anderson's OLD CROW, 43-24823, that Overstreet took over when Anderson completed his first tour.

BERLIN EXPRESS *now exhibiting three victories. It later went to Bill Fricker, coded B6-K. See color photo on page 332.*

Bill Overstreet and his BERLIN EXPRESS, *with one of the Group's most spectacular pieces of nose art. Photo on right is close up of photo on left.*

Lt. John Schlossberg admires the lovely clown art work on his JOKER! It was G4-X, S/N 44-13738.

A close up of the two seat conversion method. The rear seat canopy appears to be a shortened version of the standard "birdcage" type, and the forward is a Malcolm. Of course, the rear canopy could not be opened until the Malcolm hood was closed.

Lt. Eldrid Danner, (left), has his photo taken while Sgt. Avery Goodrich works on the Merlin. This P-51 44-13334, had a long life surviving the war as a two-seater. Danner and Goodrich also survived the war.

TEXAS RANGER, a handsome P-51B, G4-E, 43-6698, with some 60 missions, including two dive bombing. Lt. Hershel "Tex" Hill flew it to Russia and back. It was eventually lost with John Templin (POW) on 28 September 1944.

A beautiful portrait of Lt. Roland Wright's MORMON MUSTANG, by lt. Joe Black of the 362nd Sqdn. who did a walking photo tour of the flight line at the end of the war. This is a P-51D-25-NA, a late model airplane not received at Leiston until March, 1945.

Home again. 12 August and back at home base. There had been no losses, but two wrecked P-51s were left behind, their pilots returning on what ever they could hitch a ride. In this photo just after landing, Colonel Dregne is smiling, left center. John Storch is next to him talking to a ground crew member and Tommy Hayes, who did not fly the mission, is at far right not in flight gear.

Colonel Donald Graham, Group Commander until he completed his tour in October. He is standing next to the AT-6 in which Lt. Walter Corby and SSgt. Melvin Schuneman were killed on 27 January 1945.

364th pilots hashing over the Russian trip for the camera. L-R, they are Hank Pfeiffer, Henry Hermanson, John Salsman, George Morris and Gerald Tyler.

2nd Lt. Richard "Rip" Potter and his MARY MAE. We don't know if this is an accurate depiction of Mary Mae or not.

*PEABODY'S PET, 42-106854 364th Sqdn. C5-B, Walter Baron, left, landed
this airplane in Sweden in August for reasons that are still mysterious.
Sgt. Richard Eagan at right was still annoyed by this 50 years later.*

*A lovely air shot of Bob Foy's, RELUCTANT REBEL,
over the patchwork English countryside.*

"Sucking up" the gear so early as this pilot has could be embarrassing, if the aircraft should sink a bit resulting in chewed up prop tips and an annoyed Engineering Officer. But a great photo!

There has been much speculation about the identity of Lt. Col. John Lander's BIG BEAUTIFUL DOLL during the short period he commanded the 357th. No photo has been found showing the tail section. However, it is believed that it was B6-0, 44-13923, as Wendell Helwig was killed in a P-51 with this name and s/n a month or so after Landers left the group.

Another Joe Black photo, this scene of the 364th squadron dispersal area, shows these sleek warriors facing retirement. C5-X is also a D-25. These late models began to arrive sometime in March of 1945 and did not see much action. Pilot of C5-X is unknown.

PRUNE PICKER, C5-A, seen here in an earthen revetment. It went missing on 18 September 1944, during the Arnhem Affair with Robert Fandry who was KIA. Its s/n was 44-13583

Take off time on a foggy winter day in 1944/1945. Ground crews stand by to provide any assistance needed. The 362nd Squadron Cletrac, with its distinctive crane, is at right in the center photo.

364th pilot Lt. James Strode, with MA CHERIE LIZ and an unknown crewman. Strode was lost while climbing through overcast and was not seen again. He was flying P-51B 43-6978. This is probably it.

A cockpit portrait of Harold Wyatt, pilot of MAN-O-WAR.

SSgt. Robert Scott (R), Crew Chief, and Lt. Rod Starkey with REMEMBER ME? a P-51B, s/n 43-7047, Sqdn. code G4-X. Starkey scored one victory on his combat tour but tragically shot down an RAF Mosquito mistaking it for a Ju 88.

Wyatt's second MAN-O-WAR, a P-51K. both pilot and aircraft survived the war.

Joe Cannon's attractive artwork on 44-72258, a late war 363rd Sqdn. aircraft.

Lt. Lynn Drollinger an original member of the 362nd Sqdn. and one of several who were YOUNG-UNS. The P-51 is 43-6729. Known throughout the squadron as "Junior", Drollinger was shot down in this airplane on 28 March 1944 but evaded capture and returned to the ZI.

Of the 357th pilots who became double or triple aces, all were original members of the group except John Kirla, who joined the group in the spring of 1944. This is the second SPOOK. It is a late model D-20, s/n 44-72180. The use of yellow and red for the name makes it very difficult to read. The huge supply of 108 gallon drop tanks spilling out of the blister hangar is of interest.

Lt. Pete Pelon with GASH-HOUND, G4-D, s/n 44-14879.
Lt. Oliver Boch later flew it for forty missions.

SWAMP FOX was C5-A, s/n 44-15660. Its pilot, Lt. Will Foard, named his P-51 after
Revolutionary hero General Francis Marion who harassed the British throughout the Carolinas.

Lt. A.E. Smith flew 80 missions in AMERICAN GIRL to complete his combat tour.
It was 43-6637, G4-K and became RUBBER CHECK. It was destroyed in a non-fatal
accident at home base in December, 1944 after almost a year of operational flying.

Another Joe Black photo, C5-J, PLASTERED BASTARD, is a D-20. The pilot was Capt. Ivan McQuire.

CAMPUS QUEEN *was another late model aricraft, a D-20, pilot Roger Moore.*

*Lt. Joe Robinson was the pilot of "BIG STUD", G4-B (bar). This is
a 362nd Squadron aircraft but with a 363rd Squadron red rudder.*

WANDERIN' WILLIE Jr., Lt. William T. Gilbert. After Gilbert's death
in another aircraft, Jack Danner flew it the rest of his tour.

John Stern standing on the wing
of Don Bochkay's WINGED ACE
OF CLUBS. Although he is wearing a chute, his clothing suggests
he is not about to fly a mission.

FRITZ, with pilot Amos Van Fleet, is flying over a village near home base in the county of Suffolk near the end of the war.

LONESOME POLECAT, B6-H, after a runway altercation with B6-T, February, 1945.

This striking photo of THE TENDER TERROR has never been published. Pilot Lt. Ralph Mann recalls his most memorable flying experience as being on 14 January, 1945, The Big Day, when he was flying as wingman and keeping the tail clear, while Major Robert Foy shot down three enemy fighters. This P-51 D-20-NA was tail number 463755 and its code was B6-W. Like all late war 363rd Squadron P-51s it had a red rudder.

MACHINE GUNS AND OPTICAL SIGHTS

The purpose of a fighter plane is to transport its weapons to the point and time where it will destroy the enemy. No matter how capable the machine, it is useless without those weapons. In this respect, the B and C model P-51 Mustangs were deficient. They probably could be considered under-gunned. Although a .50 caliber machine gun can do fearful damage to a thin-skinned airplane, the maximum weight of metal on the target could be applied only where the fire of the four guns converged. The manual gives this as 300 yards, but this could be adjusted to fit the tastes of squadron, group, or individual pilot. Like all fighters with wing mounted guns, at any other range, only half or less of your armament is likely to score hits.

The .50 caliber Browning M2 machine gun was (and is) an excellent weapon but the installation in the P-51B and C was somewhat unorthodox. In order to keep the wing thinner, the guns lay at a 45 degree angle (half on their sides). The ammunition belt coming from outboard, turned rather sharply to feed the cartridges into the gun. As the gun's mechanism pulled the ammo along its track, considerable stress was imposed on the belt links, with either belt breakage or simply jamming of the cartridges in the feedway.

However, the system worked well enough when the aircraft was flying reasonably straight - which was not often in combat!

By the time the 357th became operational, the 354th Group had been in combat for several months and must have already encountered the problem. Prior to the Group becoming operational, Lt. Col. Don Graham was one of the Group's senior pilots who flew a mission with the 354th. During the course of the mission, Graham found himself alone except for the unwelcome company of an Fw 190. In the course of the mixup, Graham found himself close behind a 190 but none of his guns would function. Somehow, he extracted himself from the situation and escaped the attention of the 190s. Graham soon became Group Commander and in a recent letter to the author, he says he immediately began to badger 66th Fighter Wing for a solution. It is probable that the 354th Group was also badgering its higher command. Later Graham found out that all the testing at the Air Force armament test center at Eglin Field was one of strafing targets in the water involving mostly straight flight.

On the 20th of February, only a week or so after becoming operational, several pilots had minor skirmishes with enemy aircraft and claimed two. At the end of his report the mission leader reported '"Usual trouble with gun stoppages."

Sergeant Willard Bierly, a 364 Squadron Armorer, describes the P-51's armament and recalls the gun problems: "As in our P-39s in the ZI, the .50 calibers were the Browning M2 air cooled weapons. These were a short recoil, reliable, 61 pound engineering marvel that fired at the rate of 750-850 rounds per minute. The gun was originally developed by the noted arms designer, John Browning while with Winchester and refined by him at Colt where production and improvements were made in

the 1920s and '30s. With the huge quantity required for the war effort, nine industrial firms produced the gun during WWII. I'm sure we had examples of all of them.

"The B and C model Mustangs had a fault not discovered until used in combat. The feed mechanism, designed to lift 35 pounds of ammunition, was not enough to pull the belted ammo through the articulated ammo tracks during violent maneuvers resulting in many stoppages. Booster motors salvaged from B-26 turrets did the trick of providing the extra energy needed to properly feed the guns. The guns were equipped with electric heaters that were clamped over the cover plates. Difficulties were encountered due to the extreme cold until it was discovered that the firing solenoids were actually freezing. A good wrapping of tape with several coats of shellac resolved that problem. Normal ammo load was 350 rounds for the inboard guns and 280 for outboard.

"The difficulties found in the B model were not present in the D model as the guns were mounted in a vertical position and the feed tracks were more in a straight line. The ammunition first used in combat by our group was the traditional loading of armor piercing (black tip), two incendiary (blue tip), and one tracer (red tip) with this pattern repeated throughout the length of the belt. It was later discovered that this stream of tracers was as of much value to the enemy as to our pilots, so the tracers were removed and only used near the end of the belt to warn our pilots his ammunition was almost exhausted.

About March or April, 1944, the M8 silver tipped armor piercing incendiary combination projectile began to flow through the supply system. It was originally only issued to "management", Group and Squadron leaders.

The troublesome gun installation on the B & C models (left wing here). As can be seen, the weapons are mounted at an angle and the ammunition belt entered the feedway at an acute angle, causing many of the early gun stoppages.

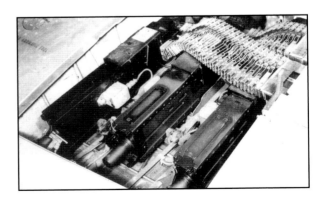

The much neater and more efficient installation in the D & K airplanes - and one more gun. Each M2 machine gun weighed 61 pounds, the plate on top of the breech cover is a heater and light colored "box" visible on the left gun is the firing solenoid which could be mounted on either side of the weapon.

As above, the tracers were used only near the end of the belt. The D model P-51 held 400 rounds for each of the two inboard guns and 270 rounds for the center and outboard guns. In event of a malfunction, it was not possible to re-charge the guns from the cockpit."

There was however, an effort made to develop a gun charger system. Little is known of this, the only document found being in an encounter report dated 11 April 1944. Lt. Mark Stepeltan with 364th Green flight were in a dogfight with 109s and 190s over the city of Leipzig. Stepelton recorded: "My guns jammed after each short burst, but due to an experimental hydraulic gun charger, was able to clear the jam and fire again. My guns jammed and were cleared at least seven times. I over ran the e/a at which time Lt. Sumner closed and observed hits on e/a which crashed and exploded. I claim one Fw 190 destroyed, shared with Lt. Sumner."

With most of the gun problems solved even in the Bs, they became quite reliable. In February, 1945, as the war was winding down, the 362nd Squadron armament section produced its usual monthly statistical analysis. 34,547 rounds had been fired, but none at air targets. No *Luftwaffe* aircraft were to be found except on the ground. Out of this total fired, there were thirteen stoppages, of which seven were failure to extract the round from the belt.

Vital to hitting anything with aircraft guns is a good optical sight or a great deal of luck. The army N-3 (in the B) and the N-9 were the usual type sights installed in the P-51s, although photo evidence makes it clear that some B models had the RAF Mk II sight. By mid summer of 1944, the British-designed K-14 computing sight was being receivedd for local installation. This marvelous piece of equipment was a giant leap forward in gun sights. During the confused and wide spread air battles that swirled over the Arnhem operation in September, Lt.

Donald Pasaka shot down two Me 109s. He closed his encounter report with this statement: "In closing, may I add that the K-14 sight is really perfect. In fact it is hard to miss after you once get it on him. I hope all of the planes are equipped with it soon."

The major new feature in the K-14 was that the pilot no longer had to calculate (guess) at the proper lead on a deflection shot. All that was required was to frame the enemy aircraft in the sight, track for one second and begin firing - the sight had calculated the lead from information fed into it by the pilot, primarily by the twist grip on the throttle which framed the target and provided range information to the sight.

Soldiers are often a conservative lot, they are reluctant to change from the old and familiar. Many pilots with considerable combat experience preferred the more simple N-9 and other optical sights. The K-14 did require a smooth touch and co-ordination to track the target, but once that was mastered, the K-14 was a marvel. It was surely responsible for many destroyed enemy aircraft which would have survived to fight another day if opposed by the old N-9.

To wrap up the gunnery discussion, we can't do better than to quote Leonard "Kit" Carson from his super book PURSUE AND DESTROY. Carson had done a lot of it in the most effective but brutal teaching arena - enemy skies.

The following was part of his chalk talk to newly arrived pilots and because of his comments on deflection shooting, was probably made before the K-14 arrived on the scene: "The day of the long range deflection shot is over, in fact it never really existed. Both the RAF and we have found that the common problem of new pilots in combat is to underestimate the range of targets in the air by a factor of two. When new pilots think they are shooting at 200 yards, it's actually closer to 400. Don't try for the

In this photo by the author, in G4-P, FLOOGIE II, the marvelous K-14 sight shows up well. The K-14 relieved the pilot of "guessing" the right amount of lead the pilot had to hold on a target for a deflection shot. He put the "pipper" on the target and the sight computed the correct "lead".

A strange composite photo of a K-14 gun sight superimposed on a photo of an Me 163, (which the 357th never encountered). In the foreground is the rubber crash pad and the dial on which the pilot set the type of German aircraft he was shooting at. At the right, the adjustment lever can be seen set between Me 109 and Fw 190. The wing spans were so similar that the lever was left set between the two and the sight was suitable for either.

big deflection shots, that is 30 degrees and up. You'll miss at least four out of five times. Get dead astern and drive in to 200 yards or less, right on down to 50 yards. I know that you were taught pursuit gunnery and deflection shooting as I was and that's all well and good but it isn't the whole story by far. In a dogfight you'll naturally wind up in a position dead astern while closing the range down to 200 yards. If you fire a couple of one second bursts from that range and position you'll nail him every time. Leave the 400 yard big deflection shots to the Hollywood movie producers, they'll have more success with it than we ever could out here. Your .50 caliber slugs have steel cores. We don't use tracer ammunition. It gives a false illusion of distance and direction. But when the steel cores of your .50 caliber ammunition hit the target, they strike sparks which appear as winking lights and you know you are scoring."

Later Carson has this to say about the K-14 sight: "It required a smooth touch on the controls to be truly effective, but was deadly accurate in most tactical situations. It could be defeated only if the target aircraft rapidly reversed its direction, momentarily tumbling the gyros when the P-51 attempted to follow."

The 364th's Lt. Osborn Howes recalls the school he attended on the K-14 sight: "My orders were to proceed, taking my own P-51 to an RAF training school up near the Scottish border to learn about the new gyro (K-14) sight. This school was located on the grounds of a grand estate, the Officer's club being the manor house, a venerable brick monster with a thick ivy coating. My living quarters, shared with three other yanks, were in a converted stable but we had running water, indoor plumbing, a fireplace and a "Bat Girl".

I'd heard of British officer's "Batmen" who were really valets in uniform, but this gender switch was very interesting! Our "Bat Girl" was a slim, shy, blonde named Dorothy, about 18 years old. She'd slip into our quarters after we had left for the flight line, make our beds, hang up our clothes, mop the floor, and generally spoil us for our return to U.S. authority.

"Squadron Leader Andrews, a worldly humorous Australian, was our C.O. and we listened, in ground school, to a series of British scientists explain the gyro principle and how it applied to the gun sight. When not in ground school, weather cooperating, we'd take off in our Spitfires, P-51s and P-47s, and fire on drone targets, first using fixed sights, then switching to the K-14 so we could see the compensating effectiveness.

"Evenings, the Officer's mess was a polyglot of Allied pilots Czechs, Poles, Norwegians, and Dutch, as well as U.S, British and all of the Commonwealth fliers, collected at the bar swapping lies and drinks and frequently forgetting dinner in favor of a jaunt to the village pub, THE BLACK SWAN nicknamed THE MUCKY DUCK by an iconoclastic Czech Spitfire pilot.

"Upon my return to Station F-373, I found most of our P-51s already had the new sights installed. When I attempted to justify my vacation by instructing one of our pilots in the technicalities of the K-14, he stopped me, saying he'd shot down two Me 109s with it the day before and he felt he could skip the science.

"So endeth the lesson. I wished that the concept of Bat Girls could be transferred as easily!"

MERLIN POWER & THE MUSTANG

The successes and the failures of the 357th Fighter Group were achieved by a combination of men and machines. The machine that THE YOXFORD BOYS took to war is so closely related to the tale of the 357th that some facts, comments and opinions on the magnificent Mustang are in order.

The image of the P-51 as the top all-around fighter of WWII seems to be secure and there are few aviation historians who would dispute this. Still, the airplane was not all that much better than the other major fighting machines that dominated the skies of Europe in the year 1944. The P-47, the Me 109 and Fw 190, the Spitfire IX (and later variants) and the Hawker Tempest were all very good at their designed tasks. However, the P-51 could match most of their strengths, could do everything well and it could do it from down among the weeds up to the rarified atmosphere (for those days) of 35,000 feet. The crucial element however, was its ability to do these things in the far corners of Europe wherever the heavies went. Phenomenal range was the key, and six or seven hour missions were not unusual. After the arrival of the Mustang, the *Luftwaffe* had no secure location where it could retreat to in order to lick its wounds and prepare to fight again.

The origins of the P-51 are thoroughly covered in several excellent books and anyone wishing the story in detail is referred to the titles listed in the bibliography. However, to provide continuity, we will sum up the origins of the airplane in as few words as possible.

In the early days of WWII when Britain stood alone, the RAF fearing that production of their standard fighters, the Spitfire and Hurricane, might not keep up with attrition, turned to Curtiss-Wright in the U.S to provide P-40s. Curtiss production however, was committed to U.S. orders so the British Purchasing Commission in the U.S. asked North American Aviation to tool up for P-40 production. Definitely not thrilled with this idea, North American countered with an offer to build a new and superior fighter and to do it in 100 days. In an age when it can take ten years to bring a new fighter to production, it seems incredible that North American rolled the prototype P-51 out of the Inglewood factory in the specified time even if it was not quite ready to fly.

Both the RAF and the USAAF purchased moderate quantities of Allison-powered Mustangs, using them for reconnaissance, low level intruder duties and ground support. Both services found them satisfactory but were less than happy with performance above 15,000 feet. The V-1710 Allison engine, with a dismally inefficient internal supercharger was of little use at the altitudes where it would have to fight in Europe. The idea of replacing the Allison with a Rolls Royce Merlin seems to have occurred to the technicians on both sides of the Atlantic about the same time, and the Merlin Mustang was created, soon to become the star of the AAF fighter forces.

However it was not just any Merlin which raised the North American air-frame from the mediocre to the best. The V-12 RR Merlin was, up until about 1941, a relatively low altitude engine but when the Merlin 61 emerged from production in the spring of 1942, the P-51 had found its power plant.

The Merlin 61 differed from the earlier engines primarily in its supercharger. In this age of high technology, the humble aircraft engine supercharger of those days seems like a simple device, merely an air pump to maintain sea level density to the cylinders to as high an altitude as possible. From the late 1920s Rolls Royce realized the need for intensive research and development of these devices, which culminated in the marvelous two stage, two speed internal supercharger with an essential after cooler to reduce the fuel-air temperature after compression. It was the Merlin 61, built as the V-1650-3 and the dash 7 by the Packard Motor Car Co. in the U.S. which made the P-51 what it was.

A centrifugal type compressor must rotate very fast to pump sufficient air and in the dash 3 engine, the ratio to crankshaft speed was about 7:1 in low blower and about 8:1 in high blower. At takeoff RPM of 3,000, the compressors were turning at about 22,000 RPM. The supercharger would shift automatically to high blower at about 19,000 feet and would downshift as the aircraft descended. This shift to low blower was somewhat violent and could grab a pilot's attention until he became used to it.

Clarence Anderson's adrenalin went up several points when he first encountered it during violent maneuvers on his first mission: "I throw my airplane about, wheel away, plummet down, look around and see nothing, then 'clunk'! Oh God, I'm hit. But where's the bastard that got me? I haul back on the stick, pulling my aircraft around just as tight as I can, damn near gray out as the blood runs to my feet - and there is no one. Then my fried brain engages. The supercharger! You dive through 16,000-17,000 feet and the P-51's supercharger cuts out automatically and when it does you get this unnerving clunk that sounds to a young pilot who has never heard a bullet punching thru metal - just like a bullet punching thru metal!" Actually, the supercharger does not "cut out" but is shifting to a lower gear. Still Bud's graphic description of the event is a classic!

During the 14 months of combat, the 357th Group received from depot and operated four different models of P-51, the B, C, D, and the K. In reality, however, there were only two as the B and C were nearly identical except for their point of origin. (the C was a product of North American's Texas plant.) The D and the K were the same except for their propellers, Hamilton Standard for the D, and Aero Products for the K. The latter had no blade cuffs making it easy to identify in photographs of the period.

Despite its many virtues, the Merlin P-51 was not without faults. Probably the most serious of these was one that many of its pilots may not have been aware of - under some circumstances the airplane was structurally weak and since the 357th lost at least five aircraft and four pilots to this cause, it is relevant to discuss the problem.

Simply put, the Merlin Mustang was considerably heavier than the earlier aircraft. The dry weight of the Allison engine at about 1310 pounds was some 300 pounds lighter than the Merlin and with the much heavier four bladed prop, larger coolant and oil radiators, plus other changes, the new airplane had lost some of its structural reserve strength. Still, the airframe was probably strong enough except for other factors which sometimes pushed the airframe beyond its limits. Landing gear doors and gun bay panels were problem areas for awhile in that they would sometimes partially open during high speed flight, causing excess air loads which led to catastrophic wing failure. Four pilots of the 357th died to this cause.

Tail sections could also separate and there was one known incident with the pilot surviving to tell a hair raising tale! The date was the 4th of October, 1944. By this date, new pilots fresh from the training fields of the ZI no longer went to Goxhill for transition into P-51s, but reported directly to their combat units where each Group's "Clobber College" handled their training.

On this date Captain Harvey Mace, a flight leader in the 362nd Squadron had sent four of his fledglings aloft on a formation flight. (Mace himself was not flying.) Two of these new lads were Lts. Richard "Rip" Potter and Ed Hyman. The day did not go well for Rip Potter. Later he told his story to his friend Jesse Frey: "Not yet on combat status, I was flying #4 position in a training flight. The leader had taken us to altitude and had us in a string formation.

"I had fallen back some as we explored the P-51 maneuverability at altitude. The leader had called me to 'pull it in'. When he rolled on his back and split-essed for the deck, I thought it would be a good time to catch up. I

didn't throttle back, in fact, I think I added throttle with the nose pointed at Merry Old England." Harvey Mace recalls: "At this point the controls stiffened up and the airplane shook so that he thought he had lost the tail. He craned his neck around in the bubble to look at the tail, it was still there - but briefly! As he looked it separated and the P-51 snapped, throwing his head through the very thick plastic of the Malcolm hood and trapping it there with the jagged edges at his throat. Only his dislocated shoulder prevented him from making the surely fatal mistake of releasing the canopy."

Jesse Frey takes up the story as told to him by Potter: "When I came to, my head is outside the canopy and the P-51 is falling, tail-less, toward the ground. I tried to reach the canopy release, but my right shoulder won't work right and my left arm was to short to reach it. I remember kicking at the instrument panel trying to push out, but to no avail. When I finally came to grips with the fact that this may be it for me, I began to think again and realized that I was still strapped in the cockpit. I released the harness with my left hand and kicked out through the canopy. I passed out again and when I came to again I was free falling, my chute not open. I couldn't pull the chute release with my right arm so I left handed it. The chute opened, I swung back and forth a few times and hit the ground."

Potter's troubles were not over yet. Ed Hyman and the rest of the flight followed him down and circled as he hit the ground. There was a stiff wind and his chute was dragging him while he attempted to get at his knife to cut the shroud lines. As he was dragged, a large farm dog had him by the foot and a farm girl was trying to get the dog off of him! Although the ambulance arrived promptly, the crew did not know he had injured his shoulder and hit his shoulder on the ambulance door and again at the hospital. It had indeed been a bad day for Rip Potter - except that he had survived.

Harvey Mace talked to Potter in the hospital and has the last word on this hairy tale: "He said he had never heard of the speed of sound or its approaching symptoms. Somewhere in his training this should have been brought out. And I, or someone, should have made all new P-51s pilots aware that a P-51 was quite capable of tearing itself apart at too fast a speed."

After a military aircraft reaches the service units, there are two groups of people who are intimately associated with it. First, of course are the pilots (or aircrew in case of multiple machines) and second are the maintainers. The latter are made up of many specialists and are the hands-on folks who fix, repair and replace, clean and paint, and who in general baby and cajole the sometimes canterous machinery into serviceable status so that its air-

crew can perform whatever the assigned mission might be - and then to bring it home, probably to be fixed again!

To close this chapter, we will have some words from both groups of people. The P-51, by today's standards was a remarkably unsophisticated machine and maintenance-wise, it was probably the star of the trio of U.S. fighters in Europe. The P-38 suffered from numerous design flaws which were not worked out until the "L" models arrived late in the war and it was a real maintenance hog with by far the worst ratio of maintenance to flight hours.

The P-47 was much better with a more reliable power plant but its turbo supercharger added to the mechanics woes. The hot section, controls, ducting and exhaust system were sources of trouble. The Mustang had a liquid cooling system that the "Jug" did not, so maybe they evened out from the point of view of the "fixer".

Leaks in the coolant system were really a minor problem if they were accessible and easily repaired unless a radiator change was required. Besides the coolant radiator in the belly, there was also a smaller oil cooler fed by air from the same scoop.

Spark plugs were a constant source of trouble and had a very short life. British plugs were preferable to U.S. plugs as they provided a slightly extended service life. Even so, plug changes were frequent, which was no great problem except for the 12 intake plugs when the engine was hot.

Major component changes such as engine, carburetor, magnetos, brakes, radiators etc. were of course, much more time consuming and were hard work in usually uncomfortable conditions and often at night. The long escort missions also piled up flight hours rapidly which brought the scheduled 25, 50, and 100 hours inspections around at amazing speed!

With a 400 hour time change on the engine, these were frequent also and many engines did not reach their 400 hour mark. With almost daily missions of approximately 65 aircraft, flown at high altitude and with engines which were often over stressed, there was ample work for the line and hangar crews which often worked well into the night to provide the airplanes for the next day's mission.

On the 5th of December, 1944, the Group with Joe Broadhead leading, became involved in violent combat with a large number of *Luftwaffe* fighters in the Berlin area. In this grand mix up ranging from 22,000 to the deck, the three squadrons claimed 18 109s and 190s while losing two (both POWs). In his diary for that day, Joe DeShay, 364 squadron hangar chief illustrates the type of mission: "Ships back in bad shape - from engine change, two carb changes, two radiators and an oil line."

A few days earlier, DeShay gives insight into another aspect of maintenance - the sheet metal men, affectionately known as "tin benders". On the 18th of December, Lechfield Airfield was the target for extensive strafing with many claims for aircraft and rolling stock destroyed. DeShay notes the following: "Mission today and ships back in bad shape. Two props out, one flak - wing change, one hole in leading edge of wing, other holes in wing. One brake out, Pete's brake line shot away." The Pete referred to was 364th squadron's leading ace Richard Peterson. DeShay's comments on both of these days probably do not include damage repaired by flight line crews on their own aircraft.

Even though the maintainers worked hard, often in miserable conditions, they had what was probably the easiest maintained aircraft in the 8th Air Force and when their labors were done they knew they had a real airplane!

On 1 September 1944, Group provided statistics on assigned aircraft, after seven months of operations which provide some highly interesting figures:

Aircraft lost: 74.
Pilots lost: 71 (includes two with 354th Grp.)
P-51s assigned (Period 30 Nov 43 thru 1 Sept 44) — 218
P-51s missing in action — 74
P-51s lost in crashes, total loss — 13
P-51s transferred (includes for battle damage) — 52
P-51s assigned, as of 31 July 44 —79
Total operational hours flown — 23,630
Total non-operational hours — 4,300
Total gasoline consumed — 2,602,132.8 gallons (U.S.)

With 115 missions, 400 operational hours and 18.5 air victories, there cannot be many men more qualified to evaluate the P-51 than Leonard K. "Kit" Carson. After his two combat tours, Carson opted to enter the research and development part of aviation, obtained his degree in Aeronautical engineering and remained in that field until his retirement, both from the USAF and from industry. In his book PURSUE AND DESTROY, he tells us: "The P-51 Mustang was not only the fighter that vanquished the *Luftwaffe*, but it was also the best performing mass-produced fighter of WWII. It was the most economical to operate, it had the longest range of any single seat Allied fighter, it was innovative, long lived, lent itself well to mass production and last but not least was the cheapest to build. In short it was the fighter the Air Force needed."

Or - as Don Gentile, great ace of the 4th Group, said of the Mustang: "This was the plane for unlimited offensive action. It could go in the front door of the enemy's home, blow down the back door and beat up all the furniture in between".

SOME CRASHES

Little is left of B6-U, 43-6999 in which Lt. Charles Campbell lost his life. The British police report states that one wing broke away in flight and the remains crashed on Rose Farm, not far from Leiston Airfield.

Details of this accident have not been found, but it appears that P-51C, 42-103348, has suffered a common ground loop, collapsing the left landing gear strut. It was repaired and wrecked again in July when the engine failed and pilot Dwaine Sanborn crash landed short of the runway.

Very little night flying was done at Leiston, but on the night of 26 April 1944, Lt. John Pugh overheated his brakes while taxiing to take off. The right brake froze and this is the result when he landed. G4-G, 42-106814 was a total wreck, but Pugh was not injured. The 8th Fighter Command Accident Board was not sympathetic and blamed 100% pilot error.

23 December 1944. Lt. Otto Jenkins took off in G4-P, s/n 44-14245, on a test flight. The coolant relief valve popped open due to an overheated engine and Jenkins put it down on the belly. It was repaired and lost on 13 January 1945 with Lt. Robert Schlicker. It carried the name FLOOGIE II.

Lt. Noel Breen in P-51, C5-Q-(bar) BABY JO suffered an engine failure in the landing pattern on 9 February 1945 and sliced through this barn in which the farmer was working. Neither Breen nor the farmer were hurt, but BABY JO was a total write-off.

Another landing mishap. After a five hour mission, all in poor weather on 10 January 1945, Lt. Rocco LePore lost control on an icy runway and PRETTY PAT ended up in a 363rd Sqdn revetment. Here the rapidly gathering crowd appears to be helping LePore from the cockpit. On 2 March, LePore was shot down in another PRETTY PAT, also C5-C, by flak while strafing some He 111s and became a POW.

This P-47 landed at Leiston on 21 May 1944, but caught fire probably from battle damage, shortly after the pilot had parked and shut down the engine. The fire soon caused all the guns to fire, spraying the airfield with .50 caliber bullets but with no reported damage. The three fire bottles indicate a futile attempt to fight the fire.

The records show that s/n 44-13681, P-51D-5 (with added dorsal fin) was salvaged due to battle damage after this 31 December 1944 crash, but no other information has been found.

A take-off accident. On 26 December 1944, Lt John Ziebell began take-off in G4-O, 44-14231, but the engine quit and he went into the trees. Amazingly, although the aircraft was totally demolished as seen here, Ziebell's injuries were minor.

Lt. Frank Gailer, landing after a mission encountered gusty cross winds on the final approach and lost control with this result to JESSIL PESSIL MOMMY, 28 September 1944.

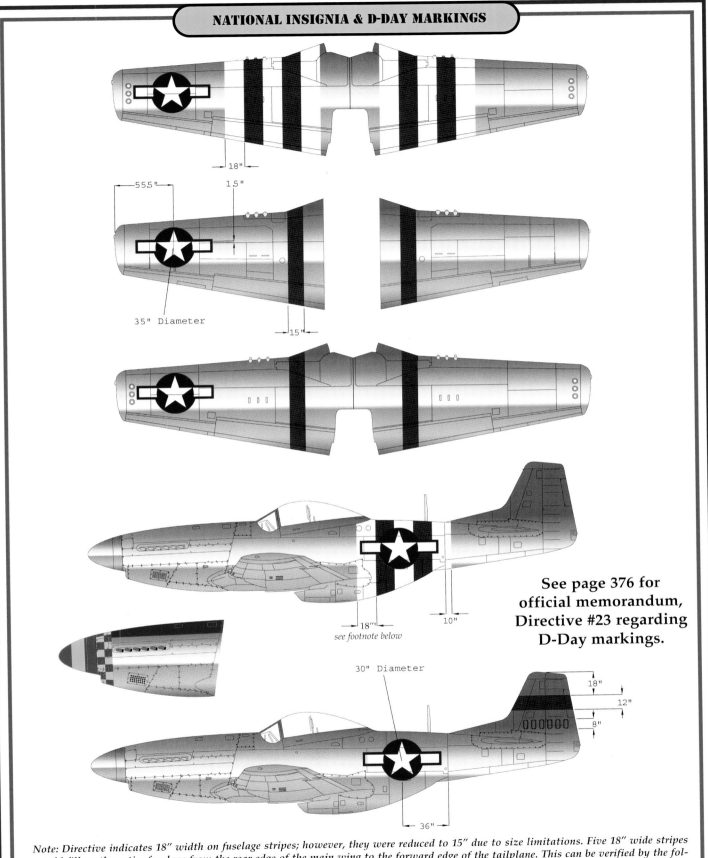

18"

555"   15"

35" Diameter

15"

See page 376 for
official memorandum,
Directive #23 regarding
D-Day markings.

18"   10"

see footnote below

30" Diameter

18"
12"
8"

000000

36"

Note: Directive indicates 18" width on fuselage stripes; however, they were reduced to 15" due to size limitations. Five 18" wide stripes would fill up the entire fuselage from the rear edge of the main wing to the forward edge of the tailplane. This can be verified by the following formula: The base roundel of the National insignia is known to be 30" in diameter and two stripes equal this in width based on available photos. Therefore, two stripes would each need to be 15" to equal the total of 30".

Thomas A. Tullis

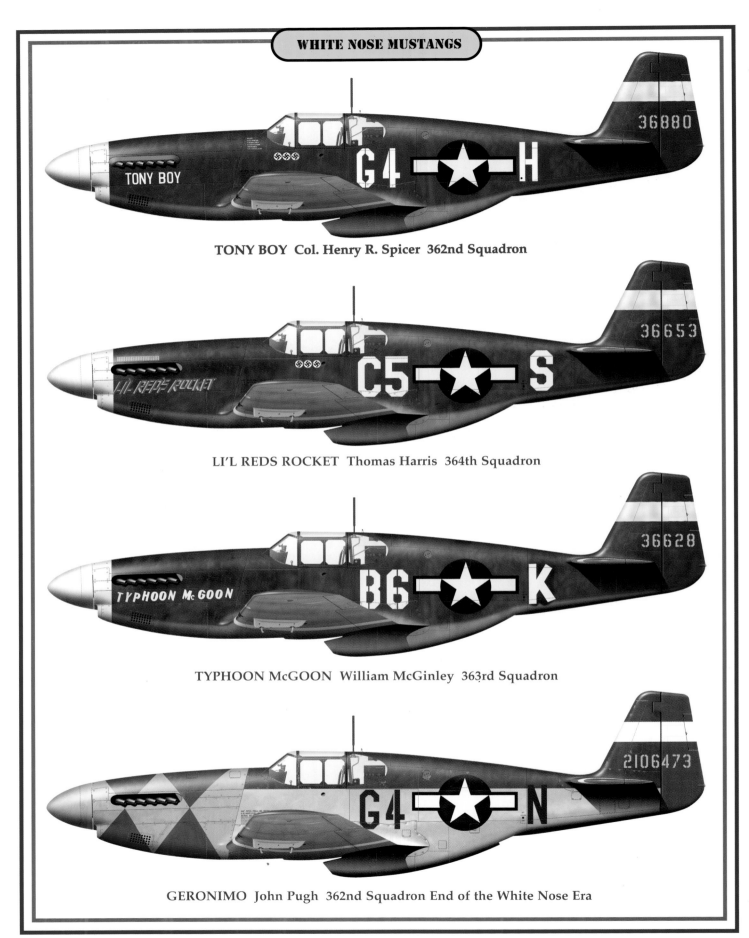

TONY BOY Col. Henry R. Spicer 362nd Squadron

LI'L REDS ROCKET Thomas Harris 364th Squadron

TYPHOON McGOON William McGinley 363rd Squadron

GERONIMO John Pugh 362nd Squadron End of the White Nose Era

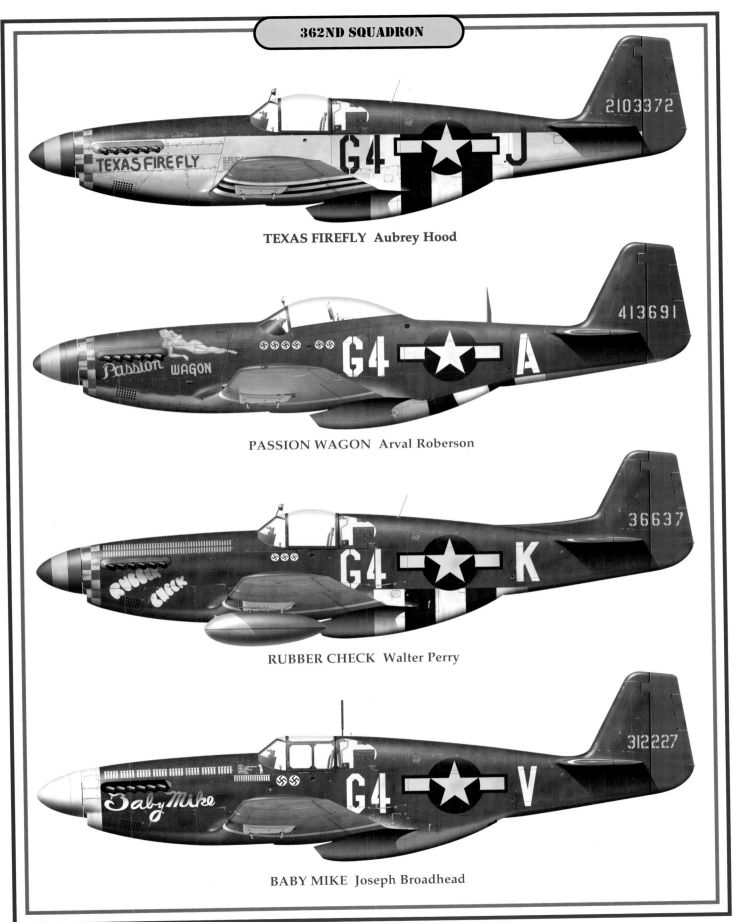

TEXAS FIREFLY Aubrey Hood

PASSION WAGON Arval Roberson

RUBBER CHECK Walter Perry

BABY MIKE Joseph Broadhead

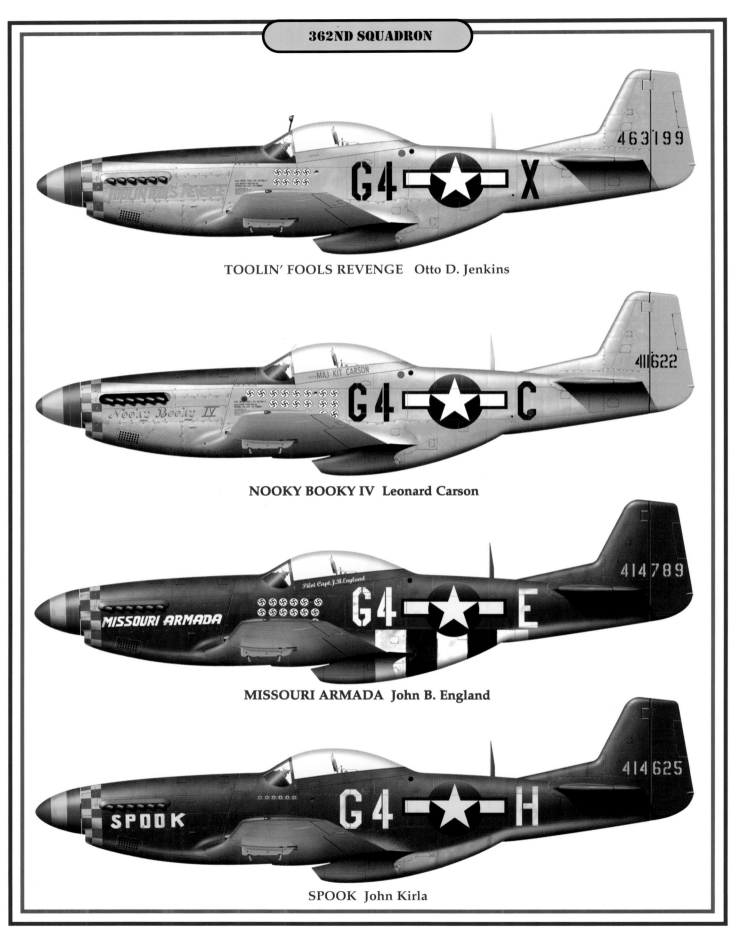

TOOLIN' FOOLS REVENGE   Otto D. Jenkins

NOOKY BOOKY IV Leonard Carson

MISSOURI ARMADA John B. England

SPOOK John Kirla

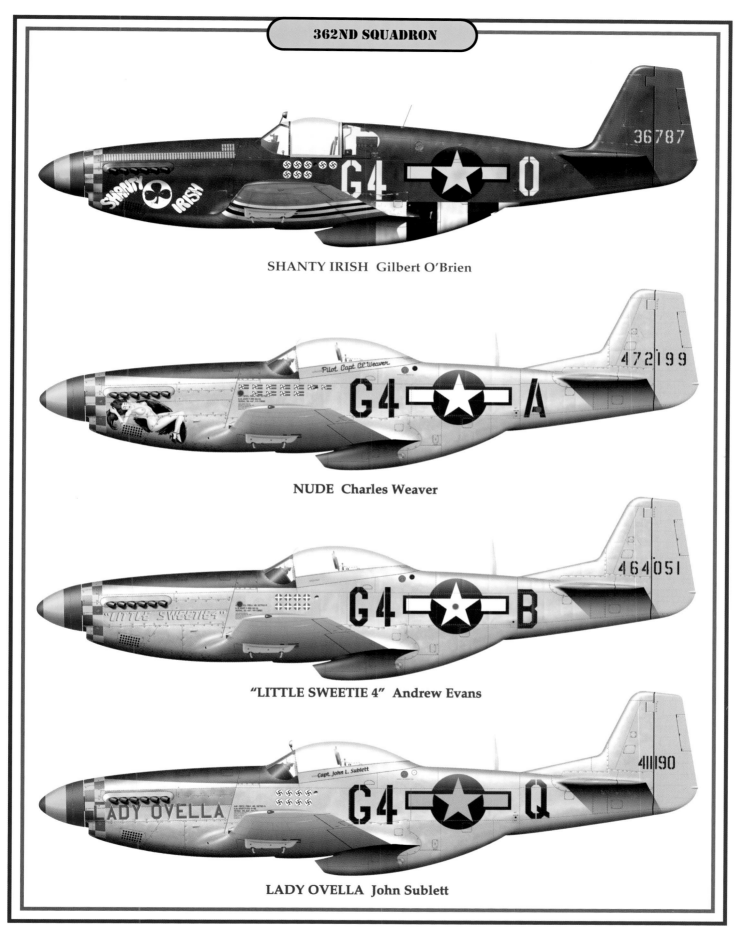

SHANTY IRISH Gilbert O'Brien

NUDE Charles Weaver

"LITTLE SWEETIE 4" Andrew Evans

LADY OVELLA John Sublett

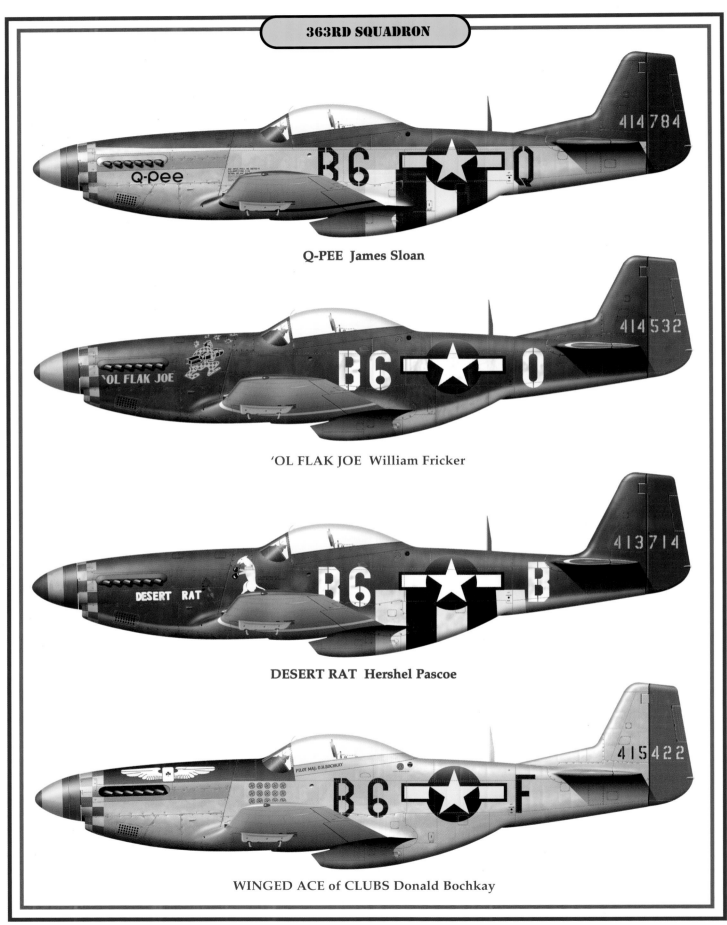

Q-PEE James Sloan

'OL FLAK JOE William Fricker

DESERT RAT Hershel Pascoe

WINGED ACE of CLUBS Donald Bochkay

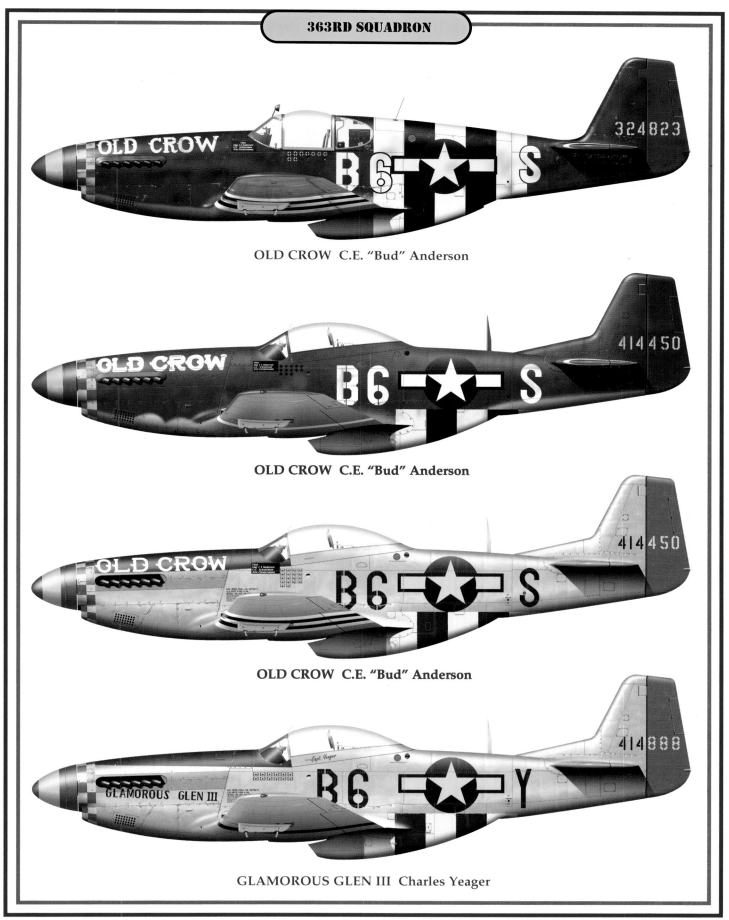

OLD CROW C.E. "Bud" Anderson

OLD CROW C.E. "Bud" Anderson

OLD CROW C.E. "Bud" Anderson

GLAMOROUS GLEN III Charles Yeager

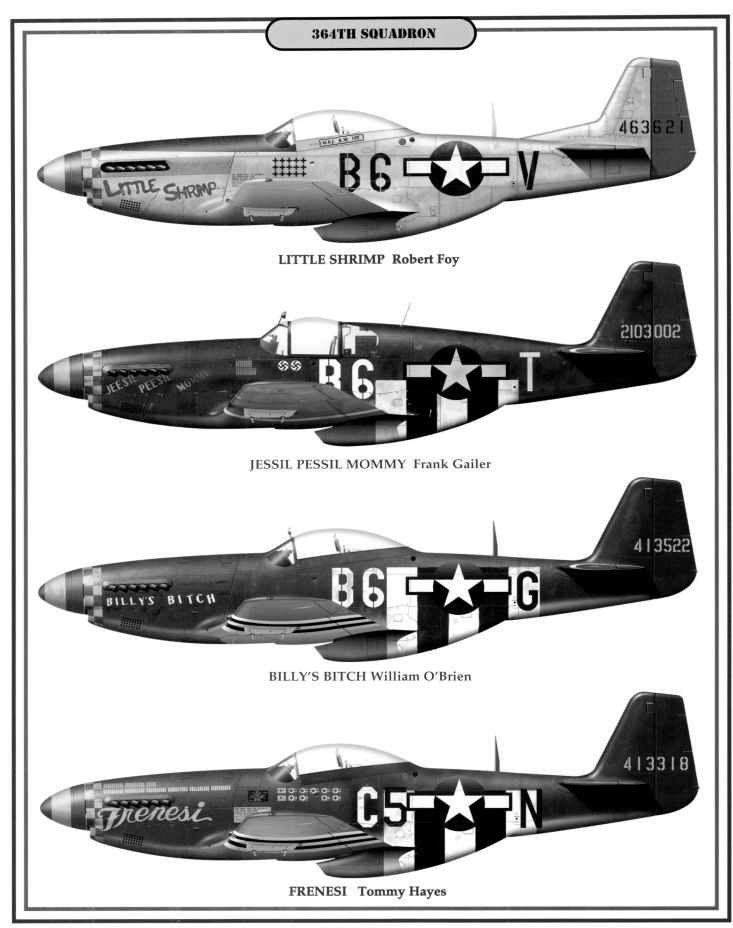

LITTLE SHRIMP Robert Foy

JESSIL PESSIL MOMMY Frank Gailer

BILLY'S BITCH William O'Brien

FRENESI Tommy Hayes

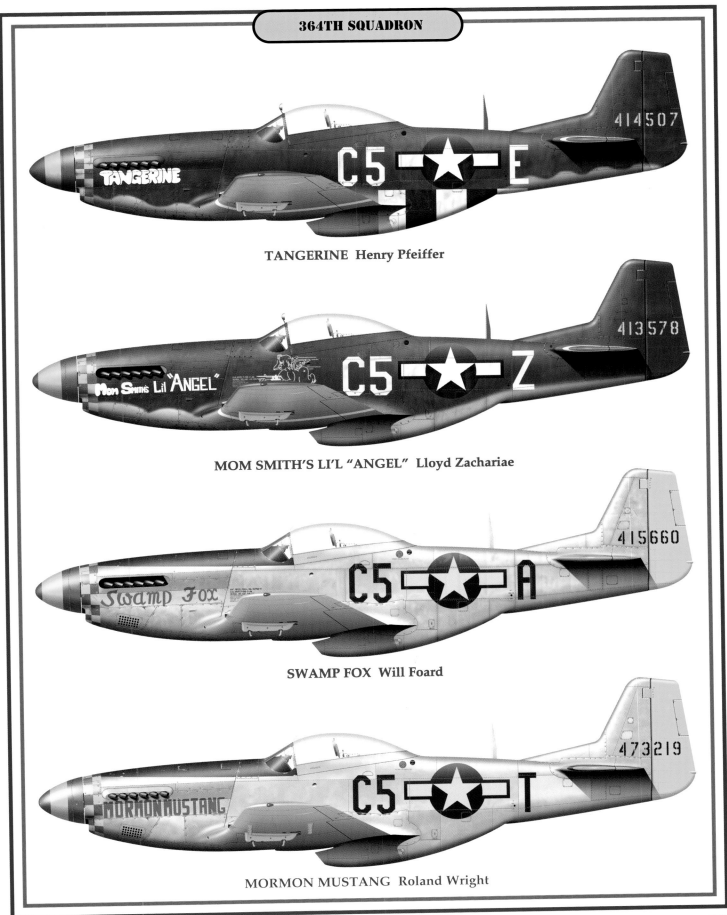

TANGERINE Henry Pfeiffer

MOM SMITH'S LI'L "ANGEL" Lloyd Zachariae

SWAMP FOX Will Foard

MORMON MUSTANG Roland Wright

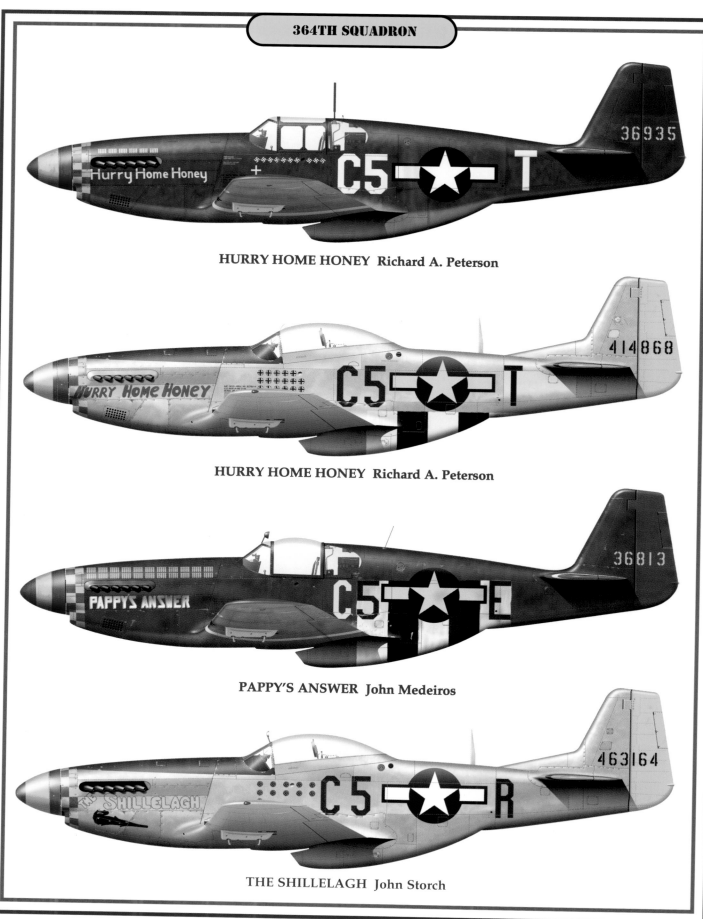

HURRY HOME HONEY Richard A. Peterson

HURRY HOME HONEY Richard A. Peterson

PAPPY'S ANSWER John Medeiros

THE SHILLELAGH John Storch

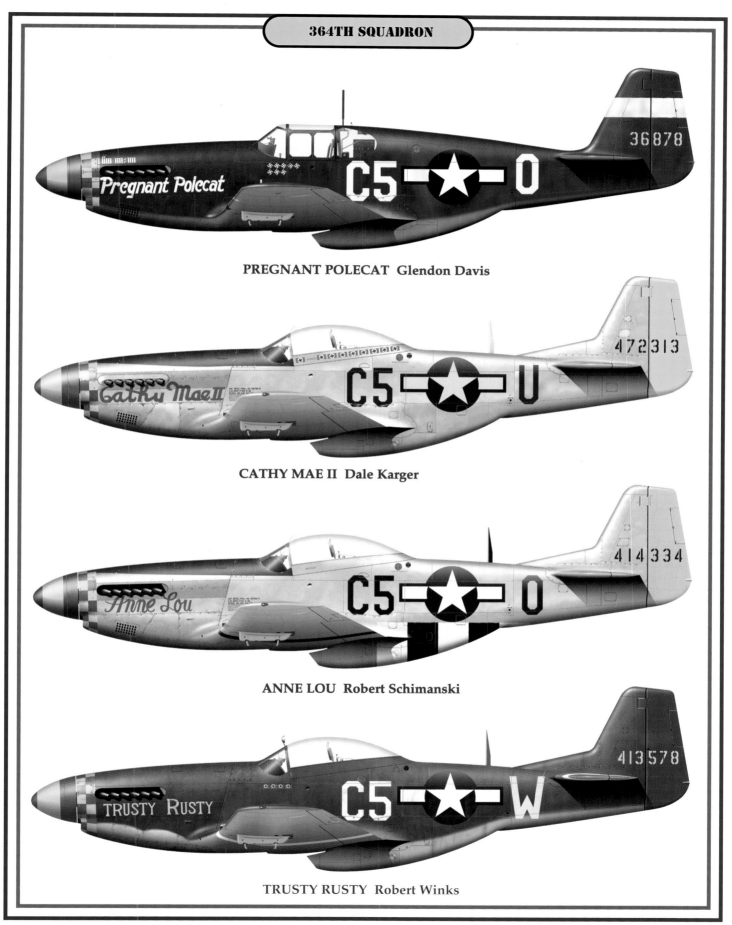

PREGNANT POLECAT Glendon Davis

CATHY MAE II Dale Karger

ANNE LOU Robert Schimanski

TRUSTY RUSTY Robert Winks

Supplied by Jeff Ethell is this great photo of Jim Gasser's MUDDY. Taken at the 355th Fighter Group base.

Lt. Joe Black in his P-51 MARY'S LI'L LAMB in this rare color cockpit shot.

This P-51B-15-NA, s/n 43-24823, had a long distinguished career with the 357th, first as Capt. Anderson's OLD CROW, then to Bill Overstreet as BERLIN EXPRESS. With a code change from B6-O to B6-K, it went to Bill Fricker and survived the war as did all three of its pilots. It was finally salvaged in the fall of 1945 in Germany. Here it is seen in close escort to an unknown bomber in its third and final form.

This is "SWEET HELEN", G4-B Harvey Mace's last P-51, the one in which he completed his tour.

*Jesse Frey's AIN'T MISBEHAVIN', G4-M at its hardstand at station F-373. This P-51
has the late war modifications of orange formation lights, and tail warning radar.*

Joe Black's G4-N, MARY'S LI'L LAMB, 44-63880, A P-51 D-20-NA.

The date is 10 November 1944, 8th Air Force had dispatched over 700 bombers to strike at airfield targets. The 96th Bomb Group out of Snetterton Heath, had bombed targets in the Weisbaden area where 337th Squadron B-17 BOOMERANG (s/n 43-38740) was hit by flak in the #2 engine. Pilot Jerry White and co-pilot R.P. "Woody" Woodson feathered the prop and dived out of formation in an attempt to put out the fire, which worked. Now they were alone and vulnerable, and called for "Little Friend" assistance. Soon FLOOGIE II, G4-P of the 362nd Squadron, 357th Fighter Group responded much to the relief of the crew of BOOMERANG. The usual pilot of FLOOGIE II was Lt. Otto Jenkins but we don't know if he was flying the P-51 that day when the Group had flown an uneventful bomber escort. In response to Woodson's hand signals, FLOOGIE II moved in close enough for Woodson to get this wonderful photo of "close escort" and BOOMERANG returned home unmolested.

An F-16C of the 162nd Fighter Squadron, 178th Fighter Wing at Springfield, Ohio in the spring of 2001. The red and yellow checks on the top of the vertical fin is carried forward from the 357th's P-51s and this aircraft also carries THE YOXFORD BOYS winged sword insignia on the side of the engine intake. Photo courtesy of Lt. Col. Tom Hitzeman, 178th Fighter Wing, Ohio ANG.

THE DESCENDANTS OF THE YOXFORD BOYS -- THE OHIO AIR NATIONAL GUARD

As the first year at Neubiberg ended in the summer of 1946, there were only a few of the wartime Yoxford Boys remaining - most had returned to the ZI to get on with the rest of their lives. Sometime in August, 1946, the news came, possibly from General "Tooey" Spaatz himself that the 357th had come to the end and would be deactivated.

On the 21st of August, orders were cut transferring the history, honors, and colors of the 357th Fighter Group to the National Guard Bureau. They in turn, passed them on to the state of Ohio. Since National Guard unit numbers normally started with the digit one, the old 357th became the 121st Fighter Group, with the Squadrons being the 162nd (old 362nd), the 164th (old 363rd) and the 166th (old 364th). The Squadron insignias were retained, but later the 162nd Squadron was required to adopt a new one, as it had been decreed that insignia could no longer bear gambling or drinking symbols. (The old 362nd Sqdn. insignia had included a pair of dice.) The current 162nd insignia bears a tiger as its main theme.

When the USAAF became the independent USAF (United States Air Force) in 1947, the National Guard units followed suit with the forming of the Air National Guard. It was mid 1948 when the 121st Fighter Group formed with its three Squadrons at Dayton, Mansfield and Columbus. These units have undergone several location changes, designation and mission changes over the years. At this writing they consist of the 178th Fighter Wing at Springfield-Beckley Municipal Airport, the 121st Air Refueling Wing (with the 166th Air Refueling Squadron) at

Rickenbacker Air National Guard Base, Columbus and the 179th Airlift Wing (with the 164th Airlift Squadron) at Mansfield-Lahm Municipal Airport.

The 178 (old 362nd) is the only one still flying fighters. Over the years since January, 1948, the 162nd has operated a cross-section of USAF fighters, starting with P-51Ds converting to H models some 28 months later. In late 1954, the unit moved to Springfield in order to fly its new jet equipment, the F-84E. The P-51 made its last flight on 9 August 1955, ending the Mustang era which had started with the 357th 11 years before.

In the following years, they flew the swept-wing F-84F and the F-100, and then to the A-7, which they were equipped with when the 357th Assn. was their guest in 1987. In 1993 they began transition to the F-16, THE FIGHTING FALCON.

In recent years, the USAF has changed the mission of the 178th from fighter to fighter training and they now train fighter pilots on the potent F-16.

The 179th Wing (with the old 363rd Squadron) switched from F-100 fighters to the airlift mission in 1975, flying the Lockheed C-130 in its various models, the C-130H at this time.

The 121st Wing (old 364th Squadron) began converting from the fighter mission with its A-7s, to that of air refueling in the early 1990s, and it now flies the USAF's mainstay tanker the KC-135.

The Airlift and Air Refueling missions are a vital part of not only the USAF's job, but that of all the military services and to all the United States.

With the 178th Fighter Wing in the F-16 training business, all three Squadrons of the old 357th are in good hands and making the wartime YOXFORD BOYS proud of their descendents.

An A-7D of the 162nd Tactical Fighter Sqdn. 178th Tactical Fighter Group at its base at Springfield, OH in August 1992. It bears the old group insignia of the 357th Fighter Group and the name SCRAPPY is that originally carried on the P-51 of Lt. Alvin Pyeatt who was KIA in March 1944. Photo courtesy of LtCol. Tom Hitzeman, 178th Fighter Wing Ohio ANG.

LEISTON AIRFIELD - 1945 TO THE NEW CENTURY

NOTE: Much of the information herein came from "90 MILES TO WAR", written in the year 2000 by Peter Saunders, a stalwart member of FOLA (Friends of Leiston Airfield).

When the Americans vacated Leiston Airfield, station F-373, it was returned to the RAF who used the site as #18 Recruit Center until May, 1946, also storing various equipment for the use of radar stations along the coast. The RAF gradually moved out in the late 1940s and early 1950s and many of the huts on the domestic sites were used as private accommodations. The airfield remained largely intact for several more years, eventually being de-requisitioned with part of it sold off in 1955 and the remainder some ten years later.

Many former YOXFORD BOYS and their families have returned to the scene which had such a major impact on their young lives and a hardcore of local (and some not so local) airfield enthusiasts are always available to serve as guides.

This author and his wife have been back to England many times, and to the airfield several times. During our first visit in 1978 with historian Roger Freeman, there were still many derelict buildings scattered among the trees and many sections of taxi strip and runways remained. The big T-2 hangars were of course long gone, but the farm owner had built a large metal building on the floor of the old 469th Service Squadron. The whole area has returned to farm land and it is still very much largely rural, and not overrun by explosive development.

There is still much to see under the guidance of Peters Saunders, Brian Boulton (a retired police inspector) and other knowledge people. The major presence in the area is a 45 acre tract occupied by THE CAKES AND ALE caravan park, a lovely leisure area for mobile RVs which also includes several rental apartments and an excellent lounge bar, THE YOXFORD BOYS.

The leisure park was put together by owner Peter Little in 1968. It occupies land along the old runway 24/06 and in what was the 363rd Squadron dispersal area. Some of the old earthen revetments are still there. There is a large scale fiberglass model of Kit Carson's NOOKY BOOKY IV on display outside the lounge bar club house.

In 1992 during a visit by about 20 veterans and wives, the Group was surprised by Warrant Officer Peter Barker and his Air Cadets (similar to Boy or Girl scouts, with an aviation orientation.) who took us to a 362nd Squadron hardstand. There they unveiled a memorial they had built, to the memory of the men who had served there. It was a most touching and appreciated gesture.

It was, however, in a rather inaccessible part of the airfield, so a local group spearheaded an effort to built a larger memorial near the site of THE CAKES AND ALE. Every spring, FOLA (Friends Of Leiston Airfield) produces a well attended memorial service complete with band, USAF dignitaries and a fly-by by P-51s, Spitfires, or AT-6s. The affair is usually attended by small and dwindling group of the original YOXFORD BOYS.

Speaking for all the veterans of the 357th Fighter Group and their families we owe a debt of gratitude to the members of FOLA, who are keeping our presence of 60 years ago very much alive.

The lovely memorial erected by "The Friends of the Leiston Airfield", dedicated to all the men of the 357th and 358th Fighter Groups who served and flew from the airfield.

357th FIGHTER GROUP REUNIONS

As World War II came to a close, the Fall of 1945 was soon upon us. Slowly the 357th Fighter Group had moved out of the Leiston Airfield in England and by means of B-17 Bomber Aircraft and Vehicle Convoy had relocated at Neubiberg, Germany to perform Air Force Occupational Duty. Soon the military point system was used to determine each man's status for departing for home and separation from the military began to dissolve the 357th Fighter Group. September and October 1945 saw the outfit come drastically apart.

It was not until twenty-two years later that Bob and Marie Grupposo of the 364th Fighter Squadron visited the De Shay's and borrowed the mailing list possessed by Joe De Shay of the men of their squadron to plan a reunion at Hartford, Connecticut. About thirty couples attended. They decided to form an organization, elected officers and established a policy to hold a reunion every three years. Usually the reunions were held in the month of September. Information as follows:

1967 the first reunion held at Hartford, Connecticut
1970 at Chicago, Illinois at which time members of all units of the 357th Fighter Group and the Supporting Units were invited to join.
1973 held at Denver, Colorado
1976 held at San Francisco, California
1979 held the second time at Denver, Colorado and called Denver II. At this time intervals between reunions changed to every two years.
1981 held at Boston, Mass.
1983 held at Charleston, W. Virginia
1985 held at San Antonio, Texas
1987 held at Dayton, Ohio
1989 held at Salt Lake City, Utah
1991 held at Marietta, Georgia
The next two reunions were held at 18 month intervals:
1993 at Long Beach, California (April)
1994 at Myrtle Beach, S. Carolina (Sept.)
Back to two year intervals:
1996 held at Louisville, Kentucky
1998 held at Colorado Springs, Colorado
2000 held at San Antonio, Texas (San Antonio II)
2001 held at Dayton, Ohio (Dayton II)

The Dayton I Reunion was the reunion with the highest attendance with 356 who were served at the Saturday evening banquet. On that occasion, the 357th Fighter Group's large Memorial was dedicated at the Wright Patterson Airfield Memorial Park.

At each reunion, the Board of Directors convened. A meeting of the General Membership was held and officers and Directors were elected. Activities for entertainment were most enjoyable.

Joe De Shay

Joe DeShay gives us the solid facts of the 357th Fighter Group Association, 1967 to 2001, but other aspects should be noted. Although many former YOXFORD BOYS have played important parts in the association of 357th alumuni, probably none were more vital that Joe and Ellen DeShay who served as association secretary, executive secretary, president and editor of the Group newsletter for the last 30 plus years. It should be pointed out that both were crucial to the success of the Association the amount of work accomplished by Ellen cannot be overstated.

From the point of view of this writer, the 357th Association and the marvelous people who make it up, from the former lowest enlisted rank to the dozen or so General Officers produced has been one of the major highlights of my life and that of my wife Margreth.

Also a major part of my life has been as the official Group historian and the great honor it has been to have the opportunity to write extensively for the last 40 years, in an attempt to put the 357th in its proper place in history. I hope that I have been able to do that.

As the Association phases out in the fall of 2001, I would like to salute all the wonderful men and women of the 357th Fighter Group and the 357th Fighter Group Assocation. They all played a major role in making it agreat life!!

Merle Olmsted
Paradise, CA. 2001

This photo by John Dibbs, one of the foremost aviation photographers of today, was taken at Stinson field, San Antonio, Texas, in May 2000 at the next to the last reunion of the 357th Fighter Group. The three men standing on the near wing are Bud Anderson, Art Vance (owner of the Green P-51) and Chuck Yeager. The author and his wife Margreth are just behind the propeller blade of GLAMOROUS GLEN III.

CHAPTER 13:
WARBIRDS

P-51 Mustangs became surplus after WWII and many were scrapped or sold to civilians. Years later, Mustangs from foreign country Air Forces's became obsolete and were also made available to the general public. The civilian owners modified these aircraft for personal use and painted them in many and varied paint schemes. Many were repainted in historically accurate markings of WWII Fighter Groups and even a particular pilot's personal aircraft markings.

Through the efforts of organizations such as the Experimental Aircraft Association and the Confederate Air Force, interest has been maintained in the preservation of these treasures of history. It is estimated that there are about 100 P-51 Mustangs still in flying condition in 2001 and many more in museums and displays around the world.

The 357th Fighter Group and its colorful WWII markings have been a frequent choice for many P-51 restoration projects. This collection is being presented so that these historical Mustangs can be seen in vivid colors and we can have a better appreciation of what they actually looked like during WWII. One must realize that the owners have taken so much pride in the restoration these aircraft may look better than the original. Some modern equipment has been added and some old has been removed so these restored aircraft are accurate but not perfect. You can compare these photographs with the black and white examples in the book.

FLIGHT OVER LEISTON

In July 2001, a combat veteran of the 357th Fighter Group had the unique experience of flying over the site of the Leiston Air Field in a Mustang. Col. "Bud" Anderson and three other WWII aces were invited to attend the annual Flying Legends Air Show at Duxford, England. Anders Saether became aware of the visit and invited Col. Anderson to fly his P-51 recently repainted in the camouflaged paint scheme of Bud's WWII OLD CROW. On 5 July 2001, Bud flew the OLD CROW from Duxford to Leiston and circled the site of the WWII home of the 357th Fighter Group. The airfield is mostly returned to agriculture but was easily recognizable. John Dibbs took some fantastic pictures from an accompanying aircraft. Bud's last flight in a Mustang from Leiston was on 15 January 1945, 56 1/2 years ago. This was a pretty nostalgic event!

In May 2000, at the 357th Fighter Group reunion in San Antonio, Texas, General Chuck Yeager in GLAMOROUS GLENN III and Col. Bud Anderson in OLD CROW fly a tight formation for a photo shoot with world-class photographer John Dibbs.

Photo credit 2001 John Dibbs and with permission of The Real McCoy's.

P-51 D B6-S OLD CROW flown by then Colonel Clarence E. "Bud" Anderson, leading ace of the 363rd Fighter Squadron and the third ranking ace of the 357th. The owner of this Mustang is Jack Roush from Livonia, Michigan.

Photo credit 2001 John Dibbs

P-51 D B6-B ISABEL III comes from New Zealand and is restored in the colors of Flt. Lt. Jack Cleland, RNZAF, an exchange officer flying with the 363rd Fighter Squadron, 357th Fighter Group. The owner of this Mustang is Sir Tim Wallis of Wanake and the pilot in the photos is Tom Middleton.

Photo credit ©2001 John Dibbs

P-51 D G4-U WEE WILLY II Captain Calvert L. Williams, 362nd Fighter Squadron, flew a Mustang like this one near the end of his combat tour. He had the distinction of being the first pilot in the 357th Fighter Group to score an aerial victory on 20 February 1944. This Mustang is owned by Steve Hinton and is based at Chino, California.

Photo credit ©2001 John Dibbs

P-51 D C5-N FRENESI was flown by then Lt. Col. Thomas L. Hayes, Commander of the 364th Fighter Squadron and later Deputy Group Commander. The pilot/owner is James Beezley Jr. of Philadelphia, PA. *Photo credit ©2002 John Dibbs*

P-51 D G4-S MOOSE was piloted by then 1st Lt. Myron Becraft, 362nd Fighter Squadron, 357th Fighter Group. This Mustang was part of The Fighter Collection and is shown being flown by the founder Stephen Grey. Home base is Duxford Airfield, England. *Photo credit ©2001 John Dibbs*

P-51 D G4-A was flown by then 1st Lt. Arval J. Roberson, 362nd Fighter Squadron, 357th Fighter Group. The pilot owner was George F. Enhorning of Wolcott, Connecticut. This P-51 flew for several years in these markings before it crashed in Chatham, MA on 29 September 1990. The pilot in this photo is the late Jeff Ethel.　　　Photo Credit Roberson Collection

P-51 D C5-T HURRY HOME HONEY was piloted by then Major Richard A. "Pete" Peterson, leading ace of the 364th Fighter Squadron and the Group's fourth ranking ace. This aicraft is owned by Charles Osborne of Louisville, Kentucky. Peterson is at the controls during the 1994, 357th Fighter Group reunion in Myrtle Beach SC. HURRY HOME HONEY was named for the manner in which Peterson's wife signed off on their letters, she would write, Hurry Home, Honey!　　　Photo credit ©2001 John Dibbs

P-51 D B6-F SPEEDBALL ALICE or the WINGED ACES OF CLUBS is a rendition of the Mustang flown by then Captain Donald H. Bochkay, 363rd Fighter Squadron, 357th Fighter Group. The pilot owner is Art Vance, a retired Federal Express Captain, from Sebastopol, California and is based at Sonoma County Airport, Santa Rosa, once the home of the 363rd Fighter Squadron in 1943. Dan Vance who often flies his dad's P-51, is shown in this photo.

Photo credit © 2001 John Dibbs

P-51 D G4-C NOOKY BOOKY IV was flown by then Major Leonard K. Carson, 362nd Fighter Squadron and the leading ace of the 357th Fighter Group. The present owner is Jean-Claude Beaudet and the P-51 is based in Sommieres, France.

Photo credit Merle Olmsted Collection

P-51D C5-T MORMON MUSTANG was flown by then Captain Roland Wright, 364th Fighter Squadron 357th Fighter Group. Eugene R. Mallette, the senior Executive of the small airline Alpine Air owns this Mustang. He is from Parker, Colorado. This aircraft flew as the MORMON MUSTANG for a considerable time but has been renamed SWEET MARY LOU, after his wife. The 357th red and yellow colors continue to be displayed.

Photo credit Gene Mallette collection

APPENDICES

A COMPILATION OF P-51 IDENTIFICATION

Aviation historians and enthusiasts always like to see a comprehensive and complete listing of all aircraft assigned to or used by any type of organization - be it airline, racing stable, or military unit. So would this writer! However, in the case of the 357th Fighter Group or most any other WWII military unit, it is not in the realm of possibility.

It seems natural to assume that any organization which operates aircraft would keep a record of all of its aircraft equipment. It also makes sense that the headquarters and three squadrons of the 357th Fighter Group would have kept such records. Although the author has a very large store of documents on the Group, no aircraft listing has surfaced in the 40 years or more of searching.

Of the 15 or so 8th Air Force fighter group histories in the author's library, only the 4th and 352nd Group have a fairly comprehensive (but apparently not complete) listing of aircraft. It appears then that original WWII records listing aircraft assigned do not exist for any group.

With only fragmentary documentary evidence available, a compiler has only two sources of information - the fading memories of the men who were there or the main source - THE PHOTOGRAPH! The problem here is that not all aircraft were photographed and of those that were, many of these are long gone or not available to the compiler.

Compounding the problem is the fact that in many many cases, any one aircraft changed its identity several times during its service life. It changed its paint scheme, its unit codes, nose art, names and pilots. The only thing that could be relied upon not to change was its tail number which gives any military aircraft its own identity. (derived from the serial number - see the chapter on paint etc.)

From the time it began to receive its P-51s late in January, 1944, until the fall of 1944, the 357th Fighter Group had about 275 P-51s assigned. There are no figures for the last six months of the war but we can assume that the Group flew at least 400 P-51s during its operational period. A great many of these are totally unknown as there are no photos of them.

The four essential items needed for a comprehensive listing are the aircraft squadron code, the serial (tail) number, aircraft name and pilot's name. There are a great many aircraft on which we have one or two of these elements, but not the others. For instance, we have a long list of names, but nothing else. In most cases these are not listed only those with most of the known elements.

We present this compilation then, as a partial list of the aircraft operated by THE YOXFORD BOYS during those amazing and often traumatic days of 1944-1945. There is no guarantee that it is free of errors. Nevertheless, it is hoped it will be of interest and useful to historians and enthusiasts.

My special thanks to Mr. James Anderson for his efforts "for the cause" and for his wonderful web site on the old 357th Fighter Group.

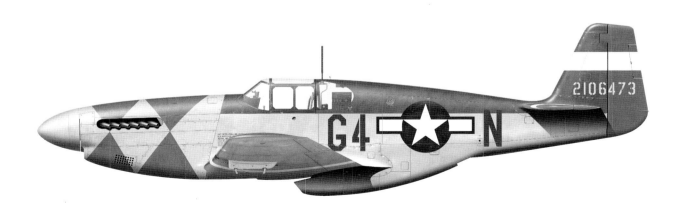

AIRCRAFT IDENTIFICATION DATA

362ND SQUADRON, CODE G4

SQDN CODE	SERIAL NUMBER	AIRCRAFT NAME	PILOT	COMMENTS
G4-A	43-12455	*BLYTHE SPIRIT*	DONALD VOGEL	MIA 7-1-44 EVADER
G4-A	44-13691	PASSION WAGON	ARVAL ROBERSON	LATER CHARLES WEAVER
G4-A	44-72199	*NUDE, no name*	CHARLES WEAVER	PROBABLY SAME COWLPANELS ON BOTH
G4-A	44-63779	*NUDE, no name*	CHARLES WEAVER	AIRCRAFT
G4-A (bar)	44-63222	*NEVADA SKAT KAT*	HARRY WILLIAMS	
G4-A	44-15620(uncertain)	UNKNOWN	WILLIAM T. GILBERT	MIA 24 DEC 44
G4-B	43-6556	*CHICAGO GUN MOLL*	ROBERT D. BROWN	
G4-B	44-13558	*SWEET HELEN II*	HARVEY MACE	
G4-B	44-64051	*LITTLE SWEETIE 4*	ANDREW EVANS	*SHE'S MY GAL*, on right side.
G4-B (bar)	44-14819	*BIG STUD*	JOE ROBINSON	
G4-C	43-6634	*NOOKY BOOKY*	LEONARD CARSON	HIS 1ST P-51, BUT NO EVIDENCE IT CARRIED THE NAME.
G4-C	44-13316	*NOOKY BOOKY II*	LEONARD CARSON	
G4-C	44-13316	*OLIVIA DeH*	RAY CONLIN	(AFTER CARSON COMPLETED TOUR)
G4-C	44-14896	*NOOKY BOOKY III*	LEONARD CARSON	SALVAGE BATTLE DAMAGE& DEC 44.
G4-C	44-11622	*NOOKY BOOKY IV*	LEONARD CARSON	TO END OF WAR.
G4-D	43-6710	*MISS MARVEL*	LLOYD MITCHELL	
G4-D	44-14849	*GASH-HOUND*	PAUL PELON	LATER OLIVER BOCH TOOK IT OVER AND FLEW 40 MISSIONS IN IT
G4-E	43-6698	*TEXAS RANGER*	HERSHEL HILL	BECAME *BOW LEGS*, MIA W/ JOHN TEMPLIN, 28 SEPT 44.
G4-E	44-14789	*MISSOURI ARMADA*	JOHN B. ENGLAND	LATER BECAME SAD SACK WITH OSCAR T. RIDLEY, PILOT.
G4-E	44-72819	*MY BONNIE*	JOE SHEA	
G4-F	43-6824	*PARKER 51*	MAURICE BAKER	
G4-F	44-15687	*THE WHISTLER*	C. R. COON (uncertain)	MIA 27 MAY 44
G4-G	42-106654	*JERSEY BOUNCE*	JAMES ROUGHGARDEN	LATER AS G4-M.
G4-G	42-106814	UNKNOWN	JOHN PUGH	CRASHED HOME BASE MINOR INJURY ACFT SALVAGED 7 May 44
G4-G	43-6448	*MAN-O-WAR*	HAROLD WYATT	Prev. G4-U.CALVERT WILLIAMS
G4-G	42-106831	*MY BONNIE*	KEN HAGAN	MIA, evader, 17 June '44
G4-G	44-13741	*BUDDY BOY*	CLIFFORD ANDERSON (Not confirmed)	MIA, 19 Sept 44 w/James Blanchard
G4-G	44-13719	*MAN O WAR*	HAROLD WYATT	MIA W/ H. CHANDLER, PITTER PAT, 30 Dec 44
G4-G	44-11683	*MAN O WAR*	HAROLD WYATT	P51K
G4-H	42-106462	*U'VE HAD IT*	JOHN ENGLAND	LATER G4-Y. LOST IN TRAINING CRASH, 4 OCT 44. POTTER BAILED.
G4-H	44-14625	*SPOOK*	JOHN KIRLA	LATER TO 359TH GROUP.
G4-H	44-72180	*SPOOK*	JOHN KIRLA	SURVIVED WAR.
G4-H	43-6880	*TONY BOY*	COL. SPICER	MIA 5 Mar 44
G4-H	43-12442	UNKNOWN		MIA WITH KONSTINTIN VOGEL, 18 MAR 44
G4-H	44-13735	UNKNOWN	JOHN ENGLAND	DAMAGED IN CRASH I OCT 44 LOST WITH MAJ GIARRIZZO, 2 NOV AS G4-N.
G4-I	43-7176	UNKNOWN		MIA WITH FRANK CONNAGHAN, 24 Apr 44, COLLISION WITH Me 110
G4-I	43-6727	*DARE DEVIL*	PAUL HOLMBERG	KIA 29 July 44
G4-I	44-13741			From Sqdn. document, see G4-G above.
G4-J	42-103372	*TEXAS FIRE FLY*	AUBREY HOOD	
G4-J	44-15527	*CHI LASSIE*	GEORGE BEHLING	MIA 14 Jan 45. POW.
G4-J	44-63863	*GEORGIA BOY TOO*	UNKNOWN	
G4-K	43-6637	*AMERICAN GIRL*	ALDEN SMITH	LATER AS *RUBBER CHECK*, PROBABLY WALTER PERRY PILOT. DESTROYED IN HOME BASE CRASH, 2 DEC 44.
G4-K	44-63195	*MARY MAE*	RICHARD POTTER	
G4-K	44-11697	*MUDDY*	JAMES GASSER	(Mother's nickname)
G4-L	43-12468	*SOUTHERN BELLE*	FLETCHER ADAMS	MIA 30 MAY 44 (NAME NOT CONFIRMED)
G4-L	44-13570	*LITTLE BEV*(not confirmed)	HENRY BEAL	FLEW IT ON THE SHUTTLE MISSION, 6 AUGUST 44. ACFT LOST WITH 363RD PILOT WILLIAM HAACK ON 9 APRIL 45.

362ND SQUADRON, CODE G4 (cont'd)

SQDN CODE	SERIAL NUMBER	AIRCRAFT NAME	PILOT	COMMENTS
G4-L	44-72077	NO NAME	OSCAR T. RIDLEY	(NOT CONFIRMED)
G4-M	42-106654	JERSEY BOUNCE		HAD BEEN G4-G, LOST 13 SEPT 44 WITH HOWARD JOHNSON, BAILED, RETURNED TO UNIT LATER TO E.A. GORDON WITH SAME NAME
G4-M	44-15267	AIN'T MISBEHAVIN'	JESSE FREY	
G4-M	44-63195	MARY MAE	RICHARD "RIP" POTTER	
G4-N	44-13735	UNKNOWN MIA	LAWRENCE GIARRIZZO	2 NOV 44 HAD BEEN G4-H
G4-N	42-106473	GERONIMO	JOHN PUGH	FLEW IT THROUGH HIS WHOLE TOUR. MIA WITH JAMES VALKWITCH, 13 SEPT 44
G4-N	44-14722	TEMPTATION	MATHEW "SMILIN' JACK" MARTIN. BAILED OUT, POW, 5 DEC 44.	
G4-N	44-63880	MARY'S LI'L LAMB	JOE BLACK	
G4-N	44-63195	FRITZ	AMOS VAN FLEET	NO OTHER DATA
G4-0	44-13741	BUDDY BOY	CLIFFORD ANDERSON	(NAME AND PILOT NOTCONFIRMED). MIA 19 SEPT 44, JAMES BLANCHARD.
G4-0	44-14231	BUDDY BOY II	CLIFFORD ANDERSON	WRECKED ON BASE 26 DEC 44, BY JOHN ZIEBELL, MINOR INJURY
G4-0	43-7184	NO NAME	NO OTHER DATA	NOT ON LOSS LIST.
G4-0	44-13517	SEBASTIAN JR.	ROBERT BECKER	CRASHED ON TAKE-OFF ITALY RETURNING FROM SHUTTLE. MAURICE BAKER UNINJURED.
G4-0	42-106783	SEBASTIAN	ROBERT BECKER	TIGER HEAD ON COWL
G4-0	44-64073	SKIN-N-BONES	ANTON SHOEPKE	
G4-0	43-6923	SWEET HELEN	HARVEY MACE	ACFT SALVAGED ON 7 AUG 44, REASONS UNKNOWN
G4-P	42-103007	SWOOSE, then JOAN	ROBERT WALLEN	ACFT BADLY DAMAGED IN GROUND ACCIDENT March/April 44
G4-P	42-106829	JOAN	ROBERT WALLEN	BECAME FLOOGIE WITH NEXT PILOT OTTO JENKINS. BELLIED IN OCT 44, BRUSSELS. SALVAGED 30 NOV 44.
G4-P	44-14245	FLOOGIE II	OTTO D. JENKINS	CRASHED NEAR BASE, 13 JAN, 45, ROBERT L. SCHLIEKER KILLED.
G4-P	44-72489	ROLLA U-BAR (GIRL'S NAME AND RANCH BRAND)	EDWARD HYMAN	TO END OF WAR. SOLD SWITZERLAND
G4-Q	43-6787	SHANTY IRISH	GILBERT O'BRIEN	THEN BECAME LITTLE FEETIE, WITH JAMES KENNEY. AFTER GROUND ACCIDENT, IT WAS CONVERTED TO A TWO SEATER AND NAMED EAGER BEAVER, WITH NEW CODE C5-H bar.
G4-Q	44-11190	LADY OVELLA	JOHN SUBLETT	CRASHED 21 MAY 45, ALFRED BIERWEILER KILLED.
G4-Q BAR	44-72710	NO OTHER DATA		
G4-Q	44-14682	WINNIE GAL		LOST IN THE SEA W/JACOB GIEL, 3 APRIL 45.
G4-R	43-6688	PASSION WAGON	ARVAL ROBERSON	DAMAGED IN GROUND ACCIDENT, UNKNOWN DATE, REPAIRED - STILL IN SERVICE Dec. 44
G4-R	44-15113	WANDERIN' WILLIE JR	WILLIAM T. GILBERT	AFTER HIS DEATH, JACK DUNN FLEW IT THE REST OF HIS TOUR. NOTE: WANDERIN' WILLIE, WAS A P-51B, BUT NO DATA.
G4-S	43-6960	SCRAPPY	ALVIN PYEATT	MIA, 16 MARCH 44
G4-S	43-6825	BETSY	HARRY ANKENY	
G4-S	44-13596	BETSY NAUGHTY AUTY BOW LEGS SCREAMIN' DEMON	HARRY ANKENY JAMES SEHL JOHN COON SAM FULLER	(NAME AND PILOT NOT CONFIRMED) MIA, 18 NOV 44
G4-S	44-15607	TICKET TO LORRAINE LI'L MARY	UNKNOWN JACK BUZZARD	KILLED IN C-47 CRASH IN ALPS, OCTOBER 45
G4-S	44-63221	MOOSE	MYRON BECRAFT	
G4-T	43-7188	UNKNOWN	ERLE TAYLOR	CRASHED ON TAKE-OFF, 13 JUNE 44 SALVAGED
G4-T	44-13552	UNKNOWN	FRED C. SMITH	
G4-T	44-63658	BLIND DATE (not confirmed)	HERMAN DELAGER	LOST IN SEA; 19 JAN 45
G4-U	43-6448	WEE WILLIE	CALVERT WILLIAMS	ACHIEVED GROUP'S FIRST VICTORY IN THIS P51B
G4-U	44-14390	NO OTHER DATA		
G4-U	44-13334	WEE WILLIE BITE ME BUFFALO BELLE	CALVERT WILLIANS ALVA MURPHY ELDRID DANNER	NOTE: THIS AIRCRAFT CONVERTED TO A 2-SEATER
G4-V	43-12227	BABY MIKE	JOSEPH BROADHEAD	WHO FLEW IT DURING HIS FIRST TOUR.

THEN TO MATHEW MARTIN FOR A FEW MISSIONS SHOT DOWN 8 Nov 44, BY ME 262, WARREN CORWIN DIED OF WOUNDS.

362ND SQUADRON, CODE G4 (cont'd)

SQDN CODE	SERIAL NUMBER	AIRCRAFT NAME	PILOT	COMMENTS
G4-V	44-14798	*MASTER MIKE*	JOSEPH BROADHEAD	2ND TOUR, THEN TO JULIAN BERTRAM, AS BUTCH BABY. FINISHED WAR IN RAF GREEN PAINT, STRIPPED IN GERMANY WITH LUFTWAFFE PAINT STRIPPER. PILOT JIM MCLANE, WHO NAMED IT DAINTIE DOTTIE
G4-W	43-6721	*UNKNOWN*	HOWARD EGLAND	FLEW IT ON SHUTTLE MISSION CRASHED ON TAKE-OFF, DUE TO CONTAMINATED FUEL. NO INJURY
G4-W	44-14152	*COOTER*	WILLIAM GRUBER	BELLIED IN HOME BASE BY JOHN ENGLAND. REPAIRED AND FLEW REST OF WAR. SALVAGED IN 1946.
G4-W	44-14672	NONE ON RIGHT SIDE	KEITH WILSON	
G4-X	43-7047	*REMEMBER ME?*	RODNEY STARKEY	CRASHED NEAR HOME BASE, 8 AUG 44. WILLIE GILBERT BAILED.
G4-X	44-13738	*JOKER!* with clown painting right side.	JOHN SCHLOSSBERG	TOTAL WRECK WITH PILOT HAROLD WYATT, (OK), 30 Sept 44.
G4-X	44-11198	*LIBBY B*	WILLIAM MOONEY	LOST 24 DEC '4, BAILED, MURDERED ON GROUND
G4-X	44-13738	UNKNOWN		BELLIED IN, HOME BASE, 1 Oct 44
G4-X	44-63199	*TOOLIN' FOOLS REVENGE*	OTTO D. JENKINS	KILLED IN THIS REVENGE ACFT, CRASH AT HOME BASE, 24 MARCH 45 NOTE: MAY HAVE BEEN JOKER, WITH JOHN SCHLOSSBERG BEFORE JENKINS GOT IT
G4-Y	42-106462	UNKNOWN		HAD BEEN ENGLAND'S YU'VE HAD IT FLOWN ON SHUTTLE MISSION BY FLT. LT. WOOLEY, RAF. SALVAGED, BATTLE DAMAGE, OCT 44.
G4-Y	43-7143	*MISS FLORIDA*	JAMES BADGER	MIA 29 JULY 44 w/ROLLIN CARTER BAILED, POW
G4-Y	44-14640	*DUCHESS*	DONALD CHEEVER	
G4-Z	43-6987	*MISS SATAN*	TOM NORRIS	RICHARD ANDERSON KILLED IN LOCAL CRASH, 13 JAN 45
G4-Z	44-13963	*MISS SATAN*	TOM NORRIS	LATER TO TOM MARTINEK, WITH NAME MORNING STAR CHARLES GOSS BAILED, 19 OCT 44, EVADER
G4-Z	43-12173	*PEG-O-MY HEART*		(NAME AS REC'D FROM 354TH GROUP)
G4-Z	44-14612	*HOT SHOT*	JOHN "HOT SHOT CHARLIE" DUNCAN	
G4-Z	UNKNOWN	*ONA IRENE*	G.A. ROBINSON	(HIS MOTHER'S NAME)
G4-Z	43-6729	*"YOUNG-UNS"*	LYNN "JUNIOR" DROLLINGER,	MIA THIS ACFT, 28 MAR 44. CODE PROBABLE, BUT NOT CONFIRMED. EVADER.

363RD SQUADRON, CODE B6

SQDN CODE	SERIAL NUMBER	AIRCRAFT NAME	PILOT	COMMENTS
B6-A	43-6712	*YARD BIRD*	ROBERT E. SMITH	
B6-A	44-14736	*PAPPY'S ANSWER* (LEFT SIDE)		PHOTO EVIDENCE SHOWS YANKS RIGHT SIDE THE TWO NAMES AT ABOUT THE SAME TIME PERIOD JOHN STERN -PILOT
B6-A	44-11331	*EXPECTANT*	FRANK GAILER JR	SHOT DOWN BY ANOTHER P-51 27 NOV 44 POW
B6-A	UNKNOWN	*SHANGHAI LI'L*	MONTGOMERY THROOP,	SQDN C.O. FROM JANUARY THROUGH MAY. HIS CREW CHIEF, GENE BARTH, SAYS IT WAS B6-A, BUT NO RECORD HAS BEEN FOUND OF ITS SERIAL NUMBER.
B6-B	43-6999	UNKNOWN	HERSHEL T. PASCOE	LATER BECAME B6-U
B6-B	44-13714	*DESERT RAT*	HERSHEL PASCOE	MIA 12 OCT 44 (POW)
B6-B	44-13887	*LITTLE JOE*	JOSEPH CANNON	LATER BECAME MARGIE MAY? PILOT UNK.
B6-B	44-72258	*LITTLE JOE*	JOSEPH CANNON	TILL END OF WAR
B6-B (bar)	44-13573	*ISABEL III* (LATER B6-V)	JACK CLELAND (FLT/LT, RNZAF)	
B6-C (bar)	43-6712	*FIGHTIN' BITIN'*		BECAME B6-W, NAME UNCERTAIN
B6-C	44-13745	*HI PHYL*	ROBERT MOORE	FLEW IT ON THE SHUTTLE. MIA 13 SEPT 44, MARION BURNETT
B6-C	44-63168	*MOUNTAINEER*	PAUL BOWLES	THRU END OF WAR.

363RD SQUADRON, CODE B6 (cont'd)

SQDN CODE	SERIAL NUMBER	AIRCRAFT NAME	PILOT	COMMENTS
B6-D	43-6686	UNKNOWN	FRANK KOKA	LANDING ACCIDENT 7 JUNE 44
B6-D	UNKNOWN	*HORSE'S ITCH*	EDWIN HIRO	FLEW THIS P-51B OR C, CODE NOT CONFIRMED, AND S/N UNKNOWN
B6-D	44-13518	*HORSE'S ITCH*	EDWIN HIRO	KIA THIS ACFT, 19 SEPT 44
B6-D	44-15529	*PONY'S EXPRESS*	FRANK KYLE	
B6-D	43-24???	*CLUB CAR*	UNKOWN	
B6-E	43-24842	*$ BLACKPOOL BAT*	GEORGE G. GEORGE	LOST IN COLLISIONPILOT KENNETH GRAEFF
B6-E	44-15161	*JOYCE DIANNE*	CARROLL OFSTHUN	MIA WITH MATHEW CRAWFORD, 2 MAR 45.
B6-E	44-14977	*THE COUNT*	CARROLL OFTHSUN	LATER BECAME B6-Y, SAME NAME
B6-E	43-6519	*OH BOBBY!*	UNKNOWN	

THE FOLLOWING DATA ON DONALD BOCHKAY'S P-51s REQUIRED A GREAT DEAL OF DETECTIVE WORK TO SORT OUT. SOME OF IT CANNOT BE PROVEN WITH PHOTO DOCUMENTATION.

SQDN CODE	SERIAL NUMBER	AIRCRAFT NAME	PILOT	COMMENTS
B6-F	42-103041.	*ALICE IN WONDERLAND*		BELIEVE THIS WAS BOCHKAY'S FIRST P-51, IT WAS A C MODEL, AND WE HAVE A CLEAR PHOTO OF HIM STANDING BY THE RUDDER. THIS AIRPLANE ARRIVED IN ENGLAND AT THE, END OF JANUARY, AND WOULD HAVE BEEN AMONG THE FIRST ONES DELIVERED TO THE 357TH. IT WAS LOST ON 8 MARCH, 44, WITH WILLIAM GAMBILL.
B6-F	43-6963	*SPEEDBALL ALICE*		(THERE IS NO PHOTO SHOWING THE TAIL NUMBER, OR THE CODE, BUT SEVERAL SHOWING THE NAME. BOCHKAY FLEW THIS FOR MANY MISSIONS, AND THE ACFT WAS SALVAGED FOR BATTLE DAMAGE IN FEB 45. FURTHER NOTE: THERE ARE RUMORS OF OTHER BOCHKAY AIRCRAFT NAMES, SUCH AS MARY ALICE, BUT NO PROOF. IT IS BELIEVED THAT ALL OF HIS P-51S CARRIED THE WINGED ACE OF CLUBS, IN VARYING SIZES, ON THE UPPER ENGINE COWL, USUALLY ON BOTH SIDES.
B6-F	44-13681	NO NAME, *WINGED ACE CLUBS OF ONLY*		BECAME PERRY LOU
B6-F	44-15422	NO NAME, *WINGED ACE CLUBS OF ONLY*		BELLIED IN HOME BASE 15 FEB 45, BY JOHN CASEY (COOLANT POP-OFF)
B6-F	44-72244	NO NAME, *WINGED ACE OF CLUBS ONY*		(THIS ACFT ENDED THE WAR, AND WAS NOTED IN STORAGE IN ENGLAND, AT SPEKE.
B6-F	44-72147	NO CONFIRMATION OF THIS AS A BOCHKAY AIRPLANE.		
B6-F	44-13573	*MARY ALICE*	ATLEE MANTHOS	HAD BEEN JACK CLELAND'S ISABEL III
B6-G	UNKNOWN	WILLIAM O'BRIEN, AN ORIGINAL MEMBER OF THE 363RD, FLEW A P-51 B OR C MODEL UNTIL JULY, 1944, WHEN HE GOT HIS D MODEL, BUT NO RECORD HAS BEEN FOUND OF THE SERIAL NUMBER OF HIS B (OR C). NAME BILLY'S BITCH. THERE WAS RATHER CRUDE NUDE FEMALE PAINTING ON LEFT SIDE (NOT DONE BY O'BRIEN!)		
B6-G	44-13522	*BILLY'S BITCH*		AFTER O'BRIEN COMPLETED HIS TOUR THIS ACFT SHOT DOWN BY FLAK, 17 AUG 44, WITH HAROLD KENNEY.
B6-H	43-6755	*KALAMAZOO KID*	CHARLES PEARSON	LOST WITH HOLSEY JOHNSON 10 FEB 45.
B6-I	UNKNOWN	*DRAGON LADY*	UNKNOWN,	P-51B, S/N NOT READABLE ON ONLY PHOTO
B6-I	44-14009	UNKNOWN		MAY HAVE BEEN JOHN SKARA'S "DOODLE BUG"
B6-J	43-6564	*7 UP HIGH*	ERNEST TIEDE	ACFT TOTALLED, LANDING ACCIDENT.
B6-J	43-6594	*DADDY RABBIT*	CHARLES PETERS	
B6-J	44-13897	*DADDY RABBIT*	CHARLES PETERS	
B6-J	44-15888	*WHOLE HAWG*	DONALD McGEE	HAD BEEN YEAGER'S GLAMOROUS GLEN III.
B6-K	43-6628	*TYPHOON McGOON*		WILLIAM McGINLEY KILLED IN THIS ACFT, COLLISION WITH GUITIERREZ 29 MAR 44
B6-K	44-15385	*MARY E.*	WARNER ROBERTS	
B6-L	42-106783	*FLYING PANTHER*		MIA WITH LOUIS NOWLIN, 15 SEPT 44
B6-L	44-15630	*JUNIOR MISS*	GLENWOOD ZARNKE	MIA WITH JIM BROWNING, FEB 45.
B6-L	44-63680	*JUNIOR MISS II*	GLENWOOD ZARNKE	
B6-M	44-13681	*PERRY LOU*	UNKNOWN	EX-BOCHKAY B6-F WRECKED BELLY LANDING DEC 44
B6-M	44-13716	UNKNOWN	BILL FRICKER	FLEW IT ON SHUTTLE
B6-N	44-15053	*ALICE MARIE II*	ED CARR	
B6-0	44-72187	*ALICE MARIE III*	ED CARR	
B6-0	42-103309	*BERLIN EXPRESS*	WILLIAM OVERSTREET	SALVAGED 12 JULY 44
B6-0	43-24823	*BERLIN EXPRESS*	WILLIAM OVERSTREET	HAD BEEN ANDERSON'S OLD CROW. AFTER OVERSTREET COMPLETED HIS TOUR, BILL FRICKER BECAME PILOT, NOW CODED B6-K

363RD SQUADRON, CODE B6 (cont'd)

SQDN CODE	SERIAL NUMBER	AIRCRAFT NAME	PILOT	COMMENTS
B6-O	44-14532	*'OL FLAK JOE*	WILLIAM FRICKER	
B6-O	44-13923	*BIG BEAUTIFUL DOLL*	JOHN LANDERS	(CODE O NOT CONFIRMED.)Wendell Helwig KILLED IN THIS ACFT 24 DEC 44. COLLISION WITH KENNETH MIX, 55TH FTR GRP.
B6-P	43-6393	*ALL AWAY II*	EDWARD SIMPSON	
B6-P	43-24766	UNKNOWN	WILLIAM FENNELL	FLEW IT ON THE SHUTTLE.
B6-P	43-6563	*GENTLEMAN JIM*	JAMES BROWNING	MIA with John CHILDS, 10 JUNE 44
B6-P	44-14937	*GENTLEMAN JIM*	JAMES BROWNING	BECAME SUPER X B6-X, BILL CURRIE PILOT, AFTER DEATH OF BROWNING
B6-Q	43-6510	*DAM-PHY-NO!*		CRASHED HOME BASE, 18 SEPT 44, PILOT NORBERT FISHER, MINOR INJURY
B6-Q	44-14784	*Q-PEE*		MIA WITH JAMES SLOAN 14 JAN 45 (POW)
B6-R	43-6644	UNKNOWN	NO DATA	
B6-R	42-103286	UNKNOWN		MIA WITH WILLIAM MICHAELY, 21 MAY 44 POW
B6-R	44-14519	NO NAME EITHER SIDE		NO OTHER DATA
B6-R	43-6858	UNKNOWN	FRANK KOKA	SHOT DOWN 7 JULY 44 KIA CODE "R" NOT CONFIRMED)
B6-S	43-6723	*OLD CROW*	C.E. ANDERSON	MIA WITH ALFRED BOYLE, 21 FEB 44
B6-S	43-24823	*OLD CROW*	C.E. ANDERSON	COMPLETED HIS FIRST TOUR IN THIS P-51B, AND SCORED MOST OF HIS VICTORIES IN IT. IT THEN WENT TO BILL OVERSTREET AS B6-K AND THEN TO BILL FRICKER
B6-S	44-14450	*OLD CROW*	C.E. ANDERSON	ANDERSON FLEW HIS 2ND TOUR IN THIS P-51 D. IT WAS SALVAGED, NOV 45.
B6-S	43-12454			NO DATA. MAY HAVE BEEN ANDERSON'S P-51 BETWEEN THE LOSS OF 6723, WITH BOYLE, AND THE DELIVERY OF 43-24823, WHICH DID NOT ARRIVE IN ENGLAND UNTIL LATE IN APRIL AND TO 357TH ABOUT 1 MAY. PURE SPECULATION ON 12454.
B6-T	44-14976	UNKNOWN		THIS ACFT WRECKED ON 30 NOV 44, W/PETER PIELICH, UNINJURED. NO VISIBLE NAME.
B6-S	44-63634	*THE GIZZARD*	GUY BENDER	AIRCRAFT FLOWN TO AMSTERDAM AFTER WAR FOR DISPLAY WITH FAKE VICTORY SYMBOLS, CAUSING MUCH CONFUSION AMONG HISTORIANS. ACFT JUNKED THERE AFTER DISPLAY
B6-T	42-103002	*JEESIL PEESIL MOMMY*	FRANK GAILER	HAD BEEN B6-Y ON SHUTTLE LANDING ACCIDENT, 26 SEPT 44
B6-T	43-6758	*COBBER*	LAWRENCE WOOD	LANDING ACCIDENT 5 MARCH 44 SALV, BATTLE DAMAGE
B6-U	43-6999	UNKNOWN	CHARLES CAMPBELL	KILLED LOCAL CRASH 17 AUG 44. HAD BEEN B6-B EARLIER.
B6-V	43-7011	UNKNOWN	STANLEY OMERNIK	MIA, 9 MAY 44, POW
B6-V	44-13712	*RELUCTANT REBEL*	ROBERT FOY	LOST 10 AUG 44, EDWARD SIMPSON. COLLISION WITH DONALD FERRON.
B6-V	44-63621	*LITTLE SHRIMP*	ROBERT FOY	FINISHED WAR IN THIS ACFT.
B6-V	44-13573	*ISABEL III*	FLT/ Lt. JACK CLELAND	RNZAF. BRIEFLY CODED B 6-B (bar), then B6-V. SURVIVED WAR.
B6-V	43-6998	*RELUCTANT REBEL*	ROBERT FOY	HIS FIRST P-51, FROM WHICH HE BAILED INTO THE SEA ON 3 MAR 44.
B6-W	43-6712	NONE		SEE B-6C (bar)
B6-W	44-13388	*BODACIOUS*	COL. DONALD GRAHAM	TO END OF HIS TOUR
B6-W	44-11672	*TEXAN* (left side) *LOVE OF MINE* (right side)	LT. COL. GUERNSEY CARLISLE	
B6-W	43-6566	NONE		GROUND ACCIDENT 28 SEPTEMBER 44 WITH PAUL BOWLES
B6-X	44-14937	*SUPER X*	WILLIAM CURRIE	HAD BEEN JIM BROWNING'S GENTLEMAN JIM B 6-P
B6-W	44-63755	*THE TENDER TERROR*	RALPH MANN	TO END OF WAR.

363RD SQUADRON, CODE B6 (cont'd)

SQDN CODE	SERIAL NUMBER	AIRCRAFT NAME	PILOT	COMMENTS
B6-X	44-14937	*SUPER X*	WILLIAM CURRIE	HAD BEEN JIM BROWNING'S GENTLEMAN JIM.
B6-X	44-1493?	*TIL THEN* (left) *MARGIE'S MAN*(RIGHT)	CLIFFORD MILLER	THIS MAY HAVE BEEN SUPER X AT A LATER DATE. LAST DIGIT OF TAIL NUMBER NOT VISIBLE. HAS A "ZOOT SUITED" FIGURE NEXT TO NAME.
B6-Y	42-103002	UNKNOWN		SEE B6-T. FISHER FLEW IT AS B6-Y ON THE SHUTTLE.
B6-Y	43-6763	*GLAMOROUS GLEN* (SPELLED AS PAINTED ON THE P-51)	CHARLES YEAGER	SHOT DOWN IN THIS ACFT ON 5 MAR 44. EVADER.
B6-Y	44-13897	*GLAMOROUS GLEN II*		LOST WITH ROYCROFT 18 OCT 44. SERIAL NUMBER BELIEVED CORRECT, BUT NOT CONFIRMED BY PHOTO EVIDENCE.
B6-Y	44-14888	*GLAMOROUS GLEN III*	CHARLES YEAGER	BECAME B6-J WHOLE HAWG, PILOT DONALD MCGEE, AFTER YEAGER COMPLETED HIS TOUR. LOST 2 MARCH 45 WITH PATRICK MALLIONE, KIA
B6-Y	44-14977	*THE COUNT*	CARROLL OFSTHUN	THE NAME WAS FROM A CARTOON CHARACTER THAT APPEARED IN THE YANK, THE UK WEEKLY NEWSPAPER.
B6-Y	44-73103	*LIL'L MISS MELBA*	DENNIS TOUPS	
B6-Z	44-13388	*PETER BEATER*	PETER PIELICH	HAD BEEN COL. GRAHAM'S BODACIOUS, B6-W
B6-Z	43-6429	UNKNOWN		LOST WITH JOE PIERCE, 21 MAY 44 CODE NOT CONFIRMED.
B6-Z	42-106458	*DOODLE BUG*	JOHN SKARA	LOST WITH JAMES WINDHAM, BAILED, 25 DEC 44.
B6-Z	44-15504	UNKNOWN		CODE NOT CONFIRMED. GROUND COLLISON WITH LONESOME POLECAT, 3 FEB 45
B6-G	44-11643	*LATE ARRIVAL*	UNKNOWN	
B6-H	44-14356	*LONESOME POLECAT*	KEEHN LANDIS	LOST FEB 1945 - PILOT DAN MYERS RESCUED

364TH SQUADRON, CODE C-5

SQDN CODE	SERIAL NUMBER	AIRCRAFT NAME	PILOT	COMMENTS
C5-A	42-106843	*ROUND TRIP JR.*	TOM McKINNEY	MIA WITH DANIEL FINLEY, 29 JULY 44 DIED AS POW
C5-A	44-13583	*PRUNE PICKER*	ROBERT FANDRAY	MIA WITH A/C SEPT 44. PRUNE PICKER CONFIRMED-LEFTSIDE
C5-A	44-13691	*GYPSY*	UNKNOWN	THIS IS EX-PASSION WAGON. TRANSFERRED FROM 362nd to 364th SQDN. ROBERSON'S NUDE AND VICTORY SYMBOLS REMAINED.
C5-A	UNKNOWN	*BUZZ BUGGY*	WILL FOARD	FORCED LANDING IN BELGIUM16 APR 45, LEFT THERE.
C5-A	44-15660	*SWAMP FOX*	WILL FOARD	TO END OF WAR.
C5-B	42-106854	*PEABODY'S PET*	WALTER BARON	LANDED SWEDEN 25 AUG 4, INTERNED
C5-B	44-14900	*MELLIE JEAN*	PAUL HATALA	BELLY LANDED 17 APR 45, NEAR PRAGUE, JAMES MONAHAN POW FOR A FEW DAYS UNTIL WAR'S END.
C5-B	44-63710	UNKNOWN	ROBERT FIFIELD	KILLED IN CRASH NEAR HOME BASE, 3 MAY 45.
C5-E	43-6801	*BOILER MAKER* WITH SHOT GLASS & BEER MUG	RAY SPARKS	LOST WITH SPARKS ON 8 MAY 44 (POW)
C5-C	42-103601	*MAZIE R*	JOHN SALSMAN	FLEW 300 COMBAT HOURS WITHOUT ABORT, TILL WAR'S END .(NAMED AT DEPOT WAR BOND DRIVE)
C5-C	44-11224	*PRETTY PAT*		WRECKED IN LANDING ACCIDENT WITH ROCCO LEPORE, 10 JAN 45.
C5-C	44-14555	*PRETTY PAT*		MIA WITH LEPORE, 2 MAR 45 (POW)
C5-C	44-63747	*WES'S WICKED WENCH*		MAY BE HOWARD WESLING
C5-D	43-6701	*TUFF TITTY*	CORDELL SUMMERS	P-51B, FROM WARTIME WATERCOLOR PAINTING
C5-D	44-14648	*PRINCESS PAT*	EDWARD FRY	MIA WITH ROBERT MULLER, 17 APR 45
C5-D	44-73125	*PRINCESS PAT II*	EDWARD FRY	
C5-D	44-63687	*EVELYN*	UNKNOWN	
C5-E	43-6813	*PAPP'S ANSWER* *PAPPY'S ANSWER*	JOHN MEDEIROS HENRY PFEIFFER	PHOTO SHOWS NAME PAPP'S ANSWER, WITH WHITE NOSE. ACFT MIA WITH JERRY JACOBS, 19 SEPT 44

364TH SQUADRON, CODE C-5 (cont'd)

SQDN CODE	SERIAL NUMBER	AIRCRAFT NAME	PILOT	COMMENTS
C5-E	44-14429	*TANGERINE*	HENRY PFEIFFER	MIA WITH BRYCE MCINTYRE, 19 SEPT 44
C5-E	44-14507	*TANGERINE*	HENRY PFEIFFER	REPLACEMENT FOR JOHN SALSMAN 44-14429 DWAINE SANDBORN
C5-F	43-12313	*BEAR RIVER BETSY*	WILLIAM REESE	KIA 21 MAY 44
C5-F	44-72927	*CANTON CAN*	VINCENT ZETTLER	
C5-F	43-12124	UNKNOWN	JACK WARREN	MIA WITH THIS ACFT, 18 MAR 44
C5-F	43-6502	UNKNOWN	WALLACE REID	BURNED ON THE RUNWAY, 29 JULY 44. FAULTY DROP TANK
C5-G	42-106978	*LADY JULIE*	MARK STEPELTON	MIA WITH WALLACE REID 4 AUG 44. POW
C5-G	44-72372	*ALIBABSANDI*	GILMAN WEBER	COMBINED NAMES OF HIS WIFE & DAUGHTERS.
C5-G	42-106721	*SERGEANT*	GILMAN WEBER	MIA WITH MORRIS GALLANT 19 JAN 45
C5-G	UNKNOWN	*TREASURE*	UNKNOWN	PHOTOS SHOW IT RAF GREEN AND LATER BARE METAL NAME BOTH SIDES.
C5-H (bar)	44-13578		HOWARD REDD	
C5-H	44-13875	UNKNOWN	ROBERT SHAW	FLEW THIS ACFT ON SHUTTLE
C5-H	44-63861	*LADY ESTHER*(RT) *ELIXER* (left)	CHESTER MAXWELL	BELLY LANDING, 25 FEB 45
C5-I	44-13783	*BOBBY MARILYN* *ROVIN` RHODA*	GEORGE MORRIS IRV SNEDEKER	WAS ROVIN' RHODA ON 17 APRIL WHEN SNEDEKER WAS shot DOWN, POW.
C5-I(bar)	44-13345	*MARY ANN*	CHARLES BURTNER	LANDED IN SWEDEN 25 AUGUST 44.
C5-I	42-106777	*TAXPAYER'S DELIGHT*	JOHN CARDER	MIA 12 MAY 44
C5-J	44-11165	*LADY NELDA*		EDWARD HAYDON THIS ACFT INVOLVED WITH HAYDON AS PILOT IN THE BATTLE WHICH KILLED THE GREAT GERMAN ACE NOWOTNY, NOV 44 HAYDON & ACFT LOST TO FLAK 20 JAN 45. POW
C5-J(bar)	44-13698	*SHADY LADY*	KIRBY BROWN	KIA IN THIS ACFT ON 13 SEPT 44.
C5-J	44-72056	*PLASTERED BASTARD*	IVAN McGUIRE	
C5-J	43-6376	*LITTLE DUCKFOOT*	GERALD TYLER	
C5-J	44-14660	*LITTLE DUCK FOOT*	GERALD TYLER	
C5-K	43-6974	*MR. PERIOD*	RICHARD C. SMITH	MIA 29 JUNE 44
C5-K	43-25039	*LI'L KITTEN*	LOUIS FECHER	
C5-L	42-106447	*SHOO SHOO BABY*	JOHN C. HOWELL	WAS C5-X ON SHUTTLE RALPH EISERT KILLED, IN THIS ACFT ON 27 FEB 45.
C5-L	44-13583	*SHOO SHOO BABY*	JOHN C. HOWELL	
C5-L	44-64099	*ARKANSAS TRAVELLER*	TOM ADAMS	
C5-M	43-6582	*GEECHEE GAL*	JOE JENKINS	WRECKED ON TAKE-OFF BY RAY SPARKS
C5-M	43-6581	UNKNOWN		CRASH ON BASE, GEAR TORN OFF 9 FEB 44
C5-M	43-6376	UNKNOWN		BELLIED IN, OZBORN HOWES, 26 SEPT 44
C5-M	42-103348	NONE VISIBLE	HOLLIS NOWLIN	WRECKED AT LEAST TWICE BY OTHER PILOTS. MAY HAVE BEEN NAMED HELLS BELLS OR VICIOUS VIV AT ONE TIME.
C5-M	44-13783	*ROVIN' RHODA* (LEFT) *4 BOLTS* (RIGHT)	IRV SNEDEKER	FOUR PILOTS NAMED THEIR P-51 "4 BOLTS" ON RIGHT SIDE, ANOTHER NAME ON LEFT.
C5-M	44-13801	UNKNOWN		HOLLIS NOWLIN FLEW IT ON THE SHUTTLE.
C5-N		NOTE: THOMAS L. "TOMMY" HAYES, WAS AN ORIGINAL MEMBER OF THE 354th SQDN, BECAME ITS COMMANDER, AND LATER DEPUTY GROUP COMMANDER. FROM THE TIME OF BECOMING OPERATIONAL, HAYES FLEW A P-51B OR A P-51C (AS DID EVERYONE ELSE) UNTIL LATE JULY WHEN HIS WELL KNOWN D MODEL "FRENESI" ARRIVED AT LEISTON. HE FLEW THIS P-51D-5 UNTIL THE END OF HIS TOUR. NO EVIDENCE HAS EVER SURFACED TO PROVIDE THE SERIAL NUMBER ON HIS FIRST ACFT, WHICH WAS ALSO WAS TITLED "FRENESI"		
C5-N	UNKNOWN	*FRENESI*	THOMAS HAYES	THIS WRITER HAS SEVERAL PHOTOS OF HAYES' P51 B, ONE SHOWING WHITE NOSE AND NAME BUT NONE SHOWING TAIL NUMBER
C5-N	44-13318	*FRENESI*	THOMAS HAYES	ONE LISTING SHOWS THIS ACFT SALVAGED FOR BATTLE DAMAGE 15 APRIL 45.
C5-0	42-106923	*DADDY'S PET* AT ONE TIME THIS P-51 WAS *"PISTOL PACKIN' MAMMA"*	HARRY HERMANSON	MAY HAVE BEEN "ALMOST" AT TIME BERNARD SEITSINGER WAS SHOT DOWN, 18 SEPT 44.
C5-0	44-14334	*ANNE LOU*	ROBERT SCHIMANSKI	
C5-0	43-6867	*PREGNANT POLECAT*	GLENDON DAVIS	BAILED, 28 APR 44. EVADER
C5-P	44-13861	UNKNOWN	PAUL FAIRWEATHER	FLEW IT ON THE SHUTTLE BECAME C5-Z, LI'L POOPSIE

364TH SQUADRON, CODE C-5 (cont'd)

SQDN CODE	SERIAL NUMBER	AIRCRAFT NAME	PILOT	COMMENTS
C5-P	UNKNOWN	*BLETHERKINSKATE*		ACCORDING TO OSBORN HOWES, THE PILOT IS A SCOTTISH TERM MEANING "IMP" OR "MISCHIEF MAKER".
C5-Q	44-11678	*BOBBY JEANNE AH FUNG GOO* (RT)	COLONEL IRWIN DREGENE	
C5-Q	44-13408	*BOBBY JEANNE AH FUNG GOO* (RT)	COLONEL IRWIN DREGNE	
NOTE: COLONEL DREGNE FLEW A P-51B FEBRUARY UNTIL JULY, BUT NO RECORD HAS BEEN FOUND OF ITS IDENTITY				
C5-Q (bar)	44-14884	*BABY JO*	HUGH MOORHOUSE	NOEL BREEN CRASHED IT INTO A BARN ON BASE.DEMOLISHED. MINOR INJURY
C5-R	42-106826	*THE SHILLELAGH*	JOHN STORCH	BECAME C5-Y, NICK FREDERICK FLEW IT ON SHUTTLE
C5-R	44-13546	*THE SHILLELAGH*	JOHN STORCH	MIA WITH ZETTERQUIST 5 DEC 44
C5-R	44-63164	*THE SHILLELAGH*	JOHN STORCH	TILL END OF WAR.
C5-S	43-6653	*LI'L RED'S ROCKET*	THOMAS HARRIS	MIA 27 MAY 44 POW
C5-T	43-6935	*HURRY HOME HONEY*	RICHARD PETERSON	LOST WITH HEYWOOD SPINKS, 20 JUNE 44
C5-T	44-13586	*HURRY HOME HONEY*	RICHARD PETERSON	BECAME C5-T BAR
C5-T (bar)	44-13586	*FLAK HAPPY*	HORACE HOWELL	BECAME C5-ZZ
C5-T	44-14868	*HURRY HOME HONEY*	RICHARD PETERSON	PROBABLY FLEW THIS ACFT TO END OF HIS TOUR
C5-T	44-14868	*MORMON MUSTANG*	ROLAND WRIGHT	AFTER PETERSON
C5-U	44-15026	*KARGER'S DOLLY* (RT)	DALE KARGER	FRED MCCALL, MIA 10 JAN 45
C5-U	44-72313	*CATHEY MAE II* (both sides)	DALE, KARGER	
C5-U	44-72167	*ALWAYS MARY*	UNKNOWN	END OF WAR, EX-78th GRP
C5-U	43-6971	UNKNOWN	BRYCE McINTYRE	FLEW IT ON SHUTTLE JAMES LEEK KILLED IN LOCAL CRASH 28 SEPT 44.
C5-V	44-13678	NONE	MORRIS STANLEY	
C5-V	44-72451	*CAMPUS QUEEN*	UNKNOWN	LATE WAR AIRCRAFT
C5-V	44-14549	*MISS JANICE*	UNKNOWN	UNCLEAR, MAY BE 649
C5-V	44-13691	*GYPSY*	UNKNOWN	HAD BEEN PASSION WAGON, G4-A
C5-W	44-13578	*TRUSTY RUSTY*	ROBERT WINKS	HAD BEEN C5-H (bar)
C5-X	42-106768	*LINDA LU*	LEROY RUDER	KIA 6 JUNE 44.
C5-X	42-106447	UNKNOWN	ROBERT L. SMITH	ON SHUTTLE HAD BEEN SHOO SHOO BABY, C5-L
C5-X	44-13821	*DEE LAURA*	MERLE ALLEN	
C5-X (bar)	44-13621	*PHILLY DILLIES*	STEVEN WASYLYK	
C5-X	42-106447	*SLIC CHIC*	UNKNOWN	Ex-John Howell
C5-Y		*SHOO SHOO BABY*		LOST WITH RALPH EISERT, 27 FEB 45, COLLISION WITH HOFFMAN NAME PARTIALLY OBSCURED
C5-Y	44-13552	*PAZDA (PIZDA?)*	UNKNOWN	NAME NOT CONFIRMED FOR THIS 'B' MODEL
C5-Y	42-106826	*MARIE*	NICK FREDERICK	
C5-Y	44-14549	*MARIE*	NICK FREDERICK	
C5-Y	44-15266	*FIREBALL*	RAY BANK	MIA 2 MAR 45. POW
C5-Z	42-103502	*PRIDE OF THE YANKS*	CHARLES SUMNER	THIS WAS ONE OF THREE P-51 CS THAT WERE NAMED BY THE WINNERS OF A WAR BOND RALLY AT WARTON AIR DEPOT.
C5-Z	44-13861	*4 BOLTS* (RIGHT) *LI'L POOPSIE* (LEFT)	DONALD KOCHER	BELLIED IN NEAR HANOVER, GERMANY, 20 APRIL 45. KOCHER PICKED UP BY US TROOPS AND RETURNED TO UNIT
C5-Z	44-15613	NO FURTHER DATA		
C5-Z	44-13586	*FLAK BAIT GREECE LIGHTNING*	HORACE HOWELL	MAY HAVE BEEN CODED C5-ZZ (DOUBLE Z TO INDICATE TWO AIRCRAFT WITH Z CODE). OR MAY HAVE Z BAR. ONLY AVAILABLE PHOTO SEEMS TO SHOW ONLY ONE Z. AIRCRAFT MIA, 3 FEB 45 WITH GEORGE KOURIS (POW). AT THAT TIME IT WAS NAMED GREECE LIGHTNING.
C5-Z	43-12159	*BAT CAVE*	CHARLES SUMNER	LOST 5 APR 45 DONOVAN/SIVERT COLLSION

357ᵀᴴ FIGHTER GROUP THE COMMANDERS

This listing of Group and Squadron Commanders ends roughly with the end of hostilities. After the move to Munich, Commander's tenures were often short and many were from outside the Group. Records of these days are also sparse. A few 357th veterans held command positions after the move, notably Lt. Col. Andrew Evans who took over from Col. Dregne, and Captain Robert D. Brown who commanded the 362nd Squadron. In many cases the dates are not exact.

GROUP COMMANDERS

Lt. Col. Loring F. Stetson Jr............. 1 Dec 1942
Lt. Col. Edwin S. Chickering............. 7 Jul 1943
Col. Henry R. Spicer................... 17 Feb 1944
Lt. Col. Donald W. Graham .... 7 Mar 1944
Lt. Col. John D. Landers.................. 11 Oct 1944
Lt. Col. Irwin H. Dregne.................. 2 Dec 1944
Lt. Col. Andrew J. Evans Jr............... 21 Jul 1945

362nd FIGHTER SQUADRON

Lt. Col. Hubert I. Egenes..................1 Dec 1942
Major Joseph E. Broadhead............... 10 Mar 1944
Major John B. England .... 25 Aug 1944
Major Leonard K. Carson .... 8 Apr 1945
Capt. Robert D. Brown .... Nov 1945

363rd FIGHTER SQUADRON

Capt. Stuart R. Lauler................. 8 Jan 1943
Capt. Clay R. Davis .... 20 May 1943
1st Lt. Wesley S. Mink .... 13 Jul 1943
Major Donald W. Graham .... 27 Sept 1943
Capt. Joe H. Giltner Jr................ Nov 1943
Major Montgomery H. Throop Jr........... 25 Jan 1944
Major Edwin W. Hiro.................... Jun 1944
Lt. Col. Guernsey I. Carlisle .... 20 Sept 1944
Major Donald C. McGee.................. Jan 1945
Major Donald H. Bochkay................ Feb 1945

364th FIGHTER SQUADRON

Capt. Varian K. White .... I Dec 1942
Major Thomas L. Hayes Jr............... May 1943
Major John A. Storch .... 14 Aug 1944
Major Donald C McGee................... May 1945

SQUADRON FIRST SERGEANTS

362nd...................... lst Sgt. Henry E. Ramm
363rd...................... lst Sgt. Marvin E. Collet
364th......................lst Sgt. Clifton Ferguson
1st Sgt. James Ackley

AERIAL VICTORY CREDITS

GROUP HEADQUARTERS				DATE	NAME		CREDIT
DATE	NAME		CREDIT	13-4	Becker, Robert M.	1LT	1
1944				13-4	Carson, Leonard K.	1LT	1
22-2	Spicer, Henry R.	COL	1	13-4	England, John B.	1LT	1
24-2	Spicer, Henry R.	COL	2	22-4	Broadhead, Joseph F.	CPT	1
8-3	Graham, Donald W.	LTC	1	24-4	O'Brien, Gilbert M.	1LT	1
16-3	Dregne, Irwin H.	MAJ	1	24-4	Adams, Fletcher F.	1LT	3
16-3	Egnes, Hubert I.	LTC	2	24-4	Beal, Henry E. Jr.	1LT	2
19-4	Haves, Thomas L. Jr.	MAJ	1	24-4	Connaghan, Frank J.	2LT	1
12-5	Dregne, Irwin H.	MAJ	1	24-4	England, John B.	1LT	3
19-5	Dregne, Irwin H.	MAJ	1	24-4	Smith, Fred C.	CPT	1
28-5	Hayes, Thomas L. Jr.	LTC	1	24-4	Williams, Calvert L.	CPT	1
29-5	Hayes, Thomas L. Jr.	LTC	1.5	30-4	Becker, Robert M.	1LT	1
14-7	Hayes, Thomas L. Jr.	LTC	1	30-4	Broadhead, Joseph E.	CPT	1
18-11	Landers, John D.	LTC	1	30-4	Brown, Rpbert D.	1LT	1
27-11	Evans, Andrew J.	MAJ	1	30-4	O'Brien, Gilbert M.	1LT	.5
2-12	Foy, Robert W.	CPT	1	12-5	Baker, Maurice F.	CPT	1
23-12	Foy, Robert W.	CPT	2	12-5	Hood, Aubrey 0.	2LT	.5
24-12	Dregne, Irwin H.	LTC	1	12-5	Norris, Thomas F.	1LT	1.5
				19-5	Adams, Fletcher F.	CPT	.5
1945				19-5	Roberson, Arval J.	1LT	.5
14-1	Dregne, Irwin H.	LTC	1	27-5	Adams, Fletcher F.	CPT	1
14-1	Evans, Andrew J.	LTC	4	27-5	England, John B.	CPT	1
14-1	Foy, Robert W.	CPT	2	27-5	Hill, Hershel L.	1LT	1
19-3	Foy, Robert W.	MAJ	1	27-5	O'Brien, Gilbert M.	1LT	1
24-3	Evans, Andrew J.	LTC	1	27-5	Pugh, John F.	1LT	1
24-3	Foy, Robert W.	MAJ	1	27-5	Smith, Alden E.	1LT	1
19-4	Hayes, Thomas L. Jr.	LTC	1	28-5	Broadhead, Joseph E.	MAJ	1
				28-5	Carson, Leonard K.	1LT	1
362nd SQUADRON				30-5	Adams, Fletcher, F.	CPT	.5
1944				30-5	Becker, Robert M.	CPT	3
20-2	Williams, Calvert L .	1LT	1	30-5	Carson, Leonard, K.	1LT	1
22-2	Adams, Fletcher F.	2LT	1	30-5	Harris, Ollie E. Jr.	1LT	1
22-2	Pyeatt, Alvin F. III	2LT	1	30-5	Mitchell, Lloyd W.	1LT	1
24-2	Rice, Donald R.	1LT	1	30-5	Norris, Thomas F.	1LT	1
25-2	Becker, Robert H.	1LT	1.5	30-5	O'Brien, Gilbert M.	1LT	1.5
25-2	Broadhead, Joseph E.	CPT	1	30-5	Roberson, Arval J.	1LT	2
25-2	Brown, Robert D.	1LT	1	30-5	Vogel, Donald W.	1LT	1
25-2	Kehrer, Merlin R.	1LT	1	29-6	Pugh, John F.	1LT	1
25-2	Lingo, Arthur M.	CPT	.5	29-6	Smith, Fred C.	CPT	1
25-2	Pyeatt, Alvin F. III	2LT	1	1-7	Holmberg, Paul E.	1LT	1
4-3	Wallen, Robert D.	LT	1	1-7	Williams, Calvert L.	CPT	1
5-3	O'Brien, Gilbert M.	2LT	1	25-7	Carson, Leonard K.	CPT	1
6-3	Broadhead, Joseph E.	CPT	1	25-7	Pugh, John F.	CPT	1
6-3	Hagan, Kenneth E.	1LT	1 (two .5)	29-7	Becker, Robert M.	CPT	.5
6-3	Perron, Davis T.	CPT	3	29-7	Carson, Leonard K.	CPT	1
6-3	Roberson, Arval J.	2LT	.5	29-7	Mace, Harvey F.	1LT	1
6-3	Starkey, Rodney M.	2LT	1	29-7	Martinek, Thomas W.	1LT	.5
6-3	Williams, Calvert L.	1LT	.5	29-7	O'Brien, Gilbert M.	1LT	1
8-3	England, John B.	1LT	1	30-7	Gates, Thomas L.	MAJ	1
16-3	England, John B.	1LT	1	30-7	Smith, Alden E.	1LT	1
18-3	Adams, Fletcher F.	2LT	1	7-8	Pugh, John F.	CPT	1
29-3	Broadhead, Joseph E.	CPT	1	18-8	Anderson, Clifford	2LT	1
8-4	Ankeny, Harry R.	1LT	1	18-8	England, John B.	CPT	.5
8-4	Carson, Leonard K.	2LT	.	18-8	Perry, Walter H. Jr.	2LT	1
8-4	Lingo, Arthur M.	CPT	1	13-9	England, John B.	CPT	2.5
8-4	Pugh, John F.	1LT	1	13-9	Fuller, Sam G.	1LT	.5
11-4	Adams,Fletcher F.	UT	2	13-9	Jenkins, Otto D.	FO	1.5
11-4	Ankeny, Harry R.	1LT	.5	13-9	Kirla, John A.	2LT	1.5
11-4	England, John B.	1LT	.5	13-9	Taylor, Erle A.	1LT	1
11-4	O'Brien, Gilbert M.	1LT	1	13-9	Templin, John S.	2LT	1
11-4	Pugh, John F.	1LT	1	18-9	Blanchard, James L .	1LT	1
11-4	Roberson, Arval J.	1LT	1				

DATE	NAME		CREDIT
18-9	Egeland, Howard B.	1LT	1
18-9	Gates, Thomas L.	MAJ	1
18-9	Mace, Harvey F.	1LT	1
18-9	Perry, Walter N. Jr.	2LT	1
18-9	Smith, Fred C.	CPT	1
18-9	Templin, John S.	2LT	1
19-9	Jenkins, Otto D.	FO	2
19-9	Kirla, John A.	2LT	1
19-9	Perry, Walter N. Jr.	2LT	1
19-9	Roberson, Arval J.	1LT	2
19-9	Sehl, James H.	1LT	1
19-9	Weaver, Charles E.	2LT	1
6-10	England, John B.	CPT	2
6-10	Gilbert, William T.	2LT	1
6-10	Jenkins, Otto D.	FO	1
6-10	Martinek, Thomas W.	1LT	1
7-10	Martinek, Thomas W.	1LT	2
2-11	Carson, Leonard K.	CPT	1
8-11	Kenney, James W.	1LT	1
27-11	Anderson, Clifford	1LT	1
27-11	Carson, Leonard K.	CPT	5
27-11	Delager, Herman H.	1LT	1
27-11	England, John B.	CPT	4
27-11	Gilbert, William T.	1LT	1
27-11	Murphy, Alva C.	CPT	2
27-11	Sublett, John L.	1LT	3
27-11	Weaver, Charles E.	1LT	2
2-12	Carson, Leonard K.	CPT	2
2-12	Delager, Herman H.	1LT	1
2-12	Murphy, Alva C.	CPT	2
2-12	Schlieker, Robert L.	2LT	1
5-12	Broadhead, Joseph E.	MAJ	1
5-12	Carson, Leonard K.	LT	1
5-12	Kirla, John A.	1LT	2
23-12	Weaver, Charles E.	1LT	1
24-12	Behling, George A.	1LT	1
24-12	Carson, Leonard K.	CPT	1
24-12	Frey, Jesse R.	1LT	1
24-12	Gilbert, William T.	1LT	2
24-12	Hyman, Edward D.	1LT	2
24-12	Jenkins, Otto D.	2LT	4
24-12	Kirla, John A.	1LT	3
24-12	Pelon, Paul A. Jr.	1LT	2

1945

DATE	NAME		CREDIT
14-1	Broadhead, Joseph E.	MAJ	1
14-1	Carson, Leonard K.	CPT	3
14-1	Cheever, Donald W.	2LT	1
14-1	Duncan, John F.	LT	2
14-1	England, John B.	MAJ	1
14-1	Frey, Jesse R.	1LT	1
14-1	Gasser, James A.	2LT	1
14-1	Kirla, John A.	1LT	4
14-1	Sublett, John L.	1LT	2
14-1	Weaver, Charles E.	1LT	2
14-1	Wyatt, Harold A.	1LT	1
2-3	Becraft, Myron A.	1LT	1
2-3	Duncan, John F.	1LT	1
2-3	Ridley, Oscar T	2LT	1
2-3	Sublett, John L.	CPT	2
20-3	Sublett, John L.	CPT	1
24-3	Duncan, John F.	1LT	1
24-3	Gruber, William W.	1LT	1
24-3	Weaver, Charles E.	CPT	1
18-4	Weaver, Charles E.	CPT	1

DATE	NAME		CREDIT
	363rd SQUADRON		
1944			
20-2	Ross, Donald H.	1LT	1
21-2	Boyle, Alfred R.	1LT	1
22-2	Rogers, Ellis A.	1LT	1
24-2	Michaely, William D.	2LT	1
4-3	Yeager, Charles F .	FO	1
5-3	Bochkay, Donald H.	1LT	.33
5-3	Peters, Charles K.	2LT	.33
5-3	Rogers, Ellis A.	1LT	1.33
6-3	Bochkay, Donald H.	1LT	1
6-3	O'Brien, William P.	CPT	.5
6-3	Pagels, Roger E.	2LT	1
6-3	Pierce, Joseph F.	1LT	1
8-3	Anderson, Clarence E.	CPT	1
16-3	Throop, Montgomery H. Jr.	CPT	1
22-3	Jones, Carter L.	2LT	1
8-4	Bochkay, Donald H.	ILT	1
11-4	Anderson, Clarence E.	CPT	1.25
11-4	Bochkay, Donald H.	ILT	.5
11-4	DeVries, Paul K.	CPT	1
11-4	Kayser, Henry R.	2LT	1.25
11-4	Kenney, Harold M.	2LT	1
11-4	Overstreet, William B.	1LT	.25
11-4	Peters, Charles K.	1LT	1
11-4	Simpson, Edward K Jr.	1LT	1.25
11-4	Throop, Montgomery H. Jr.	CPT	1
24-4	Bochkay, Donald H.	ILT	1
24-4	Browning, James W.	1LT	1
24-4	Hiro, Edwin W.	CPT	1
24-4	Pierce, Joseph F.	1LT	2
24-4	Throop,Montgomery H. Jr.	CPT	1
30-4	Anderson, Clarence E.	CPT	1
30-4	Pierce, Joseph F.	1LT	2
8-5	Anderson, Clarence E.	CPT	1
8-5	Pierce, Joseph F.	1LT	1
9-5	Wood, Lawrence 0.	1LT	1
12-5	Anderson, Clarence E.	CPT	1
12-5	DeVries,Paul K.	CPT	1
12-5	O'Brien, William P.	CPT	1
12-5	Pierce, Joseph F.	1LT	1
13-5	Moore, Robert N.	1LT	1
19-5	Foy, Robert W.	1LT	3
19-5	Hiro, Edwin W.	CPT	2
19-5	Peters, Charles K.	1LT	1
24-5	O'Brien, William P.	CPT	1
27-5	Anderson, Clarence E.	CPT	2
27-5	Browning, James W.	CPT	1
27-5	O'Brien, William P.	CPT	1
27-5	Simpson, Edward K. Jr.	1LT	1
28-5	Peters, Charles K.	1LT	1
30-5	Anderson, Clarence E.	CPT	1
30-5	Browning, James W.	CPT	1
30-5	Moore, Robert N.	1LT	1
30-5	O'Brien, William P.	CPT	2
29-6	Anderson, Clarence E.	CPT	3
29-6	Bochkay, Donald H.	CPT	1
29-6	Browning, James W.	CPT	2
29-6	Fennell, William S.	1LT	.5
29-6	Foy, Robert W.	CPT	3
29-6	Overstreet, William B.	1LT	1
29-6	Staude, Raymond W.	1LT	1
5-7	Bochkay, Donald H.	CPT	2
6-7	Simpson, Edward K. Jr.	1LT	1
6-7	Anderson, Clarence E.	CPT	1
7-7	Fennell, William S.	1LT	1
7-7	Simpson, Edward K. Jr.	1LT	1
25-7	Bochkay, Donald H.	CPT	1

DATE	NAME		CREDIT
25-7	Foy, Robert W.	CPT	1
29-7	Bochkay, Donald H .	CPT	1
29-7	Overstreet, William B.	1LT	1
30-7	Hiro, Edwin W.	MAJ	1
8-8	Moore, Robert N.	CPT	1
13-9	Gailer, Frank L.	2LT	.5
13-9	Hand, Harold 0.	LT	1
13-9	Yeager, Charles F.	1LT	.5
18-9	Dunlop, William R.	1LT	1
18-9	Fennell, William S.	1LT	.5
18-9	Fifield, Robert S.	1LT	.5
18-9	Gailer, Frank L.	2LT	.5
18-9	Hughes, Thomas E.	CPT	.5
18-9	Landis, Keehn	1LT	1
18-9	Pascoe, Hershel T.	1LT	1
19-9	Dunlop, William R.	1LT	1
19-9	Gailer, Frank L.	2LT	.5
19-9	Hand, Harold 0.	1LT	.5
19-9	Hiro, Edwin W.	MAJ	1
19-9	Pasaka, Donald J.	1LT	2
19-9	Roper, Richard C.	1LT	2
7-10	Gailer, Frank L.	1LT	1
12-10	Gailer, Frank L.	1LT	1
12-10	Roper, Richard C.	1LT	2
12-10	Yeager, Charles F.	CPT	5
2-11	Hand, Harold 0.	1LT	1
2-11	Hughes, Thomas E.	CPT	1
6-11	Yeager, Charles F.	CPT	1
18-11	Foy, Robert W.	CPT	1
27-11	Anderson, Clarence E.	CPT	2
27-11	Gailer, Frank L.	1LT	2
27-11	Sloan, James R.	1LT	1
27-11	Wolf, Raymond E.	2LT	1
27-11	Yeager, Charles F.	CPT	4
5-12	Anderson, Clarence E.	CPT	2
5-12	Bochkay, Donald H.	CPT	2
5-12	Browning, James W.	CPT	1
5-12	Carter, Johnnie L.	1LT	1
5-12	Rice, George J.	1LT	1
5-12	Stern, John P.	1LT	1
23-12	Sitzer, Saul	FO	1
24-12	Carlisle, Guernsey I.	MAJ	1
24-12	Carter, Johnnie L.	1LT	2
24-12	Crump, James T.	1LT	1
24-12	Dunlop, William R.	1LT	1
24-12	Roberts, Warner P.	1LT	1
24-12	Sloan, James R.	1LT	1

1945

DATE	NAME		CREDIT
14-1	Browning, James W.	CPT	1
14-1	Dunlop, William R.	1LT	1
14-1	Rice, George J.	1LT	1
14-1	Sloan, James R.	1LT	1
14-1	Stern, John R.	1LT	3
14-1	Taylor, James E.	2LT	1
14-1	Windham, James T.	1LT	1
14-1	Wolf, Raymond E.	2LT	1
14-1	Zarnke, Glenwood A.	1LT	1
9-2	Bochkay, Donald H	CPT	1
9-2	Carter, Johnnie L.	1LT	1
2-3	McGee, Donald C.	CPT	1
19-3	Fifield, Robert S.	CPT	1
20-3	Thorkelson, Robert L.	1LT	1
7-4	Windham, James T.	CPT	1
18-4	Bochkay, Donald H.	MAJ	1
19-4	Bowles, Paul N.	1LT	1
19-4	Fifield, Robert S.	CPT	1
19-4	Ofsthun, Carroll W.	1LT	1

364th SQUADRON
1944

DATE	NAME		CREDIT
22-2	Carder, John B.	1LT	1
22-2	Medeiros, John L.	CPT	1
22-2	Warren, Jack R.	CPT	1
24-2	Medeiros, John L.	CPT	1
2-3	Carder, John B.	1LT	1
2-3	Hayes, Thomas L. Jr.	MAJ	1
5-3	Davis, Glendon V.	CPT	2
5-3	Peterson, Richard A.	1LT	1
5-3	Stanley, Morris A.	2LT	1
6-3	Carder, John B.	1LT	1
6-3	Davis, Glendon V.	CPT	1.5
6-3	Harris, Thomas L.	2LT	1.5
6-3	Hayes, Thomas L. Jr.	MAJ	1
6-3	McKinney, Thomas M.	FO	1
6-3	Ruder, LeRoy A.	1LT	1.5
6-3	Stanley, Morris A.	2LT	1
8-3	Carder, John B.	1LT	1
8-3	Davis, Glendon V.	CPT	.5
8-3	Harris, Thomas L.	2LT	.5
8-3	Haves, Thomas L. Jr.	MAJ	1
8-3	Warren, Jack R.	CPT	1
16-3	Davis, Glendon V.	CPT	1.5
16-3	Hayes, Thomas L. Jr	MAJ	1
16-3	Peterson, Richard A.	1LT	.5
16-3	Reese, William C.	1LT	2
16-3	Warren, Jack R.	CPT	3
18-3	Peterson, Richard A.	ILT	1
11-4	Carder, John B.	1LT	1
11-4	Nowlin, Hollis R.	2LT	1
11-4	Peterson, Richard A.	1LT	1
11-4	Postle, Maurice R.	2LT	.5
11-4	Reese, William C.	1LT	1
11-4	Ruder, LeRoy A.	1LT	1
11-4	Shaw, Robert M.	1LT	1
11-4	Smith, Robert C.	1LT	1
11-4	Stepelton, Mark H.	1LT	.5
11-4	Sumner, Charles D.	1LT	.5
13-4	Davis, Glendon V.	CPT	1
13-4	Fairweather, Paul D.	1LT	.5
13-4	Postle, Maurice R.	2LT	.5
13-4	Shaw, Robert M.	1LT	1
13-4	Smith, Robert C.	1LT	.5
19-4	Carder, John B.	1LT	1
19-4	Davis, Glendon V.	CPT	1
19-4	Harris, Thomas L.	1LT	1
19-4	Stanley, Morris A.	1LT	1
24-4	Carder, John B.	1LT	1
24-4	McKinney, Thomas M.	2LT	1
24-4	Peterson, Richard A.	1LT	1
24-4	Reese, William C.	1LT	1
24-4	Sumner, Charles D.	1LT	1
30-4	McKinney, Thomas M.	2LT	.5
30-4	Peterson, Richard A.	1LT	2
12-5	McKinney, Thomas M.	1LT	1
12-5	Peterson, Richard A.	CPT	.5
12-5	Reese, Willaim C.	1LT	1
12-5	Smith, Richard C.	1LT	1
12-5	Smith, Robert C.	1LT	1
12-5	Storch, John A.	CPT	.5
12-5	Sumner, Charles D.	1LT	1
13-5	Dooley, Charles H.	1LT	.5
13-5	Peterson, Richard A.	CPT	1.5
13-5	Shaw, Robert M.	1LT	.5
13-5	Sullivan, Joseph G.	1LT	1.5
19-5	Ruder, LeRoy A.	1LT	1
19-5	Storch, John A.	CPT	1

DATE	NAME	RANK	CREDIT	DATE	NAME	RANK	CREDIT
27-5	Conklin, Cyril D.	2LT	2	2-11	Peterson, Richard A.	CPT	1
27-5	Fairweather, Paul D.	1LT	1	8-11	Haydon, Edward R.	1LT	.5
27-5	Harris, Thomas L.	CPT	2	18-11	Peterson, Richard A.	CPT	1
27-5	Ruder, LeRov A.	1LT	1	18-11	Winks, Robert P.	1LT	1
27-5	Shaw, Robert M.	1LT	1	27-11	Schimanski, Robert G.	1LT	1
27-5	Stanley, Morris A.	1LT	2	5-12	Adams, Thomas J.	1LT	1
27-5	Stepelton, Mark H.	1LT	1	5-12	Gallant, Morris E.	1LT	1
27-5	Storch, John A.	MAJ	2.5	5-12	Hatala, Paul R.	1LT	1
28-5	Howell, John C.	1LT	1	5-12	Juszczyk, Edmund J.	1LT	1
28-5	Peterson, Richard A.	CPT	1	5-12	Karger, Dale F.	1LT	2
28-5	Ruder, LeRoy A.	1LT	1	5-12	McCall, Frederick C.	1LT	2
30-5	Howell, John C.	1LT	.5	5-12	Schimanski, Robert G.	1LT	1
30-5	Shaw, Robert M.	1LT	.5	5-12	Zetterquist, Herman R.	CPT	1
14-6	Colburn, James E.	1LT	1	24-12	Bank, Raymond M.	ILT	1
14-6	Shaw, Robert M.	1LT	1	24-12	Braley, Byron K.	lLT	1
20-6	Allen, Merle F. Jr.	2LT	.5	24-12	Karger, Dale F.	ILT	1
20-6	Fecher, Louis A.	2LT	.5	24-12	McCall, Frederick C.	1LT	1
20-6	Frederick, Nicholas J.	1LT	1.5	24-12	McGuire, Ivan L.	1LT	1
20-6	Salsman, John J.	1LT	1	24-12	Schimanski, Robert G.	ILT	1
20-6	Smith, Richard C.	CPT	1	24-12	Winks, Robert P.	1LT	1
20-6	Storch, John A.	MAJ	.5				
29-6	Allen, Merle F. Jr.	2LT	.5	**1945**			
29-6	Howell, John C.	CPT	1	5-1	Adams, Thomas H.	ILT	.5
29-6	Stepelton, Mark H.	CPT	1	5-1	Snedecker, Irving F.	ILT	.5
29-6	Summer, Charles D.	CPT	2	10-1	Adams, Thomas H.	1LT	1
29-6	Tyler, Gerald E.	1LT	1	14-1	Adams, Thomas H.	CPT	2
1-7	Peterson, Richard A.	CPT	2	14-1	Bank, Raymond M.	CPT.	3
5-7	Shaw, Robert M.	1LT	1	14-1	Hatala, Paul R.	1LT	2
5-7	Tyler, Gerald E.	1LT	1	14-1	Johnson, Earl W.	ILT	1
14-7	Finley, Daniel L.	1LT	1	14-1	Karger, Dale F.	1LT	1
14-7	Frederick, Nickolas J.	1LT	1	14-1	Maxwell, Chester K.	CPT	3
14-7	Stepelton, Mark H.	CPT	1	14-1	Snedecker, Irving F.	1LT	1
6-8	Brown, Kirby M.	1LT	.5	14-1	Storch, John A.	MAJ	3
6-8	Frederick, Nickolas J.	1LT	.5	14-1	Williams, David R.	2LT	1
6-8	Shaw, Robert M.	1LT	1	14-1	Winks, Robert P.	ILT	2.5
7-8	Nowlin, Nollis R.	1LT	1.5	15-1	Winks, Robert P.	1LT	1
7-8	Storch, John A.	MAJ	.5	20-1	Karger, Dale F.	ILT	1
24-8	Hermanson, Harry H.	1LT	1	20-1	Wright, Roland R.	2LT	1
24-8	Tyler, Gerald, E.	1LT	1	2-3	Bank, Raymond M.	ILT	1
13-9	Allen, Merle F. Jr .	1LT	1	2-3	Hatala, Paul R.	CPT	.5
13-9	Howell, Horace P.	1LT	2	2-3	Howes, Osborn	ILT	1
13-9	Schimanski, Robert G.	2LT	.5	2-3	Karger, Dale F.	ILT	.5
13-9	Storch, John A.	MAJ	1.5	2-3	Murphy, Alva C.	CPT	2
18-9	Braley, Byron K.	2LT	1	2-3	Schimanski, Robert G.	CPT	1.5
18-9	Jacobs, Jerome	2LT	2	2-3	Steiger , James A.	FO	1
18-9	McGuire, Ivan L.	1LT	1	2-3	Zettler, Vincent V.	1LT	1
18-9	Moebius, Howard F.	2LT	1	24-3	Hatala, Paul R.	CPT	2
18-9	Moorhouse, Hugh J.	2LT	1	24-3	Karger, Dale F.	1LT	2
18-9	Morris, George W.	1LT	1	24-3	Schimanski, Robert G.	CPT	1
18-9	Seitzinger, Bernard K.	CPT	1	24-3	Schneider, Charles F.	FO	1
18-9	Shaw, Robert M	1LT	1	24-3	Storch, John A.	LTC	1
18-9	Smith, Robert L.	1LT	2	24-3	Wasylyk, Stephen	1LT	1
18-9	Tyler, Gerald E.	1LT	3	24-3	Weber, Gilman L.	1LT	1
19-9	Braley, Byron K.	2LT	1	24-3	Westphal, Lawrence A.	1LT	1
19-9	Jacobs, Jerome	1LT	1	24-3	Wright, Roland R.	1LT	1
19-9	Maxwell, Chester K.	2LT	2	7-4	McGuire, Ivan L.	CPT	1
19-9	McIntyre, Bryce W.	CPT	2	17-4	Steiger, James A.	FO	1
19-9	Moebius, Howard F.	1LT	2	19-4	McGuire, Ivan L.	CPT	.5
19-9	Sandborn, Dwaine A.	1LT	1	19-4	McMullen, James P.	2LT	1
19-9	Tyler, Gerald E.	1LT	1	19-4	Weber, Gilman L.	1LT	.5
6-10	Peterson, Richard A.	CPT	1				

VIGNETTES OF THE YOXFORD BOYS

Captain Donald Pickerell, Intelligence Officer, 362nd Sqdn. Post mission pilot debriefing: "Most debriefings took place as pilots came into the pilot's room after a mission. Our reports were taken individually by myself and my assistant and two clerks. If it was a wild day then it was difficult to get reports quickly, but most reports were taken informally in a hurry and then later typed out and sent to Group. The number of enemy aircraft destroyed, possibles and other pertinent information was also reported by other pilots. MIA reports were also taken at this time with as much info as possible to perhaps be of help. The pilots did not write out encounter reports in longhand and then sign them after being typed. Ordinarily they were never written by the pilots." (Author's note: The above is the reason that so many pilots in later years, when shown their encounter reports, say it is wrong in some respects. They did not write them.

Sergeant William C. Staples, Communications, 364th Sqdn., on detached duty as control tower operator at Woodbridge Emergency Landing Ground: "I do not recall the date, but on one occasion the mission was recalled due to bad weather but over 100 bombers and 35 fighters did fly the mission. On return, all of England was socked in and we lit the FIDO (fog dispersal oil burners). The wind was from the north and the fog rolled in about as fast as FIDO burned it off and we had to 'talk in' many of the planes. When the day was over we had landed all the aircraft from the mission, even though some were still on the runway. It was the most hectic day for me in the control tower but it must have been a lot worse for the aircrews, but if FIDO had not been doing its job it would have been a lot worse."

Captain Harvey Mace, flight leader, 362nd Sqdn. "I had just gotten up one morning when I heard a buzz bomb approaching the coast. I went outside in time to see the second or third round fired by the nearby triple A gun hit the bomb which exploded in a big orange and yellow flash. It was a quick kill.

"Not long after, I heard the very familiar sound of a B-17 returning from what must have an abort from the morning mission. It was quickly followed by the sound of the gun going off again. I rushed outside to see the B-17 falling out of the clouds in flames, followed by several chutes and I later heard that all ten men got out. The B-17 had the misfortune of coming in at about the same altitude and track as the buzz bombs, and gunners could not recognize the sound of the 150 mph B-17.

"Many years later I became good friends with a Brit who was selling cars in California. One day we were sitting around shooting the breeze and I decided to needle him a bit with the B-17 story. He came back with; 'You want to know something strange - I was the gun captain of that crew that shot the B-17 down.'

"I did not press a vindictive attack in view of the two Mosquitoes that we had shot down!" (author's note: This is true, 357th pilots did shoot down Mosquitoes on two occasions, mistaking them for Me 110s or Ju 88s. In one the pilot was killed, the fate of other crew unknown.)

Lt. Frank L. Gailer, 363rd Sqdn. "I was a brand new pilot in September, 1944, and was flying on Chuck Yeager's wing during the first Arnhem mission. The call came over the radio 'bandits, drop tanks'. As Chuck's tanks fell off, I jettisoned mine. Everything went strangely quiet. It was just like in the movie HELLS ANGELS - airplane going around in a great melee and no sound. Chuck's plane was pulling away rapidly and I then realized I had not switched to internal fuel. I quickly switched tanks, the engine caught and I caught up with Chuck. Talk about lucky.

"The next day, again at Arnhem, I was again on Chuck's wing and the same thing occurred! 'Bandits - drop tanks'. I dropped tanks and again Chuck pulled away. I reacted a bit quicker this time, switched tanks and caught up with Chuck. I shared my first kill with Chuck on this mission. It shows how green I was and how lucky. Chuck never chewed me out just smiled both times." (Author's note: Gailer went on to become an ace himself, later retired from USAF as a Brig/General. In the year 2000 he served as president of the American Fighter Aces Association.)

Lt. William B. Overstreet, 363rd Sqdn. Near Santa Rosa Army Airfield, CA. 28 June, 1943. "I took off as part of a flight of four P-39s to engage in general rat racing and dog fighting in vicinity of the airfield. At some point in the rat race I lost control of the airplane, possibly due to an overcontrol. The P-39 snapped to the left and then tumbled tail over nose, ending up in an inverted spin. At that moment it was obviously time to part company with the airplane. I pulled the release handle for the doors, but they did not separate, possibly due to air pressure on the doors. By getting my shoulder against one door and my knees against the other, I was able to push enough to get the door off. I got out immediately and pulled the rip cord. When the chute opened it slowed my fall at the same instant my feet hit the ground - I landed standing up, didn't even bend my knees. I landed among the wreckage of the P-39 right beside one of the prop blades and among the 37 mm ammunition. Since the chute opened below the trees, the rest of the flight went back to base and reported my demise." (Author's note: Overstreet completed an extended combat tour as a Captain and Flight Leader.)

Captain William R. O'Brien, 363rd Sqdn. flight leader. "The only real contribution I made to life at Leiston was done through Col. Spicer. When he got through with his introductory speech to the pilots, he said 'If you have a problem, my door is always open.' I took advantage of the offer to tell him I wanted those 'little bitty' coke burner stoves replaced because I had pilots down with colds. The big 'pot belly' stoves were in supply but the damn quartermaster wouldn't give them to me. Not the usual chain of command for supply requests but understandable when you think about how often the 363rd got a new commanding officer. Anyway I wanted to talk to 'the big boss'. The next

day we started getting the new stoves. I've never forgotten the way Don Graham (deputy Group Commander) looked at me when he ushered me into Spicer's office, rattlesnakes with two heads would be more welcome. I don't think Graham knew what was going on, or his attitude would have been different - I wasn't passing anyone, I just needed help. I got it and so did the whole group."

1st Lt. William R. Dunlop, 363rd Sqdn., Shot down 14 January, 1945. Note: Bill Dunlop's experiences while in POW camp on the receiving end of and RAF attack on Nuremberg. The date is unknown, probably Feb-April 1945.

"The first indication that there was a raid coming was in the 8 pm report from Ashman (one of our officers who spoke German and acted as a liaison to the camp command): Word from the German or from whatever source was routinely spread through the camp by runners. The report said a large formation of heavy bombers was on a direct course for Nuremberg. A German 'voralarm' was sounded, followed by a shelter call to get into the slit trenches outside the barracks. I stayed in the block by the window just in from the trenches, so I could go thru if the bombs came too close. 'Goon searchlights in-all directions were hurriedly rallying the night fighters, telling us that a 'big show' was near. Suddenly the searchlights went off and the BLAM of the flak guns which surrounded the camp was heard. (We had heard there were something like 90 guns on the camp periphery.) Their fire seemed directed at pathfinder planes, target selecting for the bombers following and marking our camp. The area around us became like the 4th of July.

"A line of parachute flares, in clusters of red and green, separated our camp for Nuremberg across the railroad tracks to the north of us. It was awesome and a relief that the RAF was looking out for us. Then, at about the same time, a scare as one of our men yelled 'falling flak', followed by a piece crunching into the roof next door. To the din of the flak guns was added the deep rumble of RAF 'cookies'. (We always removed our dishes from the walls because concussion from the cookies, even miles away, shook the barracks and on one occasion blew out windows.) Slowly a stream of bombers made an appearance. (Someone said there were 200-300 'Lanes' and 'Rallies' (Lancasters and Halifaxs).

"From the slit trench where I had just taken refuge I watched as the city became a deep red glow. Over the glow there was an occasional streak of white flame racing across the sky in a backdrop of numerous star like flak flashes. This was apparently burning gasoline as flak found its mark. Then the streak would tragically turn red as the plane burned. As it came closer it seemed to to be floating earthward, a twisted burning mass of wings and parts. I watched one such streak in an area where there were no flak flashes.

"A split second after the white streak, what must have been a nightfighter 'lit up' and spun in. The bomber came down in 3 pieces, trailing skirts of red and emitting a terrible death whine. I also saw a bomber hit but then the fire went out and the plane seemed to continue on its way. Most often it was the other way around. The destruction in the sky seemed part of the destruction on the ground. The fires in the city reflected from scattered high cirrus and the flak barrage smoke at something like 20,000 feet could be seen clearly. For 15-20 minutes it was

nearly unbelievable scene and then a last bomb, the flak stopped and the planes droned home. The searchlights came on again and several low flying jerry fighters were seen headed in the direction of the retreating bomber stream. Cold and wet from crouching in the trench, I hit the sack. Twenty four hours later there were still explosions, probably from delayed action bombs."

Donald W.Marner, Auto mechanic, truck driver, flight line Mechanic, 363rd Sqdn. "When I joined the 363rd in July, 1944, I was an 022 Auto Mechanic. At the time they didn't need me as a mechanic, so they put me on a 6 X 6 and told me to transport 108 gallon drop tanks from an RAF base to Leiston and then distribute about a dozen to each hardstand. At that time there were a great many tanks being used, 120 or more a day, all handled by myself. As I recall, I distributed to all three Squadrons, but my main job was to the 363rd and if I got behind, I had help from the 362nd and 364th. As I remember back, this was a glamorous job for a 22 year old for I met a lot of Crew Chiefs, Assistant Crew Chiefs and Armorers and learned all about individual P-51s, their names, their records and of course, the pilots who flew them.

"Fifty three years later, I still have many of those P-51s sitting on their hardstands, photographed in my memory, and in color too! Wouldn't it be wonderful if I could develop a photo, in color, from my memory bank?!"

Lt. William "Stubby" Gambill, 363rd Sqdn. Letter to his wife, 12 Jan 1944. (author's note: Stubby Gambill was shot down on 8 March '44 and was killed a few days later as a POW, by an Allied bomb.)
"Dear Honey,
I haven't rec'd any mail for a couple of days, but suppose it is bunching up somewhere and I will get it all at once.

'Andy''(Capt. C.E. Anderson) is at gunnery school so I am leading the flight now. We are breaking in a new boy so you know how it goes. Browning was grounded for a while because he took an unauthorized pass, but we are all together again. We took a little navigation trip today and I never got lost, so I figure I am doing better. Yeager jumped us so we had a big rat race, then buzzed a few fields here and there. It sure is good to get back in the air again, to dive, climb, and roll and play among the clouds. Almost life again.

"Guess what! Pilots get a special issue of eggs, oranges and milk, and I drew mine today for the week - five eggs and an orange. We buy fresh bread at a nearby bakery and peanut butter someplace else, and every night we have a feed of toast jam and peanut butter sandwiches - really a good deal! It reminds me of the time I fried an egg sandwich at home. I never realized how well off I was then. Peters, Hubbard and Pascoe are having a hearts game on the footlocker and the radio is making a lot of noise so I guess I better cut the gab.

"Keep good care of Dick and as I have said before, a hundred million times, I love you so very much it is useless to try to put it in words. Forever, Your Bill

John Salsman, on his P-51C-5-NT serial number 42-103601, C5-C, and crew "The MAZIE R and two others named at the Depot as a result of a war bond drive, came to the 364th Squadron. John Schultz (Crew Chief) and Dick Spicer, (Asst. Crew Chief) got the MAZIE R, and I was assigned as pilot.

Armorer was Mort Hyman. Both John and Dick got the Bronze Star for going 300 hours without an abort. Actually it went over 600 hours and at least while I flew it, never had any battle damage. It had a dash three engine with the supercharger which shifted to high blower at a higher altitude than the dash seven, and it was about ten miles per hour faster then the D model. The bird cage canopy was replaced with the English bubble canopy so it had better visibility then the P-51Ds. I had the good fortune of flying the P-51s from the A model through the H model. MAZIE R was the best of the bunch.

"Hats off to the crew, they were wonderful and probably a number of us owe our lives to them."

Lt. Harold Vartanian, 18th Weather Squadron and 362nd Ftr. Sqdn. (Author's note: Vartanian was one of several weather observers attached to the 357th. Captain Leo Miller was station Weather Officer besides Vartanian, who billeted with the 362nd Sqdn. Gene Rhoades was with Hdqers and Bob Clark with the 364th. All weather men were assigned to the 18th Weather Squadron which had 106 detachments at operational bases, as of April 1944. Normally each detachment had three officers (Observers) and eight enlisted forecasters.

Following is a letter from Vartanian to Joe DeShay, September 1993. Vartanian died in 1994. "My bunk mate in the 362nd was 'lone eagle' Kit Carson and he was a tough one to get to know intimately. Believe it or not, Colonel Egenes and maintenance officer Fred Gilbert played ten cent poker on occasion. Egenes was tough on some people like Tony Siroka and 'Pop' Nickols, the 'ole exec officer and that's how Henslee got to move up to exec officer.

"Basically, Rhoades, Clark and I alternated giving the weather briefing. Our job was to give very distilled major data of the weather picture that might save the pilot's life when he was returning from the mission, and try to give them 30 to 60 seconds of the most critical information.

"My tour with the 362nd was active, exciting, crude living conditions, rough, cold, damp, but being able to share the 'working' life of the pilots, their talk, roughhousing, shared experiences, and even being a 'ground pounder', provider of (we hoped) essential services such as weather service to provide these modern 'knights of the air' with the very best information for survival."

Merle Olmsted, 362nd, flight line mechanic, letter to his parents: "Well, I finally got airborne today for the first time in along time. Major England had finished his tour of duty and last night he was to he flown to another part of England to catch transportation home. However, the radio in the Norseman was out so we did not take off until this morning. Besides the Major, there was Captain Kirla and myself. The weather was pretty rough and since we stayed below the clouds (about 1,000 feet) I felt pretty rough myself by the time we sat down at an RAF station in order to ask where we were, which turned out to be only a few miles from the correct station. On the way back there was only Kirla and myself so I occupied the co-pilot's seat. Luckily for me he decided to climb through the clouds about 5,000 feet. Up there the sun was brilliant and when we got to 10,000 you could look down on an unending carpet of clouds. We were alone until Kirla spotted a twin engined British Oxford headed in our direction. Being a fighter pilot, he couldn't resist a few passes at our ally - although the Norseman is no fighter. A couple of times I found myself hanging from my safety belt.

"When the Britishers decided they were tired of playing, Kirla gave me the controls for a half hour or so. I guess I did alright but kept slipping off course and he had to keep pointing me in the right direction. I enjoyed the trip, we were in the air about three hours and got back just in time to miss dinner. As long as we stayed up high where it was smooth, my stomach did not wander all over the sky by itself!."

William R. "OBee" O'Brien, 362rd Sqdn. Flight leader Pilot of three aircraft named BILLIE'S BITCH: P-39Q, 42-20750; P-51B, s/n unknown; P-51D, 44-13522.
Question by Jim Anderson: "What was the origin of the name BILLIE'S BITCH for your aircraft?"
OBee: "The name BILLIE'S BITCH was chosen as appropriate for my first P-39 aircraft - Beautiful to behold, clothed in style, passionately sensitive to a gentle touch but absolutely unforgiving when not receiving full and proper attention - truly the definition of a bitch and a P-39."

William R. O'Brien; OBEE'S WAR WOUND. "I HAD A LOT OF HELP": "When stationed at Oroville, California during 1943, Al Boyle my assistant flight leader shot me by accident with a .45 caliber service pistol. The bullet went through my upper right biceps without causing bone damage. Injury was to nerves and muscle. After hospitalization and being grounded, I walked around with my arm in a sling for about a month. My right hand was inoperative. The medical decision was to let nature take its course, if the nerve endings rejuvenated themselves to restore feeling then I had a chance to be of use to the Group. John Bricker Meyers, 363rd Squadron intelligence officer, and a lawyer, had a briefcase full of court martial papers that remained unfilled. Boyle's charges were among the many. No one said a word to me about the future. Thanks to John Brick Meyers!

"Don Graham was my Squadron Commanding officer. I bled all over his pants, ruined them as I was being taken to the Oroville field dispensary. I owe him not only for the slacks but I'm sure he knew what Meyers was doing. Thanks to General Graham!

"While recovering I did a little work at Group Operations, till the Group moved to Casper, Wyoming and on to Camp Shanks, staging area for shipment to England. At Camp Shanks, Lt. Col. Edwin Chickering, Group Commander called me to his office and said: 'OBee, you know you don't have to go with us'. I replied, 'Sir, I've come too far to turn back. I want to go if only to hold someone's hat.' He replied, 'You are dismissed'. Thanks here to Colonel Chickering!

"I made it on and off the QUEEN ELIZABETH without assistance to prove to myself that I was not helpless and could do well using one arm. At Raydon Wood, our first base in England, I could shovel mud with the rest of the guys. My fingers were just numb but my arm motion was returning. Now the problem was what to do with me. During my recovery period there was little flying, I was in the position that if I didn't soon log some flying time I would loose flight pay and the Group needed pilots, not cripples. Soon the Group would receive new airplanes and combat would not be long in coming. There was only an L-4 liaison aircraft on the flight line at Raydon.

"Major John Barker MD, and the Group flight surgeon, drove with me to the closest General Hospital for a medical evaluation by a Neurologist. After demonstrating to this Captain that my freedom of motion was acceptable and being made uncomfortable while undergoing his sensitivity testing for two hours, I was asked to leave the room. I did, but kept the door ajar and heard the specialist tell Major Barker that I should be sent to the zone of interior for discharge as I was unfit for duty.

"I left the hospital with Major Barker and when getting in the jeep I asked him 'what are we going to do?' He asked me, 'OBee, can you fly an airplane?' When I said yes, he said, 'go and fly'. I asked what about the specialist, Barker said; 'He doesn't fill out the forms, I do.' May God bless John Barker as I owe him a big bunch. That had to be the finest decision demonstrating wonderful medical judgment. I was flying the L-4 that afternoon at Raydon.

"Physically, I may have encountered trouble pulling the emergency canopy release and the parachute D-ring, but no emergency occurred. Early in 1944 the first two fingers of the right were still numb, I had to use my left hand to fire the guns but later in the year all fingers had some feeling. Remember, it does not take great physical strength to fly an airplane. The RAF had several pilots missing one or more limbs.

"So, with the help of these fine people, I was able to continue with and complete my tour with the Group."

Robert Krull, 362nd Sqdn. Crew Chief: "One evening just after dark, we heard a very loud buzz bomb and ran outside and there was a buzz bomb not over 50 feet high, flying right over our area. You could see the short wings and the jet engine setting up above the bomb with about five feet of red flame coming out of the motor. It must have been hit by anti-aircraft fire as it was out of control. We all stood there and watched it go on over and after it passed we wondered just how much it cleared the big oak tree which stood by our orderly room. It went on over and soon we heard it hit the ground and explode"

(Author's note: In the period 13 June 1944 to 29 March 1945, the Germans launched 6,725 VI "buzz bombs" against England. 5,500 people were killed and 23,000 homes destroyed. 1,859 V-ls were shot down by AA guns and 1,846 by fighters. Another 230 hit barrage balloons. Starting in September, the Germans launched 1,178 V-2 rocket missiles for which there was no defense, killing 2,541 people in England. Many were also killed in Antwerp, Belgium and other places. Source: FLYING BOMB, by Peter Cooksley, Scribner & Sons, NY, 1979.

Captain George Boswell, Asst Group Intelligence Officer. Commentary on the Big Day mission, 14 Jan. 1945: "Early in the week the secret report, compiled by POW interrogators and distributed to groups, was received. All Group and Squadron leaders were carefully briefed on the contents concerning *Luftwaffe* 'Company front' tactics. Plans to counter an attack was evolved and the pilots themselves were briefed. So when the situation, almost to the letter as outlined in the report, arose, the 357th was ready. There suddenly appeared in the sky the exact formations as outlined and the plan that was worked out during one of the days when the Group was not flying by Colonel Dregne and his squadron leaders, was executed!"

Lt. Col. Loring F. Stetson, first Commander of the 357th from Dec. 1942 until July, 1943, when he took command of the 33rd Ftr. Grp in the Med. Letter to the 357th, received 23 October 1943: "Dear Don (Graham), Bob and gang laying in bed with a slight case of malaria and catching up on correspondence. How is the old outfit getting along? Damn fine, I imagine. Been having a bit of fun myself, caught me an Fw the other day. Keep giving the boys plenty of gunnery. Saves a lot of ammo not to mention wear and tear on the nerves. Our ships aren't the newest in the world but at least they don't tumble and they get the job done. Don't let the boys gripe about promotion, they haven't seen anything yet! Enjoy your salads, whiskey and women while you can. Best of luck. Stets.

Lt. Albert Lichter, 362nd Sqdn., shot down by flak on 22 Feb. 1944, bailed: "I landed in Holland near the small village of Tilburg near a canal. There was a patrol boat there with the navy waiting to pick me up. They took me aboard the boat and radioed the army to come and get me. The vehicle was a motorcycle with an enlisted man driving and an officer in the sidecar who asked me my name. I said 'Lichter' and he said, 'Oh Leister, that's a good German name, ya?' We had gone only a few miles when the cycle quit running. The enlisted man got off, waved his hand and said 'Hmm, American, nix good.' I looked at the gas tank and it said 'Harley Davidson'. A truck came along and I was taken into town and into the city jail. This was my first night as prisoner of war."

Lt. Joe Black, 362nd Sqdn., "On one of my early missions I was flying as Captain Charles Weaver's wingman. We were heading home when we ran into four Me 109s, so our flight of four P-51s dived down to intercept the enemy. Captain Weaver picked out one of the 109s with a yellow nose and immediately the enemy aircraft headed straight down with Chuck right behind it. At about 1500-2000 feet he reached a cloud layer and we went in after him. Chuck and I went through the clouds and broke out below, we were alone! Suddenly the 109 dropped down behind Chuck and opened fire with a short burst. As I turned to get a shot at him, he ducked back into the clouds. Over the radio, Chuck told me to drop back further to see if we could mouse trap him, using himself as bait. We flew above and below the cloud layer, trying our best to nail him. He would pop out of the cloud cover to take a quick shot and be gone again. On one pass he made at Chuck I was able to get off a two or three second burst, but I doubt that I hit him. All told, the Me 109 got about six tries at us and we got only one quick shot at him. After his last attempt at adding a P-51 to the tail markings on his plane, he disappeared. We hung around for a short while but he did not return.

"When we got back to Leiston, Chuck said that he thought the 109 pilot must have run low on fuel and had to break off to return to base. We were rather glad he did! It was the first time I had fired my guns at an enemy aircraft and it was too bad I didn't see any hits. We discussed the event in the mess and think the 109s were from JG 26, THE ABBEVILLE KIDS."

Dick Eagen, Crew Chief, 364th Sqdn. (Author's note: Recognition of Crew Chiefs was done by the award of the Bronze Star medal when their aircraft had flown 175 hours of operations without an abort. There is no record of how many achieved this, but the author's guess is that it was somewhere around twenty Crew Chiefs. Eagen describes how he "almost" did not get one.): "I had, as usual, preflighted my plane and it was running as smooth as could be. I had a very young pilot come out one day to fly it. The flight took off and in a short time, PEABODY'S PET (Name of his P-51) was back at my revetment. I asked the pilot what was wrong and he said the engine was running rough. I did not say anything, but after he left, I hopped in and ran the engine and it was very smooth. I went to Operations, got a certain Captain to test fly it. He did, came back and told there was nothing wrong with it. He agreed that the aborted mission was not a mechanical defect and went back to Ops and cleared me of blame. I was able to maintain my record, and did get the Bronze Star."

1st. Lt. James R. Sloan, 363rd Fighter Sqdn. Letter to the author. James R. Sloan arrived at Leiston Airfield in the late fall of 1944. Although a newcomer to the Group, Sloan was not a pilot just out of flight school - his total pilot time at the end of December was almost 2,000 hours. He was shot down on The Big Day, and spent a miserable three months as POW. Before being shot down, however, he scored one victory bringing his total to three.

Here he describes a mission that remains vivid in his memory after 50 plus years. Due to the impromptu nature of the mission, no report or even date has been found for it: "As I recall, there were four of us. Bud Anderson leading,with Jim Browning on his wing, Chuck Yeager as element lead and myself at 'Tail End Charlie'. We made rendezvous over Belgium with a Mosquito that was painted fire engine red, flown by an air force General who wanted to observed bombing results from close up, and at low level and that we did!

"The bomb run was down 'flak alley'. We were on the east side of the target area at about 2,000 feet or lower. The sight of hundreds of bombs falling simultaneously and the ensuing explosions was awesome!!

"The General was soon satisfied and departed for home. The Mosquito seemed faster than we were and went off and left us. As I recall we did some treetop buzzing on the way home. It was a short mission but spectacular!"

lst Lt. James Sloan, 363rd Fighter Sqdn. Letters to author, 1990s: "A B-17 was limping along flying due north over Northwestern Germany. The weather was not good and the ground was not visible. After a few minutes when it did not change course for England, radio contact was made. The pilot was told we could not stay with him much longer due to low fuel. His navigator insisted that they were on course for England. When we turned to head for home, the B-17 pilot told his navigator, 'We're going with the fighters, they know the course home'. The B-17 landed at our base with wounded on board and the pilot showed his considerable appreciation at the club that evening.

"I also recall an incident with a B-24, which we spotted at about 12,000 feet headed in the general direction of England. Our location was over western Germany near Belgium. The '24 attracted some light flak and it seemed to take some evasive action. It made slight altitude changes and changed direction alternately right and left. However, the left turns were always larger, soon the course of the aircraft was southerly. In the meantime, flying as Yeager's (Charles) wingman, we checked it out at very close range from every angle. All four engines were running well and there was no visible damage and there was no one

in the aircraft!! Yeager contacted Luxembourg Control and requested permission to shoot it down but it was denied. It was headed back into Germany when we left it. The serial number of the B-24 was given to Ernie DeNigres (Intelligence Officer) but I never did hear anything more about it. Was it a radio controlled ship which got away from its 'mother' ship? Did the crew bail out? Not likely as the bomb bay doors were closed and there were no other openings to leave it."

It 1st Lt. James Sloan, 363rd Squadron, letter to the author, 1990s: "One morning while doing a test flight, I saw a black and white checker-nosed P-51 (78th Fighter Group) at low altitude, smoking heavily. He was about a mile out and lined up with our longest runway. Seeing a fellow pilot in trouble leaves one with a little empty and helpless feeling. His airspeed was much too high to make a good landing, but he did manage to touch down shortly before reaching the far end of the runway. The landing gear sheared off in a ditch and both wings were partially torn off. The rest of the aircraft finally came to rest when it hit a haystack.

"It was a welcome sight to see the pilot running from the wreck and a safe distance away when there was an explosion. He was knocked down but suffered only bruises - just plain lucky!!"

Hoyt Parmer, T/Sgt, Armament Flight Chief, 362nd Sqdn., from an interview by Jim Anderson: "Each armament flight had nine Armorers who took care of the armament requirements on their eight assigned aircraft. We had three armament flights in each squadron. At preflight time I always took a quick trip around by bicycle to all of the planes in my flight to see if help was needed and then I pitched in where necessary. After a couple of incidents where guns were fired accidentally during preflight, the Flight Chief always had to be present when the guns were tested.

"If a pilot had used his guns during the mission or had any difficulty with them, all of this had to be checked out, the guns cleaned and ready for the next day's mission. The guns were always over-nighted without a round in the chamber. At preflight the firing solenoids had to be checked to see if the gun fired when the trigger was depressed. After this was determined, the guns were made 'hot' (with a round in the chamber).

"Gun camera operation was checked, as were the bomb/tank shackles. Bombs were fused if carried. We always kept a strip of tape over the muzzles to keep from picking up moisture. The guns were cleaned once a week even if not fired. They were pulled, taken to the shop and checked over. It was very damp in England - the gun bores would rust and pit easily.

"I can truthfully say that I experienced very few difficulties doing my job, as everyone knew that we were all there for the same reason and help was always there for the asking. We just had a great bunch of guys in our outfit and I don't believe that we had one bad apple in the bunch."

Arthur Schalick, TSgt, Group Communications, letter to author, 1992: "Group Communications acted as overseer of the three Squadron communications sections and also in charge of the transmitter and the receiver stations, the Leiston DF (direction finding), the Woodbridge DF station and some equipment in the control tower. We had about 36 men who were taken from the Squadrons. Ten were assigned to Woodbridge.

(Author's note: Woodbridge was one of three emergency airfields which had 10,000 foot runways and FIDO bad weather equipment.)

"The DF station at Leiston was located off base in a field behind the 363rd line area and in a special frame building that looked like a silo. The receiver station was also located off base and the transmitter station was located on base near the base hospital. It, as well as the receiver station were in a special brick building that looked like a bomb shelter. The equipment in the brick buildings handled only two frequencies so we parked two mobile units next to each building that increased our capabilities to six frequencies.

"The antennas for both the transmitters and receivers were on large square wooden towers nearly 100 feet high. Each tower had only four antennas, so we erected a mobile 75 foot tower for additional capacity. When the frequencies were changed it was necessary for someone to climb the tower on large protruding bolts There were only one or two on our staff who would tackle this job, so I did it many times. I also found the platform at the top of the transmitter tower a perfect place to take pictures and watch takeoffs and landings as it was near the end of the runway."

LETTER FROM MRS PAULEEN BALLS, Leiston school girl, Pauleen Botwright in 1944: "December, 1944: Mr Blower, then headmaster of Leiston Senior School, came into our classroom with a paper in his hand. All went quiet as this usually meant bad news. Mr Osborne, our teacher told us that Mr. Blower had something very important to tell us, but it turned into a day to remember as Mr. Blower told us that he had been asked by the Commander of the American base if some or all of the children in the school would like to go to the base just before Christmas to give the airmen a concert to cheer them up, as they were missing their families and children. We were all very excited and shouted yes!

"It was agreed that each class was to pick something suitable, as there were five classes it would mean five items, to all come together at the end to sing carols and end with the Stars and Stripes. We had only two weeks to plan them and learn the Stars and Stripes which we were told had to be word perfect and we were not to be disappointed if at the last moment it had to be cancelled as this was war time and things changed so quickly. All parents had to sign to say we could go and our work was not to suffer. The whole school was electric as we planned and practiced.

"We all had to wear our school uniform, which was to be smart and girls had to wear long white socks. The day arrived and we all waited in the school playground in pitch black (no lights due to the black out). I remember it being so quiet, as even at this late stage we were told the trucks may not come. What a cheer when they arrived. We were loaded into the trucks in blackness and an airman sat at the entrance of each truck to make sure no one moved or fell out - no seat belts in those days!

"In great excitement we were off to the base. We were helped as we jumped out of the trucks and I have a lasting memory of jumping to the side into the mud, giving me one very muddy sock. We then walked in line still in blackness to a huge hangar and the biggest surprise of all - that it was full of food. Eyes were on stalks as we looked at doughnuts, chocolate

sweets, cakes, ice cream and pop! We had never seen anything like it and went mad! We could eat and drink what we wanted. We had been on rations since 1940 and had no memory of such goodies. Then it was show time, some of us feeling under the weather with so many goodies eaten.

"The three younger classes did the first items. The tap dancing was done by evacuees from London who had attended stage school and had brought their satin costumes and shoes with them. They were real professional. The two top classes were 14 year old boys taught by Mr. Bill Newberry and the 14 year old girls taught by Miss Last. The boys did the cowboy scene with with camp fire, check shirts, jeans etc. The girls doing gypsy scene with caravan, fire and dancing.

"The younger classes thought them very daring with their off-shoulder tops, hip wiggling etc. getting lots of wolf whistles. We then all came together for Christmas carol singing everyone joining in, it went down well and we sang more than planned. We ended the evening singing the Stars and Stripes. We then cheered and clapped, all feeling about ten feet tall as we had never done anything like that before, so were very elated. We were then taken back by truck feeling very happy and full.

"The tail end of this story is that when we got back to school after Christmas break, Mr. Blower read each class the letter of thanks we had received from the Commander, but we had a dressing down from Mr. Blower as to our behavior over the food which he thought was dreadful!"

LETTER TO JOHN SKARA, (WHO HAD RETURNED TO THE ZI), FROM FELLOW 363rd PILOT, JOHN STERN, DATED 18 JANUARY, 1945:

"Hiya Johnny,

Well, as I sit here by the little coke fire, I will try to answer your letter. The weather here is a little chilly, have had a little snow, Germany is well covered. Quite a lot has happened since you left, Johnny. We have hit the Krauts several times and have about 575 now.

"We sure had a big day on the 14th, we got 57 1/2. What a sight. We were over by BIG B, it was clear as a bell. They came in about 150 strong. I was leading white flight, Foy Red, Browning Green and Dunlop Blue. After we got a hold of them and couldn't let go, it was fight it out! You never saw such a sight, every place you could look planes were going down. All over the ground you could see black pillars of smoke coming up. I got three Me 109s, Foy got three and so did Browning. The rest in the formation got singles. We got 13 in the squadron. Andy and Yeager were down around Switzerland goofing around. It was their next to last mission. They are finished now, Andy has 19 Krauts and Yeager 12.

"Browning has ten and Bochkay 13. I've got four now. The 'judge' still has only one. He was sure pissed off because he wasn't along the other day!

"The old barracks isn't the same any more. I'm the only one left. Landis is over in the 'Wheel' barracks. There are a lot of new faces all over the place. Some of them are pretty sad.

"You might be interested in what happened to your old airplane. It is scattered all over the snowy hills of France. After Hank finished with it, a boy named Windham got it. Coming back, the coolant screwed up and it caught fire. He bailed out close to Lille. It had about 450 hours on it.

"We have lost several boys. Not many you knew, I guess. Doranski, Dunlop, Gailer, Pascoe (who is a POW). Don't know about the rest except Doranski, he went down in the channel. I saw that.

"I only flew eight hours of combat in December. Spent the rest of the time running the training Squadron. Goxhill is closed. Sure was monotonous, I had to waste away some time.

"Andy is a Major now, as are Peterson and England. Landis and I are Captains, thank God! Carlisle is also about finished. I have about 40 hours more, then I'm going to take a 50 hour extension.

"Captain Evander is now a Major. I hear Overstreet is in Pinellas, Florida, George is at Punta, Pagels is at Perrin Field, Texas.

"Drop me a line and tell me what you are doing.

Good luck. (signed) Johnny Stern"

Bill Overstreet, On his fellow 363rd pilots. From: TO FLY & FIGHT: "I was the studious one in the Group, instead of doing the bars, I'd read books. There was no 'pilot' type. Eddie Simpson and Jim Browning were the gentlemanly type, just like Anderson. Ellis Rogers had a master's degree in mathematics. At Tonopah, I remember O'Brien taking off in the morning with two hours' fuel and not coming home until dark - he'd landed on the road by some bar. We all idolized Hubbard (Lloyd). We were flying loops around the Golden Gate bridge when his engine quit and he put the P-39 down in the surf, steering into the shore and didn't even scratch it or even get wet. And Irving Smith was a concert pianist, imagine that, with tuxedo and tails!

"I'm not laying any claims to being a hot pilot, but I had a feel for engines and probably saved a couple of airplanes, nursing them home. But the P-39s were temperamental and tricky to fly. You'd move the stick on a P-39 and eighth of an inch and you could throw it into a spin before you knew what was happening. (author's note: See Overstreet's bailout)

"I had a couple of other close calls. We dove into a wave of Germans and one put a 20 mm cannon shell through my canopy took my helmet right off my head but only gave me a burn. On a dive bombing mission, the release failed and I had to land with live bombs. Verrry softly!! And there was the time that I dove on a Messerschmitt and my sinuses swelled so badly that my eyes closed up. "Daddy Rabbit" talked me back to base and through the landing."

Lt. Osborn Howes, 364th Ftr. Sqdn: "During my tenure at Leiston Airfield, I was ordered to report to the Public Relations Department at SHAEF in London. Upon reporting as ordered, a Colonel informed me that since I spoke French I was to broadcast a radio message to the Free French Underground telling them what we, the 8th Air Force, were going to assist their resistance against the Germans.

"Somewhere down the line I had filled out a questionnaire indicating that I'd studied French in high school. There was nowhere on the form to fill in grades in French class. As I looked at the script given me, my face became a complete blank and I started pronouncing the words phonetically. This was enough for the Colonel to mentally give me a grade in French and he told me that I had a Parisian accent, probably to make me feel better. He thanked me for my trouble and wished me a pleasant trip back to East Anglia. At least I got a short vacation

in London and the Underground were spared the ordeal of deciphering my fractured French!"

Captain Harvey Mace, 362nd Squadron, on FIDO (Fog Intense Dispersal Operation: "After I finished my combat tour with the 357th, I was assigned to 3rd Division Headquarters as fighter controller. In a weak moment I volunteered to go along on a B-17 combat mission to see how the other half lived. True, it was just a one plane milk run reconn just barely over enemy territory. But I figure if it was far enough over enemy territory to over fly a V-2 launch where the rocket came close enough to us to read numbers, it's a combat mission!

"Anyway, we were up ten hours and on our return to England there was low thick fog over everything. The pilot called for FIDO at Manston. As we approached that base, the solid white fog below us was smooth everywhere except for a beautiful raised rectangular shape, the length and width of the huge Manston runway. All we had to do was aim our approach at the end of the block of white and after riding through the bumps of rising air from the heat of the burning gasoline, make a nice landing. It had worked as advertised, much to my relief.

"I understand that after the war Los Angeles was considering it for the new LAX airport but decided the consumption of gasoline was just too great."

2nd Lt. William Foard, 364th Fighter Squadron, from his diary 16 April 1945: "Six hour plus mission to rail yards SE of Munich. I was flying BUZZ BUGGY and the engine was running rough. I kept running up the RPMs to clean it out and smooth it but it was using extra fuel at the higher RPMs. I left the group with three other P-51s having trouble and headed home. When we got to the North Sea we were at 10,000 feet when my engine quit (WOW, I never heard such quiet!). I turned back looking for some solid ground but could see only trees sticking out of the water in flooded areas. After going through all of the procedures I could think of the engine started running half heartedly, I headed south mushing along nose high into a thick haze just barely holding altitude. At the briefing that morning we were told with much emphasis NOT TO LAND ON ANY 9th AIR FORCE BASES AND MUCK UP THEIR RUNWAYS - PUT IT DOWN IN THE DIRT.

"I got a steer for a repair base in Belgium but started running into the bomber stream returning home. I could not see very well in the haze and with the nose high I was seeing bombers go by above, below and on both sides. After dropping down below all that hardware I lost contact with the repair base. After watching each fuel tank go dry, the engine quit. Then I saw an airfield off each side of the plane. I rolled into a glide to the nearest airfield and hit the runway Just right. BUZZ BUGGY rolled to the middle and I climbed out feeling proud, when all of a sudden red lights were flashing and a jeep with a bunch of guys hanging all over it with horn blowing were bouncing across the field toward me hollering as a squadron of A-26s came roaring across the field, peeling off to land on the runway where I was feeling 'fat, dumb, and happy'. We pushed BUZZ BUGGY off the runway just as the first A-26 touched down.

"I spent a couple of days at Lyon, France, getting in the way of two mechanics trying to fix my engine. Having no experience with the Merlin, they never did get it to run right. A B-24 stopped at the base, so I bummed a ride back to England and I

got a ride back to Leiston in a truck. I was assigned a new P-51 and got to name it SWAMP FOX, for revolutionary general Francis Marion whom the British called THE SWAMP FOX due to his ability to disappear into the swamps of the Pee Dee River country.

"I flew SWAMP FOX for the remaining short period of the war."

"BALDY" WEISINGER and the new Flight Surgeon, Letter from William OBee O'Brien, dated July, 2001. (Author's note: 2nd Lt. William O'Brien was with the 328th Fighter Group at Oakland, CA early in 1943, as was his friend, "Baldy" Weisinger. We have been unable to discover his first name or if this is the correct spelling of his last name. O'Bee was on a weekend in San Francisco when he got a call from "Baldy" telling him to get back to Oakland as they had both been transferred to the 357th as Flight Leaders.) O'Bee takes up the story:

"Baldy got to Tonopah before I did and was assigned as a Flight Leader in the 362nd Squadron. He was practicing ground gunnery in preparation for the 4th Air Force gunnery meet. Unfortunately, Baldy hit the ground during a run and his body was the furthest object from the cockpit wreckage. He was very badly injured and hospitalized at March Field.

"I flew down to visit him. He was in a plaster cast from his neck to his ankles. The cast had been cut lengthwise into two halves, a top and a matching bottom. He could be turned over by placing both halves together, turning him over and remove the half you didn't need, pretty slick! He was under the care of an orthopedic surgeon whose work on Baldy was of such high quality that the staff remarked how good the doctor was in his profession.

"This was brought to Colonel Stetson's attention and when Dr. Ralph Sullivan was killed in the AT-6 crash, Stetson asked to have Baldy's surgeon assigned to his group. Stetson could get anything he wanted at the time, so Dr. Harold Snedden came to the 362nd at Tonopah.

"In a way it's sad, not only because of the loss of Baldy to us, but also the loss of Doctor Snedden's specialized talent that required that he belong to the staff of a general hospital where he could do more good. Doc Snedden served with the 362nd throughout the war as its Flight Surgeon."

MERLE C. OLMSTED

MSGT, USAF (RET) HISTORIAN, 357TH FIGHTER GRP

AN APPRECIATION, 1996

BY MERLE OLMSTED

"Ever since I began researching and writing about the 357th, some 40 years ago, 'The Group' has been an important part of my life. As the years went by and I got to know more and more of you, I realized that it was not only the combat history of 'The Group', but also its people who had become another family to me. In recent months it has been brought that it is long past time that I tell these people what I think of them. We are a dwindling group - just recently Ed Hyman, Don Kocher, Henry D'Esti, Tom Beemer, Dottie Pfeiffer and a dozen or so others have left us. It is time to say THANK YOU to all of 'The Group' for being such a marvelous assemblage of ladies and gents, and for being a major part of my life for these many years.

So I raise a symbolic tall cool one to those who have gone on to the 'Big Hangar' in the sky and to those who are still with us I say THANKS and CHEERS to all of you."

TWO GENERATIONS OF FIGHTER PILOTS

As far as is known, 1st Lt. Keehn Landis, 363rd Fighter Sqdn. was the only pilot in the 357th Group whose father was also a fighter pilot. Reed Landis, Keehn's father, was the son of a distinquished judge and commissioner of baseball, Kenesaw Mountain Landis. (the unusual first names were from the civil war battlefield). Reed Landis had been in the Illinois National Guard cavalry in 1916, but when World War I came he enlisted as an aviation cadet and was sent to England to train with the RAF. Although he was a U.S. Army officer, he remained with the British where he shot down ten German aircraft while flying SE5s with RAF 40 Squadron. Recalled to active duty in 1942, he served in several staff positions and finally as Commander of 61st Troop Carrier Wing. In the photo above, Colonel Landis is seen pinning the wings on his son Keehn at graduation with class 44A while his mother looks on. Keehn completed a full combat tour with the 363rd in January, 1945, during which he shot down an Me 109. In the below photo, Keehn is seen with his P-51 LONESOME POLECAT and his crew Cpl. Britton, SSgt. Harry Malinas and Sgt. Vince Inglise.

BIBLIOGRAPHY

Anderson, Clarence E, with Joeseph P. Hamlin, *TO FLY AND FIGHT*. St. Martin's Press, New York, 1990
Carson, Leonard K, *PURSUE AND DESTROY*. Sentry Books, 1978
Freeman, Roger A., *THE MIGHTY EIGHTH*. McDonalds, 1970
Freeman, Roger A., *THE MIGHTY EIGHTH WAR DIARY*. Janes, London, 1981
Freeman, Roger A., *THE MIGHTY EIGHTH WAR MANUAL*. Janes, London, 1984
Freeman, Roger A., *THE MIGHTY EIGHTH WARPAINT AND HERALDRY*. Arms & Armour Press, 1997
Girbig, Werner, *SIX MONTHS TO OBLIVION*. Shiffer Publishing 1989
Hess, William S.& Ivie, Thomas G., *FIGHTERS OF THE MIGHTY EIGHTH*. Motorbook International
Kaplan, Philip, *FIGHTER PILOT, A HISTORY AND A CELEBRATION*. Barnes & Noble, 1999
Mace, Harvey, *THE HIGHS AND LOWS OF FLYING*. Aviation Usk, 1994
Olmsted, Merle C, *THE YOXFORD BOYS*. Aero Publishers, Inc, Calif, 1971
Olmsted, Merle C, *THE 357TH OVER EUROPE*. Phalanx Publishing Ltd, 1994
Roeder, James, *357TH FIGHTER GROUP*. Squadron/Signal Publications, 2000.
Williamson, Murray, *STRATEGY FOR DEFEAT, THE LUFTWAFFE 1933-1945*. Chartwell Books Inc. 1986
Yeager, Chuck & Leo Janis, *YEAGER*. Bantam Books, New York, 1985

Be sure to visit the website of the General Chuck Yeager Foundation at www.chuckyeager.com

The publishers wish to thank Mark Proulx and Lorelei Kozsan for their assistance.

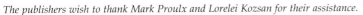

GLOSSARY AND ABBREVIATIONS

Abort - Early return, did not complete mission.
API - Type of .50 caliber ammunition - Armor piercing, incendiary.
ASR - Air Sea Rescue.
Bandits - Enemy aircraft.
Belly in - To land with landing gear retracted.
Big Friends - The bombers, B-17s and B-24s.
Bogies - Unidentified aircraft.
Bounce - To attack another aircraft.
CG - Center of gravity on an aircraft.
CW - Combat Wing, referring to bombers.
Deck - Ground surface "flying on the deck".
Deflection shot - Firing at an airborne target from any angle except dead astern.
Ditch - Crash landing in water.
DOW - Died of wounds.
Element - Two fighters, half of a flight.
EM - Enlisted men.
ETO - European Theatre of Operations.
Flak - Abbreviation for the German term for Anti-aircraft Artillery.
Flight - Four fighters, consisting of two elements.
FO - Field Order, the order detailing the mission for the day.
F/O - Flight Officer, same as army Warrant Officer.
Gaggle - A loose formation of aircraft.
Group - In 8th Air Force, a fighter group consisted of three Squadrons, a bomb group usually had four.

Hardstand - Hard-surfaced docking pad for one or two aircraft.
IP - The point at which the bombers turned onto their bomb run.
KIA - Killed in Action.
Kill - or victory, to shoot down an enemy aircraft.
Little Friends - Allied fighters.
LF - Land Fall, used in mission reports such as "Land Fall in" or "out".
May Day - From the French, a call on the R/T for assistance.
MIA - Missing in Action.
MEW - Micro Wave Early Warning, or M.E.W., radar control for aircraft.
OD - Olive Drab, a standard color for army aircraft for many years.
OCS - Officer Candidate School.
POW - Prisoner of War. (or PW)
PRU - Photo Reconnaissance Unit, or just PR referring to an aircraft.
R/T - Radio Telephone, a British term widely used in 8th AF.
RMC - Returned to Military Control (after being a POW).
RV - Rendezvous.
Section - Eight fighters or half a squadron.
Sortie - One mission by one aircraft.
Split-Ess - Or Split S, to roll inverted and dive away.
Strafe - Attack ground target with guns
THE WASH - a large inlet or bay, in north east England
U/I - Unidentified.
ZI - Zone of the Interior, the United States.
10/10 - refers to cloud cover, solid overcast. (from 1/10 to 10/10ths.)

INDEX OF AIRCRAFT

OFFICIAL MEMORANDUM REGARDING D-DAY MARKINGS

TOP SECRET
SUPREME HEADQUARTERS
ALLIED EXPEDITIONARY FORCE

OPERATION MEMORANDUM)   TOP SECRET
NUMBER   23   )   COPY NO. 75

18 April, 1944

DISTINCTIVE MARKINGS—AIRCRAFT

1. OBJECT

The object of this memorandum is to prescribe the distinctive markings which will be applied to US and BRITISH aircraft in order to make them more easily identified as friendly by ground and naval forces and by other friendly aircraft.

2. SCOPE

a. The instructions contained herein will apply to the following types of US and BRITISH aircraft:
(1) Fighters and fighter-bombers.
(2) Tactical and photographic reconnaissance aircraft.
(3) Aircraft employed in spotting for naval gunfire and field artillery.
(4) Light bombers.
(5) Medium bombers.
(6) Troop carrier aircraft, including four engine types.
(7) Glider tugs, including four engine types.
(8) Liaison aircraft and Air OP's employed in forward areas for fire spotting and adjustment or for advanced aircraft control.
(9) Coastal Command, Air Sea Rescue and disembarked Fleet Air Arm aircraft **except seaplanes and four engine aircraft which need not be marked.**
b. These instructions will **not** apply to the following classes of aircraft:
(1) Four engine bombers.
(2) Air transports.
(3) Gliders.
(4) Night fighters.
(5) Seaplanes.

3. GENERAL

a. The instructions contained herein will be effective on the day of the assault and thereafter until it is deemed advisable to change. Aircraft will be given distinctive markings as shortly before the day of the assault as it is possible to protect the effectiveness of their use.
b. These instructions are in no way intended to change the present US and BRITISH national markings now in use, namely: the USAAF white star on a white horizontal bar, and the RAF red, white and blue roundel.

4. DISTINCTIVE MARKINGS

a. Single engine aircraft.
(1) **Upper and lower wing surfaces** of aircraft listed in paragraph 2 a above, will be painted with five white and black stripes, each eighteen inches wide, parallel to the longitudinal axis of the airplane, arranged in order from center outward: white, black, white, black, white. Stripes will end six inches inboard of the national markings.
(2) **Fuselages** will be painted with five parallel white and black stripes, each eighteen inches wide, completely around the fuselage, with the outside edge of the rearmost band eighteen inches from the leading edge of the tailplane.
b. Twin engine aircraft.
(1) **Upper and lower wing surfaces** of aircraft listed in paragraph 2 a above, will be painted from the engine nacelles outward with five white and black stripes, each twenty-four inches wide, arranged in order from center outwards: white, black, white, black white.
(2) **Fuselages** will be painted with five parallel white and black stripes, each twenty-four inches wide, completely around the fuselage, with the outside edge of the rearmost band eighteen inches from the leading edge of the tailplane.
c. Four engine troop carrier aircraft and glider tugs.
(1) Same as for twin-engine aircraft, wing stripes to be outboard of the outer engine nacelles.
d. Stripes will in no case be painted over the national markings, which take precedence. Wing stripes will extend from leading edge to trailing edge of wings. Special equipment, such as deicer boots, will not be painted over.
e. Types of paint be employed.
(1) USAAF Units—as directed by the Commanding General of the Air Force concerned.
(2) RAF Units—as directed by the appropriate BRITISH agency.

5. BRIEFING

Army, Navy and Air Commanders will disseminate complete information concerning these distinctive markings to all troops under their commands no earlier before the day of the assault than will insure the complete distribution of the information.

By command of General Eisenhower:

W. B. Smith
Lieutenant General, U.S. Army
Chief of Staff

OFFICIAL
H. R. Bull,
Major General, G.S.C.,
Assistant Chief of Staff, G-3.

DISTRIBUTION:	COPY NO.
Allied Naval Commander, Expeditionary Force,	1-3
Commander-in-Chief, 21 Army Group,	4-8
Commanding General, First US Army Group,	9-10
Air Commander-in-Chief, AEAF,	11-16
The Secretary, The Admiralty,	17
The Under Secretary of Ste, The War Office (MO 3),	18
Commanding General, ETOUSA,	19
Commander-in-Chief, Home Forces,	20
The Under Secretary of State, The Air Ministry	21-23
Commanding General, USSTAF,	24
Air Officer Commanding, Bomber Command,	25
Chief of Combined Operations,	26
The Secretary, Chiefs of Staff Committee, Offices of the War Cabinet,	27
The Secretary, Combined Chiefs of Staff, Washington, D.C.	28
OPD, War Department, Washington, D.C.	29
OPD, Navy Department, Washington, D.C.	30
A.F.H.Q.	31
Supreme Commander, SHAEF,	32
Deputy Supreme Commander,	33
Chief of Staff,	34
Deputy Chief of Staff,	35
Chief Administrative Officer,	36
Adjutant General,	37
Secretary General Staff,	38
AC of S, G-1,	39
AC of S, G-2,	40-41
AC of S, G-3,	42-47
AC of S, G-4,	48-50
AC of S, G-5,	51
Chief Engineer,	52
Chief Signal Officer,	53
Public Relations Division,	54
Headquarters Commandant,	55
Spares	56-100

TOP SECRET

APPENDIX 'A'
to SHAEF OP MEMO NO. 23
dated 18 April, 1944

SAMPLE SKETCHES
OF DISTINCTIVE MARKINGS

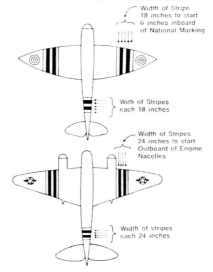

Width of Stripe
18 inches to start
6 inches inboard
of National Marking

With of Stripes
each 18 inches

Width of Stripes
24 inches to start
Outboard of Engine
Nacelles

Width of stripes
each 24 inches

NOTE: National Markings are not to be painted over by the black and white stripes.
TOP SECRET

This high quality color photo is by 362nd Squadron's Jim Frary and shows P-51D, 44-14152, Squadron code G4-W. Its pilot was Lt. William Hank Gruber. The tall man in the center is MSGT. Mac McGinnis with SSGT. Robert Currie at left.